THE LETTERS OF
Samuel Johnson

'I hope to see standing corn in some part
of the earth this summer.'—30 May 1780

Mr James Macpherson — I received your foolish
and impudent note. Whatever insult is offered me
I will do my best to repel, and what I cannot do
for myself the law shall do for me. I will not
desist from detecting what I think a cheat, from
any fear of the menaces of a Ruffian.

You want me to retract. What shall I retract? I thought your book an imposture from
the beginning, I think it upon yet surer reasons
an imposture still. For this opinion I give the
publick my reasons which I here dare you to
refute.

JOHNSON'S MATURE HAND. PART OF HIS
LETTER TO JAMES MACPHERSON, 20 JANUARY
1775 (373).

THE LETTERS OF

Samuel Johnson

WITH MRS. THRALE'S GENUINE LETTERS

TO HIM

Collected & Edited by

R. W. CHAPMAN

Sometime Fellow of Magdalen College
Oxford

VOLUME II: 1775—1782
Letters 370–821.1

OXFORD
AT THE CLARENDON PRESS

Oxford University Press, Walton Street, Oxford OX2 6DP

London New York Toronto
Delhi Bombay Calcutta Madras Karachi
Kuala Lumpur Singapore Hong Kong Tokyo
Nairobi Dar es Salaam Cape Town
Melbourne Auckland

and associated companies in
Beirut Berlin Ibadan Mexico City Nicosia

Oxford is a trade mark of Oxford University Press

Published in the United States
by Oxford University Press, New York

First published 1952
Reprinted 1984

British Library Cataloguing in Publication Data

Johnson, Samuel, 1709–1784
The letters of Samuel Johnson.
Vol. 2: 1775–1782. Letters 370–821.1
1. Johnson, Samuel, 1709–1784
2. Authors, English – 18th century –
Biography
I. Title   II. Chapman, R. W. (Robert William)
828'.609   PR3533

ISBN 0-19-818537-5

Printed in Great Britain by
Antony Rowe Ltd,
Chippenham

CONTENTS

VOLUME II

1775–1782

v

CONTENTS

LIST OF ILLUSTRATIONS

vii

ABBREVIATIONS

(See also *Authorities*, i. xv)

I. PERSONS

J(ohnson).

J(ames) B(oswell); C(harles) B(urney), F(rances) B(urney); (Francis Barber is Barber or Frank).

B(ennet) L(angton).

L(ucy) P(orter).

F(rances) R(eynolds), J(oshua) R(eynolds).

J(ohn) T(aylor); H(enry) T(hrale); H(ester) L(ynch) T(hrale) or H L P(iozzi); Q = Hester Maria ('Queeny') Thrale.

J(oseph) W(arton), T(homas) W(arton); A(nna) W(illiams).

II. PLACES

A'n = Ashbourn(e). B'm = Birmingham. B'n = Brighthelmston (Brighton). L'd = Lichfield. L'n = London. O'd = Oxford. S'k = Southwark. S'm = Streatham.

III. DATES

'51 = 1751.

IV. BOOKS, PERIODICALS, ETC.

PM = J's *Prayers and Meditations* 1785. Reprint in *JM* (see below). *Account* = *Account of the Life of . . . Johnson . . . by himself* 1805.

L = Boswell's Life of J. Undated references are to Hill–Powell (see i. xvi). Dated references are to 1791(-3, -9), and are followed by a bracketed reference to Hill (i.e. Hill–Powell). Hill standing alone = his edition of the *Letters* 1892.

BP = Boswell's *Private Papers* (see i. xvi).

1788 = HLP's *Letters to and from J.* (HLP = her own copy, Lysons = Samuel L's copy, Malone = Edmond M's copy).

Th = *Thraliana.*

JM = Hill's *Johnsonian Miscellanies* 1897.

C = J. L. Clifford's *Hester Lynch Piozzi* (*Mrs. Thrale*).

R i (etc.) = Vol. i (etc.) of A. L. Reade's *Johnsonian Gleanings*; *Reades* = his *Reades of Blackwood Hill.*

E(nglish) H(istorical) R(eview); G(entleman's) M(agazine); M(odern) L(anguage) N(otes); N(otes and) Q(ueries); R(eview of) E(nglish) S(tudies); T(imes) L(iterary) S(upplement).

Rylands 539, etc. = John Rylands Library English MSS.

viii

VOLUME II
1775–82

370. M. 2 Jan. '75. Henry Thrale.

Sotheby 30 January 1918 (not seen).—1788, No. 96 (dated June 2 but placed before the letter of Feb. 3).

Dear Sir   June 2, 1775.

I have taken the liberty of enclosing a letter, which contains a request of which I cannot know the propriety. Nothing, I suppose, can be done till the present master of the tap has given notice of his resignation; and whether even then it is fit for you to recommend, there may be reason to doubt. I shall tell Heely, that I have laid his letter before you, and that he must inform you when he is certain of the intended resignation. You will then act as you judge best. There seems to be nothing unreasonable in Heely's desire. He seems to have a genius for an alehouse, and if he can get this establishment, may thank his friend that sent him to the Marshalsea.[1]

This, I know, is a happy week; you will revel with your constituents in plenty and merriment; I must be kept at home by my wicked mistress, out of the way of so much happiness. You shall however have my good wishes. I hope every man will go from your table more of a friend than he came.

I am, &c.

371. Sa. 14 Jan. '75. James Boswell (Edinburgh).

Not traced.—Boswell 1791, i. 442 (Hill ii. 290).

Dear Sir,
You never did ask for a book by the post till now, and I

370.—The true date is clear; on 2 June J was at O'd, not therefore 'kept at home'; it was in Jan. that HT was in the habit of entertaining his constituents.

1. The debtors' prison in S'k, not far from the brewery. By arresting him, H's 'friend' has brought him into the orbit of HT's charitable interest.

371.—Seems to answer a lost letter; for on 19 Jan. JB replied that he 'did really ask

I

did not think on it. You see now it is done. I sent one to
the King, and I hear he likes it.[1]

I shall send a parcel into Scotland for presents, and intend
to give to many of my friends. In your catalogue you left
out Lord Auchinleck.

Let me know, as fast as you read it, how you like it; and
let me know if any mistake is committed, or any thing important left out. I wish you could have seen the sheets. My
compliments to Mrs. Boswell, and to Veronica, and to all
my friends.

I am, Sir, Your most humble servant,

January 14, 1775. Sam: Johnson

372. Sa. 14 Jan. '75. John Taylor (Ashbourne).

Lichfield; known to Hill only from an auction catalogue.

Dear Sir

I would send you my Journey to the Western Islands,
which will be published next Wednesday, but that I do not
know in whose care to deliver it for you.[1] It would go commodiously in any parcel which is sent weekly to the tradesmen in your town. Pray send me a direction.

I have been to see Congreve, but he was not at home, and
he thinks not, I believe, of coming to me.

I hope your health is good. I have hitherto passed the
winter with little cold or pain.

I am, Sir, Your most affectionate

Jan. 14. 1775 Sam: Johnson

the favour twice; but you have been even with me by granting it so speedily' (*L* ii.
290). The sending of a book by post was an unusual and a formidable business. JB
records, 18 Jan., the arrival of 'thirteen franks' (that is, two sheets in each). He had
to go out to supper; but 'I was lively though ill of a cold, being inspirited by Mr.
Johnson. I came home as early as I could, sat down by the drawing-room fire, and
read on till I had reached the end of the *Journey*. It was then about three in the
morning, and the fire was very low and the night very cold' (*BP* x. 85). For the
word 'book' see on 369.1.

1. See 369.2.

372.—1. See my note on 371, which shows that it was impracticable to send a book
by post in a single packet, even if franked.

373. F. 20 Jan. '75. James Macpherson.

Address: To Mr. James Macpherson. No postmark.

Adam (see note).—William Shaw, *Enquiry into the Authenticity of the Poems ascribed to Ossian*, 1781, 11; Boswell 1791, i. 449 (Hill ii. 298).

Mr James Macpherson—I received your foolish and impudent note. Whatever insult is offered me I will do my best to repel, and what I cannot do for myself the law will do for me. I will not desist from detecting what I think a cheat, from any fear of the menaces of a Ruffian.

You want me to retract. What shall I retract? I thought your book an imposture from the beginning, I think it upon yet surer reasons an imposture still. For this opinion I give the publick my reasons which I here dare you to refute.

But however I may despise you, I reverence truth and if you can prove the genuineness of the work I will confess it. Your rage I defy, your abilities since your Homer[1] are not so formidable, and what I have heard of your morals disposes me to pay regard not to what you shall say, but to what you can prove.

You may print this if you will.

Jan. 20. 1775   Sam: Johnson

373.—Of this famous letter there are four versions: (1) the original in the Adam collection: facsimile in *Catalogue* 1929, i. 57. (2) The lost MS. dictated to JB 'written down in his presence, and authenticated by a note in his own hand-writing, "*This, I think, is a true copy*"'; JB adds, by anticipation, 'I have deposited it in the British Museum.' Like other MSS. which he intended to give to the Museum, it is not there; and it has not been found elsewhere. (3) A holograph copy by J in the collection of the late A. T. Loyd. Facsimile in *L* ii. 298 (where the underline is erroneous; it was corrected by an erratum-slip). (4) A lost MS. printed by Shaw, who was the first to publish the letter, though quotations from it had appeared in the newspapers of '75.

However surprising it may be that Macpherson should keep such a document, the Adam MS. is certainly the original; it is folded for transmission (by hand, not post) and is directed on the outside. Thus the variants, due to J's imperfect recollection or other causes, though they are interesting, create no textual problem. (Chesterfield, we know, left J's letter lying about, and praised it to his friends. But the manners of the lion are not the manners of the jackal.) See Addenda, p. 528.

A good deal is known of the negotiations between M and Strahan that provoked J's defiance, and caused him to arm himself, as Hawkins tells us, with 'an oak-plant of a tremendous size' (*L* ii. 300). The documents in the case are fully set out in Dr. Powell's long note (*L* ii. 511) and need not be repeated. For the discussion of Ossian in the *Journey* see my edition (references there in Index II, s.v. Macpherson), or *L* ii. 292. In conversation J was willing to concede (*Tour* 23 Sept., 322 in my edition) that M 'has found names, and stories, and phrases, nay passages in old songs, and with them has blended his own compositions'.

1. M had published in '73, in two volumes quarto, a translation of the *Iliad* in Ossianic prose, which 'was generally ridiculed' (*DNB*).

374. Sa. 21 Jan. '75. James Boswell (Edinburgh).

Not traced.—Boswell 1791, i. 444 (Hill ii. 292).

Dear Sir,

I long to hear how you like the book; it is, I think, much liked here. But Macpherson is very furious; can you give me any more intelligence about him, or his Fingal? Do what you can, and do it quickly. Is Lord Hailes on our side?

Pray let me know what I owed you when I left you, that I may send it to you.

I am going to write about the Americans.[1] If you have picked up any hints among your lawyers, who are great masters of the law of nations,[2] or if your own mind suggests any thing, let me know. But mum,—it is a secret.

I will send your parcel of books as soon as I can; but I cannot do as I wish. However, you find every thing mentioned in the book which you recommended.

Langton is here; we are all that ever we were.[3] He is a worthy fellow, without malice, though not without resentment.

Poor Beauclerk is so ill, that his life is thought to be in danger. Lady Di. nurses him with very great assiduity.

Reynolds has taken too much to strong liquor,[4] and seems to delight in his new character.

This is all the news that I have; but as you love verses,[5] I will send you a few which I made upon Inchkenneth; but remember the condition, that you shall not show them, except to Lord Hailes, whom I love better than any man whom I know so little. If he asks you to transcribe them for him, you may do it, but I think he must promise not to let them be copied again, nor to show them as mine.

374.—1. *Taxation No Tyranny.*

2. JB disclaims the compliment: 'You rate our lawyers here too high, when you call them great masters of the law of nations.' My legal friends tell me that by 'law of nations' J means not what, since Bentham, we call international law, but 'the law of nature and of nations', that is, the common element in the laws of different nations. International law in the modern sense did not affect the problems of American taxation.   3. See 313.

4. JB in a note calls this a 'fanciful description of his friend'. JB's letters, in his later years in London, suggest that JR's habits were convivial (e.g. Tinker's edition, p. 369).

5. For J's Latin verses on Inchkenneth, which JB published in his *Tour*, see *L* v. 325, *Poems* 169.

4

I have at last sent back Lord Hailes's sheets. I never think about returning them, because I alter nothing. You will see that I might as well have kept them. However, I am ashamed of my delay; and if I have the honour of receiving any more, promise punctually to return them by the next post. Make my compliments to dear Mrs. Boswell, and to Miss Veronica.

I am, dear Sir, Yours most faithfully,

January 21, 1775.   Sam: Johnson

---

375. Sa. 28 Jan. '75. James Boswell (Edinburgh).

Not traced.—Boswell 1791, i. 446 (Hill ii. 294).

Dear Sir,

You sent me a case[1] to consider, in which I have no facts but what are against us, nor any principles on which to reason. It is vain to try to write thus without materials. The fact seems to be against you, at least I cannot know nor say[2] any thing to the contrary. I am glad that you like the book so well. I hear no more of Macpherson. I shall long to know what Lord Hailes says of it. Lend it him privately. I shall send the parcel as soon as I can. Make my compliments to Mrs. Boswell.

I am, Sir, &c.

January 28, 1775.   Sam. Johnson

375.1. Sa. 30 Jan. '75. Thomas Lawrence.

Maggs Cat. 291 (1912), 2610 (not seen).—Extract in catalogue.

I think it will be best for you to write the account of Mr. Lawrence's conduct in a few words to me, that I may send it to Mr. Chamier.

375.—1. See 377, 378, and *L* ii. 291.
    2. I am tempted to suspect the text. But cf. 457 'think or say'.

375.1.—'Mr.' Lawrence should properly be Dr. L's eldest son—if J knew which was the eldest. The eldest was probably Soulden; see 531. 2 and Index II.

5

376. F. 3 Feb. '75. Mrs. Thrale.

Sotheby 30 Jan. 1918 (not seen).—1788, No. 97.

Madam   February 3, 1775.

So many demands are made upon me, that if you give leave I will stay here till Tuesday. My pamphlet has not gone on at all. Please to send by the bearer the papers on my table; and give my love to my *brother* and *sisters.*

I am, &c.

376a. Southwark. Su. 5 Feb. ⟨'75⟩. From Mrs. Thrale.

Address: To Doctor Johnson Fleet Street.

R 539.35—

Dear Sir   Southwark 5: February

I wonder when we shall have any Leisure from our Engagements to chat with each other. Today I hear you dine with Mr Paradise, so I will take this Afternoon to go out a'visiting. Tomorrow Mr Thrale entertains two or three of the People concerned in Crossby's Affairs, so when I have sat the Dinner out, & said a few civil Things to my Company I shall go to drink Tea with Jack & Fanny Rice with whom I shall go to the Comic Mirror at Night to hear the Dialogue between Doctor *Anecdote* & Mrs *Thalia.* If you will meet me at home when I return from that Nonsense we shall have something to laugh about. On Wednesday we dine with Sir Joshua Reynolds according to an invitation he sent hither on Saturday to ask us to meet Mrs Montagu so I am like Miss Jenny in the Journey to London telling how tomorrow we see the New Pantomime & the next day dine with the Duchess of Distinction &c. I like however that you should always know where I go & what I do that you may either approve me or scold me which is the next best as the one shews your Partiality the other your Friendship for Dear Sir

Your most Obliged & faithful Servant H: L: T.

376.1. Sa. 4 Feb. '75. Edmund Hector (Birmingham).

Sotheby 5 June 1929.—

Dear Sir

You have such love to be giving, that your minds ought to learn how to refuse. But the china which is ultimately designed for another, I have no right to refuse, and I will not lessen the Lady's[1] pleasure by letting her know any thing of it.

I am glad if my book gave you any pleasure. I hope Mrs. Careless likes it too. The Scotch are angry, and the King says, I must go into that country no more.

376.1.—1. HLT, see 384.3.

Be pleased to direct the Box to me at Henry Thrale's, Esq in Southwarke.

I am, Dear Sir, Your most affectionate Servant
Feb. 4. 1775.   Sam: Johnson

376.2. ⟨Sa.⟩ 4 Feb. ⟨'75⟩. Mrs. Thrale.

James F. Drake of New York (not seen).—Extracts in Drake catalogue (? early 1930), 107; the letter is in a copy of the first edition of *Rasselas*.

'The letter speaks of the famous Club and of Mr. Hoole . . . and his play "Cleonice". . . . The letter reads in part:'

Please to send the printed pamphlets that are upon my table.

Mr. Hoole's play[1] is in rehearsal. Pepys and Tigh[2] are reading Jephsa[3] to all comers and goers, and it is told how well I liked it; so your spite is spited. . . .

Eleven of the club dined together and we made many salutary regulations.

Be pleased to frank the letter to Mr. Hector in Birmingham and send it.

377. Tu. 7 Feb. '75. Thomas Lawrence.

Henkel's catalogue 11 March 1916; copy by Elizabeth L., Isham.—Boswell 1791, i. 447 (Hill ii. 296).

Sir,   February 7, 1775.

One of the Scotch physicians is now prosecuting a corporation that in some publick instrument have stiled him *Doctor of Medicine* instead of *Physician*. Boswell desires, being

376.2.—I regret my failure to secure the full text. My notes show that I asked for a photostat, perhaps too late. The year is fixed by the reference to *Cleonice*, the coincidence with 376, and the reference to the letter to Hector, i.e. 376.1.

1. *Cleonice*.

2. The only likely Tigh I can find is Edward T of the Middle Temple, whose marriage is recorded in *GM* 8 May 1755.

3. 'Jephsa' seems to be *vox nihili*. The obvious correction is 'Jephtha' (which might be written 'Jephta'). There are several writers of that name, but none of them seems to fit. The context suggests a play; I suggest that J wrote 'Jephson', which in his hand might easily be read as 'Jephsa', and that the allusion is to Robert Jephson's *Braganza*, which was played at Drury Lane 17 Feb. '75 and published in the same year.

advocate for the corporation, to know whether *Doctor of Medicine* be not a legitimate title, and whether it can be considered as a disadvantageous distinction. I am to write to-night, be pleased to tell me.

I am, Sir, your most, &c.

Sam. Johnson

378. Tu. 7 Feb. '75. James Boswell (Edinburgh).

Not traced.—Boswell 1791, i. 447 (Hill ii. 296); Boswell Papers x. 95 (the suppressed passage).

My dear Boswell,

I am surprized that, knowing as you do the disposition of your countrymen to tell lies[1] in favour of each other, you can be at all affected by any reports that circulate among them. Macpherson never in his life offered me the sight of any original or of any evidence of any kind, but thought only of intimidating me by noise and threats, till my last answer,— that I would not be deterred from detecting what I thought a cheat, by the menaces of a ruffian,—put an end to our correspondence.

The state of the question is this. He, and Dr. Blair,[2] whom I consider as deceived, say, that he copied the poem from old manuscripts. His copies, if he had them, and I believe him to have none, are nothing. Where are the manuscripts? They can be shown if they exist, but they were never shown. *De non existentibus et non apparentibus,* says our law, *eadem est ratio.*[3] No man has a claim to credit upon his own word, when better evidence, if he had it, may be easily produced. But, so far as we can find, the Erse language was never written till very lately for the purposes of religion. A nation that cannot write, or a language that was never written, has no manuscripts.

But whatever he has, he never offered to show. If old

378.—JB had written 2 Feb. asking for 'a full and pointed account of what had passed between' J and Macpherson, and hinting rather broadly that he and Hailes were inclined to allow *Fingal* a degree of authenticity. For the sequel see 380.

1. 'My friend has, in this letter, relied upon my testimony, with a confidence, of which the ground has escaped my recollection' JB—a sentence worthy of J himself.

2. *A Critical Dissertation on the Poems of Ossian,* 1763.

3. 'What cannot be produced must be treated as non-existent.'

manuscripts should now be mentioned, I should, unless there were more evidence than can be easily had, suppose them another proof of Scotch conspiracy in national falsehood.

Do not censure the expression; you know it to be true.

Dr. Memis's question is so narrow as to allow no speculation; and I have no facts before me but those which his advocate has produced against you.

I consulted this morning the President of the London College of Physicians, who says, that with us, *Doctor of Physick* (we do not say *Doctor of Medicine*) is the highest title that a practicer of physick can have; that *Doctor* implies not only *Physician*, but teacher of physick; that every *Doctor* is legally a *Physician*, but no man, not a *Doctor*, can *practice physick* but by *licence* particularly granted. The Doctorate is a licence of itself. It seems to us a very slender cause of prosecution.

Your love of publication is offensive and disgusting, and will end, if it be not reformed, in a general distrust among all your friends.[4]

I am now engaged, but in a little time I hope to do all you would have. My compliments to Madam and Veronica.

I am, Sir, Your most humble servant,

February 7, 1775. Sam. Johnson

378.1. Th. 9 Feb. '75. John Taylor.

Sotheby 31 March 1875 (not seen; extracts in catalogue).—

'Referring to some matter in dispute.'

I do not conceive myself able to judge the question between you and that wild woman—I consider her as the slave of her own appetite, as a being that acts only by the grossest motives.

'Entreats him if the cause is tried to push it on as fast as he can that he may

---

378.—4. 'Your love . . . friends': suppressed by JB, with asterisks indicating an omission. The reference was presumably to something, suppressed likewise, in JB's letter of 2 Feb., from which two passages were omitted. JB's Journal, to which we owe the supplement of J's letter, reveals also the provocation: 'He was angry with me for begging to be allowed to read to more people than to Lord Hailes some verses on Inchkenneth which he had sent me (see 374). He said (then the quotation). This was too severe, as Lord Hailes had agreed with me that the verses should be freely shewn.' For JB's editing of his own letters see Boswell's *Letters*, ed. Tinker, 111.

rid his mind of the anxiety—is alarmed at what he says of his state of perturba-
tion—advises him not to trust himself alone, etc.'

Take great care of your health both of body and mind and
do not let melancholy thoughts lay hold on you.

379. ⟨end of Feb. '75⟩. Henry Thrale.

Adam.—1788, No. 105 (misplaced among the letters of June '75).

Dear Sir

I beg that you will be pleased to send me an attestation
to Mr. Carter's[1] merit. I am going to morrow,[2] and shall
leave the pamflet to shift for itself.

You need only say, that you have sufficient knowledge of
Mr. Carter to testify that he is eminently skilful in the art
which he professes, and that he is a man of such decency and
regularity of manners, that there will be no danger from his
example to the Youth of the Colleges, and that therefore you
shall consider it as a favour, if leave may be obtained for him
to profess horsemanship in the University.

I am, Sir, Your most humble servant, Sam: Johnson

Please to free this letter to Mrs Lucy Porter in Lichfield.

379a. Southwark. W. 1 Mar. ⟨'75⟩. From Mrs. Thrale to J at Oxford.

Address: To Samuel Johnson Esqr at Oxford. *Postmark*: 2 MR.
Franked by HT.

R 539.36—

Dear Sir   Southwark 1: March at Night
   Nothing has gone well since your Absence yet I have not wished for you:
Hester has been very sick indeed & taken up all my Thoughts. I have myself
caught a bad cold with getting up in the Night after her—so now She is
better I shall nurse myself up against you come home.
   Frank saw me that Day you sent for the Letter under the immediate
Influence of a dreadful Fright.—Harry & his Companions were gone down the

---

379.—1. For the attempt to set up this protégé of the Thrales as a riding-master at
O'd see the references, in Index II, s.vv. Carter, the three Clarendon Trustees
(Drummond, Mansfield, Markham), and Douglas. For the complicated story of the
Clarendon Bequest, which contemplated 'establishing a Riding School in the Uni-
versity', see *L* ii. 424, 527. The scheme broke down because the profits from the
Life of Clarendon (Oxford 1759), of which the bequest mainly consisted, were found
to be insufficient. This discovery led to discussion of the conduct of the University
Press, and to J's letter to Wetherell (463) on that subject.
   2. To Oxford.

Brewhouse Yard ten Minutes before, when a violent Shriek was heard & a Boy said to be scalded—he was got out immediately indeed & carried home, but died the Day after in sad Torment. His Parents are substantial Tallow Chandlers, particular Friends of ours—this was their only Son—13 Years old —& had an Estate of 100£ a Year settled on him & his heirs. So much for this Misery. God preserve the poor People's Senses!

I hope you will succeed for Carter—he is an unlucky creature, but has for once met with Friends truly assiduous in his Service: Dr Glasse is affronted at my pressing so closely for the Presentation, & says I have not due Reliance on him & Mr Herne: but we will pacify him by Bromfield's Help. Surely the Monday's Convocation will agree on some good Scheme for this poor Fellow: he dares not stir out of his House scarce except on Sundays, & then he haunts me with his doleful Looks. The dying Boy too, though given over by Evans, has still a *voracious Appetite* I hear. Oh Dear! what a World is this? May you however remain in it these very many Years, for the Sakes of hundreds—& particularly of Sir

Your most faithful & Obedient Servant H: L: Thrale

Queeney mends since her Emetic & will do very well again.

380. Sa. 25 Feb. '75. James Boswell (Edinburgh).

Not traced.—Boswell 1791, i. 456 (Hill ii. 309).

Dear Sir,

I am sorry that I could get no books for my friends in Scotland. Mr. Strahan has at last promised to send two dozen to you. If they come, put the names of my friends into them; you may cut them out,[1] and paste them with a little starch in the book.

You then are going wild about Ossian.[2] Why do you think any part can be proved? The dusky manuscript of Egg is probably not fifty years old; if it be an hundred, it proves nothing. The tale of Clanranald has no proof. Has Clanranald told it? Can he prove it? There are, I believe, no Erse manuscripts. None of the old families had a single letter in Erse that we heard of. You say it is likely that they could write. The learned, if any learned there were, could; but

380.—1. 'From a list in his hand-writing' JB. No copy with such an inscription seems to be on record. But see on 505.

2. See on 378. JB, in spite of J's reply to his former letter, returned to the charge on 18 Feb., and was brave enough to opine that the authenticity of Ossian 'is capable of being proved to a certain degree'. He mentioned 'one of the Grants', who 'seemed to hope he should be able to convince you'; reported the arrival from Egg of Ranald Macdonald with 'MSS. of Erse poetry', one of which 'does appear to have the dusky-ness of antiquity'; and told a story of Macpherson's having 'got one old Erse MS. from Clanranald'. Evidence on these MSS. is collected in *L* ii. 514.

knowing by that learning some written language, in that language they wrote, as letters had never been applied to their own. If there are manuscripts, let them be shewn, with some proof that they are not forged for the occasion. You say many can remember parts of Ossian. I believe all those parts are versions of the English; at least there is no proof of their antiquity.

Macpherson is said to have made some translations himself; and having taught a boy to write it, ordered him to say that he had learnt it of his grandmother. The boy, when he grew up, told the story. This Mrs. Williams heard at Mr. Strahan's table. Do not be credulous; you know how little a Highlander can be trusted.[3] Macpherson is, so far as I know, very quiet. Is not that proof enough? Every thing is against him. No visible manuscript; no inscription in the language; no correspondence among friends: no transaction of business, of which a single scrap remains in the ancient families. Macpherson's pretence is, that the character was Saxon. If he had not talked unskilfully of *manuscripts*, he might have fought with oral tradition much longer. As to Mr. Grant's information, I suppose he knows much less of the matter than ourselves.

In the mean time, the bookseller says that the sale[4] is sufficiently quick. They printed four thousand. Correct your copy wherever it is wrong, and bring it up. Your friends will all be glad to see you. I think of going myself into the country about May.

I am sorry that I have not managed to send the books sooner. I have left four for you, and do not restrict you absolutely to follow my directions in the distribution. You must use your own discretion.

Make my compliments to Mrs. Boswell: I suppose she is now just beginning to forgive me.

I am, dear Sir, your humble servant,

Feb. 25, 1775.   Sam. Johnson

380.—3. 'The laxity of Highland conversation' is a topic of the *Journey* (e.g. 45, 106, in my edition); and J's impression was confirmed by JB in his Journal: *L* v. 237, 336.

4. The figure 4,000 almost certainly covers the two editions printed in 1775, commonly called two issues of the first edition. There were also three pirated editions. Strahan and Cadell did not again print the book until 1785, when the publication of the *Tour* revived interest.

380.1. Feb. or Mar. '75. Joseph Palmer.

Not traced.—Susan M. Radcliffe, *Sir Joshua's Nephew* 1930, 82.
Addenda, p. 528.

381. Oxford. W. 1. Mar. '75. William Strahan.

Adam.—Hill's Boswell 1887, vi. xxxvi.

Sir

I am sorry to see that all the alterations[1] proposed are
evidence of timidity. You may be sure that I do ⟨not⟩ wish to
publish, what those for whom I write do not like to have published. But print me half a dozen copies in the original state,
and lay them up for me. It concludes well enough as it is.

When you print it, if you print it, please to frank one to
me here, and frank another to Mrs Aston at Stow Hill,
Lichfield.

The changes are not for the better, except where the facts
were mistaken. The last paragraph was indeed rather con-
temptuous, there was once more of it which I put out myself.

I am Sir Your humble Servant

March 1. 1775   Sam: Johnson

382. Oxford. F. 3 Mar. '75. William Strahan.

Adam.—Hill 1892.

Sir

Our post is so unskilfully managed that we can very rarely,
if ever, answer a letter from London on the day when we
receive it. Your pages were sent back the next post, for there
was nothing to do. I had no great difficulty in persuading
myself to admit the alterations, for why should I in defense
of the ministry provoke those, whom in their own defense
they dare not provoke.—But are such men fit to be the
governours of kingdoms?

They are here much discouraged by the last motion, and
undoubtedly every Man's confidence in Government must

381.—1. In *Taxation No Tyranny*. Of the copies in the original state there is no
trace; Strahan might be afraid to print them. But Boswell (*L* ii. 313) preserved 'a few
proof leaves . . . marked with corrections in his own hand-writing' (not found at
Malahide or Fettercairn). From these leaves, and from J's conversation, JB records
a number of suppressed passages.

be diminished, yet if Lives can be saved, some deviation from rigid policy may be excused.[1]

I expect to return some time in the next week, perhaps not till the latter end.

Do not omit to have the presentation pamflets, done and sent to Mrs Williams, and lay by for me the half dozen which you print without correction, and please to send me one by the post of the corrected books.

       I am, Sir, Your humble servant

March 3. 1775   Sam: Johnson
University College

You will send to Mr Cooper[2] and such as you think proper either in my name or your own.

383. Oxford. F. 3 Mar. '75. Mrs. Thrale.

Adam.—1788, No. 98.

Dear Madam

I am afraid that something has happened to occupy your mind disagreeably, and hinder you from writing to me, or thinking about me.

The fate of my proposal for our Friend Mr Carter will be decided on Monday. Those whom I have spoken to are all friends. I have not abated any part of the entrance, or payment,[1] for it has not been thought too much, and I hope he will have scholars.

I am very deaf, and yet cannot well help being much in company, though it is often very uncomfortable. But when I have done this thing, which, I hope, is a good thing, or find that I cannot do it, I wish to live a while under your care and protection.

The imperfection of our post makes it uncertain whether we shall receive letters, sooner than we must send them, this is therefore written while I yet do not know whether you

---

382.—1. The 'last motion' was no doubt, as Hill says, North's proposals for 'Conciliating the Differences with America', debated on 20 and 27 Feb.

2. This is, I think, Sir Grey Cooper. I have a note, and a strong recollection, that JB somewhere expresses indignation that J should be obliged to submit to revision by such a man. But I cannot find the passage, and Dr. Pottle does not recall it.

383.—1. By 'payment' J perhaps means rent for the school, see 384.1; the 'entrance' was also, I suppose, a payment. But the payments might be fees charged by Carter.

have favoured me or no. I was sufficiently discontented that I heard nothing yesterday. But sure all is well.

I am, Dearest Madam your most obedient and most humble
servant

March 3. 1775   Sam: Johnson
University College.[2]

384. Oxford. M. 6 Mar. '75. ⟨William Strahan⟩.
Harvard; known to Hill only from an auction catalogue.—

Sir

I received the pamflet, but not one scrap of a letter. I have shown it about the College, and to me at least it is commended. I shall stay here but a little while, and should be glad of about a dozen and half to give to my friends here. Please to send them by the coach on Wednesday, and on Thursday I can distribute them, and write me a little piece of a letter. I am Sir Your most humble servant
March 6. 1775   Sam: Johnson

384.1. Oxford. M. 6 Mar. '75. Mrs. Thrale.
Tregaskis (1938).—

Dear Madam

Leave was given about two hours ago to Mr. Carter to profess horsemanship in Oxford. It is expected that he wait on the Vicechancellor to receive such directions about hours, and other particulars as may make his exercises consistent with the other parts of education. If he comes before Friday I shall attend him.

I have no place for him, but several are mentioned, which he must come and examine. I doubt he must pay for that which he has. It is generally believed that he will have a sufficient number of Scholars.

I have wished to hear from you every post, and am uneasy. Sure all is well.

Mr. Thrale's letter[1] to Dr. Wetherel was very efficacious,

383.—2. J had been intimate at University College as early as '64, when he told Strahan 'the College is almost filled with my friends' (167). At his later visit of this year he seems to have been Colson's guest; see 399.

384.—This letter is clearly to Strahan, the 'pamflet' *Taxation No Tyranny*.

384.1.—1. See 379.

every body was spoken to, and every ⟨thing⟩ was done by him to promote the design.

You know I owe two guineas to Mr Carter's expedition, be so kind as to advance them, for I cannot spare them here.

Do write to me.

I am, Madam, Your most humble servant

March 6. 1775   Sam: Johnson

384.1a. Southwark. Tu. 7 Mar. ⟨'75⟩. From Mrs. Thrale to J at Oxford.

Address: To Doctor Sam: Johnson at Oxford. *Postmark*:—MR. Franked by HT.

R 539.38—

My Dear Sir   Southwark 7: March.

I am astonished & grieved that you hear nothing from me, yet I will try this one Letter more by the Post, odd as it is—while I am sending for Carter & fitting him out. I have not been well to be sure, but I have written two very long Letters with all manner of Stuff in them I forget what. Niggey has been bad too; her Illness was the beginning of mine: I got up in the Night after her, & caught a Cough which has half killed me: however I have driven it away at last, but by Methods so rough that I fainted twice in one Hour Yester Night. All will do well again though—I am pretty sure it will; no Complaint being now left but extream Weakness & Lassitude; & as I am as *stout as a Lyon* they will soon be got over. The new Pamphlet is the only Thing I can read with Pleasure—it is a most delightful Book to me, so full of Sense & so ornamented with Wit—and I warrant his Majesty says the same. Mʳ Thrale tells me some passages were expunged by desire of the Courtiers— I think he had it from Strachan.

I have seen Baretti but once since I saw you, & that only for three hours. Queeney is glad of her Holydays, & jumps incessantly now she has done being sick.

How prodigiously good you are! and how respectfully polite is Doctor Wetherell! what can be the reason that your Letters come safely hither, & mine cannot find their way to Oxford? Adieu! I will send a Letter by Carter & see if that will go. ever most faithfully Yours—H: L: Thrale.

384.1b. Southwark. Tu. 7 Mar. '75. From Mrs. Thrale to J at Oxford.

R 539.37—

My Dear Sir   Southwark 7: March 1775

I think this Letter will go safe whatever has become of the others. I am sadly mortify'd to think you have been uneasy about my writing so seldom— this is my fourth or fifth I know not which. Mʳ Carter will tell you if he can

speak between Veneration & Gratitude—how I do, & how much I feel myself
obliged by your wonderful kindness to him. I put 3 Guineas to your two
which I advanced as you desired, & do put Words in the Man's Mouth as well
as Money in his Purse, for he is cruelly deficient in Oratory, partly from
Astonishment at the Pains we take for him and partly from Fear that something must befall to allay his Happiness. I have been ill and still look so
dismally that I suppose he has settled it that I am to die, but I intend no such
matter but am nursing myself up as fast as I can.

He goes down tomorrow but without his Horses, they can be fetched when
Preliminaries are fixed; I am glad there was no need to abate the Price,
Poor Fellow! how full his Heart is! of Gratitude, Hope, Expectation &
Apprehension. How astonishingly kind to him you are! & how strange it is
that you should daily & hourly make even him love honour & esteem you
more & more!

The Letters by the Post must come to you *sometime*; to them I refer you
for Chat. I am ever

Dear Sir Your most Obliged and Faithful Servant H: L: Thrale.

I cannot think how your Letters come safe & mine miscarry so, it never was
so before. Saturday you will come home.

384.2. Oxford. W. 8 Mar. ⟨'75⟩. Mrs. Thrale (Southwark).

Address: To Henry Thrale Esq. in Southwark. *Postmarks*: OXFORD *and*
—MR.
Adam.—

Dear Madam

Yesterday (March 7) I received from you two letters,[1] of
March 1. and March 4. Such is the fidelity of somebody. I
wondered why you forgot me, and did not know but you
were angry.

I hope Mr Carter is coming. Dr Wetherel is busy thinking
on a place for him, and Mr Scot thinks he can secure him six
Scholars to begin with, and says, that rather than the Scheme
shall miscarry he will ride himself. I really hope it will do.

If he comes tonight, I will take him to the Vicechancellor
to morrow, and perhaps to some other of the heads. I shall
then have done that for which I came, and hope to get into
the tower on friday night.

Poor Boy, what a dreadful death. I hope you will let none
of your children go alone into that danger, nor go yourself.

Queeny perhaps is a little lovesick, you will see how she
recovers when I come home.

384.2.—1. For the delay of HLT's letter 379*a* of 1 Mar. (that of 4 Mar. is lost)
the Post Office was to blame; it bears the L'n postmark 2 MR.

I think Evans to blame in despairing of young Carter, he should persist in his medicines, he can but dye, and young people will recover from great weakness.

Mr Cadel says that he has yet so many of Mr Baretti's book[2] unsold, that he is not ready for a new edition, but, will, I suppose, be willing to treat when he has occasion to reprint.

I am Madam Your most obedient servant

March 8.   Sam: Johnson

384.3. Th. 23 Mar. '75. Edmund Hector (Birmingham).
Address: To Mr Hector at Birmingham. *Postmark* 23 MR. Franked by Thrale.
A. Houghton.—

Dear Sir

I omitted to return you thanks for your kind present of china, because I knew that Mrs Thrale[1] would make her own acknowledgments.

I shall think it a favour if you will take opportunity of applying to the Rector of *Kingsnorton* a parish not far from Birmingham, for the dates of the Christenings of the several children of Cornelius Ford, who formerly lived at the *Haunch* in his parish. Of those Children the eldest was Joseph born, I believe, about 1660, and the youngest Nathanael, in all they were eight. My original curiosity is after Sarah, who was my Mother.

I have lately written a pamflet concerning our American disputes, which I will take care to transmit to you.

Be pleased to make my compliments to dear Mrs Careless.

I am, Sir, Your affectionate humble Servant

March 23. 1775   Sam: Johnson

384.4. Th. 23 Mar. '75. John Taylor (Ashbourne).
Address: To The Rev: Dr Taylor Ashbourne Derbys. *Postmark*: 23 MR. Franked by Thrale.
Amos Ettinger.—

Dear Sir

I am told that your month of residence is April, and that

384.2.—2. Not his *Easy Phraseology*, 1775, which was not yet published (Campbell's Diary ed. J. L. Clifford 1947, 61). Perhaps his *Introduction to the most useful European Languages*, published by Cadell and Davies 1772.
384.3.—1. See 376.1.

you are making so⟨me⟩ attempt to defer it, till a further time
in Summer. I cannot judge of your convenience, but considering my own, I wish you to be here in April, because, I
think, I can very commodiously accompany you to Derbyshire in May, and the following months will not suit me
so well.

I am again gotten into politicks, and have written a
pamflet in answer to the American Congress. I shall send
it you.

I am, Sir, Yours &c.

March 23. 1775 Sam: Johnson

385. F. 7 Apr. '75. Thomas Fothergill (Oxford).

Not traced.—Boswell 1791, i. 470, from F's copy communicated to
B. by Warton (Hill ii. 333) and now Isham. Hill by an oversight
interpreted the date as if 'Kal. Apr.' and so misnumbered the letter.

Viro Reverendo Thomae Fothergill, S.T.P. Universitatis
Oxoniensis Vice-Cancellario.

S.P.D.

Sam. Johnson.

Multis non est opus, ut testimonium quo, te praeside,
Oxonienses nomen meum posteris commendârunt, quali
animo acceperim compertum faciam. Nemo sibi placens non
laetatur; nemo sibi non placet, qui vobis, literarum arbitris,

385.—For Lord North's letter to the University see *L* ii. 331. It grounds the
recommendation on 'the many learned labours which have since that time' ('55,
when the University made J an M.A.) 'employed the attention and displayed the
abilities of that great man', and makes no reference to J's recent political activities.
The Latin diploma (found at Malahide, and in 1938 generously given to the Bodleian
by Col. Isham) is in similar terms, with a special mention of the Dictionary. On the
general question of the relation of J's political writings to his pension see *L* i. 373,
ii. 317.

I attempt a translation: 'I need not use many words to tell you how I receive the
commendation with which the University over which you preside has transmitted my
name to posterity. Every man is glad to think well of himself; and that man must
think well of himself, of whom you, the arbiters of letters, can think well. But the
good you have done me has one drawback: henceforth any fault of mine, of commission or omission, will hurt your reputation; I must always fear that what is a
signal honour to me may one day bring discredit upon you.' My translation does
less than justice to the original. J wrote Latin almost as readily as English; some of
his best verse is in Latin. It is unfortunate that we have but little of his Latin prose,
which has some of the virtues of his English style and, from the nature of the language,
is more compact. But it is, of course, largely imitative, and so less individual than his
vernacular.

placere potuit. Hoc tamen habet incommodi tantum bene-
ficium, quod mihi nunquam posthàc sine vestrae famae
detrimento vel labi liceat vel cessare; semperque sit timen-
dum, ne quod mihi tam eximiae laudi est, vobis aliquando
fiat opprobrio. Vale.

7. Id. Apr. 1775.

385.1. Southwark. Th. 30 Mar. '75. Benjamin Wheeler
(Oxford).

A. H. Hallam Murray.—

Sir

I beg leave to lay before you an inscription which the
Editor perceives too late, to have been negligently or unskilfully copied. I have made myself so little acquainted
with the lapidary language that I am not willing to venture
upon it, nor believe myself able to set it right. If any
Gentleman used to read inscriptions will try his skill upon
it, he will do a favour to the authour of the travels, whom I
do[t] not know, to the Bookseller who has applied to me,
and to, Sir, Your most humble Servant

Sam: Johnson.

At Mr Thrale's in Southwa⟨r⟩k
March 30. 1775.

386. Sa. 1 Apr. '75. Mrs. Thrale.

Adam.—1788, No. 99.

Madam

I had mistaken the day on which I was to dine with Mr
Bruce,[1] and hear of Abissinia, and therefore am to dine this
day with Mr Hamilton.

The news from Oxford is that no tennis court can be hired
at any price, and that the Vicechancellor[2] will not write to
the Clarendon Trustees without some previous intimation

385.1.—See 387.3.

386.—1. The phrase 'dine with' does not imply that Bruce was the host. It appears
from *L* ii. 333 that it was on this day, 1 April, that J was 'in the company of a gentleman whose extraordinary travels had been much the subject of conversation'. JB
does not mention Hamilton.

2. Fothergill, 'un esprit foible', as J writes in 419.

that his request will not be unacceptable. We must therefore find some way of applying to Lord Mansfield, who with
the Archbishop of York, and the Bishop of Chester holds the
trust. Thus we are thrown to a vexatious distance. poor
Carter! do not tell him.

The other Oxford news is, that they have sent me a degree
of Doctor of Laws, with such praises in the diploma, as, perhaps, ought to make me ashamed; they are very like your
praises. I wonder whether I shall ever show them to you.

Boswel[3] will be with you. Please to ask Murphy the way
to Lord Mansfield. Dr Wetherel[4] who is now here and will
be here for some days is very desirous of seeing the Brewhouse. I hope Mr Thrale will send him an invitation. He
does what he can for Carter.

Today I dine with Hamilton, tomorrow with Hoole, on
Monday with Paradise, on tuesday with Master and Mistress,
on Wednesday with Dilly, but come back to the tower.[5]

Sic nunquam rediturus labitur annus.[6]

I am Madam Your most humble servant

Apr. 1. 1775   Sam: Johnson

Poor Mrs Williams is very bad, worse than I ever saw her.

386a. Southwark. Sa. 1 Apr. '75. From Mrs. Thrale.

Address: Doctor Sam: Johnson Fleet Street.

R 539.39—

Dear Sir   Southwark 1: April 1775.

I thank you for your Letter and shall expect you on Tuesday: I am sad sick
to day which vexes me because we have Company, & I would have been glad
to have been agreable: but my well Days are partly over I am afraid for some
Time to come. I rejoyce in your being made Doctor in due Form, and next
to praising you myself I love to hear others praise you. Mr Thrale heard me
read the Passage in your Letter about Wetherell and I suppose will *do* right,
he will *say* nothing. Poor Mrs Williams's Illness makes me quite sorry, I send

386.—3. J and JB dined with the Thrales on 8 Apr. (*L* ii. 349).

4. On 20 Apr. Thomas Campbell 'Dined at Thrale's with Dr. Johnson Barretti &
a Dean Wetherell of Oxford; who is solliciting for a riding house at Oxford' (*Diary*,
ed. Clifford 1947, 83).

5. 'The Tower was a separate room at Streatham, where Dr. Johnson slept'
HLP (1788). This, as Baretti remarked in a note quoted by Hill, was a slip; in a note
quoted by Clifford, 68, she writes that J 'became something like a regular Inmate
of the House at Southwark, where Mr. Thrale fitted him up an Apartment over the
Counting House Two Pair of Stairs high—& called it the *Round Tower*'.

6. Not traced, and possibly not a quotation.

her a separate Card. I looked for a Girl at our School today but there was
none fit for me it seems, but a blind one, and I don't want a blind Maid of all
Things. Carter is a most ill-starred Fellow: if Murphy comes I will consult
him to be sure, but it is ten to one he will not come.

Laura is so troublesome & insolent that I know not what we shall do with
her. I have been afraid to tell her Father how foolishly She behaves.

Adieu till Tuesday Dinner Time; I will be better that Day if I can. I
will be always

Sir Your Faithful and Obedient Servant H: L: Thrale.

386.1. M. 3 Apr. '75. Mrs. Thrale.

Address: To Mrs Thrale.
Newton.—

Madam

I have this morning received an invitation to dine to
morrow with Mrs Montagu, and am to dine on Thursday
at Davis's. I wish Mr Thrale would invite Dr Wetherel for
Friday, but you must have something not flesh.[1]

So I am taken hold of; I would come home at night but
you will not let me. I intend not to forget Mr Carter. You
must give Laura[2] a good scolding before her Mistress; if she
is turned out of the school, I am afraid she is ruined.

While I sit at this paper I have a summons to dine with the
Club on Friday, which I shall be expected to obey.

If Dr Wetherel were with you to morrow, I could come in
the afternoon. He lodges with Perrot and Hodgson over the
Crown office Temple. I⟨f⟩ you send me an invitation to
bring him some morning it will do. Thursday Morning
will fit.

I am, Dearest of all dear Ladies, Your servant and slave,
and admirer, and honourer,

Apr. 3. 1775.   Sam: Johnson

387. Sa. 8 Apr. '75. John Taylor (Ashbourne).

Address: To the Revd Dr Taylor at Ashborne Derbys—. Franked
by Thrale. *Postmark* 8 AP.
Loyd.—*NQ* 6 S. v. 422.

Dear Sir

When shall I come down to you? I believe I can get away

386.1.—1. Wetherell as J's friend may be probably assumed a high churchman. I
am told that fasting was not infrequently practised by devout Anglicans.

2. Carter; her Mistress was Mrs. Cummins.

pretty early in May, if you have any mind of me; If you have none, I can move in some other direction. So tell me what I shall do.

I have placed young Davenport in the greatest printing house in London,[1] and hear no complaint of him but want of size, which will not hinder him much. He may when he is a journeyman always get a guinea a week.

The patriots pelt me with answers. Four pamflets[2] I think, already, besides newspapers and reviews, have been discharged against me. I have tried to read two of them, but did not go through them.

Now and then I call on Congreve, though I have little or no reason to think that he wants[3] or wishes to see me. I sometimes dispute with him, but I think he has not studied. He has really ill health, and seems to have given way to that indulgence which sickness is always in too much haste to claim. He confesses a bottle aday.

I am Sir Your humble Servant

April 8. 1775 Sam: Johnson

387.1. Sa. 8 Apr. '75. ⟨Edward Bentham⟩.

Adam.—

Sir

It might perhaps have the appearance of romantick ambition to say, that I regret that want of opposition which made your benevolent eloquence unnecessary, but at least I may

---

387.—1. Strahan's.

2. For replies to *Taxation No Tyranny* see Courtney.

3. I suppose J means 'lacks anything that I can give him'. The starkest insensibility could not make J wholly indifferent to an old acquaintance.

387.1.—The letter is endorsed 'Dr. S. Johnson Apr. 8 75 To Dr. Bentham, T.B.'. The phrase 'rumour of opposition' suggests that someone—perhaps some vile Whig— had threatened to oppose J's degree in Convocation. Bentham was the author of a pamphlet *De Tumultibus Americanorum . . . Senilis Meditatio*, published in '76. But the reference can hardly be to *Taxation No Tyranny*, which had no 'want of opposition'. Bentham in this pamphlet records that 'Oxoniensis Academia die Oct. 26 (i.e. '75) Literas solennes ad Dnum Regem mittendas decrevit, narrantes, Quid sentirent de Tumultibus Americanis, . . . Tres tantùm Dissenserunt'. J had perhaps heard a 'rumour' of this. He had doubtless read the pamphlet. JB records 22 Mar. '76 that 'I had read yesterday in the Chaise' (driving with J to B'm) Bentham's *De Motibus Americanis*'. BP xi. 182.

⟨be⟩ allowed to rejoice at the rumour of opposition which has produced from a Mind like yours, such a testimony in my favour. Having so much of your approbation I hope to be admitted to your friendship, and shall applaud myself, if the opinion of my merit which my writings have impressed upon such a judge, is not impaired by more familiar knowledge.

I am, Sir, Your most obliged and most humble servant

April 8. 1775   Sam: Johnson

387.2. Th. 13 Apr. '75. John Taylor (Ashbourne).

Address: To the Reverend Dr. Taylor in Ashbourne Derbyshire.
Postmark: 13 AP.
Adam.—

Dear Sir

Your letter did not miscarry. When your enquiry came I consulted Mr Thrale, who told me, that less than two hundred guineas would not buy a Governours staff.[1] Mrs Thrale who is more copious, informed me, that you might for a hundred pounds be made a kind of half governour, with so many limitations and restrictions that there would ⟨be⟩ no advantage in it. I then let it out of my head. You may probably do more good with two hundred pounds in other ways.

I hope to pass some time with you in Derbyshire early in the summer. We will concert the visit, if we can, so as to accommodate us both.

How is your health? I have had of late very bad nights, and have taken physick three days together in hope of better.

I hope poor Davenport will do. His temper is well spoken of, and I have recommended him as far as I well can. He is now launched into the world, and is to subsist henceforward by his own powers. The transition from the protection of others to our own conduct is a very awful point of human existence.

I am, Sir, Your most humble servant

Apr. 13. 1775   Sam: Johnson

387.2.—1. I have not found the institution that JT aspired to govern.

387.3. Sa. 15 Apr. '75. Benjamin Wheeler (Oxford).

Address: The Revd Dr Wheeler Magdalen College Oxford. Franked by Strahan. *Postmark*: 15 AP.
A. H. Hallam Murray.—

Dear Sir

The Bookseller has just now brought me the transcript of the Stone at Genoa. I hope that between this paper and Gruter you will be able to adjust the reading. You will forgive this trouble. I know not where to find Gruter in London, if we knew how to make use of him, and perhaps we could not use him if we had him.

Be pleased to return the papers, when you have finished them, to Mr Dilly Bookseller in the Poultry.

I am, Sir, Your most humble Servant
Apr. 15. 1775.   Sam: Johnson.

388. M. 17 Apr. '75. Bennet Langton.

Fettercairn.—Boswell 1793, ii. 632 (Hill ii. 361).

Dear Sir

I have enquired more minutely about the medicine for the rheumatism which I am sorry to hear that you still want. The receipt is this

Take equal quantities of flour of sulphur, and *flour* of mustardseed, make them an electary with honey or treacle; and take a bolus as big as a nutmeg several times a day, as you can bear it, drinking after it a quarter of a pint of the infusion of the root of Lovage.

Lovage,[1] in Ray's *Nomenclature*, is Levisticum, perhaps the Botanists may know the Latin name.

Of this medicine I pretend not to judge. There is all the appearance of its efficacy, which a single instance can afford.

387.3.—See 385.1. The book was presumably published; but though we know the publisher, and the source of the faulty inscription, I have not succeeded in identifying either book or inscription. Prof. Last, who 'bends a keener eye on vacancy', very kindly tells me that the inscription was probably the 'Sententia Minuciorum'; but even with his help I find no trace of its publication in England at or near this date.

388.—1. The point is not clear to me; having given a Latin name, why should J add 'perhaps, etc.'? Does he mean that a botanist might be more familiar with the herb by its scientific than by its vernacular name? The late Latin *levisticum* is thought to be a corruption of *ligusticum*; Linnaeus used both words, to designate distinct genera.

The patient was very old, the pain very violent, and the relief, I think, speedy and lasting.

My opinion of alterative medicines is not high, but quid tentâsse nocebit ?[2] if it does harm, or does no good, it may be omitted, but that it may do good, you have I hope, reason to think is desired by,

Sir, your most affectionate humble Servant,

Apr. 17. 1775　　　　　　　　　　　　　Sam: Johnson.

389. Sa. 6 May '75. Macleod of Raasay.

Address (Boswell): To the Laird of Raasay.
Not traced.—Boswell, *Hebrides* 1785, 519 (Hill v. 412).

Dear Sir,

Mr. Boswell has this day shewn me a letter, in which you complain of a passage in 'the Journey to the Hebrides'. My meaning is mistaken. I did not intend to say that you had personally made any cession of the rights of your house, or any acknowledgement of the superiority of M'Leod of Dunvegan. I only designed to express what I thought generally admitted,—that the house of Rasay allowed the superiority of the house of Dunvegan. Even this I now find to be erroneous, and will therefore omit or retract it in the next edition.

Though what I said had been true, if it had been disagreeable to you, I should have wished it unsaid; for it is not my business to adjust precedence. As it is mistaken, I find myself disposed to correct it, both by my respect for you, and my reverence for truth.

As I know not when the book will be reprinted, I have desired Mr. Boswell to anticipate the correction in the Edinburgh papers. That is all that can be done.

I hope I may now venture to desire that my compliments may be made, and my gratitude expressed, to Lady Rasay, Mr. Malcolm M'Leod, Mr. Donald M'Queen, and all the gentlemen and all the ladies whom I saw in the island of Rasay; a place which I remember with too much pleasure

388.—2. Ovid, *Metam.* i. 397: 'it can do no harm to try.'

389.—For the offending passage see *Journey* (1924, 53); for the correspondence between Raasay and JB, *L* v. 410. The correction was made in the edition of 1785, not in the text but in a publisher's note, in which the newspaper advertisement is quoted.

and too much kindness, not to be sorry that my ignorance, or hasty persuasion, should, for a single moment, have violated its tranquillity.

I beg you all to forgive an undesigned and involuntary injury, and to consider me as,

Sir, your most obliged, and most humble servant,
London, May 6, 1775.   Sam: Johnson.

389.1. Sa. 6 May '75. Henry Thrale.

Sotheby 30 Jan. 1918 (not seen).—Described in catalogue as 'asking for news of Mrs. Thrale's health'.

389.2. Tu. 9 May '75. Mrs. Thrale.

Adam.—

Dearest Lady

When I sent last week to enquire after you, Mr Thrale sent me word that he had a testimonial of your health, *written by Madam's own hand*. I hope you are by this time, strong enough to give me the same pleasure, for next to Mr. Thrale and the young ones, your doing well is of most importance to,

Madam, Your most obliged and most humble servant
May 9. 1775   Sam: Johnson

390. F. 12 May '75. Mrs. Thrale.

Clifton College.—1788, No. 100.

And so, my dearest Mistress, you lie a bed hatching suspicions. I did not mean to reproach you, nor meant anything but respect and impatience to know how you did.

I wish I could say or send any thing to divert you, but I have done nothing and seen nothing. I dined one day with Paoli, and yesterday with Mrs Southwels,[1] and called on Congreve. Mr Twiss hearing that you talked of despoiling

---

390.—1. Hill thought this a misprint for 'Southwell'. See Index II for the family. I do not understand 'Mrs'; but 'Miss Southwells' would be normal for the modern 'the Misses Southwell'. J and others write 'Miss Colliers' for the two spinsters Collier. 'Mrs Southwels' might, alternatively, be the elder of the two sisters, who was old enough to be 'Mrs.' by courtesy.

his book of the fine print,[2] has sent you a copy to frame.
He is going to Ireland, and I have given him letters to Dr
Leland, and Mr Falkner.

Mr. Montague is so ill that the Lady is not visible but
yesterday I had I know not how much kiss of Mrs. Abington,
and very good looks from Miss Jefferies[3] the maid of Honour.

Boswell has made me promise not to go to Oxford till he
leaves London; I had no great reason for haste, and therefore
might as well gratify a friend. I am always proud and pleased
to have my company desired. Boswell would have thought
my absence a loss, and I know not who else would have considered my presence as profit. He has entered himself at the
Temple, and I joined in his bond.[4] He is to plead before the
Lords, and hopes very nearly to gain the cost of his journey.
He lives much with his friend Paoli who says a man must see
Wales to enjoy England.

I forgot till now to send Mrs Gardiner's card. She is got
out of her chamber, and has been once in the air, Dr Lawrence
says she has been very bad. Mrs Williams's pimples continue to come out and go in.[5]

The book which is now most read, but which as far as ⟨I⟩
have gone, is but dull, is Gray's letters[6] prefixed by Mason
to his poems. I have borrowed mine, and therefore cannot
lend it, and I can hardly recommend the purchase.

I have offended, and, what is stranger, have justly offended

390.—2. Richard Twiss's *Travels through Portugal and Spain* (1775, quarto) is embel-
lished with several copperplates; but this 'fine print' is doubtless that of 'the Madonna,
or our Lady of the Fish, in the Escorial', which bears the signatures 'Rafaele pinxit.
G.P. Cypriani delin. F. Bartolozzi sculp.' and a note that it cost ninety guineas.

3. Thomas Campbell reported in his diary (ed. Clifford 1947, 76) for 8 Apr. that
J 'had supped the night before with . . . Miss Jeffrys one of the maids of honour . . .
&c at M^rs. Abbingtons'.

4. Hill gives a copy of the bonds on admission and on call; the 'securities' were
Johnson and Malone.

5. 'I forgot . . . go in' om. 1788.

6. For J's opinion of this book see his *Life of Gray*, in which he praises Gray's
accounts of his various travels; *L* iii. 31, where he declares the book 'mighty dull; and,
as to the style, it is fit for the second table'; and JB's letter to Temple 10 May '75.
Though the book is called *Memoirs*, it consists mainly of letters by and to Gray;
there is not much of Mason except footnotes. It is, however, possible that J's condemnation of the 'style', which surprised JB, was aimed at Mason. But see *L* iii. 31,
where Hill quotes Mackintosh's view that Gray, like Walpole, modelled himself on
Mme de Sévigné, and in consequence had 'the double stiffness of an imitator, and
of a college recluse'.

the Nation of Rasay. If they could come hither, they would
be as fierce as the Americans. Rasay has written to Boswel
an account of the injury done him, by representing his
House as subordinate to that of Dunvegan. Boswel has his
letter and, I believe, copied my answer. I have appeased
him, if a degraded Chief can possibly be appeased, but it
will be thirteen days, days of resentment and discontent,
before my recantation can reach him. Many a dirk will
imagination, during that interval fix in my heart. I really
question if at this time my life would not be in danger, if
distance did not secure it.

Boswel[7] will find his way to Streatham before he goes, and
will detail this great affair. I would have come on Saturday,
but that I am engaged to do Dr. Lawrence a little service on
Sunday. Which day shall I come next week. I hope you will
be well enough to see me often.

I am, dearest Madam, Your most humble servant
May 12. 1775.   Sam: Johnson

391, 392. May '75. Thomas Leland, George Faulkner.
Not traced; the letters mentioned in 390.

393. Sa. 20 May '75. Mrs. Thrale.
Adam.—1788, No. 101.

Dear Madam

I will try not to be sullen,[1] and yet when I leave you how
shall I help it. Bos goes away on Monday [to morrow *erased*],
I go in a day or two after him, and will try to be well and to
be as you would have me. But I hope that when I come back
you will teach me the value of liberty.

Nurse tells me that you are all well, and she hopes all
growing better. Ralph[2] like other young Gentlemen will
travel for improvement.

390.—7. JB wrote to Temple Wed. 17 May: 'I am now at Mr. Thrale's villa at
Streatham—a delightful spot. Dr. Johnson is here too. I came yesterday to dinner,
and this morning Dr. Johnson and I return to London.'

391, 392.—For the treatment of lost letters see Introduction.

393.—1. See 393*a*.
  2. Ralph 'had been sent with a nurse to Brighton to try sea bathing' (C 126).

I have sent you six Guineas and an half. so you may laugh at neglect and parcimony.[3] It is a fine thing to have money. Peyton and Macbean are both starving, and I cannot keep them.

Must we mourn for the Queen of Denmark? How shall I do for my black cloaths which you have in the chest?

Make my compliments to every body.

I am, Madam, Your most humble servant

May 20. 1775   Sam: Johnson

I dined in a large company at a Dissenting Booksellers yesterday, and disputed against toleration, with one Doctor Meyer.[4]

393a. Streatham. Sa. 20 May ⟨'75⟩. From Mrs. Thrale.

Address: To Doctor Samuel Johnson Johnson's Court Fleet Street. *Postmark*: illegible.

R 539.40—

Dear Sir   Streatham Sat: 20: May.

Our friends Journal has half blinded me, yet I must write two Lines to wish you a good Journey: I am sure I wish you a safe return, but do not set out sullen when there is nothing to be sullen about. I could pout myself for a Penny to see my Master never come near me but on those Days that he would come if I had never been born—Saturday Sunday & Monday, & to see him delight in keeping me distressed for the Sight of him, wch now I am confined he knows I cannot get at: but I think 'tis better sing the French Song

> Mon Mari est a Paris,
> Et moi je suis a Nantes;
> Il m'a laissé sans Argent
> Et pour mon Contentement
> Je chante, Je chante, Je chante.

À propos please to pay your Debts before we part as Fordyce said in the Storm. There is 27ˢ due for Plates, and an Epitaph for that Dear Lady

393 —3. 'parcimony' is explained by 393a; I do not understand 'neglect'; his neglect of the epitaph he had not yet remedied.

4. So 1788 and, as appears, the MS. Malone in his copy corrects to 'Mayo'; and no doubt J intended Mayo. This sentence, printed in 1788 as a postscript to 393, is on a separate piece of paper pasted to the rest; there is therefore no difficulty in identifying this dinner with that at Dilly's on 7 May '73, described in *L* ii. 252. There is no other trace of a letter of 8 May '73, and I have no guess at HLP's motive for this piece of falsification, if such it be.

'The only foundation for toleration is a degree of scepticism; and without it there can be none. For if a man believes in the saving of souls, he must soon think about the means.' Fox, in Rogers's *Recollections* 1859, 49.

whose Remembrance gives me more delight than many a pretended Lover feels from that of his Mistress. Adieu and forget not

Your faithful Servant H: L: Thrale.

I shall write to you at Oxford & expect an account of poor Carter's hopes Fears &c.

394. Su. 21 May '75. Bennet Langton.

Fettercairn.—Boswell 1793, ii. 633 (Hill ii. 379).

Dear Sir

I have an old Amanuensis[1] in great distress. I have given what I think I can give, and begged till I cannot tell where to beg again. I put into his hands this morning four guineas. If you could collect three guineas more, it would clear him from his present difficulty.

I am, Sir, Your most humble Servant,

May 21. 1775   Sam: Johnson.

395. M. 22 May '75. Mrs. Thrale.

Address: To Mrs. Thrale.
Adam.—1788, No. 102.

Dearest Lady

One thing or other still hinders me, besides what is perhaps the greatest hindrance, that I have no great mind to go. Boswel went away at two this morning. Langton, I suppose, goes this week. Boswel got two and forty guineas in fees while he was here. He has, by his Wife's persuasion and mine, taken down a present for his Mother in law.

Pray let me know how the breath does. I hope there is no lasting evil to be feared. Take great care of your self. Why did you take cold? Did you pump[1] into your shoes?

I am not sorry that you read Boswel's journal.[2] Is it not

394.—1. Whether Macbean or Peyton (see 393) I do not know.

395.—1. 'A trick I used to scold him for doing' HLP.

2. HLP was here in two minds: she erased the words 'Boswel's journal', but thought better of it and wrote 'Boswel's journal' over the erasure. In 393*a* HLT had written: 'Our friends Journal has half blinded me.' The original MS., like all JB's finished journals, was very legible (Pottle and Bennett, xi); but it contained some 675 pages. See 415.

a merry piece? There is much in it about poor me. Miss, I hear, touches me sometimes in *her* memoirs.

I shall try at Oxford what can be done for Mr Carter; what can be done for his daughter[3] it is not easy to tell. Does her mother know her own distress, or is she out of her wits with pride, or does Betsy[4] a little exaggerate? It is strange behaviour.

The mourning it seems, is general. I must desire that you will let somebody take my best black cloaths out of the chest, and send them. There is nothing in the chest but what may be tumbled. The key is the newest of those two that have the wards channelled. When they are at the borough,[5] my man can fetch them.

But all this while, dear and dear Lady, take great care of yourself.

Do not buy Chandler's travels, they are duller than Twiss's. Wraxal is too fond of words, but you may read him. I shall take care that Adair's account of America may be sent you for I shall have it of my own.[6]

Beattie has called once to see me. He lives grand at the Archbishop's.[7]

Dear Lady do not be careless, nor heedless, nor rash, nor giddy. But take care of your health,

I am, Dearest Madam, Your most humble servant

May 22. 1775   Sam: Johnson

Dr Talbot,[8] which, I think I never told you, has given five hundred pounds to the future infirmary.

395.—3. Laura. The story is not in any extant letter from HLT, but is told at length in *Th* 118.

4. Cummins.

5. HLT was to send them from S'm to S'k, where Frank would collect them.

6. Because Adair's *History of the American Indians* was published ('75) by J's friends the Dillys.

7. Beattie was the guest not of the Archbishop but of his 'friend, Dr. Porteus, at Lambeth'. Forbes's *Life of Beattie*. Dr. Claude Jenkins writes: 'Porteus was chaplain as well as rector and during the time of "waiting" would be probably in the house at Lambeth rather than his rectory next door. Beattie might quite well have had a room in either, and in any case would share the hospitality of the Great Hall, like Porteus himself as chaplain.'

8. For J's interest in the projected infirmary at Hereford see E. L. McAdam and A. T. Hazen in *Huntington Library Quarterly* Apr. 1940. It is possible that J was enlisted in the scheme by Wetherell, who had become Dean of Hereford in '71.

396. W. 24 May '75. Mrs. Thrale.

Adam; known to Hill only from an auction catalogue.—

Dear Madam

I am not gone, nor can well go till I have my black cloaths, sending them after me will load me with two suits,[1] and I have no large box. I write this at random, for I hope Frank will find them at the borough.

You were a naughty thing for taking cold but you have suffered for it, and I hope will take warning. How strange it is that I am not gone. Yet one thing or another has hindered me and perhaps, if we knew ourselves, I am not heartily in haste. I had yesterday a kind of fainting fit, but it is gone and over.

For Mr Carter I will try to do something, but time and opportunity must tell what, for I am sure, I do not know.

Do, send the cloaths if you send them in a wheelbarrow. There are two suits let me have the best.

I am, Dearest of all dear Ladies, Your most humble servant
May 24. 1775   Sam: Johnson

397. Th. 25 May '75. Mrs. Thrale.

J. E. Brown (mutilated).—1788, No. 103.

Dearest Lady

The fit was a sudden faintness such as I have had I know not how often; no harm came of it, and all is well. I cannot go till Saturday, and then go I will, if I can. My Cloaths Mr. Thrale says must be made like other peoples, and they are gone to the Taylor. If I do not go, you know, how shall I come back again?

I told you, I fancy, yesterday, that I was well,[1] but I thought so little of the disorder, that I know not whether I said any⟨thing⟩ about it. . . .

I am Madam Your most humble Servant
May 25. 1775   Sam: Johnson

396.—1. This suggests that J intended a two months' stay in the country without a change of clothes.

397.—Strips have been cut from the top and bottom of the leaf, which is reduced by nearly a half. A passage is therefore lost which was on the bottom of the first page and the top of the second; of the second only the conclusion survives.

1. J seems to have omitted a negative, as often happens.

397.1. F. 26 May '75. Mrs. Thrale.

Sotheby 5 May 1930.—

Dearest Lady

I have taken the place for Monday. I could not get one for any day sooner. My cloaths came home last night but I could not depend upon them,[1] and therefore could not go to day, and for the two next days the coach is full.

I see no harm in the bark, but as your disorder is now mere weakness, I believe Meat and Drink, and Air, and Quiet will do all that is wanted. And then, *throw physick to the dogs.*

Will Sir Joseph[2] succeed this time? I am a little afraid, though his success can have very little effect.

Well then.—On Monday, I fancy I shall go, and I fancy I shall not wish to stay longer away, for I shall always think on Master and Mistress, and all the rest.

I am Madam, your most humble servant[3]
May 26. 1775.

398. Sa. 27 May '75. James Boswell (Edinburgh).

Not traced.—Boswell 1791, i. 495 (Hill ii. 379).

Dear Sir,

I make no doubt but you are now safely lodged in your own habitation, and have told all your adventures to Mrs. Boswell and Miss Veronica. Pray teach Veronica to love me. Bid her not mind mamma.

Mrs. Thrale has taken cold, and been very much disordered, but I hope is grown well. Mr. Langton went yesterday to Lincolnshire, and has invited Nicolaida to follow him. Beauclerk talks of going to Bath. I am to set out on Monday; so there is nothing but dispersion.

I have returned Lord Hailes's entertaining sheets, but must stay till I come back for more, because it will be inconvenient to send them after me in my vagrant state.

I promised Mrs. Macaulay[1] that I would try to serve her son at Oxford. I have not forgotten it, nor am unwilling to

397.1.—1. Until he had tried them on and approved the alterations? But see Addenda, p. 528.

2. Mawbey. See 407.

3. The signature has been cut away.

398.—1. See *L* v. 122, 505.

could give me some information about him, for the life which we have is very scanty, I should be glad.

I am, dear Sir, Your most affectionate humble servant,

May 3, 1777   Sam: Johnson

516. Sa. 3 May '77. John Taylor (Ashbourne).

Address: To the Reverend Dr Taylor in Ashbourne Derbyshire.
Postmark: 3 MA.
Morgan.—Hill 1892.

Dear Sir

The weather now begins to grow tempting, and brings my annual excursion into my mind. It is now an interesting question whether you intend to come hither again,[1] for if you do, I shall endeavour to accompany you back: if you let idleness prevail, and stay at home, I have my own course to take.

Mr. Lucas[2] has just been with me. He has compelled me to read his tragedy, which is but a poor performance, and yet may perhaps put money into his pocket; it contains nothing immoral or indecent, and therefore, we may very reasonably wish it success.

My nights continue to be very flatulent and restless, and my days are therefore sluggish and drowsy. After physick I have sometimes less uneasiness, as I had last night, but the effect is by no means constant; nor have I found any advantage from going to bed either with a full or an empty stomach.

Let me know what you resolve about your journey, as soon as you have taken your resolution.

I am, Sir, Your affectionate humble servant,

May. 3. 1777   Sam: Johnson.

the mere frequency of editions of *The Seasons* is enough to reject that hypothesis. I suspect that there were difficulties of copyright, or what the booksellers chose to regard as such. It is perhaps more than a coincidence that the subject of the case, Donaldson v. Becket, which in '74 had decided the vexed question of 'literary property', was a 'pirated' edition of *The Seasons*. For JB's response to J's application see *L* ii. 64, iii. 116 (his letter of 9 June), 360.

516.—1. I have no actual evidence that JT had been in L'n earlier in this year; but J had written 23 Jan.: 'I suppose you continue your purpose of residing in February' (506.2).

2. For J's revision of this play, *The Earl of Somerset*, and his disapproval of L's expression of gratitude in a Prefatory Address, see *BP* xiii. 219, *L* iii. 531, H. W. Liebert in *Papers of the Bibl. Soc. of America* xli (1947), 231. The paragraph is erased in the MS.; for JT's erasures in J's letters see Appendix D.

516a. Streatham. Sa. ⟨17 May '77⟩. From Mrs. Thrale.
R 540.63—

My Dear Sir   Streatham Sat: Night.

Tom Cotton carries your Watch, and he is a careful Creature; but I have a favour to beg: it is that you would take the Trouble to write to Dr Taylor to procure me a Ticket for the Festival at Devonshire house: his Interest cannot I think be doubted—but it must not be delayed—pray write tomorrow, & if you think a Letter from me to the D^r would be useful, say so & I'll set about instantly but write yourself at all Events—may be he could get one *two* Tickets, but if he produces only one I must beat about where I can for another. Do write however by the first Opportunity, as I really wish to see what Pleasure can do upon her Throne.

Let me have a Line from You directed either hither if you write tomorrow, or to Brighthelmstone if you favour me on Monday. Adieu! you have done a great deal more for Dodd I find that [*sic*] you did for poor R: Perreau—& so Doddy is safe.

                                        Ever most faithfully Yours H: L: Thrale.

517. M. 19 May '77. Charles O'Connor.

Not traced; copy by J. C. Walker, Isham.—Thomas Campbell, *Strictures on the . . . History of Ireland* 1790, p. 1 (extract); Boswell 1791, ii. 113 (Hill iii. 111).

Sir,

Having had the pleasure of conversing with Dr. Campbel[1] about your Character and your literary Undertaking, I am resolved to gratify myself by renewing a correspondence which began and ended a great while ago,[2] and ended, I am afraid, by my fault, a fault which, if you have not forgotten it, you must now forgive.

If I have ever disappointed you, give me leave to tell you that you have likewise disappointed me. I expected great discoveries in Irish Antiquity, and large publications in the Irish language. But the world still remains as it was, doubtful and ignorant. What the Irish Language is in itself, and to what language it has affinity are very interesting questions; which every man wishes to see resolved, that has any philological or historical curiosity. Dr. Leland begins his history too late;[3] the ages which deserve an exact enquiry are those

517.—1. See Campbell's *Diary* ed. Clifford 1947, 11, 13, for C's share in these transactions.
    2. Presumably with J's letter of '57 (107). See my note there. Was J ignorant of O'C's second work?
    3. Leland began with Henry II.

times (for⁴ such times there were) when Ireland was the school of the West, the quiet habitation of sanctity and literature. If you could give a history, though imperfect, of the Irish nation from its conversion to Christianity, to the invasion from England, you would amplify knowledge with new views and new objects. Set about it, therefore if you can, do what you can easily do, without anxious exactness. Lay the foundation, and leave the superstructure to posterity.

I am, Sir, Your most humble Servant,

May 19, 1777. Sam. Johnson

518. M. 19 May '77. Mrs. Thrale.

Adam.—1788, No. 162.

Madam

I have written to Dr Taylor, you may be sure, but the business is pretty much out of the Doctors way. His acquaintance ⟨is⟩ with the Lord Cavendishes, he barely knows the young Duke and Dutchess. He will be proud to show that he can do it, but he will hardly try, if he suspects any danger of refusal.

You will become such a Gadder, that you will not care a peny for me. However, you are wise in wishing to know what life is made of; to try what are the pleasures, which are so eagerly sought, and so dearly purchased. We must know pleasure before we can rationally despise. And it is not desirable that when you are with matronal authority talking down juvenile hopes and maiden passions, your hearers should tell you, like Miss Pitches,¹ 'You never saw a Fête'.

That you may see this show I have written because

I am, Madam, Your most humble servant

May 19. 1777 Sam: Johnson

519. M. 19 May '77. John Taylor (Ashbourne).

Loyd.—*NQ* 6 S. v. 423.

Dear Sir

I am required by Mrs Thrale to solicite you to exert your

517—4. Campbell printed 'if'. See *L* iii. 489. It can hardly be doubted that J was sure of the survival of literature in Ireland in the dark ages.
518.—1. 'Lady Pitches was haranguing about a Black Fox—"Why (says her daughter dryly) you never saw a Black Fox" ' HLP.

interest, that she may have a ticket of admission to the enter-tainment at Devonshire house. Do for her what You can.

I continue to have very troublesome and tedious nights, which I do not perceive any change of place to make better or worse. This is indeed at present my chief malady, but this is very heavy.

My thoughts were to have been in Staffordshire before now. But who does what he designs?—My purpose is still to spend part of the Summer amongst you; and of that hope I have no particular reason to fear the disappointment.

Poor Dod was sentenced last week. It is a thing almost without example for a Clergyman of his rank to stand at the bar for a capital breach of morality. I am afraid he will suffer. The Clergy seem not to be his friends. The populace that was extremely clamorous against him, begin to pity him. The time that was gained by an objection[1] which was never considered as having any force, was of great use, as it allowed the publick resentment to cool. To spare his life, and his life is all that ought to be spared, would be now rather popular than offensive. How little he thought six months ago of being what he now is.

I am Sir &c

May 19. 1777.   Sam: Johnson

519a. Brighthelmston. Su. 25 May ⟨'77⟩. From Mrs. Thrale.

Address: none (MS. mutilated). *Postmark*: 26 MA.

R 540.64—

Dear Sir   Brighthelmstone 25 May.

I am exceedingly obliged to you for your ready Assistance in getting me a Ticket for the Devonshire Fête: I find it is deferred to another Year but I have the same Thanks to pay you: I shall hope to see you at Streatham on Wednesday next fraught with a World of News—we have none here.

I am ever Most faithfully yours H: L: Thrale.

519.1. M. 2 ⟨? June '77⟩. Mrs. Thrale.

Sotheby 30 Jan. 1918 (not seen; extract in catalogue).—

I was at Mrs. Vesey's last night and so commended was my prologue[1] by five[2] Ladies—you cant think—nor I tell.

519.—1. A technical objection, on which Hill quotes the *Annual Register*.
519.1.—1. To Kelly's *A Word to the Wise*.
       2. J perhaps wrote 'fine'.

519.1a. Streatham. Tu. 3 June ⟨'77⟩. From Mrs. Thrale.
Address: Doctor Johnson Fleet Street.
R 540.65—

Dear Sir

How kind you are to be thinking of my Clothes & Queeney's! mine are a plain White Silk which I bought in Paris of a Colour peculiarly elegant—trimmed with pale Purple & Silver by the fine Madame Beauvais & in the newest & highest Fashion. My fair Daughter has no new Clothes, nor I see no Call, for we get no Tickets for the Chamberlains Box so we are to make amends by Ranelagh.

M^r & Mrs Garrick have been here, so I have heard the Eagle & the Blackbird, & a very pretty Thing it is I think: he is to get us Places for Sherridan's new Play which is a *Thing* it seems, & he is *so* civil & *so* desirous to be intimate &c. Lady Lade too is monstrous Kind & somewhat comical: She will see the School for Scandal She says—The School for Guardians has not answered. Farewell! & forget not how much & how sincerely you are beloved & respected by H: L: T.

Streatham 3: June.

519.2. W. 11 June '77. Mrs. Thrale.
Sotheby 30 Jan. 1918 (not seen; 'a list of engagements').—

519.3. Tu. 17 June '77. ⟨Edmund Allen.⟩
Newton.—Chapman, *Dr. Johnson and Dr. Dodd* 1926.

Sir

You know that my attention to Dr Dodd has incited me to enquire what is the real purpose of Government; the dreadful answer I have put into your hands.

Nothing now remains but that he whose profession it has been to teach others to dye, learn now to dye himself.

It will be wise to deny admission from this time to all who do not come to assist his preparation; to addict himself wholly to prayer and meditation, and consider himself as no longer connected with the world. He has now nothing to do for the short time that remains, but to reconcile himself to God. To this end it will be proper to abstain totally from all strong liquors, and from all other sensual indulgencies, that his thoughts may be as clear and calm as his condition can allow.

If his remissions of anguish, and intervals of devotion leave him any time, he may perhaps spend it profitably in writing

the history of his own depravation, and marking the gradual
declination from innocence and quiet, to that state in which
the law has found him. Of his advice[1] to the Clergy or admoni-
tions to Fathers of families there is no need; he will leave
behind him those who can write them. But the history of
his own mind, if not written by himself, cannot be written,
and the instruction that might be derived from it must be
lost. This therefore he must leave, if he leaves anything; but
whether he can find leisure, or obtain tranquillity sufficient
for this, I cannot judge. Let him however shut his doors
against all hope, all trifles, and all sensuality. Let him
endeavour to calm his thoughts by abstinence, and look out
for a proper director in his penitence, and may God who
would that all men should be saved, help him with his Holy
Spirit, and have mercy on him for Jesus Christ's sake.

I am Sir your most humble servant

June 17 1777   Sam: Johnson
This may be communicated to Dr Dodd.

520. F. 20 June '77. Charles Jenkinson.
Address (Boswell): To the Right Honourable Charles Jenkinson.
Not traced.—Boswell 179ɪ, ii. 138 (Hill iii. 145).

Sir,

Since the conviction and condemnation of Dr. Dodd, I
have had, by the intervention of a friend, some intercourse
with him, and I am sure I shall lose nothing in your opinion
by tenderness and commiseration. Whatever be the crime,
it is not easy to have any knowledge of the delinquent without a wish that his life may be spared, at least when no life
has been taken away by him. I will, therefore, take the
liberty of suggesting some reasons for which I wish this
unhappy being to escape the utmost rigour of his sentence.

He is, so far as I can recollect, the first clergyman of our
church who has suffered publick execution for immorality;
and I know not whether it would not be more for the interest
of religion to bury such an offender in the obscurity of perpetual exile, than to expose him in a cart, and on the gallows,
to all who for any reason are enemies to the clergy.

519.3.—1. J had perhaps been told that D planned to edify the world with moral
exhortations.

The supreme power has, in all ages, paid some attention to the voice of the people; and that voice does not least deserve to be heard, when it calls out for mercy. There is now a very general desire that Dodd's life should be spared. More is not wished; and, perhaps, this is not too much to be granted.

If you, Sir, have any opportunity of enforcing these reasons, you may, perhaps, think them worthy of consideration: but whatever you determine, I most respectfully intreat that you will be pleased to pardon for this intrusion,

Sir, Your most obedient And most humble servant,

Sam. Johnson

521. Su. 22 June '77. William Dodd.

Not traced; copy (by Edmund Allen), Newton (see Chapman, *Dr. Johnson and Dr. Dodd* 1926, 19).—Boswell 1791, ii. 138 (Hill iii. 145).

Sir,

I must seriously enjoin you not to let it be at all known that I have written this Letter,[1] and to return the Copy[2] to Mr. Allen in a Cover to me. I hope, I need not tell you that I wish it Success.—But do not indulge Hope.—Tell nobody.

521.1. Su. 22 June '77. Edmund Allen.

Address: To Mr. Allen in Bolt Court Fleetstreet.

Newton.—Chapman, *Dr. Johnson and Dr. Dodd* 1926.

Dear Sir

There was mention made of sending Dr Dod's sermon to the great Officers of State. I opposed it, but have now altered my Mind. Nothing can do harm, let every thing therefore be tried. Let Mr Jenkinson have his letter wherever he be. Let the Sermon be sent to every Body, and to the King if it can be done. He is, I believe more likely to read it, and to regard it than his Ministers. Let Lord Dartmouth have it, and Lord North.

I am Sir your humble servant

June 22. 1777   Sam: Johnson

521.—1. Dodd's letter to the King, composed by J and printed *L* iii. 144.

2. It is unlike J to keep copies of letters. But throughout this transaction he took unusual precautions. He perhaps wrote or intended 'by Mr. Allen'; that is, Allen as J's messenger was to bring back the copy of the Letter to the King in a cover directed to J.

522. Tu. 24 June '77. James Boswell (Edinburgh).

Not traced.—Boswell 1791, ii. 121 (Hill iii. 124).

Dear Sir,

This gentleman[1] is a great favourite at Streatham, and therefore you will easily believe that he has very valuable qualities. Our narrative has kindled him with a desire of visiting the Highlands, after having already seen a great part of Europe. You must receive him as a friend, and when you have directed him to the curiosities of Edinburgh, give him instructions and recommendations for the rest of his journey.

       I am, dear Sir, Your most humble servant,

June 24, 1777.   Sam. Johnson

522.1. W. 25 June '77. The Countess of Harrington.

Address: To the Right Hon. Lady H.

Not traced; copy (by Edmund Allen), Newton.—Chapman, *Dr. Johnson and Dr. Dodd* 1926, 28.

Madam

That Humanity which disposed Your Ladyship to engage me in favour of Dr Dodd, will incline You to forgive me when I take the Liberty of soliciting Your Influence in Support of my Endeavours, which, I am afraid, will otherwise be ineffectual. What could be done by the Powers which fall to my Share, has been warmly and carefully performed. The Time is now come when high Rank and high Spirit must begin their Operations. Dodd must die at last unless your Ladyship shall be pleased to represent to his Majesty how properly the Life of a Delinquent may be granted to the Petitions of that Society for the sake of which he is to be punished; that the greatest Princes have thought it the highest Part of their Praise to be easily flexible to the Side of Mercy; and that whether the Case be consider'd as political or moral, the joint Petition of Three and Twenty Thousand Supplicants, ought not to be rejected, when even after all

522.—1. William Seward; see 524.

522.1.—For Lady H's eccentricities see *DNB* (at end of life of William Stanhope 1st E. of H.).

that they desire is granted, the Offender is still to suffer perpetual Exile, perpetual Infamy, and perpetual Poverty.

I am, Madam, Yr Ladyship's Most obedient and most humble Servt.

June 25, 1777. Sam: Johnson

523. Th. 26 June '77. William Dodd.

Address (Boswell): To the Reverend Dr Dodd.

Not traced.—Boswell 1791, ii. 140, from Johnson's own copy (Hill iii. 147).

Dear Sir,

That which is appointed to all men is now coming upon you. Outward circumstances, the eyes and the thoughts of men, are below the notice of an immortal being about to stand the trial for eternity, before the Supreme Judge of heaven and earth. Be comforted: your crime, morally or religiously considered, has no very deep dye of turpitude. It corrupted no man's principles; it attacked no man's life. It involved only a temporary and reparable injury. Of this, and of all other sins, you are earnestly to repent; and may God, who knoweth our frailty and desireth not our death,[1] accept your repentance, for the sake of his Son JESUS CHRIST our Lord.

In requital of those well-intended offices which you are pleased so emphatically to acknowledge, let me beg that you make in your devotions one petition for my eternal welfare.

I am, dear Sir, Your affectionate servant,

June 26, 1777. Sam. Johnson.

524. Sa. 28 June '77. James Boswell (Edinburgh).

Not traced.—Boswell 1791, ii. 119 (Hill iii. 120).

Dear Sir,

I have just received your packet[1] from Mr. Thrale's, but have not day-light enough to look much into it. I am glad that I have credit enough with Lord Hailes to be trusted with more copy. I hope to take more care of it than of the

523.—1. J perhaps recalled the phrase in the Absolution: 'who desireth not the death of a sinner'.

524.—1. So bulky a matter as author's MS. would hardly be sent by post unless, as in this case, it could be sent free.

last. I return Mrs. Boswell my affectionate thanks for her present,[2] which I value as a token of reconciliation.

Poor Dodd was put to death yesterday, in opposition to the recommendation of the jury[3]—the petition of the city of London—and a subsequent petition signed by three-and-twenty thousand hands. Surely the voice of the publick, when it calls so loudly, and calls only for mercy, ought to be heard.

The saying that was given me in the papers[4] I never spoke; but I wrote many of his petitions, and some of his letters. He applied to me very often. He was, I am afraid, long flattered with hopes of life; but I had no part in the dreadful delusion; for as soon as the King had signed his sentence, I obtained from Mr. Chamier an account of the disposition of the court towards him, with a declaration that there was *no hope even of a respite*. This letter immediately was laid before Dodd; but he believed those whom he wished to be right, as it is thought, till within three days of his end. He died with pious composure and resolution. I have just seen the Ordinary[5] that attended him. His Address to his fellow-convicts offended the Methodists; but he had a Moravian[5a] with him much of his time. His moral character[6] is very bad: I hope all is not true that is charged upon him. Of his behaviour in prison an account[7] will be published.

I wish you joy of your country-house,[8] and your pretty garden; and hope some time to see you in your felicity. I was much pleased with your two letters that had been kept so long in store;[9] and rejoice at Miss Rasay's advancement, and wish Sir Allen success.

524.—2. JB had sent with his letter 'a ship-master's receipt for a jar of orange-marmalade'. Not even a member of parliament could be sent marmalade by the post.

3. The facts are in doubt; see *L* iii. 120.

4. JB had written 'the newspapers give us a saying of your's in favour of mercy' (*L* iii. 119); Dr. Powell quotes from the *Public Advertiser* a saying which may be what J disclaims (*L* iii. 491).   5. Of Newgate, John Villette.

5a Latrobe.   6. That is, as often, 'reputation'.

7. *A Genuine Account of the Behaviour and Dying Words of William Dodd, LL.D. By the Reverend John Villette, Ordinary of Newgate,* 1777.

8. JB had written 9 June: 'For the health of my wife and children I have taken the little country-house at which you visited my uncle, Dr. Boswell.' See *L* v. 574, *BP* xii. 135.

9. JB had enclosed in his letter of 9 June letters of '64 and '75, explaining (*L* iii. 118) why they had not been sent at the time. They are printed *L* iii. 122.

I hope to meet you somewhere toward the north, but am loath to come quite to Carlisle.[10] Can we not meet at Manchester? But we will settle it in some other letters.

Mr. Seward, a great favourite at Streatham, has been, I think, enkindled by our travels, with a curiosity to see the Highlands. I have given him letters to you and Beattie. He desires that a lodging may be taken for him at Edinburgh, against his arrival. He is just setting out.

Mr. Langton has been exercising the militia. Mrs. Williams is, I fear, declining. Dr. Lawrence says he can do no more. She is gone to summer in the country, with as many conveniences about her as she can expect; but I have no great hope. We must all die: may we all be prepared!

I suppose Miss Boswell reads her book, and young Alexander takes to his learning. Let me hear about them; for everything that belongs to you, belongs in a more remote degree, and not, I hope, very remote, to, dear Sir, Yours affectionately,

June 28, 1777.   Sam. Johnson

525. Su. 29 June '77. Bennet Langton.

Fettercairn.—Boswell 1791, ii. 122 (Hill iii. 124).

Dear Sir

I have lately been much disordered by a difficulty of breathing but am now better. I hope all your house is well.

You know we have been talking lately of St Cross at Winchester. I have an old acquaintance[1] whose distress makes him very desirous of an hospital, and I am afraid, I have not strength enough to get him into the Chartreux. He is a painter, who never rose higher than to get his immediate living, and from that at eighty three he is disabled by a slight stroke of the palsy, such as does not make him at all helpless on common occasions, though his hand is not steady enough for his art.

My request is that you will try to obtain a promise of the next Vacancy from the Bishop of Chester.[2] It is not a great

525.—10. JB had proposed a meeting there in his letter of 4 April, and repeated the suggestion in that of 9 June. He made the point that this was the only cathedral in England that J had not seen.

525.—1. Isaac De Groot, see 527.   2. Markham.

thing to ask, and I hope we shall obtain it. Dr Warton has promised to favour him with his notice, and I hope he may end his days in peace.

I am, Sir, Your most humble Servant,

June 29. 1777   Sam: Johnson

526. M. 7 July '77. William Sharp.

Not traced.—*GM* Feb. 1787; Boswell 1791, ii. 123, wrongly assigned to Edward Dilly (Hill iii. 126).

Sir   *London, 7th July,* 1777.

To the Collection of *English Poets* I have recommended the volume of Dr. Watts to be added. His name has been long held by me in *veneration*; and I would not willingly be reduced to tell of him, only, that he was born and died. Yet, of his life I know very little; and therefore must pass him in a manner very unworthy of his character, unless some of his friends will favour me with the necessary information. Many of them must be known to you; and by your influence perhaps I may obtain some instruction. My plan does not exact much; but I wish to distinguish *Watts*; a man who never wrote but for a good purpose. Be pleased to do for me what you can.

I am, Sir, your humble servant,

Sam. Johnson.

526.1. M. 7 July '77. Bennet Langton.

Address: To Mr Langton.
Fettercairn.—

Dear Sir

I thank you for calling on me, and wish to meet. I am going out to morrow but shall be at home on Saturday. My respectful compliments to Lady Rothes. I hope my Miss Jenny is better.

526.—I follow the text of *GM*, which differs from 1791 in punctuation and italics, as well as in the date, which in 1791 is 'Bolt-Court, Fleet-street, July 7, 1777' and appears at the end of the letter. The reason for these discrepancies, and for JB's erroneous attribution, is obscure. Perhaps J sent his letter to Dilly to be forwarded; if so, JB might see a copy in Dilly's possession. A further discrepancy is in Maggs catalogue 258 (525), where the date is 22 July 1777.

526.1.—For the reasons of the suppression of (parts of) letters to BL see on 240.1.

I am making a collection for a case of great distress, and hope You will favour me with a Guinea. I am, Sir, &c.

July 7. 1777   Sam: Johnson

527. Sa. 19 July '77. William Vyse.

Address (Boswell): To the Reverend Dr. Vyse, at Lambeth.
Not traced.—Boswell 1791, ii. 123; the date 9 July is a misprint of 1793 (Hill iii. 125).

Sir,

I doubt not but you will readily forgive me for taking the liberty of requesting your assistance in recommending an old friend to his Grace the Archbishop,[1] as Governour of the Charter-house.

His name is De Groot; he was born at Gloucester; I have known him many years. He has all the common claims to charity, being old, poor, and infirm, in a great degree. He has likewise another claim, to which no scholar can refuse attention; he is by several descents the nephew of Hugo Grotius; of him, from whom perhaps every man of learning has learned something. Let it not be said that in any lettered country a nephew of Grotius asked a charity and was refused.

I am, reverend Sir, Your most humble servant,

July 19, 1777.   Sam. Johnson

528. Tu. 22 July '77. James Boswell (Edinburgh).

Not traced.—Boswell 1791, ii. 125 (Hill iii. 127).

Dear Sir,

Your notion of the necessity of a yearly interview[1] is very pleasing to both my vanity and tenderness. I shall, perhaps, come to Carlisle another year; but my money has not held out so well as it used to do. I shall go to Ashbourne, and I purpose to make Dr. Taylor invite you. If you live awhile with me at his house, we shall have much time to ourselves, and our stay will be no expence to us or him. I shall leave London the 28th; and after some stay at Oxford and Lichfield, shall probably come to Ashbourne about the end of

527.—1. Cornwallis.

528.—1. JB had written 9 June: 'I ask you if it would not be wrong that I should be two years without having the benefit of your conversation.' *L* iii. 118.

your Session, but of all this you shall have notice. Be satisfied we will meet somewhere.

What passed between me and poor Dr. Dodd you shall know more fully when we meet.[2]

Of lawsuits there is no end; poor Sir Allan[3] must have another trial, for which, however, his antagonist cannot be much blamed, having two judges on his side. I am more afraid of the debts than of the House of Lords. It is scarcely to be imagined to what debts will swell, that are daily encreasing by small additions, and how carelessly in a state of desperation debts are contracted. Poor Macquarry was far from thinking that when he sold his lands he should receive nothing. For what were they sold? And what was their yearly value? The admission of money into the Highlands will soon put an end to the feudal modes of life, by making those men landlords who were not chiefs. I do not know that the people will suffer by the change, but there was in the patriarchal authority something venerable and pleasing. Every eye must look with pain on a *Campbell* turning the *Macquarries* at will out of their *sedes avitae*,[4] their hereditary Island.

Sir Alexander Dick[5] is the only Scotsman liberal enough not to be angry that I could not find trees, where trees were not. I was much delighted by his kind letter.

I remember Rasay with too much pleasure not to partake of the happiness of any part of that amiable family. Our ramble in the islands hangs upon my imagination. I can hardly help imagining that we shall go again. Pennant seems to have seen a great deal which we did not see: When we travel again let us look better about us.

You have done right in taking your unkle's house. Some change in the form of life, gives from time to time a new epocha of existence. In a new place there is something new to be done, and a different system of thoughts rises in the mind.

528.—2. JB had asked 15 July for 'an exact list of the several pieces (written for Dodd by J) when we meet'.

3. Maclean. For his suit and his debts see JB's letter of 15 July (*L* iii. 126).

4. Prof. Mynors suggests that J had in mind Tibullus II. iv. 53 sedes jubeat si vendere avitas.

5. 'Scotland . . . is still in most places so devoid of clothing, or cover from hedges and plantations, that it was well you gave your readers a sound *Monitoire* with respect to that circumstance' *L* iii. 103.

I wish I could gather currants in your garden. Now fit up a little study, and have your books ready at hand; do not spare a little money, to make your habitation pleasing to yourself.

I have dined lately with poor dear ⟨Langton⟩. I do not think he goes on well. His table is rather coarse, and he has his children too much about him. But he is a very good man.

Mrs. Williams is in the country to try if she can improve her health; she is very ill. Matters have come so about that she is in the country with very good accommodation; but, age and sickness, and pride, have made her so peevish that I was forced to bribe the maid to stay with her, by a secret stipulation of half a crown a week over her wages.

Our club ended its session about six weeks ago. We now only meet to dine once a fortnight. Mr. Dunning, the great lawyer, is one of our members.[6] The Thrales are well.

I long to know how the Negro's cause[7] will be decided. What is the opinion of Lord Auchinleck, or Lord Hailes, or Lord Monboddo?

I am, dear Sir, Your most affectionate, &c.
July 22, 1777.   Sam. Johnson

529. Tu. 22 July '77. Margaret Boswell (Edinburgh).
Not traced.—Boswell 1791, ii. 126 (Hill iii. 129).

Madam,

Though I am well enough pleased with the taste of sweet-meats, very little of the pleasure which I received at the arrival of your jar of marmalade arose from eating it.[1] I received it as a token of friendship, as a proof of reconciliation, things much sweeter than sweetmeats, and upon this consideration I return you, dear Madam, my sincerest thanks. By having your kindness I think I have a double security for the continuance of Mr. Boswell's, which is not to be expected that any man can long keep, when the influence of a lady so highly and so justly valued operates against him. Mr. Boswell will tell you, that I was always faithful to your interest, and always endeavoured to exalt you in his estimation. You must now do the same for me. We must all help one another,

528.—6. Is it gratuitous to suggest that J wrote 'number'?
        7. Knight.
529.—1. But see 533 'I have not opened my pot'.

and you must now consider me, as, dear Madam, Your most obliged, And most humble servant,
July 22, 1777.   Sam. Johnson.

530. Tu. 22 July '77. Richard Farmer (Cambridge).
Morgan.—*GM* Jan. 1835.
Address (*GM*; not now in original): To Dr. Farmer, Emanuel Coll., Cambridge.

Sir

The Booksellers of London have undertaken a kind of Body of English Poetry, excluding generally the dramas, and I have undertaken to put before each authour's works a sketch of his life, and a character of his writings. Of some, however I know very little, and am afraid I shall not easily supply my deficiencies. Be pleased to inform me whether among Mr. Bakers manuscripts, or anywhere else at Cambridge any materials are to be found. If any such collection can be gleaned, I doubt not of your willingness to direct our search, and will tell the booksellers to employ a transcriber. If you think my inspection necessary, I will come down, for who that has once experienced the civilities of Cambridge[1] would not snatch the opportunity of another visit?
                          I am, Sir, Your most humble servant,
July 22. 1777   Sam: Johnson
Bolt-court, Fleet-street

531. Tu. 22 July '77. William Vyse.
Not traced.—Malone's Boswell 1807, iii. 134.

If any notice should be taken of the recommendation which I took the liberty of sending you, it will be necessary to know that Mr. De Groot is to be found at No. 8, in Pye-street, Westminster. This information, when I wrote, I could not give you; and being going soon to Lichfield, think it necessary to be left behind me.

More I will not say. You will want no persuasion to succour the nephew of Grotius.
                          I am, Sir, Your most humble servant,
July 22, 1777.   Sam. Johnson.

530.—1. For J's visit to Cambridge in '65 see *L* i. 517, 555.
531.—See 525, 527.

531.1. ⟨'77⟩. William Vyse.

This is the lost letter in praise of Grotius, described by Vyse in his letter to Boswell of 9 June 1787 (Life iii. 125) and again in his letter to Malone of 23 Apr. 1800 (Malone's Boswell 1804, iii. 135).

'It was from Dr. Johnson, to return me thanks for my application to Archbishop Cornwallis in favour of poor De Groot. He rejoices at the success it met with, and is lavish in the praise he bestows upon his favourite, Hugo Grotius. I am really sorry that I cannot find this letter, as it is worthy of the writer.'

531.2. Sa. 26 July '77. Thomas Lawrence.
Address: To Dr Laurence.
Cecil Tildesley.—*Outlook* 11 May 1912.

Dear Sir

I send you a very handsome letter just received from Mr Lawrence.[1] There is great reason for hoping that you will live to derive pleasure from his character and conduct.

Be pleased to consider these two epitaphs,[2] which I purpose to have engraven. I am going into Staffordshire. I will send for them tonight.

I am, Sir, Your most humble Servant,
Boltcourt, July 26. 1777. Sam: Johnson.

532. Oxford. Th. 31 July '77. Henry Thrale.
Not traced.—1788, No. 163.

Dear Sir July 31, 1777.
I came hither on Monday, and find every thing much as I expected. I shall not stay long, but if you send any letters to me on Saturday, to University College, I shall receive them. Please to make my compliments to my mistress and Queeney. I have picked up some little information for my Lives at the library.[1] I know not whether I shall go forward without

531.2.—1. J is punctilious in the use of titles, and 'Mr Lawrence' is no doubt the eldest son, (probably) Soulden. The Rosenbach Co. has or had a copy of *The Rambler* inscribed by J to him. See 375.1 and Index II.

2. One was no doubt Goldsmith's, see 539.1. J habitually wrote in Latin to L, and perhaps wanted his opinion of the latinity of those epitaphs. The other might be that mentioned in 583.

532.—J was the guest of William Scott, at University College. Surtees, *Lives of Stowell and Eldon*, 23.

1. The Bodleian, not the college library.

some regret. I cannot break my promise to Boswell and the rest; but I have a good mind to come back again.

I am, &c.

532a. Streatham. Sa. 2 Aug. '77. From Mrs. Thrale to J at Oxford.

R 540.66—

Dear Sir   Streatham 2: August 1777.

Mr Thrale shewed me your Letter, so I resolved to write. What can make you so lowspirited; and lowspirited for nothing as I hope & believe; I cannot for my own part tell how to advise your going forward or invite your Return—but it would be better for *you* to go on now you are half way, or the People who expect to see you will think you whimsical. Perhaps the bad State of our Affairs abroad lowers your Spirits, but go to Dr Taylor and he'll tell you 'tis all a Trick, and that we let the Americans torment us on purpose. We have dined at Cator's; his house is splendid & his Countenance gay, but he does not like the additional Land Tax.

Mrs Montagu's young heir has the Measles in London; She nurses him and writes me fine Letters. I wish you would tell me what folks at a Distance think of the harvest—the Weather here is abominable and if you continue murmuring I shall think it affects your Chearfulness and that a rainy day is not as good as a fine one, even to you though you won't own it.

My Aunt has wrote me word She will come, I expect her in about a fortnight, my Master does not rejoyce much at the thoughts but I am less dainty—loving Talk more.

Adieu Dear Sir and assure yourself that whether Kindness or Caprice Good humour to us or Ill humour to anyone else brings you back you will be welcomed with the warmest Affection & sincerest Esteem by Mr Thrale and by Sir Your most faithful and Obedient Servant H: L: Thrale

I shall be sorry for Mr Boswell if you don't see him—but I don't value Mrs Aston of Stowe Hill.

533. Oxford. M. 4 Aug. '77. Mrs. Thrale.

Mrs. F. Bowman.—1788, No. 164.

Dear Madam

I did not mean to express much discontent nor any ill humour in my letter. When I went away I knew that I went partly because I had talked of going, and because I was a little restless. I have been searching the library for materials for my lives, and a little I have got.

Things have not gone quite well with poor Gwynne.[1] His work was finished so ill that he has been condemned to pay three hundred pounds for damages, and the sentence is considered as very mild. He has however not lost his friends, and is still in the best houses,[2] and at the best tables.

I shall enquire about the harvest when I come into a region where any thing necessary to life is understood. I do not believe that there is yet any great harm, if the weather should now mend. Reaping time will only be a little later than is usual.

Dr. Wetherel is abroad, I think at London; Mr. Coulson is here, and well. Every body that knows you enquires after you.

Boswel's project is disconcerted by a visit from a relation[3] of Yorkshire, whom he mentions as the head of his clan. Boszy, you know, makes a huge bustle about all his own motions, and all mine. I have inclosed[4] a letter to pacify him and reconcile him to the uncertainties of human Life.

I believe it was after I left your house that I received a pot of orange Marmalade from Mrs. Boswel. We have now, I hope, made it up. I have not opened my pot.

I have determined to leave Oxford to morrow and on thursday I hope to see Lichfield, where I mean to rest till Dr. Taylor fetches me to Ashbourne, and there I am likely enough to stay till you bid me come back to London.

I am, Madam, Your most humble Servant
Aug. 4. 1777   Sam: Johnson.

534. Oxford. M. 4 Aug. '77. James Boswell (Edinburgh).
Not traced.—Boswell 1791, ii. 127 (Hill iii. 130).

Dear Sir,

Do not disturb yourself about our interviews; I hope we shall have many; nor think it any thing hard or unusual, that your design of meeting me is interrupted. We have both endured greater evils, and have greater evils to expect.

533.—1. See Hill's note for his fruitless efforts to trace this affair.
    2. It is, I think, possible that by 'houses' J means colleges. See Index VII.
    3. Godfrey Bosville, 'my Yorkshire chief'. For JB's doubts and difficulties see *BP* xii. 221–3, or *L* iii. 492.
    4. To be franked by HT. See 534.

Mrs. Boswell's illness[1] makes a more serious distress. Does the blood rise from her lungs or from her stomach? From little vessels broken in the stomach there is no danger. Blood from the lungs is, I believe, always frothy, as mixed with wind. Your physicians know very well what is to be done. The loss of such a lady would, indeed, be very afflictive, and I hope she is in no danger. Take care to keep her mind as easy as is possible.

I have left Langton in London. He has been down with the militia, and is again quiet at home, talking to his little people, as, I suppose, you do sometimes. Make my compliments to Miss Veronica. The rest are too young for ceremony.

I cannot but hope that you have taken your country-house at a very seasonable time, and that it may conduce to restore, or establish Mrs. Boswell's health, as well as provide room and exercise for the young ones. That you and your lady may both be happy, and long enjoy your happiness, is the sincere and earnest wish of, dear Sir, Your most, &c.,
Oxford, Aug. 4, 1777.   Sam. Johnson

535. Lichfield. Th. 7 Aug. '77. Mrs. Thrale (Southwark).

Address: To Henry Thrale Esq. in Southwark. *Postmark*: 9 AV. Newton.—1788, No. 165.

Dear Madam

On Tuesday I left Oxford, and came to Birmingham. Mr. Hector is well, Mrs Careless was not at home; yesterday I came hither. Mrs Porter is well. Mrs Aston, to whom I walked before I sat down, is very ill, but better. Whether she will recover I know not. If she dies I have a great loss. Mr Green is well, and Mrs Adey, more I have not yet seen. At Birmingham I heard of the death of an old friend, and at Lichfield of the death of another.[1] Anni praedantur euntes.[2] One was a little older, the other a little younger than myself.

But amidst these privations, the present must still be thought on, we must act as if we were to live. My Barber a

534.—1. JB had written 28 July that his wife 'had been affected with complaints which threatened a consumption'.

535.—1. Mrs. Roebuck and Harry Jackson.

2. Horace, *Ep.* II. ii. 55, Singula de nobis anni praedantur euntes: 'Years following years steal something every day' Pope.

man not unintelligent speaks magnificently of the Harvest, and Frank whom I ordered to make his observations, noted fields of very fine shew as we passed along.

Lucy thinks nothing of my prologue for Kelly, and says she has always disowned it. I have not let her know my transactions with Dr Dod. She says she takes Miss's correspondence very kindly.

I am, Madam, Your most humble servant
Lichfield Aug. 7. 1777   Sam: Johnson

536. Lichfield. Sa. 9 Aug. '77. Mrs. Thrale.
Lichfield.—1788, No. 166.

Dear Madam

No great matter has happened since I wrote, but this place grows more and more barren of entertainment. Two whom I hoped to have seen are dead. I think that I am much more unwieldy and inert than when I was here last; my Nights are very tedious. But a light heart &c.[1]

Lucy says "When I read Dod's Sermon to the prisoners I said, Dr Johnson could not make a better".

One of Lucy's Maids is dreadfully tormented by the taenia or long worm. She has taken many medicines without effect, and it is much wished that she could have the Knightsbridge powder. I will pay for it, if you, dear Madam, will be so kind as to procure it, and send it with directions. Can it be franked?[2] If it cannot, the best way will be to unite it with something of greater bulk. I have promised Lucy to give her Cook's last Voyage, for she loves prints; but the last Voyage cannot be well understood without some knowledge of the former. If you will lend us Hawkesworth's Books, they shall be carefully returned. If you will do this for us, the powders may be easily put up with the Books.

Please to make my compliments to Master, and to Queeney.

I am Madam Your most humble servant
August 9. 1777 Lichfield   Sam: Johnson

536.—1. 'A light heart lives long', Shakespeare, *L.L.L.* v. ii.
2. There was at this time a limit of two ounces; see Hill's note. That is why J sent JB a copy of his *Journey* in 'thirteen franks' (*BP* x. 85). The alternative that J here suggests is 'the carrier'.

537. Lichfield. W. 13 Aug. '77. Mrs. Thrale.

O. R. Barrett.—1788, No. 167.

Dear Madam

Such tattle as filled your last sweet Letter prevents one great inconvenience of absence, that of returning home a stranger and an enquirer. The variations of life consist of little things. Important innovations are soon heard, and easily understood. Men that meet to talk of Physicks or Metaphysicks, or law or history may be immediately acquainted. We look at each other in silence only for want of petty talk upon slight occurrences. Continue therefore to write all that You would say.

——'s ——[1] I think, is in the Library in one volume in large octavo. It never was printed but once.

You have Lord Westcote and every body when I am away, and you go to Mr. Cator's, and you are so happy.—

Miss Turton, and Harry Jackson are dead. Mrs Aston is I am afraid, in great danger. Mr Green, Mr Garrick, and Mr Newton are all well. I have been very faint and breathless since I came hither, but fancy myself better this day. I hope Master's Walk will be finished when I come back and I shall perambulate it very often.

There seems to be in this country scarcely any fruit, there never indeed was much,[2] but great things have been said of the harvest, and the only fear is of the weather. It rains here almost every day.

I dined yesterday with the corporation, and talked against a workhouse[3] which they have in *contemplation*—there's the word now—I do not know that they minded me, for they said nothing to me.

I have had so little inclination to motion that I have always gone the shortest way to Stowhill, and hardly any where else, so that I can tell you nothing new of Green's Museum, but I design to visit him, and all friends.

537.—1. One might be tempted to guess that the erasure hid 'Cook's Voyage'; but why should HLP erase that? It is, moreover, a large quarto, and J 'was bred a bookseller'. The whole paragraph is erased, but the rest can be read.

2. For the penury of English horticulture see *L* iv. 205.

3. Hill has a very interesting note on the horrors of workhouses in J's time.

I hope for a letter to morrow, for you must not forget that
I am, Madam, Your most humble Servant

Aug. 13. 1777 Lichfield   Sam: Johnson

Why cannot Queeney write?

537a. Streatham. W. 13 Aug. ⟨'77⟩. From Mrs. Thrale to
J at Lichfield.

R 540.67 (imperfect)—

Dear Sir
                                            Streatham 13: August
Since I wrote last I have dined at Sir Joshua's on Richmond Hill, where we
were invited to meet the Pepyses, the Patersons, the Garricks &c. there was
Mr Langton, Lady Rothes and their two pretty Babies; I think Miss Langton
for an infant of four Years old the most elegant Creature I have seen, and
little George is a fine Fellow too: but very troublesome they were with their
Prattle, every word of which their Papa repeated in order to explain; however
Miss Reynolds with great composure put them under the Care of a Maid &
sent them a walking while we dined; very little to the Satisfaction of the
Parents, who expressed some uneasiness lest they should overheat themselves
as it was a hot day. In the mean Time Mr Garrick was taken Ill, and after
suffering a good deal from Sickness in his Stomach desired a Table to himself
near the open Window: by the Time he was settled, the Children returned;
and Lady Rothes who did not much like they should lose their dinner so, had
got some Scraps of the Second Course—Cheesecakes & such like ready for
them at their Return. She then directed them to go to Mr Garrick's Table,
and *eat fair.* He was sick before, and I actually saw him change Colour at
their approach, however he was civiller to them than anybody there except
myself. Pepys—who had heard you give a Specimen of the *Langtonian* Mode
of Life at our house whispered me that he wished them all at the Rope-Walk—
& added can one ever come to this oneself? I really never had such difficulty
to forbear laughing.

538. Lichfield. Sa. 23 Aug. '77. Mrs. Thrale.
Sotheby 6 Dec. 1904 (not seen).—1788, No. 168.
An extract (My master ... pounds a year) in Quaritch cat. 253 of 1906.

Dear Madam   Lichfield, August 23, 1777.
At Lichfield? Yes; but not well. I have been trying a
great experiment with ipecacuanha, which Akensyde had
inclined me to consider as a remedy for all constrictions of the
breath. Lawrence indeed told me that he did not credit him,
and no credit can I find him to deserve. One night I thought
myself the better for it, but there is no certainty. On Wednesday night I took ten grains; the night was restless. On
Thursday morning I took ten grains; the night again was

restless. On Friday night I took twenty grains, which Aken-syde mentions as the utmost that on these occasions he has *ventured* to give; the night was perhaps rather worse. I shall therefore take truce with ipecacuanha. Tell me, if you can, what I shall do next.

Mr. Thrale's heart may be at rest. It is not fine Mrs. Anne that has been caught by the taenia, but Mrs. Anne tumbled down stairs last night, and bruised her face. Both maid and mistress are very grateful to you for the kindness with which you procured the powders, and directed their use. They have not yet been tried. It has been washing week; and I suppose every body shrinks a little from such rough remedies, of which at last the success is doubtful. However it will, I think, be tried in all its formalities.

My master may plant and dig till his pond is an ocean, if he can find water, and his parterre a down. I have no doubt[1] of a most abundant harvest; and it is said that the produce of barley is particularly great. We are not far from the great year of a hundred thousand barrels, which, if three shillings be gained upon each barrel, will bring us fifteen thousand pounds a-year. ⟨Whitbread⟩[2] never pretended to more than thirty pounds a-day, which is not eleven thousand a-year. But suppose we shall get but two shillings a barrel, that is ten thousand a-year. I hope we still have the advantage. Would you for the other thousand have my master such a man as ⟨Whitbread⟩?[2]

I showed dear Queeney's letter to Mrs. Aston and Mrs. Porter, they both took her remembrance of them very kindly.

It was well done by Mr. Brooke to send for you. His house is one of my favourite places. His water is very commodious, and the whole place has the true old appearance of a little country town. I hope Miss goes, for she takes notice.

The races are next week. People seem to be weary of them, for many go out of town I suppose to escape the cost of entertaining company. Dr. Taylor will probably come, and probably take me away; and I shall leave[3] Mrs. Aston.

538.—1. 'hear no doubts' Quaritch.

2. Whitbread HLP (*bis*).

3. If the text is sound J must mean 'T will probably come, in his carriage, for the races, and will probably carry me off to stay with him; if so, I shall desert Mrs. A.' But I think it possible that J wrote not 'leave', but 'have', i.e. have her company. 539 shows

Do not you lose, nor let Master lose, the kindness that you have for me. Nobody will ever love you both better than, dear Madam, Your, &c.

539. Lichfield. W. 27 Aug. '77. Mrs. Thrale (Southwark).
Address: To Henry Thrale Esq. in Southwark. *Postmark*: 29 AV. Lady Charnwood.—1788, No. 169.

Dear Madam

Our Correspondence is not so vigorous as it used to be; but now you know the people at Lichfield, it is vain to describe them, and as no revolutions have happened, there is nothing to be said about them. We have a new Dean whose name is Proby, he has the manners of a Gentleman, and some spirit of discipline which brings the cathedral into better method. He has a lady[1] that talks about Mrs Montague and Mrs Carter.

On next Saturday I go to Ashbourne, and thither must my Letters be sent, if you are pleased ever to write to me.

When I came hither, I could hardly walk, but I have got better breath, and more agility. I intend to perambulate Master's dominions every day at least once. But I have miserable, distressful, tedious nights. Do you think they will mend at Brighthelmston?

When I come to Ashbourne I will send my dear Queeney an account how I find things, for I hope she takes an interest in Dr. Taylor's prosperity.

This is race week, but Mrs. Aston, Mrs. Porter, and myself have no part in the course, or at the ball. We all sit at home and perhaps pretend to wonder that others go, though I cannot charge any of us with much of that folly. Mrs. Gastrel who wraps her head in a towel, is very angry at the present mode of dress and feathers.

But amidst all these little things there is one great thing. The Harvest is abundant, and the weather *a la merveille.*[2]

that she, like J and LP, stayed at home. JT, if he came, could not return on the same day, and is thought of as at the races and the ball. The two words are in J's hand very similar.

539.—1. Hill heard at L'd this squib against Mrs. Proby: 'She would far sooner from the steeple fling her, Than let a tradesman touch her high born finger.'

2. A slip for 'à merveille'; I cannot find authority for 'à la m.' at any date.

No season ever was finer. Barley, Malt, Beer, and Money. There is the series of Ideas. The deep Logicians call it a sorites. I hope my Master will no longer endure the reproach of not keeping me a Horse.

The Puppies played us a vile trick when they tore my letter, but I hope my loss will be repaired to morrow. You are in the way of business and intelligence, and have something to write. I am here in unactive obscurity, and have little other pleasure, than to perceive that the poor languishing Lady is glad to see me. I hope, dearest Lady, you will be glad to see me too, and that it will be long before disease lays hold upon You.

I am, Dear Madam, Your most humble servant
Lichfield Aug. 27. 1777.   Sam: Johnson.

539a. Streatham. Th. 28 Aug. '77. From Hester Maria Thrale to J at Ashbourne.

R 540.68—Lansdowne, *Queeney Letters* 1934, 10.

Sir   Streatham Aug^st 28th: 1777
   I think both the Ladies and you did me great honour to take notice of my Letter: I have now been at Town Malling, and think it a very pretty odd old fashioned Place: the Cascade out of the Wall and that down by the Ponds are quite charming, and Mr Brooke was vastly civil and gave Mama some fine old China, and sent some to Susan who is his Godaughter. I liked it all much upon the whole, but it seems there have been Alterations made by which my Mother thinks it not mended. I hope Doctor Taylor is well and all his pretty Animals, Jigg and Jessamy in particular, but I should have named Mrs Sally first and given my kind Service to her.
                    I am Sir Your most humble Servant H: M: Thrale.

539b. Streatham. Sa. 30 Aug. ⟨'77⟩. From Mrs. Thrale to J at Ashbourne.

R 540.69—

Dear Sir   Streatham 30: August.
   You will find Letters enough from me at Ashburn; I believe I began directing there sooner than I had need: I grieve that your nights are so bad, but can think of nothing that is likely to mend them unless the Sea may do something —by its roar. We have agreed to go at Michaelmas and not before. Mr Thrale has listed Burney to be of the Party; that Man is mighty pleasing, & mighty inoffensive.—He was here for a Week, and Pepys came with his Wife to spend two Days. I received a Letter from Seward one of the Evenings and my Master bid me read it out:—I did so—he mentioned Bachygraig in the

Letter, and said that though some few of my Trees had been felled, the Wood was still extreamly luxuriant, and the Neighbours of Opinion that more Light should yet be let in.—I said I was very sorry any Trees had been felled, and that it was well Mr Thrale had resolved to cut no more, for that I had rather my right hand suffered mutilation than those Woods. Burney & Pepys, surprized at the Emotion with which I said this cried out both in a Breath—then I am sure they are safe enough, for Mr Thrale is a very unlikely man to touch the *sacred Groves*. Nobody has touched anything replies my Master but two or three old Pollards which I think She should have been ashamed, not proud of in her Woods. I wish Seward had been hanged before he had written of such Stuff. I desired he would let me know said I, for they shall not if I can help it be thinned without my Consent, and I never *will* consent—till I am much changed at least. The two Men stared, & my Master was silent & sullen; but no matter, the more People know that 'tis against my Will they are cut, the less danger they will be in of falling. Make no Answer to this part of my Letter I beg of you—no need of your getting into the Quarrel till Things are worse than they are now. The Harvest is best Friend to my poor Woods however, at least that can do more for their Preservation than anything else.

Adieu and be as well as ever you can & come home disposed with the same kind partiality you have so long felt for your most Faithful & Obedient Servant H: L: Thrale.

539.1. Lichfield. F. 29 Aug. '77. Joseph Nollekens.

Address: To Mr Nollikens in Mortimer Street, Oxford Road London.
Postmark: 29 AV.
Fettercairn.—

Sir

I have at last sent you what remains,[1] to put to poor dear Goldsmiths monument, and hope to see it erected in the abbey.

You promised me a cast of the head.[2] If it could be sent to Lichfield directed to Mrs Lucy Porter before I leave the country I should be glad, though the matter is not of such Consequence, as that you should incommode yourself about it.

I hope Mrs Nollikens and our Friends[3] in Italy are all well,

539.1.—I cannot account for JB's failure to publish this letter (505.2 he might think negligible). Perhaps he got it too late for 1791 and inadvertently missed it in his revision. For his suppressions in general see App. E, II § 5.

1. See 505.2.
2. J's own; see Index II, s.v. Nollekens.
3. Welch and his daughter.

and that we shall all have some time or other a joyful Meeting. I am, Sir, Your most humble Servant

Sam: Johnson

Natus Hibernia, Forneiae Longfordiensis, in loco cui nomen Pallas, Nov. xxix, mdccxxxi.

Eblanae literis institutus,
Obiit Londini, Apr. iv. mdcclxxiv.

540. Ashbourne. Sa. 30 Aug. '77. James Boswell (Edinburgh).

Not traced.—Boswell 1791, ii. 128 (Hill iii. 131).

Dear Sir,

I am this day come to Ashbourne, and have only to tell you, that Dr. Taylor says you shall be welcome to him, and you know how welcome you will be to me. Make haste to let me know when you may be expected.

Make my compliments to Mrs. Boswell, and tell her, I hope we shall be at variance no more.

I am, dear Sir, Your most humble servant,

August 30, 1777. Sam. Johnson.

541. Ashbourne. M. 1 Sept. '77. James Boswell (Edinburgh).

Not traced.—Boswell 1791, ii. 128 (Hill iii. 131).

Dear Sir,

On Saturday I wrote a very short letter, immediately upon my arrival hither, to shew you that I am not less desirous of the interview than yourself. Life admits not of delays; when pleasure can be had it is fit to catch it: Every hour takes away part of the things that please us, and perhaps part of our disposition to be pleased. When I came to Lichfield, I found my old friend Harry Jackson dead. It was a loss, and a loss not to be repaired, as he was one of the companions of my childhood. I hope we may long continue to gain friends, but the friends which merit or usefulness can procure us, are not able to supply the place of old acquaintance, with whom the days of youth may be retraced, and those images revived which gave the earliest delight. If you and I live to be much older, we shall take great delight in talking over the Hebridean Journey.

In the mean time it may not be amiss to contrive some other little adventure, but what it can be I know not; leave it, as Sidney says,
      'To virtue, fortune, time,[1] and woman's breast;'
for I believe Mrs. Boswell must have some part in the consultation.

One thing you will like. The Doctor, so far as I can judge, is likely to leave us enough to ourselves. He was out to-day before I came down, and, I fancy, will stay out till dinner. I have brought the papers about poor Dodd, to show you, but you will soon have dispatched them.

Before I came away I sent poor Mrs. Williams into the country, very ill of a pituitous defluxion, which wastes her gradually away, and which her physician declares himself unable to stop. I supplied her as far as could be desired,[2] with all conveniencies to make her excursion and abode pleasant and useful, but I am afraid she can only linger a short time in a morbid state of weakness and pain.

The Thrales, little and great, are all well, and purpose to go to Brighthelmston at Michaelmas. They will invite me to go with them, and perhaps I may go, but I hardly think I shall like to stay the whole time; but of futurity we know but little.

Mrs. Porter is well; but Mrs. Aston, one of the ladies at Stowhill, has been struck with a palsy, from which she is not likely ever to recover. How soon may such a stroke fall upon us!

Write to me, and let us know when we may expect you.
          I am, dear Sir, Your most humble servant,
Ashbourne, Sept. 1, 1777.   Sam. Johnson.

541.—1. 'wine' 1791, an error which Malone regarded as 'a mistake in the transcript'. We now know that there were in general no transcripts; JB, like HLP and other editors of his time, sent the originals to the printer. (See however App. B, or i. 427.) But *t* in J's hand is almost the same as the first element of *w*, so that *tim* (*t* and four 'minims') is virtually identical with *win* (*w* and three 'minims'). For other points arising out of the quotation see *L* iii. 131, 493.

2. This hardly seems the appropriate word. It is perhaps just possible that J wrote 'devised'. The corruption of 'vif' to 'fir' would be an example of that scribal transposition of which Housman in his *Horatiana* cites many ancient examples. For the 'conveniencies' see 528.

541.1. Ashbourne.—Th. 4 Sept. '77. Hester Maria Thrale.
Lansdowne.—Lansdowne, *Johnson and Queeney* 1932, 7.

Dear Miss,   Ashbourne, Sept. 4, 1777

And so between you and your Mamma, the postman has brought me no letter.[1] Such usage—but this it is to be away. However I will shift a little longer as I can.

Dr. Taylor has put a very elegant iron palisade[2] before his house; he has emptied his pool of the mud, and laid it upon the ground behind it. He thinks he has now six feet of water. I see but few deer, and hardly any fowls. The Doctor has transferred his attention to other things, and is become one of the sons of Harmony. To his Harpsichord he has added a very magnificent organ, a very fine hautbois, and if I count right, three fiddles. I hear that he makes the organist teach him to play, and hope to see you and him at the same instrument, like Miss Burney[3] and Master Wesley.

The walk in the garden is covered with new gravel which will be continued to the waterfal, which now roars tolerably well.

The Cattle prosper pretty well, a Cow has just been sold to Mr. Chapplin a great breeder in Lincolnshire for one hundred and twenty pounds, and for the other Cow one hundred and thirty have been refused. The young Bull is said to be bigger than his sire. The horses are all well, but some of the cows are diseased, one in the udder, and one in the foot.

The Doctor thinks he shall get his lawsuit against Mrs. Rudd.

Tell Mamma that I hear every where of full crops though we have at present in Derbyshire bad weather, and that I reckon on us to grow next year so rich, that what is now iron shall then be silver.[4]

541.1.—1. This is surprising, since HLT (539*b*) wrote that she had posted to A'n on 30 Aug., and apparently earlier. But J often complains of the A'n post. 542*a*, moreover, though directed to A'n, has the L'd postmark, and was presumably forwarded thence.   2. This improvement no longer embellishes the Mansion.

3. Dr. Scholes has no hesitation in identifying 'Miss Burney' as CB's eldest daughter Esther. She had married in '70 her cousin Charles Rousseau B; J might easily forget that. She was eminent as a harpsichordist. 'Master Wesley' might be Charles or Samuel; Charles was the better-known performer at this date, but since he was born in '57 he would hardly be 'Master' in '77; Samuel was born in '66.

4. J perhaps thought of the four ages of classical mythology, in which the course of the world's decadence was from golden to silver, to bronze, to iron.

Mr. Langley and his Lady are well, but the Doctor and they are no friends. I know not whether I ever told that my cousin Mr. Flint's wife is dead.

Neither at Lichfield nor Ashbourne is there any fruit and I am afraid you have not much upon all your Walls.

I hear no good of poor Mrs. Williams. Mrs. Porter is better than she uses to be. Mrs. Aston does not mend.

I cannot boast of mending myself, nor much expect that Brighthelmston will mend me, yet I hope to pass a little time with you there.

I am Dearest Miss, Your most humble servant,

Sam: Johnson

542. Ashbourne. Sa. 6 Sept. '77. Mrs. Thrale.
Sotheby 30 Jan. 1918 (not seen).—1788, No. 170.

Dearest Lady   Sept. 6, 1777.

It is true that I have loitered, and what is worse, loitered with very little pleasure. The time has run away, as most time runs, without account, without use, and without memorial. But to say this of a few weeks, though not pleasing, might be borne, but what ought to be the regret of him who, in a few days, will have so nearly the same to say of sixty-eight years? But complaint is vain.

If you have nothing to say from the neighbourhood of the metropolis, what can occur to me in little cities and petty towns; in places which we have both seen, and of which no description is wanted? I have left part of the company[1] with which you dined here, to come and write this letter; in which I have nothing to tell, but that my nights are very tedious. I cannot persuade myself to forbear trying something.

As you have now little to do, I suppose you are pretty diligent at the Thraliana, and a very curious collection posterity will find it. Do not remit the practice of writing down occurrences as they arise, of whatever kind, and be very punctual in annexing the dates. Chronology you know is the

542.—1. HLT's journal of the tour of '74 records that 15 July 'we were visited by the Dyott family' and 18 July 'we dined at Mr. Gell's'. Broadley, *Dr. Johnson and Mrs. Thrale*, 169, 173. These meetings are noted also in J's journal, *L* v. 430.

eye of history;[2] and every man's life is of importance to himself. Do not omit painful casualties, or unpleasing passages,
they make the variegation of existence; and there are many
transactions, of which I will not promise with Aeneas, *et haec
olim meminisse juvabit.*[3] Yet that remembrance which is not
pleasant may be useful. There is however an intemperate
attention to slight circumstances which is to be avoided, lest
a great part of life be spent in writing the history of the rest.
Every day perhaps has something to be noted, but in a
settled and uniform course few days can have much.

Why do I write all this, which I had no thought of when I
begun? The Thraliana drove it all into my head. It deserves
however an hour's reflection, to consider how, with the least
loss of time, the loss of what we wish to retain may be prevented.

Do not neglect to write to me, for when a post comes
empty, I am really disappointed.

Boswell, I believe, will meet me here.

> I am, dearest Lady, Your, &c.

542a. Streatham. Sa. 6 Sept. ⟨'77⟩. From Mrs. Thrale to
J at Ashbourne (see note on 541.1).

Address: To Doctor Johnson at the Revd Dr Taylors Ashbourne
Derbyshire. *Postmark*: LITCHFIELD.

R 540.70—

My Dear Sir   Streatham Saturday 6: Sep^r

I begin to be angry, uneasy at least in good earnest: you are used to be so
punctual in writing even though there was nothing to be said: Sure it is Time
to come home almost is it not? and you not yet got to Ashbourne where you
said you should be this Day sevennight. So here's a whole Week without a
Line. Sure you have not been taking Opium or Ipecacuanha or any dangerous
Medecine again—sure you have not. Have Patience with the bad Nights
till you get them into Sussex, & try whether the Sea will wash them away.
We have Venison & Pine Apple & not a Creature in London to come & eat
them. I thank you for the Account you give of the harvest & now wish only
for one of yourself, tho' I think if anything ailed you too we should all hear

---

542—2. Prof. Donald F. Bond of Chicago refers me to Ozell's translation, 1704, of
Perrault's *Characters*, i. 43: 'Geography and Chronology . . . are the two Eyes of
History', and to Desfontaines, *Jugemens*, 1744, i. 170: 'La Chronologie, l'un des deux
yeux de l'histoire'.

3. Virgil, *Aen.* i. 203, 'An hour will come, with pleasure to relate Your sorrows
past, as benefits of fate' (Dryden).

of it but too soon, so sedulous are the News Papers to keep your Name vibrating.

Farewell Dear Sir & be pretty well & write to your most faithful & Obedient Servt H: L: Thrale.

My Master works hard at his Pond. Is poor Mrs Aston dying? & does that detain you at Lichfield? I have sent a hundred Letters to Ashburn thinking you were there, so I can't charge myself with any neglect.

543. Ashbourne. M. 8 Sept. '77. Mrs. Thrale.

Sotheby 15 Feb. 1926.—1788, No. 171.

Dear Madam

Surely the same vexatious interruption of our correspondence happens now that happened once when I was at Oxford. I write often, yet you seem not to have my Letters. I charged Frank with trusting some other hand to the post-office, this he denies, and indeed I have answers to other letters.

I came hither on Saturday, Aug 30. The books[1] were not then come; but I suppose according to Davies's letter, they came that evening. Of the receipt of the Powders I wrote word, and told that the girl delayed a little while to take them. From this place I wrote to Miss last Thursday, and to you last Saturday. Nothing has been mentioned by you of which I have not taken proper notice, except that I have said nothing of ⟨Sir John⟩.[2] Many instances there are of the vanity of human solicitude, and it is not strange to find another. We were all planning out for him some mode of life, and disease was hovering over him. If he dies his Mother will lose what has engaged her care, and incited her Vanity. The Son and the estate go away together. But Life occupies us all too much to leave us room for any care of others beyond what duty enjoyns; and no duty enjoyns sorrow or anxiety that is at once troublesome and useless. I would readily help the poor Lady, but, if I cannot do her good by assisting her I shall not disturb myself by lamenting her. Yet I suppose, his death will be as hard a blow as is commonly felt. Let me know, if you hear how he goes on. I go on but uneasily.

543.—1. See 536. Davies was not the publisher, but was no doubt employed as a friendly member of the trade.

2. 'Sir John Lade' HLP, which is certainly right.

I am in hopes of seeing Mr. Boswel, and then he may perhaps tell me something to write, for this is but a barren place. Not a mouse stirring.[3]

I am, Madam, Your most humble Servant

Ashbourne. Sept. 8. 1777   Sam: Johnson.

544. Ashbourne. Th. 11 Sept. '77. James Boswell (Carlisle).
Not traced.—Boswell 1791, ii. 131 (Hill iii. 135).

Dear Sir,

I write to be left at Carlisle, as you direct me, but you cannot have it. Your letter, dated Sept. 6, was not at this place till this day, Thursday, Sept. 11;[1] and I hope you will be here before this is at Carlisle. However, what you have not going, you may have returning; and as I believe I shall not love you less after our interview, it will then be as true as it is now, that I set a very high value upon your friendship, and count your kindness as one of the chief felicities of my life. Do not fancy that an intermission of writing is a decay of kindness. No man is always in a disposition to write; nor has any man at all times something to say.

That distrust which intrudes so often on your mind is a mode of melancholy, which, if it be the business of a wise man to be happy, it is foolish to indulge; and if it be a duty to preserve our faculties entire for their proper use, it is criminal. Suspicion is very often an useless pain. From that, and all other pains, I wish you free and safe; for I am, dear Sir,

Most affectionately yours,

Ashbourne, Sept. 11, 1777.   Sam. Johnson.

545. Ashbourne. Sa. 13 Sept. '77. Mrs. Thrale.
Not traced.—1788, No. 172; Boswell 1791, ii. 131, an extract (Hill iii. 134).

Dear Madam,   Ashbourne, Sept. 13, 1777.

Now I write again, having just received your letter dated the 10th.

543.—3. *Hamlet* i. i. 10.

544.—J's prediction was fulfilled. His letter 'was forwarded to my house at Edinburgh' JB.

1. JB did not print this letter, which is merely recorded in his journal (under 5 Sept.), *BP* xii. 223.

You must not let foolish fancies take hold on your imagination. If Queeney grows tall, she is sufficiently bulky, and as much out of danger of a consumption as nature allows a young maiden to be. Of real evils the number is great, of possible evils there is no end. ⟨Lady Lade⟩[1] is really to be pitied. Her son in danger; the estate likely to pass not only from her, but to those on whom, I suppose, she would least wish it bestowed, and her system of life broken, are very heavy blows. But she will at last be rich, and will have much gratification in her power, both rational and sensual.

Boswell, I believe, is coming. He talks of being here to-day. I shall be glad to see him. But he shrinks from the Baltick expedition,[2] which I think is the best scheme in our power. What we shall substitute, I know not. He wants to see Wales, but except the woods of Bachycraigh what is there in Wales? What that[3] can fill the hunger of ignorance, or quench the thirst of curiosity? We may perhaps form some scheme or other, but, in the phrase of Hockley in the Hole,[4] it is a pity he has not a better bottom.

Tell my young mistress that this day's letter is too short, and it brings me no news either foreign or domestick.

I am going to dine with Mr. Dyot, and Frank tells sternly, that it is past two o'clock.

I am, dearest Madam,
Your, &c.

546. Ashbourne. Sa. 13 Sept. '77. Elizabeth Aston (Lichfield).

Address: To Mrs Aston at Stow hill Lichfield. *Postmark* illegible. Pembroke.—Croker's Boswell 1831, iii. 499.

Dear Madam,

As I left you so much disordered, a fortnight is a long time to be without any account of your health. I am willing to flatter myself that you are better, though you gave me no

545.—1. So HLP, Lysons; suppressed in 1788.

2. JB had written 9 Sept.: 'I shrink a little from our scheme of going up the Baltick. I am sorry you have already been in Wales; for I wish to see it.'

3. For 'Wales? What that' JB printed 'Wales, that'.

4. For Hockley see *L* iii. 134, and for 'bottom' Hill's note on 545, from which it appears that in the language of the ring the word meant what is to-day called 'guts'. JB's magnanimity in quoting this passage deserves remark.

reason to believe that you intended to use any means for your recovery. Nature often performs wonders, and will, I hope, do for you more than you seem inclined to do for yourself.

In this weakness of body with which it has pleased God to visit you, he has given you great cause of thankfulness, by the total exemption of your Mind from all effects of your disorder. Your Memory is not less comprehensive or distinct, nor your reason less vigorous and acute, nor your imagination less active and spritely than in any former time of your life. This is a great Blessing as it respects enjoyment of the present, and a Blessing yet far greater as it bestows power and opportunity to prepare for the future.

All sickness is a summons. But as you do not want exhortations, I will send you only my good wishes, and intreat you to believe the good wishes very sincere, of,

Dear Madam,

Your most humble servant,

Ashbourne Sept. 13. 1777   Sam: Johnson.

547. Ashbourne. M. 15 Sept. '77. Mrs. Thrale.

Not traced.—1788, No. 173.

Dear Madam,   Sept. 15, 1777.

Do you call this punctual correspondence? There was poor I writing, and writing, and writing, on the 8th, on the 11th,[1] on the 13th; and on the 15th I looked for a letter, but I may look and look. Instead of writing to me you are writing the Thraliana. But—he *must be humble who would please.*[2]

Last night came Boswell. I am glad that he is come. He seems to be very brisk and lively, and laughs a little at....[3] I told him something of the scene at Richmond.[4] You find, now you have seen the *progenies Langtoniana,* that I did not praise them without reason; yet the second girl is my favourite.

You talk of pine-apples and venison.[5] Pine-apples it is sure

547.—1. We have no letter of this date.

2. The same quotation from Prior's 'Chloe Jealous' is in 421.

3. 'Langton' HLP: Hill confidently restored 'Taylor'. HLP is not always right (see, e.g. 262, 304; other examples are in my article 'Piozzi on Thrale' in *NQ* 23 Oct. 1943); and here she might be deceived by the context.

4. See 537*a*.   5. See 542*a*.

we have none; but venison, no forester that lived under the green-wood-tree ever had more frequently upon his table. We fry, and roast, and bake, and devour in every form.

We have at last fair weather in Derbyshire, and every where the crops are spoken of as uncommonly exuberant. Let us now get money and save it. All that is paid is saved, and all that is laid out in land or malt. But I long to see twenty thousand pounds in the bank, and to see my master visiting this estate and that, as purchases are advertised. But perhaps all this may be when Colin's forgotten and gone.⁶ Do not let me be forgotten before I am gone, for you will never have such another, as,

Dearest dear Madam,
Your most humble servant.

547a. Streatham. Tu. 16 Sept. ⟨'77⟩. From Mrs. Thrale to J at Ashbourne.

R 540.71.—

Dear Sir   Streatham 16: September

I have now had two sweet Letters again, & I thank you for them heartily. My Imagination does play me Tricks now & then about my Children, which however my extreme Ill Fortune in losing so many vindicates, and vindicates severely.

Mr Boswell will make Ashbourne alive better than three Hautboys & the Harpsichord; and in Sewards Phrase will *do more* for one. A propos Mr Seward is come back, but in such Pain with his Teeth & Face that he can neither talk in the Day nor he says—sleep in the Night. He only tells that he likes Scotch Hospitality and Welch Castles—that Myddelton is erecting an Urn I think to your Memory at Gwynynnog & that your Friend the Schoolmaster at Beaumaris remembers your meeting with Delight.

My Aunt is coming from Bath, but if my Uncle was coming from the Grave —my Master says he would stick to his Word & go to Brighthelmstone on the 30th. You have it seems longer Journeys in *Contemplation* but remember Mr Boswell has a Wife & Children, and you have Friends at Streatham who love you more than many a Man is loved by his Wife & Children. Tis Penance to write even to you with this pen, so for the present—Adieu—I go over every Stroke twice.

I am ever most faithfully Sir Your Obedient Servant H: L: Thrale. Never forget our Compliments to Doctor Taylor.

547.—6. Rowe, 'Colin's Complaint': 'While Colin forgotten and gone No more shall be talked of or seen; Unless when beneath the pale moon, His ghost shall glide over the green.'

548. Ashbourne. Th. 18 Sept. '77. Mrs. Thrale.

Mrs. F. Bowman.—1788, No. 174.

Dear Madam

Here is another Birthday.[1] They come very fast. I am now sixty eight. To lament the past is vain, what remains is to look for hope in futurity. Queeney has now passed another year. I hope every year will bring her happiness.

Boswel is with us in good humour and plays his part with his usual vivacity. We are to go in the Doctors vehicle and dine at Derby to morrow.

Do you know any thing of Boltcourt? Invite Mr. Levet to dinner and make enquiry what family he has, and how they proceed. I had a letter lately from Mrs. Williams. Dr Lewis visits her, and has added Ipecacuanha to her bark. But I do not hear much of her amendment. Age is a very stuborn Disease. Yet Levet sleeps sound every Night. I am sorry for poor Sewards pain, but he may live to be better.

Mr. ⟨Myddelton⟩'s[2] erection of an urn looks like an intention to bury me alive. I would as willingly see my friend, however benevolent and hospitable quietly inurned. Let him think for the present of some more acceptable memorial.

Does nobody tell ⟨Lady Lade⟩[3] that a warmer climate and a clearer air is likely to help her son, and that it may ⟨be⟩ convenient to run away from an English Winter, before he becomes too weak for travel. It appears to me not improbable that change of air and the amusement and exercise of easy journeys might enable one so young to overcome his disease.

Dr Taylor has another Buck. You must not talk to us of Venison. Fruit indeed we have little, and that little not very good. But what there is, has been very liberally bestowed.

Mr. Langley[4] and the Doctor still live on different sides of the street.

We have had for some time past such Harvest weather, as a Derbyshire Farmer dares scarcely hope. The Harvest has this year been every where a Month backward, but so far as I

548.—1. For J's feelings about his birthday, in this and other years, see references at *L* iii. 157.

2. So HLP, Lysons; suppressed in 1788. See 547*a*. For JB's projected monument at Auchinleck see *L* v. 380.

3. So HLP, Lysons; suppressed in 1788.

4. So HLP, Lysons; 'L——' 1788; there are traces of the initial and of the second *l*.

can hear, has recompensed the delay by uncommon plenty.
Next year will, I hope, complete Mr. Thrales wish of an
hundred thousand barrels. Ambition is then to have an end,
and he must remember, that Non minor est Virtus quam
quærere, parta tueri.[5] When he has climbed so high, his care
must be to keep himself from falling.

I am, dear Madam,

Your &c.,

Sam: Johnson

September the 18th 1777 Ashbourne

548a. Streatham. Sa. 18 Sept. ⟨'77⟩. From Mrs. Thrale to
J at Ashbourne.

R 540.72—

Dear Sir   Streatham 18: Sept^r.

I am glad Mr Boswell is with you—nothing that you say for this Week at
least will be lost to Posterity. If I do not write to you, and if I do work at the
Book with the foolish name You are not the more out of my Head for *that*.

Yesterday was Queeneys Birthday *you know*; I may wish you Joy of *that* I
suppose, and hope that you as well as I may live to see many of them and
happy ones: I treated the Men and Maidens with a Dance and they were
happy. Dignan the Cook came down on purpose to make one, but got drunk
too soon, tumbled down Stairs and broke a Rib; but he will do very well
again and dance next Year. It is utterly impossible to find one Word to say,
in a Place where no Revolutions happen even among the Poultry. You will
bring us some thing to chat about, and I hope you will bring us yourself pretty
well after all. May no Misfortunes happen to me till *Colin's forgotten* &c and
we find a better in his Place—both those Events will happen the same Day.

I wish it may be possible that Langton's second Daughter can exceed the
elder in Beauty & Sprightliness, that which I saw was a mighty lovely Girl.
I asked Lady Rothes how She did that day as She had not been very well when
She was here you know, & She seemed to be strangely mobbled. Madam says
She, in a pretty loud Voice, I have a *Poul*tice on now.—it has cured my
Master of his Passion however.—This was at Richmond. I have not seen them
since. Adieu dear Sir—and continue your kindness for Mr Thrale, & for
Hetty, & for Susan, and for Sophy, & for Ciceley, and for all that belongs to
Your most Faithful & Obedient

H: L: Thrale.

Give a thousand Compliments to Mr Boswell, and tell Dr Taylor I always
send some to him, for if I *say* Lilly Lolly—I *mean* my Service to Doctor
Taylor. I hope you remember that nonsense or you will think me mad.

Mr Seward & Mr Thrale call to me from the Lawn to send their Compliments to you & to Mr Boswell.

548.—5. Ovid, *Ars Amat.* ii. 13: to keep is as good as to get.

549. Ashbourne. Sa. 20 Sept. '77. Mrs. Thrale.

Adam.—1788, No. 176.

Dear Madam

I do not remember what has happened that you write on mourning paper and use black wax.

Boswel liked Seward better as he knew him more, and seems well pleased to be remembered by him and my Master.

Pretty dear Queeney I wish her many and many happy Birthdays. I hope you will never lose her, though I should go to Lichfield, and though she should sit the thirteenth in many a company.[1]

You have nothing to say because you live at Streatham, and expect me to say much when I return from Lichfield and Ashbourne places to be considered as abounded[2] in Novelty, and supplying every hour materials for history. It is as much as I can do to furnish every post with a letter, I keep nothing behind for oral communication.

I took Boswel yesterday to see Keddleston,[3] and the silk mils, and china work at Derby, he was pleased with all. The Derby China is very pretty, but I think the gilding is all superficial, and the finer pieces are so dear, that perhaps silver vessels of the same capacity may be sometimes bought at the same price, and I am not yet so infected with the contagion of China-fancy, as to like any thing at that rate which can so easily be broken.

Master is very inconstant to Lady R——. Did he not hold out against forty such repellents from Mrs P——?[4] He grows nice I find let him try whether nicety will make him happy.

Boswel has spent more money than he expected, and I must supply him with part of his expences home. I have not

549.—1. In 1788, No. 175, dated 18 Sept., is the following: 'Something always happens when you go to Lichfield; and our sitting down thirteen to table yesterday made my fool's nerves flutter for Queeney.'

2. 'abounding' 1788, no doubt rightly correcting a slip.

3. During a previous visit Lord Scarsdale had dined with JT, see 418. But J may have known him otherwise; on this occasion JT was not of the party, though he lent his chaise (*L* iii. 160). I note that 'we talked of Mr. Langton' (*L* iii. 161). Now Lord S had married Lord Portmore's daughter, and Lord P was BL's friend.

4. The dashes are J's. HLP's supplements are 'Rothes' (see 548*a*) and 'Mrs. Percy'. For Mrs. P see on 288.

much with me, and beg Master to send me by the next post a note of ten pounds, which I will punctually return, not in opportunities of beneficence, though the noblest payments in the world, but in money or Bank paper. Do not let him forget me.

Do not suppose that I wrote this letter on purpose to borrow. *My soul disdains it.* I did not think on it when I began to write. When I miss a post I consider myself as deviating from the true rule of action. Seeing things in this light,[5] I consider every letter as something in the line of duty, upon this foot I make my arrangements, and under whatever circumstances of difficulty, endeavour to carry them into execution, for having in some degree pledged myself for the performance I think the reputation both of my head and my heart engaged, and reprobate every thought of desisting from the undertaking.

Howel tells of a few words in Spanish, the true utterance of which will denominate the Speaker bueno Romanciador,[6] the last sentence will un bueno politico. He that can rattle these words well together may say all that political controversy generally produces.

I am, Madam, Your most humble servant
Sam: Johnson

Nay, but do enquire after Bolt court.

Sept. 20. 1777 Ashbourne.

549a. Streatham. ⟨Sa. 20 Sept. '77.⟩ From Mrs. Thrale to J at Ashbourne.

R 540.73—

Dear Sir

Lest Mr Seward should have neglected to put my last Letter in the Post I write again today;—for Seward seems to turn Humourist I think, and talk of nothing but himself. Horrible Accidents have happened lately among the great Folks; Lord Harcourt was walking about his Woods & Grounds with a

549.—5. 'this light', 'the line', 'this foot', 'under whatever circumstances', 'pledged myself', and 'reprobate' are all underlined; but the underlines seem not to be J's. For J's views on some of these phrases see *L* iii. 196. HLP's note is: 'A ridicule of the Newspaper Language, the cant phrases of the Day.'

6. *Epistolae Ho-Elianae*, 1 August 1623 ('Buen Romancista, a good speaker of Spanish'; Hill quotes the shibboleth).

favourite Spaniel whom he was heard to call very loud, & seen to follow; but he was seen & heard no more till he & his Dog were found many Hours after drowned in a Well surrounded with Bushes; it is supposed the Spaniel fell in & he endeavouring to draw him out fell after him. Sir Edward Hawke's Son too yesterday riding thro' Knightsbridge, a Post Chaise ran against him, drove its Pole into his Body, & he died on the Spot—without a Groan.

Sir John Lade is better—Elliott the Physician has frighted him into more Care they say, & it is to be hop'd He may go on to one & Twenty. So the World runs on. My Master has Prosperity in Sight, & in Possession; and lets no Cares for the future disturb his golden Dreams: everybody tells me of some new Plan of Expence, he tells me nothing himself, but I hear it on all Sides, & shall I suppose see it anon. I am pleased you have Mr Boswell at Ashburne, it would be a fine House for Burney, now 'tis so musical; I beg you to give my best Compliments both to the Doctor & Mr Boswell. Your Friend Levett came here Yesterday unluckily we dined out; Father Prior too from the Paris Benedictines and another Monk came here to dinner, but Abbess & Armstrong managed very prudently & pleased them all. Mr Levett staid till today & returned to Town with Mr Thrale. The Fryars are to spend next Sunday & Monday with us.

My Master was gone to an Annual Meeting of the Election Folks—to which I sent all the Fruit I could strip the Garden of. I was gone to London to buy finery for Brighthelmston, that I may have my Share of the *Years of Plenty* but nobody was displeased & all went well. I hope you will not be long away. My Master's Bridle must be held by a stronger hand than that of Your most faithful & Obedient

H: L: Thrale.

He is grown so grand now he is quite touchy if one speaks to him.

550. Ashbourne. M. 22 Sept. '77. Mrs. Thrale.

Adam.—1788, No. 177.

Dear Madam

Now to sit down to tell me a long newspaper story about Lord Harcourt and his dog.[1]—I hoped when you had seen Levet, you would have learned something that concerned me.

I hope Master has been so kind as to send me the ten pounds else I shall be forced to borrow at Ashbourne or Lichfield.

Boswel has been this morning with me to see Ilam[2] Garden, he talks of going away this week, and I shall not

<hr>

550.—1. See 549a.
   2. For the visit to 'Islam' see *L* iii. 187.

think of staying here much longer though the wind whistles very prettily. My Nights, are still such as I do not like, but complaint will not mend them.

If Sir John[3] holds life to one and twenty, he will probably live on, for his constitution if it does not grow weaker will become firmer.

The harvest in Staffordshire has been such for plenty, and so well gathered as to be mentioned with admiration. Make your most of these golden years, and buy liberally what will now be liberally allowed. I hope to partake a little of the general abundance.—But I am now sixty eight. Make good use, my dear Lady of your days of health and spriteliness, sixty eight is coming fast upon you. Let it not find you wondering what is become of all the past.

If Aunt[4] comes now she can do but little harm, for she will hardly go with you to Brighthelmston, and she cannot long trouble you at Streatham.

I hope soon to come to Lichfield, and from Lichfield to London.

Taylor and Bos. send their compliments with those of
     Madam, Your most humble servant
Sept. 22. 1777 Ashbourne   Sam: Johnson

550.1. Ashbourne. ⟨Tu. 23 Sept. '77.⟩ James Boswell.

Address: To James Boswel Esq
R. H. Isham.—Pottle, *Catalogue of Boswell Papers* 1931, No. 466.

Mr Boswel's company is desired at the Blackmore's head.

551. Ashbourne. Th. 25 Sept. '77. Mrs. Thrale.

Adam.—1788, No. 178.

Dear Madam
 Boswel[1] is gone, and is I hope pleased that he has been here; though to look back on any thing with pleasure is not

550.—3. Lade (suppressed in 1788).   4. See 479.
550.1.—The date is fixed by *BP* xiii. 58 and Letter 552.
551.—1. HLP erased the name, but changed her mind and rewrote it.

very common. He has been gay and good humoured in his usual way, but we have not agreed upon any other expedition. He had spent more money than he intended, and I supplied him; my deficiences are again made up by Mr Thrales bill, for which I thank him.

I will send directions to the Taylor to make me some cloaths according to Mr Thrale's direction, though I cannot go with you to Brighthelmston, having loitered away the time I know not how, but, if you would have me I will endeavour to follow you, which upon the whole, perhaps may be as well. I am here now on the 25th and am obliged by promise to take Lichfield in my way, so that the 30th will come upon me too soon.

The Levet[2] that has been found in the register must be some other Levet; I dare say our Friend does not in his heart believe that it is he.

I am glad that the Benedictines found you at last. Father Wilkes, when he was amongst us, took Oxford in his way. I recommended him to Dr Adams, on whom he impressed a high opinion of his Learning: I am glad that my cell[3] is reserved. I may perhaps some time or other visit it, though I cannot easily tell why one should go to Paris twice. Our own beds are soft enough.[4] Yet my Master will tell you that one wants to be doing some thing. I have some thing like a longing to see my Masters Performances, a pleasure which I shall hardly have till he returns from Brighthelmston. I beg that before you go you will send the Bibliographia Britannica[5] to my habitation.[6]

I am Dear Madam, Your most humble servant,

Sam: Johnson

Let your next be sent to Lichfield.

Ashbourne. Sept. 25 1777

551.—2. In HLT's letter dated 18 Sept. (see on 549) is: 'My husband bids me tell you that he examined the register, and that Levet is only seventy-two years old.'

3. 'A cell is always kept ready for your use, he' (Cowley, the Benedictine prior) 'tells me.' 1788, loc. cit.

4. In 1788, loc. cit., a conversation is reported between the Thrales, Father Cowley, and Lord Mulgrave on the softness and dirt of French beds.

5. A slip for Biographia, see 561.1.

6. He does not call it his house, perhaps because he did not own it; he rented it from Allen. See on 605.1.

551a. London. F. 26 (misdated 25) Sept. ⟨'77⟩. From Mrs. Thrale to J at Ashbourne.

Address: To Dr Sam: Johnson at the Rev: Dr Taylor's Ashburn Derbys.
Postmark: 26 *and* 27 SE (one stamped in error?). Franked by HT.

R 540.74—

Dear Sir   a Shop in Dean Street Soho. Fryday Septr 25.

I have this Moment been at Bolt Court myself to pick up News such as you like: Mrs Des Moulines however wrote to you it seems two Days ago so now you know all without my help: Mr Levett was dusting Books, he hears Mrs Williams mends a little under Dr Lewis's Care—The fine Weather may also contribute something. Mr Levett believes Matters go tolerable about Mrs DesMoulines Son because She makes no Complaints. With regard to News paper Stories you put me in Mind of the Man in the Spanish Dialogues; & I am ready to answer with M^r A—Se no hazeis Caso de mis Nuevas que quereis que os diga? Nothing can I say with Certainty but that we go next Tuesday the 30 to Brighton & that I am ever most Faithfully Sir Your humble Servant

H: L: Thrale

Compliments to Dr Taylor.

552. Ashbourne. Sa. 27 Sept. '77. Mrs. Thrale.
Mrs. F. Bowman.—1788, No. 179.

Dear Madam

I think I have already told you that Bos is gone. The day before he went we met the Duke and Dutchess of Argyle in the street, and went to speak to them while they changed horses,[1] and in the afternoon Mrs. Langton and Juliet,[2] stopped in their way to London, and sent for me, I went to them and sent for Boswel whom Mrs Langton had never seen.

And so, here is this post without a letter. I am old, I am old, says Sir John Falstaff.[3] 'Take heed, my dear, youth flies

---

552.—1. Hill rightly guessed that the omission of the incident from the *Life* was intentional. See *BP* xiii. 58 (23 Sept.): 'The Duke and Duchess of Argyll stopped at Ashbourne to change horses, going to London. Dr. Johnson and I waited on the Duke, who was civil to us both. . . . The Duchess was courteous to the Doctor. But, as at Inveraray, would take hardly any notice of me.' JB perhaps thought he had said enough of her in the *Tour*.

2. 'After dinner the Doctor and I waited on Langton's Mother and one of her sisters, who stopped at the Blackamoor's head Inn' (*BP* xiii. 59). See 550.1. Hill sagely remarks that A'n is not on the road from Lincolnshire to L'n. The ladies were probably on their way between L'n and Scotland.

3. *II Henry IV*, ii. iv. 294.

apace.'⁴ You will be wanting a letter sometime. I wish I
were with you, but I cannot come yet.—

<blockquote>
Glacies et frigora Rheni
Me sine sola vides. Ah! ne te frigora lædant
Ah tibi ne glacies teneras secet aspera plantas! Ecl. x.⁵
</blockquote>

I wish you well; B⟨urney⟩⁶ and all, and shall be glad to
know your adventures. Do not however think wholly to
escape me, you will, I hope, see me at Brighthelmston. Dare
you answer me as Brutus answered his evil genius?⁷ I know
not when I shall write again now you are going to the world's
end. Extra anni solisque vias,⁸ where the post will be a long
time in reaching you. I shall notwithstanding all distance
continue to think on you, and to please myself with the hope
of being once again

Madam, Your most humble servant,

Sept. 27. 1777 Ashbourne   Sam: Johnson.

553. Ashbourne. M. 29 Sept. '77. Mrs. Thrale.

Adam.—1788, No. 180.

Dear Madam

And so because you hear that Mʳˢ Desmoulines¹ has
written, you hold it not necessary to write, as if she could
write like you, or I were equally content with hearing from
her. Call you this backing your Friends?² She did write,
and I remember nothing in her letter, but that she was

552.—4. Not traced.

    5. Virgil, *Ecl.* x. 47. HLP in her edition restored the text (*nives* for *glacies* and
teneras glacies). 'While you (alas, that I should find it so!) To shun my sight your
native soil forgo, And climb the frozen Alps, and tread the eternal snow. Ye frosts
and snows her tender body spare. These are not limbs for icicles to tear' Dryden.

    6. 'B——' 1788, original erased. My collator read the last letter as *g*, but Lysons's
'Burney' is certainly right, see 539*b*. HLP supplies 'Baretti', forgetting that he had
walked out in '76.

    7. 'Why, I will see thee at Philippi then' (*Julius Caesar*, IV. iii).

    8. Virgil, *Aen.* vi. 796: 'Beyond the solar year, without the starry way' Dryden.

553.—1. See 551*a*.

    2. 'Call you that backing of your friends?' (*I Henry IV*, II. iv. 168).

known, what remains is only to follow it. Daily business adds no more to wisdom, than daily lesson to the learning of the teacher. But of how few lives does not stated duty claim the greater part.

Far the greater part of human minds never endeavour their own improvement. Opinions once received from instruction or settled by whatever accident, are seldom recalled to examination; having been once supposed to be right, they are never discovered to be erroneous, for no application is made of any thing that time may present, either to shake or to confirm them. From this acquiescence in preconceptions none are wholly free, between fear of uncertainty, and dislike of labour every one rests while he might yet go forward, and they that were wise at thirty three, are very little wiser at forty five.

Of this speculation you are perhaps tired, and would rather hear of Sophy. I hope before this comes, that her head will be easier, and your head less filled with fears and troubles, which you know are to be indulged only to prevent evil, not to encrease it.

Your uneasiness about Sophy is probably unnecessary, and at worst your other children are healthful, and your affairs prosperous. Unmingled good cannot be expected, but as we may lawfully gather all the good within our reach, we may be allowed to lament after that which we lose. I hope your losses are at an end, and that as far as the condition of our present existence permits, your remaining life will be happy.

I am, Madam, your most obliged and most humble servant
Lichfield Aug. 5. 1775   Sam: Johnson

430. Lichfield. Sa. 5 Aug. '75. Mrs. Desmoulins.
Address: To Mrs Desmoulins in Chelsea. *Postmark*: illegible.
Adam.—*Corresp.* of D. Garrick 1831, ii. 72.

Madam

Mr Garrick has done as he is used to do. You may tell him that Dr Hawkesworth and I never exchanged any letters worth publication; our notes were commonly to tell when

430.—Hill suggests that G may have contemplated a memoir of H. But his inquiry might be connected with the abortive proposals for a posthumous collection of H's works; see Index II.

we should be at home, and I believe were seldom kept on either side. If I have any thing that will do any honour to his memory, I shall gladly supply it, but I remember nothing.

　　　　　　　I am, Madam, Your humble servant,

Lichfield. August. 5. 1775　　　　　　Sam: Johnson

431. Su. 27 Aug. '75. James Boswell (Edinburgh).
Not traced (see Addenda, p. 528).—Boswell 1791, i. 496 (Hill ii. 381).

Dear Sir,

I am now returned from the annual ramble into the middle counties. Having seen nothing that I had not seen before, I have nothing to relate. Time has left that part of the island few antiquities; and commerce has left the people no singularities. I was glad to go abroad, and, perhaps, glad to come home; which is, in other words, I was, I am afraid, weary of being at home, and weary of being abroad. Is not this the state of life? But, if we confess this weariness, let us not lament it; for all the wise and all the good say, that we may cure it.

For the black fumes[1] which rise in your mind, I can prescribe nothing but that you disperse them by honest business or innocent pleasure, and by reading sometimes easy and sometimes serious. Change of place is useful; and I hope that your residence at Auchinleck will have many good effects. . . .

That I should have given pain to Rasay, I am sincerely sorry; and am therefore very much pleased that he is no longer uneasy. He still thinks that I have represented him as personally giving up the Chieftainship. I meant only that it was no longer contested between the two houses, and supposed it settled, perhaps, by the cession of some remote generation, in the house of Dunvegan. I am sorry the advertisement was not continued for three or four times in the paper.

431.—1. JB had written 'My mind has been somewhat dark this summer. I have need of your warming and vivifying rays; and I hope I shall have them frequently. I am going to pass some time with my father at Auchinleck.' JB in his 'Review of my Life during the Summer Session' (*BP* x. 227) wrote, 'I do not remember any portion of my existence flatter than these two months.' No letter from J; 'so that my mind wanted it's great sun'. 'I could do nothing but what I was obliged to do; so kept no Journal.' For the visit to Auchinleck see the letter of 2 Sept. to Temple. His stepmother got on his nerves; 'I have appeared good-humoured; but it has cost me drinking a considerable quantity of strong beer to dull my faculties' (*L* ii. 382).

That Lord Monboddo[2] and Mr. Macqueen should controvert a position contrary to the imaginary interest of literary or national prejudice, might be easily imagined; but of a standing fact there ought to be no controversy: If there are men with tails, catch an *homo caudatus*; if there was writing of old in the Highlands or Hebrides, in the Erse language, produce the manuscripts. Where men write, they will write to one another, and some of their letters, in families studious of their ancestry, will be kept. In Wales there are many manuscripts.

I have now three parcels of Lord Hailes's history, which I purpose to return all the next week: that his respect for my little observations should keep his work in suspense, makes one of the evils of my journey. It is in our language, I think, a new mode of history, which tells all that is wanted, and, I suppose, all that is known, without laboured splendour of language, or affected subtilty of conjecture. The exactness of his dates raises my wonder. He seems to have the closeness of Henault without his constraint.

Mrs. Thrale was so entertained with your *Journal*, that she almost read herself blind.[3] She has a great regard for you.

Of Mrs. Boswell, though she knows in her heart that she does not love me, I am always glad to hear any good, and hope that she and the little dear ladies will have neither sickness nor any other affliction. But she knows that she does not care what becomes of me, and for that she may be sure that I think her very much to blame.

Never, my dear Sir, do you take it into your head that I do not love you; you may settle yourself in full confidence both of my love and my esteem; I love you as a kind man, I value you as a worthy man, and hope in time to reverence you as a man of exemplary piety. I hold you as Hamlet[4] has it, 'in my heart of heart', and therefore, it is little to say, that I am,

Sir, Your affectionate humble servant,
London, August 27, 1775.   Sam. Johnson

431.—2. JB had written that M and Donald Macqueen had supped with him; 'they joined in controverting your proposition, that the Gaelick of the Highlands and Isles of Scotland was not written till of late.'

3. See on 395.
4. III. ii.

83

432. Tu. 29 Aug. '75. Mrs. Thrale.

A. Houghton.—1788, No. 140.

Madam

Here is a rout and bustle; and a bustle, and a rout; as if nobody had ever before forgotten where a thing was laid.[1] At last there is no great harm done both Colson and Scot have copies; and real haste there is none. You will find it some day this week and any day will serve, or perhaps we can recollect it between us.

About your memory we will, if you please, have some serious talk. I fret at your forgetfulness, as I do at my own. We will try to mend both; yours at least is, I should hope, remediable. But, however it happens, we are of late never together.

Am I to come to morrow to the Borough, or will any call on me? This sorry foot! and this sorry Doctor Laurence who says it is the Gout! But then he thinks every thing the gout, and so I will try not to believe him. Into the sea,[2] I suppose, you will send it, and into the sea I design it shall go.—Can you remember, dear Madam, that I have a lame foot? I am sure I cannot forget it, if you had one so painful you would *so* remember it. Pain is good for the memory.

I am, Dear Madam, Your most humble Servant

Aug. 29. 1775   Sam: Johnson

432.1. W. 30 Aug. '75. James Boswell (Edinburgh).

Not traced.—Boswell 1791, i. 498 (Hill ii. 384; overlooked by Hill in *Letters*).

Sir,

If in these papers,[1] there is little alteration attempted, do not suppose me negligent. I have read them perhaps more closely than the rest; but I find nothing worthy of an objection.

Write to me soon, and write often, and tell me all your honest heart.

I am, Sir, Your's affectionately,

August 30, 1775.   Sam: Johnson

432.—1. The missing document was probably connected with the affair of Carter and the riding-school.   2. At B'n. See on 433.

432.1.—1. Lord Hailes's MS.

433. Sa. 9 Sept. '75. Lucy Porter (Lichfield).

The Misses Pennant (not seen); copy by Thomas Harwood, *c.* 1820, at Pembroke.—Croker's Boswell 1831, iii. 263.

Dear Madam

I have sent your Books[1] by the Carrier, and in Sandys's Travels you will find your glasses.

I have written this post to the ladies at Stow-hill, and you may, the day after you have this, or at any other time, send Mrs. Gastrel's Books.

Be pleased to make my Compliments to all my good friends.

I hope the poor dear hand is recovered, and you are now able to write, which, however, you need not do, for I am going to Brighthelmston,[2] and when I come back, will take care to tell you. In the mean time take great care of your health, and drink as much as you can.

I am, Dearest Love, Your most humble servant
London. Sept. 9. 1775.   Sam: Johnson

434. Sa. 9 Sept. '75. Mrs. Aston and Mrs. Gastrell.

Not traced; known only from the reference in 433.—

435. Th. 14 Sept. '75. James Boswell (Edinburgh).

Not traced; copy by one of JB's children, Isham.—Boswell 1791, i. 498 (Hill ii. 384).

My Dear Sir,

I now write to you, lest in some of your freaks and humours you should fancy yourself neglected. Such fancies I must entreat you never to admit, at least never to indulge, for my regard for you is so radicated and fixed that it is become part of my mind, and cannot be effaced but by some cause uncommonly violent. Therefore, whether I write, or not, set your thoughts at rest. I now write to tell you that

433.—Mr. Clifford, who had seen the original, told me that Croker's text is substantially accurate.

1. See 444.

2. Since they started for France on 15 Sept. (C 130), we may probably infer that the visit to B'n was cancelled.

I shall not very soon write again, for I am to set out to morrow on another journey.

.   .   .   .

Your friends are all well at Streatham, and in Leicester fields.[1] Make my compliments to Mrs. Boswell if she is in good humour with me.

I am, Sir, &c.

September 14th, 1775.   Sam. Johnson

436. Calais. M. 18 Sept. '75. Robert Levet.

Not traced.—Boswell 1793, ii. 257 (Hill ii. 385).

Dear Sir   Sept. 18, 1775, Calais.

We[1] are here in France, after a very pleasing passage of no more than six hours. I know not when I shall write again, and therefore I write now, though you cannot suppose that I have much to say. You have seen France yourself.[2] From this place we are going to Rouen, and from Rouen to Paris, where Mr. Thrale designs to stay about five or six weeks. We have a regular recommendation to the English resident,[3] so we shall not be taken for vagabonds. We think to go one way and return another, and see[4] as much as we can. I will

435.—1. Sir Joshua Reynolds and his nieces.

436.—1. The party was the same as had visited Wales in '74, with Baretti added. Both J and HLT kept journals of the tour, which lasted nearly two months. Of the former only a fragment survived the 'precipitate burning of his papers a few days before his death' (*L* ii. 389): this was the second of three or more small volumes, and covers the period 10 Oct. to 5 Nov. JB acquired this MS. from J's executors, and printed it; it is now in the British Museum, and has been carefully re-edited by Dr. Powell: *L* ii. 389-401. HLT's much fuller journal was unknown until the acquisition by the John Rylands Library of a great mass of HLP's papers; it was edited, with her later French journal of '84, by Drs. Tyson and Guppy in 1932, as *The French Journals of Mrs. Thrale and Doctor Johnson.*

2. L 'became early in life a waiter at a coffee-house in Paris' (*GM*, quoted *L* i. 243).

3. 'the English resident' is, I suppose, not what we now call 'the English colony' ('English' being a substantive), of whom, in fact, the travellers seem to have seen little, but an individual ('resident' being the substantive). If that is so, I am told the ambassador must be intended, though (see *OED*) that is an unusual application of the word 'resident'. HLT recorded (20 Oct.) 'we . . . had applied . . . to the English Ambassador' for leave to attend 'the fine Playhouse erected . . . for the Entertainment of the King, Queen, &c.'. He was Lord Stormont (*French Journals* 128).

4. I print Hill's conjecture *see* for the *for* of 1793, which seems certain. For the corruption cf. 416, where 'from' was read in 1788 as 'seem'.

try to speak a little French;[5] I tried hitherto but little, but
I spoke sometimes. If I heard better, I suppose I should
learn faster.

> I am, Sir, Your humble servant,
> Sam. Johnson.

437. Paris. Su. 22 Oct. '75. Robert Levet.

Not traced.—Boswell 1793, ii. 257 (Hill ii. 385).

Dear Sir   Paris, Oct. 22, 1775.

We are still here, commonly very busy in looking about us.
We have been to day at Versailles. You have seen it, and I
shall not describe it. We came yesterday from Fontainbleau,
where the Court is now. We went to see the King and Queen
at dinner, and the Queen was so impressed by Miss,[1] that she
sent one of the gentlemen to enquire who she was. I find all
true that you have ever told me of Paris. Mr. Thrale is very
liberal, and keeps us two coaches, and a very fine table; but
I think our cookery very bad.[2] Mrs. Thrale got into a con-
vent of English nuns,[3] and I talked with her through the
grate, and I am very kindly used by the English Benedictine
friars.[4] But upon the whole I cannot make much acquain-

436.—5. J usually fell back on Latin: *L* ii. 404. 'Though Johnson understood French
perfectly, he could not speak it readily . . . yet he wrote it, I imagine, pretty well.'
If J's 'hitherto' refers only to the present occasion, his opportunities had been limited;
they did not reach Calais until the afternoon of the 17th, where, however, they 'had
an excellent Dinner which a Capuchin Fryar enlivened by his Company' (*French
Journals* 71).

437.—1. HLT records 19 Oct. that they watched 'Monsieur et Madame dine
together'. They, like the King and Queen, 'sat like two people stuffed wth straw;
and only spoke to enquire after our Niggey, about whom the Queen had likewise
before been very inquisitive'.

2. J noted in Paris 10 Oct. 'Their meals are gross'. HLT abounds in the same
sense, complaining that the meat was sometimes not hung long enough, sometimes
much too long; 'besides that every sort of Food being dress'd so very much, & no
Flavour of the Food remaining, they are driven to the Necessity of superadding
something else which is commonly Garlick, Vinegar, Cheese & Salt.' She does,
however, mention the plenty of fish and game; and in her journal of 1784: 'my Maid
will not easily forget the French Cuisine; I never saw a Creature so enjoy herself'
(*French Journals* 103, 130, 195). In her *Anecdotes* (102 = *JM* i. 216) she quotes J as
saying 'They have few sentiments, but they express them neatly; they have little meat
too, but they dress it well.' Hill is inclined to reject this anecdote as inconsistent;
perhaps he is needlessly suspicious. See also *L* ii. 402.

3. HLT 16 Oct. gives a long account of this visit.

4. Especially the Prior, Cowley, and Father Wilkes, both of whom were in England
in '77. See *L* ii. 390, *French Journals* 97, 223, and Index II, s.v. Wilkes.

tance here, and though the churches, palaces, and some private houses are very magnificent, there is no very great pleasure after having seen many, in seeing more; at least the pleasure, whatever it be, must some time have an end, and we are beginning to think when we shall come home. Mr. Thrale calculates that as we left Streatham on the fifteenth of September, we shall see it again about the fifteenth of November.[5]

I think I had not been on this side of the sea five days before I found a sensible improvement in my health. I ran a race in the rain this day, and beat Baretti. Baretti is a fine fellow, and speaks French, I think, quite as well as English.

Make my compliments to Mrs. Williams; and give my love to Francis, and tell my friends that I am not lost.

I am, dear Sir, Your affectionate humble, &c.

Sam. Johnson.

437.1. ⟨Nov. '75. Jane Burke⟩.
Earl Fitzwilliam, Wentworth Woodhouse.—*TLS* 2 July 1938.

Madam

Among those who really share your pleasures and your troubles, give me leave to condole with you upon the death of a Friend whom I loved much, and whom you undoubtedly loved much more. His death has taken from us the benefit of his counsel, and the delight of his conversation, but it cannot without our own fault, deprive us of the influence of his virtues, or efface the pleasing remembrance of his Worth his Integrity, and his Piety.

I am, Madam, your most humble servant,

Sam: Johnson

438. Th. 16 Nov. '75. James Boswell (Edinburgh).
Not traced.—Boswell 1791, i. 499 (Hill ii. 387).

Dear Sir,
I am glad that the young Laird[1] is born, and an end, as I

437.—5. HLT concludes her journal 'at Dover Saturday—11th: Nov[r] 1775'.

437.1.—Endorsed by Edmund Burke 'Mrs. Burke on her Father's death'. Christopher Nugent died 12 Nov. '75 (*TLS* 21 Jan. 1939, 42, correcting *DNB*).

438.—1. JB had written 24 Oct. to announce 'the birth of my Son, on the 9th instant; I have named him Alexander, after my father.'

hope, put to the only difference that you can ever have with Mrs. Boswell.[2] I know that she does not love me, but I intend to persist in wishing her well till I get the better of her.

Paris is, indeed, a place very different from the Hebrides, but it is to a hasty traveller not so fertile of novelty, nor affords so many opportunities of remark. I cannot pretend to tell the publick any thing of a place better known to many of my readers than to myself. We can talk of it when we meet.[3]

I shall go next week to Streatham, from whence I purpose to send a parcel of the 'History' every post. Concerning the character of Bruce,[4] I can only say, that I do not see any great reason for writing it, but I shall not easily deny what Lord Hailes and you concur in desiring.

I have been remarkably healthy all the journey, and hope you and your family have known only that trouble and danger which has so happily terminated. Among all the congratulations that you may receive, I hope you believe none more warm or sincere, than those of,

dear Sir, Your most affectionate,

November 16, 1775.   Sam. Johnson.

439. Th. 16 Nov. '75. Lucy Porter (Lichfield).

Fettercairn.—Boswell 1791, i. 500 (Hill ii. 387).

Dear Madam

This week I came home from Paris. I have brought you a little box[1] which I thought pretty, but I know not whether it is properly a snuff box, or a box for some other use. I will send it when I can find an opportunity. I have been through the whole Journey remarkably well. My fellow travellers

---

438.—2. 'This alludes to my old feudal principle of preferring male to female succession' JB. See 448.

3. JB had written: 'Shall we have "*A Journey to Paris*" from you in the winter? You will, I hope, at any rate be kind enough to give me some account of your French travels very soon, for I am very impatient.'

4. Hailes had written to JB 'I intend soon to give you "The Life of Robert Bruce", which you will be pleased to transmit to Dr. Johnson. I wish that you could assist me in a fancy which I have taken, of getting Dr. Johnson to draw a character of Robert Bruce, from the account that I give of that prince.' JB surmised that H was referring to a part of his *Annals*, 'and not a separate work' (*L* ii. 386).

439.—1. Perhaps the 'snuff-box' for which J paid '24L' (livres) at the Palais Marchand on 17 Oct. (*L* ii. 393).

were the same whom you saw at Lichfield, only we took Baretti with us. Paris is not so fine a place as you would expect. The palaces and Churches however are very splendid and magnificent, and what would please you, there are many very fine pictures, but I do not think their way of life commodious or pleasant.

Let me know how your health has been all this while. I hope the fine summer has given you strength sufficient to encounter the Winter.

Make my compliments to all my friends, and if your fingers will let you, write to me, or let your maid write, if it be troublesome to you.

I am, Dear Madam, Your most affectionate humble servant,
Nov. 16. 1775. Sam: Johnson

440. Th. 16 Nov. '75. John Taylor (Ashbourne).
Loyd.—Malone's Boswell 1811, ii. 418 (an extract); NQ 6S. v. 422.

Dear Sir

I came back last tuesday from France. Is not mine a kind of life turned upside down? Fixed to a spot when I was young, and roving the world when others are contriving to sit still, I am wholly unsettled. I am a kind of ship with a wide sail, and without an anchor.

Now I am come home, let me know how it is with you. I hope you are well, and intend to keep your residence this year. Let me know the month, and I will contrive to be about you. Our Friendship has now lasted so long, that it is valuable for its antiquity. Perhaps neither has any other companion to whom he can talk of his early years. Let me particularly know the state of your health. I think mine is the better for the journey. The French have a clear air and a fruitful soil, but their mode of common life is gross, and incommodious, and disgusting. I am come home convinced that no improvement of general use is to be gained among them.

I am, Dear Sir, Your affectionate servant,
London. Nov. 16. 1775 Sam: Johnson.

440.—I noted that this letter, though it is a complete sheet of two leaves, bears no direction. J wrote four letters on 16 Nov., and doubtless they were sent in covers franked by HT or Strahan.

441. Th. 16 Nov. '75. Edmund Hector (Birmingham).

Sotheby 5 June 1929.—*NQ* 6S. iii. 401.

Dear Sir

On Tuesday I returned from a ramble about France, and about a month's stay at Paris. I have seen nothing that much delighted or surprised me. Their palaces are splendid, and their Churches magnificent in their structure, and gorgeous in their ornaments, but the city in general makes a very mean appearance.

When I opened my letters, I found that you had very kindly complied with all my requests. The Bar[1] may be sent in a box directed to me at Henry Thrale Esq in Southwark. The whole company[2] that you saw went to France together, and the Queen was so pleased with our little girl, that she sent to enquire who she was.

We are all well, but I find, my dear Sir, that you are ill. I hope it does not continue true that you are almost a cripple. Would not a warm bath have helped you? Take care of yourself for my sake as well as that of your other friends. I have the best claim to your attention, if priority be allowed any advantages. Dear Mrs. Careless, I know, will be careful of you. I can only wish you well, and of my good wishes you may be always certain, for

I am, Dear Sir, Your most affectionate

Fleet Street. Nov. 16. 1775   Sam: Johnson

442. F. 15 Dec. '75. Elizabeth Montagu.

Not traced.—Croker's Boswell 1831, iii. 295.

Madam   15th Dec. 1775.

Having, after my return from a little ramble to France, passed some time in the country,[1] I did not hear, till I was told by Miss Reynolds, that you were in town; and when I did hear it, I heard likewise that you were ill. To have you detained among us by sickness is to enjoy your presence at

441.—1. I have no clue to the Bar. Perhaps something of B'm metal-work.

    2. In his Welsh journal of '74 J noted that on 20 Sept. 'We breakfasted with Hector'.

442.—1. At S'm.

too dear a rate. I suffer myself to be flattered with hope that only half the intelligence is now true, and that you are now so well as to be able to leave us, and so kind as not to be willing.

I am, madam, your most humble servant,

Sam: Johnson

443. Su. 17 Dec. '75. Elizabeth Montagu.

C. T. Jeffery.—Croker's Boswell 1831, iii. 296.

Madam

All that the esteem and reverence of mankind can give you, has been long in your possession, and the little that I can add to the voice of Nations, will not much exalt you; of that little however you are, I hope, very certain.

I wonder, Madam, if you remember Coll in the Hebrides?[1] The Brother and Heir of poor Coll has just been to visit me, and I have engaged to dine with him on Thursday. I do not know his lodging, and cannot send him a message, and must therefore suspend the honour which you are pleased to offer, to

Madam, Your most humble Servant,

Decr 17, 1775   Sam: Johnson

444. ⟨Sa. 23?⟩ Dec. '75. Lucy Porter (Lichfield).

Address: To Mrs Lucy Porter in Lichfield. *Postmark*: 2 ⟨? 3⟩ DE. Franked by Thrale.

Fettercairn.—Boswell 1791, i. 500, dated 'December, 1775' (Hill ii. 388).

Dear Madam

Some weeks ago I wrote to You to tell you that I was just come home from a ramble, and hoped that I should have heard from you. I am afraid Winter has laid hold on your fingers, and hinders you from writing. However let somebody write, if you cannot, and tell me how you do, and a

443.—1. J implies, no doubt with reason, that Mrs. M had read his book.

444.—I guess that J wrote just before Christmas; Saturday was a post-day.

little of what has happened at Lichfield among our Friends. I hope you are all well.

When I was in France, I thought myself growing young, but am afraid that cold weather will take part of my new vigour from me. Let us however take care of ourselves, and lose no part of our health by negligence.

I never knew whether you received the Commentary on the New Testament and the Travels,[1] and the glasses.

Do, my dear Love, write to me, and do not let us forget each other. This is the season of good wishes, and I wish you all good. I have not lately seen Mr. Porter, nor heard of him. Is he with you?

Be pleased to make my compliments to Mrs. Adey, and Mrs. Cobb, and all my friends, and when I can do you any good let me know.

  I am, Dear Madam, Yours most affectionately
Dec. 1775   Sam: Johnson.

445. Th. 21 Dec. '75. Elizabeth Montagu.

Princeton.—Croker's Boswell 1831, iii. 296.

Madam,

I know not when any letter has given me so much pleasure or vexation, as that which I had yesterday the honour of receiving. That you, Madam, should wish for my company, is surely a sufficient reason for being pleased; that I should delay twice, what I had so little right to expect even once, has so bad an appearance, that I can only hope to have it thought, that I am ashamed.

You have kindly allowed me to name a day. Will you be pleased, Madam to accept of me any day after Tuesday? Till I am favoured with your answer, or despair of so much condescention I shall suffer no engagement to fasten itself upon me.

  I am, Madam, Your most obliged, and most humble servant,
Thursday, Dec. 21, 1775.   Sam: Johnson.

444.—1. See 433.

446. Sa. 23 Dec. '75. James Boswell (Edinburgh).

Not traced.—Boswell 1791, i. 515 (Hill ii. 411).

Dear Sir,

Never dream of any offence,[1] how should you offend me? I consider your friendship as a possession, which I intend to hold till you take it from me, and to lament if ever by my fault I should lose it. However, when such suspicions find their way into your mind, always give them vent, I shall make haste to disperse them, but hinder their first ingress if you can. Consider such thoughts as morbid.

Such illness as may excuse my omission to Lord Hailes I cannot honestly plead. I have been hindered I know not how, by a succession of petty obstructions. I hope to mend immediately, and to send next post to his Lordship. Mr. Thrale would have written to you if I had omitted; he sends his compliments, and wishes to see you.

You and your lady will now have no more wrangling about feudal inheritance. How does the young Laird of Auchinleck? I suppose Miss Veronica is grown a reader and discourser.

I have just now got a cough, but it has never yet hindered me from sleeping: I have had quieter nights than are common with me.

I cannot but rejoice that Joseph[2] has had the wit to find the way back. He is a fine fellow, and one of the best travellers in the world.

Young Col brought me your letter. He is a very pleasing youth. I took him two days ago to the Mitre, and we dined together. I was as civil as I had the means of being.

I have had a letter from Rasay, acknowledging, with great appearance of satisfaction, the insertion in the Edinburgh paper. I am very glad that it was done.

446.—1. JB had written, 5 Dec., a letter introducing young Maclean of Col. (*L* ii. 406). 'Not having heard from him for a longer time than I supposed he would be silent', JB wrote again 18 Dec.: 'Sometimes I have been afraid that the cold which has gone over Europe this year like a sort of pestilence has seized you severely: sometimes my imagination, which is upon occasions prolific of evil, hath figured that you may have somehow taken offence at some part of my conduct' (*L* ii. 410). JB's journal further tells us that on the same day he wrote also 'to Mr. Thrale in case of his being ill' (*BP* ix. 42). This explains the allusion to HT in J's reply.

2. Ritter; who, as JB explains in a note, 'after having left me for some time, had now returned to me'—as Frank returned to J.

My compliments to Mrs. Boswell, who does not love me; and of all the rest, I need only send them to those that do; and I am afraid it will give you very little trouble to distribute them.

I am, my dear, dear Sir, Your affectionate humble servant,
December 23, 1775.   Sam. Johnson.

446.1. Dec. '75. John Taylor.

Address (Maggs): To the Rev. Dr. Taylor (franked by Thrale).
Maggs Cat. 247 (1909), 382 (not seen).—Extract in catalogue.

(Respecting the Claim of a Mr. Wood):

If the lawyers judge your claim untenable, or even disreputable (?) I would not have you bring into the Courts etc.

447. Streatham. W. 10 Jan. '76. James Boswell (Edinburgh).

Not traced.—Boswell 1791, ii. 1 (Hill ii. 412).

Dear Sir,

I have at last sent you all Lord Hailes's papers. While I was in France, I looked very often into Henault; but Lord Hailes, in my opinion, leaves him far, and far, behind. Why I did not dispatch so short a perusal sooner, when I look back, I am utterly unable to discover: but human moments[1] are stolen away by a thousand petty impediments which leave no trace behind them. I have been afflicted, through the whole Christmas, with the general disorder, of which the worst effect was a cough, which is now much mitigated, though the country, on which I look from a window at Streatham, is now covered with a deep snow. Mrs. Williams is very ill: every body else is as usual.

Among the papers, I found a letter to you, which I think you had not opened; and a paper for 'The Chronicle',[2] which

446.1.—'Mr. Wood' should perhaps be 'Mrs. Wood' (q.v. in Index II); 'disreputable' I suppose is a misreading of 'disputable'.

447.—1. I cannot feel happy about this phrase. If 'moments' is moments of time, 'human' seems inapplicable. Perhaps 'moments' is 'impulses', though the latest quotation for such a sense in *OED* is 1691. J himself gives a definition 'actuating power', for which he quotes Hooker and others. Discussing a reading in Pope, he said 'Of moment, is momentous; of moments, temporary' (*L* iii. 347).

2. For JB's habit of 'inserting' papers in *The London Chronicle* see references in Pottle, *Index to BP*, or *Lit. Career of JB* 236–50.

I suppose it not necessary now to insert. I return them both.

I have, within these few days, had the honour of receiving Lord Hailes's first volume, for which I return my most respectful thanks.

I wish you, my dearest friend, and your haughty[3] lady, (for I know she does not love me,) and the young ladies, and the young Laird, all happiness. Teach the young gentleman, in spite of his mamma, to think and speak well of,

Sir, Your affectionate humble servant
Jan. 10, 1776.   Sam. Johnson

448. M. 15 Jan. '76. James Boswell (Edinburgh).

Not traced.—Boswell 1791, ii. 4 (Hill ii. 415).

Dear Sir,

I was much impressed by your letter,[1] and, if I can form upon your case any resolution satisfactory to myself, will very gladly impart it: but whether I am quite equal to it, I do not know. It is a case compounded of law and justice, and requires a mind versed in juridical disquisitions. Could you not tell your whole mind to Lord Hailes? He is, you know, both a Christian and a Lawyer. I suppose he is above partiality, and above loquacity: and, I believe, he will not think the time lost in which he may quiet a disturbed, or settle a wavering mind. Write to me, as any thing occurs to you; and if I find myself stopped by want of facts necessary to be known, I will make enquiries of you as my doubts arise.

If your former resolutions should be found only fanciful, you decide rightly in judging that your father's fancies may claim the preference; but whether they are fanciful or rational, is the question. I really think Lord Hailes could help us.

Make my compliments to dear Mrs. Boswell; and tell her,

447.—3. I am tempted to suspect that J wrote 'naughty'; his initial *b* and *n* are very similar, so that 'now' and 'here' have been confused.
448.—1. The letter by which J was 'much impressed' is not quoted in the *Life*, where it is replaced (ii. 413) by a fresh 'state of the question'. In his journal JB describes his letter as 'long, serious, and earnest'; it was written 2 Jan., and enforced two days later by 'a Postscript still stronger'. The whole 'made three gilt sheets'. He adds 'My Wife wrote also', a rare intervention. Her letter is not mentioned in the *Life* until J's reference to it 457, ii. 422 (*BP* xi. 56, 57, 61).

that I hope to be wanting in nothing that I can contribute, to bring you all out of your troubles.

I am, dear Sir, most affectionately, Your humble servant, London, Jan. 15, 1776.   Sam. Johnson

449. M. 15 Jan. '76. John Taylor (Ashbourne).

Address: The Revd Dr Taylor at Ashborne Derbys.—Franked by Thrale. *Postmark*: 16 IA.
E. Byrne Hackett 1925; known to Hill only from an auction catalogue.

Dear Sir

You gave me but an uncomfortable account of your health, and as I have not heard from you since, I am afraid you are worse, let me know whether you are well, and when we shall see you.

You will not wonder, that I am curious about your cause. My advice still[1] is, if you are likely to lose it, that you should not try it; but as I know not the nature of the settlement, I cannot tell whether you are likely to lose it. It is easy to conceive that such a woman would have power enough over such a man, to dictate his will. Have you had the opinions of Dunning, and the rest of your council? If you have you will begin to judge what you may expect. Do not let an event to disturb you, about which you have so little need to care.

                    I am, Sir, your most humble servant
London. Jan 15. 1776   Sam: Johnson

450. Sa. 3 Feb. '76. James Boswell (Edinburgh).

Not traced.—Boswell 1791, ii. 4, dated 1773 but placed s.a. 1776 (Hill ii. 416).

Dear Sir,

I am going to write upon a question which requires more knowledge of local law, and more acquaintance with the general rules of inheritance, than I can claim; but I write, because you request it.

449.—1. As in 446.1.

Land is, like any other possession, by natural right wholly in the power of its present owner; and may be sold, given, or bequeathed, absolutely or conditionally, as judgement shall direct, or passion incite.

But natural right would avail little without the protection of law; and the primary notion of law is restraint in the exercise of natural right. A man is therefore, in society, not fully master of what he calls his own, but he still retains all the power which law does not take from him.

In the exercise of the right which law either leaves or gives, regard is to be paid to moral obligations.

Of the estate which we are now considering, your father still retains such possession, with such power over it, that he can sell it, and do with the money what he will, without any legal impediment. But when he extends his power beyond his own life, by settling the order of succession, the law makes your consent necessary.

Let us suppose that he sells the land to risk the money in some specious adventure, and in that adventure loses the whole: his posterity would be disappointed; but they could not think themselves injured or robbed. If he spent it upon vice or pleasure, his successors could only call him vicious and voluptuous; they could not say that he was injurious or unjust.

He that may do more, may do less. He that, by selling or squandering, may disinherit a whole family, may certainly disinherit part, by a partial settlement.

Laws are formed by the manners and exigencies of particular times, and it is but accidental that they last longer than their causes: the limitation of feudal succession to the male arose from the obligation of the tenant to attend his chief in war.

As times and opinions are always changing, I know not whether it be not usurpation to prescribe rules to posterity, by presuming to judge of what we cannot know; and I know not whether I fully approve either your design or your father's, to limit that succession which descended to you unlimited. If we are to leave *sartum tectum*[1] to posterity, what we have without any merit of our own received from

450.—1. Technical in Roman law for a building in good repair.

our ancestors, should not choice and free-will be kept un-
violated? Is land to be treated with more reverence than
liberty?—If this consideration should restrain your father
from disinheriting some of the males, does it leave you the
power of disinheriting all the females?

Can the possessor of a feudal estate make any will? Can
he appoint, out of the inheritance, any portions to his
daughters? There seems to be a very shadowy difference
between the power of leaving land, and of leaving money to
be raised from land; between leaving an estate to females,
and leaving the male heir, in effect, only their steward.

Suppose at one time a law that allowed only males to
inherit, and during the continuance of this law many estates
to have descended, passing by the females, to remoter heirs.
Suppose afterwards the law repealed in correspondence with
a change of manners, and women made capable of inheritance; would not then the tenure of estates be changed?
Could the women have no benefit from a law made in their
favour? Must they be passed by upon moral principles for
ever, because they were once excluded by a legal prohibition?
Or may that which passed only to males by one law, pass
likewise to females by another?

You mention your resolution to maintain the rights of
your brothers:[2] I do not see how any of their rights are
invaded.

As your whole difficulty arises from the act of your
ancestor, who diverted the succession from the females, you
enquire, very properly, what were his motives, and what was
his intention; for you certainly are not bound by his act
more than he intended to bind you, nor hold your land on
harder or stricter terms than those on which it was granted.

Intentions must be gathered from acts. When he left the
estate to his nephew, by excluding his daughters, was it, or
was it not, in his power to have perpetuated the succession
to the males? If he could have done it, he seems to have
shewn, by omitting it, that he did not desire it to be done;
and, upon your own principles, you will not easily prove
your right to destroy that capacity of succession which your
ancestors have left.

450.—2. JB in a note explains that by 'brothers' he intended 'all the heirs male'.

If your ancestor had not the power of making a perpetual settlement; and if, therefore, we cannot judge distinctly of his intentions, yet his act can only be considered as an example; it makes not an obligation. And, as you observe, he set no example of rigorous adherence to the line of succession. He that overlooked a brother, would not wonder that little regard is shewn to remote[3] relations.

As the rules of succession are, in a great part, purely legal, no man can be supposed to bequeath any thing, but upon legal terms; he can grant no power which the law denies; and if he makes no special and definite limitation, he confers all the powers which the law allows.

Your ancestor, for some reason, disinherited his daughters; but it no more follows that he intended his act as a rule for posterity, than the disinheriting of his brother.

If therefore, you ask by what right your father admits daughters to inheritance, ask yourself, first, by what right you require them to be excluded?

It appears, upon reflection, that your father excludes nobody; he only admits nearer females to inherit before males more remote; and the exclusion is purely consequential.

These, dear Sir, are my thoughts, immethodical and deliberative;[4] but, perhaps, you may find in them some glimmering of evidence.[5]

I cannot, however, but again recommend you to a conference with Lord Hailes, whom you know to be both a Lawyer and a Christian.

Make my compliments to Mrs. Boswell, though she does not love me.

I am, Sir, Your affectionate servant,

Feb. 3, 1773.   Sam: Johnson.

450.—3. J perhaps wrote 'remoter'.

4. 'deliberative' is in its normal use incompatible with 'immethodical'. J means, I suppose, that his thoughts are set out as they occur in the process of deliberation. He gives 'hesitate' as a sense of the verb; and in the *Preface to Shakespeare* (p. 30 in the Oxford edition by Raleigh) 'deliberatively' is opposed to 'dogmatically'.

5. J was not in a position to supply any 'evidence' in the ordinary sense; he could work only on JB's materials. I was at one time tempted to think that he wrote 'Guidance', which could be misread as 'Evidence'. But 'evidence' can mean 'evidentness', so that a 'glimmering of evidence' is a ray of light.

451. Tu. 6 Feb. '76. John Wesley.

Not traced; copy by Thomas Harwood, *c.* 1820, at Pembroke.—
GM 1797, i. 455.

Sir   Feb. 6. 1776.

When I received your Commentary on the Bible I durst
not at first flatter myself that I was to keep it, having so
little claim to so valuable a present; and when Mrs. Hall
informed me of your kindness, was hindered from time to
time from returning you those thanks, which I now entreat
you to accept.

I have thanks likewise to return you for the addition of
your important suffrage to my argument on the American
question.[1] To have gained such a mind as yours, may justly
confirm me in my own opinion. What effect my paper has
had upon the publick, I know not; but I have no reason to be
discouraged. The Lecturer was surely in the right, who,
though he saw his audience slinking away, refused to quit
the Chair, while Plato[2] staid.

I am, Reverend Sir, Your most humble servant,

Sam: Johnson.

452. F. 9 Feb. '76. James Boswell (Edinburgh).

Not traced.—Boswell 1791, ii. 7 (Hill ii. 419).

Dear Sir,

Having not any acquaintance with the laws or customs of
Scotland, I endeavoured to consider your question upon
general principles, and found nothing of much validity that
I could oppose to this position. 'He who inherits a fief
unlimited by his ancestor, inherits the power of limiting it

451.—1. Hill quotes passages from W's *A Calm Address to our American Colonies*
(late in '75), in which he urged that 'no governments under Heaven are so despotic
as the republican', and other writings of his on the question; he quotes also an anonymous reply (*GM* Dec. '75, 561), the writer of which pointed out that Wesley, of all
men, ought to know better than to 'expect any good to arrive from a calm address to
men . . . under the dominion of enthusiasm'.

2. Cicero (*Brutus* 191) tells the story of 'Antimachus clarus poeta', who when reading his long poem was deserted by all his audience except Plato; 'legam, inquit,
nihilo minus; Plato enim mihi unus instar est centum milium.' J has the same
allusion 608: 'Plato is a Multitude.'

452.—JB wrote again 30 Jan. (*BP* xi. 83) enclosing a letter from Lord Hailes and
'begging to hear from him again' (*L* ii. 419).

according to his own judgement or opinion.' If this be true you may join with your father.

Further consideration produced another conclusion, 'He who receives a fief unlimited by his ancestors, gives his heirs some reason to complain if he does not transmit it unlimited to posterity'. For why should he make the state of others worse than his own, without a reason? If this be true, though neither you nor your father are about to do what is quite right, but[1] as your father violates (I think) the legal succession least, he seems to be nearer the right than yourself.

It cannot but occur that 'Women have natural and equitable claims as well as men, and these claims are not to be capriciously or lightly superseded or infringed'. When fiefs implied military service, it is easily discerned why females could not inherit them; but that reason is now at an end. As manners make laws, manners likewise repeal them.

These are the general conclusions which I have attained. None of them are very favourable to your scheme of entail, nor perhaps to any scheme. My observation, that only he who acquires an estate may bequeath it capriciously, if it contains any conviction includes this position likewise, that only he who acquires an estate may entail it capriciously. But I think it may be safely presumed, that 'he who inherits an estate inherits all the power legally concomitant'. And that 'He who gives or leaves unlimited an estate legally limitable, must be presumed to give that power of limitation which he omitted to take away, and to commit future contingencies to future prudence.' In these two positions I believe Lord Hailes will advise you to rest; every other notion of possession seems to me full of difficulties, and embarrassed with scruples.[2]

If these axioms be allowed, you have arrived now at full liberty without the help of particular circumstances, which, however, have in your case great weight. You very rightly observe, that he who by passing by his brother gave the inheritance to his nephew, could limit no more than he gave, and by Lord Hailes's estimate of fourteen years purchase, what he gave was no more than you may easily entail accord-

---

452.—1. 'though . . . but' is not modern English; but we say 'though . . . yet'.
　2. For J's distrust of scruples see 454, 458, and references at *L* ii. 421.

ing to your own opinion, if that opinion should finally prevail.

Lord Hailes's suspicion that entails are encroachments on the dominion of Providence, may be extended to all hereditary privileges and all permanent institutions; I do not see why it may not be extended to any provision but for the present hour, since all care about futurity proceeds upon a supposition, that we know at least in some degree what will be future. Of the future we certainly[3] know nothing; but we may form conjectures from the past; and the power of forming conjectures, includes, in my opinion, the duty of acting in conformity to that probability which we discover. Providence gives the power of which reason teaches the use.

I am, dear Sir, Your most faithful servant,
February 9, 1776. Sam. Johnson.

I hope I shall get some ground now with Mrs. Boswell; make my compliments to her, and to the little people.

Don't burn papers; they may be safe enough in your own box,—you will wish to see them hereafter.

453. Tu. 13 Feb. '76. Archibald Hamilton.
Address: To Mr Hamilton.
Sotheby 18 Nov. 1929.—Nichols, *Lit. Anecd.* 1815, ix. 805.
Dear Sir

I am afraid that by altering the first article of the Dictionary at your desire, I have given occasion to an unhappy difference between you and Dr Calder, who has been with me, and seems to think himself in danger of losing the revision of the work. For this consequence I should be very deeply sorry. I considered the redundance which I lopped away not as the consequence of negligence or inability, but as the ⟨? result⟩ of superfluous diligence, naturally exerted on the first article. He that does too much soon learns to

452.—3. That is, 'know nothing for certain'.
453.—See Nichols, op. cit., for C's abortive attempt to produce a new edition of Chambers's *Cyclopaedia*. The work was ultimately undertaken by Abraham Rees, and published in five volumes '79–'86. Strahan's name appears first on all the title-pages except the last (produced after his death); Hamilton's appears in all volumes, with a large number of other proprietors. See 456, and for a long account of the controversy Nichols, *LI* iv. 799–819. N prints an 'expostulatory address' from C to J, dated 10 Feb., the MS. of which was catalogued by Tregaskis in 1935 (Cat. 453, 37). See also in Vol. iii. the letter to Hawkesworth of 20 Jan. ⟨?'73⟩.

do less. By his own account, however, it appears that ⟨he⟩ has shown what I think an improper degree of turbulence and impatience. I have advised him, and he has promised, to be hereafter less tenacious of his own determination, and more pliable to the direction of the proprietors and the opinion of those whom they may consult. I entreat therefore that all the past may be forgotten, that he may stand where he stood before, and be permitted to proceed with the work in which he is engaged. Do not refuse this request to
Sir, your most humble Servant,

Febr. 13. 1776   Sam: Johnson

454. Th. 15 Feb. '76. James Boswell (Edinburgh).

Not traced.—Boswell 1791, ii. 9, dated 1775 but placed s.a. 1776 (Hill ii. 420).

Dear Sir,

To the letters which I have written about your great question I have nothing to add. If your conscience is satisfied, you have now only your prudence to consult. I long for a letter, that I may know how this troublesome and vexatious question is at last decided.[1] I hope that it will at last end well. Lord Hailes's letter was very friendly, and very seasonable, but I think his aversion from entails has something in it like superstition. Providence is not counteracted by any means which Providence puts into our power. The continuance and propagation of families makes a great part of the Jewish law, and is by no means prohibited in the Christian institution, though the necessity of it continues no longer. Hereditary tenures are established in all civilised countries, and are accompanied in most with hereditary authority. Sir William Temple[2] considers our constitution as defective, that there is not an unalienable estate in land connected with a peerage; and Lord Bacon[3] mentions as a

454.—1. See JB's note: 'I was freed by Dr. Johnson from scruples of conscientious obligation, and could, therefore, gratify my father.'

2. Temple recommends 'a fixed Resolution in the Crown to create no Baron who shall not at the same time entail Four thousand Pounds a Year upon that Honour whilst it continues in his Family'—and so on, up to £8,000 for a duke. 'Essay on Popular Discontents' in *Miscellanea* Part iii, 1701, 87.

3. *An Advertisement touching an Holy War* (vii. 22 in Spedding 1859): 'No nobles, no gentlemen, no freemen, no inheritance of land, no stirp of ancient families.'

proof that the Turks are Barbarians, their want of *Stirpes*, as he calls them, or hereditary rank. Do not let your mind, when it is freed from the supposed necessity of a rigorous entail, be entangled with contrary objections, and think all entails unlawful, till you have cogent arguments, which I believe you will never find; I am afraid of scruples.

I have now sent all Lord Hailes's papers, part I found hidden in a drawer in which I had laid them for security, and had forgotten them. Part of these are written twice, I have returned both the copies. Part I had read before.

Be so kind as to return Lord Hailes my most respectful thanks for his first volume; his accuracy strikes me with wonder; his narrative is far superior to that of Henault, as I have formerly mentioned.

I am afraid that the trouble, which my irregularity and delay has cost him, is greater, far greater, than any good that I can do him will ever recompense, but if I have any more copy, I will try to do better.

Pray let me know if Mrs. Boswell is friends with me, and pay my respects to Veronica, and Euphemia, and Alexander.

I am, Sir, Your most humble servant,

Feb. 15, 1775   Sam. Johnson.

455. Sa. 17 Feb. '76. John Taylor (Ashbourne).

Address: Rev^d Dr Taylor Ashbourn Derbyshire. Franked by Strahan.
Postmark: 17 FE.
Loyd.—*NQ* 6S. v. 423.

Dear Sir

The Case which you sent me contains such vicissitudes of settlement and rescission that I will not pretend yet to give any opinion about it. My advice is, that it be laid before some of the best Lawyers, and branched out into queries, that the answer may be more deliberate, and the necessity of considering made greater.

Get it off your hands and out of your head as fast as you can. You have no evidence to wait for; all that can be done may be done soon.

Your health is of more consequence. Keep yourself

455.—See 461.

cheerful. Lye in Bed with a lamp, and when you cannot sleep, and are beginning to think, light your candle and read. At least light your candle, a man is perhaps never so much harrassed by his own mind in the light as in the dark.

Poor Caleb Harding is dead. Do's not every death of a Man long known begin to strike deep? How few dos the Man who has lived sixty years now know of the friends of his youth? At Lichfield there are none but Harry Jackson and Sedgwick, and Sedgwick when I left him, had a dropsy.

I am, I think, better than usual, and hope you will grow better too.

I am Sir Your most affectionate,

Febr. 17. 1776   Sam: Johnson

456. M. 19 Feb. '76. John Calder.

Sotheby (reference mislaid; dated 15 Feb. in catalogue; not seen).— Nichols, *Lit. Illustr.* 1822, iv. 811.

Sir,   Feb. 19, 1776.

I saw Mr. Strahan on Saturday, and find that Mr. Hamilton had shewn him my letter. Mr. Strahan is, as I feared, so angry and so resolute that I could not impress him in your favour, nor have any hope from him. If anything is done it must be with the other Proprietors. I am sorry for it.

I am, Sir, Your very humble servant,

Sam: Johnson.

457. Sa. 24 Feb. '76. James Boswell (Edinburgh).

Not traced; copy by JB, Isham.—Boswell 1791, ii. 10 (Hill ii. 422).

Dear Sir,

I am glad that what I could think or say has at all contributed to quiet your thoughts. Your resolution not to act, till your opinion is confirmed by more deliberation, is very just. If you have been scrupulous, do not now be rash. I hope that as you think more, and take opportunities of talk-

456.—See on 453.

457.—JB had written 20 Feb. 'You have illuminated my mind and relieved me from imaginary shackles of conscientious obligation. Were it necessary, I could immediately join in an entail upon the series of heirs approved by my father; but it is better not to act too suddenly.'

ing with men intelligent in questions of property, you will
be able to free yourself from every difficulty.

When I wrote last, I sent, I think, ten packets.[1] Did you
receive them all?

You must tell Mrs. Boswell[2] that I suspected her to have
written without your knowledge, and therefore did not
return any answer, lest a clandestine correspondence should
have been perniciously discovered. I will write to her
soon. . . .

I am, dear Sir, Most affectionately yours,

Feb. 24, 1776. Sam. Johnson

458. Tu. 5 Mar. '76. James Boswell (Edinburgh).

Not traced.—Boswell 1791, ii. 11 (Hill ii. 423).

Dear Sir,

I have not had your letter half an hour; as you lay so
much weight upon my notions, I should think it not just to
delay my answer.

I am very sorry that your melancholy should return, and
should be sorry likewise if it could have no relief but from
my company. My counsel you may have when you are
pleased to require it; but of my company you cannot in the
next month have much, for Mr. Thrale will take me to
Italy,[1] he says, on the first of April.

Let me warn you very earnestly against scruples. I am

457.—1. Of Hailes's MS. JB's copy of the *Journey* was sent in 'thirteen franks'.

2. 'A letter to him on the interesting subject of the family settlement, which I
had read.' See 448, and for J's letter to her 481.

458.—The course of correspondence as given in *L* ii. 422–3 is this: (1) B to J 20 Feb.
(see on 457); (2) J to B 24 Feb. (457); (3) B to J: 'I wrote to Dr. Johnson on the 20th of
February, complaining of melancholy, and expressing a strong desire to be with him;
informing him that the ten packets (see 457) came all safe; that Lord Hailes was
much obliged to him, and said he had almost wholly removed his scruples against
entails'; (4) J to B 5 Mar. (458), written within 'half an hour' of the receipt of (3).
The normal course of post was four days. It is surprising that successive editors
should have acquiesced in this sequence; JB's journal for Th. 29 Feb. shows that it
was on that day, not on 20 Feb., that he wrote the letter which J received 5 Mar.
(*BP* xi. 108). JB's account of this letter in his journal is more revealing than that
in the *Life*: 'I . . . wrote an earnest letter to Dr. Johnson; but was sensible that I
might appear weak and troublesom to him. I trusted to his kindness for me, and his
knowledge from experience of dejection of mind.' See Addenda, p. 528.

1. For the projected Italian tour, frustrated by Harry Thrale's death, see references
in Index II, s.v. Thrale, and *L* iii. 19, 470.

glad that you are reconciled to your settlement, and think it a great honour to have shaken Lord Hailes's opinion of entails. Do not, however, hope wholly to reason away your troubles; do not feed them with attention, and they will die imperceptibly away. Fix your thoughts upon your business, fill your intervals with company, and sunshine will again break in upon your mind. If you will come to me, you must come very quickly, and even then I know not but we may scour the country together,[2] for I have a mind to see Oxford and Lichfield before I set out on this long journey. To this I can only add, that

I am, dear Sir, Your most affectionate humble servant,
March 5, 1776.   Sam: Johnson

459. W. 6 Mar. '76. John Douglas.

Address: To the Reverend Dr Douglas.
B.M.—Hill 1892.

Sir

This Gentleman[1] has been approved by the Vicechancellor and Proctors of Oxford, as a Man properly qualified to profess Horsemanship in that place. The Trustees of the Clarendon legacy have consented to issue Money for the credit of a Riding house, and the Bishop of Chester delays the payment till he knows the state of the account between the Trustees and the University, for he says very reasonably, that he knows not to give, till he knows how much they have.

Upon application to the Dean of Hereford, I was told that you, dear Sir, have in your hand the accounts between them. If you would be pleased to examine them, and appoint this Gentleman a time when he may wait on you for the result to carry to the Bishop, you will put an end to a business, in which I have interested myself very much, as it will restore

458.—2. JB arrived in L'n 15 Mar., and saw J next day: 'Before leaving England I am to take a jaunt to Oxford, Birmingham, my native city Lichfield, and my old friend, Dr. Taylor's, at Ashbourn, in Derbyshire. I shall go in a few days, and you, Boswell, shall go with me' (*L* ii. 428). (This quotation is perhaps unhistorical; J had no need to tell JB that L'd was his native city or Taylor his old friend.) For the jaunt see *L* ii and *BP* xi, 19–29 Mar. (especially xi. 133).

459.—1. Carter; see on 379. The Bishop of Chester was Markham, the Dean of Hereford, Wetherell. For Douglas's connexion with the matter see on 463. See also 461.1. It is, I think, surprising that J should designate C 'gentleman'. But see on 408.1, 'Captain' C.

prosperity to a family that has suffered great difficulties a long time.

I am, Dear Sir, Your most humble servant

March 6th. 1776   Sam: Johnson

460. Th. 7 Mar. '76. Edmund Hector (Birmingham).

Sotheby 5 June 1929.—*NQ* 6S. iii. 401.

Dear Sir   March 7. 1776

Some time ago you told me that you had unhappily hurt yourself; and were confined, and you have never since let me hear of your recovery. I hope however that you are grown, at least are growing well. We must be content now to mend very gradually, and cannot make such quick transitions from sickness to health, as we did forty years ago. Let me know how you do, and do not imagine that I forget you.

I forget whether I told you that at the latter end of the summer I rambled over part of France. I saw something of the vintage, which is all I think that they have to boast above our country, at least, it is their great natural advantage. Their air, I think, is good, and my health mended in it very perceptibly.

Our Schoolfellow Charles Congreve is still in town, but very dull, very valetudinary, and very recluse, willing, I am afraid, to forget the world, and content to be forgotten by it, to repose in that sullen sensuality, into which men naturally sink, who think disease a justification of indulgence, and converse only with those who hope to prosper by indulging them. This is a species of Beings with which your profession must have made you much acquainted, and to which I hope acquaintance has made you no friend. Infirmity will come, but let us not invite it; Indulgence will allure us, but let us turn resolutely away. Time cannot be always defeated, but let us not yield till we are conquered.

I had the other day a letter from Harry Jackson who says nothing, and yet seems to have something which he wishes to say. He is very poor. I wish something could be done for him.

I hope dear Mrs. Careless is well, and now and then does

460.—Cf. 749 for J's wistful praise of the Burneys' 'consanguineous unanimity'.

not disdain to mention my name. It is happy when a Brother and Sister live to pass their time at our age together. I have nobody to whom I can talk of my first years. When I go to Lichfield I see the old places, but find nobody that enjoyed them with me. May she and you live long together.

I am Dear Sir, Your affectionate humble servant

Sam: Johnson

461. Th. 7 Mar. '76. John Taylor (Ashbourne).
Morgan.—Hill 1892.

Dear Sir   March 7, 1776.

You will not write to me, nor come to see me, and you will not have me within reach long for We are going to Italy in the Spring.

I called the other day upon poor Charles Congreve, whom I had not seen for many months. He took no notice of my absence, nor appeared either glad or sorry to see me, but answered every thing with monosyllables, and seemed heavy and drowsy, like a man muddled with a full meal; at last I enquired the hour, which gave him hopes of being delivered from me, and enabled him to bounce up with great alacrity and inspect his watch. He sits in a room about ten feet square, and though he takes the air every day in his chaise, fancies that he should take cold in any other house, and therefore never pays a visit.

Do you go on with your suit? If you do, you had surely better come to town and talk with Council.[1] Unless skilful men give you hopes of success,[2] it will be better not to try it, you may still triumph in your ill success. But supposing that by the former compact between you and Wood, she had it for her life, she had as much as she ought to have. I never well understood the settlement which he and you concerted

461.—In this letter the names Congreve and Wood, and the paragraph ending 'What a wretch it is!', are erased. The name near the end of that paragraph is effaced; I noted that it is a short word, and that the first letter might be *P*. Perhaps it is 'Rudds'? For JT's lawsuit see Thomas Taylor's *Life of John Taylor* (n.d., 1910), 63. For JT's erasures in J's letters see Appendix D.

1. The Latin words *concilium* and *consilium* appear in English in a great many forms. In the eighteenth century the distinction between *council* and *counsel* was hardly fixed, though it is observed by J in his Dictionary.

2. J had urged (449) that JT had 'little need to care'. Perhaps he now suggests that JT may 'triumph' in his own prudence and forbearance, if he decides to do nothing.

between you. Do you know what is become of her, and how she and the ⟨ ⟩ live together? What a wretch it is!

I would be glad to take my usual round and see my friends before I set out, but I am afraid it will hardly be convenient,[3] therefore write to me.

I am, Dear Sir, your most humble servant,
Sam: Johnson.

461.1. Sa. 9 Mar. '76. John Douglas.
Address: To the Rev^d Dr Douglas at Windsor. Franked by Thrale.
Postmark: 9 MR.
O. D. Young.—

Dear Sir

The Vicechancellor and Proctors of Oxford have approved, a Master of Horsemanship recommended by me, as a proper man to put in practice the design for which Lord Clarendon[1] left a provision. The Trustees have been consulted and have agreed to issue Money for the erection of a Ridinghouse, and the business is at a stand only till the Bishop of Chester can be informed how ⟨much⟩ money the Book has produced. For this information I have ⟨? been⟩ directed by the Dean of Hereford, the late Vicechancellor to apply to you; and I make it my earnest request that you will be pleased to lay out your first hours of leisure upon the settlement of the account, and transmit the result either to the Bishop, or to
Sir, Your most humble servant
March 9. 1776   Sam: Johnson

462. Tu. 12 Mar. '76. James Boswell (Edinburgh).
Not traced.—Boswell 1791, ii. 12 (Hill ii. 424).

Dear Sir

Very early in April we leave England, and in the beginning of the next week I shall leave London for a short time; of this I think it necessary to inform you, that you may not be disappointed in any of your enterprises. I had not fully resolved to go into the country before this day.

461.—3. 462 shows that the decision to visit the Midlands was hastily taken.

461.1.—This letter is virtually a duplicate of 459. Perhaps J had reason to think the former letter wrongly addressed.
    1. A slip for Cornbury.

Please to make my compliments to Lord Hailes; and mention very particularly to Mrs. Boswell my hopes that she is reconciled to,

Sir, Your faithful servant,

March 12, 1776.   Sam. Johnson.

463. Tu. 12 Mar. '76. Nathan Wetherell (Oxford).

Address (Boswell): To the Reverend Dr. Wetherell, Master of University College, Oxford. See Addenda, p. 528.
Not traced; copy by JB, Isham.—Boswell 1791, ii. 12 (Hill ii. 424).

Dear Sir,

Few things are more unpleasant than the transaction of business with men who are above knowing or caring what

463.—JB 'got the letter and copied it' at University College on 21 Mar.; Wetherell had agreed to this 'if Dr. Johnson consented. I obtained his consent last night' (*BP* xi. 177). JB tells us that 'on enquiry into the matter' (of the proposed riding-school) J 'found that the scheme was not likely to be soon carried into execution; the profits arising from the Clarendon press being, from some mismanagement, very scanty. This having been explained to him by a respectable dignitary of the church, who had good means of knowing it, he wrote a letter', &c. (*L* ii. 424). Dr. Powell (ib. 527) is right in identifying the 'dignitary' with John Douglas, and the letter sent by J to Wetherell as D's reply to 459 and 461.1. His conjecture is confirmed by JB's copy. D had in 1763 edited for the Oxford Press the *Diary and Letters of Henry, Fourth Earl of Clarendon*; Dr. P at one time suspected that he was the editor also of the *Life of Lord Clarendon* 1759, on which the Trustees mainly depended for their funds (see on 379). That would explain why, as 461.1 shows, the accounts for this book were in his hands. The history of the trade in J's time is yet to be written. In the chapter on Authors and Booksellers in *Johnson's England* (Oxford 1933; ii. 310–30) I did the best I could with somewhat scanty materials. On the important matter of discounts in particular the evidence is still meagre and has never, I believe, been collected or analysed. So far as it goes, it seems to bear out J's account. Some years ago I made some examination of the minutes and accounts preserved in the archives of the Delegates of the Press. There I found that in 1758 the Delegates appointed Payne of Castle Street their Warehouse-keeper or Publisher in London. The discounts allowed were fixed on a complicated sliding scale, which was altered from time to time. In 1770, however, 'the Booksellers' in general were allowed 15 per cent. on books over ten shillings; the rates on cheaper books were higher; but the Press then published few cheap books. In '74, on Payne's resignation, the Delegates appointed to succeed him Elmesly for books in the learned languages, Cadell for the rest (so J's 'Mr. Cadell' is more than a type). On 21 Mar. '76 it was reported that C would sell 'the Modern Books' at 15 per cent., but could not at that rate 'put back such books in his sale'. I am not clear of the full implications of this phrase; but I suppose C was unwilling to push the sale of Oxford books after the first year or so. He was invited to say on what terms he 'will bona fide consent to put the University publications into his Sale and bring them to a fair Market'. I found no record of any answer. But in '79 Elmesly (Cadell is not named) was to have 20 per cent. on all books; and in '80 there is mention of '20 per cent to booksellers'.

they have to do, such as the Trustees for Lord Cornbury's institution will perhaps appear when you have read Dr. Douglas's[1] letter.

The last part of the Doctor's letter is of great importance. The complaint which he makes I have heard long ago, and did not know but it was redressed. It is unhappy that a practice so erroneous has not yet been altered; for altered it must be, or our press will be useless with all its privileges. The Booksellers who like all other men have strong prejudices in their own favour are enough inclined to think the practice of printing and selling books by any but themselves an encroachment on the rights of their fraternity and have need of stronger inducements to circulate academical publications than those of one another; for of that mutual co-operation by which the general trade is carried on, the University can bear no part. Of those whom he neither loves nor fears and from whom he expects no reciprocation of good offices, why should any man promote the interest but for profit. I suppose with all our scholastick ignorance of mankind we are still too knowing to expect that the Booksellers will erect themselves into Patrons and buy and sell under the influence of a disinterested zeal for the promotion of learning.

To the Booksellers if we look for either honour or profit from our press, not only their common profit but something more must be allowed, and if books printed at Oxford are expected to be rated at a high price, that price must be levied on the publick, and paid by the ultimate purchaser not by the intermediate agents. What price shall be set upon the book is to the Booksellers wholly indifferent provided that they gain a proportionate profit by negotiating the Sale.

Why Books printed at Oxford should be particularly dear I am however unable to find. We pay no rent, we inherit many of our instruments and materials; lodging and victuals are cheaper than at London, and therefore workmanship ought at least not to be dearer. Our expences are naturally less than those of Booksellers, and in most cases communities are content with less profit than individuals.

It is perhaps not considered through how many hands a Book often passes, before it comes into those of the reader,

463.—1. JB suppressed the name.

113

or what part of the profit each hand must retain as a motive for transmitting it to the next.

We will call our primary Agent in London Mr. Cadel who receives our books from us, gives them room in his warehouse and issues them on demand. By him they are sold to Mr. Dilly a wholesale Bookseller who sends them into the Country, and the last seller is the Country Bookseller.[2] Here are three profits to be paid between the Printer and the Reader, or in the stile of commerce between the Manufacturer and the Consumer; and if any of these profits is too penuriously distributed the process of commerce is intercepted.[3]

We are now come to the practical question, what is to be done? You will tell me with reason that I have said nothing till I declare how much according to my opinion of the ultimate price ought to be distributed through the whole succession of Sale.

The deduction I am afraid will appear very great. But let it be considered before it is refused. We must allow for profit between thirty and thirty five per cent. between six and seven shillings in the pound, that is for every book which costs the last buyer twenty shillings we must charge Mr. Cadel with something less than fourteen. We must set the copies at fourteen shillings each and superadd what is called the quarterly book[4] or for every hundred books so charged we must deliver an hundred and four.

The profit will then stand thus.

Mr. Cadel who runs no hazard and gives no credit will be paid for warehouse room and attendance by a shilling profit on each Book, and his chance of the quarterly Book.

Mr. Dilly who buys the Book for fifteen shillings and who will expect the quarterly book if he takes five and twenty will sell it to his country customer at sixteen and sixpence

463.—2. See *Johnson's England* ii. 315, where I suggest that J simplifies the picture to his purpose. In fact, Cadell was himself a retailer, Dilly at once a retailer and a publisher (for example, of Boswell's *Life*). Nor, of course, does J mean that there were no retailers in London; but the position of the London retailer as such was the same as the country bookseller's.

3. 'interrupted' 1791.

4. The term is obsolete, but this form of discount persists ('26 as 25', and even '13 as 12'). If Cadell took 104 copies and sold them all in small quantities the odd four would be his perquisites.

by which at the hazard of loss and the certainty of long credit, he gains the regular profit of ten per cent. which is expected in the wholesale trade.

The Country Bookseller buying at sixteen and six-pence and commonly trusting a considerable time gains but three and sixpence, and if he trusts a year, not much more than two and sixpence, otherwise than as he may perhaps take as long credit as he gives.

With less profit than this, and more you see he cannot have, the Country Bookseller cannot live; for his receipts are small, and his debts sometimes bad.

Thus Dear Sir I have been incited by Dr. Douglas's letter to give you a detail of the circulation of Books which perhaps every man has not had opportunity of knowing and which those who know it, do not perhaps always distinctly consider.

March 12, 1776.

I am, &c.
Sam. Johnson.

463.1. Sa. 16 Mar. '76. Mrs. Thrale.

Rosenbach 1929.—

Dearest Madam

When you have read the two letters which I have enclosed you will, I am afraid, be of opinion that the last spark of hope[1] is now extinguished. If the 150 L could be had, which is doubtful, the condition upon which it will be offered, of employing it in some purchase permanently useful, we cannot perform, and on any other terms they cannot honestly grant it.

You will be pleased to return this letter that I may show it to Dr Wetherel, at Oxford. I shall not go till tuesday, for Gwin neglected to get places in the coach. Boswel will either accompany or follow me.

In the Closet there is an Italian Palmerin[2] of England,

463.1.—HLP has written at the head of this letter: 'Qu. if this shod not be inserted because it mentions Heely, Dr. J's Cousin?' The motive does her credit, though Heely did not deserve consideration.   1. Of the riding-school.

2. JB noted, 27 Mar., 'He had with him upon this jaunt a Volume of *Il Palermino* [sic] *d'Inghilterra*, a romance praised by Cervantes. But Dr. Johnson did not like it much. He read it for the language, by way of preparation for Italy' (*BP* xi. 206). For the book see *L* iii. 468.

and the key of the Closet is in the tabledrawer at the window. Please to send it me.

Poor Carter's case is truly worthy of commiseration. Peyton was not worse this morning. Heely has yet got no employment.

Sunt lacrymae rerum, et mentem mortalia tangunt.[3]

I am, Madam, Your most obliged and most humble Servant

March 16. 1776   Sam: Johnson

464. Lichfield. Sa. 23 Mar. '76. John Taylor (Ashbourne).
Adam.—Hill 1892.

Dear Sir

I came hither last night, and found your Letters. You will have a note from me on Monday, yet I thought it better to send a Messenger today. Mr Boswel is with me, but I will take care that he will hinder no business, nor shall he know more than you would have him.[1] Send when you please, we shall be ready.

I am, Sir, Your humble servant

Lichfield. Saturday. March 23. 1776   Sam: Johnson

If you care not to send, let me know, we will take a chaise.

464.1. Lichfield, Sa. 23 Mar. '76. Mrs. Thrale.
Newton.—

Dear Madam

On Thursday we set out[1] so late that we got only to Henley,[2] early in the morning on Friday we reached Birmingham. I dined with some Quaker Friends,[3] and sent Mr Boswel with Hector to Bolton's, while I sat with Mrs. Careless. When it was dark we went to Lichfield, To day Mr Boswel went to Mr Garrick, who shewed him the City, while I

463.1.—3. Virgil, *Aen.* i. 462: 'Mortality hath her tears; the woes of man touch the heart of man.' Jackson.

464.—1. Of JT's projected lawsuit?

464.1.—Note by HLP on the original: 'This Letter was written I suppose during the very Hour in which my dear Boy was ill and died—they sent for Dr. Johnson that Night I believe—he lov'd the Child!'

1. From Oxford, 'in a post-chaise to pursue our ramble' (*L* ii. 451).
2. In Warwickshire.   3. Lloyd.

waited on Mrs Aston. I have taken him to Mr Green's, and to morrow he sees the Cathedral. We shall struggle hard to be with you in the next week.

I am, Madam, Your most humble servant

Lichfield. March 23. 1776   Sam: Johnson

465. Lichfield. M. 25 Mar. '76. Mrs. Thrale.

Adam.—1788, No. 141.

Dear Madam

This letter will not, I hope, reach you many days before me, in a distress which can be so little relieved, nothing remains for a friend but to come and partake it.

Poor dear sweet little Boy. When I read the letter[1] this day to Mrs Aston, she said 'such a death is the next to Translation'. Yet, however I may convince myself of this, the tears are in my eyes, and yet I could not love him as you loved him, nor reckon on him for a future comfort, as you and his Father reckoned upon him.

He is gone, and we are going. We could not have enjoyed him long, and shall not long be separated from him. He has probably escaped many such pangs as you are now feeling.

Nothing remains but that with humble confidence We resign ourselves to almighty Goodness, and fall down without irreverent murmurs before the Sovereign Distributer of good and evil, with hope that though sorrow endureth for a night, yet joy may come in the Morning.[2]

465.—1. Not 'your letter'; HLT was in no condition to write herself; and see her note on 464.1. The letter announcing Harry Thrale's sudden death on the afternoon of 23 Mar. (C 135) 'was from Mr. Thrale's clerk, and concluded, "I need not say how much they wish to see you in London". He said, "We shall hasten back from Taylor's."' J received this letter while at breakfast 25 Mar. (*L* ii. 468–9). There seems to have been no question of cancelling the visit to A'n; so J looks forward to seeing the Thrales not 'many days' after the arrival of his letter, that is, after 27 Mar. He and JB reached L'n on the 29th 'and stopped at Messieurs Dillys . . . from whence he hurried away, in a hackney coach, to Mr. Thrale's, in the Borough'—only to find that 'the coach was at the door' waiting to take HLT, Queeney (who also had been alarmingly ill) and Baretti to Bath (*L* iii. 5). See on 470a, where I suggest that it was 465 that moved HT to tears.

2. Ps. 30. 5; in the Prayer Book 'heaviness may endure for a night, but joy cometh in the morning'. All the versions I have examined (per me vel per alium) have either 'heaviness' or 'weeping' (ad vesperum demorabitur fletus: et ad matutinum laetitia Vulgate). The late Dr. F. E. Hutchinson told me that 'sorrow' is in a marginal note in the Douay Version. J read the Bible in many tongues, and quotes or translates indifferently.

I have known you, Madam, too long to think that you want any arguments for submission to the supreme will, nor can my consolation have any effect but that of showing that I wish to comfort you. What can be done you must do for yourself. Remember first that your Child is happy, and then, that he is safe not only from the ills of this world, but from those more formidable dangers which extend their mischief to eternity. You have brought into the world a rational Being, have seen him happy during the little life that has been granted him, and can have no doubt but that his Happiness is now permanent and immutable.

When you have obtained by Prayer such tranquillity as nature will admit, force your attention, as you can, upon your accustomed duties, and accustomed entertainments. You can do no more for our dear Boy, but you must not therefore think less on those whom your attention may make fitter for the place to which he is gone.

I am Dearest, dearest Madam Your most affectionate humble servant,
Lichfield. March 25. 1776   Sam: Johnson

465.1. Lichfield. Mon. 25 March '76. James Boswell (Lichfield).

Not traced.—*Boswell Papers* xi. 199.

'Mrs. Gastrel had asked after me, for I received a card in the Doctor's handwriting to come and dine with her.'

466. Sa. 30 Mar. '76. Mrs. Thrale (Bath).

Address: To Mrs. Thrale.
Newton.—1788, No. 142.

Dear Madam

Since, as Mr. Baretti informs us our dear Queeney is grown better, I hope you will by degrees recover your tranquillity. Only by degrees and those perhaps sufficiently slow, can the pain of an affliction like yours be abated. But though effects are not wholly in our power, yet Providence always gives us something to do, many of the operations of nature may by human diligence be accelerated or retarded. Do not indulge your sorrow, try to drive it away by either pleasure or pain; for opposed to what you are feeling many pains will become pleasures. Remember the great precept, *Be not solitary, be not idle.*[1]

But above all resign yourself and your children to the Universal Father, the Authour of Existence, and Governour of the Universe, who only knows what is best for all, and without whose regard not a Sparrow falls to the Ground.[2]

That I feel what friendship can feel I hope I need not tell you. I loved him as I never expect to love any other little boy, but I could not love him as a parent. I know that such a loss is a laceration of the mind. I know that a whole system of hopes, and designs, and expectations is swept away at once, and nothing left but bottomless vacuity. What you feel, I have felt, and hope that your disquiet will be shorter than mine.

Mr. Thrale sent me a letter from Mr. Boswel,[3] I suppose, to be inclosed. I was this day with Mrs. Montague, who with everybody else laments your misfortune.

I am, dearest Madam, Your most dutiful servant
March 30. 1776   Sam: Johnson

467. M. 1 Apr. '76. Mrs. Thrale (Bath).
Address: To Mrs. Thrale.
Adam.—1788, No. 143.

Dearest Madam

When you were gone Mr Thrale soon sent me away.[1] I came next day, and was made to understand that when I was

466.—1. Quoted, as in 338, from Burton's *Anatomy*.
    2. St. Matthew x. 29.
    3. JB's letter of condolence, now in the Adam collection, is addressed to Mrs. Thrale and dated from 'Mr. Dillys in the Poultry Friday 29 March 1776'; it was sent by the penny post to S'k (Tinker 157). HLT wrote from Bath 1 April: 'Shall I beg you to tell Mr Boswell that I feel myself but too much affected by his Friendship.'

467.—1. JB 'called at his house in the evening' (of 29 Mar.) 'having promised to acquaint Mrs. Williams of his safe return', and was surprised to find J at home 'and, as I thought, not in a very good humour'. JB suggests that HLT's hurrying away showed a lack of respect for 'the Imlac who had hastened from the country to console a distressed mother, who he understood was very anxious for his return' (see on 465). But he does not say that J expressed any resentment (*L* iii. 6).

wanted I should be sent for; and therefore I have not gone yesterday or to day, but I will soon go again whether invited or not.

You begin now I hope to be able to consider that what has happened might have had great aggravations. Had you been followed in your intended travels[2] by an account of this afflictive deprivation, where could have ⟨been⟩ the end of doubt, and surmise, and suspicion, and self condemnation, you could not easily have been reconciled to those whom you left behind, or those who had persuaded you to go. You would ⟨have⟩ believed that he died by neglect, and that your presence would have saved him. I was glad of your letter from Marlborough, and hope you will try to force yourself to write. If grief either caused or aggravated poor Queeney's ilness, you have taken the proper method for relieving it. Young minds easily receive new impressions.

Poor Peyton expired this morning. He probably during many years for which he sat starving by the bed of a Wife not only useless, but almost motionless, condemned by poverty to personal attendance, and by the necessity of such attendance chained down to poverty, he probably thought often how lightly he should tread the path of life without his burthen. Of this thought the admission was unavoidable, and the indulgence might be forgiven to frailty and distress. His Wife died at last, and before she was buried he was seized by a fever, and is now going to the grave.

Such miscarriages when they happen to those on whom many eyes are fixed, fill histories and tragedies and tears have been shed for the sufferings, and wonder excited by the fortitude of those who neither did nor suffered more than Peyton.

I was on Saturday at Mrs. Montague's who expressed great sensibility of your loss, and have this day received an invitation to a supper and a ball, but I returned my acknowledg-

---

467.—2. A non-committal phrase. On 29 Mar. J thought that the Italian tour should and would take place; 'their loss was an additional reason for their going abroad'; but that he could not press it, lest he be suspected of a selfish motive (*L* iii. 6). On 4 Apr. J told JT 'the Expedition still proceeds' (469). HLT's letter from Marlborough, therefore, which has not been found, did not raise the question; and her first letter from Bath (1 Apr., see on 466 and 468) was wholly devoted to her loss and her fears for Q.

ments to the Ladies, and let them know, that I thought, I should like the ball better another week.[3]

I am, Dear Madam, Your most obedient servant

Apr. 1. 1776   Sam: Johnson

467a. Bath. M. 1 Apr. '76. From Mrs. Thrale.

R 539.51—

My Dear Sir   Bath 1: April 1776.

Shall I beg you to tell Mr Boswell that I feel myself but too much affected by his Friendship; Yours has long been the best Cordial to my Heart, it is now almost the only one. I cold bathe here, & endeavour all I can to excite Appetite, & force Attention; I owe every Thing to Mr Thrale's indulgent Tenderness, and will bring him home the best Wife I can: how has it happened that every body has been so kind?

My dear Queeney will be spared me, I see She will; if by patient Endurance of the great Calamity I forbear to provoke further Punishment from Heaven— her Danger has shewn me I have still something left to lose. Pray for her perfect Recovery Dear Sir, or you never more will have any Comfort of your

Faithful & Affectionate friend Hester L: Thrale.

468. Th. 4 Apr. '76. Mrs. Thrale (Bath).

Adam.—1788, No. 144.

Dearest Madam

I am glad to hear of pretty Queeney's recovery,[1] and your returning tranquillity.[2] What we have suffered ought to make us remember what we have escaped. You might at as short a warning have been taken from your children, or Mr Thrale might have been taken from us all.

Mr Thrale, when he dismissed me, promised to call on me; he has never called, and I have never seen him.[3] He said that he would go to the house,[4] and I hope he has found something that laid hold on his attention.

467.—3. Hill notes that J had not scrupled to go to the L'd theatre on the day on which he heard of Harry's death (*L* ii. 471). But 'another *week*' suggests that J is not thinking of that as a reason for his refusal; his letter was written on the Monday before Easter.

468.—1. See 467a.

2. See 467a. J may have had also a later letter, not preserved.

3. JB records that on 5 Apr. 'Mr. Thrale and I sat with him' (*L* iii. 22). 'Poor Thrale, orbus et exspes, came for comfort and sat till seven when we all went to Church' (*PM* 7 Apr.).

4. Presumably the House of Commons, not the 'Brewhouse'. The earliest clear example in *OED* of *house* in this sense (without help from the context) is 1845.

I do not wish you to return, while the novelty of the place does any good either to you or Queeney, and longer I know you will not stay, there is therefore no need of soliciting your return. What gratification can be extracted from so sad an event, I derive from observing that Mr Thrale's behaviour has united you to him by additional endearments. Every evil will be more easily born while you fondly love one another, and every good will be enjoyed with increase of delight *past compute* to use the phrase of Cumberland. May your love of each other always encrease.

I am, Dearest Madam, Your most obedient servant
April. 4. 1776   Sam: Johnson

469. Th. 4 Apr. '76. John Taylor (Ashbourne).

Address: To the Reverend Dr. Taylor in Ashbourn Derbyshire.
Adam.—Hill, *J.M.* 1897, ii. 447.

Dear Sir

I was sorry, and so was Mr Boswel, that we were summoned away so soon. Our effort of travelling in the Evening was useless.[1] We did not get home till friday morning. Mrs. Thrale and her girl are gone to Bath. The blow was very heavy upon them.

The Expedition[2] however still proceeds, so that I shall be but a short time here. If Mr Langdon will be so kind as to send the barley[3] next week, I can deliver it to Boswel, I wish he would ⟨put⟩ a peck more in a separate bag, for I would not break the main bulk, and yet I cannot well help it, unless I have a little more.

Mr Boswel is in the room, and sends his respects.

Let me know whether you design to come hither before I am to go, and if you come we will contrive to pass a few hours together.

I am, Sir, Your most humble servant
No 8 Bolt Court,[4] Fleet Street.   Sam: Johnson
(not Johnson's Court.) Apr. 4. 1776

469.—1. They had reached A'n on 26 Mar. and left after dinner the next day, but got no farther than Loughborough; on the 28th they slept at St. Albans (*L* iii. 2, 4).
   2. See on 467.
   3. No doubt the Siberian barley of 421; the 'main bulk' was for S'm.
   4. JB had called at Johnson's Court on 16 Mar. and 'found he was removed' (*L* ii. 427).

470. Tu. 9 Apr. '76. Mrs. Thrale.

Adam.—1788, No. 145.

Dear Madam

Mr Thrale's alteration of purpose[1] is not weakness of resolution; it is a wise man's compliance with the change of things, and with the new duties which the change produces. Whoever expects me to be angry will be disappointed. I do not even grieve at the effect. I grieve only at the cause.

Your business for the present is to seek for ease, and to go where you think it most likely to be found. There cannot yet be any place in your mind, for mere curiosity. Whenever I can contribute to tranquillity, I shall readily attend, and hope never to add to the evils that may oppress you. I will go with you to Bath,[2] or stay with you at home.

I am very little disappointed. I was glad to go, to places of so much celebrity, but had promised to myself no raptures, nor much improvement. Nor is there anything to be expected worth such a sacrifice as you might make.

Keep yourself busy, and you will in time grow cheerful; new prospects may open, and new enjoyments may come within your reach. I surely cannot but wish all evil removed from a house, which has afforded my miseries all the succour which attention and benevolence could give. I am sorry not to owe so much, but to repay so little. What I can do, you may with great reason expect from, Dearest Madam, Your most obliged and most humble servant

Apr. 9. 1776   Sam: Johnson

470a. Southwark. Tu. ⟨9 Apr. '76⟩. From Mrs. Thrale.

R 539.53—

Tuesday.

Every day every hour makes me more happy in your Friendship—it ought to take up a larger part of my Mind than I can just now afford it—nothing however out of my own Bosom is half so dear to my Heart as that is. I went to Streatham today, & left Baretti trying to perswade Mr Thrale to go *some*

470.—1. HLT and Q had returned by Easter Sunday 7 Apr. There is no mention of them in the *Life* for this day; but in his journal JB notes that 'Mr. Thrale sat by me' at St. Paul's; 'Mrs. and Miss Thrale were also here' (*BP* xi. 231). The decision not to go to Italy may have been imparted to J on that day. For his 'philosophical calmness' in bearing this disappointment, see *L* iii. 27.

2. J accompanied them to Bath 15 Apr.

where on the Continent—we should look so ridiculous he said. I hope our dear Master has more Wit however than to be bullied or coaxed out of a Resolution which his own good Sense originally suggested & Your Judgment has confirm'd in a Letter which is such a proof of Benevolence as I have not met before. I cannot tell you how much I am your obliged Friend Servant &c

H: L: Thrale

They are just come home, my Master holds his purpose & Baretti teizes no more; Mr Thrale says he has behaved well enough upon the whole, and that as he says he has been at some Expence on the Occasion, that Matter shall be made straight to him.

Mr Thrale has seen your Letter[1] & shed Tears over the reading it—they are the first he has shed.—I can say no more. You dine at our House to morrow. Jackson is put off.

471. Th. 11 Apr. '76. Frances Reynolds.

Rupert Colomb.—Croker's Boswell 1831, iii. 398.

Dearest Madam

To have acted with regard to you in a manner either unfriendly or disrespectful would give me great pain, and I hope will be always very contrary to my intention. That I staid away was merely accidental. I have seldom dined from home; and I did not think my opinion necessary to your information in any proprieties of behaviour.

The poor parents of the Child are much grieved, and much dejected. The Journey to Italy is put off, but they go to Bath on Monday. A visit from you will be well taken, and I think your intimacy is such, that you may very properly pay it in a morning. I am sure it will be thought seasonable and kind, and wish you not to omit it.

I am Dear Madam Your most humble servant

Apr. 11. 1776   Sam: Johnson

472. Th. 11 Apr. '76. The Earl of Hertford.

Not traced.—GM 1850, 33, 292 (endorsement dated 11 May).

My Lord

Being wholly unknown to your lordship, I have only this apology to make for presuming to trouble you with a request

470a.—1. She refers, I think, not to 470 but to 465.

472.—The *GM* prints also the answer, noted on J's letter: 'Lord C. presents his compliments to Mr. Johnson, and is sorry that he cannot obey his commands, having already on his hands many engagements unsatisfied' (C. = Chamberlain).

—that a stranger's petition, if it cannot be easily granted, can be easily refused. Some of the apartments are now vacant in which I am encouraged to hope that, by application to your lordship, I may obtain a residence. Such a grant would be considered by me as a great favour, and I hope that to a man who has had the honour of vindicating his Majesty's government, a retreat in one of his houses may be not improperly or unworthily allowed. I therefore request that your lordship will be pleased to grant such rooms in Hampton Court as shall seem proper to,

My lord, Your lordship's most obedt. and most humble servant,

Bolt Court, Fleet Street,   Sam. Johnson.
April 11, 1776.

473. Sa. 13 Apr. '76. John Taylor (Ashbourne).

Address: To the Reverend Dr. Taylor in Ashbourn, Derbyshire.
University of Rochester, N.Y.—Hill 1892.

Dear Sir

I have not yet carried the cases.[1] I would have the value of the Estate truly told. This trial[2] takes up the Attorney general for the present, and there is little hope of his attention to any thing else. And upon the whole, I do not see that there is any haste. The opinion is as good and useful a month hence, unless you found Mr Rudd[3] alienating the land. I am going with Mr Thrale to Bath on Monday. Our Italian journey is deferred to another year, perhaps totally put off on their part. They are both extremely dejected. I think, his grief is deepest. If you put off your coming to town, I will give you notice when we return, but if your coming is necessary, I will come from Bath to meet you.

I am, Sir, Your most humble Servant,
                                        Sam: Johnson.
Bolt court (not Johnson's court) Fleet street
Apr. 13. 1776

473.—1. There were two, as appears from 475.

2. The Attorney-General, Thurlow, was engaged in the trial of the notorious 'Duchess of Kingston' for bigamy.

3. The name is erased; but Mr. Metzdorf tells me that the reading is not in doubt.

474. M. 15 Apr. '76. Frances Reynolds.

Address: To Miss Reynolds.

Rupert Colomb.—Croker's Boswell 1831, iii. 409 (part only); Hill, 1897, ii. 448.

Dearest Madam

When you called on Mrs. Thrale, I find by enquiry that she was really abroad; the same thing happened to Mrs. Montague, of which I beg you to inform her, for she went likewise by my opinion. The Denial, if it had been feigned would not have pleased me. Your visits however are kindly paid, and very kindly taken.

Pray tell Sir Joshua, that I have examined Mr Thrale's Man, and find no foundation for the Story of the Alehouse and mulled Beer. He was at the Play two nights before, with one of the chief men in the Brewhouse, and came home at the regular time.

This, I believe is true, for Mrs Thrale told me that she had sent him to her friend Murphy's play,[1] and if more had been to be told, I should then have heard it.

We are going to Bath this morning but I would not part without telling you the real state of your visit.

I am, dearest Madam, Your most humble servant

Apr. 15. 1776.   Sam. Johnson

475. Bath. ⟨*c.* 22 April '76.⟩ James Boswell (London).

Not traced; copy by one of JB's children, Isham.—Boswell 1791, ii. 66 (Hill iii. 44).

Dear Sir

Why do you talk of neglect?[1] When did I neglect you? If you will come to Bath, we shall all be glad to see you. Come, therefore, as soon as you can.

But I have a little business for you at London. Bid Francis look in the paper-drawer of the chest of drawers in

474.—1. This might be either *The Way to Keep Him* (Drury Lane '60, revived there 20 Mar. '76) or *Three Weeks After Marriage* (Covent Garden '64, revived there 30 Mar. '76).

475.—1. JB's journal here is defective. In the *Life* he writes: 'I had never seen that beautiful city (Bath), and wished to take the opportunity of visiting it, while Johnson was there. Having written to him, I received the following answer' (n.d., but that might be JB's copyist's fault. JB's Register records the receipt of the letter 23 Apr.) The 'talk of neglect' was perhaps cover for a self-invitation.

my bed-chamber, for two cases;[2] one for the Attorney-General, and one for the Solicitor-General. They lie, I think, at the top of my papers; otherwise they are somewhere else, and will give me more trouble.

Please to write to me immediately, if[3] they can be found. Make my compliments to all our friends round the world, and to Mrs. Williams at home.

I am, Sir, your, &c.
Sam. Johnson.

Search for the papers as soon as you can, that, if it is necessary, I may write to you again before you come down.

475.1. M. 29 Apr. '76. John Taylor.
Sotheby 31 Mar. 1875 (not seen).—

476. M. 6 May '76. Mrs. Thrale (Bath).
A. Ettinger.—1788, No. 147.

Dearest Madam   May 6, 1776
On Friday night, as you know, I left you about eleven o'clock. The moon shone, but I did not see much of the way, for I think I slept better than I commonly do in bed. My companions were civil men, and we despatched our journey very peaceably. I came home at about seven[1] on Saturday very little fatigued.

To-day I have been at home. To-morrow I am to dine, as I did yesterday, with Dr. Taylor. On Wednesday I am to dine with Oglethorpe; and [and] Thursday with Paoli. He that sees before him to his third dinner, has a long prospect.

My political tracts are printed, and I bring Mr. Thrale a copy when I come. They make but a little book.

Count Manucci is in such haste to come, that I believe he will ⟨not⟩ stay for me; if he would, I should like to hear his remarks on the road.

475.—2. JT's, for Thurlow and Wedderburn. See 473.
  3. That is, 'to tell me if'.

476.—1. J's account of his journey reads as if he reached L'n on Saturday morning. But as late as '85 the record between L'n and B'm, approximately the same distance, was 19 hours (*Johnson's England* 1933, i. 140). Hill quotes evidence that in '84 L'n and Bristol were under 16 hours apart. But there was substantial improvement between '76 and '84.

Mr. Baretti has a cold and hoarseness, and Mrs. Williams says that I have caught a cold this afternoon.

> I am, &c.,
> Sam: Johnson.

476a. Bath. W. 8 May ⟨'76⟩. From Mrs. Thrale.
R 539.54—

Bath 8: May.

My Dear Sir   you dine with General Oglethorpe.

I believe I should not have forborne writing so long but that my Spirits have been strangely disordered since you went by hearing that the Girls at Kensington had the Chicken Pox, which though a trifling Thing in any other Family, might for ought I know prove fatal in my ill fated House. She sends word however that they are perfectly recover'd & able to walk to Streatham &c.—so I believe one Night's crying will do—& that I have already had.

Count Manucci is a Goose Cap *not* to wait for you; one good only will attend his coming sooner, I shall make Seward who speaks Italian shew him what is to be seen by pretty Men in the Cards & Dancing Way, & Seward leaves Bath this Day sevenight.

The Politicians sigh here, & the Wits laugh at General Howe's walking out of Boston, & General Washington's walking in; but everybody agrees that Peace will soon be made, and an excellent Topick of Conversation taken from us all. While my Children can keep their Lives & Healths how little do I care? I am hastening to the State of Mind of old Alderman Plumbe I think—You remember his *kind* Expression concerning his own Family & all the rest of the World.

Your Friendship is however too serious & solid a Good to be thought on while one is even *half* in Jest—I am therefore most seriously & certainly Dear Sir Your Faithful and Obliged Servant H: L: Thrale.

Give all our Compliments to Doctor Taylor if you please, & tell me when you will return to us. We will have Count Manucci near us, but he has not done quite civilly never to write.

477. Sa. 11 May '76. Mrs. Thrale (Bath).
Adam.—1788, No. 148.

Dear Madam

That you may have no superfluous uneasiness I went this afternoon to visit the two Babies at Kensington, and found them indeed a little spotted with their disorder, but as brisk and gay as health and youth can make them. I took a paper of sweetmeats, and spread them on the table. They took great delight to show their governess the various animals that were made of sugar, and when they had eaten as much as was fit the rest were laid up for tomorrow.

Susy sends her duty and love with great propriety. Sophy sends her duty to you, and her love to Queeney and Papa. Mr Evans came in after me. You may set your heart quite at rest, no babies can be better than they appear to be. Dr Taylor went with me, and we staid a good while. He likes them very much. Susy said her Creed in French.

Dr Taylor says I must not come back till his business is adjusted, and indeed it would not be wise to come away without doing what I came hither only to do. However I expect to be dismissed in a few days, and shall bring Manucci with me.

I dined yesterday with Langton ⟨. . .⟩[1] just going to bed. His three children are very lovely. ⟨. . .⟩ longs to teach him a little economy. I know not how his money goes, for I do not think that Mrs Williams and I had our due share of the nine guineas.

He begins to reproach himself with neglect of George's education, and censures that idleness or that deviation by the indulgence of which he has left uncultivated such a fertile mind. I advised him to let the child alone, and told him that the matter was not great, whether he could read at the end of four years or of five, and that I thought it not proper to harrass a tender mind with the violence of painful attention. I may perhaps procure both father and son a year of quiet, and surely I may rate myself among their benefactors.

I am, Madam, Your most humble servant

May 11. 1776 Sam: Johnson

478. Tu. 14 May '76. Mrs. Thrale (Bath).

Sotheby 10 May 1949.—1788, No. 149.

Dear Lady

Since my visit to the Younglings nothing has happened but a little disappointment in Dr. Taylor's affairs which, he says, must keep me here a while longer. Mr. Wedderburn has given his opinion to day directly against us. He thinks

477.—1. The erasures are troublesome; 'Langton' is clear; then follows about half a line, which seems to end 'just going to bed'. The second name I could not read; Malone in his copy of 1788 filled the blank with 'Boswell'.

of the claim much as I think. We sent this afternoon for a
solicitor, another Scrase,[1] who gave the same sentence with
Wedderburn, and with less delicacy. The Dr tried to talk
him into better notions, but to little purpose, for a man is
not much believed in his own cause. At last finding the Dr
somewhat moody I bid him not be disturbed, for he could
not be injured till the death of Mrs. Rudd, and her life was
better than his. So I *comforted and advised him.*[2]

I know not how You intend to serve me, but I expect a letter
to-morrow, and I do not see why Queeney should forget me.

Manucci must, I believe, come down without me. I am
ashamed of having delayed him so long, without being able
to fix a day; but you know, and must make him know that
the fault is not mine.

⟨Boswel⟩[3] goes away on thursday, very well satisfied with
his journey. Some great men have promised to obtain him
a place, and then a fig for my father, and his new wife.

I have not yet been at Borough, nor know when I shall go
unless you send me. There is in the exhibition of Exeter exchange, a picture of the house at Streatham, by one Laurence,
I think,[4] of the Borough. This is something, or something like.[5]

Mr. Welch sets out for France tomorrow, with his
younger daughter. He has leave of absence for a year, and
seems very much delighted with the thought of travelling,
and the hope of health.

I am, Madam, Your most humble servant,

May. 14. 1776   Sam: Johnson.

478.—1. I have not found that Charles Scrase had a namesake in the profession;
perhaps J means someone like him in prudence and experience.

2. *Clarissa* (Mowbray to Belford, 7 Sept.; ed. 1810, viii. 95). 'What was there
in one woman more than another? Hey, you know, Jack!—And thus we comforted
and advised him.' The quotation was current in the S'm circle; see references in
Hill, and add 304.1*c*.

3. 'Boswell' HLP; a blank in 1788. JB's kaleidoscopic journal of this L'n visit
contains frequent mentions of his hopes from his friend Lord Mountstuart. See
references in Pottle, *Index*, s.v. Bute, fourth Earl. On 6 May: 'Lord Mountstuart's;
the Duke of Queensberry there. "What shall we do for our friend?" Saw the mode
of getting a place.' 10 May: 'Then to Lord Mountstuart's. I said, "I am indifferent
as to how small an office it is, if you get me an independency from my father"' (*BP*
xi. 270, 276). Writing to Temple on 1 May he calls Mountstuart 'my *Maecenas*'.

4. J's comma does not mean, as it naturally would to-day, that his doubt extends
to the painter's name; he is doubtful only whether Laurence was of S'k. See Index II.

5. *OED* records this colloquialism as early as 1702, where one would least expect
to find it: in a translation of Cicero's *De Finibus*.

479. Th. 16 May '76. Mrs. Thrale (Bath).

Bergson.—1788, No. 150.

Dear Madam

This is ⟨my⟩ third letter,[1] well—sure I shall have something to morrow. Our business stands still. The Doctor says I must not go; and yet my stay does him no good. His Solicitor says he is sick, but I suspect he is sullen. The Doctor in the mean time has his head as full as yours at an Election. Livings and preferments, as if he were in want with twenty children, run in his head. But a man must have his head on something small or great.

For my part, I begin to settle and keep company with grave aldermen. I dined yesterday in the poultry[2] with Mr. Alderman Wilkes, and Mr. Alderman Lee, and Counsellor Lee, his Brother. There sat you the while, so sober, with your Woodwards and your Harringtons[3] and my Aunt[4] and her turnspit, and when they were gone, you think by chance on Johnson what is he doing? What should he be doing? he is breaking jokes with Jack Wilkes upon the Scots. Such Madam, are the vicissitudes of things. And there was Mrs. Knowles the Quaker that works the sutile[5] pictures, who is a great admirer of your conversation. She saw you at Mr Shaw's, at the election time. She is a Staffordshire Woman, and I am to go and see her. Staffordshire is the nursery of art, where the⟨y⟩[6] grow up till they are transplanted to London.

479.—1. 477 and 478 being still unanswered. HLT had answered 476 on 8 May, and wrote again 16 May.

2. With the Dillys. For this (the most famous of all dinner-parties?) see *L* iii. 68.

3. In 1788 HLP reduced these gentlemen to initials, and in the original the rest is thoroughly erased. But J wrote the names at the top of his second page, and as the paper is transparent they can be read at the top of the first, which is left blank. 'The dull duty of an editor' has its occasional compensations.

4. In her published 'letter' (1788 No. 151) dated 16 May, HLT writes: 'I *must* be civil to my aunt, who is exceedingly kind to me.' Mr. Clifford would identify her with Sidney Arabella Cotton, who lived at Bath.

5. J uses the word in *Idler* 13: '*sutile pictures* which imitate tapestry'. HLP printed *futile*, and was laughed at. Michael Lort wrote to Percy 17 Apr. '88: 'I desired a sight of the original letter in order to determine a wager. There it plainly appeared that a dash had been put across the long *s*, perhaps by the printer or corrector of the press' (Nichols, *LI* vii. 494). I have seen only a photograph; but I think the letter is certainly ſ, which is not very like J's *f*; the appearance of the cross-bar is suspicious.

6. J elsewhere writes *the* for *they*. An alternative possibility is that he omitted a word, e.g. *artists*.

Yet it is strange that I hear nothing from you. I hope you are not angry, or sick. Perhaps you are gone without me for spite to see places. That is natural enough, for evil is very natural, but I shall vex, unless it does you good.

Stevens seems to be connected with Tyrwhit in publishing Chatterton's poems; he came very anxiously to know the result of our enquiries,[7] and though he says, he always thought them forged, is not quite pleased to find us so fully convinced.

I have written to Manucci to find his own way, for the *Law's delay*[8] makes it difficult for me to guess when I shall be, able to ⟨be,⟩ otherwise than by my inclination, Madam,

> Your most humble Servant

May 16. 1776   Sam: Johnson

480. Th. 16 May '76. Joshua Reynolds.

Address: To Sir Joshua Reynolds.
Fettercairn.—Boswell 1793, ii. 448 (Hill iii. 81).

Dear Sir

I have been kept away from You, I know not well how, and of these vexatious hindrances I know not when there will be an end. I therefore send you the poor dear Doctor's[1] epitaph. Read it first yourself, and if you then think it right, show it to the Club. I am, you know, willing enough to be corrected. If you think any thing much amiss, keep it to yourself, till we come together. I have sent two copies,[2] but prefer the card. The dates must be settled by Dr Percy.

> I am, Sir, Your most humble Servant,

May 16. 1776   Sam: Johnson

479.—7. 'On Monday, April 29, he and I made an excursion to Bristol', (from Bath) 'where I was entertained with seeing him enquire upon the spot, into the authenticity of "*Rowley's Poetry*"' (*L* iii. 50). See also *L* iii. 478, and Dr. Powell's article in *RES* referred to there. The point is that Tyrwhitt originally believed the poems genuine; Steevens, if 'connected' with Tyrwhitt, would share his embarrassment. T, says Nichols, 'changed his opinion after his volume was actually completed at the press' (*LA* ix. 530). See also 485.
  8. *Hamlet* III. i.

480.—1. Goldsmith. For the epitaph, and the 'round robin' praying J to write it in English, see *L* iii. 82.
  2. For a difference between them see 491.

481. Th. 16 May '76. Margaret Boswell (Edinburgh).

Not traced.—Boswell 1791, ii. 93 (Hill iii. 85).

Madam,

You must not think me uncivil in omitting to answer the letter[1] with which you favoured me some time ago. I imagined it to have been written without Mr. Boswell's knowledge, and therefore supposed the answer to require, what I could not find, a private conveyance.

The difference with Lord Auchinleck is now over; and since young Alexander has appeared, I hope no more difficulties will arise among you; for I sincerely wish you all happy. Do not teach the young ones to dislike me, as you dislike me yourself; but let me at least have Veronica's kindness, because she is my acquaintance.

You will now have Mr. Boswell home; it is well that you have him, he has led a wild life.[2] I have taken him to Lichfield, and he has followed Mr. Thrale to Bath. Pray take care of him, and tame him. The only thing in which I have the honour to agree with you is, in loving him; and while we are so much of a mind in a matter of so much importance, our other quarrels will, I hope, produce no great bitterness.

I am, Madam, Your most humble servant,
May 16, 1776.   Sam. Johnson.

482. Sa. 18 May '76. Mrs. Thrale (Bath).

Donald F. Hyde.—1788, No. 152.

Dear Madam

Then You are neither sick nor angry.[1] Don't let me be

481.—1. See on 457.

2. We cannot suppose that J meant to tell tales. He may have intended a friendly warning. He can hardly have failed to guess, at least, something of JB's debaucheries during this visit, from the tone of the conversation, which JB was always steering to the subjects of concubinage and fornication. See the journal *passim*, and especially Prof. Pottle's note, *BP* xi. 232, on the nature of certain pages of it that are missing. The entry for 10 Apr. reveals that J had rebuked him, and that he had written him 'a letter to defend myself against his severity'. Of this there is nothing in the *Life*. Prof. Pottle suggests the possibility that 'he finally reached the stage of a confession and was severely scolded'; this might be in the missing pages. A further lacuna occurs in the journal for 10 Apr., which Prof. Pottle thinks contained an account of a reconciliation.

482.—1. In 479 he had written 'it is strange that I hear nothing from you, I hope you are not angry, or sick'. The very long letter printed in 1788 and dated 16 May was no doubt based, at least, on an original of this date. She explains that 'I had no

defrauded of Queeney's Letter.[2] Yesterday Seward was with
me, and told me what he knew of you. All good. To day I
went to look into my places at the borough. I called on Mr
Perkins in the counting house. He crows, and triumphs; as
We go on, we shall double our business. The best brown
malt he can have laid in at thirty and sixpence, and great
stores he purposes to buy. Dr Taylor's business stagnates
but he resolves not to wait on it much longer. Surely I shall
get down to you next week.

B⟨oswel⟩[3] went away on Thursday night, with no great
inclination to travel northward, but who can contend with
destiny? He says, he had had a very pleasant journey;[4] he
paid another visit, I think, to ⟨Mrs Rudd⟩, before he went
home ⟨to his own Deary⟩. He carries with him two or three
good resolutions, I hope they will not mould upon the road.
Who can be this new friend[5] of mine? The letter you sent me
was from Mr. Twisse, and the book, if any come, is Twisse's
travels to Ireland, which you will, I hope, unty and read.

I enclose some of the powders[6] lest you should lose your
patient by delay.

I am, Madam, Your most humble Servant

May 18. 1776   Sam: Johnson

482a. Bath. Tu. 21 May '76. From Mrs. Thrale.
Address: To Dr Sam Johnson Bolt Court Fleet Street London. *Post-
mark*: 23 MA. Franked by HT.
R 539.55—
Dear Sir
    It is so much better that this Letter should be useless, than that you should
be disappointed of a Letter when you want one, that I will write though I

notion of your staying away from us so long, or you should not surely have wanted
a letter'.
    482.—2. HLT had written 'expect a long letter from Queeney'.
    3. 'Boswell' and 'Mrs. Rudde' HLP. She had no doubt forgotten her good-
natured suppression of 'to his own Deary', the preservation of which we owe to
Lyseus; the initial *t* and final *y* are discernible at the end of an otherwise complete
erasure.
    4. Not, of course, to Scotland; the reference is to JB's travels in J's company.
    5. HLT's letter dated 16 May describes at some length a 'hot-headed Irishman',
'a flashy friend here who is much your adorer'; he is not named in that letter, but
in 482*a* 'his name is Musgrave'. See on 483.
    6. The extant letters give no clue to this. Her original letter of 16 May perhaps
asked him to *bring* the powders.

think you are now on the road. The new Friend we talked of is an Irishman, rich, young, handsome, hotheaded & I fancy vicious enough: not however without some parts & some Literature, & has an enthusiastick Regard for you:—he was sure he said today after some pause—yes he was sure he could shed his Blood for you. It is equally impossible not to like the Man, and not to laugh at him, his Name is Musgrave. I hope Doctor Taylor will not lose his Tranquillity, his Cause I fear will be lost—but the less one has left, the more one ought to cultivate the remainder; and try to compare ones-self with those that have less still.

I had a better Claim to a larger Estate which I had been longer nursed up in the hopes of. I did fret after it too for a while, till a worse Calamity cured me, I think I can now say from my heart that It gives me no pain at all.—The price of Malt however now gives me no pleasure; when our debts are once paid, my Desires as to Money Matters are over.

Farewell Dear Sir, and continue me Your Friendship, every Absence from you shews me if I was not sure enough of it before, that I am

Your most faithful and Obedient Servant H: L: Thrale.

Bath Tuesday 21: May 1776

483. W. 22 May '76. Mrs. Thrale (Bath).

Adam.—1788, No. 153.

Dear Madam

On friday and saturday I dined with Dr Taylor who is in discontent, but resolved not to stay much longer to hear the opinions of Lawyers who are all against him. Who can blame him for being weary of them?

On Sunday I dined at Sir Joshua's house on the hill,[1] with the Bishop of St. Asaph.[2] The Dinner was good, and the Bishop is knowing and conversible. Yesterday at the Doctor's again—very little better—in the evening came in Dr Crane who enquired after you.

All this while the Doctor is hurt only in his vanity. He thought he had supplanted Mrs Wood, and Mrs Wood has found the means of defeating him. He really wanted nothing more than to have the power of bequeathing a reversion to Mr. Green's son, who is very nearly related to Wood. This purity of intention however he cannot prove, and the transaction in itself seems pactum iniquum. I do not think that he can, or indeed that he ought to prevail.

Woodward, I hear, is gone to Bristol, in deep dudgeon at Barret's declaration against Chatterton's productions. You

483.—1. Richmond Hill.   2. Shipley.

have now only Harington, whom you can only make a silent
admirer. I hope my friend[3] buzzes a little about you to keep
me in your head, though I think, I do my part pretty well
myself, there are very few writers of more punctuality.

I wish Queeney joy of her new watch, and next time I
write intend myself the honour of directing my letter to her.
Her hand is now very exact, and when use has made it free,
may be very beautiful.

I am glad of Mr Thrale's resolution to take up his restes[4]
in person. He is wise in keeping the trade in his own hands,
and appearing on proper occasions as the principal agent.
Every man has those about him who wish to sooth him into
inactivity and delitescence, nor is there any semblance of
kindness more vigorously to be repelled, than that which
voluntarily offers a vicarious performance of the tasks of life,
and conspires with the natural love of ease against diligence
and perseverance.

While I was holding my pen over the last period I was
called down to Father Wilks the Benedictine, and Father
Brewer, a Doctor of the Sorbon, who are come to England,
and are now wandering over London. I have invited them
to dine with me tomorrow. Father Cowley is well, and Mrs
Strickland[5] is at Paris. More news than this I have not yet
learned. They stay, I think, here but a little time.

I have sent your last parcel of powders, and hope soon to
come myself.

I am, Madam, Your most humble servant

May. 22. 1776　　　　　　　　　　　　　　Sam: Johnson

483.1. Th. 23 May '76. Mrs. Thrale (Bath).

Sotheby 30 Jan. 1918 (not seen; extract in catalogue).—

Yesterday Father Wilkes of the Benedictines and another
of the same monastery dined with me. Mr Baretti luckily
came in.

483.—3. The (still nameless, see on 482) Irishman, Sir Richard Musgrave.
　　4. 'When the master brewer goes round to his victuallers once a year, in order to
examine the state of the trade, and the stock left on the hands of the alehouse-
keeper, the expression used in the profession is, *that he takes up his restes*; a word
borrowed from the French, and means the remainder—*les restes*' (*HLP* (1788)).
　　5. They had seen much of this lady when in Paris. See HLT's *French Journals,
passim.*

484. W. 29 May '76. William Adams (Oxford).

Adam.—*Morrison Autographs* 1885, ii. 342.

Sir

The Gentleman[1] who brings this is a learned Benedictine, in whose monastery I was treated at Paris with all the civilities, which the Society had means or opportunity of showing. I dined in their refectory, and studied in their library, and had the favour of their company to other places, as curiosity led me. I therefore take the liberty of recommending him to You, Sir, and to Pembroke college, to be shown that a lettered Stranger is not treated with less regard at Oxford than in France, and hope that You and my fellow collegians will not be unwilling to acknowledge some obligation for benefits conferred on one who has had the honour of studying amongst you.

I am Sir, Your most humble servant

May. 29. 1776 Sam: Johnson

484a. Southampton. Th. 30 May ⟨'76⟩. From Mrs. Thrale.

R 539.56—

Dear Sir Star Inn at Southampton 30: May.

In return for the obliging Care you have taken to write by every Opportunity, I now date a Letter to you from Southampton, with the Sight of which Mr Thrale has kindly treated me this day. We have seen Wilton in peace and I have escaped your teizing me with mock Connoissance, yet I wished for you sincerely at every *other* place, and most at Stonehenge; I am sadly behindhand sure in never having read or heard much said of that astonishing Thing. I read Scott's Amwell because you bid me; it is a dull Performance, resembling all the descriptive Poems one has read for these twenty Years; but I really wish you would read Law's Spirit of Prayer to please me, and *give a good Account of it*, as your foolish Friend says whose Name I have forgotten: Mrs Brown lent it me, but I want to hear what you think of it—it is at least not like every other book. Doctor Harrington suspects Soame Jenyns to be a false Brother I find: I was of that Opinion from the first, but durst not speak, because I am learning to be always on the good natured Side You know.

I hope Doctor Taylor will find your Company make him some Amends for the uneasiness this Woman has caused; being moody only drives one's Friends away, and every Year's vexation makes one want them more: His is just such a Grief as may be alleviated by Conversation & Amusement.

Be pleased to give him our best Compliments, I hope we shall soon see him

484.—1. Father Wilks.

at Streatham; but what shall I do for Servants? I shall be like the Old Hero in History who found all his Domesticks transformed to Birds & fled away when he returned from the Wars.—If you have any pity for me do not come home till I have got my house a little to rights, & if you can hear of a *Butler* or a *Footman* or a *Maid*, or almost anything do send them to me. My Master will have Henderson in Town, & Sam must be like Scrub in the Stratagem till he gets Help.

Tomorrow we go to Portsmouth; is not Mr Thrale very kind to carry me about so? but I know you love him always & so no more just now.

I am Sir Your most faithful and Obedient Servant H: L: Thrale.

485. M. 3 June '76. Henry Thrale.

Sotheby 30 Jan. 1918 (not seen).—1788, No. 154.

Dear Sir   June 3, 1776.

You are all, I suppose, now either at one home or the other, and all I hope well. My mistress writes as if she was afraid I should make too much haste to see her. Pray tell her that there is no danger. The lameness, of which I made mention in one of my notes, has improved to a very serious and troublesome fit of the gout. I creep about and hang by both hands. Johnny Wilcocks[1] might be my running footman. I enjoy all the dignity of lameness. I receive ladies and dismiss them sitting. *Painful pre-eminence.*[2]

Baretti is at last mentioned in one of the Reviews,[3] but in a manner that will not give him much delight. They are neither angry nor civil.

Catcot has been convinced by Barret, and has written his recantation to Tyrwhitt, who still persists in his edition of the poems, and perhaps is not much pleased to find himself mistaken.[4]

You are now, I suppose, busy about your *restes*;[5] I heartily wish you, dear Sir, a happy perambulation, and a good account of the trade; and hope that you and my mistress, as you come by, will call upon, Sir, Your, &c.

485.—1. Perhaps a character in comedy.

2. Addison's *Cato* III. v.

3. In the *Monthly Rev.* for May '76, 423, is a brief review of *Easy Phraseology*. The reviewer condemns Baretti for the common fault of such books: 'at the same time that they are instructing our youth in the French or Italian, they seldom fail to teach them bad English'. He adds, however, that 'this book, barring the Author's vanity ...', is not the most contemptible of the kind'.

4. See on 479.

5. See 483.

486. Tu. 4 June ⟨'76⟩. Mrs. Thrale.

Sotheby 30 Jan. 1918 (not seen).—1788, No. 155.

Dear Madam   June 4, at night.

The world is indeed full of troubles, and we must not chuse for ourselves. But I am not sincerely sorry that in your present state of mind you are going to be immediately a mother. Compose your thoughts, diversify your attention, and attend your health.

If I can be of any use, send for me; I think I can creep to the end of the court, and climb into a coach, though perhaps not very easily; but if you call me, very willingly. If you do not send for me, let me, pray let me know as oft as you can how you do.

I am glad that my master is at his *restes*, they will help to fill up his mind.

Pray let me know often how you do.

I am, dearest Lady, Your, &c.

487. W. 5 June '76. Mrs. Thrale.

Adam.—1788, No. 156.

Dearest Lady

You will have a note which I wrote last night. I was thinking as I lay awake that you might be worse, but I hope you will be every moment better and better. I have never had any overpowering pain, nor been kept more awake than is usual to me; but I am a very poor creeper upon the earth, catching at any thing with my hands to spare my feet. In a day or two I hope to be as fit for Streatham as for any other place. Mr Thrale it seems called last night when I was in bed, and yet I was not in bed till near twelve, for I sit up lest I should not sleep. He must keep well, for he is the pillar of

486.—Both 1788 (where this letter is placed as of '76) and the sale catalogue gives the date with no year. The references to J's gout and HT's *restes* seem to fix it as of '76. The reference in 487 to 'a note which I wrote last night' also fits. But HLT's next child, Cecilia, was born 8 Feb. '77; and according to her 'Children's Book' (1 July) she did not suspect her condition until the end of June. J had perhaps heard an inaccurate account of the 'cholera morbus' which had attacked her. His 488 of 6 June, which also lacks the year in its date, but seems clearly to belong to '76, makes the same assumption: 'cheerfulness at that time is reckoned a good thing'. HLP's note, written many years later, on J's 'mother', is simply 'To Cecilia Margaret Mostyn'. If J wrote 'immediately', he perhaps meant 'without any (unusual) interval'. For J's use of the word see 739.1.

the House,[1] and you must get well or the house will hardly
be worth propping.

　　I am, Dearest Madam, Your most humble servant,

June 5. 1776　　　　　　　　　　　　Sam: Johnson.

488. Th. 6 June ⟨'76⟩. Mrs. Thrale.

Hyde.—1788, No. 157.

My dear Lady

　　How could you so mistake me? I am very desirous that
the whole business should be as You would have it, only
cheerfulness at that time is reckoned a good thing.

　　My feet grow better, and I hope, if you send a carriage, to
mount it on Monday. This gout has a little depressed me,
not that I have suffered any great pain; I have been teized
rather than tortured; but the tediousness and the imbecill-
ity have been unpleasant. However I now recover strength
and do not yet despair of kicking the Moon.[1]

　　Could not you send me something out of your garden?
Things have been growing, and you have not been consuming
them. I wish I had a great bunch of asparagus for Sunday.

　　Take great care of our Queeney, and of yourself, and
encourage yourself in bustle and variety, and cheerfulness.
I will be ready to come as soon as I can, but the pain is now
twinging me. Let me know, my sweetest Lady, very often
how you do. I thought it late before I heard today.

　　I am, Dear Madam, your most humble Servant

June 6.　　　　　　　　　　　　　　Sam: Johnson

488a. Streatham. Th. ⟨? 6 June '76⟩. From Mrs. Thrale.

Address: Dr Sam Johnson Fleet Street.

R 539.59—

Dear Sir　　　　　　　　　　　　　　　Thursday Morning

　　I have slept and perspired, and am surprizingly mended thank God: today
I quit my bed, tomorrow or next day at furthest, my Chamber; & on Monday

487.—1. In 642 J calls him 'columen domus'.

488.—The allusions are obscure. See on 486. HLT's 488a, dated 'Thursday Morning', seems to be of 6 June '76. She reports herself better, and hopes to see J 'on
Monday' (see 489). This then should be the letter which J received 'late' on 6 June.
But nothing in 486 or 487 seems to fit her allusion to 'the *great Affair*'. It is possible
that 486 as we have it is incomplete. Whatever the misunderstanding, J in 488 dis-
misses it as past.

　　1. See 488b.

I hope to meet you in the Library if you can come thither with as little Trouble as I, though I shall be weak enough even then. How can you say what you do about the *great Affair*, & yet be so sincerely kind to me as you are? what else can this World afford me? Reason as you well know gives only Stubbornness, Religion itself only Patience; the Birth of another Son—Poor Amends—is the only Event that can give present Consolation, or future hope of Happiness in *this Life*. Indeed my sweet Queeney grows every day more precious to me, and any harm happening to her would be a most severe Grief to me, but the Pleasure I receive from her is now at its height, it is not the Pleasure one receives from the Possession of a Son to continue one's Family. So Farewell, & let me see you on Monday if you can come with ease to yourself; & believe that next to my own *very Household*, Your Friendship is the dearest Thing to your faithful & Obliged Servant

H: L: Thrale.

pray direct Jacob where to get me some Oil of Box—for to complete my Woes I have got the Toothach, but that signifies little,—*graviora tuli.*

488b. Streatham. F. 7 or Sat. 8 ⟨June '76⟩. From Mrs. Thrale.

R 539.57

Dear Sir

Saturday 7:

I mend gradually and get better on the whole but am as weak as a Cat now, not as strong as a Lyon: The Coach shall come on Monday, but do not you come home in it unless you are pretty well: what should we do together if both should want nursing? for I have here no Superfluity of Conveniencies at present, nor have had Time or Ability to get any about me.

Nemesis heard you talk of kicking the Moon, & so gave you the Twinge at the end of your Letter; for my Part I am miserably meek. You will serve me (bad as you are) as you did Dr Delap, I suppose, & give me a *Glass of Wine* when you *do* come.

Adieu I am ever your most faithful Servant

H: L: Thrale

489. Sa. 8 June ⟨'76⟩. Mrs. Thrale.

Adam.—1788, No. 158.

Dear Madam

My feet disappointed me last night; I thought they would have given me no disturbance, but going up stairs, I fancy, fretted them, and they would not let me be easy. On Monday I am afraid I shall be a poor walker, but well enough to talk, and to hear you talk. And then you know, what care We?

Mr Norton[1] called on me yesterday, he is at Sayer's print-

489.—1. Not identified. HLT's 489a, 'Sat: Even:' (i.e. presumably 8 June '76), 'Mr. Hector has a Card sent him . . . You must bring our Birmingham Friend with You', tempts the guess that J wrote 'Hector'. But the word is clearly 'Norton'.

shop in Fleet-street, and would take an invitation to diner very kindly.

Poor Mr Levet has fallen down and hurt himself dangerously.

Of the Monks I can give no account. I had them to dinner, and gave each of them the *Political tracts* and furnished Wilkes with letter,[2] which will, I believe, procure him a proper reception at Oxford.

I am, Dearest Lady, Your most—and most &c

June 8.   Sam: Johnson

489a. Streatham. Sa. and Su. ⟨? 8 and 9 June '76⟩. From Mrs. Thrale.

Address: Dʳ Sam: Johnson Fleet Street.

R 540.60—

Dear Sir   Sat: Even:

  I do mend apace, and will be alive on Monday if you'll come, but this vile Disorder has so sunk my Spirits which did not want sinking that I have been a poor Soul indeed. Mʳ Hector has a Card sent him, less from Compliment than true kindness. I shall lose the Sight of the Monks. When I get better I will call the World about me, even the D'Avenants coming today has done me good—& I wished them further too just at first. You must bring our Birmingham Friend with You, but I can't sit up at Night now—*& cry King George.* Adieu till tomorrow. I am Your most

                        Obliged & Faithful Servant H: L: Thrale.

This was finished o' Sunday Morning in bed.

489.1. Sa. 15 June '76. Frances Reynolds.

Address: To Miss Reynolds.

Rupert Colomb.—Hill, J 1897, ii. 449.

My dearest Dear

  When I am grown better, which is, I hope, at no great distance, for I mend gradually, We will take a little time to ourselves, and look over your dear little production,[1] and try to make it such as we may both like. I will not forget it, nor neglect it, for I love your tenderness.

  I am, Dear Madam, Your most humble servant

June 15. 1776   Sam: Johnson

489.—2. J perhaps intended 'a letter', or 'letters'. The only recorded letter is 484.
489.1.—1. See Index II for J's criticisms of FR's literary efforts. She was also an artist; but 'look over' suggests a manuscript.

490. F. 21 June '76. Frances Reynolds.

Address: To Miss Reynolds.
B.M.—Croker's Boswell 1831, iii. 447.

Dear Madam

You are as naughty[1] as you can be. I am willing enough to write to you when I have any thing to say. As for my disorder, as Sir Joshua saw me, I fancied he would tell you, and that I needed not tell you myself.

Of Dr. Goldsmith's Epitaph,[2] I sent Sir Joshua two copies, and had none myself. If he has lost it, he has not done well. But I suppose I can recollect it, and will send it to you.

I am Madam Your most humble servant

June 21. 1776   Sam: Johnson

All the Thrales are well, and Mrs Thrale has a great regard for Miss Reynolds.

491. Sa. 22 June '76. Joshua Reynolds.

Address: To Sir Joshua Reynolds.
Fettercairn—Boswell 1793, ii. 449 (Hill iii. 82).

Sir,

Miss Reynolds has a mind to send the Epitaph[1] to Dr. Beattie, I am very willing, but having no copy, cannot immediately recollect it. She tells me you have lost it. Try to recollect and put down as much as you retain; you perhaps may have kept what I have dropped. The lines for which I am at a loss are something of *Rerum civilium sivè naturalium*.[2] It was a sorry trick to lose it, help me if you can.

I am, Sir Your most humble Servant

June 22. 1776   Sam: Johnson.

The gout grows better, but slowly.

490.—1. This is in answer to FR's letter printed by Croker, iii. 446, in which she wrote of 'the rule you have certainly prescribed to yourself of writing to some sort of people just such a number of lines'. J's letters to her are in fact almost all very short.

2. FR had written 'Be so good as to favour me with Dr. Goldsmith's Epitaph; and if you have no objection, I should be very glad to send it to Dr. Beattie. . . . My brother says he has lost' it. See 480, 491.

491.—1. See 480, 490.

2. 'These words must have been in the other copy. They are not in that which was preferred.' JB. See Addenda, p. 529.

491.1. Sa. 22 June '76. Bennet Langton.

Address: To Benet Langton Esq.
Fettercairn—

Dear Sir

I am better, but gain ground slowly. However, at this
rate of amendment, I can probably wait on You at the latter
end of next week.

I hope that Lady Rothes and all the pretty little people
are well. When you would see me favour me with a not at
Mr Thrales'. I am Sir, Your most humble Servant
June 22. 1776.   Sam: Johnson

492. Tu. 25 (? misdated 23) June '76. John Taylor (Ashbourne).

Address: To the reverend Dr Taylor in Ashbourne Derbyshire.
Postmark: 25 IV.
Loyd.—*NQ* 6 S. v. 423.

Dear Sir   June 23. 1776.
    The Gout is now grown tolerable; I can go up stairs pretty
well, but am yet aukward in coming down.

Some time ago I had a letter from the Solicitor,[1] in which
he mentioned our cause with respect enough, but persists in
his opinion, as I suppose, your Attorney has told you. He is
however convinced that nothing fraudulent was intended:[2]
I would be glad to hear what the Attorney says.

Mr. Thrale would glad⟨l⟩y have seen you at his house.
They are all well.

Whether I shall wander this summer, I hardly know. If I
do, tell me when it will be the best time to come to you.

I hope you persevere in drinking, My opinion is that I

491.1.—For the reasons of the suppression of (parts of) letters to BL see on 240.1.

492.—Hill points out that the show of hands in the City election (see below) was on
24 June, and suggests that this letter is misdated. It was probably written, or
finished, on the date of its postmark.

  1. Hill identifies this with the 'solicitor, another Scrase', of 478. But Sir Frank
MacKinnon confirmed me on the opinion that J means the Solicitor-General,
Wedderburne. See 475. By 'the Attorney' J probably means JT's regular attorney,
who had given him no encouragement (479); but he may mean Thurlow, whom also
JT intended to consult (473, 475).

  2. 'The Solicitor' had no doubt written that JT's 'pactum iniquum' (483) was
innocent in intention.

have drank too little, and therefore have the gout, for it is of my own acquisition, for neither my father had it nor my mother.

Wilkes and Hopkins have now polled two days, and I hear that Wilkes is two hundred behind.[3]

Of this sudden Revolution in the Prince's household,[4] the original cause is not certainly known. The quarrel began between Lord Holderness, and Jackson, the part of Jackson was taken by the Bishop, and all ended in a total change.

I am, Sir, Your affectionate, &c.

Sam: Johnson

493. Tu. 2 July '76. James Boswell (Edinburgh).

Not traced.—Boswell 1791, ii. 94 (Hill iii. 86).

Dear Sir,

These black fits,[1] of which you complain, perhaps hurt your memory as well as your imagination. When did I complain that your letters were too long?[2] Your last letter, after a very long delay, brought very bad news.

[Here a series of reflections upon melancholy, and—what I could not help thinking strangely unreasonable in him who had suffered so much from it himself,—a good deal of severity and reproof, as if it were owing to my own fault, or that I was, perhaps, affecting it from a desire of distinction.]

Read Cheyne's '*English Malady*'; but do not let him teach you a foolish notion that melancholy is a proof of acuteness. . . .

To hear that you have not opened your boxes of books[3] is

492.—3. In the end Hopkins was elected Chamberlain of the City of London with 2,600 votes, Wilkes polling 1,513 (*GM* 1776, 285).

On the Monday Hopkins led by 55, on the Tuesday by 368. So J's information, though not quite accurate, was up to date (*Morning Post* 26 June).

4. Hill quotes a letter of Horace Walpole, 5 June, describing this palace revolution. The Bishop was Markham.

493.—1. JB had written 25 June 'an account of having been afflicted with a return of melancholy or bad spirits'.

2. JB had written: 'You have formerly complained that my letters were too long.' In a footnote he supports this: 'Baretti told me that Johnson complained of my writing very long letters to him when I was upon the continent; which was most certainly true; but it seems my friend did not remember it.'

3. JB had written: 'The boxes of books which you sent to me are arrived; but I have not yet examined the contents.' In a footnote he explains: 'Upon a settlement of our account of expences on our Tour to the Hebrides, there was a balance due to me, which Dr. Johnson chose to discharge by sending books.'

very offensive. The examination and arrangement of so many volumes might have afforded you an amusement very seasonable at present, and useful for the whole of life. I am, I confess, very angry that you manage yourself so ill. . . .

I do not now say any more, than that I am, with great kindness and sincerity, dear Sir, Your humble servant,
July 2, 1776   Sam. Johnson

It was last year determined by Lord Mansfield, in the Court of King's Bench, that a negro cannot be taken out of the kingdom without his own consent.[4]

493a. Streatham. Tu. 2 July ⟨'76⟩. From Mrs. Thrale.
Address: Dr Johnson.
R 540.61—

As Mr Baretti comes down today Dr Johnson will be so good to wait five Minutes for him at the Bunhouse & bring him down. Mr Thrale is gone to Rickmansworth.

2 July.

494. Sa. 6 July '76. James Boswell (Edinburgh).
Not traced.—Boswell 1791, ii. 95 (Hill iii. 88).

Dear Sir,

I make haste to write again, lest my last letter should give you too much pain. If you are really oppressed with overpowering and involuntary melancholy, you are to be pitied rather than reproached. . . .[1]

Now, my dear Bozzy, let us have done with quarrels and with censure. Let me know whether I have not sent you a pretty library. There are, perhaps, many books among them which you never need read through; but there are none which it is not proper for you to know, and sometimes to

493.—4. JB had sent 'Mr. Maclaurin's paper for the negro', Joseph Knight, 'who claims his freedom in the Court of Session'. For J's exertions on his behalf see *L* iii. 200; and for the case of the other negro, James Somerset, *L* iii. 87.

494.—1. JB records: 'And thus on Saturday the 24 of August I have once more brought up my Journal, which had fallen sadly behind. My low spirits this summer have been very severe upon me. I complained to Dr. Samuel Johnson. He first wrote to me rather harshly, but soon wrote in a gentler strain. I have been too long without writing to him.' JB did not answer 493, and did not write again until 18 July: 'Your letter of the second of this month was rather a harsh medicine; but I was delighted with that spontaneous tenderness, which, a few days afterwards, sent forth such balsam as your next brought me.'

consult. Of these[2] books, of which the use is only occasional, it is often sufficient to know the contents, that, when any question arises, you may know where to look for information.

Since I wrote, I have looked over Mr. Maclaurin's plea, and think it excellent. How is the suit carried on? If by subscription, I commission you to contribute, in my name, what is proper. Let nothing be wanting in such a case. Dr. Drummond,[3] I see, is superseded. His father would have grieved; but he lived to obtain the pleasure of his son's election, and died before that pleasure was abated.

Langton's lady has brought him a girl,[4] and both are well; I dined with him the other day. . . .

It vexes me to tell you, that on the evening of the 29th of May I was seized by the gout, and am not quite well. The pain has not been violent, but the weakness, and tenderness were very troublesome, and what is said to be very uncommon, it has not alleviated my other disorders. Make use of youth and health while you have them; make my compliments to Mrs. Boswell. I am, my dear Sir, Your most affectionate

July 6, 1776.   Sam. Johnson.

495. Th. 11 July '76. Francis Fowke.

Not traced; copy by Thomas Harwood, *c.* 1820, at Pembroke.—Warner, *Original Letters* 1817, 205.

Sir   July 11. 1776.

I received some weeks ago a collection of papers, which contain the trial of my dear friend Joseph Fowke, of whom I cannot easily be induced to think otherwise than well, and who seems to have been injured by the prosecution and the sentence. His first desire is, that I should prepare his narrative for the press; his second, that if I cannot gratify him by

494.—2. J perhaps wrote 'those'. In the first edition of the *Journey* the two words seem often to have been confused.

3. 'The son of Johnson's old friend, Mr. William Drummond. He was a young man of such distinguished merit, that he was nominated to one of the medical professorships in the College of Edinburgh, without solicitation, while he was at Naples. Having other views, he did not accept of the honour, and soon afterwards died' JB.

4. J's godchild Jenny.

495.—For J's acquaintance with Joseph Fowke, and F's trial and conviction for conspiracy in '75, see *L* iii. 471.

publication I would transmit the papers to you. To a compliance with his first request I have this objection; that I live in a reciprocation of civilities with Mr. Hastings, and therefore cannot properly diffuse a narrative, intended to bring upon him the censure of the publick. Of two adversaries, it would be rash to condemn either upon the evidence of the other; and a common friend must keep himself suspended, at least till he has heard both.

I am therefore ready to transmit to you the papers, which have been seen only by myself; and beg to be informed how they may be conveyed to you. I see no legal objection to the publication; and of prudential reasons, Mr. Fowke and you will be allowed to be fitter judges.

If you would have me send them, let me have proper directions; if a messenger is to call for them, give me notice by the post, that they may be ready for delivery.

To do my dear Mr. Fowke any good would give me pleasure; I hope for some opportunity of performing the duties of friendship to him, without violating them with regard to another.

I am, Sir, Your most humble Servant,
Sam: Johnson.

496. Sa. 3 Aug. '76. Joshua Reynolds.

Address: To Sir Joshua Reynolds.
Fettercairn.—Boswell 1793, ii. 459 (Hill iii. 90).

Sir

A young Man whose name is Paterson offers himself this evening to the Academy. He is the Son of a Man for whom I have long had a kindness, and who is now abroad in distress. I shall be glad that you will be pleased to show him any little countenance, or pay him any small distinction. How much it is in your power to favour or to forward a young man I do not know, nor do I know how much this candidate deserves favour by his personal merit, or what hopes his proficiency

496.—Sir Walter Lamb, Secretary to the Royal Academy of Arts, wrote: 'Charles Patterson was admitted a student in painting on the 4th. October 1776. I conceive that Reynolds was asked to favour his admission and give him some special attention and encouragement while he was working in the Schools.' The conditions of admission were not onerous.

may now give of future eminence. I recommend him as the Son of my Friend. Your character and station enable you to give a young man great encouragement by very easy means. You have heard of a Man who asked no other favour of Sir Robert Walpole, than that he would bow to him at his levee.[1]

I am, Sir, Your most humble Servant,

Aug. 3. 1776   Sam: Johnson.

497. Sa. 3 Aug. ⟨'76⟩. Frances Reynolds.

Address: To Mrs. Reynolds.
Adam; copy by F.R. ('I believe in 74'), Rupert Colomb.—*Morrison Autographs* 1885, ii. 342.

Dearest Madam

To do what you desire with your restrictions is impossible. I shall not see Mrs Thrale till tuesday in the afternoon. If I write, I must give a stronger reason than you care to allow. The company is already very numerous, but yet there might I suppose be found room for a girl, if the proposal could be made. Even writing if you allow it, will hardly do, the penny post does not go on Sunday, and Mr Thrale does not always come to town on Monday. However let me know what you would have done.

I am Madam Your most humble servant

Aug. 3.   Sam: Johnson

497.1. Sa. 31 Aug. '76. ⟨? Thomas Cadell.⟩

Johnson House.—

Sir

Mr Stockdale desires me to mention to You a small literary project, of which, I hope You will have no ill opinion.

496.—1. I have not traced this anecdote, and Mr. W. S. Lewis cannot help me.

497.—Hill assigns this letter to '76, since it must have been written on a Saturday, at latest on a Sunday. It may have been sent with 496. (On Sun. 3 Aug. '77 J was in Oxford.)

497.1.—This letter is in a frame, with an inscription describing it as to Cadell and dating it 31 May '78. On removing the frame I satisfied myself that the date is 31 Aug. '76. The ascription to Cadell is traditional, or more probably conjectural; it is perhaps more likely that J wrote to Strahan.

Stockdale's published works are numerous; he added no history of Spain to the list.

He proposes to write, in three octavo volumes, a short history of Spain. We have none in our language but translations. It is a very interesting story, and contains many important revolutions and events. I have given Mr Stockdale such hints as occurred to me. Of his abilities for the performance You must judge by his works.

I am, Sir, Your most humble Servant

Aug. 31. 1776   Sam: Johnson

498. Sa. 21 Sept. '76. John Ryland.

Address: To Mr Ryland.
W. Marchbank.—Hill 1892.

Sir

I have procured this play[1] to be read by Mrs. Thrale, who declares that no play was ever more nicely secured from the objection of indelicacy.

If it can be got upon the stage, it will I think, succeed, and may get more money, than will be raised by the impression of the other works.

In selling the copy to the printer, the liberty of inserting it in the volumes may be retained.

I am, Sir, Your most humble servant,

Septr. 21, 1776   Sam: Johnson

498.1. M. 23 Sept. '76. Robert Levet.

Address: To Mr Levett.
Adam.—

Dear Sir

Mr Thrale ⟨ ? ⟩ to enquire after you, and this is the answer. You must contrive to be more particular when we return. We are going to Brighthelmston, but shall hardly stay long so late in the year. Francis and his Wife have both given great satisfaction by their behaviour.

I am Sir Your humble servant

Sept. 23. 1776   Sam: Johnson

498.—1 By Hawkesworth. For the abortive scheme of a posthumous collection of H's works see Index II.

499. Brighthelmston. M. 14 Oct. '76. 〈William Strahan.〉
Elkin Mathews 1924.—Hill's Boswell vi. xxxvii.

Sir

I wrote to you about ten days ago, and sent you some copy.[1] You have not written again. That is a sorry trick.

I am told that you are printing a Book for Mr. Professor Watson[2] of Saint Andrews, if upon any occasion, I can give any help, or be of any use, as formerly in Dr Robertson's[3] publication, I hope you will make no scruple to call upon me, for I should be glad of an opportunity to show that my reception at Saint Andrews has not been forgotten.

I am, Sir Your humble Servant

Oct. 14. 1776.   Sam: Johnson

500. Brighthelmston. M. 21 Oct. '76. Robert Levet.
Not traced.—Boswell 1793, ii. 461 (Hill iii. 92).

Dear Sir

Having spent about six weeks at this place, we have at length resolved upon returning. I expect to see you all in Fleet-street on the 30th of this month.

I did not go into the sea till last Friday, but think to go most of this week, though I know not that it does me any good. My nights are very restless and tiresome, but I am otherwise well.

I have written word of my coming to Mrs. Williams. Remember me kindly to Francis and Betsy.

I am, Sir, Your humble servant,

Brighthelmstone, Oct. 21, 1776.   Sam: Johnson

500.1. W. 30 Oct. '76. John Hoole.
Sotheby 15 Feb. 1932.—

Dear Sir

I am just come from Brighthelmston, and have heard of

499.—1. See 510.

2. Watson's *History of Philip II* was 'printed for W. Strahan and T. Cadell' and published 1777.

3. Nothing more seems to be known, than is revealed by this passage, of any help given by J to R's 'publication'. But Strahan was both printer and publisher of R's *Charles V* 1769. Hill quotes Forbes's *Life of Beattie* for the statement that Strahan 'corrected the phraseology of both Hume and Robertson'. No doubt he had J's help in correcting R.

dear Mrs Hoole's dreadful illness. I am just told that she is
thought better, and sincerely wish her a complete recovery.
Take care of your own health in the mean time. Mrs
Williams sends her compliments.

I am Sir, Your most humble Servant

Oct. 30. 1776   Sam: Johnson

501. Th. 14 Nov. '76. John Ryland.

Christie 5 June 1888 (not seen).—Hill 1892.

Dear Sir,

The selection[1] made in this parcel is indicated partly in
a catalogue by the words *print* or *omit*, and partly by the
same words written in red ink at the top of those pieces
which are not in the catalogue. I purpose to send the rest
very soon, and I believe you and I must then have two or
three interviews to adjust the order in which they shall
stand.

I am, Sir, Your most humble servant,

Nov. 14, 1776.   Sam: Johnson.

502. Sa. 16 Nov. '76. James Boswell (Edinburgh).

Not traced.—Boswell 1791, ii. 98 (Hill iii. 93).

Dear Sir

I had great pleasure in hearing that you are at last on good
terms with your father.[1] Cultivate his kindness by all honest
and manly means. Life is but short; no time can be afforded
but for the indulgence of real sorrow, or contests upon
questions seriously momentous. Let us not throw any of our
days away upon useless resentment, or contend who shall
hold out longest in stubborn malignity. It is best not to be
angry, and best, in the next place, to be quickly reconciled.
May you and your father pass the remainder of your time in
reciprocal benevolence!

＊　　＊　　＊　　＊　　＊　　＊

501.—1. Of Hawkesworth's writings; see on 498.

502.—1. JB had written 21 Oct. (from Auchinleck *BP* xii. 66) 'informing him that
my father had . . . paid a large debt for me'—the sum was £1,000—'and that I had
now the happiness of being upon very good terms with him'.

Do you ever hear from Mr. Langton? I visit him sometimes, but he does not talk. I do not like his scheme of life;
but, as I am not permitted to understand it, I cannot set
any thing right that is wrong. His children are sweet babies.

I hope my irreconcileable enemy, Mrs. Boswell, is well.
Desire her not to transmit her malevolence to the young
people. Let me have Alexander, and Veronica, and Euphemia, for my friends.

Mrs. Williams, whom you may reckon as one of your well-
wishers, is in a feeble and languishing state, with little hope
of growing better. She went for some part of the autumn
into the country, but is little benefited; and Dr. Lawrence
confesses that his art is at an end. Death is, however, at a
distance; and what more than that can we say of ourselves?
I am sorry for her pain, and more sorry for her decay. Mr.
Levett is sound, wind and limb.

I was some weeks this autumn at Brighthelmston. The
place was very dull, and I was not well: the expedition to the
Hebrides was the most pleasant journey that I ever made.
Such an effort annually would give the world a little
diversification.

Every year, however, we cannot wander, and must therefore endeavour to spend our time at home as well as we can.
I believe it is best to throw life into a method, that every
hour may bring its employment, and every employment have
its hour. Xenophon[2] observes, in his 'Treatise of Oeconomy',
that if every thing be kept in a certain place, when any thing
is worn out or consumed, the vacuity which it leaves will
shew what is wanting; so if every part of time has its duty,
the hour will call into remembrance its proper engagement.

I have not practised all this prudence[3] myself, but I have
suffered much for want of it; and I would have you, by
timely recollection and steady resolution, escape from those
evils which have lain heavy upon me. I am, my dearest
Boswell, Your most humble servant,
Bolt-court, Nov. 16, 1776.   Sam. Johnson

502.—2. *Oeconomicus* viii. 10: ἡ γὰρ χώρα αὐτὴ τὸ μὴ ὂν ποθήσει.

3. In *PM* 9 Jan. '74 J deplores 'a life immethodical, and unsettled' as 'the chief
cause of my deficiency'.

503. Su. 1 Dec. '76. Thomas Percy.
Address: To the Reverend Dr Percy.
Dyce-Forster.—Hill 1892.

Dear Sir

Mr Langton and I shall wait on you at St. James's[1] on Tuesday.

I must entreat your attention to a business of more importance. The Duke[2] is President of the Middlesex hospital; Could you obtain from him the admission of a Patient, the Son of Mr Thomas Coxeter, a Gentleman and a Man of Letters? The unhappy Man inherits some claim from his Father to particular notice; and has all the claims common to others, of disease and want.

I shall apply no where else till I hear from you: Be pleased to answer this request as soon as you can. I am, Sir, Your most humble Servant, Sam Johnson. Dec. 1, 1776.

504. M. 2 Dec. ⟨'76⟩. Thomas Percy.
Address (Hill): To the Reverend Dr Percy.
Not traced.—Hill 1892.

Thomas Coxeter of little Carter lane, in Doctors Commons.

His disease I could not gather from his sister's accounts so as to name it. He has had a scorbutick humour which I believe has fallen back upon his vitals.

I have got a cold which, I hope, will not hinder me from dining at your table, and returning you thanks for this favour. Dec. 2.

504.1. M. 16 Dec. '76. Thomas Percy.
Historical Society of Pennsylvania.—

Reverend Sir

At this time when donatives are distributed at Northumberland House, with such unexampled liberality, I beg leave to recommend Mrs Elizabeth Coxeter, a Gentlewoman, and very poor, as not unfit to partake of the Duke's beneficence.

I am, Sir, Your most humble Servant,
Dec. 16, 1776.   Sam: Johnson
I am just come home, and am going to Dr. Laurence.

503.—1. Percy during his month of waiting as Chaplain to the King was entitled to invite his friends to dine at the Chaplain's table; see 504. (Gaussen, *Percy* 1908, 173.)
   2. Of Northumberland, Percy's patron.

505. Sa. 21 Dec. '76. James Boswell (Edinburgh).

Not traced.—Boswell 1791, ii. 99 (Hill iii. 94).

Dear Sir,

I have been for some time ill of a cold, which, perhaps, I made an excuse to myself for not writing, when in reality I knew not what to say.

The books[1] you must at last distribute as you think best, in my name, or your own, as you are inclined, or as you judge most proper. Every body cannot be obliged, but I wish that nobody may be offended. Do the best you can.

I congratulate you on the increase of your family, and hope that little David is by this time well, and his mamma perfectly recovered. I am much pleased to hear of the re-establishment of kindness between you and your father.[2] Cultivate his paternal tenderness as much as you can. To live at variance at all is uncomfortable; and variance with a

505.—1. JB had written 16 Nov. that Strahan had sent him—nearly two years after publication—twelve copies 'handsomely bound' of the *Journey*, instead of a larger number (variously stated, see references in Index VI) promised, which JB 'supposed were to be only in sheets'. S seems to have been inordinately afraid of damaging the sale. But JB's letter of acknowledgement to him (7 Feb. '77, Tinker 168) makes no complaint of delay. The copy sent to Lord Monboddo is in Prof. Tinker's collection. I have not heard that any other is known. See Addenda, p. 529.

2. JB quotes copiously, *L* iii. 101, from his reply, 14 Feb. '77, to 502 and 505. But he does not quote from the last leaf, which has happily survived, of that long letter. The discovery at Malahide of large parts of the copy for the *Life* proved that it was at some date in two sections: JB's MS. proper, and the documents which he included. No documents were found at Malahide. It looks as if this section had been further subdivided; for though Prof. Abbott found at Fettercairn most of the other letters from J printed in the *Life*, he did not find J's letters to JB, which like JB's to J are almost all still to seek. Four of JB's letters to J, however, were found at Malahide; one of these is the fragment mentioned above. Prof. Pottle remarks (*BP* xii. 236): 'It is significant that, though the fragmentary letter appears in the *Life*, the portion now recovered is there omitted; and no one of the other three is to be found in the *Life* at all.' It is tempting to think that JB failed to quote this part of his letter of 14 Feb. just because he had mislaid it; but that cannot be so, since he *does* quote (*L* iii. 102) the elaborate subscription. The whole leaf will be found (with a facsimile) at *BP* xii. 241. The passage dealing with his father, which we must suppose JB to have suppressed from filial piety, is as follows: 'You form too agreable a notion of the terms on which I am with my Father. Happily there is no longer any substantial difference. But there is a coldness which is very discouraging; an inattention to me and my Wife and my children that is unnatural. I do not suspect my Stepmother of foul play in money matters. But I beleive she estranges my Father from me and mine, with an assiduity that is too successful. Is not that culpable? What do you think of their never asking my Wife and children to come to Auchinleck?' See also *L* iii. 95. For the *latest* Malahide finds see Addenda, p. 529.

father is still more uncomfortable. Besides that, in the whole dispute you have the wrong side; at least you gave the first provocations, and some of them very offensive. Let it now be all over. As you have no reason to think that your new mother has shewn you any foul play, treat her with respect, and with some degree of confidence; this will secure your father. When once a discordant family has felt the pleasure of peace, they will not willingly lose it. If Mrs. Boswell[3] would but be friends with me, we might now shut the temple of Janus.

What came of Dr. Memis's cause? Is the question about the negro[4] determined? Has Sir Allan[5] any reasonable hopes? What is become of poor Macquarry? Let me know the event of all these litigations. I wish particularly well to the negro and Sir Allan.

Mrs. Williams has been much out of order; and though she is something better, is likely, in her physician's opinion, to endure her malady for life, though she may, perhaps, die of some other. Mrs. Thrale is big, and fancies that she carries a boy; if it were very reasonable to wish much about it, I should wish her not to be disappointed. The desire of male heirs is not appendant only to feudal tenures. A son is almost necessary to the continuance of Thrale's fortune; for what can misses do with a brewhouse? Lands are fitter for daughters than trades.

Baretti[6] went away from Thrale's in some whimsical fit of disgust, or ill-nature, without taking any leave. It is well if he finds in any other place as good an habitation, and as many conveniences. He has got five-and-twenty guineas by translating Sir Joshua's Discourses into Italian, and Mr. Thrale gave him an hundred in the spring; so that he is yet in no difficulties.

Colman[7] has bought Foote's patent, and is to allow Foote for life sixteen hundred pounds a year, as Reynolds told me, and to allow him to play so often on such terms that he may

505.—3. In the surviving leaf (see above) of JB's reply of 14 Feb. he writes, 'My Wife is quite well; but cannot forgive your supposing that she still retains hostile dispositions towards you.'

4. Joseph Knight.   5. Maclean.

6. On 6 July. See C 144, *L* iii. 96.

7. See references in *L* iii. 97.

gain four hundred pounds more. What Colman can get by this bargain, but trouble and hazard, I do not see.

I am, dear Sir, Your humble servant,

Dec. 21, 1776. Sam. Johnson

505.1. Tu. 24 Dec. '76. William Strahan.

Address: To William Strahan Esq.
Fettercairn.—Boswell 1791, ii. 101 (Hill iii. 97); an extract; overlooked by Hill in *Letters*.

Sir

I have read over Dr Blair's first Sermon, with more than approbation to say it is good is to say too little.

Be so kind as to frank this Letter to Mrs Lucy Porter in Lichfield.

I intended to have come to you to day but something has hindred me. I will come on Saturday or Monday, or both.

I am, Sir, Your most humble Servant

Dec. 24. 1776 Sam Johnson

505.2. Tu. 24 Dec. '76. Joseph Nollekens.

Address: Mr Nollikens.
Fettercairn.—

Sir

I have sent the inscription.[1] Where there are dots : : : there must be a space left for the dates which we have ⟨not⟩ yet got at. My compliments and good wishes come with this both to You and Mrs Nollikens, from Sir, Your most humble Servant

Dec. 24. 1776 Sam: Johnson

505.3. Sa. 11 Jan. '77. Mrs. Thrale.

Adam.—

Tempora mutantur.[1] I am to dine to day (Saturday) with Sir Joshua and Dr Warton on Sunday with Dr Lawrence, on Monday I am engaged to Miss Way, on Tuesday to Mrs Gardiner; on Wednesday I dine with Mr Langton and the Bishop of Chester;[2] on Thursday with Mr Paradise and Mr

505.2.—1. For Goldsmith, see 539.1.

505.3.—1. See Index IIIB. 2. Markham.

Bryant. Thus, dearest Lady, am I hindred from being with you and Miss Owen. Mrs Montague talks of you, and says she will come see you. but I hope, I shall come before her. Jan. 11. 1777.

505.3a. Streatham. Su. 12 ⟨Jan. '77⟩. From Mrs. Thrale.
Address: Mr Johnson Bolt Court Fleet Street.
R 540.94—

Dear Sir   Streatham Sunday 12.
  I am always pleased when you are busy and bustling in the World: when you have fulfilled all your Engagements and are tired with rattling about, it will be time enough to come home to your Mistress whom Pain makes peevish of late, and whose Nights are growing very insupportable.
  Mrs Montagu's Visit—at any Time a Favour, will now be a Charity:— I hope She will come too for the Sake of Miss Owen who longs to see her, & who deserves something for staying with me so: it is a vast Comfort to have a Lady about one—and I have had none so long. Adieu! and wish me good Wishes from your heart as I am ever
                                    Sir Your most Faithful &c. H: L: T.

506. W. 15 Jan. '77. Mrs. Thrale.
Adam.—1788, No. 159.

Omnium rerum vicissitudo.[1] The Night after last Thursday was so bad, that I took ipecacuanha the next day. The next night was no better. On Saturday I dined with Sir Joshua. The night was such as I was forced to rise and pass some hours in a chair, with great labour of respiration. I found it now time to do something and went to Dr Lawrence, and told him I would do what he should order without reading the prescription. He sent for a Chirurgeon and took about twelve ounces of blood, and in the afternoon I got sleep in a chair.

At night when I came to lie down, after trial of an hour or two I found sleep impracticable, and therefore did what the Doctor permitted in a case of distress. I rose and opening the orifice let out about ten ounces more. Frank and I were but awkward, but with Mr Levet's help we stopped the

---

506.—1. Terence, *Eunuchus* II. ii. 45: Omnium rerum heus vicissitudo est. In the Highlands J had quoted from Gifford's *Contemplation* 'the sad vicissitude of things', which was perhaps a reminiscence of Terence. *L* v. 117.

stream, and I lay down again, though to little purpose, the difficulty of breathing allowed no rest. I slept again in the day time in an erect posture. The Doctor has ordered me a second bleeding, which, I hope, will set my Breath at liberty. Last night I could lie but a little at a time.

Yet I do not make it a matter of much form. I was to day at Mrs Gardiner's. When I have bled to morrow I will not give up Langton,[2] nor Paradise. But I beg you will fetch me away on Fryday. I do not know but clearer air may do me good; but whether the air be clear or dark, let me come to You.

I am, Madam, Your most humble servant Sam: Johnson Wednesday Jan 15 one in the morning 1777. To sleep, or not to sleep.

351. Thursday ⟨? 16 Jan. '77⟩. Mrs. Thrale.

Address: To Mrs Thrale.
Sotheby 15 Feb. 1932.—1788, No. 95.

Madam   Thursday.

Master is very kind in being very angry, but he may spare his anger this time. I have done exactly as Dr. Lawrence ordered, and am much better at the expence of about thirty-six ounces of blood. Nothing in the World! For a good cause I have six and thirty more. I long though to come to Streatham, and you shall give me no solid flesh for a week; and I am to take Physick. And hey boys up go we.[1] I was in bed all last night, only a little sitting up. The box goes to *Calcutta*.

I am Dearest dearest Madam, Your most &c.

Sam: Johnson

Let me come to you to morrow.

506.—2. J was to dine with L on Wed. (505.3). Though 506 is dated 1 a.m. Wed., he writes as if on Tuesday.

351.—This letter appears in 1788 among those of '74. But it is clearly the answer to HLT's 506*a*, which is as clearly the answer to 506. HLP in choosing '74 may have recalled that J had in that year sent a copy of his *Journey* to Hastings in Calcutta. The 'box' of this letter I cannot identify.

1. The *Oxford Dict. of Quotations* 1935 quotes Quarles, *The Shepherd's Oracles*: 'We'll cry both arts and learning down, And hey! then up go we.'

506a. ⟨*c.* 16 Jan. '77.⟩ From Mrs. Thrale.

Address: To Doctor Johnson Bolt Court Fleet Street.

R 540.86—

Here is Dr Burney come & says You are very ill: Oh sad! Oh sad! indeed I am very sorry; and I unable to nurse You—for Goodness Sake do as Dr Lawrence would have you & be well before you come home—and pray don't be bleeding yourself & doing yourself harm. My Master is very angry already.

506.1. F. 17 Jan. ⟨'77⟩. Thomas Barnard.

Earl of Crawford.—

Mr. Johnson, not being to dine at the Club this day, as he intended, waits on the Dean of Derry to take leave, and wish him a prosperous voyage.

Friday Jan: 17th

Charade!

My first, shuts out Theives from yr house or yr Room,
My second, expresses a Syrian perfume,
My whole, is a Man in whose converse is shar'd,
The strength of a Bar, and the sweetness of Nard.

506.2. Th. 23 Jan. '77. John Taylor.

Address: To the Rev^d Dr Taylor in Ashbourne Derbyshire. *Postmark*: 23 IA.

Adam.—

Dear Sir

I am desired by Mrs Williams to return thanks for the excellent Turkey and Hare, with the Turkey she made one feast and with the Hare she intends to make another.

You told me in your last nothing of your health. I hope it is as you wish. I was lately seized with a difficulty of breathing, which forced me out of bed, to pass part of the night in a chair. Dr Laurence has taken away, as is reckoned, about thirty six ounces of blood, and by purging and lower diet, I begin to breathe better than I have done for many months past.

I suppose you continue your purpose of residing in

506a.—This letter must be later than Mar. '76, when J moved to Bolt Court.

506.1.—The year depends on 506 and 351, which tell us that J was to go to S'm on the Friday.

February. Mrs Thrale expects a little one in about three weeks. I shall be glad to see you come up well and cheerful, and hope we may pass a good part of the time pleasantly together.

I am, Sir, your most affectionate

Bolt court. Jan. 23. 1777 Sam: Johnson

506.2a. Streatham. W. 12 Feb. ⟨'77⟩. From Mrs. Thrale.
Sotheby 4 Feb. 1919 (not seen).—Described in catalogue.

'Announcing the birth of her daughter Cecilia.'

506.3. Th. 13 Feb. '77. Bennet Langton.
Address: To Benet Langton Esq.
Fettercairn.—

Sir Thursday Febr. 13. 1777
I suppose you do not doubt of my having written for Mr Parr.[1]

If you dine with the Bishop of Chester to morrow, it will be kind to take up me. If you come down Holbourn, and through Chancery Lane, you lose but little ground. If I receive no answer, I shall expect you till three to morrow.

My Compliments &c. I am Sir Your most &c.

Sam: Johnson

507. Tu. 18 Feb. '77. James Boswell (Edinburgh).
Not traced.—Boswell 1791, ii. 106 (Hill iii. 104).

Dear Sir,
It is so long since I heard any thing from you,[1] that I am not easy about it; write something to me next post. When

---

506.3.—For the reasons of the suppression of (parts of) letters to BL see on 240.1.

1. Parr's doctorate is now as inseparable from his name as Johnson's from his; but he did not receive the degree until '81. The letter 'for Mr Parr' was no doubt the letter J is known to have written in support of P's successful application for the head-mastership of Colchester Grammar School (*DNB*). It has not been traced.

507.—1. 'By the then course of the post, my long letter of the 14th had not yet reached him' JB. Throughout their correspondence the normal course of post between L'n and Edinburgh was four days. This is ascertained by JB's practice of noting the dates of receipt in his journal. His letter dated 14 Feb. was in fact 'finished' 17 Feb. (*BP* xii. 133). See on 505.

you sent your last letter every thing seemed to be mending,
I hope nothing has lately grown worse. I suppose young
Alexander continues to thrive, and Veronica is now very
pretty company. I do not suppose the lady is yet reconciled
to me, yet let her know that I love her very well, and value
her very much.

Dr. Blair is printing some sermons. If they are all like the
first, which I have read, they are *sermones aurei, ac auro magis
aurei.*[2] It is excellently written both as to doctrine and
language. Mr. Watson's book seems to be much esteemed.

* * * * * *

Poor Beauclerk still continues very ill. Langton lives on
as he is used to do. His children are very pretty, and, I
think, his lady loses her Scotch. Paoli I never see.

I have been so distressed by difficulty of breathing, that I
lost, as was computed, six-and-thirty ounces of blood in a
few days. I am better, but not well.

I wish you would be vigilant and get me Graham's 'Telemachus' that was printed at Glasgow, a very little book, and
'*Johnstoni Poemata*',[3] another little book, printed at Middle-
burg.

Mrs. Williams sends her compliments, and promises that
when you come hither, she will accommodate you as well as
ever she can in the old room.[4] She wishes to know whether
you sent her book[5] to Sir Alexander Gordon.

My dear Boswell, do not neglect to write to me, for your
kindness is one of the pleasures of my life, which I should be
very sorry to lose.

I am, Sir, Your humble servant,

Feb. 18, 1777.   Sam. Johnson

507.—2. This eluded me (as all my predecessors?) until Mr. C. S. Lewis reminded me
of Sappho's description (122 Bergk, 41 Lobel) of a girl as χρύσω χρυσοτέρα. This fragment is preserved by Demetrius of Phalerum *de Elocutione* 127, 162; and Dr. Paul
Maas directed me to look in the sixteenth-century versions, or in early phrase-books.
In the version by Franciscus Maslovius, 1557, I found (f. 17ᵛ), among examples of
happy hyperbole, 'illa Sapphica . . . χρυσοῦ χρυσοτέρα'. Erasmus (*Adagia*, p. 923 in
the 1699 folio) renders it 'auro auratior'. J might get it from Dryden, quoting
Casaubon, in *The Original and Progress of Satire* (Ker ii. 72).

3. This was the book J had failed to buy at Aberdeen. *L* v. 95.

4. In '75 J 'had been so good as to assign me a room in his house, where I might
sleep occasionally' (L ii. 375). The privilege had been transferred to the house in
Bolt Court to which J moved in '76.

5. Presumably the *Miscellanies* of 1766.

508. Tu. 25 Feb. '77. George Steevens.

Not traced.—Boswell 1791, ii. 102 (Hill iii. 100).

Dear Sir,

You will be glad to hear that from Mrs. Goldsmith, whom we lamented as drowned, I have received a letter full of gratitude to us all, with promise to make the enquiries[1] which we recommended to her.

I would have had the honour of conveying this intelligence to Miss Caulfield, but that her letter is not at hand, and I know not the direction. You will tell the good news.

I am, Sir, Your most, &c.,

February 25, 1777.   Sam. Johnson

509. Sa. 8 Mar. '77. Elizabeth Aston (Lichfield).

Address (Croker):
Sotheby 16 Dec. 1870 (not seen).—Croker's Boswell 1831, iii. 468.

Dear Madam   Bolt-court, Fleet-street, 8th March, 1777.

As we pass on through the journey of life, we meet, and ought to expect, many unpleasing occurrences, but may likewise encounter as ⟨many⟩ unexpected. I have this morning heard from Lucy of your illness. I heard indeed in the next sentence that you are to a great degree recovered. May your recovery, dearest madam, be complete and lasting! The hopes[1] of paying you the annual visit is one of the few solaces with which my imagination gratifies me; and my wish is, that I may find you happy.

My health is much broken; my nights are very restless, and will not be made more comfortable by remembering that

508.—1. It was originally contemplated that J should be Goldsmith's biographer. For the vexed course of that undertaking see Miss Balderston's acute and laborious study, *The History and Sources of Percy's Memoir* 1926, or L iii. 100. 'Mrs. Goldsmith' was 'in all probability the widow of Henry' (Balderston, op. cit. 21).

509.—There are quotations from this letter in Sotheby 16 Dec. 1870, 272, and 8 July 1878, 166. The latter conspires with Croker in reading 'occurrences' where the former has 'circumstances'. In what immediately follows (not quoted 1870) 1878 has 'but may likewise encounter as unexpected'; Croker has 'but many likewise encounter us unexpected'. The *OED* has no example of *encounter* with an inanimate subject. I believe that Croker's is a plausible misreading, that 1878 is right, and that J intended 'but may likewise encounter as many unexpected'.

1. J may have written 'hope'. As his final *s* is often vestigial, so he often ends a word with a tiny flourish which simulates that vestige.

one of the friends whom I value most is suffering equally with myself.

Be pleased, dearest lady, to let me know how you are; and if writing be troublesome, get dear Mrs. Gastrel to write for you. I hope she is well and able to assist you; and wish that you may so well recover, as to repay her kindness, if she should want you. May you both live long happy together!

I am, dear madam, your most humble servant,

Sam. Johnson.

510. Tu. 11 Mar. '77. James Boswell (Edinburgh).
Not traced.—Boswell 1791, ii. 107 (Hill iii. 105).

Dear Sir,

I have been much pleased with your late letter, and am glad that my old enemy, Mrs. Boswell, begins to feel some remorse.[1] As to Miss Veronica's Scotch, I think it cannot be helped. An English maid you might easily have; but she would still imitate the greater number, as they would be likewise those whom she must most respect. Her dialect will not be gross. Her Mamma has not much Scotch, and you have yourself very little. I hope she knows my name, and does not call me *Johnston*.[2]

The immediate cause of my writing is this:—One Shaw, who seems a modest and a decent man, has written an Erse Grammar, which a very learned Highlander, Macbean, has, at my request examined and approved.

The book is very little,[3] but Mr. Shaw has been persuaded by his friends to set it at half a guinea, though I had advised only a crown, and thought myself liberal. You, whom the authour considers as a great encourager of ingenious men, will

510.—1. JB had written 24 Feb.: 'She is to send you some marmalade of oranges of her own making.'

2. 'My illustrious friend observed, that many North Britons pronounced his name in their own way' JB. See *L* iii. 488, v. 341.

3. Shaw's *Analysis of the Galic Language* contains only 156 pages; it is, however, a large quarto. The subscribers include Lord Eglinton, who took ten copies, and many of J's friends (e.g. JB, BL) but not himself. In his introduction, p. xxiii, Shaw writes 'To the advice and encouragement of Dr. Johnson . . . the Public is indebted for these sheets', and thanks JB for his good offices. The book was printed by Strahan 'for the Author'. See 499.

receive a parcel of his proposals[4] and receipts. I have undertaken to give you notice of them, and to solicit your countenance. You must ask no poor man, because the price is
really too high. Yet such a work deserves patronage.

It is proposed to augment our club from twenty to thirty,
of which I am glad; for as we have several in it whom I do not
much like to consort with,[5] I am for reducing it to a mere
miscellaneous collection of conspicuous men, without any
determinate character.

*   *   *   *   *   *

I am, dear Sir, Most affectionately yours,
March 11, 1777.   Sam. Johnson

My respects to Madam, to Veronica, to Alexander, to
Euphemia, to David.

511. Sa. 15 Mar. '77. Elizabeth Aston (Lichfield).
Pembroke.—Croker's Boswell 1831, iii. 470.

Dearest Madam

The letter with which I was favoured ⟨by⟩ the kindness of
Mrs Gastrel has contributed very little to quiet my solicitude.
I am indeed more frighted than by Mrs Porter's account.
Yet since you have had strength to conquer your disorder so
as to obtain a partial recovery, I think it reasonable to believe
that the favourable season which is now coming forward,
may restore you to your former health. Do not, dear Madam,
lose your courage, nor by despondence or inactivity give way
to the disease. Use such exercise as you can bear, and excite
cheerful thoughts in your own mind. Do not harrass your
faculties with laborious attention, nothing is in my opinion
of more mischievous tendency in a state of body like yours,
than deep meditation, or perplexing solicitude. Gayety is a
duty when health requires it. Entertain yourself as you can
with small amusements or light conversation, and let nothing
but your Devotion ever make you serious.

510.—4. JB replied 4 Apr.: 'I have received Mr. Shaw's Proposals . . ., which I can
perceive are written *by the hand of a* MASTER.' He quotes J's part of the Proposals
iii. 107.

5. 'On account of their differing from him as to religion and politicks' JB. See
references at *L* iii. 106. Members of the obscure Johnson Club (privileged to meet
in Gough Square) have been heard to quote J's description of their more conspicuous
but less appropriated rival.

But while I exhort you, my dearest Lady, to merriment, I am very serious myself. The loss or danger of a friend is not to be considered with indifference; but I derive some consolation from the thought that you do not languish unattended, that you are not in the hands of strangers or servants, but have a Sister at hand to watch your wants and supply them.

If at this distance I can be of any use by consulting Physicians or for any other purpose I hope you will employ me. I have thought on a journey to Staffordshire, and hope in a few weeks to climb Stowhill, and to find there the pleasure which I have so often found.

Let me hear again from you.

I am, Dear Madam, Your most humble servant,

March 15. 1777   Sam: Johnson

512. W. 19 Mar. '77. Mrs. Thrale.

Leverton Harris.—1788, No. 160.

Madam

Be pleased to procure the Bearer credit for a linen gown, and let her bring the bill to me.

Did you stay all night at Sir Joshua's? and keep Miss up again? Miss Owen had a sight—all the Burkes—the Harris's —Miss Reynolds—what has she to see more? and Mrs. Horneck and Miss.—

You are all young and gay and easy. But I have miserable nights, and know not how to make them better; but I shift pretty well a-days, and so have at you all at Dr. Burney's to morrow.[1]

I never thought of meeting you at Sir Joshua's, nor knew that it was a great day. But things, as sages have observed happen unexpectedly, and you thought little of seeing me this fortnight except to morrow. But go where you will, and see if I do not catch you. When I am away, every body runs

512.—1. FB in her diary for Jan. 1788 records at length her feelings on borrowing a copy, 'still unpublished', of the *Letters*. 'Our name once occurs' (in the first volume): 'how I started at its sight!—'Tis to mention the party that planned the first visit to our house: Miss Owen, Mr. Seward, Mrs. and Miss Thrale, and Dr. Johnson. How well shall we ever, my Susan, remember that morning!' (*Diary* iv. 15). See also *Early Diary* ii. 153.

away with you, and carries you among the grisettes,[2] or
whither they will. I hope you will find the want of me
twenty times before you see me.

I am Madam Your most humble servant

March 19. 1777 Sam: Johnson

512a. Brighthelmston. Sa. 5 Apr. ⟨'77⟩. From Mrs. Thrale.

Address: To Doctor Johnson Bolt Court Fleet Street London. *Postmark*: 7 AP. Franked by HT.

R 540.62—

Dear Sir   Brighthelmstone Saturday 5: April

As we had no Engagements in Town for these two last Days of the holyday
Week, Mr Thrale perswaded us to come down hither to him, and take a Dip
in the Sea by way of refreshing ourselves & washing off London Smoak;—but
how was I astonish'd this Morning to see my Master's Death in all the
London Papers! the first Person I feared it might make uneasy was you, I
therefore make haste to write that you may be satisfied he is alive & well,
and just going out on horseback this Moment with Tom Cotton & Seward who
are here. We shall return to Streatham on Tuesday at farthest, and expect
the Pleasure of your Company on Wednesday as we settled it when we met
last. Doctor Taylor comes o' Thursday but you live with us till you go to
Litchfield. This Report of Mr Thrale's Death half shocks me though I see
him alive. Where can the Jest be of frighting a Man's Friends so foolishly?
I feel for Lady Lade too, who does not want something to flutter her Spirits.
Our House is dressing up against the Season, & will be very neat: one Pretence
for my coming hither is to give Directions about the doing it. Farewell till
Wednesday, when I hope you will see my Master as live as a Lark notwithstanding all this Nonsense: The Sea freshens up Queeney after her raking
very cleverly.

I am most faithfully H: L: Thrale

Sir Joshua Reynolds was painted at Paradise's that Evening. Miss Owen says
so as well as me.

512.1. ⟨F.⟩ 4 Apr. ⟨'77⟩. John Perkins.

O. T. Perkins.—

Mr Johnson sends compliments to Mr Perkins, and though
he believes this foolish newspaper to be false, yet desires to
know when Mr Perkins heard of Mr Thrale, and what he can
tell of the ground of the report.   Apr. 4.

512.—2. I think 'grisettes' means 'bluestockings'. The eponymous stockings were rather
grey than blue; Stillingfleet 'literally wore grey stockings' at Mrs. Vesey's assemblies.
Forbes, *Beattie* 1806, i. 210, quoted in *OED*.

512.1.—The date is ascertained by 512*a*.

513. W. 9 Apr. '77. Henry Thrale.

Sotheby 30 Jan. 1918 (not seen).—1788, No. 161

Dear Sir   April 9, 1777.
     This is a letter of pure congratulation. I congratulate you,
     1. That you are alive.[1]
     2. That you have got my mistress fixed again after her
excentricities.
     3. That my mistress has added to her conquests the Prince
of Castiglione.
     4. That you will not be troubled with me till to-morrow,[2]
when I shall come with . . .
     5. That . . . will go away in the evening.
                                                        I am, &c.

514. Sa. 12 Apr. '77. John Ryland.

Address: To Mr Ryland.
Adam.—Hill 1892.

Sir
     I have sent you the papers. Of this parcel I have ejected
no poetry. Of the letters there are some which I should be
sorry to omit, some that it is not proper to insert, and very
many which as we want room or want matter we may use or
neglect. When we come to these we will have another selection. But to these I think our present plan of publication
will never bring us. His poems with his play will I think
make two volumes. The Adventurers will make at least one,
and for the fourth, as I think you intend four which will
make the subscription a Guinea, if you subscribe, we have so
much more than we want that the difficulty will ⟨be⟩ to
reject.
     If Mrs Hawkesworth sells the copy, we are then to con-
sider how many volumes she sells, and if they are fewer than
we have matter to fill, we will be the more rigorous in our
choice.
     I am for letting none stand that are only relatively good

513.—1. See 512*a*, 515, and *Public Advertiser* 5 Apr.: 'We are authorised to assure
our Readers, that the Paragraph concerning the Death of Henry Thrale Esq; has
no Foundation in Truth.'
     2. J had been expected on the Wednesday. His companion was Taylor. See 512*a*.
514.—For the projected edition of Hawkesworth's works see references in Index II.

as they were written in youth. The Buyer has no better bargain when he pays for mean performances, by being told that the authour wrote them young.

If the Lady can get an hundred pounds a volume, I should advise her to take it. She may ask more. I am not willing to take less.

If she prints them by subscription the volumes should be four, if, at her own expence, I still do not see considering the great quantity of our matter how they can be fewer. But in this I shall not be obstinate.

I have yet not mentioned Swift's Life,[1] nor the Novel[2] which together will go far towards a volume.

Who was his Amanuensis? that small hand strikes a reader with terrour. It is pale as well as small.

Many little things are, I believe, in the Magazines, which should be marked and considered. I do not always know them but by conjecture.

The poetry I would have printed in order of time, which he seems to have intended by noting the dates, which dates I should like to preserve, they show the progress of ⟨his⟩ Mind, and of a very powerful Mind. The same ⟨. . . .⟩[3] may be generally observed in the prose pieces.

What we have to consider, and what I have considered are the Authour's credit, and the Lady's advantage.

I should be glad to talk over the whole, when you can spend an hour or two with, Sir, Your most humble servant
Apr. 12. 1777   Sam: Johnson

515. Sa. 3 May '77. James Boswell (Edinburgh).
Not traced.—Boswell 1791, ii. 110 (Hill iii. 108).

Dear Sir,

The story of Mr. Thrale's death,[1] as he had neither been sick nor in any other danger, made so little impression upon me, that I never thought about obviating its effects on any

---

514.—1. Hawkesworth had published Swift's *Works* in 1755; the first volume of that edition contained his *Life*.
   2. *Almoran and Hamet; an Oriental Tale*, 1761.
   3. The MS. is defective; perhaps 'rule' or 'plan'.

515.—1. See 513. Though JB had read the contradiction as well as the false report, he was still (24 Apr.) 'in a state of very uneasy uncertainty.... How could you omit to write to me on such an occasion? I shall wait with anxiety.'

body else. It is supposed to have been produced by the
English custom of making April fools, that is, of sending one
another[2] on some foolish errand on the first of April.

Tell Mrs. Boswell that I shall taste her marmalade cautiously at first, *Timeo Danaos et dona ferentes*.[3] Beware, says
the Italian proverb,[4] of a reconciled enemy. But when I find
it does me no harm, I shall then receive it and be thankful for
it, as a pledge of firm, and, I hope, of unalterable kindness.
She is after all, a dear, dear lady.

Please to return Dr. Blair thanks for his sermons. The
Scotch write English wonderfully well.

*   *   *   *   *   *

Your frequent visits[5] to Auchinleck, and your short stay
there are very laudable and very judicious. Your present
concord with your father gives me great pleasure; it was all
that you seemed to want.

My health is very bad, and my nights are very unquiet.
What can I do to mend them? I have for this summer
nothing better in prospect than a journey into Staffordshire
and Derbyshire, perhaps with Oxford and Birmingham in
my way.

Make my compliments to Miss Veronica; I must leave it to
her philosophy to comfort you for the loss of little David.[6]
You must remember, that to keep three out of four is more
than your share. Mrs. Thrale has but four out of eleven.

I am engaged to write little Lives, and little Prefaces, to
a little edition of the English Poets.[7] I think I have persuaded
the booksellers to insert something of Thomson,[8] and if you

515.—2 The words are not necessarily reciprocal in sense; cf. 184 'one will tell another'.

3. Virgil, *Aen.* ii. 49.

4. Prof. d'Entrèves tells me that this, though hardly proverbial, is a commonplace
in Italian, e.g. Machiavelli, *Il Principe*, c. 7.

5. JB had written 'I am going to Auchinleck to stay a fortnight with my father.
It is better not to be there very long at one time. But frequent renewals of attention
are agreeable to him.' Dr. Pottle kindly furnishes the explanation: J's 'frequent
visits' and 'short stay' are not opposite, they are complementary. J approves JB's
policy: 'make your visits frequent, and keep them short'. For the long and unsuccessful visit in the autumn of '76 (14 Sept.–20 Oct.) see on 505.

6. JB 4 Apr. had reported the death of his infant son.

7. JB had seen an advertisement: 'Pray tell me about this edition' (24 Apr.).

8. In the event the collection included all T's poems except his dramas, which
were excluded by its plan. Why the booksellers needed any 'persuasion' has not, I
believe, been explained. It has been assumed that T's popularity had waned; but

perform it. If they desire to give him an English education, it should be considered whether they cannot send him for a year or two to an English school. If he comes immediately from Scotland, he can make no figure in our Universities.[2] The schools in the north, I believe, are cheap; and, when I was a young man, were eminently good.

There are two little books published by the Foulis, Telemachus[3] and Collins's Poems,[4] each a shilling; I would be glad to have them.

Make my compliments to Mrs. Boswell, though she does not love me. You see what perverse things ladies are, and how little fit to be trusted with feudal estates. When she mends and loves me, there may be more hope of her daughters.

I will not send compliments to my friends by name, because I would be loath to leave any out in the enumeration. Tell them, as you see them, how well I speak of Scotch politeness, and Scotch hospitality, and Scotch beauty, and of every thing Scotch, but Scotch oat-cakes and Scotch prejudices.

Let me know the answer of Rasay, and the decision relating to Sir Allan.[5]

I am, my dearest Sir, with great affection, Your most obliged and most humble servant,

May 27, 1775.   Sam. Johnson

398.1. Sa. 27 May '75. ⟨John Taylor⟩.
Buffalo Public Library (not seen).—Hill, *JM* 1897, ii. 447.
Dear Sir

On Monday I purpose to be at Oxford, where I shall perhaps stay a week, from whence I shall come to Birmingham, and so to Lichfield. At Lichfield my purpose is to pass a week or so, but whether I shall stay there in my way to Ash-

---

398.—2. 'Men bred in the universities of *Scotland* cannot be expected to be often decorated with the splendours of ornamental erudition' (*Journey* 1924, 146). By 'ornamental erudition' J, I suppose, means 'imitatio veterum', translations, or original compositions, in the ancient languages.

3. George Graham's.

4. The book is now in the library of Columbia University; it is inscribed 'To Samuel Johnson LLD from his most affectionate and grateful friend James Boswell'.

5. For Sir Allan Maclean's lawsuit see *L* ii. 380, iii. 101, 126.

bourne, or in ⟨returning⟩ from it, you may, if you please,
determine. When I come thither I will write to you or
perhaps I may find a letter at Mrs. Porter's.

I am, Sir, Your affectionate servant,

May 27, 1775   Sam: Johnson

399. Oxford. Th. 1 June '75. Mrs. Thrale.
Adam.—1788, No. 104.

Dear Madam

I know well enough what you think, but I am out of your
reach. I did not make the epitaph[1] before last night and this
morning I have found it too long. I send you it as it is to
pacify you, and will make it shorter. It is too long by near
half. Tell me what you would be most willing to spare.

Dr Wetherel went with me to the Vicechancellor,[2] to
whom we told the transaction with my Lord of Chester,[3]
and the Vicechancellor promised to write to the Archbishop.[4]
I told him that he needed have no scruples he was asking
nothing for himself, nothing that would make him richer,
or them poorer, and that he acted only as a Magistrate and
one concerned for the interest of the University. Dr
Wetherel promises to stimulate him.

Don't suppose that I live here, as we live at Streatham.
I went this morning to the Chapel at six, and if I was to stay
would try to conform to all wholesome rules. Pray let Harry
have the peny which I owe him for the last morning.[5]

Mr Colson is well, and still willing to keep me, but I shall
not delight in being long here. Mr Smollet of Loch Lomond
and his Lady have been here. We were very glad to meet.

Pray let me know how you do, and play no more tricks, if
you do, I can yet come back and watch you.

I am, Madam, Your most humble servant

June 1. 1775   Sam: Johnson

399.—1. HLT in 393*a* (and perhaps again in a lost letter) had reminded him of his
promise to write an epitaph for Mrs. Salusbury. See on 403.

2. Fothergill, Provost of Queen's. The Provost's Lodgings are on the other side
of the High Street, almost opposite University College, where J was staying with
Colson and conspiring with the Master, Wetherell.

3. Markham.

4. Of York, Drummond.

5. 'for calling Dr. Johnson up' HLP.

400. Oxford. M. 5 June '75. Mrs. Thrale.
Sotheby 15 Feb. 1926.—1788, No. 107.

Madame

Trois jours sont passés sans que ⟨je⟩ reçoive une lettre; point de nouvelles, point d'amitie, point de querelles. Un silence si rare, que veut il? J'ai vous ai envoyé l'épitaphe, trop longue à la veritè, mais on la raccourcira sans trop de peine. Vous n'en avez dit pas un mot. Peutêtre que je suis plus heureux ce soir.

J'ai epuisé ce lieu, ou je n'étudie pas, et ou si on ôte l'étude, il n'y a rien, et je ne trouve guere moyen d'echaper. Les voitures qui passent par cy, passent dans la minuit; les chaises de poste me couteront beaucoup. J'envoye querer une passage plus commode.

Je dinerai demain chez le Vicechancelier, j'espere de trouver des choses un peu favorables à nôtre ami infortunè, mais je n'ai null confiance.

Je suis, Madame, Votre tres obeissant Serviteur,
Juin 5. 1775.   Sam: Johnson

401. Oxford. Tu. 6 June '75. Mrs. Thrale.
Sotheby 30 Jan. 1918 (not seen).—1788, No. 108.

Madam   June 6, 1775.

Such is the uncertainty of all human things, that Mr. C——[1] has quarrelled with me. He says, I raise the laugh upon him, and he is an independent man, and all he has is his own, and he is not used to such things. And so I shall have no more good of C——, of whom I never had any good but flattery, which my dear mistress knows I can have at home.

That I had no letters yesterday I do not wonder; for yesterday we had no post.[2] I hope something will come

401.—1. Colson. Philip Fisher in 1833 told Croker 'that he was present at this quarrel. Coulson was going out on a country living, and talking of it with the same pomp, as to Lord Stowell (*ante*, p. 425). Johnson chose to imagine his becoming an archdeacon, and made himself merry—Dr. Fisher thought too merry—at Coulson's expense; at last they got to warm words, and Johnson concluded the debate by exclaiming emphatically—"Sir, having meant you no offence, I will make you no apology".' (Croker, p. 458 in the 1848 edition; his reference, 425, is to another anecdote.)

2. Hill remarks that since no post left L'n on Sunday, J could not get a letter before Tuesday. He adds (writing *c.* 1892), 'At the present day a letter posted in the morning receives its answer in the evening.' In this century we have made some

to-day. Our post is so ill-regulated that we cannot receive letters and answer them the same day.

Here I am, and how to get away I do not see; for the power of departure otherwise than in a post-chaise depends upon accidental vacancies in passing coaches, of which all but one in a week pass through this place at three in the morning. After that one I have sent, but with little hope: yet I shall be very unwilling to stay here another week.

I supped two nights ago with Mr. Bright, who enquired after Harry and Queeney, to whom I likewise desire to be remembered.

Suppose I should grow like my mistress, and when I am to go forward, think eagerly how and when I shall come back, would that be a strange thing? Love and reverence have always had some tendency to produce conformity.

Where is Mr. Baretti? Are he and Queeney plague and darling as they are used to be? I hope my sweet Queeney will write me a long letter, when I am so settled that she knows how to direct to me, and if I can find any thing for her cabinet, I shall be glad to bring it.

What the Vice Chancellor says respecting Mr. Carter, if he says any thing, you shall know to-morrow, for I shall probably leave him too late for this day's post.

If I have not a little something from you to-day, I shall think something very calamitous has befallen us. This is the natural effect of punctuality. Every intermission alarms. Dearest dear Lady, take care of yourself. You connect us, and rule us, and vex us, and please us. We have all a deep interest in your health and prosperity.

I am, &c.

402. Oxford. W. 7 June (misdated July) '75. Mrs. Thrale. Tregaskis 1925.—1788, No. 122 (misplaced).

Dearest Madam

What can be the reason that I hear nothing from you or

return to the slower methods of the eighteenth; but for urgent matters we now use the telephone.

402.—Misdated July (J seems to have had a trick of confusing June and July: 788, 973) and so misplaced 1788. It was careless of HLP to make J confer with the Vice-Chancellor at A'n.

from your house? Are you well? Yet while I am asking the question I know not when I shall be able to receive your answer, for I am waiting for the chance of a place in a coach which will probably be come and gone in an hour.

Yesterday the Vicechancellor told me that he has written to the Archbishop of York; His letter, as he represented it to me, was very proper and persuasive. I believe we shall establish Mr Carter, the riding Master of Oxford.

Still I cannot think why I hear nothing from you.

The Coach is full. I am therefore at full leisure to continue my letter, but I have nothing more to say of business, but that the Vicechancellor is for adding to the riding school a house and stable for the master; nor of myself but that I grieve and wonder, and hope and fear about my dear friends at Streatham. But I may have a letter this afternoon—Sure it will bring me no bad news. You never neglected writing so before. If I have a letter to day I will go away as soon as I can; if I have none, I will stay till this may be answered, if I do not come back to town.

   I am, Madam, Your most obedient Servant
July 7. 1775.   Sam: Johnson

403. Oxford. W. 7 June '75. Mrs. Thrale.
Lichfield.—1788, No. 109.

Dearest Lady

Your letter which ought to have come on tuesday came not till wednesday. Well, now I know that there is no harm I will take a chaise and march away towards my own country.

You are but a goose at last. Wilton[1] told you that there is room for 350 letters, which are equivalent to twelve lines.[2] If you reckon by lines the inscription has 17. if by letters

403.—1. 'the Statuary' HLP.

 2. When J sent the epitaph on 1 June (399) he presumably kept a copy to 'make it shorter', and so was able on 7 June to give the number of letters. This may explain the slight differences between the version in *Th* 7 and that in *Anecdotes* 1786 (= *JM* i. 236). Both versions contain, in 17 lines, some 544 letters. An autograph version, substantially identical with that of *Th*, is in the Rylands Library (Eng. MS. 543). See the *Bulletin* for Jan. 1932, 60. The late H. W. Bromhead (*The Heritage of St. Leonard's Parish Church, Streatham*, 1932, 36) reported that 'after careful counting I find only 547 letters and 23 stops (= 570) in the inscription as it stands'; the discrepancy need not disturb us. See also 405, 408.

579. so that one way you must expel five lines, the other 229 letters. This will perplex us, there is little that by my own choice I should like to spare, but we must comply with the stone.

Coulson and I are pretty well again. I grudge the cost of going to Lichfield, Frank and I in a post chaise. Yet I think of thundering away to morrow. So you will write your next dear letter to Lichfield.

This letter is written on Wednesday after the receipt of yours,[3] but will not be delivered to the post till to morrow. I wish Ralph better, and my Master and his boys[4] well. I have pretty good nights.

I am, Madam, Your most humble servant

June 7. 1775   Sam: Johnson

403a. Streatham. W. 7 June ⟨'75⟩. From Mrs. Thrale to J at Oxford.

R 539.41—

Dear Sir   Streatham 7: June

I had a kind Letter from you Yesterday in a Foreign Tongue for which I thank you very sincerely in my own: I will try this one Letter to Oxford just to say all is well, & the next shall be directed either to Lichfield or Doctor Taylor's as you are most likely to be at one of them next Week. I will send one to Lichfield at a venture. Mr Thrale vexes me about this foolish Election: Norton is vastly unpopular—& not likely to succeed at all, & my Master will ask the Southwark folks to be for *him* whereas Young Vincent would do just as well for *public Purposes* & be better received than the Son of Sir Fletcher, whose very Name they abhor; & whom to exclude they will even admit of Sir Joseph that has disobliged them; It is however vain to vex, but when I see you I will tell you the whole: if you had been at home you would have done no good, for Mr Thrale promised his Interest at an accidental Meeting before he had Time to ask Advice.

Ralph is gone. The other Children are well, and so am I, and so I hope are you; be happy if you can—and when you find yourself very restless change your Place. Mrs D'Avenant has coaxed me to go down with her for one Week to see her Sister at Lewes, & bathe Mrs D'Avenant in the Sea for her health, we are to *leave our Husbands* at home; I shall see the Child's Situation—so that is an Inducement—whenever we set out I will tell you & when we return, you will be just finishing your Visits, and return to the Iron Dominion of Your most Faithful & Obedient Servant H: L: Thrale.

403.—3. Not 403a, which does not mention the epitaph, but a lost letter written on 5 June.

4. 403a suggests that the reference is not to brewing but to politics.

403.1. W. 7 June '75. Philip Fisher.

Address: To the Reverend Mr. Fisher-Hyde.—Maggs Cat. 262 (1910), extract.

I beg the favour of you, that you will remember to give the Earse books[1] with the proper message to the librarian,[2] and enable me to return his thanks.

I mentioned them yesterday to the Vice-Chancellor.

I am Sir Your most humble Servant

Sam: Johnson

404. Lichfield. Sa. 10 June '75. Mrs. Thrale.

Sotheby 30 Jan. 1918 (not seen).—1788, No. 110.

Dear Madam June 10, 1775.

On Thursday morning I took a post-chaise, and intended to have passed a day or two at Birmingham, but Hector had company in his house, and I went on to Lichfield, where I know not yet how long I shall stay, but think of going forward to Ashbourne in a short time.

Neither your letters nor mine seem to have kept due time; if you see the date of the letter in which the epitaph was enclosed, you will find that it has been delayed. I shall adjust the epitaph some way or other. Send me your advice.

Poor Miss Porter has been bad with the gout in her hand. She cannot yet dress herself.

I am glad that Ralph is gone;[1] a new air may do him good. I hope little Miss promises well.

I will write you a longer letter on Monday, being just now called out according to an appointment which I had forgotten.

I am, &c.

405. Lichfield. Su. 11 (? M. 12) June '75. Mrs. Thrale.

Not traced.—1788, No. 111.

Dearest Lady June 11, 1775.

I am sorry that my master has undertaken an impractic-

403.1.—1. See 360. 2. Price.

404.—1. To B'n. This reference seems to show that her letter of 7 June (403*a*) had reached him (forwarded from O'd). She wrote 'Ralph is gone'. Other parts of her letter are answered in 405 and 406.

405.—Perhaps J fulfilled his intention (404) of writing on Monday, and misdated this letter 'June 11' for 12; note 'on Saturday'. For the question whether he avoided writing on Sundays see Appendix F.

able interest;[1] but it will be forgotten before the next election. I suppose he was asked at some time when he could not well refuse.

Lady Smith is settled at last here, and sees company at her new house.—I went on Saturday. Poor Lucy Porter has her hand in a bag, so disabled by the gout that she cannot dress herself. She does not go out. All your other friends are well.

I go every day to Stowhill: both the sisters are now at home. I sent Mrs. Aston a *Taxation*, and sent it nobody else, and Lucy borrowed it. Mrs. Aston since that enquired by a messenger when I was expected. I can tell nothing about it, answered Lucy; when he is to be here I suppose she'll know.

Every body remembers you all.[2] You left a good impression behind you. I hope you will do the same at ....[3] Do not make them speeches. Unusual compliments, to which there is no stated and prescriptive answer, embarrass the feeble, who know not what to say, and disgust the wise, who knowing them to be false, suspect them to be hypocritical. Did I think when I sat down to this paper that I should write a lesson to my mistress, of whom I think with so much admiration?

As to Mr. Carter, I am inclined to think that our project will succeed. The Vice-Chancellor is really in earnest. He remarked to me how necessary it must be to provide in places of education a sufficient variety of innocent amusements,[4] to keep the young men from pernicious pleasures.

When I did not hear from you, I thought whether it would not be proper to come back and look for you. I knew not what might have happened.

Consider the epitaph,[5] which, you know, must be shortened, and tell what part you can best spare. Part of it, which tells

405.—1. See 403*a*, 407.

2. HT, HLT, and Q had visited L'd with J in July '74 (*L* v. 428).

3. Probably Lewes. See 403*a*, 406. J seems to be reflecting on HLT's universal complaisance in the Welsh tour, when she declared she was 'obliged to be civil for two'—or according to FB, 'for four' (*L* v. 440).

4. Hill quotes Bentham on fishing 'as a relief from the weary monotony of existence' when he was an undergraduate at Queen's in the sixties, and Burke on the virtues of games.

5. See on 403.

the birth and marriage, is formulary, and can be expressed only one way; the character we can make longer or shorter; and since it is too long, may choose what we shall take away. You must get the dates for which you see spaces left.

You never told me, and I omitted to enquire, how you were entertained by Boswell's Journal. One would think the man had been hired to be a spy upon me.[6] He was very diligent, and caught opportunities of writing from time to time. You may now conceive yourself tolerably well acquainted with the expedition. Folks want me to go to Italy,[7] but I say you are not for it. However write often to,

   Madam, Your, &c.

406. Lichfield. Tu. 13 June '75. Mrs. Thrale.

Folger Library.—1788, No. 112.

Dearest Lady.

I now write at Mrs Cobb's where I have dined and had custard. She and Miss Adey send their compliments. Nothing considerable has happened since I wrote, only I am sorry to see Miss Porter so bad; and I am not well pleased to find that after a very comfortable intermission, the old flatulence distressed me again last night. The world is full of ups and downs, as I think I once told you before.

Lichfield is full of Box clubs. The Ladies have one for their own sex. They have incorporated themselves under the appellation of the amicable Society,[1] and pay each twopence a week to the box. Any woman who can produce the weekly twopence is admitted to the Society, and when any of the poor Subscribers is in want, she has six shillings a week, and I think when she dies five pounds are given to her children. Lucy is not one, nor Mrs. Cobb. The subscribers are always

---

405.—6. 'It seems very improbable that Johnson wrote this', Hill. I have no doubt that the passage is genuine. It is entirely in his vein, and very unlike a forgery. HLP was not a scrupulous editor; but neither was she a forger. I do not think that her improvement, or even fabrication, of her own letters deserves that name. See on 408.

   7. For the projected tour to Italy see on 458.

406.—1. Information on this Society will be found in a pamphlet by the late William Bennett, Birmingham 1934.

quarrelling, and every now and then a Lady in a fume with-draws her name. But they are an hundred pounds before-hand.

Mr Green has got a cast of Shakespeare, which he holds to be a very exact resemb⟨l⟩ance.

There is great lamentation here for the death of Coll. Lucy is of opinion that he was wonderfully handsome.

Boswel[2] is a favourite, but he has lost ground, since I told them that he is married, and all hope is over.

Be so kind as to let me know when you go to Lewes and when you come back that I may not fret for want of a letter, as I fretted at Oxford. Pay my respects to my dear Master.

I am Madam Your most humble servant

Lichfield June 13. 1775   Sam: Johnson

406a. Streatham. F. 16 June ⟨'75⟩. From Mrs. Thrale to J at Lichfield.

Address: To Doctor Sam: Johnson at Lichfield. *Postmark*: 17 IV. Franked by HT.

R 539.42—

Dear Sir   Streatham Fryday 16: June.

The Election is over, & Mawbey victorious; I was wrong however in being so cold a friend to Mr Norton: for Vincent is a Patriot at last, & as such gave his Votes to Sir Joseph when matters drew towards a Conclusion. My Master is apt to be right and I apt to be perverse & self opinionated. There is how-ever to be a Scrutiny. Mr Thrale is right in another Affair, he has found out that the Letter of the Epitaph may be made less, and then the Stone will hold more; he will not have your Writing or my Mother's Praises curtailed he says. All this you may be sure obliges me & I am in the best humour now, as well as the best Health in the World.

Pitches's eldest Daughter will die, the Parents are grievously distress'd.

Queeney says I must tell you how a Guinea hen that was missing & we thought her lost, is come home with twelve young ones—the prettiest little Creatures you ever saw. I write so often I can have nothing to say though

La Conversation des Amis ne tarit pas

says even Rochefoulcoult.

I am ever most faithfully Yours H L Thrale.

They say Ralph mends. I long to go see, but Mrs D'Avenant is not yet stout enough to travel so far.

406.—2. JB was still unknown to the ladies of L'd, which he first visited in '76.

407. Lichfield. Sa. 17 June '75. Mrs. Thrale.

Rosenbach 1927.—1788, No. 113.

Dear Madam

Write to me something every post, for on the stated day[1] my head runs upon a letter. I will answer Queeney. Bad nights came again, but I took Mercury, and hope to find good effects. I am distressfully and frightfully deaf. Querelis jam satis datum.[2]

So we shall have a fine house[3] in the winter, as we already have in the summer. I am not sorry for the appearance of a little superfluous expence. I have not yet been at Ashbourne, and yet I would fain flatter myself that you begin to wish me home, but do not tell me so, if it be not true, for I am very well at Stowhill.

Mrs. Porter will be glad of a memorial from you, and will keep the workbag carefully, but has no great use for it, her present qualifications for the niceties of needlework, being dim eyes and lame fingers.

Of the harvest about us, it is said, that the much is expected from the wheat, more indeed than can be easily remembred. The Barley is promising enough but not uncommonly exuberant. But this is of itself a very good account, for no grain is ever dear, when wheat is cheap. I hope therefore that my Master may without fear or danger build this year, and dig the next. I do not find that in this part of the country rain has been much wanted.

If you go with Mrs. D——,[4] do not forget me amidst the luxuries of absolute dominion, but let me have kind letters full of yourself, of your own hopes and your own fears and your own thoughts, and then go where you will. You will find your journey however but a barren business; it is dull to live neither scolding nor scolded, neither governing nor governed. Now try.

I expected that when the interest of the county had been

407.—1. See Appendix F.

2. 'Enough of complaint.' Not traced, and perhaps not a quotation. If a classical quotation, I am told it cannot be an iambic dimeter (where a spondee in the second foot is not allowed), but may be part of a trimeter.

3. At S'k, where HT was enlarging the house.

4. 'D'Avenant' HLP; see on 405.

divided, Mawbey[5] would have had very ⟨little⟩ difficulty and am glad to find that Norton opposes him with so much efficacy, pray send me the result.

I am, Madam, Your most obedient Servant
Lichfield June 17. 1775   Sam: Johnson

407.1. Lichfield. Sa. 17 June '75. Edmund Allen (London).
Address: To Mr Allen Printer in Boltcourt Fleetstreet London.
Postmark: 19 IV.
Jeffery.—

Dear Sir

I wrote to you and to Sir Joshua yesterday, but wrote by the bypost,[1] and lest it should have miscarried have written again, and inclosed a ⟨   ⟩[2] which you may take to Sir Joshua. You will see by it that your success is earnestly desired, by

Sir Your most humble Servant
Lichfield June 17. 1775   Sam: Johnson.

408. Lichfield. M. 19 June '75. Mrs. Thrale.
Lichfield.—1788, No. 115; *Times Literary Supplement* 17 Jan. 1929 supplies a suppressed passage. See 408.1.

Dear Madam

I hope it is very true that Ralph mends,[1] and wish you were gone to see that you might come back again.

Queeney revenges her long tasks upon Mr Baretti's hen, who must sit on Duck eggs a week longer than on her own. I hope she takes great care of my Hen, and the Guinea hen and her pretty little brood.[2]

I was afraid Mawbey would succeed, and have little hope from the scrutiny. Did you ever know a scrutiny change the account?

407.—5. Mawbey, who had been a member for S'k '61–'74, stood for the county at the general election of '74 without success. In '75, on the death of Sir Francis Vincent, he tried again, and was opposed by the late member's son and by Norton, son of the Speaker of the House of Commons, who thus 'divided the interest of the county'. Mawbey was returned with 1,385 votes to Norton's 1,285, Vincent a bad third. Manning and Bray, *History of Surrey* 1814, 222. See 405, 406a.

407.1.—I have not discovered the nature of the application referred to here and in 408.1.   1. See Appendix F.   2. J omitted a word.

408.—1. See 404, 406a.   2. See 406a.

Miss Adey does not run after me, but I do not want her, here are other Ladies.

> Invenies alium, si te hic fastidit Alexis.[3]

Miss ⟨Turton⟩[4] grows old; and Miss Vyse has been ill, but I believe, she came to me as soon as she got out. And I can always go to Stowhill. So never grieve about me. Only flatulencies are come again.

Do you read Boswel's Journals? He moralised, and found my faults, and laid them up to reproach me. Boswel's narrative is very natural, and therefore very entertaining, he never made any scruple of showing it to me. He is a very fine fellow. He has established Rasa's Chieftainship in the Edinburgh papers,[5] and quieted all commotion in the Hebridean world. These little things are great to little Man.[6]

Small letters[7] will undoubtedly gain room for more words, but words are useless if they cannot be read. The lines need not all be kept distinct, and some words I shall wish to leave out, though very few. It must be revised before it is engraved. I always told you[8] that Mr Thrale was a man take him for all in all, you ne'er will look upon his like,[9] but you never mind him nor me, till time forces conviction into your steely bosom. You will perhaps find all right about the house and the windows.

Pray always suppose that I send my respects to Master, and Mr. Baretti,[10] and Queeney, and Harry, and Susey, and Sophy.

408.—3. Virgil, *Ecl.* ii. 73 (Alexim): 'And find an easier love, though not so fair', Dryden. Mr. Laithwaite reports that J probably wrote 'Alexis', possibly 'Alexin'.

4. Erased, but the initial and the medial *t* are visible.

5. See on 389.

6. This paragraph was erased in the original, and further hidden by a piece cut from another letter and pasted over the erasure. In 1788, accordingly, the recto of the superpositious piece ('Your dissertation . . . when we meet', see 408.1) is printed as part of 408, a *callida junctura* in both space and context. For HLP's oscillations between preserving and suppressing J's praises of JB see 395, 415. Her malice, it is fair to note, was not strong enough to reach consistency. For J's account of the journal cf. 405. The quotation, 'These little things', is from Goldsmith, *The Traveller*, l. 41.

7. See 403, 406*a*.

8. J refers to her admission, 406*a*, that HT was right and she wrong about Mawbey's election (see on 407). He suggests that her fears about 'building' (which may be inferred from 407) may also prove groundless.

9. *Hamlet* I. ii (adapted).

10. Heavily erased by HLP, who also pasted a scrap of paper over the erasure. Mr. Laithwaite, Secretary of the Johnson Society of Lichfield, steamed off the patch and was able to fill the lacuna.

Poor Lucy mends very slowly, but she is very good humoured, while I do just as she would have me.

Lady Smith has got a new postchaise, which is not nothing to talk on at Lichfield. Little things here serve for conversation. Mrs Aston's Parrot pecked my leg, and I heard of it some time after at Mrs Cobb's.

> —We deal in nicer things
> Than routing armies, and dethroning kings.[11]

a week ago Mrs Cobb gave me sweetmeats to breakfast, and I heard of it last night at Stowhill.

If you are for small talk.

> —Come on, and do the best you can
> I fear not you, nor yet a better man.[11]

I could tell you about Lucy's two cats, and Brill her brother's old dog, who is gone deaf, but the day would fail me. Suadentque cadentia sidera somnum.[12] So said Aeneas but I have not yet had my diner. I have begun early for what would become of the nation if a Letter of this importance should miss the post? Pray write to

Dear Madam Your most obedient and most humble Servant

Lichfield. June 19. 1775   Sam: Johnson

408.1. n.d. Mrs. Thrale.

Lichfield; pasted by Mrs. Piozzi to the original of 408, and printed (the recto only) as if part of that letter.—*Johnson, Boswell, and Mrs. Piozzi, a suppressed Passage Restored*, 1929.

Recto

Your dissertation upon Queeney is very deep. I know not what to say to the chief question. Nature probably has some part in human characters, and accident has some part, which has most we will try to settle when we meet.

408.—11. Not traced.

   12. Virgil, *Aen.* ii. 9 and iv. 81 (somnos) 'And setting stars to kindly rest invite', Dryden.

408.1.—When in 1929 I was allowed to remove this fragment from 408, on which HLP had foisted it, I disclosed the fragmentary verso, which gives us a clue to the date. HLT's 'dissertation upon Queeney' has not been found; it might naturally arise out of their adventures at the Regatta (see 409). But what J writes of 'Shakespeare' and 'Liz' is clearly in answer to her letter of 29 June, 411a. She reported that

Verso

as to hold a horse, and that is in the possession of ⟨
Shakespeare. However, I am sure Mr Langton will g⟨
and he is but a little further off. When Liz. is tr⟨avelling
one hundred and thirty miles,[1] he may as well trav⟨el twenty more to find a welcome. If every thing fails, ⟨
⟩ or Christmas.

408.2. Lichfield. M. 19 June '75. Edmund Allen.

Address: To Allen Printer in Boltcourt, Fleetstreet London. *Postmark*: (probably) 21 iv.
Newton.—

Dear Sir

I have recommended you, as you desire, both to Sir
Joshua, and to Mr Davies, and hope that you will find the
effect of my good will. I had it not in my thoughts that Mr
Davies could ask for the place being no printer. They will
both have their letters by the post that brings this.

Please to make my compliments to Mrs Allen. Whenever
you think I can do any good, make no difficulty to call upon,
Sir, Your most humble Servant
Lichfield. June 19. 1775   Sam: Johnson

409. Lichfield. W. 21 June '75. Mrs. Thrale.

Adam.—1788, No. 115.

Dear Madam

Now I hope you are thinking. Shall I have a letter from
Lichfield? Something of a letter you will have how else can
I expect that you should write? and the morning on which I
should miss a letter, would be a morning of uneasiness, not-

Carter, the indigent riding-master, could not afford to keep Lizard, an old stallion
('the well-known war-horse who carried Duke William over the plains of Culloden'
HLP, quoted *L* ii. 528), and might be forced to sell him. 'I would myself be foolish
enough to purchase old Lizard, if I knew any good Body that would give him his
Keep when I had done. This is what I have half a hope for from Dr. Taylor.' J
replies that the only adequate stall is preoccupied by Shakespeare, whose purchase
by JT he had reported 1 July (413). In the *Catalogue of the Pictures exhibited by the
Society of Artists* for '63, No. 44, 'Mr. Gilpin', is 'Portrait of Lizard the pillar horse
in Capt. Carter's riding-school' (*pillar* 1 d. in *OED*). I suspect that 408.1 may have
been part of 414, q.v.

1. J seems to say that Langton is farther from S'm than A'n is. My edition (1810)
of *Cary's New Itinerary* gives the distance from L'n to A'n as 139 miles, L'n to
Spilsby 130.

withstanding all that would be said or done by the Sisters of Stowhill, who do and say whatever good they can. They give me good words, and cherries, and strawberries. Lady Smith, and her Mother and sister were visiting there yesterday, and Lady Smith took her tea before her Mother.

Mrs Cobb is to come to Miss Porters this afternoon. Miss Adey comes little near me. Mr Langley of Ashbourne was here to day in his way to Birmingham, and every body talks of you.

The Ladies of the amicable society are to walk in a few days from the townhall to the Cathedral in procession to hear a sermon. They walk in Linen gowns, and each has a stick with an acorn, but for the acorn they could give no reason, till I told them of the civick crown.[1]

I have just had your sweet letter, and am glad that you are to be at the regatta.[2] You know how little I love to have you left out of any shining part of life. You have every right to distinction and should therefore be distinguished. You will see a show with philosophick superiority, and therefore may see it safely. It is easy to talk of sitting at home contented when others are seeing or making shows. But not to have been where it is supposed, and seldom supposed falsely, that all would go if they could; To be able ⟨to⟩ say nothing when every one is talking; to have no opinion when every one is judging; to hear exclamations of rapture without power to depress; to listen to falsehoods without right to contradict, is, after all, a state of temporary inferiority,[3] in ⟨which⟩ the mind is rather hardened by stubornness, than supported by fortitude. If the world be worth wining[4] let us enjoy it, if it is to be despised let us despise it by conviction. But the world is not to be despised but as it is compared with something better. Company is in itself better than solitude and pleasure better than indolence. Ex nihilo

409.—1. The *corona civica* of the Romans was of oak-leaves. See 406.

2. See the letters following. Hill quotes *Annual Register*, *GM*, Walpole's letters, &c., for descriptions of this 'entertainment borrowed from the Venetians'.

3. When JB said there was not half a guinea's worth of pleasure in seeing the Pantheon, J replied: 'But, Sir, there is half a guinea's worth of inferiority to other people in not having seen it' (*L* ii. 169).

4. 'If the World be worth thy Winning, | Think, O think, it worth Enjoying. | Lovely *Thais* sits beside thee, | Take the Good the Gods provide thee.' Dryden, *Alexander's Feast*.

nihil fit, says the moral as well as natural philosopher. By doing nothing and by knowing nothing no power of doing good can be obtained. he must mingle with the world that desires to be useful. Every new scene impresses new ideas, enriches the imagination, and enlarges the power of reason, by new topicks of comparison. You that have seen the regatta will have images which we who miss it must want, and no intellectual images are without uses. But when you are in this scene of splendour and gayety, do not let one of your fits of negligence steal upon you. Hoc age,[5] is the great rule whether you are serious or merry, whether you are stating the expences of your family, learning science or duty from a folio, or floating on the Thames in a fancied dress. Of the whole entertainment let me not hear so copious nor so true an account from any body as from you.

I am, Dearest Madam, Your most obedient and most humble servant,

Lichfield June 21. 1775   Sam: Johnson

410. Lichfield. F. 23 June '75. Mrs. Thrale.
Houghton.—1788, No. 118.

Dear Madam

So now you have been at the regatta, for I hope you got tickets somewhere, else you wanted me, and I shall not be sorry, because you fancy You can do so well without me, but however I hope you got tickets, and were dressed fine and fanciful, and made a fine part of the fine show, and heard musick, and said good things, and staid on the water four hours after midnight, and came well home, and slept, and dreamed of the regatta, and waked, and found yourself in bed, and thought now it is all over, only I must write about it to Lichfield.

We make a hard shift here to live on without a regatta. The cherries are ripe at Stowhil, and the currants are ripening, and the Ladies are very kind to me. I wish however you would go to Surry[1] and come back, though I think it wiser

409.—5. 'Hoc age', 'get on with the job', is an injunction frequent in Latin comedy, and often inculcated in Chesterfield's letters.

410.—1. 'Sussex' HLP; the same mistake in 411. She had intended to go to Lewes and did go to B'n.

to stay till the improvement in Ralph may become perceptible, else you will be apt to judge by your wishes and your imagination. Let us in the mean time hope the best. Let me but know when you go, and when you come back again.

If you or Mr Thrale would write to Dr Wetherel about Mr Carter, it will please Wetherel, and keep the business in motion. They know not otherwise how to communicate news if they have it.

As to my hopes and my wishes I can keep them to myself. They will perhaps grow less, if they are laughed at. I needed not tell them, but that I have little else to write, and I needed not write but that I do not like to be without hearing from you, because I love the Thrales and the Thralites.

I am, Madam, Your most humble Servant

June 23, 1775   Sam: Johnson

411. Lichfield. M. 26 June '75. Mrs. Thrale.
Sotheby 30 Jan. 1918 (not seen).—1788, No. 118.

Dear Madam   June 26, 1775

That the regatta[1] disappointed you is neither wonderful nor new; all pleasure preconceived and preconcerted ends in disappointment; but disappointment, when it involves neither shame nor loss, is as good as success; for it supplies as many images to the mind, and as many topicks to the tongue. I am glad it failed for another reason, which looks more sage than my reasons commonly try to look; this, I think, is Queeney's first excursion into the regions of pleasure, and I should not wish to have her too much pleased. It is as well for her to find that pleasures have their pains; and that bigger misses who are at Ranelagh when she is in bed, are not so much to be envied as they would wish to be, or as they may be represented.

So you left out the . . . s,[2] and I suppose they did not go.

411.—1. For the successes and failures of the regatta see 1788, No. 117, dated 24 June: if it will divert the Lichfield ladies, 'the hour has been happily spent that wrote the *immortal letter of the regatta*'. This document, which contains nearly 2,000 words, is rejected by Mr. Clifford (301, note 1) as too good to be true; it abounds in literary allusions. Much of it might have been written from memory; but it is no doubt based on a lost original written on 24 June.

2. 'Rices' HLP.

It will be a common place for you and Queeney fourscore years hence; and my master and you may have recourse to it sometimes. But I can only listen. I am glad that you were among the finest.

Nothing was the matter between me and Miss . . . .[3] We are all well enough now. Miss Porter went yesterday to church, from which she has been kept a long time. I fancy that I shall go on Thursday to Ashbourne, but do not think that I shall stay very long. I wish you were gone to Surry[4] and come well back again, and yet I would not have you go too soon. Perhaps I do not very well know what I would have; it is a case not extremely rare. But I know I would hear from you by every post, and therefore I take care that you should every post day hear from me.

I am, &c.

411a. Streatham. Th. 29 June '75. From Mrs. Thrale to J at Ashbourne.

Address: To Mr S. Johnson at Dr Taylor's Ashbourn Derbys. *Postmark*: 2⟨9⟩ IV. Franked by HT.

R 539.43—

Dear Sir   Streatham 29: June 1775.

The Time is absolutely fixed for our going to Brighthelmstone, and on Tuesday next the 4th of July we set out, and on Saturday the 8th or Monday the 10th at farthest—we return. M^{rs} D'Avenant indeed does not go; her Husband's Relations grow more & more tyrannical, and will not let her stir but strictly where they please; however as I longed to see Ralph, and my Master has somewhat particular to say to Scrase, and I would wish to see what Condition the House is in against we go all together in September: he has promised to drive me down (if I will take little Jack) and give me a dip in the Sea: we must be at home by the 10th—so now manage your matters accordingly and let me see you improved by your Journey.

Now I wonder whether you go to Ashbourne or no; but I suppose you will too for a little little while—and if you do, & if you think proper to mention such a Thing, and if Doctor Taylor be as charitable as he is rich, I will tell you how he may do a good Thing.

Poor Carter when I saw him last told me all his Heart; The Man at whose Livery Stable in the Borough his Horses have stood for these last five Years, finding our Friend backward in his Payments insisted on half the Profits of

411.—3. 'Seward' HLP, who writes the same note on her own question 'Why does Miss **** never find a place in the letters from Lichfield. I thought her a mighty elegant amiable country lady.'

4. For Sussex, as in 410.

the Riding House, and finding that likewise but a small matter, insisted on Prince and Lizard being mortgaged to him: They however continuing to eat—and to get but little towards feeding themselves—Weston (The Stable Man) now insists on their being sold—and poor Carter is quite broken hearted about it: for if our Oxford Project answers—what shall we do without Lizard in particular? who though inestimable as a Pillar Horse, and the most useful Creature living for Learners, is from his Age & long disuse so incapable of course and common Work that he is likely to sell for a Trifle at publick Auction: Weston however being a true Creditor, swears they shall both be sold for what they will fetch; and I would myself be foolish enough to purchase old Lizard, if I knew any good Body that would give him his keep when I had done. This is what I have half a hope of from Dr Taylor,

> Whose ample Lawns are not ashamed to feed
> The milky Heifer and deserving Steed.

and Lizard would recompense his Charity by leaving him a beautiful Colt or Filley for a Favourite. What an unlucky Wretch this Carter is by the by! to lose his Horses just at the only Time he was ever in the way to want them. Well but Dr Glasse has really been very good, and with him he has got a Settlement which will bring his Family Bread till he goes to Oxford—so as he was got a little in Heart, I told him of his Wife & Daughter's Insolence & folly; which made him cry again, & he said he was an unhappy Man! & that disarmed my Wrath—& so let's have no more of him.

When will you come home? I shall be wondrous glad to see you—though I write every thing so I shall have nothing to tell: but I shall have you safe in your Bow Window to run to, when any thing comes in my head, and you say that's what you are kept for you know.

H: L: T.

412. Lichfield or Ashbourne. Th. 29 June '75. Richard Greene (Lichfield).

Puttick and Simpson 10 March 1862 (363) (not seen); known to Hill only from this catalogue.

'Making an appointment.'

413. Ashbourne. Sa. 1 July '75. Mrs. Thrale.

Mrs. F. Bowman.—1788, No. 119.

Dear Madam   Ashbourne, July 1, 1775

On Thursday, I came to Dr. Taylor's, where I live as I am used to do, and as you know.[1] He has gotten nothing new, but a very fine looking glass, and a Bull bitch. The less Bull is now grown the bigger. But I forgot; he has bought old Shakespeare the Racehorse for a Stalion. He has likewise

413.—1. From her stay there in '74.

some fine iron gates[2] which he will set up somewhere. I have
not yet seen the old Horse.

You are very much enquired after, as well here as at
Lichfield.

This I suppose will go after you to Sussex,[3] where I hope
you will find every thing either well, or mending. You never
told me whether you took Queeney with you; nor ever so
much as told me the name of the little one.[4] May be, you
think, I don't care about you.

I behaved myself so well at Lichfield, that Lucy says I am
grown better, and the Ladies at Stow hill, expect I should
come back thither before I go to London, and offer to entertain me if Lucy refuses.

I have this morning received a letter from Mrs Chambers
of Calcutta. The Judge has a sore eye and could not write.
She represents all as going on very well, only Chambers does
not now flatter himself that he shall do much good.

I am, &c.,

Sam: Johnson

413a. Streatham. M. 3 July '75. From Mrs. Thrale to J
at Ashbourne.

R 539.44—

Dear Sir   Streatham 3: July 1775.

I receive your Letter tonight, I go to Sussex tomorrow Morning: I so
little think of leaving Queeney behind that I forgot to say She went with
me. This Post has brought me disagreeable Accounts of poor Ralph; he has
had another Struggle with his Teeth it seems, a Fever & Diarrhea but is
mending again.

I wrote to the Dean of Hereford & he has returned me a very obliging
Answer; nothing however to fill me with hope of poor Carter's Success. They
wait for Lord Mansfield's Concurrence & Markham's: I wish we could get at
Lord Mansfield, of Markham's good Offices I think we are sure and the Archbishop is—in King James's Phrase—*as kind as you can desire.* Doctor Glasse
however will keep Life & Soul together till something is settled, for I fancy
it will be done sometime. I am sorry Doctor Taylor has just bought a Stallion.
—Carter is as unlucky as he thinks himself. This Rain has been very seasonable, I hope there will be a plentiful Harvest—but nobody talks loudly neither
about the growth of the Barley.

413.—2. The iron gates have disappeared.
    3. See 411a.   4. Frances Anna (4 May).

I am glad Dr Taylor remembers us with kindness, we shall ever remember him with Respect. I love the old Bull best—whoever is largest he will be handsomest. I hope he is able to preserve his Authority. I should be sorry to have that matter decided without Henderson being present.

        I am ever Dear Sir Most faithfully Yours H: L: T.

414. Ashbourne. ⟨July '75⟩. Mrs. Thrale.

Not traced.—1788, No. 120.

Now, thinks my dearest Mistress to herself, sure I am at last gone too far to be pestered every post with a letter: he knows that people go into the country to be at quiet; he knows too that when I have once told the story of Ralph, the place where I am affords me nothing that I shall delight to tell, or he will wish to be told; he knows how troublesome it is to write letters about nothing; and he knows that he does not love trouble himself, and therefore ought not to force it upon others.

But, dearest Lady, you may see once more how little knowledge influences practice, notwithstanding all this knowledge, you see, here is a letter.

Every body says the prospect of harvest is uncommonly delightful; but this has been so long the Summer talk, and has been so often contradicted by Autumn, that I do not suffer it to lay much hold on my mind. Our gay prospects have now for many years together ended in melancholy retrospects. Yet I am of opinion that there is much corn upon the ground. Every dear year encourages the farmer to sow more and more, and favourable seasons will be sent at last. Let us hope that they will be sent now.

The Doctor and Frank are gone to see the hay. It was cut on Saturday, and yesterday was well wetted; but to day has its fill of sunshine. I hope the hay at Streatham was plentiful, and had good weather.

414.—This letter, the original of which is untraced, has no date in 1788. But it is there placed between 413 of 1 July and 415 of 6 July, doubtless where it belongs. In 411 J threatened to write by every post, and if he kept his word there is a gap to be filled between 413 and 415; the contents of the letter are also apt. I have suggested above that 408.1 may have been part of 414, though I cannot suggest from what place in 414 it may have been cut away. There is no date on 408.1; but HLP might cut away more than she needed for insertion in 408. I have no record that 414 ever came into the market; but I am reluctant to hint that HLP might cover her traces by destroying it when she had printed it.

Our lawn is as you left it, only the pool is so full of mud that the water-fowl have left it. Here are many calves, who, I suppose, all expect to be great bulls and cows.

Yesterday I saw Mrs. Diot at church, and shall drink tea with her some afternoon.

I cannot get free from this vexatious flatulence, and therefore have troublesome nights, but otherwise I am not very ill. Now and then a fit; and not violent. I am not afraid of the waterfall. I now and then take physick; and suspect that you were not quite right in omitting to let blood before I came away. But I do not intend to do it here.

You will now find the advantage of having made one at the regatta. You will carry with you the importance of a publick personage, and enjoy a superiority which, having been only local and accidental, will not be regarded with malignity. You have a subject by which you can gratify general curiosity, and amuse your company without bewildering them. You can keep the vocal machine in motion, without those seeming paradoxes that are sure to disgust; without that temerity of censure which is sure to provoke enemies; and that exuberance of flattery which experience has found to make no friends. It is the good of publick life that it supplies agreeable topicks and general conversation. Therefore wherever you are, and whatever you see, talk not of the Punick war;[1] nor of the depravity of human nature; nor of the slender motives of human actions; nor of the difficulty of finding employment or pleasure; but talk, and talk, and talk of the regatta, and keep the rest for, dearest Madam,

Your, &c.,

415. Ashbourne. Th. 6 July '75. Mrs. Thrale.
Adam.—1788, No. 121.

Dear Madam

Dr Taylor says he shall be very glad to see you all here again, if you have a mind of retirement. But I told him that he must not expect you this summer, and ⟨he⟩ wants to know—why?

414.—1. J's dislike of the subject was a standing joke; L iii. 206. He was provoked by the extravagant praise of Roman republican institutions and virtues that was part of the Whigs' stock-in-trade.

I am glad you have read Boswel's journal[1] because it is something for us to talk about, and that you have seen the Hornecks, because that is a publick theme. I would have you see and read and hear, and talk it all, as occasion offers.

Pray thank Queeney for her letter. I still hope good of poor Ralph, but sure never poor rogue was so troubled with his teeth. I hope occasional bathing, and keeping him about two minutes with his body immersed, may promote the discharge from his head, and set his little brain at liberty. Pray give my service to my dear friend Harry, and tell him that Mr Murphy does not love him better than I do.

I am inclined to be of Mr Thrale's mind about the changes in the state. A dissolution of the parliament would in my opinion, be little less than a dissolution of the government, by the encouragement which it would ⟨give to⟩[2] every future faction to disturb the publick tranquillity. Who would ever want places and power if perseverance in falsehood, and violence of outrage were found to be certain and infallible means of procuring them? Yet I have so little confidence in our present statesmen, that I know not whether any thing is less likely, for being either absurd or dangerous.

About your estate I have little to say. Why it should not be settled upon your children I do not see, and I do not see on the other side, why you should diminish your own power over it. I think there is hardly sufficient reason for you, as distinct from Mr Thrale, either to promote or oppose the settlement. To oppose it, if he desires it, there can be surely no reason. I love you all too well, not to wish that whatever is done, may be best. It will be prudent to hear Mr Scrase's opinion. In matters of business the most experienced man must have great authority.[3]

I am Dearest Lady Your most humble servant
Ashbourne. July. 6. 1775   Sam: Johnson.

415.—1. The words 'Boswel's Journal' were written on a piece of paper pasted over the original. The letter was at one time in my possession, and on removing the pasted scrap I was able to read 'Boswel's'. Here, as in 395, HLP changed her mind. See on 408.

2. Added in another hand.

3. This paragraph was omitted in 1788. A full account of the decision, and of Scrase's advice, is in *Th* 317.

415a. Brighton. ⟨? Sa 8⟩ July ⟨'75⟩. From Mrs. Thrale to
J at Ashbourne.

Address: To Dʳ Sam Johnson at Doctor Taylors Ashbourne Derbys.
Postmarks: 10 IY *and* 11 IY. Franked by HT.
R 539.46—

My Dear Sir   Brighton
   This poor unfortunate Child will dye at last. The Matter which discharged
from his Ear was it seems a temporary Relief, but that was all over when I
came down & the Stupor was returned in a most alarming Manner: he has
however violent fits of Rage—proceeding from Pain I guess—just as Lucy &
Miss Anna had—Kipping says the Brain is oppressed of which I have no doubt.
What shall I do? What can I do? has the flattery of my Friends made me too
proud of my own Brains? & must these poor Children suffer for my Crime?
I can neither go on with this Subject nor quit it.—I have heard no more of
Mʳ Thrale's Intentions about my Estate &c. & you know I am not inquisitive.
He spends whole Hours with Scrase engaged in some Business—he does not
tell me what. I opened the Ball last Night—tonight I go to the Play: Oh that
there was a Play or a Ball for every hour of the four & twenty.
   Adieu! my head & my heart are so full I forgot to say how glad I shall be
to see you. as I am with the truest Regard
                              Sir Your most faithful Servant H: L: Thrale

416. Ashbourne. Su. 9 July '75. Mrs. Thrale.

E. D. North 1920.—1788, No. 126 (misplaced, for the date see 417).
Dear Madam
   I am sorry that my poor little friend Ralph goes on no
better. We must see what time will do for him.
   I hope Harry is well. I had a very pretty letter from
Queeney, and hope she will be kind to my Hen and her ten
chickens, and mind her Book.
   I forget whether I tell some things, and may perhaps tell
them twice, but the matter is not great, only, as you observe,[1]
the more we write, the less we shall have to say, when
we meet.
   Are we to go all to Brighthelmston in the Autumn, or
have you satiated yourself with this visit? I have only one
reason[2] for wishing you to go, and that reason is far enough
from amounting to necessity.

416.—The date is incomplete, but this letter seems clearly to be that which in 417
J says he wrote on 9 July.

   1. In the undated letter numbered 125 in 1788 is this remark: 'what shall we
have to talk if all the facts are sent flying so between Ashbourne and Streatham?'
   2. See 424.

That Dr Delap's³ simplicity should be forgiven for his benevolence is very just, and I will not ⟨now⟩ say anything in opposition to your kind resolution. It is pity that any good man should ever from violence be ridiculous.

This letter will be short, for I am so much disordered by indigestion of which I can give no account, that it is difficult to write more than that I am,

Dearest Lady, Your most humble Servant

Ashbourne. July 1775   Sam: Johnson

416a. Streatham. 'Sa. 9 July' ⟨'75⟩. From Mrs. Thrale to J at Ashbourne. (9 July was a Sunday.)

R 539.45—

Dear Sir   Streatham Saturday 9: July

    I came home very late last Night and found your sweet Letters all three lying on the Table: I would not have come home at all but Mr Thrale insisted on it—so I have left this poor Child to dye at Brighthelmstone. Doctor Pepys says he will write every Post & Kipping too. What signifies their writing? What signifies anything? the Child will die & I fear in sad Torments too— he is now exactly as Lucy was. The discharge at the Ear stopping on a sudden, they bathed him exactly as you would have bid them yourself—by Bromfield's advice indeed but all to no purpose: they are now blistering away about the Ear, Head & Neck, & if he should give them time to do all they intend he will have a Fontanelle cut in his Arm.

    Now it is not the Death of this Boy that affects me so; he is very young, & had he lived would probably have been a greater Misfortune to me: but it is the horrible Apprehension of losing the others by the same cruel Disease that haunts my affrighted Imagination & makes me look upon them with an Anxiety scarce to be endured. If Hetty tells me that her Head achs, I am more shocked than if I heard She had broken her Leg.

    Poor old Captain Conway is dead. Carter is dolorous still: The Horse is in Westons Possession at present, nobody would bid above five pounds for him, so Mr Weston was forced to take him back: as he is now at the Expence of keeping him I will not buy him to ease Weston's Pocket & empty my own, but whenever he is going to be parted with I shall step in & save him for Carter.—I enclose you the Dean's Letter which Carter gave me back today.

    When we came home last Night here to Streatham, the first Man I saw was Perkins; my Spirits were already low, & I feared there was some sad News from London; but it was only a Story about that Crossby who broke in our Debt last Winter, & who has some concerns at Derby—you may remember Avis saying he was struck dumb or stupid or something about it. I warrant

416.—3. Suppressed in 1788; 'Dr. Delap's' and (in margin) 'I have quite forgotten' HLP; that is, she had forgotten the incident—misled, perhaps, by her own text, which had printed 'seem, or ever' for J's 'from violence'.

you recollect his Expression which I have forgotten. Pray tell me if your Relation Mr Flint has all his Children alive? there was a sweet little Girl among them very like my poor Lucy—& afflicted with Headachs: do enquire whether She be living or no: I took an Interest in her from the Resemblance, & was not without many Apprehensions for her Life. I have forgotten her name if it was not Lucy—I think it was.

        I am ever Sir Your most faithful Servant H L T.

417. Ashbourne. Tu. 11 July '75. Mrs. Thrale.
Sotheby 30 Jan. 1918 (not seen).—1788, No. 123 (dated in the text).
Dear Madam   Ashbourne

    I am sure I write and write, and every letter that comes from you charges me with not writing. Since I wrote to Queeney I have written twice to you, on the 6th and the 9th, be pleased to let me know whether you have them or have them not. That of the 6th you should regularly have had on the 8th, yet your letter of the 9th seems not to mention it; all this puzzles me.

    Poor dear . . .!¹ He only grows dull because he is sickly; age has not yet begun to impair him; nor is he such a chameleon as to take immediately the colour of his company. When you see him again, you will find him reanimated. Most men have their bright and their cloudy days, at least they have days when they put their powers into act, and days when they suffer them to repose.

    Fourteen thousand pounds make a sum sufficient for the establishment of a family, and which, in whatever flow of riches or confidence of prosperity, deserves to be very seriously considered. I hope a great part of it has paid

417.—HLT wrote two letters reporting that she had no hope of Ralph's recovery. The first, 415*a*, dated merely 'Brighton', must have been written on 8 July at latest, since she reached S'm that night; the postmarks show that it reached L'n 10 July and left for A'n 11 July. This letter, then, J had not received when he wrote 417. The second, 416*a*, is dated 'Streatham Saturday 9: July' and reports 'I came home very late last Night and found your sweet Letters all three lying on the Table'. These would be 414 and 415, and perhaps also 413, though that letter she had received, and answered 3 July, before she left for B'n.

    1. HLP has no note here. But in the undated letter which in 1788 follows 418 (419*a*) she writes: 'You account very tenderly for * * * *'s dullness'; and her note on this is 'Berenger'.

    Her description of a bore who had allowed his talent to rust does not well fit what we know of Richard Berenger; it is possible that her memory in 1788 was at fault. Hill guessed William Seward to be meant.

debts, and no small part bought land.[2] As for gravelling and walling and digging, though I am not much delighted with them, yet something, indeed much, must be allowed to every man's taste. He that is growing rich has a right to enjoy part of the growth his own way. I hope to range in the walk, and row upon the water, and devour fruit from the wall.

Dr. Taylor wants to be gardening. He means to buy a piece of ground in the neighbourhood, and surround it with a wall, and build a gardener's house upon it, and have fruit, and be happy. Much happiness it will not bring him; but what can he do better? If I had money enough, what would I do? Perhaps, if you and master did not hold me, I might go to Cairo, and down the Red Sea to Bengal, and take a ramble in India. Would this be better than building and planting? It would surely give more variety to the eye, and more amplitude to the mind. Half fourteen thousand would send me out to see other forms of existence, and bring me back to describe them.

I answer this the day on which I had yours of the 9th, that is on the 11th. Let me know when it comes.

I am, &c.

417a. Streatham. Tu. 11 July ⟨'75⟩. From Mrs. Thrale to J at Ashbourne.

Address: To Doctor Sam: Johnson at the Rev: Dr Taylor's Ashbourne Derbys. *Postmark*: 11 IY. Franked by HT.

R 539.47—

Dear Sir

I have dismal Letters from Pepys and Kipping too; though the Doctor has some faint hopes, probably for want of Experience in the Disorder. He cuts a Seton in the Neck. Young Practitioners in Physick as in Life will try to do Something, Old Practitioners in both know that there is little to be done, and so relinquish Hope too soon perhaps. I am pleased that Ralph is in the hands of Pepys. Kipping the Apothecary of the Place lost one Child by this Disorder and has one alive who is an Ideot.

Now am I in a greater Passion because I can't get this Letter to the Post without a purpose Messenger than I have been for all my Misfortunes put together. What a perverse & foolish Being is Your faithful & Obedient H: L: Thrale

Streatham Tuesday 11: July

417.—2. 'Debts yes land no' HLP. There is no mention of £14,000 in any extant letter up to this date; but in 419*a* she writes: 'I will keep the Story of the 14000£ till we meet.'

418. Ashbourne. W. 12 July '75. Mrs. Thrale,

Adam.—1788, No. 124.

Dear Madam   Ashbourn. Wednesday July 12. 1775

On Monday[1] I was not well, but I grew better at night, and before morning was, as the Doctors say, out of danger.

We have no news here, except that on saturday Lord Scarsdale dined with the Doctor. He is a very gentlemanlike man. On Sunday Mr Green paid a visit from Lichfield, and having nothing to say, said nothing and went away.

Our great Cattle, I believe, go on well, but our deer have died, all but five does and the poor Buck. We think the ground too wet for them.

I have enclosed a letter from Mrs Chambers[2] partly, perhaps wholly, for Mr Baretti's amusement and gratification, though he has probably a much longer letter of his own, which he takes no care to send me.

Mr Langley and the Doctor still continue at variance, and the Doctor is afraid, and Mr Langley not desirous of a reconciliation. I therefore step over at bytimes; and of bytimes I have enough.

Mrs Dale has been ill, and at fourscore has recovered. She is much extenuated, but having the Summer to favour her, will, I think, renew her hold on life.

To the Diots I yet owe a visit. Mr Gell is now rejoicing at fifty seven for the birth of an heir male—I hope here is news. Mr O——[3] and the Doctor seem to be making preparations for war.

Now I flatter myself that you want to know something about me. My spirits are now and then in an uneasy flutter, but upon the whole, not very bad.

We have here a great deal of rain, but this is a very rainy region. I hear nothing but good of the harvest; but the expectation of [*sic*] higher of the wheat than of the barley, but

418.—1. It is perhaps surprising that J should on Wednesday report an ailment not noticed in a letter of Tuesday. But I see no reason to doubt the dates; 418 is fully dated, and 417, though dated only 'the 11th', seems clearly to belong to July '75.

2. She had been B's pupil.

3. 'Mr. O' is the 'Okeover' of 422*a*; Mr. Metzdorf has read Ok . . . er.

I hope there will be barley enough for us and Mr Scrase, and Lady Lade,[4] and something still to spare.

    I am Dearest, Sweetest Lady, Your most obedient servant,

                                        Sam: Johnson

Be pleased to send Mrs Chambers's Letter to Mrs Williams.[5]

419. Ashbourne. Th. 13 July '75. Mrs. Thrale.

Rosenbach 1927.—1788, No. 127.

Dearest Madam   July 13. 1775

    In return for your three letters[1] I do not find myself able to send you more than two; but if I had the prolixity of an emperour,[2] it should be all at your service.

    Poor Ralph. I think what they purpose to do for his relief is right, but that it will be efficacious I cannot promise.

    Your anxiety about your other Babies[3] is, I hope, super-fluous. Miss and Harry are as safe as ourselves, they have outlived the age of weakness; their fibres are now elastick, and their headachs when they have them are from accidental causes, heat, or indigestion.

    If Susy had been at all disposed to this horrid malady, it would have laid hold on her, in her early state of laxity and feebleness. That native vigour which has carried her happily through so many obstructions to life and growth, will, I think, certainly preserve her from a disease, most likely to fall only on the weak.

    Of the two small ladies it can only be said, that there is no present appearance of danger, and of fearing evils merely possible there is no end. We are told by the Lord of Nature that 'for the day its own evil is sufficient'.[4]

    Now to lighter things, and those of weight enough to

418.—4. 1788 reduces the names to S— and L—; Lysons notes 'Scrase' and 'Lade', which are consistent with the traces in the erased original. For HT's debts to them see C 93.

    5. The postscript is not in 1788.

419.—1. HLT's 'three letters' no doubt include 416*a* and 417*a*; J's 'two' are 418 and 419 in one cover.

    2. Hill suggests that J was thinking of Dogberry's 'If I were as tedious as a King, I could find it in my heart to bestow it all of your worship' (*Much Ado* III. v).

    3. See 416*a*.

    4. St. Matthew vi. 34: in the A.V., 'Sufficient unto the day is the evil thereof.' J's wording is closer to the Vulgate: 'sufficit diei malitia *sua*.'

another. I am still of opinion that we shall bring the Oxford
riding School to bear. The Vicechancellor is indeed un
esprit foible, and perhaps too easily repressed, but Dr.
Wetherel is in earnest. I would come back through Oxford,
but that at this time there is nobody there. But I will not
desist. I think to visit them next term.

Do not let poor Lizard[5] be degraded for five pound. I
sent you word that I would spend something upon him, and
indeed for the money which it would cost to take him to
Taylor or Langton and fetch him back, he may be kept while
he stands idle, a long time in the Stable.

Mrs Williams has been very ill, and it would do her good,
if you would send a message of enquiry, and a few strawberries or currants.

Mr Flints little girl is alive and well, and pretty, as, I
hope, yours, my dear Lady, will long continue.

The hay harvest is here very much incommoded by daily
showers, which, however, seem not violent enough to beat
down the corn.

I cannot yet fix the time of coming home. Dr Taylor
and I spend little time together, yet he will not yet be persuaded to hear of parting.

I am Dearest Lady Your most obliged and obedient

Sam: Johnson

419a. Brighthelmston. ⟨? *c.* 13 July '75⟩. From Mrs. Thrale
to J (? at Ashbourne).

R 538.13—1788, No. 125 (omitting the postscript).

Dear Sir

The Letters are all come, & very kind Letters they are, & I always wish
them longer and less frequent: for when you once turn the page I am sure of
a Disquisition or an Observation, or a little Scold or something—when you
write less than 20 Lines at once 'tis only a Scrap sent from the next Week's
Chat, for what shall we have to talk if all the facts are sent flying so between
Ashbourne & Streatham? I will keep the Story of the 14000£ till we meet,

419.—5. See on 408.1.

419a.—The MS. of this letter resembles most of the MSS. of the published letters
of 1788, which are manifestly not originals sent to J. Its claim to be such depends
mainly on the postscript, since the MS. does show traces of thread. With Mr.
Clifford I give it the benefit of the doubt (C 300, 301). The date is also uncertain.
For an account of Ralph's last illness see *French Journals* 236.

so I will all Family Concerns, unless little Queeney sends her *Country Post* as usual to give Information of a new *Sail of Ducks* or some such Important Intelligence, which will not greatly interfere with my Project. At present the last Paragraph of your last long Letter is much in my Head—& Mr Thrale say'd when we read it together, that you should not travel alone if he could once see this dear little Boy quite well, or see me well perswaded (as many are) that nothing ails him.

Why what an uncomfortable Reflexion it is at last that those who are best qualified to travel, & tell what they have seen at their Return should be almost always obliged for one Reason or another to stay at home.

My great delight like yours would be to see how Life is carried on in other Countries, how various Climates produce various Effects, and how different Notions of Religion & Government operate upon the human Manners & the human Mind: for 'tis they at last which cause all the distinction between National Characters, as the Method in which our Bones & Fibres are disposed creates all the Variety observed in the human Figure: yet I do not commend those Voyagers who teize one with too much of such Stuff to shew their own Profundity, any more than I like a Painter who exhibits none but Anatomical Figures. I think however we have had little to lament of on that Side lately, as counting Pictures & describing Ruins seems to have been the sole Business of modern Travellers—but when *we* go to *Cairo* one shall take one Department, another shall take another, and so a pretty Book may be made out amongst us that shall be commended, and censured, and cuffed about the Town for a Twelve Month, if no new Tub takes the Whale's Attention. Well! now all this is Nonsense and Fancy and Flight you know, for my Master has his great Casks to mind, and I have my little Children, but he has really half a mind to cross the Water for half a Year's Frisk to Italy or France if we could leave Matters so that we might not be frighted or called back to any Vexation. For digging, walling or planting we should be better qualified at our return, and we would shake off our Superflux of Science to Dear Dr Taylor—to whom make in the mean time our best Compliments with Love to his Jigg & Jessamy—I should not expect to see their superiors in any Country, but the foreign Ass we admired at Blenheim might measure against either of them as well as I remember.

You account very tenderly for ——s dullness, it was perhaps only accidental: but if a Man will never add to his original Stock by reading, and keep on living away upon what he set out with, Dullness in Conversation must finally ensue: a besieged Town is always obliged to capitulate at last if strongly invested and all foreign Supplies cut off, however well stored with Provision when the Blockade begun. Mr Thrale said he was more agreable this Afternoon, but I told him Starving produced a Feaver always in the last Stage of a Life losing by Famine, and his Friends Warmth in Conversation was occasioned by nothing better. Would it not be wiser to talk of the Regatta than make such Welch Speeches as these?—but nobody was by.

I said I would write nothing of Family Matters but here is a Letter from Sussex come that will make me write of nothing else. The Child is very bad I am sure, but I had better go and see, for the Suspense is terrible & these nasty Posts!

The Illness of this Boy frights me for all the Rest, if any of them have a Head ach it puts me in an Agony, a broken Leg would less affect my peace. So many to have the same Disorder is dreadful: what can be the meaning of it? Sophy complained yesterday, but I hope it was on purpose to fright me. Send me some comfortable Words do Dear Sir and believe me ever Your Obliged & faithful Ser^t H: L: Thrale

Here is some confusion with the paper—but I stick it together with Thread. They intend to cut a Seton it seems.

420. Ashbourne. Sa. 15 July '75. Mrs. Thrale.

Tregaskis 1921.—1788, No. 128.

Dear Madam

You are so kind, every post, that I now regularly expect your favours. You have indeed more materials for writing than I; here are only I and the Doctor, and of him I see not much. You have Master, and young Master, and Misses ⟨about 3 words erased⟩[1] besides Geese, and Turkies, and Ducks, and Hens.

The Doctor says, that if Mr Thrale comes so near as Derby,[2] without seeing us, it will be a sorry trick. I wish, for my part, that he may return soon, and rescue the fair captives from the tyranny of B⟨arett⟩i.[3] Poor B⟨arett⟩i! do not quarrel with him, to neglect him a little will be sufficient. He means only to be frank, and manly, and independent, and perhaps, as you say, a little wise. To be frank he thinks is to be cynical, and to be independent, is to be rude. Forgive him, dearest Lady, the rather, because of his misbehaviour, I am afraid, he learned part of me. I hope to set him hereafter a better example.

Your concern for poor Ralph,[4] and your resolution to visit him again, is too parental to be blamed. You may perhaps do good, you do at least your duty, and with that we must be contented, with that indeed, if we attained it, we ought to be happy; but who ever attained it?

You have perceived by my letters, that without knowing more than that the Estate was unsettled, I was inclined to a

420.—1. Perhaps HLP suppressed a mention of Baretti, as in 408.

2. See 416*a*.

3. 'Baretti' HLP; the 'B—i' of 1788 was a merely formal disguise. HLT's account of B's 'misbehaviour' has not survived in a letter to J. But see *Th* 43.

4. See 419*a*.

settlement. I am likewise for an entail. But we will consult men of experience, for that which is to hinder my dear Harry from mischief when he comes of age, may be done with mature deliberation.⁵

You have not all the misery in the world to yourself, I was last night almost convulsed with flatulence, after having gone to Bed I thought so well—but it does not much trouble me when I am out of bed. To your anxiety about your children I wrote lately what I had to say. I blame it so little, that I think you should add a small particle of anxiety about me, for

I am Dearest Madam Your most obedient servant Ashbourne July 15. 1775.   Sam: Johnson

421. Ashbourne. M. 17 July '75. Mrs. Thrale.
Adam.—1788, No. 129.

Dear Madam

The post is come without a letter; now could I be so sullen—but *He must be humble who would please.*¹ Perhaps you are gone to Brighthelmston,² and so could not write. However it be, this I feel, that I have no letter but then I have sometimes had two, and if I have as many letters as there come posts, nobody will pity me if I were to complain.

How was your hay made? The Doctor has had one part well housed; another wetted and dried till it is hardly worth the carriage; and now many acres newly mown, that have hitherto had good weather. This may be considered as a foreign article, the domestick news is that our Bulbitch has puppies, and that our six calves are no longer to be fed by hand, but to live on grass.

Mr Langley has made some improvements in his garden. A rich man might do more; but what he has done is well.

You have never in all your letters touched but once upon my Master's summer projects. Is he towering into the air, and tending to the center? Is he excavating the earth, or

420.—5. The paragraph is deleted in the original, but marked 'stet'. For HLT's will see on 415.

421.—1. Prior, 'Chloe Jealous': 'She should be humble who would please; And she must suffer who can love.'

2. She went there 13 July, to find Ralph dead. C 127.

covering its surface with edifices? Something he certainly is doing, and something he is spending. A Genius never can be quite still. I do not murmur at his expences, a good Harvest will supply them.

We talk here of Polish oats,[3] and Siberian barley, of which both are said to be more productive, and to ripen in less time, and to afford better grain than the English. I intend to procure specimens of both, which we will try in some spots of our own ground.

The Doctor has no great mind to let me go. Shall I tease him and plague him till he is weary of me? I am, I hope, pretty well, and fit to come home. I shall be expected by all my Ladies to return through Lichfield, and to stay there a while, but if I thought you wanted me, I hope, you know what would be done, by, Dearest, dearest Madam, Your most humble servant

July 17. 1775   Sam: Johnson

421a. Streatham. Tu. 18 July ⟨'75⟩. From Mrs. Thrale to J at Ashbourne.

R 539.48—

Dear Sir   Streatham Tuesday 18: July.

I am once more returned home from my melancholy Expedition to Bright-helmstone, and finding these five Children well, have resolved to be thankful to God and chearful among my Friends again till new Vexations arise. Baretti has been very good, and taken care of my little ones like a Nurse while I was away, & has not failed writing me &c. & I am sorry I was so peevish with him. I came home Yesterday. Mr Thrale has been in Town ever since I was gone, but would not come home to me last Night but went to Ranelagh I hear, however I will not be peevish any more, for it torments nobody but myself. I see no Letter from you, but Baretti says there is one, only Mr Thrale has put it in his Pocket—it enclosed Mrs Chambers's Letter from India which Mr Baretti rejoyces over with his whole heart.

I want you to hear my long Conversation with Mr Scrase at Brighthelm-stone. I have not pleased myself much, and doubt much whether I have pleased you: however that I might not omit or enlarge I wrote down the Heads of what had been said, when I returned home at Night immediately after the Talk—not caring to trust either my Memory or my Veracity—so you & I may both be sure that what I read to you is true: I have named you

421.—3. Hill refers to *GM* 1771, 520, for Siberian barley, and 1783, 852, for Poland oats. See 422, 469.

and Cator my Trustees, & that is the wisest thing I have done in it: Your Assistance *I command* you know, and I hope your Inclinations are not averse to the Charge—I only fear there is nothing for you to do. Farewell My Dear Sir and let us see you *sometime*; I think you shall never run away so again: I lost a Child the last Time you were at a distance

I am ever Most faithfully Your humble Servant H: L: Thrale.

422. Ashbourne. Th. 20 July '75. Mrs. Thrale.

Sotheby 4 June 1908 (not seen).—1788, No. 130.

Dear Madam   Ashbourne, July 20, 1775.

Poor Ralph! he is gone; and nothing remains but that you comfort yourself with having done your best. The first wish was, that he might live long to be happy and useful; the next, that he might not suffer long pain. The second wish has been granted. Think now only on those which are left you. I am glad you went to Brighthelmstone, for your journey is a standing proof to you of your affection and diligence. We can hardly be confident of the state of our own minds, but as it stands attested by some external action; we are seldom sure that we sincerely meant what we omitted to do.

Dr. Taylor says, that Mr. Thrale has not used us well, in coming so near[1] without coming nearer. I know not what he can say for himself, but I know that he can take shelter in sullen silence.

There is, I think, still the same prospect of a plentiful harvest. We have in this part of the kingdom had rain to swell the grain, and sunshine to ripen it. I was yesterday to see the Doctor's Poland oats. They grow, for a great part, four feet high, with a stalk equal in bulk and strength to wheaten straw. We were of opinion that they must be reaped, as the lower joints would be too hard for fodder. We will try them.

Susy was always my little girl. See what she is come to;

422.—The tone of this letter led Hill to comment on 'the childless Johnson's natural ignorance of the feelings of a parent'. Hill could not know that if Ralph had lived he must have been an idiot. But the assumption of J's 'natural ignorance' was gratuitous, and is confuted by ample evidence. For HLT's own attitude see 421*a*, which also was unknown to Hill.

1. As to Derby, see 420.

you must keep her in mind of me, who was always on her side. Of Mrs. Fanny[2] I have no knowledge.

You have had two or three of my letters to answer, and I hope you will be copious and distinct, and tell me a great deal of your mind; a dear little mind it is, and I hope always to love it better, as I know it more.[3]

I am, &c.

422a. Streatham. Th. 20 July ⟨'75⟩. From Mrs. Thrale to J at Ashbourne.

R 539.49 (imperfect)—

Dear Sir   Streatham Thursday 20: July.

I am very glad you find me diligent in writing every Post; it is so exceedingly pleasing to have any one care whether one writes or no, that it would be a sign of a sad Spirit to forbear giving that Pleasure for the sake of momentary Indulgence. Your Account of your health pleases me upon the whole vastly well: but why do you fancy we were wrong to omit bleeding? if your Breath be good I would rather let bleeding alone, it never does anything towards calming the Spirits, or removing that vile Flatulence which is now I think your only positive Complaint. I rejoyce to hear you are not afraid of the Waterfall. I am myself once more tranquil and chearful and thankful to God for all his Mercies—*To enjoy is to obey.*

The Weather is wonderfully seasonable, & great Crops are to be expected. The Barley in Sussex looks dwarfish but My Master says it was very Fine about Derby—he went on earnest Business & staid but one Day. He did see Bakewell's Cattle however, & said our Friend the Doctor's struck him as much more beautiful—will not that make amends for his not going to Ashbourn?

I am glad poor Mrs Dale has recovered; I love her for past kindness & recent Civility, & should be obliged to you if you would tell her so. I have sent Mrs Williams a pretty Pine Apple & a Bunch of Hothouse Grapes, & will call on her when I go to Town some Day. Mr Gell is himself a Proof of the Doctrine he despises—Future Rewards & Punishments. If there were no World after this,—Children would not be taken from me & given to him. He is a hateful Fellow!

Your speaking of Okeover reminds me of his Friend Gilpin, he dined here the other day but did not court Queeney. She is very well just now.

422.—2. The letter to which this alludes has not been found. Hill assumed that HLT's baby Frances Anna is meant. A possible alternative is Fanny Rice.

3. This paragraph is quoted in Sotheby's catalogue. The punctuation of the extract, clearly J's, proves that the cataloguer read the MS., not 1788, as, to save the trouble of decipherment, cataloguers often do. The catalogue reads 'have had', no doubt rightly, for 'have' of 1788. It is no doubt wrong in reading 'diligent' for 'distinct'.

423. Ashbourne. F. 21 July '75. Mrs. Thrale.

Adam.—1788, No. 131.

Dear Lady   Ashbourn July 21. 1775

When you write next, direct to Lichfield, for I think to move that way on tuesday, and in no long time to turn homewards, when we will have a serious consultation, and try to do everything for the best.

I shall be glad of a letter from dear Queeney, and am not sorry that she wishes for me. When I come we will enter into an alliance defensive at least.

Mr Baretti very elegantly[1] sent his pupil's letter to Mrs Williams without a cover, in such a manner that she knew not whence it was transmitted.

I do not mean to bleed but with your concurrence,[2] though I am troubled with eruptions, which I cannot suppress by frequent physick.

As my Master staid only one day,[3] we must forgive him, yet he knows he staid only one day because he thought it not worth his while to stay two.

You and Baretti are friends again.[4] My dear Mistress has the quality of being easily reconciled, and not easily offended. Kindness is a good thing in itself; and there are few things that are worthy of anger, and still fewer that can justify malignity.

Nothing remains for the present but that you sit down placid and content, disposed to enjoy the present and planning the proper use of the future liberalities of Providence. You have really much to enjoy, and without any wild

---

423.—Three paragraphs, that about bleeding and the last two, are deleted in the MS. but restored with a *stet*. In this letter J replies to 421*a*. She had written 'I see no Letter from you, but Baretti says there is one, only Mr. Thrale' (who was in L'n) 'has put it in his Pocket': i.e. 418. It is to be remembered that J's letters were addressed to 'Henry Thrale Esq.'.

1. 'Ironical' HLP. I at one time guessed, wrongly, that Mr. Adam and I had overlooked a misreading of 1788, and that J wrote 'negligently'. I had this excuse, that J seldom uses that kind of irony. But see 578 and 999. The 'elegance' consisted, perhaps, in so refolding the letter that it could be redirected; HT's absence had left them without a frank.

2. See 414 for J's deference to his mistress in this article.

3. 'He went on earnest Business & staid but one Day.' HLT 20 July. See 420.

4. See 421*a* for her praise of Baretti, which is hardly consistent with her catalogue of his crimes in *Th* 43.

indulgence of imagination much to expect. In the mean time, however, life is gliding away, and another state is hastening forwards. You were but five and twenty[5] when I knew you first, and you are now — What I shall be next September I confess I have lacheté enough to turn aside from thinking.

I am glad that you read Boswel's journal, you are now sufficiently informed of the whole transaction, and need not regret that you did not make the tour of the Hebrides.

You have done me honour in naming me your Trustee,[6] and have very judiciously chosen Cator. I believe our fidelity will not be exposed to any strong temptations.

I am Madam Your most humble servant

Sam: Johnson

424. Ashbourne. M. 24 July '75. Mrs. Thrale.
Gabriel Wells.—1788, No. 132.

Dear Madam

Be pleased to return my thanks to Queeney for her pretty little letter. I hope the Peacock will recover. It is pity we cannot catch the fellow, we would make him drink at the pump. The victory over the poor wild cat delights me but little. I had rather he had taken a chicken than lost his life.

To morrow I go to Lichfield. My company would not any longer make the Doctor happy. He wants to be rambling with his Ashbourn Friends. And it is perhaps time for me to think of coming home. Which way I shall take, I do not know.

Miss says that you have recovered your spirits, and that you all are well. Pray do not grudge the trouble of telling me so your own self, for I do not find my attention to you and your sensations, at all lessened, by this time of absence which always appears to my imagination much longer than when I count it.

Now to morrow I expect to see Lucy Porter, and Mrs. Adey, and to hear how they have gone on at Lichfield. and

423.—5. 'But two or three and twenty' HLP. The words 'and you are now —' (J's blank, not an erasure) are omitted in 1788.
6. 'I have named you and Cator my Trustees.' HLT 18 July. See on 415.

then for a little I shall wander about, as the birds of passage circle and flutter, before they set out on the main flight.[1]

I have been generally without any violent disorder of either mind or body, but every now and then ailing, but so that I could keep it to myself.

Are we to go to Brighthelmston this autumn? I do not enquire with any great solicitude. You know one reason,[2] and it will not be easy to find another, except that which brings all thither that go, unwillingness to stay at home, and want of power to supply with either business or amusement the cravings of the day. From this distress all that know either You or me, will suppose that we might rescue ourselves, if we would, without the help of a bath in the morning and an assembly at night.

I am, Madam, Your most humble Servant

July 24. 1775   Sam: Johnson

425. Lichfield. W. 26 July '75. Mrs. Thrale.
Adam.—1788, No. 133.

Dear Madam   Lichfield July 26. 1775
Yesterday I came hither; after dinner I went to Stowhill; there I was pampered, and had an uneasy night, Physick today put me out of order; and for some time I forgot that this is post night.

Nothing very extraordinary has happened at Lichfield since I went away. Lucy Porter is better, and has got her lame hand out of the bag. The rest of your friends I have not seen.

Having staid long enough at Ashbourn I was not sorry to leave it. I hindred some of Taylor's diversions and he supplied me with very little. Having seen the neighbouring places I had no curiosity to gratify, and having few new things, we had little new talk.

424.—1. One may be tempted to think that this refers to the French tour of the autumn. In 419*a* she writes that HT 'has really half a mind to cross the water for half a Year's frisk to Italy or France'. But as yet J's horizon seems to have been bounded by B'n. By 'wander about' he perhaps means no more than short visits to B'm or O'd on his way home from L'd. See 425.

2. See 416. Perhaps one need look for no better reason than J's solicitude for HLT's health and spirits. But Mr. Clifford suggests that J was thinking of consultations with Scrase; see C 128.

When I came I found Lucy at her book. She had Hammond's commentary on the Psalms before her. He is very learned, she says, but there is enough that any body may understand.

Now I am here I think myself a great deal nearer London than before, for though the distance is not very different, I am here in the way of Carriages, and can easily get to Birmingham, and so to Oxford, but I know not which way I shall take, but some way or other I hope to find that may bring me back again to Streatham; and then I shall see what have been my Master's goings on; and will try whether I shall know the old places.

As I lift up my head from the paper, I can look into Lucy's Garden. Her walls have all failed. I believe she has had hardly any fruit but Gooseberries, but so much verdure looks pretty in a town.

When you read my letters I suppose you are very proud to think how much you excel in the correspondence: but you must remember that your materials are better. You have a family, and friends, and hopes, and fears, and wishes, and aversions, and all the ingredients that are necessary to the composition of a Letter. Here sit poor I, with nothing but my own solitary individuality; doing little, and suffering no more than I have often suffered; hearing nothing that I can repeat; seeing nothing that I can relate; talking, when I do talk, to those whom you can not regard, and at this moment hearing the curfew[1] which you cannot hear.

I am Dearest, dearest Lady, Your most humble servant

Sam: Johnson

426. Lichfield. Sa. 29 July '75. Mrs. Thrale.
Adam.—1788, No. 135.

Madam

The rain caught me at Stowhill, and kept me till it is very late. I must however write for I am enjoined to tell you how much Mrs Lucy was pleased with your present, and to entreat you to excuse her from writing because her hand is not yet recovered. She is very glad of your notice, and very thankful.

425.—1. The eight o'clock curfew at St. Mary's was silent for six years, but was resumed in December 1945.

Lucy may thank you if she will, but you shall have no thanks from me, for Wisdom—and critical eruptions—and advanced life—such Stuf.[1] I remember to have read in a book called the *Catholicon*, that all evil begins *ab undecimo*.[2] What then must be the evil of *three times eleven* or thirty three.[3] However I have burnt the letter.[4]

What you tell me of your *Reste* and ten thousand pounds, has more sense in it. Will it not be now in our power to pay Mr Scrase ?[4]

I am very desirous that Mr L⟨ester⟩[5] should be sent for a few weeks to Brighthelmston. Air, and Vacancy, and novelty, and the consciousness of his own value, and the pride of such distinction, and delight in Mr Thrale's kindness would as Cheney[6] phrases it, afford all the relief that human art can give, or human nature receive. Do not read this slightly, you may prolong a very useful life.

Whether the pineapples be ripe or rotten, whether the Duke's Venison be baked or roasted, I begin to think it time I were at home. I have staid till perhaps nobody wishes me to stay longer except the Ladies on the hill, who offer me a lodging, and though not ill, am unsettled enough to wish for change of place, even though that change were not to bring me to Streatham. But thither I hope I shall quickly come, and find you all well, and gay, and happy, and catch a little gayety and health, and happiness among you.

I am, Dearest of all dear Ladies, Your most humble servant,
July 29. 1775　　　　　　　　　　　　　　　　Sam: Johnson

427. Lichfield. Tu. 1 Aug. '75. Mrs. Thrale.

Adam.—1788, No. 136.

Dear Madam

I wonder how it could happen. I forgot that the post went out yester night, and so omitted to write. I therefore

---

426.—1. It is not clear whether the letter containing the 'Stuf'—as to the nature of which I can only guess—was HLT's own or an enclosure.

2. The quotation, which I have not found, is perhaps from the Latin *Catholicon* 1460 (a vast work) rather than the *Catholicon Anglicum*, 1483.

3. HLT was actually 34 in Jan. '75.

4. These two paragraphs omitted in 1788.

5. 'Lester, a Clerk' HLP. I could not read the erasure fully, but the f is clear.

6. Not traced. See Cheyne in Index III.

send this by the bypost, and hope it will come that I may not lose my regular letter.

This was to have been my last letter from this place but Lucy says I must not go this week. Fits of tenderness with Mrs Lucy are not common, but she seems now to have a little paroxysm, and I was not willing to counteract it. When I am to go I shall take care to inform you.

The Lady at Stowhill says, how comes Lucy to be such a sovereign; all the tow⟨n⟩ besides could not have kept you.

America[1] now fills every mouth, and some heads; and a little of it shall come into my letter. I do not much like the news. Our troops have indeed the superiority, five and twenty hundred have driven five thousand from their intrenchment but the Americans fought skilfully; had coolness enough in the battle to carry off their men; and seem to have retreated orderly for they were not persued. They want nothing but confidence in their leaders and familiarity with danger. Our business is to persue their main army, and disperse it by a decisive battle and then waste the country till they sue for peace. If we make war by parties and detachments, dislodge them from one place, and exclude them from another, we shall by a local, gradual, and ineffectual war, teach them our own knowledge, harden their obstinacy, and strengthen their confidence, and at last come to fight on equal terms of skill and bravery, without equal numbers.

Mrs Williams[2] wrote me word that you had honoured her with a visit, and *behaved lovely*.

Mr Thrale left off digging his pool, I suppose for want of water. The first thing to be done is by digging in three or four places to try how near the springs will rise to the surface; for though we cannot hope to be always full, we must be sure never to be dry.

Poor Sir L⟨yn⟩ch[3] (!) I am sorry for him. It is sad to give a family of children no pleasure but by dying. It was said of Otho. Hoc tantum fecit nobile quod periit.[4] It may be changed to Sir ⟨Lynch⟩, hoc tantum fecit utile.

427.—1. The battle of Bunker's Hill, 17 June. Horace Walpole, writing on 3 Aug., calls it an 'equivocal success'.

2. See 422*a*.   3. 'Sir Lynch Cotton (my Uncle)' HLP.

4. Ausonius, *De XII Caesaribus*: 'His death was his only noble act'; Otho committed suicide.

If I could do Mr Carter any good at Oxford, I could easily stop there, for through it, if I go by Birmingham I am likely to pass; but the place is now a sullen solitude. Whatever can be done, I am ready to do; but our operations must for the present be at London.

I am, Madam, Your most humble servant,

August 1. 1775   Sam: Johnson

428. Lichfield. W. 2 Aug. '75. Mrs. Thrale.

Lichfield.—1788, No. 137.

Madam   Lichfield August 2. 17⟨75⟩

I dined to day at Stowhill, and am come away to write my letter. Never surely was I such a writer before. Do you keep my letters? I am not of your opinion that I shall not like to read them hereafter, for though there is in them not much history of mind or any thing else, they will, I hope, always be in some degree the records of a pure and blameless friendship, and in some hours of langour and sadness may revive the memory of more cheerful times.

Why you should suppose yourself not desirous hereafter to read the history of your own mind[1] I do not see. Twelve years on which you now look, as on a vast expanse of life will probably be passed over uniformly and smoothly, with very little perception of your progress, and with very few remarks upon the way. That accumulation of knowledge which you promise to yourself, by which the future is to look back upon the present, with the superiority of manhood to infancy, will perhaps never be attempted, or never will be made, and you will find as millions have found before you, that forty five[2] has made little sensible addition to thirty three.

As the body after a certain time gains no increase of height, and little of strength, there is likewise a period though more variable by external causes, when the mind commonly attains

---

428.—1. For J's insistence on the importance of recording 'the state of your own mind', and for his aspirations to keep a journal, see references at *L* ii. 217. 'A man loves to review his own mind' (*L* iii. 228).

2. It was a commonplace that 45 was the limit of human improvement. See *L* iv. 115, 432, for Dean Barnard's verses on the theme: 'I lately thought no man alive Could e'er improve past forty-five, And ventured to assert it. The observation was not new', &c.

its stationary point, and very little advances its powers of reflection, judgement, and ratiocination. The body may acquire new modes of motion, or new dexterities of mechanick operation, but its original strength receives not improvement; the mind may be stored with new languages, or new sciences, but its power of thinking remains nearly the same, and unless it attains new subjects of meditation, it commonly produces thoughts of the same force and the same extent, at very distant intervals of life, as the tree unless a foreign fruit be ingrafted gives year after year productions of the same form and the same flavour.

By intellectual force or strength of thought is meant the degree of power which the mind possesses of surveying the subject of meditation with its circuit of concomitants, and its train of dependence.

Of this power which all observe to be very different in different minds, part seems the gift of nature, and part the acquisition of experience. When the powers of nature have attained their intended energy, they can be no more advanced. The shrub can never become a tree. And it is not unreasonable to suppose that ⟨they⟩ are before the middle of life in their full vigour.

Nothing then remains but practice and experience; and perhaps why they do so little may be worth enquiry.

But I have just looked and find it so late, that I will enquire against the next post night.

I am, Madam, Your most humble Servant
Sam: Johnson

429. Lichfield. Sa. 5 Aug. '75. Mrs. Thrale.

Morgan.—1788, No. 138.

Dear Madam

Instead of forty reasons for my return one is sufficient; That you wish for my company.[1] I purpose to write no more

429.—1. HLP printed a letter dated 9 Aug. It is of doubtful authenticity, but a postscript, 'Sophy is very sick, and we all wish you would come home', is no doubt genuine. I find no actual evidence that J was at S'm before 17 Aug. (C 129); but the lack of further letters suggests an earlier return. We hear nothing of visits to B'm or O'd.

till you see me. The Ladies at Stowhill, and Greenhill[2] are unanimously of opinion, that it will be best to take a post-chaise, and not be troubled with the vexations of a common carriage. I will venture to suppose the Ladies at Streatham to be of the same mind.

You will now expect to be told why you will not be so much wiser as you expect when you have lived twelve years longer.

It is said and said truly, that Experience is the best teacher, and it is supposed that as life is lengthened, experience is encreased. But a closer inspection of human life will discover that time often passes without any incident which can much enlarge knowledge or rectify judgement. When we are young, we learn much, because we are universally ignorant, we observe everything because every ⟨thing⟩ is new. But after some years the occurrences of daily life are exhausted; one day passes like another, in the same scene of appearances, in the same course of transactions; we have to do what we have often done, and what we do not try because we do not wish to do much better, we are told what we already know, and therefore what repetition cannot make us know with greater certainty.

He that has early learned much, perhaps seldom makes with regard to life and manners much addition to his knowledge, Not only because as more is known there is less to learn, but because a mind stored with images and principles, turns inwards for its own entertainment, and is employed in sorting those ideas which run into confusion, and in recollecting those which are stealing away, practices by which wisdom may be kept but not gained. The merchant who was at first busy in acquiring money, ceases to grow richer, from the time when he make it his business only to count it.

Those who have families or employments are engaged in business of little difficulty but of great importance, requiring rather assiduity of practice than subtilty of speculation, occupying the attention with images too bulky for refinement, and too obvious for research. The right is already

429.—2. These ladies must be Mrs. Cobb and Miss Adey. Mr. Laithwaite of L'd tells me that their house, 'The Friary', is in or near the 'small, rather indefinite, area' known as Green Hill.

discontented that I wrote only Madam[3] to her, and dear Madam to Mrs Williams. Without any great dearness in the comparison,[4] Williams is I think, the dearer of the two. I am glad that she mends, but I am afraid she cannot get the start of the season, and Winter will come before she is prepared for it.

But at Streatham there are dears and dears, who before this letter reaches them will be at Brighthelmston, wherever they be, may they have no uneasiness but for want of me.

Now you are gone I wonder how long you design to stay, pray let me know when you write to Lichfield, for I have not lost hope of coming to you, yet that purpose may chance to fail. But my comfort is, that you cannot charge me with forgetting you when I am away. You perhaps do not think how eagerly I expect the post.

M^{rs} ⟨Langton⟩[5] grows old, and has lost much of her undulation and mobility. Her voice likewise is spoiled. She can come upon the stage now only for her own benefit. But Juliet is airy and cheerful, and has I hope done lamenting the inconstancy of Man. My Mistress is represented as unable to bear them company. There was not time for many questions, and no opportunity of winding and winding them, as Mr Richardson[6] has it, so as to get truth out without questions. I do not indeed know that I am any great Winder. I suspect a Winder to be always a Man vacant, and commonly little-minded. I think my dear little Mistress no great proficient at winding, though she could wind if she would, contemnit potius quam nescit.[7]

553.—3. Cf. 262 for Miss Langton's indignation on the same ground. In Trollope's *The Duke's Children* (1880), ch. 13, Mrs. Finn regards a hostile letter from the Duke of Omnium, written in the third person, as 'worse even than if he had called her, Madam without an epithet'. For some discussion of these fine shades see RWC on 'The Formal Parts of Johnson's Letters' in *Essays on the Eighteenth Century*, Oxford 1945.

4. The comma might mislead a modern reader; 'in the comparison'(we should rather say 'by comparison') of course belongs to what follows.

5. Suppressed in 1788, and illegible; but HLP's supplement is certain. She adds: 'A Joke—She was too fond of theatrical conversation.—It teized Mr. Johnson to hear her.' For Mrs. L and her daughter see 552.

6. *Sir Charles Grandison* (ed. 1753), i. 36 (258): 'I have winded and winded about him . . . but all to no purpose.'

7. The late Prof. E. Bensly referred me to Tacitus, *De Oratoribus* 2: omni eruditione imbutus contemnebat potius litteras quam nesciebat, 'was rather scornful than ignorant of literature'.

Dr Taylor desires always to have his compliments sent. He is, in his usual way very busy,—getting a Bull to his cows and a Dog to his bitches. His waterfall runs very well. Old Shakespeare is dead and he wants to buy another horse for his mares. He is one of those who finds every hour *something new to wish or to enjoy*.[8]

Boswel[9] while he was here saw Keddleston and the Silkmils, and took Chatsworth in his way home. He says, his Wife does not love me quite well yet, though we have made a formal peace. He kept his journal very diligently, but then what was there to journalise. I should be glad to see what he says of ⟨   ⟩.[10] I think I told you that I took him to Ilam.

Why should you suspect me of forgetting lilly lolly?[11] Now you will see the Shellys, and perhaps hear something about the Cottons,[12] and you will bathe, and walk, and dress, and dance and who knows how little you will think on,

Madam, Your most humble servant

Michaelmass day 1777 Ashbourn.   Sam: Johnson

553a. Brighthelmston. Th. 2 Oct. '77. From Mrs. Thrale to J at Ashbourne (see note on 553*b*).

Not traced.—*Brighton Herald* 17 Oct. 1857.

Here we are, not very elegantly accommodated, but wishing sincerely for you to share either our pleasure or our distresses. 'Tis fine bathing, with rough breakers, and my Master longs to see you exhibit your strength in opposing them, and bids me press you to come, for he is tired of living so long

553.—8. 'Blest madman, who could every hour employ / With something new to wish or to enjoy' (Dryden, *Absalom and Achitophel* 553).

9. Erased and restored, as in 551.

10. The suppression is effected by a thorough erasure, on which are twelve asterisks (not nine as in 1788); these may indicate the number of letters. HLP's suppressions (on which see RWC, 'Piozzi on Thrale', *NQ* 23 Oct. 1943) are often capricious, so that any conjecture based on motive is precarious. Her own supplement, 'Dr. Taylor and his beasts', seems too long; but 'Taylor's beasts' is nearly 12 letters. It is in any case likely to be a mere guess, and there seems no great motive for suppression; see, however, 547. I have thought of 'Chatsworth', which would fit well with Keddlestone and Ilam. Dr. Pottle very ingeniously guesses 'the Duchess'— of Argyle, see 552.

11. See 548*a*, and for the whole story Hayward 1861², ii. 76, quoted by Hill.

12. For the Shelley–Cotton connexion see *Th.* 298.

553a.—This letter was in the possession of Cecilia Thrale (Mostyn) and was sold at her death. I quote it from C 155.

without you; and Burney says if you dont come soon he shall be gone, and he does love you, or he is a vile ——. But one woman in the water today,

> '*Una* et haec audax'

Was your most faithful and obliged
H. L. Thrale.

553b. Brighthelmston. Sa. ⟨? 4 Oct. '77.⟩ From Mrs. Thrale to J at Ashbourne.

Address (see note): To Doctor Johnson at the Rev^d Dr Taylors Ashbourne Derbyshire. *Postmark*: LITCHFIELD.

R 540.75—

Dear Sir   Brighthelmston Saturday Night.

Lest you should not have had my last Letters, and as you kindly say you love to hear from me, I write again, though I am not well tonight. We go on how we can, these nasty Lodgings gave me Cold, but we get into our own house on Wednesday next. Miss Owen is with us, so is Doctor Burney, but nobody can supply your Place—& my Master says so—he longs for you more than I do, for I see no Wit in coming to be distress'd for a Habitation; he does I suppose or he would not have been here.

Dr Pepys sucks his hat as Relhan did; the Master is tutoring his Young Wife, in the Neighbourhood of London, Mrs Smith *works at* Dr Burney, but he says he don't like Conversation out of an Alembick, Lord Lucan is here but not his Lady, Miss Burgoyne is here for a Week very ill indeed: Mrs Nesbitt's palpitation is accompanied by Spasms now both in her Throat & Side; I think a rigid Milk Regimen might alleviate, but the Doctors prescribe Heating Medecines, Oyl of Amber, &c. & they are most likely to be right. I really am not well myself, my Throat is sore, and if People offer *me Cake* I am inclined to *push them away.*

Farewell Dear Sir let us hear from you soon, & see you before it is long, & never see with less kindness than at present the Letters of Your most faithful Servant
H: L: Thrale.

554. Ashbourne. M. 6 Oct. '77. Mrs. Thrale (Brighthelmston).

Adam.—1788, No. 183.

Dear Madam

You are glad that I am absent, and I am glad that you are sick.[1] When you went away what did you do with your Aunt? I am glad she liked my Susey, I was always a Susey, when

553b.—The postmark seems to indicate that the letter was sent to L'd and forwarded by LP. The original is complete, the direction on the fourth page as usual. The original direction to L'd has disappeared, no doubt because it was on a franked cover. (HT always, I think, writes 'Derbys', not 'Derbyshire'.)

554.—1. 'For Harriet' HLP.

nobody else was a Susy. How have you managed at your new place?[2] Could you all get lodgings in one house, and meat at one table? Let me hear the whole series of misery, for as Dr Young says, *I love horrour*.[3]

Methinks you are now a great way off, and, if I come, I have a great way to come to you. And then the Sea is so cold, and the rooms are so dull. Yet I do love to hear the sea roar and my Mistress talk. For when she talks Ye Gods, how she will talk.[4] I wish I were with you, but we are now near half the length of England asunder. It is frightful to think how much time must pass between writing this letter and receiving an answer, if any answer were necessary. Taylor is now going to have a Ram, and then after aries and taurus we shall have gemini. His oats are now in the wet, here is a deal of rain. Mr Langdon bought at Nottingham fair fifteen tun of Cheese, which at an ounce apiece will suffice after dinner for 480000 men.[5] This all the news that the place affords. I purpose soon to be at Lichfield, but know not just when, having been defeated of my first design. When I come to town I am to be very busy about my Lives. Could not you do some of them for me?

I am glad Master huspelled you, and run you all on rucks,[6] and drove you about, and made you stir. Never be cross about it. Quiet and calmness you have enough of, a little hurry stirs life, and brushing o'er adds motion to the pool. Dryden.[7] Now *Pool*, bring[8] My Masters excavations into my head. I wonder how I shall like them, I should like not to see them, till we all see them together. He will have no waterfal to roar like the Doctors. I sat by it yesterday and read, Erasmus's Militis Christiani Enchiridion. Have you got that Book?

554.—2. 'Since their own house was not ready, they were forced to take uncomfortable lodgings for a few days' C 155. See 553a.

　　3. Not traced.　　　　　　　　4. From Lee's *The Rival Queens*. See on 294.

　　5. J reckons the ton at 2,000 lb., which was not uncommon at that time.

　　6. 'unspelled . . . rocks' 1788; HLP restores the text. The meaning is much the same as that of the second half of the sentence. For a full discussion see *TLS* 6 Dec. 1934; both words are in *OED*.

　　7. 'Dryden' is J's, not as one might be tempted to suppose a Piozzian interpolation. On the contrary, in 552, 'Ecl. x' is omitted in 1788. *Cymon and Iphigenia* 30: 'Nor Love is always of a vicious Kind, / But oft to virtuous Acts inflames the Mind, / Awakes the sleepy Vigour of the Soul, / And, brushing o'er, adds Motion to the Pool.'

　　8. 'brings' 1788.

Make my compliments to dear Queeny. I suppose she will dance at the rooms, and your heart will go one knows not how. I am

Dearest and dearest Lady Your most humble servant
Ashbourne. Oct. 6. 1777   Sam: Johnson

554a. Brighton. Sa. 11 Oct. '77. From Mrs. Thrale to J at Ashbourne (see note on 553*b*).

Address: To Doctor Johnson at the Revd Dr Taylors in Ashburn Derby Shire. *Postmark*: LITCHFIELD.
R 540.76.—

Dear Sir   Brighton 11 : Octr 77.

If you love my Letters I am sure I love yours better, so there we are quit : It is a long Way from Ashbourne to Brighton, yet you will travel it I think; for as Seward says a Man must be somewhere, and The Sea roars away so finely that the King shall say 'Let him roar again, Let him roar again. Seward is not with us, but Murphy is; Dr Burney leaves us tomorrow; Mr Murphy & he like one another much, and who wonders at that, for if Murphy does tell a Story or quote a Couplet he does not says Burney speaking to me—mouth it out like *Your* Master in Chancery.

Doctor Pepys, *my* Master in Chancery's Brother grows duller & prouder every day since the Birth of his Daughter Lady Harriott Leslie—for so She is called. Boswell I suppose could tell why. The Shelleys are silly and civil as usual & the Company comes & goes but the height of the Season is over.

Old Mitchell looks plump and fills his Subscriptions, and writes Latin Pamphlets about America, but I cannot bear to be civil to him, my Master too looks rather colder on him than he did last year.

Dr Taylor's Cows and Bulls make a Figure even in the News papers we read here; Dr Delap asks us every day where you are, & though we always say at Ashburn, he is never a whit nearer knowing when one has done. How very odd it is that that Man should play well at Whist! I can sit and wonder at it.

I can write no more just now I am really so very sick—but 'tis no harm; so farewell Dear Sir, and come or write or something, for it is dismall to hear so seldom as we now must absolutely do. I am ever most faithfully Your Obedient Servant

H: L: Thrale.

555. Ashbourne. M. 13 Oct. '77. Mrs. Thrale (Brighthelmston).

Mrs. F. Bowman.—1788, No. 185.

Dear Madam

Yes I do love to hear from you.[1] Such pretty kind letters

555.—1. See 553*b*.

as you send. But it gives me great delight to find that my Master misses me. I begin to wish myself with you more than I should do if I were wanted less. It is a good thing to stay away till one's company is desired, but not so good to stay after it is desired.

You know, I have some work to do. I did not set to it very soon, and if I should go up to London with nothing done, what would be said, but that I was —— who can tell what? I therefore stay till I can bring something to stop their mouths, and then ——.

Though I am still at Ashbourne I receive your dear Letters that come to Lichfield, and you continue[2] that direction, for I think to get[3] thither as soon as I can.

One of the Does died yesterday, and I am afraid, her Fawn will be starved, I wish Miss Thrale had it to nurse, but the Doctor is now all for cattle, and minds very little either Does or Hens.

How did you and your Aunt part? Did you turn her out of doors to begin your journey, or did she leave you by her usual shortness of visits. I love to know how you go on.

I cannot but think on your kindness and my Masters. Life has upon the whole fallen short, very short, of my early expectation, but the acquisition of such a Friendship, at an age when new Friendships are seldom acquired, is something better than the general course of things gives Man a right to expect. I think on it with great delight, I am not very apt to be delighted.

I am, Madam Your most obedient Servant
Sam: Johnson

556. Ashbourne. Th. 16 Oct. '77. Mrs. Thrale.
A. Houghton.—1788, No. 186.

Dearest Lady

I am just going out and can write but little, how you should be long without a letter I know not, for I seldom miss

---

555.—2. 'continue' is imperative. Hill prints 'do you continue', perhaps needlessly
   3. My collator passed 'get', but a former owner of the MS. read 'go'.

a post. I purpose now to come to London as soon as I can, for I have a deal to look after, but hope I shall get through the whole business.

I wish you had told me your adventure, or told me nothing. Be civil to Lord ⟨Lucan⟩,[1] he seems to be a good kind of man. Miss may change her mind, and will change it, when she finds herself get more credit by dancing than by Whist,[2] and though she should continue to like as she likes now, the harm is none.

Do not yet begin, dear Madam, to think about *the last*.[3] You may well dance these dozen years, if you keep your looks as you have yet kept them, and I am glad that Hetty has no design to dance you down.

The poor Pools.[4] I am sorry for the Girl, she seems to be doomed before her time to weakness and solitude.[5] What is that Bedrider[6] the Supervisor? He will be up again. But life seems to be closing upon them.

I hope you still continue to be sick, and my dear Master to be well.

I am no sender of compliments, but take them once for all, and deliver them to be kept as rarities, by Miss Owen, Mrs. Nesbit, Miss Hetty, and Doctor Burney.

Still direct to Lichfield, for thither I am hastening, and from Lichfield to London, and from London, I hope to Brighthelmston, and from Brighthelmston qua terra patet.[7]

I am Dearest of all dear Ladies,

                    Your most humble Servant,

Ashbourne Oct. 16.   Sam: Johnson.

556.—1. So Lysons; the traces are consistent with J's initial *L*.

2. 'Miss Thrale never could be brought to love dancing' Baretti.

3. Hill sees here an allusion to the famous passage in the concluding *Idler*.

4. The word is fairly clear, and is confirmed by HLP ('Pooles') and Lysons.

5. J wrote 'solidude', not I think 'solictude', i.e. 'solicitude', which is the reading of 1788.

6. 'Bedrider' may equally be 'Bedrides'. HLP corrects to 'What is it that', and notes 'bedrids, or makes bedridden'. J does not very often capitalize a verb; but 'bedrides' is an unusual word. *OED* does not recognize *bedrider*, nor any verbal back-formation from *bedridden* (which is not a true participle).

7. 'Qua terra patet, fera regnat Erinnys.' See on 318.

556a. Brighthelmston. Th. 16 ⟨Oct.' 77⟩. From Mrs. Thrale to J at Ashbourne.

R 540.77—

Dear Sir

What in the World is become of you? I know not where to direct, so I enclose my Letter to Mʳ Levett and let him manage for me: We go on here as usual, invite Company to Dinner & daudle in the Rooms at Night, yet my Master & Miss Owen call that Pleasure, & I like it better now I play at Cards, it is a *little* more interesting than before. Dʳ Delap has laid fast hold of Murphy, & set him to read a new Play that he is preparing for the Stage—he takes it to the bathing Machines, and reads it to the roaring of the Sea: 'tis all about Hercules I hear & Dejanira.

I have seen the famous J. Wilkes, he came hither to wait on Murphy: I like him not: he professed himself a Lyar and an Infidel, and I see no Merit in being either. He told a parcel of Stories which he said were as well to be thought false as true & such sort of Gabble from an old decrepit Wretch with one foot in the Grave gave me nothing but Offence, so we parted.

Mʳ Beauclerck is here, & is said to be a charming Creature too; Foote is gone or else one might have written Verses on them like those on Homer, Virgil and Milton—but their Bons Mots still circulate about the Town & about the Rooms, & we are all happy to retail them & to hear them retailed.

Mʳ Thrale is come in to my Room & has read so far of my Letter,—why says he These are the Persons we are all running after—Ay quoth I, and old Satan is the Person that even *they* are running after; so you see clearly what good humour I am in.

Hamilton keeps asking after you all day long: You have had many Enquiries made indeed concerning you, Delap never has done with the Subject. Burney is gone & Seward not arrived. Old Blakeney puffs his Cheeks as usual. Queeney will not dance, and the People twit me that I will not let her, because I dance myself—even Miss Owen who lives with us believes that to be the Case from Queeney's Manner & management. Farewell & believe me ever Most faithfully Yours

H: L: Thrale.

556b. Brighthelmston. Sa. 18 Oct. ⟨'77⟩. From Mrs. Thrale to J at Ashbourne.

R 540.78—

Dear Sir   Brighthelmston 18: October

You are very kind with your Letters & your Friendship, and we have great Reason to be very proud of both.

I had a shocking Accident befell me just after your Cover of yesterday was freed; it was the last Thing I did before I went down to dinner, where I hastily swallowed a Chicken Bone that stuck so long in the Passage as to make it necessary to send for a Surgeon with the Whalebone & Sponge from which

I expected immediate Relief, & my Spirits did not suffer though my Throat did, till one ineffectual Effort had been tried: I was then alarm'd of Course, but a second Operation forced it down, and removed all Danger at once.

The Throat is still excessively sore and I feel just as I have often felt with a common sore Throat & that's all. Miss Owen's comical Indignation at the Bustle made by all our Acquaintance sending & calling &c. made me laugh today—Why now says She in our Country there are no Surgeons at hand, & one has a hasty Pudden made on the Occasion, & if one can't eat *that*, one may choak *I think*.

Well when I was at the worst I would scarcely have changed Places with Mrs Burney: She is the Doctors second Wife you know, & had a fine Daughter —a great Fortune—by her former husband, whom She has kept some Years in France and about two or three Months ago She went over to fetch this Girl home, and I have seen some of her Letters to her Husband expressing the happiness She was enjoying at Paris in Company of this fine Daughter: how She delayed her Return because this Daughter so introduced her into high Company &c., but no sooner was Burney gone home to his Family—(for he has four or five grown-up Girls of his own by another Wife that live with *him*) —but he writes me word that Mrs Burney was coming over from Dieppe to Brighthelmston *all alone*, in great Distress, her fine Daughter having eloped from her at Paris—& so in fact She *did* come yesterday, expecting to find the D^r with us, but he was gone; & greater, & more real Distress have I seldom seen. Poor Thing! but She resolved not to go home however, but to a Friend's House where She would stay She said till her Husband came to fetch her, for She could not bear to go tell *her Story* among his Girls—& receive their Consolations. So here's a Story that will fill your Mind for the Moment as it did mine fifty Times fuller than all the Chat of the Steyne, or the Small Talk of the Rooms, and that touches my heart ten times nearer than Dr Delap's Death of Dejanira that he persecutes Mr Murphy with.

Wilkes has invited Mr Thrale to a Dinner of Rakes—Beauclerck, Lord Kelly & the Men of *Worth & honour* that are here, & here are plenty too: says Murphy looking at me—*he dares not go.* I would not have him go said I gravely; I am not fond of trying my Power over my husband, nor wish to exert it at all for a new Topknot—but if I could keep him out of such Company —I should think I did him an Act of real Friendship. So who says I have no Spirit Mr Johnson? I got severely rallied for my Prudery & at last lost my Labour for he does go, but I know *I* did right & they may all look to themselves. You know me most faithfully Y^rs H: L: T.

557. Lichfield. W. 22 Oct. '77. Mrs. Thrale (Brighthelmston).

Sotheby 10 May 1949—1788, No. 187.

Dear Madam,

I am come at last to Lichfield, and am really glad that I am got away from a place where there was indeed no evil but very little good. You may I believe write once to Lichfield after you receive this, but after that, it will be best to direct to London.

Your throat is, I suppose, well by this time. Poor Mrs. ⟨Burney⟩[1] it is impossible to think on without great compassion. Against a blow so sudden and so unexpected, I wonder that she supports herself. The consolations of ⟨Burney's⟩ girls must indeed be painful. She had intended to enjoy the triumph of her daughter's superiority. They were prepared to wish them both ill, and their wishes are gratified. There is in this event a kind of system of calamity, a conflagration of the soul. Every avenue of pain is invaded at once. Pride is mortified, tenderness is wounded, hope is disappointed. Whither will the poor Lady run from herself?

My visit to Stowhill has been paid. I have seen there a collection of Misery. Mrs. Aston paralytick, Mrs. Walmsley lame, Mrs. Hervey blind, and I think another Lady deaf. Even such is life.

I hope dear Mrs. Aston is a little better; it is however very little. She was, I believe, glad to see me, and to have any body glad to see me is a great pleasure.

I will tell while I think on it, that I really saw with my own eyes Mr. Chaplin of Lincolnshire's letter for Taylor's Cow, accompanied with a draught on Hoare for one hundred and twenty six pounds to pay for her. Frank says the young Bull is not quite so big as the old one. Taylor, I think, says he is bigger.

I have seen but one new place this journey, and that is Leek in the Morlands.[2] An old Church, but a poor Town.

The days grow short, and we have frosts; but I am in all weathers, Madam,

　　　　　　　　　　　Your most humble Servant
Lichfield Oct. 22, 1777.　　　　　　　Sam: Johnson.

557.—1. 'Burney' HLP and Lysons, confirmed by 560 and 556*b*. On 'her daughter's' HLP notes 'her own daughter's'. For the 'calamity' see 556*b* and Index II.

2. That is 'Moorlands', a district of North Staffordshire.

558. Lichfield. Sa. 25 Oct. '77. Mrs. Thrale (Brighthelmston).

Adam.—1788, No. 188.

Dear Madam   Lichfield Oct. 25. 1777

Cholmondely's[1] story shocks me, if it be true, which I can hardly think, for I am utterly unconscious of it, I am very sorry, and very much ashamed.

I am here for about a week longer, and then I purpose to hasten to London. How long do you stay at Brighthelmston? Now the Company is gone why should you be the lag. The Season of Brewing will soon be here, if it ⟨is⟩ not already come. We have here cold weather, and loud winds.

Miss Porter is better than is usual, and Mrs Aston is, I hope, not worse, but she is very bad, and being, I fancy, about sixty eight, is it likely that she will ever be better?

It is really now a long time that we have been writing and writing, and yet how small a part of our minds have we written? We shall meet, I hope, soon, and talk it out.

You are not yet sixty eight, but it will come, and perhaps you may then sometimes remembe⟨r⟩ me.

In the mean time do not think to be young beyond the time, do not play Agnes,[2] and do not grow old before your time nor suffer yourself to be too soon driven from the stage. You can yet give pleasure by your appearance, show yourself therefore, and be pleased by pleasing. It is not now too soon to be wise, nor is it yet too late to be gay.

Streatham is now I suppose the eighth wonder of the world, I long to see it, but do not intend to go till, as I once said before, my Master and You and I, and no body else shall be with us, perambulate it together.

Cicely, I warrant you, will do well enough. I am glad you are so sick—and nobody to pity—Now for another pretty little Girl—But we know not what is best.

I am Dearest Lady Your most humble servant

                              Sam: Johnson

Pay my respects to Miss Owen

558.—1. The famous story of J's rudeness and apology is not dated in *Anecdotes*, from which JB quotes it, *L* iv. 345. But in *Tb* (189) it appears in a collection of anecdotes written Dec. '77, and it was no doubt in a lost letter of HLT to J, to which he now replies.

2. 'Agnes in Moliere's play' HLP: *L'École des Femmes*. Cf. 725.

559. Lichfield. M. 27 Oct. '77. Mrs. Thrale (Brighthelmston).

Adam.—1788, No. 189.

Dear Madam

You talk of writing and writing as if you had all the writing to yourself. If our Correspondence were printed I am sure Posterity, for Posterity is always the authours favourite, would say that I am a good writer too. Anch' io sonô Pittore.[1] To sit down so often with nothing to say, to say something so often, almost without consciousness of saying, and without any remembrance of having said, is a power of which I will not violate my modesty by boasting, but I do not believe that every body has it.

Some when they write to their friends are all affection, some are wise and sententious, some strain their powers for efforts of gayety, some write news, and some write secrets, but to make a letter without affection, without wisdom, without gayety, without news, and without a secret is, doubtless, the great epistolick art.[2]

In a Man's Letters you know, Madam, his soul lies naked, his letters are only the mirrour of his breast, whatever passes within him is shown undisguised in its natural process. Nothing is inverted, nothing distorted, you see systems in their elements, you discover actions in their motives.

Of this great truth sounded by the knowing to the ignorant, and so echoed by the ignorant to the knowing, what evidence have you now before you. Is not my soul laid open in these veracious pages? do not you see me reduced to my first principles? This is the pleasure of corresponding with a friend, where doubt and distrust have no place, and everything is said as it is thought. The original Idea is laid down in its simple purity, and all the supervenient conceptions, are spread over it stratum super stratum, as they happen to be formed. These are the letters by which souls are united, and by which Minds naturally in unison move each other as they are moved themselves. I know, dearest Lady, that in the

---

559.—1. According to King's *Classical Quotations* the attribution to Correggio is doubtful.

2. For J's serious views on 'the great epistolick art' see quotations in Hill's *Lives* iii. 206 (*Pope* ¶ 273).

perusal of this such is the consanguinity of our intellects, you will be touched as I am touched. I have indeed concealed nothing from you, nor do I expect ever to repent of having thus opened my heart.

I am, Madam, Your most humble servant,
Lichfield Oct. 27. 1777   Sam: Johnson

560. Lichfield. W. 29 Oct. '77. Mrs. Thrale (Brighthelmston).

Lichfield.—1788, No. 190.

Dear Madam

Though after my last letter I might justly claim an interval of rest, yet I write again to tell you that for this turn you will hear but once more from Lichfield. This day is Wednesday, on Saturday I shall write again and on Monday I shall set out to seek adventures, for you know, None but the Brave deserve the Fair.[1]

On Monday we hope to see Birmingham, the seat of the mechanick arts, and know not whether our next stage will be Oxford, the mansion of the liberal arts, or London the residence of all the arts together. The Chymists call the world Academia Paracelsi,[2] my ambition is to be his fellow student, to see the works of Nature, and hear the lectures of Truth. To London therefore—London may perhaps fill me, and I hope to fill my part of London.

In the mean time let me continue to keep the part which I have had so long in your kindness and my Master's, for if that should grow less I know not where to find that which may supply the diminution. But I hope what I have been so happy as to gain, I shall have the happiness of keeping.

I always omitted to tell you that Lucy's Maid[3] took the worm powder with strict regularity, but with no great effect. Lucy has had several letters from you, but cannot prevail on herself to write. But she is very grateful.

560.—1. Dryden, *Alexander's Feast* ('deserves').

2. My 'physical friends' are unable to find me the origin of this phrase. Yet J has it elsewhere (*Life of Pope* ¶ 291), and it must have been notorious. P was just the kind of impostor to claim the material universe as the proper study of his 'university'.

3. See 536.

Mrs Walmsley has been at Stowhill, and has invited me when I come to Bath, to be at her house. Poor Mrs Aston either mends not at all, or not perceptibly; but she does ⟨not⟩ seem to grow worse.

Last year you gained 14000L. I long to know what are the prices of malt and hops, and what is prospect for the year approaching. I hope Master will soon put Viri's money into the Funds, and pay Lady Lade and her son, if that be not done already. I suppose Sir John is by this time recovered, and perhaps grown wiser, than to shake his constitution so violently a second time.[4]

Poor Mrs. ⟨Burney⟩![5] One cannot think on her but with great compassion. But it is impossible for her husband's daughters not to triumph, and the husband will feel, as Rochefoucault[6] says, *something that does not displease him.* You and I, who are neutral, whom her happiness could not have depressed, may be honestly sorry.

I am Dear Madam Your most humble servant
Sam: Johnson.

561. Lichfield. M. 3 Nov. (misdated Oct.) '77. Mrs. Thrale (Brighthelmston).

Sotheby 30 Jan. 1918 (not seen).—1788, No. 182; quotation in Maggs's Cat. 365, 1918, 416.

Dear Madam   Lichfield, October 3, 1777.
This is the last time that I shall write, in this excursion, from this place. Tomorrow I shall be, I hope, at Birmingham; from which place I shall do my best to find the nearest way home. I come home, I think, worse than I went; and do not

---

560.—4. HLP suppressed this paragraph except the last sentence, in which she suppressed 'Sir John'.

5. The first and last letters are legible.

6. Rochefoucauld, *Réflexions* § 105 (in the edition of 1692): 'Dans l'adversité de nos meilleurs amis, nous trouvons toûjours quelque chose qui ne nous déplaist pas.' Swift's *Verses on the Death of Dr. Swift* were 'Occasioned by reading the following Maxim in Rochfoucault' (as above). Lines 7–10 of that poem are: 'In all Distresses of our Friends / We first consult our private Ends; / While Nature, kindly bent to ease us, / Points out some Circumstance to please us.'

561.—Maggs's cataloguer, who clearly referred to the original, confirms the erroneous date, which caused HPL to misplace the letter.

like the state of my health. But, *vive hodie*,[1] make the most[2] of life. I hope to get better, and —— sweep the cobwebs.[3] But I have sad nights. Mrs. Aston has sent me to Mr. Green to be cured.

Did you see Foote at Brighthelmstone?—Did you think he would so soon be gone?—Life, says Falstaff, is a shuttle.[4] He was a fine fellow in his way; and the world is really impoverished by his sinking glories.[5] Murphy ought to write his life, at least to give the world a Footeana.[6] Now, will any of his contemporaries bewail him? Will Genius change *his sex* to weep?[7] I would really have his life written with diligence.

It will be proper for me to work pretty diligently now for some time. I hope to get through, though so many weeks have passed. Little lives and little criticisms may serve.

Having been in the country so long, with very little to detain me, I am rather glad to look homewards.

I am, &c.

561.1. Th. 6 Nov. '77. Mrs. Thrale.

Lord Charnwood—1788, but cancelled in proof. Broadley, *Dr. Johnson and Mrs. Thrale* 1910, 113, from the proof-sheets then in his possession.

Dear Lady

I am this evening come to Boltcourt, after a ramble in which I have had very little pleasure and now I have not

561.—1. Martial i. 16: Sera nimis vita est crastina, vive hodie, 'Tomorrow is too late, live today'.

2. 'best' Maggs.

3. Miss M. H. Dodds came to my rescue here with a childish recollection of a nursery rhyme about an old woman with a broom. 'Old woman, old woman, old woman', said I / 'Whither, ah! whither, whither so high?' / 'Oh! I'm sweeping the cobwebs off the sky.' Miss Dodds could give no source; her contribution to learning is the more remarkable. I find it in J. O. Halliwell (Phillipps)'s *Nursery Rhymes* 1842, 72, with a note of the source as *Musick's Handmaid* 1673. Almost the same phrase recurs 839.

4. *Merry Wives* v. i.

5. As of the setting sun?

6. *CBEL* cites an anonymous memoir, 1777, of 'Samuel Foote, Esq., the English Aristophanes', which as it comprehends his 'Bon Mots, Repartees, and Good Things' might have borne J's title. No formal biography appeared until 1805.

7. Hill refers to *L* iii. 374 for the famous interview in which J detected a would-be Pindar who, in compliment to a Duchess, made 'genius' feminine. But that was in '79. The words here look like a quotation, but I have not found it.

You to talk to, nor My Master. I carried bad health out,
and have brought it home. What else I bring is abundance
of compliments to You from every body. Lucy I cannot
persuade to write to You, but she is very much obliged.

Be pleased to write word to Streatham that they should
send me the Biographia Britannica, as soon as is possible.

I believe I owe Queeny a Letter, for which I hope she
will forgive me. I am apt to omit things of more importance.

Let me hear from You now quick. Our letters will pass
and repass like shuttlecocks.

I am Dearest Madam Your most humble Servant
Boltcourt. Nov. 6. 1777   Sam: Johnson

561.a. Brighthelmstone. Sa. 8 (misdated 7) Nov. ⟨'77⟩.
From Mrs. Thrale.

R 540.79—

Dear Sir   Brighthelmstone Saturday 7: Novʳ
   Today I received your two obliging Letters, one from Litchfield and the
other from London: I am sorry the State of your health does not please you
but as Baretti used to say of the Dyce at Back Gammon—We must have them
as they are. Mʳˢ Nesbitt has her Palpitation now once a fortnight, attended
with great Pain & Spasms; She is now ill in Bed after it, yet it seems not to
affect her general Health. She grows fat, looks very well and has good
Appetite, Rest, &c. between whiles. I begin to think the less Medecine is
used in Chronical Cases the better, you and She may lose all your Complaints
at the Age of 72 like Mʳ Scrase & begin the World anew.
   Did I tell you that my Master grew ashamed of his Wife's Peruke since we
came here & made me pull it off & dress my own hair, which looks so well now
it is dressed that he begins innocently to wonder why he ever let me wear a
Wig. I remember well however the why, the when, & the where. My Mother
thought it a good Scheme to keep young married Women at home, like the old
Story of singing the Cat's Tail, it is now laid aside again—I mean the Wig, and
I did think to have burnt it for Joy of the great News from America but there
comes no Confirmation of it they say.
   My Master stands over me and bids me say, that if you are pretty *fresh* and
well, and have a Mind to save his Credit, and take a frolick, you might come
hither on Fryday the fourteenth of this Month, dine with us on the Saturday,
with Beauclerck on Sunday, Hamilton on Monday, & return with us to
Streatham on the Tuesday the eighteenth which is the Day we have fixed
upon to leave this Place. Mʳ Thrale says you will not understand what is
meant by *saving his Credit*, but it is because he had promised those two
Gentlemen the Pleasure of seeing you this Season.

Mr Thrale is *fresh and well himself* I am sure, he hunts and eats and sleeps very comfortably, and has got the *Vive hodie* pretty strongly impressed upon *him*: we spend our Money merrily I know, I fret sometimes about it, but I never grumble: and desire you will make no Answer[1] to this part of my Letter, for Prosperity fanneth Wrath, & I caught my Master listening this very Day at the Door when Scrase & I had a Teste a Teste.

Adieu and believe me ever Most faithfully your humble Servant

H: L: Thrale.

562. M. 10 Nov. (misdated Oct.) '77. Mrs. Thrale (Brighthelmston).

Newton.—1788, No. 184.

Dear Madam

And so supposing that I might come to town and neglect to give you notice, or thinking some other strange thought, but certainly thinking wrong, you fall to writing about me to Tom Davies, as if he could tell you any thing that I would not have you know. As soon as I came hither I let you know of my arrival, and the consequence is that I am summoned to Brighthelmston through storms and cold and dirt and all the hardships of wintry journeys. You know my natural dread of all those evils, yet to shew my Master an example of compliance, and to let you know how much I long to see you, and to boast how little I give way to disease, my purpose is to be with you on Friday.

I am sorry for poor Nezzy,[1] and hope she will in time be better; I hope the same for myself. The rejuvenescency of Mr. Scrase gives us both reason to hope, and therefore both of us rejoice in his recovery. I wish him well besides as a friend to my Master.

I am just come home from not seeing my Lord Mayor's shew, but I might have seen at least part of it. But I saw Miss Wesley[2] and her Brothers. She sends her compliments. Mrs. Williams is come home, I think, a very little better.

561.1*a*.—1. This suggests that J's letters, which were addressed 'To Henry Thrale Esq', were liable to be read by him. Cf. 421*a*, where HLT writes that he had carried off one of J's letters to her in his pocket.

562.—This letter, like 561, was misdated by J and misplaced by HLP.
  1. Nesbit.
  2. Hill sought in vain for a spinster sister of John W. But no doubt Charles W's children are meant; see *Th.* 220.

Every body was an enemy to that Wig.[3]—We will burn it, and get drunk, for what is joy without drink. Wagers are laid in the city about our success, which is yet as the French call it, problematical.[4] Well, but seriously I think I shall be glad to see you in your own hair, but do not take too much time in combing, and twisting, and papering, and unpapering, and curling, and frizzing, and powdering, and getting out the powder, with all the other operations required in the cultivation of a head of hair. Yet let it be combed at least once in three months, on the quarter-day; I could wish it might be combed once at least in six weeks, if I were to indulge my wishes, but what are wishes without hopes, I should fancy the operation performed—one knows not when one has enough—perhaps—every morning.

    I am, Dearest Lady, Your most humble servant
Oct. 10. 1777   Sam: Johnson.

563. Th. 20 Nov. '77. Elizabeth Aston (Lichfield).
Address: To Mrs Aston Stow Hill Lichfield. Franked by Thrale.
Postmark: 20 NO.
Pembroke.—Croker's Boswell 1831, iv. 62.

Dear Madam,   London, Nov. 20, 1777.
    Through Birmingham and Oxford I got without any difficulty or disaster to London, though not in so short a time as I expected, for I did not reach Oxford before the second day. I came home very much incommoded by obstructed respiration, but by vigorous methods am something better. I have since been at Brighthelmston, and am now designing to settle.
    Different things, Madam, are fit for different people. It is fit for me to settle, and for you to move. I wish I could hear of you at Bath,[1] but I am afraid that is hardly to be expected

562.—3. Baretti's story (quoted by Hill), that she gave up her wig for Piozzi's sake, seems to be as worthless as most of his comments. There is no evidence that they met before '78 (C 158).

4. The word came to English from French. It is in J's dictionary, with quotations from White (probably Francis W, a seventeenth-century bishop), Boyle, and Swift. But in the sense in which it is here used, though common in the seventeenth century, it seems to be rare in the eighteenth; *OED* has only one quotation (1793) and one for '——ic' (1768), which is not in J's.

563.—1. Her sister Mrs. Walmesley lived at Bath.

from your resolute inactivity. My next hope is that you will endeavour to grow well where you are. I cannot help thinking that I saw a visible amendment between the time when I left you to go to Ashbourne, and the time when I came back. I hope you will go on mending and mending, to which exercise and cheerfulness will very much contribute. Take care therefore, dearest Madam, to be busy and cheerful.

I have great confidence in the care and conversation of dear Mrs. Gastrel. It is very much the interest of all that know her, that she should continue well, for she is one of few people that has the proper regard for those that are sick. She was so kind to me that I hope I never shall forget it, and if it be troublesome to you to write I shall hope that she will do me another act of kindness by answering this letter, for I beg that I may hear from you by some hand or another.

I am, Madam, Your most obedient servant,

Sam: Johnson.

564. Th. 20 Nov. '77. Lucy Porter (Lichfield).

Address: To Mrs Lucy Porter Lichfield. Franked by Thrale. *Postmark*: 20 NO.
Adam.—Croker's Boswell 1831, iv. 62.

Dear Love   London Nov. 20. 1777

You ordered me to write you word when I came home. I have been for some days at Brighthelmston and came back on Tuesday night.

You know that when I left you I was not well, I have taken physick very diligently and am perceptibly better, so much better that I hope by care and perseverance to recover, and see you again from time to time.

Mr Nollikens the statuary has had my direction to send you a cast of my head. I will pay the carriage when we meet. Let me know how you like it, and what the Ladies of your rout say to it. I have heard different opinions. I cannot think where you can put it.

I found every body here well. Miss[1] has a mind to be womanly, and her womanhood does not sit well upon her.

Please to make my compliments to all the Ladies and all

564.—1. Q was just thirteen years old.

the Gentlemen to whom I owe them, that is, to a great part
of the town.

I am, Dear Madam, Your most humble servant
Sam: Johnson

565. Tu. 25 Nov. '77. James Boswell (Edinburgh).

Not traced.—Boswell 1791, ii. 177 (Hill iii. 210).

Dear Sir

You will wonder, or you have wondered, why no letter has
come.from me. What you wrote at your return, had in it
such a strain of cowardly caution as gave me no pleasure.
I could not well do what you wished; I had no need[1] to vex
you with a refusal. I have seen Mr. ——,[2] and as to him have
set all right, without any inconvenience, so far as I know, to
you. Mrs. Thrale had forgot the story. You may now be at
ease.

And at ease I certainly wish you, for the kindness that you
showed in coming so long a journey to see me. It was pity
to keep you so long in pain, but, upon reviewing the matter,
I do not see what I could have done better than as I did.

I hope you found at your return my dear enemy and all her
little people quite well, and had no reason to repent your
journey. I think on it with great gratitude.

I was not well when you left me at the Doctor's, and I
grew worse; yet I staid on, and at Lichfield was very ill.
Travelling, however, did not make me worse; and when I
came to London I complied with a summons to go to
Brighthelmston, where I saw Beauclerk, and staid three days.

Our club has recommenced last Friday, but I was not there.
Langton has another wench. Mrs. Thrale is in hopes of a
young brewer. They got by their trade last year a very large
sum,[3] and their expences are proportionate.

Mrs. Williams's health is very bad. And I have had for
some time a very difficult and laborious respiration, but I am

565.—1. It is perhaps wanton to suspect this word; but if J wrote 'mind' the corruption would not be difficult.

2. Beauclerck. JB describes, but does not quote, the offending passage from his
letter of 29 Sept., *L* iii. 195, 210. He defended himself in his letter of 29 Nov., *L*
iii. 211.

3. See 560.

better by purges, abstinence, and other methods. I am yet however much behind-hand in my health and rest.

Dr. Blair's sermons are now universally commended, but let him think that I had the honour of first finding and first praising his excellencies. I did not stay to add my voice to that of the publick.

My dear friend, let me thank you once more for your visit; you did me great honour, and I hope met with nothing that displeased you. I staid long at Ashbourne, not much pleased, yet aukward at departing. I then went to Lichfield, where I found my friend at Stowhill very dangerously diseased. Such is life. Let us try to pass it well, whatever it be, for there is surely something beyond it.

Well, now I hope all is well, write as soon as you can to, dear Sir,

Your affectionate servant,

London, Nov. 25, 1777. Sam. Johnson.

565.1. Tu. 16 Dec. '77. Thomas Johnson.

Clifton College.—

Dear Tom

Our good friend Mr. Rann very kindly requires that I should give you some token of reconciliation. Neither You nor I have any time to spare for quarrels or grudges. I desire you to think no more of what you may have done wrong with respect to me, and to consider me as

Your affectionate Kinsman and Friend
Sam: Johnson

My service to your Wife
Dec. 16. 1777

566. Sa. 27 Dec. '77. Jane Gastrell (Lichfield).

Pembroke.—Croker's Boswell 1831, iv. 67.

Dear Madam

Your long silence portended no good, yet, I hope, the danger is not so near as our anxiety sometimes makes us fear. Winter is indeed to all those that any distemper has enfeebled a very troublesome time but care and caution may pass

safely through it, and from Spring and Summer some relief
is always to be hoped.

When I came hither, I fell to taking care of myself, and by
physick and opium had the constriction that obstructed my
breath very suddenly removed. My nights still continue very
laborious and tedious, but they do not grow worse.

I do not ask you, dear Madam, to take care of Mrs. Aston,
I know how little you want any such exhortation, but I
earnestly entreat her to take care of herself. Many lives are
prolonged by a diligent attention to little things, and I am
far from thinking it unlikely that she may grow better by
degrees. However, it is her duty to try, and when we do our
duty we have reason to hope.

I am, Dear Madam, Your most humble servant,
Bolt court Fleet street Dec. 27. 1777　　Sam: Johnson.

567. Sa. 27 Dec. '77. James Boswell (Edinburgh).

Not traced.—Boswell 1791, ii. 180 (Hill iii. 214).

Dear Sir,

This is the time of the year in which all express their good
wishes to their friends, and I send mine to you and your
family. May your lives be long, happy, and good. I have
been much out of order, but, I hope, do not grow worse.

The crime[1] of the schoolmaster whom you are engaged to
prosecute is very great, and may be suspected to be too
common. In our law it would be a breach of the peace, and
a misdemeanour: that is, a kind of indefinite crime, not capital,
but punishable at the discretion of the Court. You cannot
want matter: all that needs to be said will easily occur.

Mr. Shaw, the author of the Gaelick Grammar, desires me
to make a request for him to Lord Eglintoune,[2] that he may
be appointed Chaplain to one of the new-raised regiments.

All our friends are as they were; little has happened to
them of either good or bad. Mrs. Thrale ran a great black
hair-dressing pin into her eye; but by great evacuation[3] she

567.—1. See JB's letter 29 Nov., *L* iii. 212.
2. Lord Eglinton and JB were intimate.
3. The late Sir Humphry Rolleston told me that J means not a local remedy but,
as elsewhere, purges.

kept it from inflaming, and it is almost well. Miss Reynolds has been out of order, but is better. Mrs. Williams is in a very poor state of health.

If I should write on, I should, perhaps, write only complaints, and therefore I will content myself with telling you, that I love to think on you, and to hear from you; and that I am, dear Sir, Yours faithfully,

December 27, 1777.   Sam. Johnson.

568.—Sa. 24 Jan. '78. James Boswell (Edinburgh).

Not traced.—Boswell 1791, ii. 182 (Hill iii. 215).

Dear Sir

To a letter so interesting[1] as your last, it is proper to return some answer, however little I may be disposed to write.

Your alarm at your lady's illness was reasonable, and not disproportionate to the appearance of the disorder. I hope your physical[2] friend's conjecture is now verified, and all fear of a consumption at an end: a little care and exercise will then restore her. London is a good air for ladies;[3] and if you bring her hither, I will do for her what she did for me—I will retire from my apartments, for her accommodation. Behave kindly to her, and keep her cheerful.

You always seem to call for tenderness.[4] Know then, that in the first month of the present year I very highly esteem and very cordially love you. I hope to tell you this at the beginning of every year as long as we live; and why should we trouble ourselves to tell or hear it oftener?

Tell Veronica, Euphemia, and Alexander, that I wish them, as well as their parents, many happy years.

You have ended the negro's cause[5] much to my mind.

568.—1. JB 8 Jan. (L iii. 215) had given a 'particular account' of his wife's illness—the tuberculosis of which she died.

2. Alexander Wood, the 'Surgeon Wood' of JB's journal at this time.

3. The late Sir Humphry Rolleston was unable to suggest any ground for a theory that L'n had a good climate for diseases of women; and Mrs. B's was not specifically feminine. It has crossed my mind that in J's hand 'ladies' is a not very difficult misreading of 'invalids'.

4. JB had written that he 'never stood more in need of his consoling philosophy' (L iii. 215).

5. Joseph Knight. For JB's account of the cause see L iii. 212. It was decided on 15 Jan. See Index II.

Lord Auckinleck and dear Lord Hailes were on the side of liberty. Lord Hailes's name reproaches me; but if he saw my languid neglect of my own affairs, he would rather pity than resent my neglect of his. I hope to mend, *ut et mihi vivam et amicis.*[6]

                      I am, dear Sir, Your's affectionately,
January 24, 1778.   Sam. Johnson.
My service to my fellow-traveller, Joseph.

569. W. 28 Jan. '78. Thomas Cadell.

Address (Hill): To Mr. Cadell.
Not traced.—Hill 1892.

Sir

    If you should obtain what Mr. Davies tells me you design to ask, the office of Bookseller and Printer to the royal Academy, I take the liberty of requesting, and I request with great earnestness, that for any thing to be printed for the Academy, you will make use ⟨of⟩ Mr. Allen's press in Bolt court. Mr. Allen has hitherto done the work without payment, and having so long laboured only to his loss, it is reasonable that he should at last have some profit, at least some recompense.

    Mr. Allen's business is not extensive, and he will be glad of work which greater Printers do not want, nor value, and if you continue him in the employment you will confer a great favour upon,

                      Sir, Your most humble servant,
Jan. 28, 1778.   Sam: Johnson.

570. F. 30 Jan. '78. —— (Oxford).

Not traced.—Hill's Boswell 1887, v. 454.

Sir,

    Poor Mr. Gwyn is in great distress under the weight of the late determination against him, and has still hopes that some

568.—6. Mr. Vernon Rendall suggests that this is a conflation of Horace, *Ep.* I. xviii. 107: et mihi vivam, and *Sat.* I. vi. 70: si et vivo carus amicis.

569.—C obtained the office. Whether he employed Allen I have not discovered.

570.—This appeal was no doubt addressed to one of J's 'academical friends'. See Addenda, p. 529. For Gwynn's backslidings see references in Index II.

mitigation may be obtained. If it be true that whatever has by his negligence been amiss, may be redressed for a sum much less than has been awarded, the remaining part ought in equity to be returned, or, what is more desirable, abated. When the money is once paid, there is little hope of getting it again.

The load is, I believe, very hard upon him; he indulges some flattering opinions that by the influence of his academical friends it may be lightened, and will not be persuaded but that some testimony of my kindness may be beneficial. I hope he has been guilty of nothing worse than credulity, and he then certainly deserves commiseration. I never heard otherwise than that he was an honest man, and I hope that by your countenance and that of other gentlemen who favour or pity him some relief may be obtained.

> I am, Sir, Your most humble servant,
> Sam: Johnson.

Bolt Court, Fleet Street, Jan. 30, 1778.

571. Tu. 3 Feb. '78. Saunders Welch (Rome).

Address (Boswell): To Saunders Welch, Esq. at the English Coffee-House, Rome.
Not traced.—Boswell 1791, ii. 269 (Hill iii. 217).

Dear Sir

To have suffered one of my best and dearest friends to pass almost two years in foreign countries without a letter, has a very shameful appearance of inattention. But the truth is, that there was no particular time in which I had any thing particular to say; and general expressions of good will, I hope, our long friendship is grown too solid to want.

Of publick affairs you have information from the newspapers wherever you go, for the English keep no secret; and of other things, Mrs. Nollekens informs you. My intelligence could therefore be of no use; and Miss Nancy's letters made it unnecessary to write to you for information: I was likewise for some time out of humour, to find that motion, and nearer approaches to the sun, did not restore your health so fast as I expected. Of your health, the accounts have lately been more pleasing; and I have the gratification of imaging to myself a length of years which I hope you have gained, and of which the enjoyment will be improved, by a vast accession of images and observations which your journeys and various residence have enabled you to make and accumulate. You have travelled with this felicity, almost peculiar to yourself, that your companion is not to part from you at your journey's end; but you are to live on together, to help each other's recollection, and to supply each other's omissions. The world has few greater pleasures than that which two friends enjoy, in tracing back, at some distant time, those transactions and events through which they have passed together. One of the old man's miseries is, that he cannot easily find a companion able to partake with him of the past. You and your fellow-traveller have this comfort in store, that your conversation will be not easily exhausted; one will always be glad to say what the other will always be willing to hear.

That you may enjoy this pleasure long, your health must have your constant attention. I suppose you purpose to return this year. There is no need of haste: do not come hither before the height of summer, that you may fall gradually into the inconveniences of your native clime. July seems to be the proper month. August and September will prepare you for the winter. After having travelled so far to find health, you must take care not to lose it at home; and I hope a little care will effectually preserve it.

Miss Nancy has doubtless kept a constant and copious journal. She must not expect to be welcome when she returns without a great mass of information. Let her review her journal often, and set down what she finds herself to have omitted, that she may trust to memory as little as possible, for memory is soon confused by a quick succession of things; and she will grow every day less confident of the truth of her own narratives, unless she can recur to some written memorials. If she has satisfied herself with hints, instead of full representations, let her supply the deficiencies now while her memory is yet fresh, and while her father's memory may help her. If she observes this direction, she will not have travelled in vain; for she will bring home a book with which she may entertain herself to the end of life. If it were not now too late, I would advise her to note the impression which the first sight of any thing new and wonderful made upon her mind. Let her now set her thoughts down as she can recollect them; for faint as they may already be, they will grow every day fainter.

Perhaps I do not flatter myself unreasonably when I imagine that you may wish to know something of me. I can gratify your benevolence with no account of health. The hand of time, or of disease, is very heavy upon me. I pass restless and uneasy nights, harassed with convulsions of my breast, and flatulencies at my stomach; and restless nights make heavy days. But nothing will be mended by complaints, and therefore I will make an end. When we meet, we will try to forget our cares and our maladies, and contribute, as we can, to the chearfulness of each other. If I had gone with you, I believe I should have been better; but I do not know that it was in my power.

                    I am, dear Sir, Your most humble servant,
Feb. 3, 1778.   Sam. Johnson.

572. Th. 19 Feb. 1778. Lucy Porter (Lichfield).

Sotheby 17 March 1930.—Croker's Boswell 1831, iv. 72.

Dear Madam

I have several little things to mention which I have hitherto neglected.

You judged rightly in thinking that the Bust[1] would not please. It is condemned by Mrs. Thrale, Mrs. Reynolds, and Mrs. Garrick, so that your disapprobation is not singular.

These things have never cost me any thing, so that I do not much know the price. My Bust was made for the Exhibition, and shown for the honour of the Artist, who is a man of reputation above any of the other Sculptors. To be modeled in clay costs, I believe, twenty guineas, but the casts when the model is made, are of no great price, whether a guinea or two guineas I cannot tell.

572.—1. By Nollekens, see 564.

About Mrs. Thrale's table linen I was mistaken. She bought three table cloaths for twenty five pounds each, which coming to seventy five pound, caused the mistake.

When you complained for want of Oysters, I ordered you a barrel weekly for a month, you sent me word sooner that you had enough, but I did not countermand the rest. If you could not eat them, you could give them away. When you want any thing send me word.

I am very poorly, and have very restless and oppressive nights, but always hope for better. Pray for me.

I am, your most humble servant

Feb. 19 1778.   Sam: Johnson

572a. Southwark. F. 20 ⟨? Feb. '78⟩. From Mrs. Thrale.

Address: Doctor Johnson Fleet Street.
R 540.107—

Dear Sir   Fryday 20.
    Every body keeps telling me you are ill, some to vex me I suppose & some to please themselves: I have got a little Rash or I would have come to see you again. The Plaisterers are got to Streatham, & we cannot go home even as soon as I mention'd to you, if Air therefore is likely to help your Complaint, do not wait for us but run to Oxford or somewhere out of London for a while. Doctor Jebb called on me yesterday, & we talked of every thing, & we talked of you; & yet he did not tell the old Story.
    He says he did wear a Blister on his Breast when he was abroad, but it did him no good; however his Complaint was not the same to yours he thinks. He spoke very highly of Doctor Lawrence, & very sweetly of you; & I like him better & better, though he was always a Favourite. I see you will not go to Mrs Montagu's tomorrow, & unless my Rash mends I must not neither.
    I am to meet Mrs Walsingham & Soame Jenyns at a Conversation next Wednesday. The Dutchess of Beaufort's desiring *leave* to visit me forsooth was so very fine a thing that I doubt not but I told you of it like the Character in Murphy's Comedy that cries—Make me thankful! a Card from a Dutchess!
    The King spoke to me too yesterday, said I spent little Time in London because I lived so near it. Was not that fine too? but I wish I had not caught this tingling Rash on his Majesty's cold Stair case as I waited for my Chair.— Do let me have a Line under your own hand saying something kind to Your ever Faithful and Obedient

H: L: T.

572b. Southwark. M. ⟨? 16 or 23 Feb. '78⟩. From Mrs. Thrale.

Address: Dʳ Johnson.
R 540.106—

My Dear Sir   Monday Morn.
   I would not write but come if I was well, but I have caught Cold in some of my Frolicks & am more than three Parts ill.
   Let me know if I may fancy you mending. Tomorrow Sennight please God you shall come home—we have lived apart long enough at least for Your ever Faithful & Obedᵗ

                                                                        H: L: T.

---

573. Th. 5 Mar. '78. Elizabeth Montague.

Huntington.—Croker's Boswell 1831, iv. 75.

Madam
   And so you are alarmed, naughty Lady; You might know that I was ill enough when Mr Thrale brought You my excuse. Could You think that I missed the honour of being at ⟨your⟩ table for any slight reason? But You ⟨have⟩ too many to miss any one of us, and I am ⟨proud⟩ to be remembred at last.
   I am much better. A little cough ⟨still re⟩mains which will not confine me. To houses, ⟨like yours⟩ of great delicacy I am not willing to bring it.
   Now, dear Madam, we must talk of business. Poor Davies, the bankrupt Bookseller, is soliciting his Friends to collect a small sum for the repurchase of part of his household stuff. Several of them give him five guineas. It would be an honour to him, to owe part of his relief to Mrs Montague.
   Let me thank You, Madam, once more for your enquiry; You have perhaps among your numerous train, not ⟨one⟩ that values a kind word or a kind look more than
                          Madam, Your most humble Servant,
March 5–1778   Sam: Johnson

573.—The MS. is torn; the supplements are said to be in a contemporary hand (Reginald Blunt, *Mrs. Montagu* [1923], ii. 155).

574. F. 6 Mar. '78. Elizabeth Montague.

Not traced.—Croker's Boswell 1831, iv. 75.

Madam,   6th March, 1778.

I hope Davies, who does not want wit, does not want gratitude, and then[1] he will be almost as thankful for the bill as I am for the letter that enclosed it.

If I do not lose, what I hope always to keep, my reverence for transcendent merit, I shall continue to be with unalterable fidelity,

Madam, Your most obliged, and most humble servant,

                                                    Sam: Johnson.

574.1. William Adams. See Addenda, p. 530.

574.2. W. 22 Apr. '78. Richard Clark.

Address: To —— Clark Esq   C. S. Cow.—

Dear Sir

I think myself very much favoured by your invitation. Mr Langton will fix the day.

I have a request to make which, I hope, is not improper, nor such as will give you much trouble. There is in Christ's Hospital, a little boy one George Angel, whose Grandfather I once knew, and who has hardly any friend left, but a Lady who happened to be his Godmother. This little boy desires himself and his Godmother desires for him, that he may be put into the Grammar School; which we hope, Sir, to effect by your influence, and that You will be pleased to exert your influence in his favour, is very warmly desired by,

Sir, Your most obedient and most humble Servant,

Apr. 22. 1778   Sam: Johnson

575. Th. 23 Apr. '78. James Boswell (Edinburgh).

Not traced; copy by JB, Isham (see Addenda, p. 529) (no variants).
—Boswell 1791, ii. 218 (Hill iii. 277).

Sir,

The debate[1] between Dr. Percy and me is one of those

574.—1. I suspect that J wrote 'that'; his 'in' and 'at' are not seldom confused.

574.2.—The dinner was at the Old Bailey, see 576. Clark lived to be ninety-two, and described the occasion to Croker.

575.—1. For the quarrel, and the reconciliation effected by JB, see *L* iii. 275–8.

foolish controversies, which begin upon a question of which neither party cares how it is decided, and which is, nevertheless, continued to acrimony, by the vanity with which every man resists confutation. Dr. Percy's warmth proceeded from a cause which, perhaps, does him more honour than he could have derived from juster criticism. His abhorrence of Pennant proceeded from his opinion that Pennant had wantonly and indecently censured his patron.[2] His anger made him resolve that for having been once wrong, he never should be right. Pennant has much in his notions that I do not like; but still I think him a very intelligent traveller. If Percy is really offended, I am sorry; for he is a man whom I never knew to offend any one. He is a man very willing to learn, and very able to teach; a man, out of whose company I never go without having learned something. It is sure that he vexes me sometimes, but I am afraid it is by making me feel my own ignorance. So much extension of mind, and so much minute accuracy of enquiry, if you survey your whole circle of acquaintance, you will find so scarce, if you find it at all, that you will value Percy by comparison. Lord Hailes is somewhat like him: but Lord Hailes does not, perhaps, go beyond him in research; and I do not know that he equals him in elegance. Percy's attention to poetry has given grace and splendour to his studies of antiquity. A mere antiquarian is a rugged being.

Upon the whole, you see that what I might say in sport or petulance to him, is very consistent with full conviction of his merit.

I am, dear Sir, Your most, &c.,

April 23, 1778.   Sam. Johnson.

575a. Streatham. Su. ⟨? Apr. or May '78⟩. From Mrs. Thrale.

Address: To Dr Johnson Bolt Court Fleet Street.
R 540.80—

My Dear Sir   Sunday.

On Wednesday you shall be fetched either by my Master's Coach or mine: he grudges every Candle's End just now in a manner that would be comical

575.—2. The Duke of Northumberland.

if one was at leisure to laugh. In the mean Time Perkins has no mercy; the less—as he injures our Safety—ay and Prosperity too, tho' I sometimes think my Master will never recover so as to enjoy himself again, there is so settled a Gloom—so total a Self Desertion impressed upon his Countenance & Mind. Perkins dines here today, says he pays every body with a high hand & that the People all say there is no Money to be had at any house but ours, I mean Coopers & Ironmongers & common Tradesmen belonging to the Brewhouse. If therefore you see my Master before I do—conjure him not to fret so, when he really has every Reason to be thankful. What shall I do tho' when Burney's fine Harpsichord comes home? he grudges my new Bed so that it makes him half mad, & the other will be twice the Money of my poor Bed.—Oh Dear me! but he is woeful cross; & glad at heart shall I be to have you with us— for we *grind* sadly else. till then adieu & believe me ever Yrs

H: L: T.

576. Th. 30 Apr. '78. Mrs. Thrale.

Adam.—1788, No. 191.

Dear Madam

Since I was fetched away from Streatham the journal stands thus

Saturday, Sir J. R.   Sunday, Mr. Hoole.
Monday, Lord Lucan.   Tuesday, Gen. Paoli.
Wednesday Mr Ramsay.   Thursday, Old Bailey.
Fryday, Club.   Saturday Sir J. R.
Sunday Lady Lucan.[1]

Monday, pray let it be Streatham, and very early, do now let it be very early. For I may be carried away—just like Ganymede of Troy.

I hope my Master grows well, and my Mistress continues bad. I am afraid the Ladies will be gone, and I shall say

She's gone, and never knew how much I lov'd her.[2]

Do now let me know whether you will send for me—early

576.—The chronology is thus: Sa. 25 Apr. Reynolds (*L* iii. 315); Su. 26 Hoole; M. 27 Lucan; Tu. 28 Paoli (*L* iii. 324); W. 29 Ramsay (*L* iii. 331); Th. 30 R. Clark (see 574.1); F. 1 May Club (JB was not present: *L* iii. 337. The *Annals* of the Club (24) show that in '78 JB attended once only, 3 April). Sa. 2 May Reynolds (*L* iii. 337); Su. 3 May Lady Lucan.

1. Hill quotes Rogers, *Table-Talk* 1856, 10. Lady Spencer, her daughter, remembered that her mother 'would say "Nobody dines with us to-day; therefore, child, we'll go and get Dr. Johnson" '.

2. Not traced.

—on Monday. But take some care, or your letter will not come till tuesday.

I am, Dearest Lady, Your most humble servant
Apr. 30. 1778   Sam: Johnson

577. ⟨F. 15 May '78.⟩ Mauritius Lowe.
Address (*Examiner*): Mr. Lowe, Hedge Lane.
Not traced.—*Examiner* 24 May 1873.

Sir

I spoke at the Exhibition to Sir Joshua and Mr. Garrick, and found them both cold enough. Mr. Garrick, however, seemed to relent, and I think you have reason to expect something from him; but he must be tenderly handled. I have just, however, received what will please and gratify you. I have sent it just as it came. Write to return thanks.

Your humble servant,
Sam: Johnson.

577a. Streatham. ⟨? 20 June '78.⟩ From Mrs. Thrale.
Address: Mr Johnson.
R 539.52—

My Dear Sir—   written during Labour.
Do huff my Master & comfort him by Turns according to your own Dear Discretion: he has consulted you now, & given you a Right to talk with Him about his ill Tim'd Melancholy and do keep your Influence over him for all our Sakes. God be praised I have nothing to fear at present for my own Life or my Child's: all is regular & natural but very lingering & tedious—where there is no Danger however one does not value Pain—especially when *the Fit's off.* Living or dying sick or well I am ever your most Obliged & Faithful
H: L: T.

577.1. Tu. 30 June '78. ——.
Sotheby 25 Apr. 1843, 175 (not seen).—

'A letter of interest, unaddressed.'

577.—The date is Hill's conjecture based on a letter of this date from L to Garrick thanking him for £10. *Garrick Corr.* ii. 306. The exhibition was no doubt the spring exhibition of the R. Academy.

578. F. 3 July '78. James Boswell (Edinburgh).

Not traced.—Boswell 1791, ii. 274 (Hill iii. 362).

Dear Sir,

I have received two letters[1] from you, of which the second
complains of the neglect shown to the first. You must not
tye your friends to such punctual correspondence. You have
all possible assurances of my affection and esteem; and there
ought to be no need of reiterated professions. When it may
happen that I can give you either counsel or comfort, I hope
it will never happen to me that I should neglect you; but you
must not think me criminal or cold if I say nothing, when I
have nothing to say.

You are now happy enough. Mrs. Boswell is recovered;
and I congratulate you upon the probability of her long life.
If general approbation will add any thing to your enjoyment,
I can tell you that I have heard you mentioned as *a man
whom every body likes*. I think life has little more to give.

——[2] has gone to his regiment. He has laid down his
coach, and talks of making more contractions of his expence:
how he will succeed I know not. It is difficult to reform a
household gradually; it may be better done by a system
totally new. I am afraid he has always something to hide.
When we pressed him to go to ——, he objected the necessity
of attending his navigation; yet he could talk of going to
Aberdeen,[3] a place not much nearer his navigation. I believe
he cannot bear the thought of living at —— in a state of
diminution; and of appearing among the gentlemen of the
neighbourhood *shorn of his beams*.[4] This is natural, but it is
cowardly. What I told him of the encreasing expence of a
growing family seems to have struck him. He certainly had
gone on with very confused views, and we have, I think,

578.—1. That of 25 May is described, *L* iii. 359; that of 18 June is quoted there, but
the opening part, which doubtless contained the 'complaint of neglect', is not given.

2. Langton. The two following blanks no doubt represent his home at Langton.
His 'navigation' was the Wey Canal in Surrey, *L* ii. 136.

3. BL had perhaps talked of living at Aberdeen as a place of cheap education.
'not much nearer' is a form of irony very rare in J. Other examples are in 423 and
999, where Malone conjectured 'mortification', and Hill also doubted the text; but
'consolation' is confirmed by the MS.

4. 'shorn of his beams' is *Paradise Lost* i. 596; but the context shows, as Hill saw,
than J is thinking of a passage which he quotes from Dryden in the Dictionary s.v.
shorn: 'Shorn of his beams, a man to mortal sight.'

shown him that he is wrong; though, with the common deficience of advisers, we have not shown him how to do right.

I wish you would a little correct or restrain your imagination, and imagine that happiness, such as life admits, may be had at other places as well as London. Without asserting[5] Stoicism, it may be said, that it is our business to exempt ourselves as much as we can from the power of external things. There is but one solid basis of happiness; and that is, the reasonable hope of a happy futurity. This may be had every where.

I do not blame your preference of London to other places, for it is really to be preferred, if the choice is free; but few have the choice of their place, or their manner of life; and mere pleasure ought not to be the prime motive of action.

Mrs. Thrale, poor thing,[6] has a daughter. Mr. Thrale dislikes the times, like the rest of us. Mrs. Williams is sick; Mrs. Desmoulins is poor. I have miserable nights. Nobody is well but Mr. Levett.

I am, dear Sir, Your most, &c.

London, July 3, 1778.   Sam. Johnson.

578.1. Streatham. Th. 17 July '78. Richard Clark.

Address: To Richard Clerk Esq Sheriff of London Great Broad Street. Guildhall.—

Dear Sir

I know your kindness for literature, and therefore have not much difficulty in soliciting your help, even though You cannot give it but with considerable trouble.

578.—5. Malone's conjecture 'affecting' (*Life* 1807, iii. 391) is, I think, more than probable. In J's note on *Henry V* III. v. 40 the correction 'affected' for 'asserted' is certain. Malone in a note adds 'the original letter being burned in a mass of papers in Scotland, I have not been able to ascertain whether my conjecture is well founded'. For the question whether M wrote 'burned', or as the late Rupert Gould plausibly suggested 'buried', with all its implications, see Pottle, *Catalogue* 1931, and RWC, 'Boswell's Archives', in *Essays and Studies* xvii, 1931. Both of these were written before the discoveries at Fettercairn, and before some of those at Malahide, which greatly reduced the antecedent probability of any wholesale destruction, by fire or otherwise, of JB's archives. The *latest* (1946) Malahide finds seem decisive.

  6. See 565.

578.1.—For the subject of J's inquiry see his Life of Dryden, ¶ 116 in Hill's edition. There J repeats his opinion that Settle was the last 'of these bards'. Clark referred

In the Life of Dryden, of which I have written a great part it will be necessary to say something of Settle, who had once the honour of being his Antagonist. Settle, as I have learned, was the City Poet, and the last who bore that title. If You have the power of making the necessary enquiries I would wish to know.

The history of the office—when or how it began—The succession of City Laureats—their salary—their employment —When Settle obtained it—how long he held it—

Settle died in the Chartreux. I would wish to know the year of his reception, and of his death. But unless You have some very ready means of obtaining this knowledge, I will not trouble you about it, for I think, I can find means of obtaining what is known at the Chartreux. The account of the City Poet will be a great addition to my Work.

I am, Sir, Your most humble Servant
July. 17. 1778 Streatham in Surrey.   Sam: Johnson

579. M. 27 July '78. William Strahan.

Not traced; copy by WS, Isham (No variants).—Boswell 1791, ii. 275, dated in B's text (Hill iii. 364).

Sir,
It would be very foolish for us to continue strangers any longer. You can never by persistency make wrong right. If I resented too acrimoniously, I resented only to yourself. Nobody ever saw or heard what I wrote. You saw that my anger was over, for in a day or two I came to your house. I have given you longer time; and I hope you have made so good use of it, as to be no longer on evil terms with, Sir, Your, &c.

Sam. Johnson.

the question to one Thomas Whittell, who wrote to J from the Guildhall 26 Aug. His letter is in the collection of Mr. Arthur Houghton of New York; a photostat is in the Bodleian. W could find no record of a City Poet so styled, but there were records of City Chronologers; and from the fact that the office had been held by 'Ben: Johnson and Frans Quarles' he inferred that the chronology was in verse. W found nothing about Settle, and in his view 'the last City Chronologer was Mr. Cromwell Bradshaw who surrendered his place on the 4th ffebruary 1669'.

579.—JB remarks (*L* iii. 364) that 'it is unnecessary to relate' the circumstances of this 'difference'.

580. M. 27 July '78. James Elphinston.

Not traced.—Shaw's *Memoirs* of Johnson 1785, 168; Elphinston, *Forty Years' Corresp.* 1791, ii. 246.

Sir

Having myself suffered what you are now suffering, I well know the weight of your distress, how much need you have of comfort, and how little comfort can be given. A loss, such as yours, lacerates the mind, and breaks the whole system of purposes and hopes. It leaves a dismal vacuity in life, which affords nothing on which the affections can fix, or to which endeavour may be directed. All this I have known, and it is now, in the vicissitude of things, your turn to know it.

But in the condition of mortal beings, one must lose another. What would be the wretchedness of life, if there was not something always in view, some Being, immutable and unfailing, to whose mercy man may have recourse. Τὸν πρῶτον κινοῦντα ἀκίνητον.[1]

Here we must rest. The greatest Being is the most bene-volent. We must not grieve for the dead as men without hope,[2] because we know that they are in his hands. We have, indeed, not leisure to grieve long, because we are hastening to follow them. Your race and mine have been interrupted by many obstacles, but we must humbly hope for an happy end.

I am, Sir, Your most humble servant,

July 27, 1778.   Sam: Johnson.

580.1. ⟨'78.⟩ John Nichols.

Address: To Mr Nichol.

B.M.—*GM* Jan. 1785; Boswell 1791, ii. 345 (Hill iv. 36); overlooked by Hill in *Letters*.

In the Life of Waller Mr Nichols will find a reference to

580.—For JB's failure to notice this letter see Appendix E, II § 2.

1. Aristotle, *Metaph.* iii. 8; τὸ πρῶτον κινοῦν ἀκίνητον αὐτό 'the prime mover is itself unmoved'. Sir David Ross suggests that forgetting αὐτό, and unconsciously personalizing or christianizing Aristotle's thought, J supposed ἀκίνητον masculine not neuter and made 'prime mover' masculine to suit.

2. I Thessalonians iv. 13. J is quoting the Burial Service: 'who hath taught us, by his holy Apostle Saint Paul, not to be sorry, as men without hope, for them that sleep in him.'

the *Parliamentary Hist.*[1] from which a long quotation is to be inserted. If Mr Nichols cannot easily find the book, Mr Johnson will send it from Streatham.

Clarendon[2] is here returned.

581. M. 27 July ʼ78. John Nichols.
Address: To Mr Nichol.
B.M.—*GM* Jan. 1785.

Sir

You have now all *Cowley.* I have been drawn to a great length, but Cowley or Waller never had any critical examination before. I am very far advanced in *Dryden*, who will be long too. The next great life I purpose to be *Milton's.*

It will be kind if you will gather the Lives of *Denham, Butler*, and *Waller*, and bind them in half binding in a small volume,[1] and let me have it to shew my friends, as soon as may be. I sincerely hope the press shall stand no more.

I am, Sir, Your most humble servant,

July 27, 1778   Sam: Johnson.

581.1. W. 29 Aug. ʼ78. Bennet Langton (Warley).
Address: To Captain Langton at Warly Camp.
Fettercairn.—

Dear Sir

I received your letter, and thought You very kind in writing so soon, but one little hindrance or other making it difficult for me to fix a time for the visit which I am extremely desirous of making, I omitted to write. I have now another hindrance having lamed one of my knees so much, that I shall get no credit in the field. When it is well, I purpose to come, and will certainly send you word two or three days before. I am not indifferent about it, but shall grieve very

580.1.—1. *Life of Waller* ¶ 26: W's speech of 6 July 1641, quoted from *Parl. Hist.* ii. 869.
   2. Clarendon's 'character of Waller, both moral and intellectual', is quoted in the *Life* ¶ 91.
581.—1. Perhaps this was one of the 'books' for which HLT thanks him in 589.1*a*.
581.1.—For the reasons of the suppression of (parts of) letters to BL see on 240.1.

much if I miss the sight, when by your friendship I can have it with so much convenience.

I have lately heard from Boswel who seems to be in his *old lunes*.[1] He wants to come to town. I hope your Lady and all the rest got well through their Journey. I am, Dear Sir, Your most obliged and most humble Servant

Aug. 29. 1778   Sam: Johnson

582. ⟨Aug. '78⟩. John Nichols.

Address: To Mr Nichols.
B.M.—*GM* Jan. 1785.

Sir

You have now the life of *Dryden* and you see it is very long. It must however have an Appendix.

1 The invocation to the Georgicks from Milbourne[1] (this in the small print).

2 Dryden's remarks on Rymer, which are ready transcribed.[2]

3. Dryden's letter from Lambeth,[3] which is promised me.

I am Sir &c.,

[Sam: Johnson.]

582.1. Th. 13 Oct. '78. Thomas Lawrence.

Address: To Dr Laurence.
Adam.—

Dear Sir

I am much distressed in the night and have lately had such an account of Musk that I wish to try it, unless you think it improper. If you consent to the use of it, my request is that you will send your servant, or my servant with a note, to

---

581.1.—1. *Merry Wives* IV. ii. 22.

582.—1. *Life of Dryden* ¶¶ 148, 357: 'The invocation before the *Georgicks* is here inserted from Mr. Milbourne's version, that, according to his own proposal, his verses may be compared with those which he censures.'

2. Ibid. ¶ 358: 'Mr. Dryden, having received from Rymer his *Remarks on the Tragedies of the last Age*, wrote observations on the blank leaves, which, having been in the possession of Mr. Garrick, are by his favour communicated to the publick that no particle of Dryden may be lost.'

3. Ibid. ¶ 406: 'The original of the following letter [from D to his sons in Rome] is preserved in the Library at Lambeth.' J had it from Vyse.

Apothecaries Hall, to buy it. I may then expect to have it good. It is, I find four pound an ounce, I would have a dram.

I am, Sir Your most humble servant

Oct. 13. 1778   Sam: Johnson

---

583. Th. 15 Oct. '78. Mrs. Thrale (Brighthelmston).
Adam.—1788, No. 192.

Dearest Madam

You that are among all the Wits, delighting and delighted, have little need of Entertainment from me whom you left at home unregarded and unpitied, to shift in a world to which you have made me so much a stranger, yet I know how you will pretend to be angry if I do not write a letter which when you know the hand you will perhaps lay aside to be read when you are dressing to morrow, and which when you have read it, if that time ever comes you will throw away into the draw⟨er⟩ and say—Stuff!

As to Dr Collier's Epitaph,[1] Nollikens has had it so long, that I have forgotten how long. You never had it. So you may set the Streatfields at defiance.

There is a print[2] of Mrs Montague, and I shall think myself very ill rewarded for my love and admiration if she does not give me one, she will give it nobody in whom it will excite more respectful sentiments. But I never could get any thing from her but by pushing a face, and so, if you please, you may tell her.

I hope you will let Miss Stratfield know how safe you keep

583.—1. HLT's friend Dr. Arthur C died 23 May '77. But the epitaph cannot be one on him, for 'you never had it'; such an epitaph must have been submitted to her before it was sent to be engraved. Now in *Th* for '76 HLT quotes C's 'Greek Epitaph on his favourite dog Pompey'; a little later she adds (20 Nov.) 'I have since heard with pleasure that he picked up a more useful Friend—a Mrs Streatfield a Widow, high in Fortune. . . . Her Children I find he has been educating' (*Th* 15, 17). Sophia S's Greek was the wonder of the world. Perhaps J was asked to cause Nollekens to make a statue of Pompey and inscribe the epitaph on it?

2. The petition was granted. In the Sale Cat. 1785 of J's library lot 662 (the last) is (under heading 'Prints Framed and Glazed'): '3. Mrs. Montague, &c.' General Oglethorpe paid £3. 5s. for the lot. The print was no doubt that by J. R. Smith, '76; that by Bartolozzi is '92.

her book.[3] It was too fine for a Scholar's talons. I hope she gets books that she may handle with more freedom, and understand with less difficulty. Do not let her forget me.

When I called the other day at Burneys, I found only the young ones at home, at last came the Doctor and Madam from a dinner in the country, to tell how they had been robbed as the⟨y⟩ returned. The Doctor saved his purse but gave them three guineas and some silver, of which they returned him three and sixpence unasked to pay the turnpike.

I have sat twice to Sir Joshua, and he seems to like his own performance.[4] He has projected another in which I am to be busy, but we can think on it at leisure.

Mrs Williams is come home better, and the habitation is all concord and Harmony; only Mr Levet harbours discontent.

With Dr Lawrence's consent I have for the two last nights taken Musk, the first night was a worse night than common, the second a better, but not so much better as that I dare ascribe any virtue to the medicine. I took a scruple each time.

Now Miss has seen the Camp, I think, she should write me some account of it. A Camp, however familiarly we may speak of it, is one of the great scenes of human life. War and peace divide ⟨the⟩ business of the world. Camps are the habitations of those who conquer kingdoms or defend them.

But what are Wits, and Pictures, and Camps and Physics? There is still a nearer concern to most of us. Is my Master come to himself? Does he talk and walk and look about him, as if there were yet something in the world for which it is worth while to live? or does he yet sit and say nothing? He was mending before he went, and surely has not relapsed. To grieve for evils is often wrong, but it is much more wrong to grieve without them. All sorrow that lasts longer than its cause is morbid, and should be shaken off as an attack of melancholy, as the forerunner of a greater evil than poverty or pain.

583.—3. Perhaps a volume from her collection of the classics, finely bound in red morocco, which has been dispersed in our time.

4. For a discussion of these two portraits see *L* iv. 450.

I never said with Dr Dodd that *I love to prattle upon paper*,[5] but I have prattled now till the paper will not hold much more, than my good wishes, which I sincerely send you.

I am, Madam, Your most humble servant,

Octr 15. 1778   Sam: Johnson

583a. Brighthelmston. (?) F. 16 Oct. ⟨'78⟩. From Mrs. Thrale.

Address: To Dr Johnson Fleet Street London. *Postmark*: 17 oc. Franked by HT.

R 540.82—

Dear Sir

    In answer to the beginning of your Letter I reply that it was given me on the Walks while I was talking with the Duchess of Devonshire, who had desired to be introduced to me;—and I went from her into a Shop to read it.— This happened but three hours ago so I did not lay it aside at least. I read to Mrs Montagu the passage which concerned her, and She desired me to tell You that She has long known you had a Superior Genius, but that nothing could have proved it plainer than your making her at this Time of Day proud of her Face by desiring her Print which shall be sent you framed & glazed very soon.

    Miss Streatfield does not forget you, we talk of you often, and we went today together to see Ruins and wished for your Company.

    My Master mends but it is gradually: he is not yet a good Tête a Tête but he behaves tolerably in Company—every body however says he is *strangely broke*. The post waits. Hester shall write soon. I am ever most faithfully & Gratefully Yours

H: L: Thrale

584. Sa. 17 Oct. '78. Thomas Cadell.

Sotheby 10 May 1875 (not seen); known to Hill only from this catalogue.—

    'Apologises for the delay in returning the proof sheets, mentioning those of the *Life of Dryden.*'

583.—5. Dodd's published prattlings are numerous and multifarious. HLP repeats the phrase, 589.1*a*.

584a. Tunbridge Wells. M. 19 Oct. ⟨'78⟩. From Mrs. Thrale.

Address: To Dr Johnson Fleet Street London. *Postmarks*: TUNBRIDGE WELLS *and* 20 OC. Franked by HT.
R 540.83—

19. Monday

Though it is so much the fashion to print private Correspondence I suppose yours & Hester's will escape. Mrs Montagu cannot bear Evelina—let not that be published—her Silver-Smiths are Pewterers She says, & her Captains Boatswains. The Attorney General says you must all have commended it out of a Joke. My Master laughs to see me Down among the Dead Men & I am happy to see him laugh.

All goes on well at the Brewhouse I hear: & the Money that was borrowed when the Leaves were coming out will be paid—or may be—before they are fallen: neither must this be published.

I am called to a Dinner not of our making but Mrs Streatfields: the Montagus & Crewes meet us so Farewell & do nothing without Dr Lawrence's Advice in the Absence of Your H: L: T.

585. Sa. 24 Oct. '78. Mrs. Thrale (Tunbridge Wells).
Address: To Henry Thrale Esq at Tunbridge Wells (redirected to London). *Postmarks*: 24 *and* 26 OCT.
Newton.—1788, No. 193.

Dearest Lady

I have written Miss such a long letter that I cannot tell how soon I shall be weary of writing another, having made no new discoveries since my last either in art or Nature which may not be kept till we see each other. And sure that time is not far off. The Duchess[1] is a good Duchess for courting you while she stays, and for not staying to court you, till my courtship loses all its value. You are there as I would have you, except your humours. When my Master grows well, must you take your turn to be melancholy? You appear to me to be now floating on the spring tide of Prosperity; on a tide not governed by the moon, but as the moon governs your heads, on a tide therefore which is never likely to ebb but by your own faults? I think it very probably in your power to lay up eight thousand pounds a year for every year to come, encreasing all the time, what needs not be encreased, the splendor of all external appearance. And surely such a

585.—1. 'I forget what this alludes to. We were at Tunbridge I see by the Duchess' HLP; of Devonshire, see 583*a*.

state is not to be put into yearly hazard, for the pleasure of *keeping the house full*, or the ambition of *outbrewing Whitbread*. Stop now and you are safe, stop a few years and you may go safely on hereafter if to go on shall seem worth the while.

I am sorry for Mrs. Montague;[2] we never could make any thing of the Lawyer, when we had him among us. Montague has got some vanity in her head. Vanity always oversets a Lady's Judgement. I have not told unless it be Williams, and I do not know that I have told her. If Streatfield[3] has a little kindness for me, I am glad. I call now and then on the Burneys, where you are at the top of mortality.——When will you come home?

Two days ago Dr. Lawrence ordered a new medicine which I think to try to night, but my hopes are not high. I mean to try however, and not languish without resistance.

Young Desmoulines is taken in *an undersomething* of Drury Lane; he knows not, I believe, his own ⟨desig⟩nation.[4]

My two clerical friends Darby and Worthington have both died this month. I have known Worthington long, and to die is dreadful. I believe he was a very good Man.

I am Madam Your most &c most &c

London Oct. 24. 1778   Sam: Johnson.

585.1. Sa. 24 Oct. '78. Hester Maria Thrale (Tunbridge Wells).

Lansdowne.—Lansdowne, *Johnson and Queeney* 1932, 10.

My dearest Love,   London, 24 Oct. 1778

I was in hopes that your letter about the camp would have been longer, and that you would have considered yourself as surveying in a camp perhaps the most important scene of human existence, the real scene of heroick life. If you are struck with the inconveniencies of the military in a camp where there is no danger, where all the materials of pleasure

585.—2. Suppressed in 1788; 584*a* shows that Mrs. M and the Attorney-General (Wedderburn, J's 'the Lawyer') could see nothing in *Evelina*.

3. See 583*a*.

4. MS. torn; 'designation' is perhaps more likely than 'denomination', which is supplied by another hand, and is printed in 1788.

are supplied, and where there is little but jollity and festivity, reflect what a camp must be surrounded by enemies in a wasted or a hostile country, where provisions can scarcely be had, and what can be had must be snatched in haste by men who when they put the bread into their mouths, are uncertain whether they shall swallow it.

Sir Robert Cotton, whose degradation seems to touch you, is not the greatest man that has inhabited a tent. He is not considered out of Cheshire, nor perhaps in it, as standing on even ground with Alexander and Darius; Cæsar and Pompey; Tamerlane and Bajazet; Charles, Peter, and Augustus. These and many more like these, have lived in a camp like Sir Robert Cotton.

In a camp you ⟨see⟩ what is the lowest and most portable accommodation with which Life can be contented; what shelter it is that can be most expeditiously erected and removed. There is in a camp what human wit sharpened by the greatest exigencies has been able to contrive, and it gives ladies the particular pleasure of seeing evils which they are not to share.

I am, Sweeting, Your most humble servant

Sam: Johnson

585.1a. Brighthelmston. W. 28 Oct. ⟨'78⟩. From Mrs. Thrale.

R 540.84—

My Dear Sir　　　　　　　　　　　　Brighthelmston Wednesday 28 Oct^r
Your Letter followed us hither as soon as we arrived; the sweet Society at Tunbridge is all broken up, and some being driven one way, & some another, we find ourselves on this Coast; a barren one enough at all Times, & seeming more barren now to me who have left such a pleasing Set of Talkers so lately. Mr Thrale talks of ten Days here, & I am apprehensive it will be fifteen: he has already seen Beauclerck & Hamilton who enquire much for You; all my Fear is lest you may supply my Place in your Friendship while I am dipping in the Sea or my Master's while he is following Sir John Shelley's Pack of Dogs over the Sussex Downs—that would indeed dispirit one but we will talk of something else.

All human Kind would fain be Wits &c.—The Duchess of Devonshire, who has every thing that Heaven can give except Health and a Son, will absolutely try for Celebrity among the Wits, & to that Humour I am indebted for all her Civilities I suppose. She talked of coming here in a Week, and said She hoped to find *me* here; in the mean Time here is Master Pepys—whom I think an agreeable Man, & Mrs Montagu—a natural Converser—here is Mrs Byron too who says She tryed hard for your heart one Day at Stretham but found it impregnable either from Situation or Garrison.

Sophy Streatfield is so very lovely and singleminded a Creature that I am ready to say as you once kindly said to me of Doctor Bathurst, that you would not have trusted us with each other's Acquaintance: I like her Mother too vastly better than I thought I should. Mrs Greville has a commanding Manner & loud Voice. Why She downs every body I am sure; You never told me that She was so Lofty a Lady, nor did Dr Burney who knows her better. These Burneys are a sweet Family, I love them all, we have a Centre of Unity indeed for we all worship you alike; the D^r writes me word how happy you make them in sitting to chat some times.

Next to my Husband & Children whom should I love best but theirs and my best Friend; next to Him I do love this Dear Creature Mr Scrase: He rides out with his little Dogs about him & is fresh and comfortable & active & kind. My Master means to make him an Offer of his Money back. Please God we may yet be happy even on *my* Terms which are very Insolent too. Every Debt discharged, 20,000£ laid up, and a Son—added to my five Wenches which must be always healthy.

You have done Hester no small honour in writing such a Letter to her as would be fit for the Prince of Wales.

Farewell! if I stay here to get *fourteen Dips for my Thumb* I shall write you many a foolish before I tell you plainly how much I am

H: L: T.

Poor Doctor Worthington! I hope his Death was a Gain to himself it could not I think be a Loss to any of his Acquaintance; My Master will read my Letter, he says the poor Doctor must have died Dropsical, and that I must absolutely add that Mrs Greville is said to have formed her Manner upon yours, and now I will keep you no longer than to add his kindest Compliments lest my Letter should grow like Mrs Chapone's—five Sheets long with a Postscript of six.

586. Sa. 31 Oct. '78. Mrs. Thrale (Brighthelmston).

Address: To Henry Thrale Esq at Brighthelmston Sussex. *Postmark*: 31 OC.
Bodleian.—1788, No. 194.

Dear Madam

Your letter seemed very long a-coming, and was very welcome at last, do not be so long again.

Long live Sir John Shelly that lures my Master to hunt. I hope he will soon shake off the black dog, and come home as light as a feather. And long live Mrs G⟨reville⟩,[1] that downs

586.—Most of the allusions in this letter are explained by 585.1*a*.
    1. 'Greville' HLP *bis*; in the first occurrence this is confirmed by the traces.

my Mistress. I hope she will come home as flexible as a rush. I see my wish is rather ambiguous, it is to my Mistress that I wish flexibility. As to the imitation imputed to Mrs G⟨reville⟩, if she makes any thing like a copy, her powers of imitation are very great, for I do not remember that she ever saw me but once. If she copies me she will lose more credit by want of judgement, than she will gain by quickness of apprehension.

Of Mrs. Byron[2] I have no remembrance; perhaps her voice is low.

Miss Burney is just gone from me. I told her how you took to them all, but I told her likewise how You took to Miss S⟨...⟩.[3] All poysons have their antidotes.

Sir Joshua has finished my picture, and it seems to please every body, but I shall wait to see how it pleases You.

Of your conditions of happiness do not set your heart upon any but what Providence puts in your own power. Your debts you may pay ⟨...⟩[4] much you may lay up. The Rest you can only pray for. Of your Daughters three are out of the danger of childrens distempers, the other two have hardly yet tried whether they can live or no. You ought not yet to count them among your settled possessions.

Is it true that Mrs. D⟨avenant⟩ is enceinte?[5] it will give her great influence.

Today Mrs Williams and Mrs Desmoulines had a scold, and Williams was going away, but I bid her *not turn tail*, and she came back, and rather got the upper hand.

I wish you would come back again to us all; you will find nobody among your fine Ladies that will love you as You are loved by

Dearest Lady, Your most humble Servant

Oct. 31. 1778 Sam: Johnson.

586.—2. J means, I suppose, that her attempts upon his heart might have failed because he had not heard them.

3. HLP having covered the name with a pasted strip, wrote 'S——' on it; 1788, however, prints 'Miss . . .'. Her gloss 'Streatfield' is doubtless right.

4. After this word HLP has covered about half a line with a strip on which she has written 'much', so as to read 'pay—much'. The strip leaves, at the beginning, what looks like 'I'; J perhaps wrote 'I know not how much' or the like.

5. 'No' HLP.

587. Sa. 31 Oct. '78. Bennet Langton (Warley).

Address: To Captain Langton at Warley-camp.
Fettercairn.—Boswell 1791, ii. 276 (Hill iii. 365).

Dear Sir

When I recollect how long ago I was received with so much kindness at Warley Common, I am ashamed that I have not made some enquiries after my friends.

Pray how many Sheepstealers[1] did you convict, and how did you punish them? When are you to be cantoned in better habitations? The air grows cold, and the ground damp. Longer stay in the camp cannot be without much danger to the health of the common Men, if even the Officers can escape.

You see that Dr Percy is now Dean of Carlisle, about five hundred a year with a power of presenting himself to some good Living. He is provided for.

The session of the Club is to commence with that of the parliament. Mr. Banks desires to be admitted, he will be a very honourable accession.

Did the King please you? The Coxheath Men, I think, have some reason to complain;[2] Reynolds says your Camp is better than theirs.

I hope you find yourself able to encounter this weather; take care of your own health; and as you can, of your Men. Be pleased to make my compliments to all the Gentlemen whose notice I have had, and whose kindness I have experienced.

I am, Dear Sir, Your most humble Servant,
Oct. 31. 1778   Sam. Johnson.

588. M. 2 Nov. '78. Benjamin Wheeler (Oxford).

Address (Boswell): To the Reverend Dr Wheeler, Oxford.
Not traced.—Boswell 1791, ii. 277 (Hill iii. 366).

Dear Sir

Dr. Burney, who brings this paper, is engaged in a History

587.—1. BL had 'presided at a court-martial', 593.
2. The complaint was premature. The king, who had visited Warley 20 Oct., visited Coxheath 23 Nov. *Ann. Reg.* xxi. 1. 237.

of Musick; and having been told by Dr. Markham[1] of some MSS. relating to his subject, which are in the library of your College, is desirous to examine them. He is my friend; and therefore I take the liberty of intreating your favour and assistance in his enquiry: and can assure you, with great confidence, that if you knew him he would not want any intervenient solicitation to obtain the kindness of one who loves learning and virtue as you love them.

I have been flattering myself all the summer with the hope of paying my annual visit to my friends, but something has obstructed me: I still hope not to be long without seeing you. I should be glad of a little literary talk; and glad to shew you, by the frequency of my visits, how eagerly I love it, when you talk it. I am, dear Sir, Your most humble servant, London, Nov. 2, 1778. Sam. Johnson.

589. M. 2 Nov. '78. Edward Edwards (Oxford).

Address (Boswell): To the Reverend Dr. Edwards, Oxford.
Not traced.—Boswell 1791, ii. 277 (Hill iii. 367).

Sir

The bearer, Dr. Burney, has had some account of a Welsh Manuscript[1] in the Bodleian library, from which he hopes to gain some materials for his History of Musick; but, being ignorant of the language, is at a loss where to find assistance. I make no doubt but you, Sir, can help him through his difficulties, and therefore take the liberty of recommending him to your favour, as I am sure you will find him a man worthy of every civility that can be shewn, and every benefit that can be conferred.

But we must not let Welsh drive us from Greek. What comes of Xenophon?[2] If you do not like the trouble of

---

588.—1. No doubt the great M, who as Dean would have been familiar with the musical MSS. at Christ Church. It is, indeed, surprising that J should so name him; he is always 'the Bishop of Chester' in the letters of '75–'76 about the Carter affair, and in Dec. '77 he had become Abp. of York. J is, as a rule, punctilious in the use of titles. I note, however, that in 419 he calls the Dean of Hereford 'Dr. Wetherel'; 'Wetherel' is frequent—he knew him intimately; but 'Dr. Wetherel' is parallel to 'Dr. Markham' here.

589.—1. Not identified.
   2. See 974.

publishing the book, do not let your commentaries be lost; contrive that they may be published somewhere.

I am, Sir, Your humble servant,

London, Nov. 2, 1778.   Sam. Johnson.

589.1. M. 2 Nov. '78. Charles Burney.

Address: To Dr Burney.

Miss Blanche Burney (endorsed 'From Dr Johnson Novr 2d 1778 No 5').—

Dear Sir

I have sent your letters, and hope they may be useful. But Mr Warton can help You through all your difficulties, his acquaintance is large, and his influence powerful.

What could Madam Frances mean by leaving her little book behind her? I hope Mrs Burney grows well, and wish you a happy Journey.

I am Sir Your most affectionate

Nov. 2. 1778   Sam: Johnson

589.1a. Streatham (?). Su. 8 Nov. ⟨'78⟩. From Mrs. Thrale.

Address: To Dr Johnson Bolt Court Fleet Street. *Postmark*: PENNY POST. 8 NO.

R 540.81 (endorsed by J: 'Mrs. Thrale—78'—'79' erased).—

Tomorrow the Coach shall come for you, but can I wait so long to thank you for my books?[1] I am very proud of them, indeed I am; and they are so elegant every body envies me.

The Pepyses are here, but leave us tomorrow. Lord Westcote who is a good Tory delights in your prefaces, & would read nothing else. I am called to Breakfast & must *prattle* upon *paper* no longer. So there is another Parson to be hanged—& your Friend Hervey will make a fourth I find—but that's too odious to think on. Adieu till tomorrow. I am sure

I am your most & most

H: L: T.

589.1a.—1. See 581.

589.2. Sa. 7 Nov. '78. William Strahan.

Address: To William Strahan, Esq.

Not traced.—C. K. Shorter, *Unpublished Letters of S. J.*, 1915.

Sir   November 7, 1778

I have a friend that wants a hundred pounds. Will you send by a safe hand. I will be glad if you will find me the bill for it. There is my old reckoning with Mr. Cadell. Do look it out at last. If I can promise the hundred pounds for next week it will be sufficient.

                                  I am, Sir Your humble Servant
                                                    Sam: Johnson

590. M. 9 Nov. '78. Mrs. Thrale (Brighthelmston).

Adam.—1788, No. 195.

Dear Madam

The Lord Mayor has had a dismal day. Will not this weather drive you home? Perhaps you know not any body that will be glad to see you. I hope our Well will yield water again, and something fuller you will find the pond; but then all the trees are naked, and the ground damp. But the year must go round.

While you are away, I take great delight in your letters, only when you talk so much of obligations to me you should consider how much you put me into the condition of *honest Joseph*.[1]

Young Desmoulins thinks he has got something, he knows not what at Drury Lane; his Mother talk⟨s⟩ little of it. Sure it is not a *humm*.[2] M⟨r⟩ Levet who thinks his ancient rights invaded, stands at bay, *fierce as ten furies*.[3] M⟨rs⟩ Williams growls and scolds, but Poll[4] does not much flinch. Every body is in want.[5] I shall be glad to see Streatham again, but

589.2.—I have no clue to J's friend in need. The 'old reckoning' is no doubt that for the *Journey*; see Index VI, s.a. '75.

590.—1. Joseph Leman in Richardson's *Clarissa*, who protests to Lovelace 'I hardly know whether you are in jest, or earnest, when your Honner calls me honnest so often': 1748, iii. 38, Letter iii dated 9 April.   2. Hoax.

   3. *Paradise Lost* ii. 671.   4. Carmichael.

   5. I do not understand the point; but the reading is not in doubt.

I can find no reason for going to Brighthelmston, but that of seeing my Master and you three days sooner.

I am, Madam, Your most humble servant

Nov. 9. 1778   Sam: Johnson

---

591. Sa. 14 Nov. '78. Mrs. Thrale (Brighthelmston).
Newton.—1788, No. 197.

Dearest Madam

Then I really think I shall be very glad to see you all safe at home. I shall easily forgive my Master his long stay, if he leaves the dog behind him. We will watch as well as we can that the dog shall never be let in again, for when he comes the first thing he does is to worry my Master. This time he gnawed him to the bone. Content, said Rider's almanack, makes a man richer than the Indies.[1] But surely he that has the Indies in his possession may without very much philosophy make himself content. So much for my Master and his dog, a vile one it is, but I hope if he is not hanged, he is drowned, with another lusty shake he will pick my Master's heart out.

I have begun to take valerian; the two last nights I took half an ounce each night; a very loathsome quantity. Dr. Lawrence talked of a decoction, but I say, all or nothing. The first night I thought myself better but the next it did me no good.

Young Desmoulines says he is settled at a weekly pay of 25 shillings, about forty pounds a year.[2] Mr. Macbean has no business. We have tolerable concord at home, but no love. Williams hates every body. Levet hates Desmoulins and does not love Williams. Desmoulins hates them both. Poll loves none of them.

591.—1. 'Contentment swells a Mite into a Talent, and makes a Man richer than the *Indies*' appears, under 'Observations for October', in *Rider's British Merlin* for 1730 and other years.

  2. J's reckoning that the theatre was active for 32 weeks in the year is, I am told, approximately correct.

Dr Burney had the luck to go to Oxford, the only week in the year when the library is shut up.[3] He was however very kindly treated, as one Man is translating Arabick, and another Welsh for his service. Murphy told me that you wrote to him about Evelina. *Francis* wants to read it.

And on the 26. Burney[4] is to bring me. Pray why so. Is it not as fit that I should bring Burney?—My master is in his old lunes,[5] and so am I. Well, I do not much care how it is, and yet—At it again[6]—

Pray make my compliments to Mr Scrase. He has many things which I wish to have, his knowledge of Business, and of law. He has likewise a great chair. Such an one my Master talked of getting, but that vile black Dog.——

Mrs Queeney might write to me, and do herself no harm, she will neglect me till I shall take to Susy, and then Queeney may break her heart, and who can be blamed? I am sure I stuck to Queeney as long as I could.

Does not Master talk how full his canal will be when he comes home. Now or never. I know not how the soil was laid; if it slopes towards the canal, it may pour in a great deal of water, but I suspect it slopes the wrong way.

This is but the 14th day; there are twelve more to the twenty sixth. Did you ever hear of notching a stick? however we have it in Horace truditur dies die;[7] as twelve days have gone, twelve days will come.

Hector of Birmingham just looked in at me. He is come to his only niece, who is ill of a cancer, I believe, with very little hope, for it is knotted in two places.

I think at least I grow no worse, perhaps valerian may make me better. Let me have your prayers.

I am Dearest Lady Your most obedient servant

Nov. 14. 1778 Sam: Johnson.

591.—3. Hill has a long and entertaining (though for the most part irrelevant) note on the stated days for closing the Bodleian and on the inefficient conduct of the University's libraries. For CB's visit see 588 and letters following.

4. In her published letter dated 11 Nov. (1788, No. 196) HLT writes: 'Burney shall bring you on the 26th'; see 592.

5. *Merry Wives* IV. ii. 22.

6. 'Building!' HLP.

7. *Odes* II. xviii: 'Day tramples day' (Marris).

592. Sa. 21 Nov. '78. Mrs. Thrale (Brighthelmston).

Address: To Henry Thrale Esq at Brighthelmston Sussex. *Postmark*:
21 NO.
Adam.—1788, No. 198.

Dear Madam

I will write to you once more before you come away but—
nil mihi rescribas[1]—I hope soon to see you. Burney and I
have settled it, and I will not take a postchaise merely to
show my independence.

Now the dog is drowned I shall see both you and my
Master just as You are used to be, and with your being as
You have been, your friends may very reasonably be satisfied.
Only, be better if you can.

Return my thanks, if you please, to Queeny for her letter.
I do not yet design to leave her for Susy, but how near is the
time when She will leave me, and leave me to Susy or any
body else that will pick me up.

> —Currit enim ferox
> Aetas, et illi quos tibi demserit
> Apponet annos.[2]—

Queeny,[3] whom you watched while I held her, will soon think
our care of her very superfluous.

Miss Biron, and, I suppose, Mrs Biron, is gone. You are
by this time left alone to wander over the Steene, and listen
to the waves. This is but a dull life, come away and be busy
and count your poultry, and look into your dairy, and at
leisure hours learn what revolutions have happened at
Streatham.

I believe I told you that Jack Desmoulines is rated upon
the Book at Drury Lane five and twenty shillings a week.

Baretti has told his musical scheme[4] to Burney, and Burney

592.—1. Ovid, *Her.* i. 2: 'Don't answer; come in person'.

2. Horace, *Odes* II. v, on a girl too young for love: 'Soon she herself will dog thy
feet: / That pride of youth that reckons gain / The years thou mournest, passes fleet, /
And Lalage will chase her swain' (Marris).

3. 'When he took her in his arms, an Infant' HLP.

4. This was 'a translation . . . of the *Carmen Seculare* of Horace, which had this
year been set to musick, and performed . . . in London' (*L* iii. 373). 'Philidor and
Baretti's project it was' HLP. For J's share in the publication see *Poems* 187,
RWC in *TLS* 16 Aug. 1941.

will neither grant the question nor deny.[5] He is of opinion, that, if it does not fail, it will succeed, but, if it does not succeed he conceives it must fail.

It is good to speak dubiously about futurity. It is likewise not amiss to hope.

Did I ever tell you that George Strahan[6] was married? It so fell out that George fell in love with a girl whose fortune was so small that he perhaps could not mention it to his Father; but it happened likewise by the lottery of love, that the Father liked her so well, as of himself to recommend her to George. Such coincidence is rare.

Come, now, do come home as fast as you can,
Come with a whoop, come with a call,
Come with a good will, or come not at all.[7]
I am, Madam, Your most obedient

Nov. 21. 1778   Sam: Johnson

592a. Brighthelmston. Sa. 21 Nov. ⟨'78⟩. From Mrs. Thrale.

R 540.85—

Dear Sir   Brighthelmston Sat: 21: Nov.
    And so I heard of you at Reynolds's with Burney Baretti &c. I was glad on't: you will be content to come home & be quiet by & by; I have a grand Rout tonight, Lady Shelley Lady Poole and Militia Officers in plenty. Old Rose Fuller's Heir, Nephew to my *dear old Huh* is a very studious pretty young Fellow, & wishes I would introduce him to you, after I have made him worthy that honour he says. Lord Robert Manners visits us too. Dearee Me! how I am got all among the Quality of late—Make me thankful—like Murphy's Uncle. I hear Baretti is hard at it, not to

Sow the Sea and plough the Sands

I hope; for we are growing mighty Classical: Mason is to produce something he calls Sappho, & She is to leap into the Sea for our Entertainment—this will be a good *maxim* & a good *Fact*. Mr Scrase finds us in Sallads, Fruit &c. it is very strange how he has such pears at this Time of Year. I wish you had one of them, but what would *one* Pear do for you.
    My Master bids me say that he is just come home from a lovely Hunt, & a lovely Talk with Gerard Hamilton all about you. poor Hamilton!

592.—5. Not traced.
    6. Suppressed in 1788; 'Young Strahan' HLP.
    7. This is from the nursery rhyme 'Girls and boys come out to play'. See J. O. Halliwell, *Nursery Rhymes of England* 1842, 109.

His Head it noddeth so—that by my fay
I think it soon will fly from his old Crag away.
Tis five o'Clock & Dinner waiting Adieu

Ever Ever—H: L: T.

593. Sa. 21 Nov. '78.   James Boswell (Edinburgh).
Not traced.—Boswell 1791, ii. 278 (Hill iii. 368).

Dear Sir

It is indeed a long time since I wrote, and I think you have some reason to complain; however, you must not let small things disturb you, when you have such a fine addition to your happiness as a new boy,[1] and I hope your lady's health restored by bringing him. It seems very probable that a little care will now restore her, if any remains of her complaints are left.

You seem, if I understand your letter, to be gaining ground at Auchinleck, an incident that would give me great delight.

* * * * * *

When any fit of anxiety, or gloominess, or perversion of mind, lays hold upon you, make it a rule not to publish it by complaints, but exert your whole care to hide it; by endeavouring to hide it, you will drive it away. Be always busy.

The Club is to meet with the parliament; we talk of electing Banks,[2] the traveller; he will be a reputable member.

Langton has been encamped with his company of militia on Warley-common; I spent five days amongst them, he signalized himself as a diligent officer, and has very high respect in the regiment. He presided when I was there at a court-martial; he is now quartered in Hertfordshire; his lady and little ones are in Scotland. Paoli came to the camp and commended the soldiers.

Of myself I have no great matter to say, my health is not

593.—See *L* iii. 366 for JB's brief description of three letters, parts of which J now answers.

1. James.

2. JR wrote to B 11 Dec. informing him of his election, 'he need not add unanimously, as one black ball would have excluded him' (*Letters*, ed. F. W. Hilles, 1929, 67).

restored, my nights are restless and tedious. The best night that I have had these twenty years was at Fort-Augustus.[3]

I hope soon to send you a few lives to read.

I am, dear Sir, Your most affectionate,

Nov. 21, 1778.   Sam. Johnson.

594. M. ⟨23 Nov. '78⟩. John Nichols.

B.M.—*Gent. Mag.* Jan. 1785.

Mr Johnson will hope for Mr Nichols' company to tea, about six this afternoon, to talk of the Index,[1] and settle the terms.

Monday.

595. Th. 26 Nov. '78. John Nichols.

Address: To Mr Nichols.

B.M.—*Gent. Mag.* Jan. 1785.

Sir

I am very well contented that the Index is settled, for though the price is low, it is not penurious.

Mr. Macbean having been for some time out of business, is in some little perplexities, from which twelve guineas will set him free. This, we hope, you will advance, and during the continuance of the work subject to your inspection he desires a weekly payment of sixteen shillings, the rest to remain till it is completed.

I am Sir Your most humble servant,

Nov. 26 1778   Sam: Johnson.

595.1. Sa. 5 Dec. '78. Thomas Lawrence.

Maggs Cat. 337 (1915), 797 (not seen).—Extract in catalogue.

I perceive that our business has not been properly done. I suppose the Will must be returned, that the exemplification may be verified. If you will send me the paper and necessary directions I will send them away to-night.

593.—3. 30 Aug. '73. He had recalled this 'sweet uninterrupted sleep' in *PM* for 6 Apr. '77.

594.—1. To 'Johnson's Poets', see 595 and Index VI. The *Index to the Poets* was compiled by Macbean (*General Index to the GM* 1821, iii. xx).

596. M. 7 Dec. '78. ⟨Thomas Fitzmaurice.⟩

Sotheby 21 Dec. 1928.—Hill 1892.

Sir,

Good wishes are the necessary consequence of friendship, and of my good wishes, I hope, you make no doubt. But now you have a son I know not well what more to wish you except more sons, and a few daughters; the sons to be all brave and the daughters all beautiful, and both sons and daughters to be wise and good.

Now you have a son what can you want? You have a mother to rejoice in her grandson, and a Lady to partake in all your felicities. With Lady Shelburn I once had the honour of conversing, and entreat you, Sir, to let her know that I have not forgotten it; to your Lady I am a stranger, but who can doubt the excellence of her, who⟨m⟩ you have chosen, and who has chosen you?

If encrease of happiness cannot be expected it still remains to wish the continuance, and very long it will continue, if there be any power in the desires of,

Sir, Your most humble servant,

Dec. 7, 1778. Sam: Johnson.

597. ⟨Dec. '78.⟩ John Nichols.

B.M.—*GM* Jan. 1785 (date added by Nichols); Boswell 1791, ii. 345 (Hill iv. 36).

Sir

By some accident, I laid your note upon Duke, up so safely that I cannot find it. Your informations have been of great use to me. I must beg it again, with another list of our authours, for I have laid that with the other. I am Sir &c.

I have sent Stepney's Epitaph. Let me have the revises as soon as can be.

596.—Though the address is lost this letter is clearly to Fitzmaurice, see references in Index II.

598. Th. 29 Dec. '78. John Hussey.

Address: To the Rev^d Mr Hussey.
D. Nichol Smith (mutilated, lacking the subscription, signature, and
date given by Boswell; endorsed 'from Dr. Johnson previous to my
departure for Aleppo'); JB's copy, Isham.[1]—Boswell 1791, ii. 279 (Hill
iii. 369).

Dear Sir
    I have sent you the Grammar, and have left you two
Books more by which I hope to be remembred.[2] Write my
name in them. We may perhaps see each other no more.
You part with my good wishes, nor do I despair of seeing you
return. Let no opportunities of vice corrupt you, Let no
bad examples seduce You. Let the blindness of Mahometans
confirm you in Christianity. God bless you.
    I am, dear Sir, Your affectionate humble servant,
December 29, 1778.   Sam: Johnson

598.1. ⟨? '78.⟩ Edmund Burke.

Not traced.—Percival Stockdale, *Memoirs* 1809, ii. 129.

    S 'once' (he thought, in '78) asked J to recommend him to Burke. 'Dr.
Johnson gave me his letter of recommendation to read; it was a short, but
kind one. I have often regretted that I did not keep a copy of it. I, at this
time, took several occasions to express my dislike of the measures of government;... to this circumstance, a humorous, and ironical remark in the doctor's
letter alluded....'

To his political heresies, I wish that *you* were more an
enemy.

599. Sa. 2 Jan. '79. Elizabeth Aston (Lichfield).

Pembroke.—Croker's Boswell 1831, iv. 237.

Dear Madam
    Now the new year is come of which I wish you and dear
Mrs. Gastrel many and many returns, it is fit that I give you
some account of the year past. In the beginning of it I had
a difficulty of breathing and other ilness from which however
I by degrees recovered and from which I am now tolerably
free. In the spring and summer I flattered myself that I
should come to Lichfield, and forebore to write till I could

598.—1. JB's variants are typical: 'remembered', 'example', 'Goᴅ'.
    2. See Addenda, p. 529.

tell of my intentions with some certainty, and, one thing or other[1] making the Journey always improper, as I did not come, I omitted to write, till at last I grew afraid of hearing ill news. But the other day Mr. Prujean called, and left word that you, dear Madam, are grown better, I know not when I heard any thing that pleased me so much. I shall now long more and more to see Lichfield, and partake the happiness of your recovery.

Now you begin to mend you have great encouragement to take care of yourself, do not omit any thing that can conduce to your health, and when I come I shall hope to enjoy with you and dearest Mrs. Gastrel many pleasing hours.

Do not be angry at my long omission to write, but let me hear how you both do, for you will write to nobody to whom your welfare will give more pleasure, than to,

Dearest Madam, Your most humble servant,

Sam: Johnson.

London. Bolt court, Fleet street Jan 2. 1779

600. Sa. 2 Jan. '79. Lucy Porter (Lichfield).

Sotheby 17 March 1930.—Croker's Boswell 1831, iv. 238.

Dearest Love

Though I have so long omitted to write, I will omit it no longer. I hope the new Year finds you not worse than you have formerly been; and I wish that many years may pass over you without bringing either pain or discontent. For my part, I think my health, though not good, yet rather better than when I left you.

My purpose was to have paid you my annual visit in the Summer, but it happened otherwise, not by any journey another way, for I have never been many miles from London, but by such hindrances as it is hard to bring to any account.

Do not follow my bad example but write to me soon again, and let me know of you what you have to tell; I hope it is all good.

Please to make my compliments to Mrs Cobb, Mrs Adey,

599.—1. Here and elsewhere J refrains from alleging the obvious excuse, that he had been busy with the *Lives*. There had no doubt been periods of inactivity; but a man less scrupulous than J would have told himself and others that he had worked very hard.

and Miss Adey, and all the Ladies and Gentlemen that frequent your Mansion.

If you want any books, or any thing else that I can send you, let me know. I am

Dear Madam, Your most humble servant,

Boltcourt Fleetstreet Jan. 2. 1779   Sam: Johnson.

600.1. Streatham. Th. 21 Jan. '79. Eva Maria Garrick.

Tregaskis (1938).—

Mr Johnson sends his compliments to Mrs Garrick, and desires to know how she does.

601. Tu. 2 Feb. '79. Eva Maria Garrick.

Maggs 1926.—Hill 1892.

Dr¹ Johnson sends most respectful condolence to Mrs Garrick, and wishes that any endeavour of his could enable² her support a loss which the world cannot repair.

Febr. 2, 1779

602. M. 15 Feb. '79. Frances Reynolds.

Rupert Colomb.—Croker's Boswell 1831, iv. 240.

Dearest Madam

I have never deserved to be treated as you treat me, when you employed me before, I undertook your affair, and succeeded, but then I succeeded by chusing a proper time, and a proper time I will try to chuse again.

I have about a week's work to do, and then I shall come to live in town, and will first wait on you in Dover street. You are not to think that I neglect you, for your Nieces will tell you how rarely they have seen me. I will wait on you as soon as I can, and yet you must resolve to talk things over without anger, and you must leave me to catch opportunities; and be

601.—1. For the title see 927.1.

2. *OED* gives no example of 'enable' without 'to'; but in the light of the construction of 'help' it seems not impossible.

602.—Refers no doubt to FR's differences with her brother. Hill quotes Leslie and Taylor's *Reynolds* (i. 183) for an instance of their causes, and Northcote's *Reynolds* (i. 203) for Johnson's efforts to compose them.

assured, Dearest Dear, that I should have very little enjoyment of the day in which I had rejected any opportunity of doing good to you.

I am, dearest Madam, Your humble servant,

Febr. 15. 1799   Sam: Johnson.

603. M. 1 Mar. '79. John Nichols.

B.M.—*GM* Jan. 1785; Boswell 1791, ii. 345 (Hill iv. 36).

Sir

I have sent Philips[1] with his epitaphs to be inserted.

The fragment of a Preface is hardly worth the impression but that we may seem to do something. It may be added to the life of Philips.[2]

The Latin Page is to be added to the life of Smith.[3]

I shall be at home to revise the two sheets of Milton.

I am, Sir, Your most humble Servant

March 1. 1779   Sam: Johnson

604. Th. 4 Mar. '79. Elizabeth Aston (Lichfield).

Pembroke.—Croker's Boswell 1831, iv. 241.

Dear Madam

Mrs Gastrel and You are very often in my thoughts, though I do not write so often as might be expected from so much love and so much respect. I please myself with thinking that I shall see you again, and shall find you better. But futurity is uncertain, poor David[1] had doubtless many futurities in his head, which death has intercepted, a death, I believe, totally unexpected; he did not in his last hour seem to think his Life in danger.

My old complaints hang heavy on me, and my nights are

603.—1. John not Ambrose.

2. J appended to the *Life of Philips* (ed. Hill i. 320) 'A prefatory Discourse to the Poem on Mr. Philips'. This was by Edmund Smith, and had been 'transcribed from the Bodleian manuscripts'.

3. At the end of the *Life of Smith* (ed. Hill ii. 21) is another quotation from a Bodleian MS.: 'Ex Autographo [sent by the author to Mr. Urry].' J was no doubt attracted by the concluding sentence: 'Pembrochienses voco ad certamen Poeticum.'

604.—1. Garrick.

very uncomfortable and unquiet; and sleepless nights make heavy days. I think to go to my Physitian, and try what can be done. For why should not I grow better as well as you?

Now you are better, pray, dearest Madam, take care of yourself. I hope to come this Summer and watch you. It will be a very pleasant journey if I can find you and dear Mrs. Gastrel well.

I sent you two barels of oysters. If you would wish for more, please to send your commands to,

Madam, Your most humble servant,

Sam: Johnson.

Bolt court, Fleet street. March 4. 1779

605. Th. 4 Mar. '79. Lucy Porter (Lichfield).

D. F. Pennant.—Croker's Boswell 1831, iv. 241.

My dear Love

Since I heard from you, I sent you a little print, and two barrels of Oysters, and I shall have some little books to send you soon.

I have seen Mr Pearson, and am pleased to find that he has got a living. I was hurried when he was with me, but had time to hear that my Friends were all well.

Poor Mrs Adey was, I think, a good woman and therefore her death is the less to be lamented; but it is not pleasant to think, how uncertain it is, that when Friends part, they will ever meet again.

My old complaints of flatulence, and tight and short breath oppress me heavily; my nights are very restless. I think of consulting the Doctor to morrow.

This has been a mild Winter, for which I hope you have been the better. Take what care you can of yourself and do not forget to drink. I was somehow or other hindred from coming into the country last summer, but I think of coming this year.

I am Dear Love, Your most humble Servant

Sam: Johnson.

Bolt court Fleet street, March 4. 1779

605.1. 9 Mar. '79. John Taylor (Ashbourne).

Address: To the Rev^d Dr Taylor in Ashbourne Derbyshire. *Postmark*:
9 MR.
Sotheby 2 March 1940.—

Dear Sir

When You went away You desired me to remind You of
your health; if any Mementos of mine could do You good,
You should not want them, though I should write the same
advice by every post. I have not indeed any advice to give
You but that you keep your mind from disturbance, by
attending to such things as You can supervise without
anxiety. Utter inattention is a state both wretched and
dangerous, and too much is likewise pernicious. Attention
should be some thing less than anxiety, as exercise is some
thing less than labour.

About meat and drink I have no counsel to give; I wish
you could take more of both without oppression. Whatever
oppresses must be hurtful.

I am afraid that You have not gotten your casting weights.
They will supply you with very commodious exercise, if you
do not tire yourself with them, and throw them quite away.
Keep yourself cheerful, yet not forgetting that every decay
is sent us to remind us of another world, and of the shortness
of life. I am glad your Sunday is changed to Monday.[1]

I will in a post or two write to Mr Langley, and tell him
all that he ought to know. I am glad that we talked about it.

I have very unquiet and tedious nights. I am come home[2]
for a few weeks to be a little in the world. but I like walking
so little, that I can scarcely persuade myself to go out doors.
Take care of yourself, and consult Dr Butter. Heberden's
talk was rather prudential than medical, You might however
perceive from it how much he thought peace of mind
necessary to your reestablishment. I am Dear Sir, Your
affectionate Servant

March 9. 1779 London.   Sam: Johnson

605.1.—1. JT had perhaps intended travelling on a Sunday. For J's views on Sunday
travelling see 329 (p. 366). The practice is included, in *Persuasion*, among the
symptoms of Mr. Elliot's depravity.

2. The word 'home', which often (Hill, in a note on 551, seems to imply, always)
means one of the Thrale houses, here means Bolt Court.

606. W. 10 Mar. '79. Mrs. Thrale.

A. Houghton.—1788, No. 199.

And so, dear Madam, it is a Mumm[1] to see who will speak first. I will come to see You on Saturday only let me know whether I must come to the borough, or am to be taken up here.

Baretti's golden dream is now but silver.[2] He is of my mind, he says, that there is no money for diversions. But we make another onset on Friday, and this is to be the last time this season.

I got my lives, not yet quite printed, put neatly together, and sent them to the King,[3] what he says of them I know not. Mr Barnard could not speak to him. If the King is a Whig, he will not like them; but is any King a Whig?

So far I had gone when—in came Mr Thrale, who will have the honour of bringing it.

     I am, Madam, Your most humble Servant
March 10. 1779   Sam: Johnson

606a. Streatham. Th. ⟨11 Mar. '79⟩. From Mrs. Thrale.

Address: Doctor Johnson Fleet Street.

R 540.87—

              Streatham Thursday.
Ah Dear Sir & how kind you are! & how indulgent to the Caprices of your saucy Mistress! I had a mind you should write first sure enough.

My Master is come home in high good humour considering that the Ministry hiss on the black Dog as hard as ever they can; but here is Weather to answer every Tax on Malt I do think. I will fetch you or send the Coach to your House at 3 o Clock next Saturday when I hope you will come fraught with News to the most ignorant and most faithful of all your Friends
              H: L: T.

607. Sa. 13 Mar. '79. James Boswell (Edinburgh).

Not traced.—Boswell 1791, ii. 281 (Hill iii. 372).

Dear Sir

Why should you take such delight to make a bustle, to

606.—1. That is, a contest at 'playing mum'; to play mum is to be silent. *OED*.

2. See 592. Hill quotes Walpole on the financial stringency due to the American war; the Government had to pay eight per cent. for money.

3. HLP first reduced this to 'K——' then restored it; but she suppressed the sentence about Barnard, the king's librarian.

write to Mr. Thrale[1] that I am negligent, and to Francis[2] to do what is so very unnecessary. Thrale, you may be sure, cared not about it; and I shall spare Francis the trouble, by ordering a set both of the Lives and Poets[3] to dear Mrs. Boswell, in acknowledgement of her marmalade. Persuade her to accept them, and accept them kindly. If I thought she would receive them scornfully, I would send them to Miss Boswell, who, I hope, has yet none of her mamma's ill-will to me.

I would send sets of Lives, four volumes, to some other friends, to Lord Hailes first. His second volume lies by my bed-side; a book surely of great labour, and to every just thinker of great delight. Write me word to whom I shall send besides; would it please Lord Auchinleck? Mrs. Thrale waits in the coach.

I am, dear Sir, &c.,

March 13, 1779.   Sam. Johnson.

608. Th. 18 Mar. '79. Mrs. Thrale.

Sotheby 30 Jan. 1918 (not seen).—1788, No. 200.

Dear Madam,   March 18, 1779.

There is some comfort in writing, when such praise is to be had. Plato is a multitude.[1]

On Monday I came late to Mrs. Vesey. Mrs. Montague was there; I called for the print,[2] and got good words. The evening was not brilliant, but I had thanks for my company. The night was troublesome. On Tuesday I fasted, and went to the Doctor: he ordered bleeding. On Wednesday I had the teapot,[3] fasted, and was blooded. Wednesday night was

607.—1. JB had written on 22 Jan. and 2 Feb. without getting an answer; he wrote again 23 Feb. 'complaining of his silence, as I had heard he was ill, and had written to Mr. Thrale, for information concerning him'.

2. J had promised JB the proofs of the *Lives*, and JB had written to Frank 'to take care of them for me'.

3. 'He sent a set elegantly bound and gilt, which was received as a very handsome present' JB. It was handsome indeed, for it comprised in the end 68 volumes. See 701, 714.

608.—1. See on 451.

2. See 583.

3. My medical advisers are unable to give a technical sense to this term. I am reluctant to think that 'teapot' for Wednesday and Friday implies that J drank no tea on Thursday. He probably means that he ate and drank little except tea on 'teapot' days.

better. To-day I have dined at Mr. Strahan's at Islington, with his new wife. To-night there will be opium. To-morrow the teapot. Then heigh for Saturday. I wish the Doctor would bleed me again. Yet every body that I meet says I look better than when I was last met.

                I am, dearest Lady, Your, &c.

608a. Th. 1 Apr. 〈'79〉. From Mrs. Thrale.

Address: Doctor Johnson Bolt Court Fleet Street.
R 540.88—

Dear Sir—   Thursday 1: April.
   I *think* you promised to come home o' Tuesday, & I *think* that is the Day General Paoli & Mr Boswell dine with us; Dr Burney takes charge of this Note which is chiefly meant to coax you out of a Line to say how you do.
   News I have none, it is none to say that I am Most sincerely Dear Sir Your most Humble Servt

                              H: L: Thrale

608.1. F. 9 Apr. '79. Mrs. Thrale.

Address: To Mrs Thrale.
Adam.—

Madam

   An unexpected invitation will keep me here to Monday, but do, dear, sweet, fine, kind, &c &c &c &c &c &c send for me before sunrise on Monday. I have sent you the books.

       I am, Dearest Lady, Your most, and most &c
Friday Apr. 9 1779   Sam: Johnson

609. W. 13 Apr. '79. Thomas Cadell.

Address: To Mr. Cadel.
Newton.—Hill 1892 (misdated 3 April).

Sir

   The Duty of Man is not the right.[1] Nelson is bound in sheepskin, a thing I never saw before. I was bred a Bookseller, and have not forgotten my trade.

609.—1. J perhaps means that C has sent the wrong edition of (Allestree's?) *Whole Duty of Man*, and that sheepskin insults the dignity of Nelson's *Festivals*: presents, possibly, for LP. For his powers as a bookbinder see *L* i. 56. See also 1121, iii. 258.

Do not let us teize one another about books.² That they are lent about I suppose is true, but it must be principally by those that have bought them, which would have been done much less, if you had united every writer's life to his works, for then the borrower must have carried away near twenty volumes³ whereas he now takes but four. I will venture to say that of those which I have given very few are lent. But be that as it may, you must supply me with what I think it proper to distribute among my friends. Let us have no dispute about it. I think myself not well used.

　　　　　　　　　　I am Sir Your very humble servant,

Apr. 13. 1779　　　　　　　　　　　　　Sam: Johnson.

610. M. 26 Apr. '79. James Boswell (London).

Address (Boswell): To Mr. Boswell.

Not traced.—Boswell 1791, ii. 292 (Hill iii. 391).

Mr. Johnson laments the absence of Mr. Boswell, and will come to him.

Harley-street.

610.1. Tu. 27 Apr. '79. Edmund Burke (London).

See Addenda, p. 529.

611. Su. 2 May '79. John Nichols.

B.M.—*GM* Jan. 1785; Boswell 1791, ii. 346 (Hill iv. 36).

Please to get me the last edition of Hughes's Letters; and try to get Dennis upon Blackmore, and upon Cato, and any thing of the same writer against Pope. Our materials are defective.

As Waller professed to have imitated Fairfax, do you think a few pages of Fairfax would enrich <u>our edition</u>?¹ Few

609.—2. Author's or presentation copies, see Index VII. The original intention *was* to prefix each 'Preface' to its author's works; for proof of this see Chapman-Hazen. The booksellers might retort that J's slowness had compelled them to the change of plan. But they still did not sell the *Prefaces* separately. He was always high-handed in demanding 'books', being no doubt aware that he was paid less than his work was worth.

　　3. In fact the 'Poets' corresponding to the four volumes of 'Prefaces' comprise 22 out of the 56 volumes of the collection.

610.—J was dining at Allan Ramsay's (67 Harley Street: Hill, quoting Cunningham). JB was in bed 'with an inflamed foot'.

611.—1. The underline in the MS. (which might, of course, not be J's) is perhaps an allusion to the booksellers' 'indecent' description of the edition as 'Johnson's Poets', See 670.

readers have seen it,[2] and it may please them. But it is not necessary.

May 2, 1779.   Sam: Johnson

612. M. 3 May '79. John Wesley (Edinburgh).

Address (Boswell): To the Reverend Mr. John Wesley. Not traced.—Boswell 1791, ii. 294 (Hill iii. 394).

Sir

Mr. Boswell, a gentleman who has been long known to me, is desirous of being known to you, and has asked this recommendation, which I give him with great willingness, because I think it very much to be wished that worthy and religious men should be acquainted with each other.

I am, Sir, Your most humble servant,

May 3, 1779.   Sam. Johnson.

613. Tu. 4 May '79. Elizabeth Aston (Lichfield).

A. Houghton.—Croker's Boswell 1831, iv. 265.

Dear Madam

When I sent You the little books, I was not sure that You were well enough to take the trouble of reading them, but have lately heard from Mr. Greene[1] that you are much recovered. I hope You will gain more and more strength, and live many and many years, and I shall come again to Stowhill, and live as I used to do, with You and dear Mrs. Gastrel.

I am not well, my Nights are very troublesome, and my breath is short, but I know not that it grows much worse. I wish to see You. Mrs Hervey has just sent to me to dine with her, and I have promised to wait on her to morrow.

Mr. Green comes home loaded with curiosities, and will be able to give his friends new entertainment. When I come,

---

611.—2. By 'it' J means Fairfax's translation of Tasso's 'Godfrey of Bulloigne'. A substantial extract from the poem was appended to the *Life of Waller* (ed. Hill, ¶¶ 5, 154).

612.—Wesley was then 'in the course of his ministry at Edinburgh' (*L* iii. 394).

613.—1. Croker misread the MS. and created a fictitious 'Mr. Greeves'.

it will be great entertainment to me, if I can find You and Mrs. Gastrel well, and willing to receive me.

I am, Dearest Madam, Your most humble Servant

May 4. 1779   Sam: Johnson

614. Tu. 4 May '79. Lucy Porter (Lichfield).

Address: Miss Lucy Porter Lichfield. Franked by Strahan. *Postmark*: 5 MA.

Fettercairn.—Boswell 1791, ii. 293 (Hill iii. 393).

Dear Madam

Mr. Green has informed me that You are much better. I hope I need not tell You that I am glad of it. I cannot boast of being much better, my old nocturnal complaint still persues me, and my respiration is difficult, though much easier than when I left You the summer before last. Mr and Mrs Thrale are well, Miss has been a little indisposed, but she is got well again. They have since the loss of their boy had two daughters, but they seem likely to want a Son.

I hope you had some books which I sent You. I was sorry for poor Mrs Adey's death, and am afraid You will be sometimes solitary, but endeavour, whether alone or in company, to keep yourself cheerful. My friends likewise die very fast, but such is the state of Man.

I am, Dear Love, Your most humble Servant,

May 4. 1779   Sam: Johnson.

614.1. Tu. 4 May '79. John Taylor (Ashbourne).

Address: Revd Dr Taylor Ashburn Derbyshire. Franked by Strahan. *Postmarks*: 5 *and* 6 MA.

Harvard.—

Dear Sir

It is a long time since I wrote to you, but alas! what have two sick old Friends to say to one another? commonly nothing but that they continue to be sick. This at least is my case. Your last letter gave me hopes that it is less yours. But though we may be by intervals better, we know that we are in the main growing worse. This decline may however be hastened or retarded, and I hope we shall both retard it, as far as the laws of Nature permit. You are so regular that

I know not what to advise more than you already do. I believe a moderate use of the weights[1] will be useful, but nequid nimis, Fatigue is dangerous.

Mr Green of Lichfield has been here, and is returned loaded with Sir Ashton Levers Superfluities. He said nothing of the affair of Wood, nor was it mentioned.

I am, Dear Sir, Your most humble Servant

May 4. 1779   Sam: Johnson

615. Th. 20 May '79. Mrs. Thrale.

Rylands.—1788, No. 201.

Dear Madam,   May 20, 1779.

The vicissitudes of things, and the eddies of life, are now carrying you southward,[1] and me northward. When shall we meet again?

I must beg of you to send Mr. Watson's[2] papers to my house, directed for him, and sealed up. I know not whether he does not think himself in danger of piracy.

Take care that Susy[3] sees all that Sophy has seen, that she may tell her travels, and give them a taste of the world. And take care, and write to me very often, till we meet again; and keep Master in good thoughts of me. *Vale.*

615a. Brighthelmston. W. 26 May ⟨'79⟩.   From Mrs. Thrale to J at Lichfield.

Address: To Doctor Sam: Johnson at Lichfield. *Postmark*: 29 MA. Franked by HT.

R 540.89—

Dear Sir   Brighthelmston Wednesday 26: May

Though we mean to leave this place on Monday next, and though it is barren enough of Conversation or Subjects of Amusement yet I must date one Letter from it—'tis so *natural* to write to Lichfield from Brighthelmstone. The Bishop of Peterborough however—who is here on account of a sick Child visits us; he & his Lady spent the Evening with us last Night, and so did two

614.1.—1. See 605.1.

615.—1. The Thrales took Q, Susan, and FB to B'n (FB's *Diary*, letter of 26 May).

2. Hill was in error in stating that 'the last volume' of Watson's *Philip II* was published in '79. He was probably misled by the fact that the first edition, '77, is in two volumes quarto, the third, '79, in three volumes octavo. The 'papers' of this letter were perhaps the MS. of *Philip III*, which was published posthumously in '83.

3. Susan was the elder, but Sophy had seen B'n before, see 615a.

or three of the Militia Officers & their Ladies. The Bishop is a Gentleman-like Man, and Mrs Hinchliffe rather agreeable. Doctor Delap is getting ready His Play against the Town fills for the Winter Season—he says I shall read it, an honour you will envy me no doubt: the Shelleys & he have quarrell'd, which is not lucky for either of them as they are situated.

Sophy shews Susan the Wonders of the Deep very ludicrously; & they are both at this moment employed in writing to some of their Schoolfellows to tell them how happily they live here.

Miss Burney & Hester profess hard Study & steady Secresy, they are both very well, so is my Master & so is Dear Sir Your ever Faithful & Obliged

H: L: Thrale.

616. Lichfield. Sa. 29 May '79. Mrs. Thrale.

Adam.—1788, No. 202.

Madam

I have now been here a week, and will try to give you my Journal, or such parts of it as are fit in my mind for communication.

On friday. We¹ set out about twelve, and lay at Daventry.²

On Saturday. We dined with Mr Rann at Coventry. He intercepted us at the town's end. I saw Tom Johnson who had hardly life to know that I was with him. I hear he is since dead. In the Evening I came to Lucy, and walked to Stow hill; Mrs Aston was gone or going to Bed. I did not see her.

Sunday. After diner I went to Stow hill, and was very kindly received. At night I saw my old friend Brodhurst—you know him—the play fellow of my infancy, and gave him a Guinea.

Monday. Dr Taylor came, and we went with Mrs Cobb to Greenhill Bower.³ I had not seen it perhaps for fifty years. It is much degenerated. Every thing grows old. Taylor is to fetch me next Saturday.

616.—1. It does not appear who J's fellow traveller was. Perhaps only Frank, though 'we dined' seems against that.

2. J's favourite route was by O'd and B'm; on this occasion they took the direct (Liverpool) road, via St. Albans, Daventry, Coventry, and Coleshill. They travelled 'post', as 623 shows.

3. Hill quotes Harwood's *Hist. of Lichfield*, 352, for the traditional junketings on this 'open mount' on Whit Monday, but does not note that in '79 Whit Monday fell on the 24 May, the 'Monday' of J's 'journal'.

Mr Green came to see us, and I ordered some physick.

Tuesday. Physick, and a little company. I dined I think, with Lucy both Monday and Tuesday.

Wednesday ⎫ I had a few visits, from Peter Garrick
Thursday ⎬ among the rest, and dined at Stow hill.
          ⎭ My breath very short.

Friday. I dined at Stow hill. I have taken Physick four days together.

Saturday. Mrs Aston took me out in her chaise, and was very kind. I dined with Mrs Cobb and came to Lucy with whom I found, as I had done the first day, Lady Smith and Miss Vyse. I find that Dr Vyse talks here of Miss Stratfield.[4]

This is the course of my life. You do not think it much makes me forget Streatham. However it is good to wander a little, lest one should dream that all the world was Streatham, of which one may venture to say *None but itself can be its parallel.*[5]

I am Dear Madam, Your most humble servant
Lichfield May 29. 1779   Sam: Johnson

616.1. Ashbourne. Th. 10 June '79. Mrs. Thrale.

Address: To Henry Thrale Esq in Southwark. *Postmark*: 12 IV. Adam.—

Dear Madam

I am surprised to find that I can be away and write so seldom, but I have very little to say. Mr Green was much delighted with his afternoon at your house, and returned home much enriched by Mr Lever.[1]

Poor Lucy is so much enfeebled in her feet that she cannot walk to church, and what is far worse, has her hearing very much impaired. I wish Miss would write to her. She will be glad.

616.—4. Streatfield. HLP (for whose jealousy of the lovely Sophia see C 173) suppressed this sentence.

5. 'None but thyself can be thy parallel': Theobald, *Double Falsehood* iii. 1; quoted by Pope, *Dunciad* (iii. 271 in the *Dunciad Variorum* 1729). Joseph Warton traced this 'marvellous line' (as Pope called it in derision) to Seneca's *Hercules Furens* 84: Quaeris Alcidae parem ? / Nemo est nisi ipse.

616.1.—1. 'Sir Ashton Lever' in 614.1, correctly.

Mrs Aston is better than when I left her two years ago; but she eats almost nothing. Everybody else is as when you left us.

I have tried Phlebotomy and Physick but with no great success, but, I think, I am not worse.

Here is Dr Taylor, better in his health likewise than he was. He eats little, but drinks by measure a full quart of water every dinner, which he says has quite cured the swelling of his legs. I dined two days ago with the old set of friends, male and female.

I am Dear Madam, Your most humble servant
Ashbourne June 10. 1779   Sam: Johnson

617. Ashbourne. Sa. 12 June '79. Mrs. Thrale.

Adam.—1788, No. 203 (misdated 14 June).

Dear Madam

Your account of Mr. Thrale's ilness[1] is very terrible, but when I remember that he seems to have it peculiar to his constitution, that whatever distemper he has, he always has his head affected, I am less frighted. The seizure was, I think, not apoplectical, but hysterical, and therefore not dangerous to life. I would have you however consult such Physitians as you think, you can best trust. Bromfield seems to have done well, and by his practice appears not to suspect an apoplexy.[2] That is a solid and fundamental comfort. I remember Dr. Marsigli an Italian Physician whose seizure was more violent than Mr. Thrale's, for he fell down helpless, but his case was not considered as of much danger, and he went safe home, and is now a professor at Padua. His fit was considered as only hysterical.

617.—This letter is dated 14 June in 1788. The error must be accidental, for 618 is also dated 14 June.

1. 'It *was* apoplectical—he had dined with his simple sister Mrs. Nesbit, who had so lately lost her husband—and since these letters were printed have I found out that talking the dead brother in law's affairs over it was fully certain that he died insolvent, and Mr. Thrale knowing how he was bound for him, felt the Black Dog's bite in his heart directly. but of all this dear Dr. Johnson and I had no suspicion' HLP. Her letter giving the news is lost; for a full account see *Th* 389.

2. 'Bromfield knew it was an apoplexy' HLP.

I hope Sir Philip[3] who franked your letter comforts you as well as Mr Seward. If I can comfort you, I will come to you, but I hope you are now no longer in want of any help to be happy.

I am, Dearest Madam, Your most humble Servant,
June 12. 1779. Ashbourne.   Sam: Johnson.

The Dr sends his compliments, he is one of the people that are growing old.

618. Ashbourne. M. 14 June '79. Mrs. Thrale.
Adam.—1788, No. 204.

Dear Madam

How near we all are to extreme danger. We are [are] merry or sad, or busy or idle, and forget that Death is hovering over us. You were a dear Lady for writing again. The case as you now describe it is worse than I conceived it when I read your first letter. It is still however not apoplectick, but seems to have something worse than hys⟨t⟩erical, a tendency to a palsy, which I hope, however, is now over. I am glad that you have Heberden, and hope We are all safer. I am the more alarmed by this violent seizure, as I can impute it to no wrong practices or intemperance of any kind, and therefore know not how any defence or preservatives can be obtained. Mr Thrale has certainly less exercise than when he folowed the foxes, but he is very far from unweildiness or inactivity, and further still from any vitious or dangerous excess. I fancy however he will do well to ride more.

Do, dear Madam, let me know every post, how he goes on. Such sudden violence is very dreadful, we know not by what it is let loose upon us, nor by what its effects are limited.

If my coming can either assist or divert, or be useful to any purpose, let me but know. I will soon be with you.

617.—3. Jennings Clerk.

Mrs Kennedy, Queeny's Baucis,[1] ended last week a long life of disease and poverty. She had been married about fifty years.

Dr Taylor is not much amiss, but always complaining.

I am, Madam, Your most humble servant
Ashbourne, June 14. 1779   Sam: Johnson
Direct the next to Lichfield

618.1. Ashbourne.   M. 14 June '79.   Nathan Wetherell (Oxford).

Address: To the Reverend Dr Wetherel in Oxford. *Postmark*: 16 iv. Huntington.—

Sir

Dr Taylor one of the Prebendaries of Westminster has lately lost by sudden death a Curate who had served his living of Bosworth in Leicestershire more than twenty years. The allowance is fifty pounds a year. If Mr Maurice of your College has not something better, he may perhaps think it worth his acceptance, and I beg that You will propose it to him. It is a large parish, but there are two Curates.

My first wish is to accommodate Mr Maurice, but upon his refusal, any Gentleman whom You shall be pleased to recommend will be received by Dr Taylor. As the want is immediate and pressing, it must be supplied with speed. A little delay might be perhaps endured in favour of Mr Maurice, but if a stranger comes it will be expected that he should come quickly.

You will be pleased to direct your answer to Dr Taylor in Ashbourne, Derbyshire, for perhaps I may not stay her⟨e⟩ long enough to receive it.

I am Sir, Your most humble Servant
Ashbourne June 14. 1779   Sam: Johnson.

618.—1. 'Old Kennedy and his wife were two of the greatest scholars in England. They were imagining at what time the sun shone first upon the Earth, instead of minding how to live upon it themselves. Miss Thrale (whom we called Queeney) said humourously that they resembled Baucis and Philemon in Ovid, and it was very true, for so they did' HLP. She is thinking of K's *Scripture Chronology*, in which J had a hand. *L* i. 547, Chapman-Hazen 145.

619. Lichfield. *c.* 18 June (misdated 15 July) '79. Henry Thrale.

Address: To Henry Thrale Esq in Southwark. *Postmark*: LITCHFIELD. Bergson.—1788, No. 209.

Dear Sir

Though I wrote yesterday to my Mistress, I cannot forbear writing immediately to You, my sincere congratulation upon your recovery from so much disorder, and your escape from so much danger. I should have had a very heavy part in the misfortune of losing You, for it is not likely that I should ever find such another friend, and proportionate at least to my fear must be my pleasure.

As I know not that You brought this disease upon yourself by any irregularity[1] I have no advice to give you. I can only wish, and I wish it sincerely, that You may live long and happily, and long count among those that love you best, Dear Sir,

Your most humble Servant

July 15, 1779   Sam: Johnson

620. Ashbourne. Th. 17 June '79. Mrs. Thrale.

Seen.—1788, No. 205.

Dear Madam

It is certain that your first letter did not alarm me in proportion to the danger, for indeed it did not describe the danger as it was. I am glad that you have Heberden, and hope his restoratives and his preservatives will both be effectual. In the preservatives dear Mr. Thrale must concur, yet what can he reform? or what can he add to his regularity

---

619.—Hill, who had not seen the MS., naturally corrected the date to 15 June, supposing 'I wrote yesterday' to refer to 618 of 14 June. But this will hardly do, for the postmark is 'Litchfield', and on 17 June (620) he wrote 'I go to Lichfield to-morrow'. Probably J on arrival at L'd found a letter of good news and at once wrote 619. The (L'n) date-stamp is not legible in my photostat. Since J was confused about the date, 'yesterday' may refer to 620.

1. HLT writing 22 June (*Tb* 391) is loud in her praise of 'my dear Master' for his regularity and temperance; 'few People live in such a State of Preparation for Eternity I think'. In the sequel she sings a different tune.

620.—I have mislaid my note of the original of this letter, which, however, I have collated.

and temperance? He can only sleep less. We will do however all we can. I go to Lichfield to morrow with intent to
hasten to Streatham.

Both Mrs. Aston and Dr. Taylor have had strokes of the
palsy. The Lady was sixty eight, and at that age has gained
ground upon it. The Dr. is you know not young and he is
quite well, only suspicious of every sensation in the peccant
arm. I hope My dear Master's case is yet slighter, and that
as his age is less, his recovery will be more perfect. Let him
keep his thoughts diverted, and his mind easy.

I am, Dearest and dearest, Your most humble Servant
Asbourne. June 17. 1779   Sam: Johnson.

620a. Streatham. Th. 17 June ⟨'79⟩. From Mrs. Thrale
to J at Lichfield.

Address: To Dᴿ Sam: Johnson at Lichfield. *Postmark*: 17 ɪᴠ. Franked
by HT.

R 540.90—

Dear Sir   Streatham Thursday 17.
   Heberden finds Mᴿ Thrale vastly better, & says the Swellings in his Head &
Neck would be still more useful, if they would make themselves into Abscesses
& discharge; he gets new ones every day I think as the old ones disperse. His
Spirits mend apace now, & his good humour returns with his looks, they were
quite dreadful last Sunday, but the Convalescence since then has been
prodigiously rapid. Your last Letter pleases me exceedingly & I thank you
ten thousand Times for it; I could not bear to see you so long apparently
insensible to the distress my poor Mind has been in.
   Mᴿ Thrale must be careful not to sleep so much, he is intemperate in that
to be sure, & his present Lethargick disposition requires great force to counteract it—however he calls Company about him very judiciously, & that is the
best thing to prevent his sleeping. Lord & Lady Gage, Sᴿ Sampson & Lady
Gideon & I know not who beside dine here next Saturday: The Bishop & his
Lady are gone to Cambridge but they gave us one agreable day first, though
Mᴿ Thrale's apparent dejection damped all our Resolutions to be gay.—Gay
indeed! as if there could be Gayety in this World without Madness! but
Farewell; we shall now soon meet again: something always *does* happen
though when you leave us for long.
   I am ever most sincerely & faithfully Dear Sir your Oblig'd & Obedient
                                             H: L: T.

620.1. Ashbourne. Th. 17 June '79. ⟨Charles Burney.⟩

F. A. Pottle.—

Sir

I am extremely obliged to you for your attention, and intelligence. It was happy that you happened to be at Streatham, when this dreadful attack was made. You will do what you can, and I hope soon to come and help you. I am Dear Sir Your obliged humble Servant

June 17. 1779   Sam: Johnson

621. Lichfield. Sa. 19 June '79. Mrs. Thrale.

Sotheby 30 Jan. 1918 (not seen).—1788, No. 206.

Dear Madam   Lichfield, June 19, 1779.

Whether it was that your description of dear Mr. Thrale's disorder was indistinct, or that I am not ready at guessing calamity, I certainly did not know our danger—our danger, for sure I have a part in it, till that danger was abated.

I am glad that Dr. Heberden,[1] and that you perceive so plainly his recovery. He certainly will not be without any warning that I can give him against pernicious practices. His proportion of sleep, if he slept in the night, was doubtless very uncommon; but I do not think that he slept himself into a palsy. But perhaps a lethargick is likewise a paralytical disposition. We will watch him as well as we can. I have known a man, who had a stroke like this, die forty years afterward without another. I hope we have now nothing to fear, or no more than is unalterably involved in the life of man.

I begin now to let loose my mind after Queeney and Burney.[2] I hope they are both well. It will not be long before I shall be among you; and it is a very great degree of pleasure to hope that I shall be welcome.

I am, dear Madam, Your, &c.

620.1.—This letter was clearly to CB; see *Th* 390 (and especially note 2 on that page).

621.—1. See 620*a*.

2. FB wrote 20 July: 'Dr. Johnson gives us a Latin lesson every morning. . . . I am sure I fag more for fear of disgrace than for hope of profit. To devote so much time to acquire something I shall always dread to have known is really unpleasant enough' (*Diary* i. 235). See 636.

622. Lichfield. W. 23 June '79. Henry Thrale.

Sotheby 15 Feb. 1926.—1788, No. 207.

Dear Sir

To show you how well I think of your health I have sent you an hundred pounds[1] to keep for me. It will come within one day of quarter day, and that day You must give me. I came by it in a very uncommon manner, and would not confound it with the rest.

My wicked Mistress talks as if she thought it possible for me to be indifferent[2] or negligent about your health or hers. If I could have done any good, I had not delayed an hour to come to you, and I will come very soon to try if my advice can be of any use, or my Company of any entertainment.

What can be done, You must do for yourself do not let any uneasy thought settle in your mind. Chearfulness and exercise are your great remedies. Nothing is for the present worth your anxiety. Vivite laeti[3] is one of the great rules of health. I believe it will be good to ride often but never to weariness, for weariness is itself a temporary resolution of the nerves, and is therefore to be avoided. Labour is exercise continued to fatigue, Exercise is labour used only while it produces pleasure.

Above all keep your mind quiet, do not think with earnestness even of your health, but think on such things as may

---

622.—1. J used HT as a banker, and evidently exacted interest on his deposits; this explains 'that day'. But what was this money acquired 'in a very uncommon manner'? Hill thought it might be a payment for the *Lives*. But that could hardly be regarded as 'uncommon', or made a mystery at S'm, where the terms for the *Lives* must have been discussed. I have suggested (*RES* xix. 76, Oct. 1943) that a payment for the *Journey* may be referred to (see 589.2, 713). The terms for that book are perhaps not certainly known, though I infer from 713 that they were two hundred pounds or guineas. (The actual payment *is* known: £100 in '76 and £150 in '84; see on 713.) In my *RES* article I further call attention to L iii. 19, where J says 'I do not see that I could make a book upon Italy; yet I should be glad to get two hundred pounds, or five hundred pounds, by such a work'—which may be thought to confirm the figure of two hundred for the *Journey*. But I remained—as I remain—dissatisfied; and in conclusion hazarded the guess that this payment came from Government. The *Political Tracts* had been collected in '76, and there might be a belated honorarium.

2. See 620a.

3. This is in Seneca, *Hercules Furens* 178. Mr. Vernon Rendall, to whom I owe the reference, adds that it is quoted in Burton's *Anatomy*. Hill notes that J had 'perhaps' (he might have said 'certainly') seen Bishop Hacket's motto in L'd Cathedral: 'Inservi Deo et laetare', 'Serve the Lord in gladness'.

please without too much agitation, among which, I hope, is Dear Sir, Your most obliged and most humble Servant Lichfield. June 23. 1779   Sam: Johnson

623. Lichfield. Th. 24 June '79. Mrs. Thrale.
Sotheby 15 Feb. 1926.—1788, No. 208.

Dear Madam

Though I wrote yesterday to Mr. Thrale I think,[1] I must write this day to you, and I hope this will be the last letter, for I am coming up as fast as I can; but to go down cost me seven guineas, and I am loth to come back at the same charge.

You really do not use me well in thinking that I am in less pain on this occasion than I ought to be. There is nobody left for me to care about but you and my Master, and I have now for many years known the value of his Friendship, and the importance of his life, too well not to have him very near my heart. I did not at first understand his danger, and when I knew it, I was told likewise that it was over—and over I hope it is for ever. I have known a Man seized in the same manner, who, though very irregular and intemperate, was never seized again, Do what you can, however, to keep my Master cheerful and slightly busy till his health is confirmed, and if we can be sure of that let Mr. Perkins go to Ireland and come back, as opportunity offers, or necessity requires, and keep yourself airy and be a *funny little thing*.[2]

    I am, Madam, Your most humble Servant
June 24. 1779   Sam: Johnson

623a. Streatham. Th. 24 June '79. From Mrs. Thrale to J at Lichfield.
Address: To Dr Sam: Johnson at Lichfield. *Postmark*: 24 IV. Franked by HT.
R 540.91—

Dear Sir—   Thursday 24 June 1779.

You have been exceedingly kind, and I have been exceedingly cross; & now my Master is got well, & my Wrath over, I ask your Pardon sincerely.—Heber-

623.—1. 1788 punctuates 'Thrale, I think I' and that is the sense, though in modern punctuation J's comma would refer 'think' to what precedes.

2. My collator did not suspect the word. But Hill was probably right in his conjecture that J wrote 'funny'. Even if the underline is his (it might be hers) the words need not be a quotation; they might be a S'm joke.

den thinks all quite safe, & by the way of adding to Security has cut a Fontanel which pleases not my dainty Husband at all, but health must be preferred before Delicacy.

The Publick Concerns grow interesting; even the Opposition Men are willing to lend their Help. Sir Philip went to Court yesterday for the first Time these ten Years, & told the King that tho' his Sword was grown rusted of late, he would be happy to whet it again for his Majesties Service:—so offered to raise a Regiment of Light Dragoons in his County, Hampshire, for the Defence of the Sea Coasts. He pleases himself in the Thoughts of your applauding him, but came disgusted from the Levee too I think as he saw nothing there but Scotchmen he says.

Miss Burney & Hester tell me they mind their Book; I shall make Hetty write to Mrs Porter now, but really She was so alarmed about her father for a Week or ten days, that She could think of nothing else poor dear.

I beg you to make my proper Comp^ts to the Gentlemen & Ladies who have not yet forgotten the Kindnesses they Shewed to Dear Sir Your most Faithful and Obedient Servant

H: L: Thrale.

623.1. Lichfield. Sa. 26 June '79. Mrs. Thrale.

Lady Charnwood.—*Cornhill Mag.* Nov. 1927.

Dearest Lady

Now I find that you are pacified, I can more cheerfully tell you that I shall leave this place next Monday, to find from Birmingham the easiest way home, and when I come I will tell you what little I have to tell, which I hope my dear Masters health will allow you leisure to hear. But you will now have the whole tale to yourself, and a very interesting tale it is.

Taylor was well enough content to see me go. The Ladies at Stowhil are sorry to part and Lucy shows some tenderness. But I hope to be welcome at Streatham, and hope nothing will make Streatham less pleasing to me. I am, Dearest & Dearest, Your most humble Servant

Lichfield June 26. 1779   Sam: Johnson

623.1a. Streatham. Sa. 26 June '79. From Mrs. Thrale to J at Lichfield.

R 540.92—

Dear Sir   Streatham 26: June 1779

My Master received your kind Letter and Bill yesterday & locked them safe from the French & Spaniards who are now seriously however absurdly expected to make an early Descent either on England or Ireland when they have demolished Sir Charles Hardy & his Fleet.

Mr Thrale in the mean Time regains his Health, his Spirits recover more slowly but they will come about as the phrase is.

I enclose a Letter from Hester to Mrs Porter. I have not been inattentive to Compting House Business since [since] Mr Thrale's Illness, though I do not *live* there; I drove however a Parcel of Workmen off yesterday with a high hand, just as you would have had me.

My dear Master is easily subdued just now, & I fear no Subalterns, *as I told them.* Our Trade is in admirable order, but these Wars & Taxes tear us to pieces: it is not true that Individuals perceive no difference between living in a prosperous & in a sinking State, we all do feel the difference, & tis a folly to deny it.

Farewell my Dear Sir and continue to love us, & to take a part in all that belongs to Your ever Faithful & Obedient

H: L: T.

Seward was not with me when the blow was struck; but he came at 5 o' clock the next Morning—we were all up all the Night.

624. Su. 27 June '79. Frances Reynolds.

Not traced; copy by FR, dated 27 July 1779, Rupert Colomb.—Croker's Boswell 1831, iv. 269.

Dear Madam   London, June 27, 1779.

I have sent what I can for your German friend. At this time it is very difficult to get any money,[1] and I cannot give much, I am, Madam, Your most affectionate and most humble servant,

Sam: Johnson

625. Tu. 13 July '79. Charles Dilly.

Address (Boswell): To Mr. Dilly.

Not traced.—Boswell 1791, ii. 294, dated in JB's text (Hill iii. 394).

Sir,

Since Mr. Boswell's departure I have never heard from him; please to send word what you know of him, and whether you have sent my books to his lady. I am, &c.,

Sam. Johnson.

624.—1. For the financial stress of the time see 606.

625.—JB 'did not write to Johnson, as usual, upon my return to my family; but tried how he would be affected by my silence'. The ruse was successful; J did much what he had scolded JB for doing with more provocation; see 607. See also JB's reaction to 626.

626. Tu. 13 July '79. James Boswell (Edinburgh).

Not traced.—Boswell 1791, ii. 295 (Hill iii. 395).

Dear Sir

What can possibly have happened, that keeps us two such strangers to each other? I expected to have heard from you when you came home; I expected afterwards. I went into the country, and returned; and yet there is no letter from Mr. Boswell. No ill I hope has happened; and if ill should happen, why should it be concealed from him who loves you? Is it a fit of humour, that has disposed you to try who can hold out longest without writing? if it be, you have the victory. But I am afraid of something bad; set me free from my suspicions.

My thoughts are at present employed in guessing the reason of your silence: you must not expect that I should tell you any thing, if I had any thing to tell. Write, pray write to me, and let me know what is, or what has been the cause of this long interruption.

I am, dear Sir, Your most affectionate humble servant
July 13, 1779.   Sam. Johnson.

626.1. Th. 29 July '79. Thomas Lawrence.

Maggs Cat. 343 (1916), 290 (not seen).—Extract in catalogue.

Something has happened that will detain me in the Country[1] on Saturday. We will therefore take some day next week for our business.

627. Tu. 3 Aug. '79. John Taylor (Ashbourne).

Address: To the Revd Dr Taylor at Ashbourne Derbyshire.
Loyd.—*NQ* 6 S. v. 461.

Dear Sir

Since my return hither I have applied myself very diligently to the care of my health. My Nights grew better at your house, and have never since been bad; but my breath was very much obstructed; yet I have at last got it tolerably free. This has not been done without great efforts. Of the last

626.—JB replied 17 July pleading 'a supine indolence of mind'. But see on 625.
626.1.—1. That is, at S'm.

fifty days I have taken mercurial physick, I believe, forty, and have lived with much less animal food than has been my custom of late.

From this account you may, I think, derive hope and comfort. I am older than You, my disorders had been of very long continuance, and if it should please God that this recovery is lasting, You have reason to expect an abatement of all the pains that encumber your life.

Mr. Thrale has felt a very heavy blow. He was for some time without reason, and I think without utterance. Heberden was in great doubt whether his powers of mind would ever return. He has however perfectly recovered all his faculties and all his vigour. He has a fontanel in his back. I make little doubt but that, notwithstanding your dismal prognostication You may see one another again.

He purposes this autumn to spend some time in hunting on the downs of Sussex. I hope You are diligent to take as much exercise as You can bear. I had rather you rode twice a day than tired yourself in the morning. I take the true definition of exercise to be labour without weariness.

When I left you, there hung over you a cloud of discontent which is I hope dispersed. Drive it away as fast as you can. Sadness only multiplies self.[1] Let us do our duty, and be cheerful.

Dear Sir, your humble Servant

August 3. 1779 Sam: Johnson

627a. Streatham. Tu. 17 ⟨Aug. '79⟩. From Mrs. Thrale. R 540.58—

Tuesday 17.

With a trembling hand do I acknowledge your last kind Letter which I received in my Bed;—and till today have not been able to sit up long enough to thank you for it—Ah Dear Sir how very, very Ill I have been!

Well! but though I have lost the little Companion entrusted to my Care, though I have lost my Strength, my Appetite &c. you have not lost your Friend; for here I am once more at my Bureau; & here comes Lady Lade too, who tells me you will soon be in Town & then I shall see you sure.

No Evil without some Good however; had we gone to Spa this would have happened, and happen'd on board a Ship—What a providential Escape!

Poor Mr Thrale looks like Death again, & Dr Bromfield was obliged to

627.—1. It is possible that J, who often omits small words, intended 'itself'.

repeat some *Specifics* to prevent further Mischief, but this I have told no
Creature—not his Sister—& my master himself either has forgotten it, or
thinks I don't know. As soon as ever I can travel I must make him go some
where, Change of Scene is actually necessary to his Recovery—I knew I
should be ill when I wrote to you last, & wished he would have gone at Your
kind Invitation—but the Languor of his Disorder & the fear of leaving me &
all together prevented him. See how we all stand as in a Battle, somebody
dropping at every Moment, yet each hoping to escape that Stroke so likely
to destroy his Neighbour! for my own part I lately fancied my Campaign
quite over—May the remainder but prove as Innocent as that already past.—
I shall receive my Summons with a trembling yet strong Hope of unconcluding
Happiness.—And believe me Dear Sir whatever of good I wish for myself,
I wish with equal Earnestness for You, as I am with the purest and most
perfect Friendship Your ever Faithful & Obedient Servant

H: L: T.

627.1. Tu. 24 Aug. '79 (misdated 1777). Lucy Porter (Lichfield).

Beyer (1927).—

Dear Madam

I suppose you are all frighted at Lichfield and indeed the
terrour has been very general, but I am still of opinion that
there is not yet any danger of invasion. The French fleet
were within sight of Plymouth, but no gun was, I believe
fired on either side. I had a note from Mr Chamier (the
under Secretary of State) yesterday, that tells me. *The
combined fleets* (of French and Spaniards) *are not in sight of
land. They are supposed to be driven out of the channel by the
Easterly wind.*

The English fleet under Hardy is much inferiour to that
of the Enemy in number of vessels, but our Ships are said
to have greater guns, and to be better manned. The Battle,
whenever it happens, will be probably of greater consequence
than any battle in our time. If the French get the better we
shall perhaps be invaded, and must fight for ourselves upon
our own ground, if Hardy prevails all danger of that kind is
at an end. If we are invaded the King is said to have resolved
that he will head his own army.

Do not pay any regard to the newspapers; you will only
disturb yourself. When there is any thing worth telling you,
I design to let you know it. At present, it is the general

627.1.—The date is ascertained by the reference to invasion. See 635.

opinion that the first action of consequence will be a great naval battle, and till that is over, all other designs, whatever they are, will be suspended.

I am, Dear Madam, your humble Servant

London. Aug. 24. 1777   Sam: Johnson.

628. Streatham. Th. 9 Sept. '79. James Boswell (Edinburgh).

Not traced.—Boswell 1791, ii. 296 (Hill iii. 396).

My Dear Sir

Are you playing the same trick[1] again, and trying who can keep silence longest? Remember that all tricks are either knavish or childish; and that it is as foolish to make experiments upon the constancy of a friend, as upon the chastity of a wife.

What can be the cause of this second fit of silence, I cannot conjecture; but after one trick, I will not be cheated by another, nor will harass my thoughts with conjectures about the motives of a man who, probably, acts only by caprice. I therefore suppose you are well, and that Mrs. Boswell is well too; and that the fine summer has restored Lord Auchinleck. I am much better than you left me; I think I am better than when I was in Scotland.

I forgot whether I informed you that poor Thrale has been in great danger. Mrs. Thrale likewise has miscarried,[2] and been much indisposed. Every body else is well; Langton is in camp. I intend to put Lord Hailes's description of Dryden[3] into another edition, and as I know his accuracy, wish he would consider the dates, which I could not always settle to my own mind.

Mr. Thrale goes to Brighthelmston, about Michaelmas, to be jolly and ride a hunting. I shall go to town, or perhaps to Oxford. Exercise and gaiety, or rather carelessness, will, I hope, dissipate all remains of his malady; and I likewise hope by the change of place, to find some opportunities of

628.—1. JB had in fact written again 22 July: 'my letter was a pretty long one . . . but he, it should seem, had not attended to it.'

2. See 627a, *Tb* 400.

3. J omitted to do this in the revised edition of 1783.

growing yet better myself. I am, dear Sir, Your humble servant,

Streatham, Sept. 9, 1779.   Sam. Johnson.

629. M. 4 Oct. '79. Mrs. Thrale.
Bergson.—1788, No. 210.

Dear Madam

I had intended to send You such a card as I have inclosed, when I was alarmed by hearing that my Servant had told in the house, for servants never tell their Masters, his opinion that for the two last days Mr Thrale was visibly worse. His eyes are keen, and his attention upon such occasions vigorous enough.

I therefore earnestly wish that before You set out, even though You should lose a day, You would go together to Heberden, and see what advice he will give You. In this doubtful pendulous state of the distemper, advice may do much, and Physicians, be their power less or more, are the only refuge that we have in sickness. I wish You would do yet more, and propose to Heberden a consultation with some other of the Doctors, and if Laurence is at present fit for business, I wish he might be called, but call somebody. As You make yourselves of more importance, You will be more considered. Do not go away with any reason to tax yourselves with negligence. You are in a state in which nothing that can be done, ought to be omitted. We now do right or wrong for a great stake. You may send the Children and Nurses forward to morrow, and go Yourselves on Wednesday. Little things must not now be minded, and least of all must You mind a little money. What the world has, is to be sold, and to be enjoyed by those that will pay its price. Do not give Heberden a single Guinea, and subscribe a hundred to keep out the French, we have an invasion more formidable, and an enemy less resistible by power and less avoidable by flight. I have now done my duty.

I am, dearest Lady, Your humble servant
Monday Oct. 4. 1779   Sam: Johnson.

630. Tu. 5 Oct. '79. Mrs. Thrale.

Sotheby 30 Jan. 1918 (not seen).—1788, No. 211.

Dear Madam   Oct. 5, 1779.

When Mr. Boswell[1] waited on Mr. Thrale in Southwark, I directed him to watch all appearances with close attention, and bring me his observations. At his return he told me, that without previous intelligence he should not have discovered that Mr. Thrale had been lately ill.

It appears to me that Mr. Thrale's disorder, whether grumous or serous,[2] must be cured by bleeding; and I would not have him begin a course of exercise without considerable evacuation. To encrease the force of the blood, unless it be first diluted and attenuated, may be dangerous. But the case is too important for my[3] theory.

The weakness in my ankles left them for a day, but has now turned to a pain in my toe, much like that at Brighthelmstone. It is not bad, nor much more than troublesome; I hope it will not be greater, nor last long.

You all go with the good wishes of, dear Madam,
Your, &c.,

631. F. 8 Oct. '79. Mrs. Thrale (Brighthelmston).

Adam.—1788, No. 212.

Dear Madam

I begin to be frighted at your omission to write, do not torment me any longer, but let me know where you are,[1] how you got thither, how you live there and every thing else, that one friend loves to know of another.

I will show you the way.

On Sunday the gout left my ankles, and I went very commodiously to Church. On Monday night I felt my feet uneasy. On Tuesday I was quite lame. That night I took

630.—1. JB paid a second visit to L'n this year, staying for about a fortnight in Oct. The journal of this 'Jaunt' is lost, and the visit to S'k is not recorded in the *Life* (*BP* xiii. 291).

2. The distinctions, according to J's own definitions of these terms, is roughly that between thick and thin.

3. J perhaps wrote 'any'.

631.—1. They visited Tunbridge Wells as well as B'n. FB describes their journey (5 Oct.) to Tunbridge Wells by Knowle and Tunbridge. At T. W. they found Mrs. and Miss Streatfield at Mount Ephraim. By 12 Oct. they were at B'n. *Diary* i. 247.

an opiate, having first taken physick and fasted. Towards morning on Wednesday the pain remitted Bozzy[2] came to me, and much talk we had. I fasted another day, and on Wednesday night could walk tolerably. On Thursday finding myself mending, I ventured on my dinner, which I think has a little interrupted my convalescence. To day I have again taken physick and eaten only some stewed apples. I hope to starve it away. It is now not worse than it was at Brighthelmston.

This, Madam, is the history of one of my toes; the history of my head would perhaps be much shorter. I thought it was the gout on Saturday. It has already lost me two dinners abroad, but then I have not been at much more charges for I have eaten little at home.

Surely I shall have a letter to morrow.

I am Madam, Your most humble servant

London Oct. 8. 1779   Sam: Johnson

632. M. 11 Oct. '79. Mrs. Thrale (Brighthelmston).

Huntington.—1788, No. 213.

Dear Madam

I thought ⟨it⟩ very long till I heard from you, having sent a second letter[1] to Tunbridge, which I believe you cannot have received. I do not see why you should trouble yourself with Physicians, while Mr. Thrale grows better. Company and bustle will I hope, compleat his cure. Let him gallop over the downs in the morning, call his friends about him to dinner, and frisk in the rooms at night, and outrun time, and outface misfortune.[2]

Notwithstanding all authorities against bleeding Mr. Thrale bled himself well ten days ago.

You will lead a jolly life, and perhaps think little of me, but I have been invited twice to Mrs Vesey's Conversation, but have not gone. The Gout that was in my ankles, when Queeney criticised my gait, passed into my toe, but I have hunted it, and starved it, and it makes no figure. It has

631.—2. 'I had several interviews with him, which it is unnecessary to distinguish particularly' (*L* iii. 400).

632.—1. Either 631 or a missing letter.

2. Perhaps a quotation.

744. Lichfield. Sa. 27 Oct. '81. Mrs. Thrale (Streatham).
Address: To Mrs Thrale at Streatham Surry. *Postmark*: 29 oc.
Bergson.—1788, No. 268.

Dearest dear Lady,

Your Oxford letter[1] followed me hither with Lichfield put
upon the direction in the place of Oxford, and was received
at the same time as the letter written next after it. All is
therefore well.

Queeny is a naughty captious girl, that will not write
because I did not remember to ask her. pray tell her that I
ask her now, and that I depend upon her for the history of
her own time.

Poor Lucy's ilness has left her very deaf, and I think,
very inarticulate. I can scarcely make her understand me
and she can hardly make me understand her. So here are
merry doings.[2] But she seems to like me better than she did.
She eats very little, but does not fall away.

Mrs Cobb and Peter Garrick are as You left them. Garrick's legatees[3] at this place are very angry that they receive
nothing. Things are not quite right, though we ⟨are⟩ so far
from London.[4]

Mrs Aston is just as I left her. She walks no worse, but I
am afraid speaks less distinctly as to her utterance; her mind
is untouched. She eats too little, and wears away. Her
extenuation is her only bad symptom. She was glad to
see me.

That naughty Girl Queeny, now she is in my head again.
How could she think that I did not wish to hear from her, a
dear Sweet.—But he must suffer who can love.[5]

All here is gloomy, a faint struggle with the tediousness of
time, a doleful confession of present misery, and the approach
seen and felt of what is most dreaded and most shunned.
But such is the lot of Man. I am, Dearest Madam,

Your most humble Servant

Oct. 27. 1781   Sam: Johnson.

744.—1. 741*a*.   2. See 640 for the phrase.
   3. Hill quotes Davies, *Life of Garrick* ii. 427, for G's will. HLP erased the words
'Garrick's legatees', but printed them.
   4. Hill quotes *London, a Poem*: 'Resolved at length, from vice and LONDON far, |
To breathe in distant fields a purer air.'
   5. Prior, see 421.

745. Lichfield. W. 31 Oct. '81. Mrs. Thrale (Streatham).
Address: To Mrs Thrale at Streatham Surrey. *Postmark*: 2 NO.
Adam.—1788, No. 269.

Dear Madam

It almost enrages me to be suspected of forgetting the discovery of the papers relating to Cummins's claim.[1] These papers we must grant the liberty of using, because the Law will not suffer us to deny them. We may be summoned to declare what we know, and what we know is in those[2] papers. When the evidence appears, Lady Lade[3] will be directed by her Lawyers to submit in quiet. I suppose it will be proper to give at first only a transcript.

Your income diminished as it is, you may without any painful frugality make sufficient. I wish your health were as much in your power, and the effects of abstinence were as certain as those of parcimony. Of your regimen I do not think with much approbation; it is only palliative, and crops the disease but does not eradicate it. I wish you had at the beginning digested full meals in a warm room, and excited the humour to exhaust its power upon the surface. This, I believe, must be done at last.

Miss Seward has been enquiring after Susan Thrale of whom she has heard so much from Mrs Cummins as excites her curiosity. If my little dear Perversity continues to be cross, Susy may be my Girl too, but I had rather have them both. If Queeney does not write soon she shall have a very reprehensory letter.

I have here but a dull scene. Poor Lucy's health is very much broken. She takes very little of either food or exercise, and her hearing is very dull, and her utterance confused. But she will have *Watts's Improvements of the Mind.* Her

---

745.—1. 'Cummins' is lightly erased, but is printed in 1788. The claimant is probably distinct from the schoolmistress named below. J (in this letter) writes both 'Cummins', but HLP corrected the second to 'Cumyns'. Mr. Clifford finds in a letter from HLT to Perkins, probably of this time, references to 'Cummins and his wife. . . . The whole acc^t. is now going to Dr. Johnson . . . so the poor People will get Justice at last I doubt not.' The claim was perhaps on the brewery. It appears from HLT's letter, as well as from J's, that Lady Lade was involved.

2. 'those' should perhaps be 'these'. In my edition of the *Journey* I call attention to several places where the words, almost identical in J's hand, have probably been confused, and one (p. 141, l. 21) where 'these' of 1775 seems impossible.

3. Suppressed in 1788.

mental powers are not impaired, and her social virtues seem to encrease. She never was so civil to me before.

Mrs Aston is not that I perceive worse than when I left her, but she eats too little, and is somewhat emaciated. She likewise is glad to see me, and I am glad that I have come.

Here is little of the sunshine of life, and my own health does not gladden me. But to scatter the gloom I went last night to the ball, where, you know, I can be happy even without you. On the Ball which was very gay I looked a while, and went away. I am

Dear Madam Your most humble servant
Lichfield Oct. 31. 1781   Sam: Johnson

746. Lichfield. Sat. 3 Nov. '81. Mrs. Thrale.
Sotheby 11 Feb. 1929.—1788, No. 271.

Dearest Madam

You very kindly remind me of the dear home[1] which I have left, but I need none of your aids to recollection, for I am here gasping for breath, and yet better than those whom I came to visit. Mrs Aston has been for three years a paralytic crawler, but, I think, with her mind unimpaired. She seems to me such as I left her, but she now eats little, and is therefore much emaciated. Her sister thinks her, and she thinks herself passing fast away.

Lucy has had since my last visit a dreadful ilness, from which her Physicians declared themselves hopeless of recovering her, and which has shaken the general fabrick, and weakened the powers of life. She is unable or unwilling to move, and is never likely to have more of either strength or spirit.

I am so visibly disordered that a medical man who only saw me at Church sent me some pills. To those whom I love here I can give no help, and from those that love me, none can I receive. Do you think that I need to be reminded of Home and You?

The time of the year is not very favourable to excursions. I thought myself above assistance or obstruction from the

---

746.—1. In her published letter dated 'Nov. 2' she writes 'Come home, however, for 'tis dull living without you.' J cannot on 3 Nov. have read a letter posted 2 Nov.

seasons,[2] but find the autumnal blast sharp and nipping and the fading world an uncomfortable prospect. Yet I may say with Milton that I do not *abate* much *of heart or hope.*[3] To what I have done I do not despair of adding something, but *what it shall be I know not.*[4]

I am, Madam, Most affectionately yours,

Lichfield November 3. 1781   Sam: Johnson

746.1. Lichfield.   W. 7 Nov. '81.   Hester Maria Thrale (Streatham).

Address: To Miss Thrale at Streatham Surry.
Lansdowne.—Lansdowne, *Johnson and Queeney* 1932, 24.

My dear Sweeting,   Lichfield, Nov. 7, 1781

How could you suppose that by not asking you to write,[1] I meant to show dislike or indifference? It had been more reasonable to suppose that having asked you often, and having had no reason to change my mind, I considered it as a general compact that we should write to one another. The truth is that I did not reflect or remember that I had not asked you.

I am not sorry that this little suspicion has been discovered, because it gives me an opportunity of telling you that before you mingle in the crowd of life I wish you to exterminate captiousness from your mind, as a very powerful and active cause of discontent, of such discontent as is very often without reason, and almost always without remedy. Captiousness is commonly the resentment of negative injuries, or offences of omission, of which the ill intention cannot be proved, and should therefore very rarely be supposed. As the provocations of captiousness can seldom be declared, they operate in sullen silence, and undermine those friendships which could perhaps have withstood the battery of an open quarrel. Captiousness is a slow poison which destroys confidence and kindness by imperceptible corrosion. The

746.—2. For J's claim to be superior to the weather see references in *L* i. 332.

3. Milton, 'To Mr. Cyriack Skinner': 'Yet I argue not | Against heavns hand or will, nor bate a jot | Of heart or hope.'

4. Mr. Page suggests that J had in mind *Lear* ii. iv. 283: 'I will do such things,— | What they are yet I know not,—but they shall be | The terrors of the earth'.

746.1.—1. See 743*a*, 744.

captious man often determines wrong though he always determines against himself, and after years passed in gloom and malevolence, often discovers at last that he was never injured. The rule to be observed is, never to impute to design those negligences or omissions which can be imputed to forgetfulness, nor ever to resent as deliberate and malignant enmity, such offences as may be the effect of accidental levity or hasty petulance.

This, my lovely Dear, is a very grave and long lesson, but do not think it tedious, I have told you not many things more worthy of your attention and memory.

I have been this day returning my visits, and am going as I suppose, to Ashbourne tomorrow; I do not suppose my stay will be long, and hope that you will not be sorry to see me again.

Dear Miss Your most humble servant,

Sam: Johnson

747. Ashbourne. Sa. 10 Nov. '81. Mrs. Thrale.

F. Leverton Harris.—1788, No. 272.

Dear Madam

Yesterday I came to Ashbourne, and last night I had very little rest. Dr Taylor lives on Milk, and grows every day better, and is not wholly without hope of Lincoln.[1] Every ⟨? one⟩ enquires after you and Queeney, but whatever Burney may think of the celerity of fame,[2] the name of Evelina had never been heard at Lichfield, till I brought it. I am afraid my dear Townsmen will be mentioned in future days as the last part of this nation that was civilised. But the days of darkness are to be soon at an end, the reading Society ordered it to be procured this week.

Since I came into this quarter of the earth I have had a very sorry time, and I hope to be better when I come back. The little padock and plantations here are very bleak. The Bishop of Chester[3] is here now with his Father in law; he sent us a message last night, and I intend to visit him.

747.—1. HLP good-naturedly suppressed 'of Lincoln'—i.e. the deanery then vacant.

2. J had in mind the classical sense, report or rumour, the swiftness of which was proverbial, e.g. Virgil *Aen.* iv. 173 'Fama, malum qua non aliud velocius ullum.'

3. Porteus.

Most of your Ashbourne friends are well. Mr. Kennedy's daughter has married a Shoemaker, and he lives with them and has left his parsonage.

I am Madam Your most humble Servant
Ashbourne Nov. 10. 1781   Sam: Johnson.

748. Ashbourne. M. 12 Nov. '81. Mrs. Thrale.

Goodspeed.—1788, No. 273.

Dear Madam

I have a mind to look on Queeny as my own dear Girl, and if I set her a bad example,[1] I ought to counteract it by good precepts, and he that knows the consequences of any fault is best qualified to tell them. I have through my whole progress of authorship honestly endeavoured to teach the right, though I have not been sufficiently diligent to practise it, and have offered Mankind my opinion as a rule, but never proposed my behaviour as an example.

I shall be very sorry to lose Mr Perkins,[2] but why should he so certainly die? Nesbitt needed not have died if he had tried to live. If Mr Perkins will drink a great deal of water the acrimony that corrodes his bowels will be diluted, if the cause be only acrimony, but I suspect dysenteries to be produced by animalcula, which I know not how to kill.

If the medical man[3] did me good, it was by his benevolence, for his pills I never touched. I am, however, rather better than I was.

Dear Mrs ⟨Biron⟩,[4] she has the courage becoming an Admirals Lady, but courage is no virtue in her cause.

I have been at Lichfield persecuted with solicitation to read a poem,[5] but I sent the authour word, that I would never review the work of an anonymous authour, for why should I put my name in power of one who will not trust me

748.—1. For J on precept and practice see *L* v. 210.

    2. See 743*a*, 749*a*.   3. See 746.
    4. The erasure is almost complete, but the reading is not in doubt. After 'her' is a smaller erasure, or perhaps only a blot; if an erasure, I cannot guess what was erased. Mr. Hyde thinks it may be 'bad'. By 'is no virtue' J perhaps means 'has no virtue', that is, no efficacy.

    5. Hill guessed that this was Erasmus Darwin's *Loves of the Plants*, published anonymously 1789. He was at L'd in '81; and Edgeworth (*Memoirs* 398) stated that parts of the poem were shown from time to time in MS. Sir Charles Darwin tells me he knows of no family tradition of any intercourse between the two men.

with his own. With this answer Lucy was satisfied, and I think it may satisfy all whom it may concern.

If Crutchly[6] did nothing for life but add weight to its burden, and darkness to its gloom, he is kindest to those from whom he is furthest. I hope when I come not to advance perhaps your pleasures, though even of that I should be unwilling to despair, but at least not to encrease your inconveniencies, which would be a very unsuitable return for all the kindness that you have shown to,

Madam, Your most humble servant

Ashbourne Nov. 12, 1781   Sam: Johnson

749. Ashbourne. W. 14 Nov. '81. Mrs. Thrale.
Not traced.—1788, No. 274.

Dearest Madam   Ashbourne, Nov. 14, 1781.

Here is Doctor Taylor, by a resolute adherence to bread and milk, with a better appearance of health than he has had for a long time past; and here am I, living very temperately, but with very little amendment. But the balance is not perhaps very unequal: he has no pleasure like that which I receive from the kind importunity with which you invite me to return. There is no danger of very long delay. There is nothing in this part of the world that can counteract your attraction.

The hurt in my leg has grown well slowly, according to Hector's prognostick,[1] and seems now to be almost healed: but my nights are very restless, and the days are therefore heavy, and I have not your conversation to cheer them.

I am willing however to hear that there is happiness in the world, and delight to think on the pleasure diffused among the Burneys. I question if any ship upon the ocean goes out attended with more good wishes than that which carries the fate of Burney.[2] I love all of that breed whom I can be said

748.—6. C had disappointed HLT, who had thought of him as a husband for FB (*Tb* 496). FB herself (14 Sept.) describes 'the conclusion of Mr. Crutchley's most extraordinary summer career at Streatham' (*Diary* ii. 105). HLT wrote to FB Sunday 12 Nov. 'Crutchley left us on Monday'. For the transfer of his attentions to Q see C 205.

749.—1. See 742.
 2. James. FB in a letter to HLT dated 'Chesington, Nov. 4', placed in the *Diary* (i. 428) as of '80, but evidently of '81, describes how the news came of his appointment

to know, and one or two whom I hardly know I love upon
credit, and love them because they love each other. Of this
consanguineous unanimity I have had never much experience; but it appears to me one of the great lenitives of life;
but it has this deficience, that it is never found when distress
is mutual—He that has less than enough for himself has
nothing to spare, and as every man feels only his own neces-
sities, he is apt to think those of others less pressing, and to
accuse them of with-holding what in truth they cannot give.
He that has his foot firm upon dry ground may pluck another
out of the water; but of those that are all afloat, none has
any care but for himself.

We do not hear that the deanery[3] is yet given away, and,
though nothing is said, I believe much is still thought about
it. *Hope travels through*——[4]

I am, dearest of all dear ladies, Your, &c.

749a. Su. 18 Nov. ⟨'81⟩. From Mrs. Thrale to J at Ashbourne.

R 540. 105—

Dear Sir   Sunday 18. Nov.

Your last Letter gave a better Account of you than the preceding ones,
and Doctor Taylor too! I am glad he is so pert: a long Time it is now since
I began to think very ill of his Health, but croaking does no Good, and had
better be left off. Perkins observes Sir Richard Jebb's Rules to a Degree that
does him honour, and he mends in proportion to the Care he takes: I will not
ring People's Knell so another Time.

Seward & Pepys have visited us; nobody else since I wrote last, & they
brought me nothing very considerable from the great Mart of Society as one
of them called it. Mr Cator called Yesterday indeed, and gave such a deplor-
able Account of Baretti as shocked me, & produced the five Guineas which I
always meant to give him through your hands. He is in the Country with
Mr Cator who sollicits for him very diligently, & contributes ten Guineas a
Year: he would I think have fain perswaded me to make my five ten; but if
one is to do *all one can do* for a professed Enemy—how does one deserve to
have a Friend? I thought five enough. You however are the Person who is
expected to relieve his Distress, and you are to ask the King to give him a
pension I think;—it put me in mind of Mrs & Miss Morris.

to the frigate *Latona*. HLT in her reply, dated '12 November, 1781' (*Diary* ii.
108) quotes J's of 14 Nov. on 'consanguineous unanimity'. The quotation is not ver-
batim; but in one phrase—'*where* distress is mutual'—it may correct an error of 1788.

749.—3. 'of Lincoln' Lysons; this is probably a comment, not, as in 747, a supplement.
   4. Pope, *Essay on Man* ii. 273: 'Hope travels through, nor quits us when we die.'

What honour you do my Queeney! taking her for your own indeed, & writing her such sweet Letters! accept my truest and tenderest Thanks for all your Friendship and Kindness to Dear Sir Your Obliged & faithful Servant

H: L: Thrale.

750. Ashbourne. Sa. 24 Nov. '81. Mrs. Thrale.

Sotheby 4 June 1908 (not seen).—1788, No. 275.

Dear Madam   Ashbourne, Nov. 24, 1781.

I shall leave this place about the beginning of next week, and shall leave every place as fast as I decently can, till I get back to you, whose kindness is one of my great comforts. I am not well, but have a mind every now and then to think myself better, and I now hope to be better under your care.

It was time to send Kam to another master; but I am glad that before he went he beat Hector,[1] for he has really the appearance of a superior species to an animal whose whole power is in his legs, and that against the most defenceless of all the inhabitants of the earth.

Dr. Taylor really grows well, and directs his compliments to be sent. I hope Mr. Perkins will be well too.

But why do you tell me nothing of your own health? Perhaps since the fatal pinch of snuff I may have no care about it. I am glad that you have returned to your meat, for I never expected that abstinence would do you good.

Piozzi, I find, is coming in spite of Miss Harriet's prediction,[2] or second sight, and when *he* comes and *I* come, you will have two about you that love you; and I question if either of us heartily care how few more you have. But how many soever they may be, I hope you keep your kindness for me, and I have a great mind to have Queeney's kindness too.

Frank's wife has brought him a wench; but I cannot yet get intelligence of her colour, and therefore have never told him how much depends upon it.

The weather here is chill, and the air damp. I have been

750.—1. 'The Greyhound' HLP.

2. In her published letter dated 'Nov. 2' HLT writes: 'Instead of trying the Sortes Virgilianae for our absent friends, we agreed after dinner to-day to ask little Harriet what they were doing now who used to be our common guests at Streatham. Dr. Johnson (says she) is very rich and wise, Sir Philip is drown'd in the water—and Mr. Piozzi is very sick and lame, poor man! What a curious way of deciding!'

only once at the waterfall, which I found doing as it used to
do, and came away. I had not you nor Queeney with me.

Your, &c.

751. Ashbourne. M. 26 Nov. '81. Edmund Allen.
Address (Croker): To Edmund Allen, *Bolt Court.*
Not traced.—Croker's Boswell 1848, 699.

Dear Sir,   Ashbourne, Nov. 26, 1781.
   I am weary enough of the country to think of Bolt Court,
and purpose to leave Ashbourne, where I now am, in a day or
two, and to make my way through Lichfield, Birmingham,
and Oxford, with what expedition I decently can, and then
we will have a row[1] and a dinner, and now and then a dish of
tea together.
   I doubt not but you have been so kind as to send the
oysters to Lichfield, and I now beg that you will let Mrs.
Desmoulins have a guinea on my account.
   My health has been but indifferent, much of the time I
have been out,[2] and my journey has not supplied much
entertainment.
   I shall be at Lichfield, I suppose, long enough to receive a
letter, and I desire Mrs. Desmoulins to write immediately
what she knows. I wish to be told about Frank's wife and
child.
I am, dear Sir, Your most humble servant,
Sam: Johnson.

751.—This letter was communicated to Croker by Cunningham (the editor of
Walpole's letters). With it Cunningham had found a memorandum by Allen, which
Croker quotes: 'October 15, 1781, Dr. Johnson set out about 9 A.M. to Oxford, Lichfield, and Ashbourne. December 11, 1781, Dr. Johnson returned from Derbyshire.'
The text is suspect. Hill could make nothing of 'row', since it is unlikely that J
could contemplate going on the river in December, and no other sense seems to fit.
I suspect 'I have been out'; but there perhaps J omitted some words.
   1. Dr. Onions shares Hill's doubts (see above). The aquatic sense is not recorded
in *OED* until 1847. J's household was not always harmonious; but that sense seems
even less probable.
   2. The possibility occurs that J might write or intend 'out of sorts', which at this
date could mean 'in low spirits' and so would not be vain repetition. Alternatively,
perhaps he dropped a negative; he had been lame, and so had not been 'out' of doors
very much.

751.1. Ashbourne. W. 28 Nov. '81. Hester Maria Thrale (Streatham).

Address: To Miss Thrale at Streatham Surry.
Lansdowne.—Lansdowne, *Johnson and Queeney* 1932, 26.

My dearest Love,   Ashbourne, Nov. 28, 1781
 The day after tomorrow will carry me back to Lichfield, whence I purpose to find the way to London with all convenient speed. I have had a poor, sickly, comfortless journey, much gloom and little sunshine. But I hope to find you gay, and easy, and kind, and I will endeavour to copy you, for what can come of discontent and dolour? Let us keep ourselves easy and do what good we can to one another.

 Dr. Taylor says that he has a bigger Bull than he ever had, and the cow which he sold for an hundred and twenty guineas, has brought the purchaser a calf for which he asks a hundred pounds. The Dr. has been unsuccessful in breeding horses, for he has had sixteen fillies without one colt, an accident beyond all computation of chances. Such is the uncertainty of life. He is, I believe, yet in hopes of the deanery.

> Thus we sigh on from day to day
> And wish and wish the soul away.[1]

He is however happier than if he had no desire. To be without hope or fear, if it were possible would not be happiness; it is better that life should struggle with obstructions, than stagnate and putrefy. Never be without something to wish, and something to do.

 I believe I shall be at Lichfield long enough to receive a letter from you, and therefore hope that you will send one, for I have great pleasure in being Madam,
                              Your most humble servant
                                             Sam: Johnson

752. Lichfield. M. 3 Dec. '81. Mrs. Thrale.

Mrs. F. Bowman.—1788, No. 276.

Dear Madam
 I am now come back to Lichfield, where I do not intend to stay long enough to receive another letter. I have little to do

751.1.—1. Not traced.

here but to take leave of Mrs Aston. I hope not the last leave. But Christians may ⟨say⟩ with more confidence than Sophonisba

> Havremo tosto lungo lungo spatio
> Per stare insieme, et sarà forse eterno.[1]

My time past heavily at Ashbourne, yet I could not easily get away though Taylor, I sincerely think, was glad to see me go. I have now learned the inconveniences of a winter campaign. But I hope home will make amends for all my foolish sufferings.

I do not like poor Burney's vicarious[2] captainship. Surely the tale of Tantalus was made for him. Surely he ⟨will⟩ be in time a Captain like another captain, of a Ship like another Ship.

You have got Piozzi again, notwithstanding pretty Harriet's dire denunciations. The Italian translation[2a] which he has brought you will find no great accession to your library, for the writer seems to understand very little English. When we meet we can compare some passages. Pray contrive a multitude of good things for us to do when we meet, something that may *hold all together*.[3] Though if any thing makes *me* love you more, it is going from you.

I am, &c.,

Lichfield Dec. 3. 1781   Sam: Johnson.

753. Birmingham. Sa. 8 Dec. '81. Mrs. Thrale.

Sotheby 30 Jan. 1918 (not seen).—1788, No. 277.

Dear Madam   Birmingham, Dec. 8, 1781.

I am come to this place on my way to London and to Streatham. I hope to be in London on Tuesday or Wednesday, and at Streatham on Thursday, by your kind conveyance. I shall have nothing to relate either wonderful or delightful. But remember that you sent me away, and turned me out into the world, and you must take the chance of finding me better or worse. This you may know at present, that my affection for you is not diminished, and my expecta-

---

752.—1. Trissino, *Sofonisba*: 'Ma tu pur cerca mantenerti in vita; | Che tosto avremo un lungo lungo spazio | Di stare insieme, e sarà forse eterno': HLP partly corrected J's misquotation.

2. See 749. B's command was 'during the absence of . . . Captain Conway' (Scholes, *Dr. Burney* 1948, ii. 26).   2a Possibly the verses of 767.

3. Perhaps a quotation; but the underline might be HLP's.

tion from you is encreased. Do not neglect me, nor relinquish me.[1] Nobody will ever love you better or honour you
more than,

Madam, Your, &c.

754. W. 26 Dec. ⟨'81⟩. John Nichols.
Address: To Mr Nicols.
B.M.—*GM* Jan. 1785.

Mr. Johnson being much out of order sent in search of the
book but it is not found. He will, if he is better look himself
diligently tomorrow. He thanks Mr. Nichols for all his
favours.
Dec. 26.

754.1. W. ⟨'81⟩. Charles Wesley.
Adam.—Telford *Life of Charles Wesley* 1886, 200.

Sir

I beg that you, and M^{rs}, and Miss Wesley will dine with
your Brother, and Mrs Hall, at my house in Bolt court,
Fleet street, tomorrow.

That I have not sent sooner, if you knew the disordered
state of my health, you would easily forgive me.

I am, Sir Your most humble servant

Wednesday. Sam: Johnson

755. Tu. 1 Jan. '82. Lowe.
Not traced; known to Hill only from an auction catalogue the
reference to which he had mislaid. The catalogue tells us no more
than that the letter was 'to Mr. Lowe'.

756. Sa. 5 Jan. '82. James Boswell (Edinburgh).
Not traced.—Boswell 1791, ii. 412 (Hill iv. 136).

Dear Sir

I sit down to answer your letter on the same day in which
I received it, and am pleased that my first letter of the year

753.—1. This is perhaps the first hint of J's fear of an estrangement.

755.—Hill assumed this letter to be to Mauritius Lowe; it might be to the unidenti-
fied L of 740.

756.—JB had written 'one letter to introduce Mr. Sinclair . . . and informed him in
another, that my wife had again been affected with alarming symptoms of illness'.

is to you. No man ought to be at ease while he knows himself in the wrong; and I have not satisfied myself with my
long silence. The letter relating to Mr. Sinclair, however
was, I believe, never brought.

My health has been tottering this last year; and I can give
no very laudable account of my time. I am always hoping to
do better than I have ever hitherto done.

My journey to Ashbourne and Staffordshire was not
pleasant; for what enjoyment has a sick man visiting the
sick? Shall we ever have another frolick like our journey to
the Hebrides?

I hope that dear Mrs. Boswell will surmount her complaints; in losing her you would lose your anchor, and be
tost, without stability, by the waves of life.[1] I wish both
her and you very many years, and very happy.

For some months past I have been so withdrawn from the
world, that I can send you nothing particular. All your
friends, however, are well, and will be glad of your return
to London.

I am, dear Sir, Yours most affectionately,
January 5, 1782. Sam. Johnson.

[756.1. Sa. 5 Jan. '82.

See 787.1. I learn at the eleventh hour that I had printed this letter twice.
My excuse is that one of two copyists read the date as Jan. instead of June.
I leave the marking unaltered, for fear of deranging references.]

756.2. Sa. 5 Jan. '82. Thomas Lawrence.

Huntington.—

T. Laurentio, Medico. S.

A corpore pessime habitus ad te confugio, Vir doctissime.
Leviora incommoda prætereunda censeo, quod me maxime

756.—1. 'The truth of this has been proved by sad experience' JB; he lost his wife
in June '89.

756.2.—J describes his asthma and sleeplessness, and asks L's approval of bleeding.
'inderdum' is J's slip for 'interdum', and 'occurendum' with one *r* is his spelling.

angit, ut potero, dicam. Ubi in lecto decubui, post somnum brevem, plerumque brevissimum, sensu quodam quasi materiæ intus turgescentis pectus tentatur; ita ut, quanquam nullus dolor aut lacerat aut pungit, somnus prorsus pellatur, et capite de culcitra levato, inter stragula sedere necesse sit. Hinc crebra suspiria, interdum singultus, spirandi labor difficilis. Eo res venit ut lectum horream, neque luce perfrui possim. His malis quo sit modo occurrendum tuum esto judicium. mihi quidem vena secanda videtur, quod tamen nisi tuo jussu haud libenter fecerim. Quid possit purgatio per alvum, etiam mercurio adhibito, vano experimento satis tentavi. Si sanguis mittendus est, te praesente missum velim, nequid vel metu vel audacia peccetur.

Ad me ne venias, postquam haec legeris, adero.
Nonis Jan. 1782

756.3. Su. 6 Jan. '82. Mrs. Thrale.
Address: To Mrs Thrale.
Rylands.—*R.L. Bull.* Jan. 1932, 34.

Dear Madam

I wrote my complaint to Dr Laurence, and then went to him. A Chirurgeon was called, and sixteen ounces taken away. I durst not have done so much by myself, but it was right. I had no faintness though I fasted, and had an Elysian night compared to some nights past.

     I am Madam Your most obedient servant
Jan 6. 1782   Sam: Johnson

757. Th. 17 Jan. '82. Thomas Lawrence.
Address: to Dr Lawrence.
R. G. Pruden.—Boswell 1791, ii. 413 (Hill iv. 137).

Sir

Our old friend Mr Levett, who was last night eminently cheerful, died this morning. The man who lay in the same room hearing an uncommon noise got up: and tried to make him speak, but without effect, he then called Mr Holder the apothecary, who though, when he came, he thought him dead; opened a vein but could draw no blood. So has ended the long life of a very useful, and very blameless man.

I am Sir Your most humble servant

Jan: 17. 1782   Sam: Johnson

757.1. M. 21 Jan. ⟨'82.⟩ Thomas Lawrence.
Address: To Dr. Laurence. Huntington.—

T. Laurentio Medico. S.   Jan. 21. 17 (sic)

Mihi somnus hac nocte fuit saepe quidem intermissus, ita vero placidus, ut somnijs continuatis, et sibi constantibus otium praeberet; neque cubanti quidquam tussis molestiarum fecit. At gravem me sentio et oppleto similem, spiritumque duco solutiorem non tamen liberum. Pectus quodammodo aestuare pergit. Nescio an ausim venam iterum secandam offerre, cum tamen nihil sentiam aut debile aut vacuum, quid sit magnopere extimiscendum[1] non video. Te hoc remedium arrepturum non dubito, si quod ego in me sentio, in te ipse sentires. Quod fecisti morbo obstitit, quem tamen non vicit. Vive, valeque.

758. M. 28 Jan. '82. Mrs. Thrale.
Address: To Mrs Thrale.
Sotheby 5 May 1930.—1788, No. 291 (misdated 28 June 1781 and placed as if of June 1782).

Dearest Lady

I was blooded on Saturday, I think, not copiously enough, but the Doctor would permit no more. I have however his consent to bleed again today. Since I left you, I have eaten very little, on Friday, chiefly broath, on Saturday nothing but some bread in the morning, on Sunday nothing but some bread and three roasted apples. I try to get well and wish to see you, but if I came, I should only cough and cough. Mr Steevens, who is with me, says that my hearing is returned. We are here all three sick, and poor Levet is gone.

Do not add to my other distresses any [any] diminution of kindness for,

Madam, Your most humble Servant

Jan 28. 1782   Sam: Johnson

757.1.—Another description of asthma, convulsions, and sleeplessness. J proposes a second bleeding.   1. A slip for 'extimescendum'.

758.1. Jan. '82. ———
E. Byrne Hackett.—

         in Boult Court Fleet street of january 1782
On Thursday the 17th died very suddenly Mr Robert Levet, a very useful, and charitable practitioner in Physick, in full possession of every power both of Body and mind, though he is supposed to have been at least Eighty years old. He was born near Hull in Yorkshire, but his relations are not known.

758.2. Tu. 29 Jan. '82. John Perkins.
Address: To Mr Perkins
O. T. Perkins.—

Sir

     I have been ill, but can now venture out and will call on You this afternoon for a little private conversation, if You are to be at home; Fix what hour You please, I can wait on You any time after dinner. I am,

               Sir, Your most humble Servant
Jan. 29. 1782   Sam: Johnson

759. M. 4 Feb. '82. Margaret Strahan.
Address: To Mrs Strahan.
Fettercairn.—Boswell 1791, ii. 415 (Hill iv. 140).

Dear Madam

     Mrs Williams showed me your kind letter. This little habitation is now but a melancholy place, clouded with the gloom of disease and death. Of the four inmates one has been suddenly snatched away, two[1] are oppressed by very afflictive and dangerous ilness; and I tried yesterday to gain some relief by a third bleeding from a disorder which has for some time distressed me, and I think myself today much better.

758.1.—This document, which I have not seen (I owed my copy to R. B. Adam), is said to have been written by Francis Barber to Johnson's dictation. It is scarcely a letter; it is in fact clearly 'copy' for the obituary notice which was printed in *GM* Jan. 1782: 'In Bolt-Court, Fleet-str. at the house of his friendly patron Dr. Johnson, Mr. Rob. Levet, a very useful, skilful, and charitable practitioner in physic, in full possession of every power both of body and mind, though supposed to have been 80 years old. He was born near Hull in Yorkshire.' The brevity of the original may perhaps excuse its inclusion here.

759.—1. AW and Mrs. Desmoulins; *L* iv. 170.

I am glad, dear Madam, to hear that you are so far recovered as to go to Bath. Let me once more[2] entreat you to stay till your health is not only obtained but confirmed. Your fortune is such as that no moderate expence deserves your care, and you have a husband who, I believe does not regard it. Stay therefore till you are quite well. I am, for my part, very much dejected,[3] but complaint is useless. I hope God will bless You, and desire you to form the same wish for me.

I am, Dear Madam, Your most humble Servant,

Febr. 4. 1782　　　　　　　　　　　　　　　Sam: Johnson.

759.1. M. 4 Feb. '82. Thomas Lawrence.

Address: To Dr Laurence.

Rosenbach 1925.—

Dear Sir

This last phlebotomy has, I think, done me good. I had this morning a very kindly sweat.

Please to send me your papers,[1] which I am sorry that you should mention with an apology, as if you suspected me of forgetting the disproportion between what I can do for you, and what You can do for Me. I am, Sir,

　　　　your most obliged and most humble servant

Feb. 4. 1782　　　　　　　　　　　　　　　Sam: Johnson

759.2. Sa. 9 Feb. '82. Hester Chapone.

Castle Howard.—*Hist. MSS. Comm. Report* XV (1897), Part vi, 573.

Madam Since I had the honour of receiving this manuscript[1] I know not that I have been otherwise than very ill for a single day. I intended to have written to you, but even that I delayed with the natural expectation of another day. My purpose was to have read the piece as soon as I grew better. You may assure yourself and the authour that since I learned to unlock(?)[2] it, I have never opened it, and that

---

759.—2. As in 728.　　　　　　　　　　　3. 'deserted' 1791.

759.1.—1. In *PM* for 18 Mar. J notes that he read 'part of Dr. Laurence's book de Temperamentis'. In the entry for the next day it is called 'Laurence's paper'; it was no doubt a medical work in manuscript.

759.2.—1. Of Lord Carlisle's tragedy.　　　2. The *Report* read 'overlook'.

if he does me the honour to send it again when I am better
it shall not be again returned unread.

I am, Madam, Your most humble Servant,

Febr. 9, 1782. Sam: Johnson

I entreat to see it again.

760. Th. 14 Feb. '82. Charles Patrick.

Not traced; copy by Thomas Harwood, *c.* 1820, at Pembroke.—*GM*
May 1789, i. 383.

Sir, Bolt court, Fleet-street, Feb. 14, 1782.

Robert Levet, with whom I have been connected by a
friendship of many years, died lately at my house. His death
was sudden, and no will has yet been found; I therefore gave
notice of his decease in the papers, that an heir, if he has any,
may appear. He has left very little; but of that little his
brother is doubtless heir, and your friend may be perhaps his
brother. I have had another application from one who calls
himself his brother; and I suppose it is fit that the claimant
should give some proof of his relation. I would gladly know,
from the gentleman that thinks himself R. Levet's brother,

In what year, and in what parish, R. Levet was born?

Where or how was he educated?

What was his early course of life?

What were the marks of his person; his stature; the colour
of his eyes?

Was he marked by the small-pox?

Had he any impediment in his speech?

What relations had he, and how many are now living?

His answer to these questions will show whether he knew
him; and he may then proceed to shew that he is his brother.

He may be sure, that nothing shall be hastily wasted or
removed. I have not looked into his boxes, but transferred
that business to a gentleman in the neighbourhood, of
character above suspicion.

Sam: Johnson.

760.—Harwood notes that the original 'does not give the direction; but was in possession of Richard Beatniffe Esq the Recorder of Hull'. The reply, giving an account
of L's relatives, is recorded in the Adam Catalogue, iii. 237. It is by one John
Thompson, and is dated 21 Feb. See Addenda, p. 530.

761. Sa. 16 Feb. '82. Mrs. Thrale.

Donald F. Hyde.—1788, No. 278.

Dearest Lady

I am better, but not yet well, but Hope springs eternal.[1]
——As soon as I can think myself not troublesome, You may
be sure of seeing ⟨me⟩, for such a place to visit no body ever
had. Dearest Madam, do not think me worse than I am, be
sure at least that whatever happens to me, I am with all the
regard that admiration of excellence and gratitude for kindness can excite,

Madam, Your most humble Servant

Febr. 16. 1782   Sam: Johnson

762. Su. 17 Feb. '82. Mrs. Thrale.

Sotheby 30 Jan. 1918 (not seen).—1788, No. 280.

Dear Madam   Feb. 17, 1782.
Sure such letters would make any man well. I will let
them have their full operation upon me; but while I write I
am not without a cough. I can however keep it quiet by
diacodium, and am in hope that with all other disturbances
it will go away, and permit me to enjoy the happiness of being,

Madam, your, &c.

763. Th. 21 Feb. '82. Mrs. Thrale.

Adam.—1788, No. 281.

Dearest Madam

I certainly grow better, I lay this morning with such success, that I called before I rose for dry linen. I believe I have
had a crisis.

Last night caled Sir Richard Jebb, and many people call or
send, I am not neglected nor forgotten. But let me be
always sure of your kindness. I hope to try again this week
whether your house is yet so cold, for to be away from you,
if I did ⟨not⟩ think our separation likely to be short, how
could I endure. You are a dear, dear Lady, and your kind
attention is a great part of what Life affords to,

Madam, Your most obliged and most humble servant,

Febr. 21. 1782 Bolt court.   Sam: Johnson

761.—1. 'Hope springs eternal in the human breast': Pope, *Essay on Man*, i. 95.

764. W. 27 Feb. '82. Edmond Malone.

Address: To Mr Malone No 55 Queen Anne Street. East.
Adam.—Boswell 1791, ii. 416 (Hill iv. 141).

Sir

I have for many weeks been so much out of order, that I have gone out only in a coach to Mrs Thrale's, where I can use all the freedom that sickness requires. Do not therefore take it amiss that I am not with you and Dr Farmer. I hope hereafter to see you often.

I am Sir Your most humble servant

Febr. 27. 1782   Sam: Johnson

765. Sa. 2 Mar. '82. Lucy Porter (Lichfield).

Fettercairn.—Boswell 1791, ii. 416 (Hill iv. 142).

Dear Madam

I went away from Lichfield ill, and have had a trouble-some time with my breath, for some weeks I have been dis-ordered by a cold of which I could not get the violence abated, till I had been let blood[1] three times. I have not, however, been so bad, but that I could have written, and I am sorry that I neglected it.

My dwelling is but melancholy, both Williams, and Des-moulins and myself are very sickly: Frank is not well, and poor Levet died in his bed the other day by a sudden stroke. I suppose not one minute passed between health and death. So uncertain are human things.

Such is the appearance of the World about me; I hope your scenes are more cheerful. But whatever befals us, though it is wise to be serious, it is useless and foolish, and perhaps sinful to be gloomy. Let us therefore keep ourselves as easy as we can; though the loss of Friends will be felt, and poor Levet had been to me[2] a faithful adherent for thirty years.

Forgive me, my dear Love, the omission of writing; I hope to mend that and my other faults. Let me have your prayers.

Make my compliments to Mrs Cobb, and Miss Adey and Mr. Pearson, and the whole company of my friends.

I am, My dear, Your most humble servant

London. March 2. 1782   Sam: Johnson

765.—1. This was for long the regular idiom.   2. 'to me' om. 1791.

766. Sa. 2 Mar. '82. Edmond Malone.

Address: To Edmond Malone Esq.
Adam.—Boswell 1791, ii. 416 (Hill iv. 141).

Dear Sir

I hope, I grow better, and shall soon be able to enjoy the kindness of my friends. I think this wild adherence to Chatterton[1] more unaccountable than the obstinate defence of Ossian. For Ossian there is a national pride, which may be forgiven though it cannot be applauded: for Chatterton there is nothing but the resolution to say again what has once been said.   I am Sir Your humble servant
March 2. 1782   Sam: Johnson

766.1. Sa. 2 Mar. '82. John Taylor (Westminster).

Address: To the Reverend Doctor Taylor.
J. D. Hughes (1934).—Hill, *JM* 1897, ii. 452.

Dear Sir

I am sorry to hear that You are not well, I have had a very troublesome night myself, I fancy the Weather may hurt us; if that is the case, we may hope for better health as the year advances.

I had a letter last night from Mr Langley, which I will show you to morrow; which will I believe incline You to doubt Mr Flint's veracity, yet I believe it will be best for the Girls[1] to take the money offered them, but You shall consider it to morrow. I am Sir Yours &c.
March 2. 1782   Sam: Johnson
I shall come to morrow early in the evening

766.2. W. 13 Mar. '82. Thomas Laurence.

Huntington.—

T. Laurentio Medico. S.
     Malae valetudinis diuturnitate fatigatus, tuam artem, Vir

766.—1. M explains in a note that he had sent J his *Cursory Observations* on the Rowley controversy, published later in the year.

766.1.—1. Collier.

766.2.—J appeals 'a second time' (iterum) to Lawrence. This is not his second letter, see 756.2, 757.1; but he regards this as a second illness. His cough is better, his asthma much worse; he compares it to the weights piled on the chests of prisoners who refused to plead. L hopes, he knows, that gout will come to the rescue; but why wait for gout, which may not come, or if it comes may not rescue? He begs L to allow bleeding.

doctissime, tuamque amicitiam in auxilium iterum voco. Tussis, aliquanto sedatior, me nec saepe nec graviter vexat, ad minimum tamen frigoris tactum recrudescit. Tanti vero non est ut illi pluribus immorer; longe majores parit molestias spirandi actio laboriosa and (sic) impedita, quae quanto fiat taedio, doloris enim nihil habet, latine enarrare haud promptum cuivis est. Mihi enim in lecto recubanti ferenda est pars aliqua diri cruciatus quo tacentis Rei contumaciam aggestis in pectus ponderibus Majores expugnabant. Arteria saliens interea saepe interquiescit, cujus morae quid vel indicant, vel minentur tuum erit reputare.

Haec omnia incommoda eo gravius fero, quo facilius ea sublevari posse confido. Si quid enim vel sentiendo percipere vel judicando aestimare possim, praesens et tutum remedium in chirurgi cuspide est. Tibi, ut scio, spes est, podagram aliquando auxilio venturam, at quamdiu Podagra erit expectanda quae fortasse non veniet, et si venerit, fortasse nihil opis est allatura. Ego olim, cum podagra maxime saeviit, et pede et pectore simul laboravi.

Oro igitur, Vir doctissime, atque obtestor, sanguinem mitti ne vetes. Nimis caute res hactenus acta est; nunc vero, ne vel metu peccetur vel temeritate, optarem venam, te praesente, ante meridiem ⟨sec⟩ari, sanguinemque sisti tuo arbitrio, horis autem pomeridianis te visam, ut judices an sit tuta altera missio, quae solutâ fasciâ facile fiet.

Haec scribo primâ nocte ad te cras, mane perferenda; Vale. Mart. 13. 1782

767. Th. 14 Mar. '82. Mrs. Thrale.

Sotheby 30 Jan. 1918 (not seen).—1788, No. 282.

Dearest of all dear Ladies   March 14, 1782.
    That Povilleri[1] should write these verses is impossible. I am angry at Sastres.

Seven ounces! Why I sent a letter to Dr. Lawrence, who is ten times more *timorsome* than is your Jebb, and he came and stood by while one vein was opened with too small an orifice, and bled eight ounces and stopped. Then another

767.—1. Poverilli.

vein was opened, which ran eight more. And here am I sixteen ounces lighter, for I have had no dinner.

I think the loss of blood has done no harm; whether it has done good, time will tell. I am glad that I do not sink without resistance.

I am, dear Madam, Your, &c.

767.1. Th. 14 Mar. '82. ⟨John Taylor.⟩

Sotheby 5 June 1929.—

Dear Sir

In some frames of Mind almost every thing is wrong. You are shocked at refusing what I did not much desire, and I am now so much shocked at seeming to covet what was originally bought as a good bargain for another, that, though I have sent the price (10–7–0) I had rather not have the pot, for I shall have less liking to it for thinking it was not properly bought at first for me. If chance brings another bargain in your way let me have that, otherwise I had rather you took this again.

I have had a tolerable night and Dr Lawrence is now with me.

I am Sir your most &c

March 14. 1782.   Sam: Johnson

767.5. ⟨Th. 14 Mar. '82.⟩ Thomas Lawrence.

Address: To Dr Lawrence.

Adam.—

Mr Johnson has sent the volumes that were at hand. The first volume Sir J: Hawkins took back, the third he will send to morrow. Dr Lawrence needs not be in haste to return the books, Sir John will be glad that he reads them.

Mr Johnson feels no consequence from the loss of blood.

767.1.—*PM* 22 Mar. 'At night I wrote to Taylor about the pot.' See 793.

767.5.—To save the trouble and risk of altering many references at a late stage I have kept my original number; but the letter seems to have been written on 14 Mar.; see the references, in 767.2 of 15 Mar., to bleeding and 'Historia Musices'. Hawkins's *History of Music* was published in five volumes in 1776.

767.2. F. 15 Mar. '82. Thomas Lawrence.

Huntington.—

T. Laurentio Medico. S.

Postquam, omnibus rebus benignissime peractis, a me hesternâ die decesseras, tota corporis compages melius habere visa est, spiritus erat facilis, vires minime imminutae. Vel escae vel potus perpauxillum sumsi, ne venas vacuas replerem. prima nocte me tussis creberrima ita exercuit, ut succum papaveris mellitum e pharmacopolio comparandum ducerem; sedata tamen paulo post sine ope papaveris me cubitum dimisit, ubi somnus tantis blanditiis excepit, ut a prima ad octavam horam ne somniasse quidem meminerim. Hinc ut omnia sint et Tibi et mihi fausta et laeta faxit Deus. Vale.

Historiae Musices[1] quod heri ad manum non fuit, nunc mitto; non est ut reddere festines, vix quicquam vidimus aut suavius aut uberius. Vale et fruere.

Ut me visas, nisi tibi commodum fuerit, non est opus.

Mart. 15. 1782

767.3. Sa. 16 Mar. '82. Mrs. Thrale.

Address: To Mrs Thrale.

Rylands.—*R.L. Bull.* Jan. 1932, 35.

Madam

This last Phlebotomy has, I think, done what was wanted, and what would have been done at first with a little courage. But a little cold chills me, and a little chill renews the cough. I took diacodium last night, and repented. To night I hope to be wiser, but who can answer for himself till night.

I hear, dear Madam, that you are not well, pray take you care. Set me right with Sir Richard,[1] whom I cannot guess how I offended. I will come back to you as soon as is fit, but

767.2.—J reports great relief from bleeding, and sound, dreamless sleep. This letter is an admirable specimen of his fluent Latin. One is tempted to wish HLT had been a better scholar, so that he might sometimes have gossiped in Latin to her.

1. The reference might seem to be to the volumes published at this date of Burney's book; but see 767.5, where Hawkins's must be meant; Burney's third volume did not appear till 1789.

767.3.—1. Jebb.

I am to be here on Wednesday. I hope however to see you sooner.

I am, Madam, Your most humble servant

March 16. 1782   Sam: Johnson

767.4. M. 18 Mar. '82. Charles Burney.

Address: To Dr Burney.

W. R. Benjamin.—

Dear Sir

I have taken great liberties by shortening your paper, but have, I hope, omitted nothing important. A long apology is a tedious thing. I am Dr Sir &c Sam: Johnson.

March 18. 1782

767.5. See after 767.1.

768. Tu. 19 Mar. '82. Lucy Porter (Lichfield).

Address: To Mrs Lucy Porter in Lichfield. *Postmark*: 19 MR. Fettercairn.—Boswell 1791, ii. 417 (Hill iv. 142).

Dear Madam

My last was but a dull letter, and I know not that this will be much more cheerful, I am however willing to write because You are desirous to hear from me.

My disorder has now begun its ninth week, for it is not yet over. I was last thursday blooded for the fourth time, and have since found myself much relieved, but I am very tender and easily hurt, so that since we parted I have had little[1] comfort, but I hope that the Spring will recover me, and that in the Summer I shall see Lichfield again, for I will not delay my visit another year to the end of autumn.

I have by advertising[2] found poor Mr Levet's Brothers in Yorkshire, who will take the little that he has left; it is but little, yet it will be welcome, for I believe they are of very low condition.

767.4.—The obvious guess is that CB had written a 'long apology' for his delay; his first volume was published in '76, the second 29 May '82. But vol. ii seems to contain no such thing; perhaps there was a newspaper advertisement.

768.—1. 'but little' 1791.

2. See 758.1.

To be sick, and to see nothing but sickness and death is but a gloomy State, but I hope better times, even in this world will come, and whatever this world may withold or give, we shall be happy in a better state. Pray for me, my dear Lucy.

Make my compliments to Mrs. Cobb, and Miss Adey, and my old friend Hetty Bailey, and to all the Lichfield Ladies. I am, dear Madam, Yours affectionately

Sam: Johnson.

Bolt court, Fleet street. March 19. 1782

769. Tu. 19 Mar. '82. Elizabeth Aston.

Not traced; known only from a mention in *PM* for this day.

770. W. 20 Mar. '82. Bennet Langton (Rochester).

Address: To Captain Langton in Rochester. *Postmark*: 20 MR. Fettercairn.—Boswell 1791, ii. 419 (Hill iv. 145).

Dear Sir

It is now long since we saw one another, and whatever has been the reason neither You have written to me, nor I to You. To let friendship dye away by negligence and silence is certainly not wise. It is voluntarily to throw away one of the greatest comforts of this weary pilgrimage of which when it is, as it must be taken finally away he that travels on alone will wonder how his esteem could possibly[1] be so little. Do not forget me, You see that I do not forget You. It is pleasing in the silence of solitude to think, that there is One at least however distant of whose benevolence there is little doubt, and whom there is yet hope of seeing again.

Of my Life, from the time when[1] we parted, the history is very[1] mournful. The Spring of last year deprived me of

770.—On 28 Mar. J recorded in *PM*: 'I have in ten days written to Aston, Lucy, Hector, Langton, Boswel; perhaps to all by whom my Letters are desired' (we have all these letters except 769 to Miss Aston). It is rash to infer from this, with Hill, that 'he was beginning to doubt' HLT's affection. He had not written to Burney or to the Reynoldses, and she, like them, was a neighbour, whom he expected to see. There is, however, ample evidence that a radical change in their relations was impending. BL's reply 21 Mar. is printed in the Adam Catalogue iii. 149. He invites J to visit him at his house in Rochester, which J did in July '83.

1. 1791 is unusually inaccurate here, omitting three words: 'possibly', 'when', 'very'.

Thrale, a man whose eye for fifteen years had scarcely been turned upon me but with respect or tenderness; for such another friend the general course of human things will not suffer man to hope. I passed the Summer at Streatham but there was no Thrale, and having idled away the summer with a weakly body and neglected mind I made a journey to Staffordshire on the edge of winter. The season was dreary, I was sickly, and found the Friends sickly whom I went to see. After a sorrowful sojourn I returned to a habitation possessed for the present by two sick women, where my dear old friend Mr. Levet to whom, as he used to tell me, I owe your acquaintance,[2] died a few weeks ago suddenly in his bed. There passed not, I believe a minute between health and death. At night, as at Mrs. Thrale's I was musing in my chamber, I thought with uncommon earnestness, that however I might alter my mode of life, or whithersoever I might remove,[3] I would endeavour to retain Levet about me, in the morning my servant brought me word that Levet was called to another state, a state for which, I think, he was not unprepared, for he was very useful to the poor. How much soever I valued him, I now wish that I had valued him more.

I have myself been ill more than eight weeks of a disorder from which at the expence of about fifty ounces of blood, I hope, I am now recovering.

You, dear Sir, have I hope a more cheerful scene you see George fond of his book, and the pretty Misses airy and lively, with my own little Jenny[4] equal to the best, and in whatever can contribute to your quiet or pleasure, You have Lady Rothes ready to concur. May whatever You enjoy of good be encreased, and whatever You suffer of evil be diminished. I am, Dear Sir, your humble Servant

Sam: Johnson

Bolt court, Fleet street. March 20. 1782

770.—2. *L* i. 247.

3. J assumes BL's knowledge of a 'removal', certain or probable. By Aug. S'm had actually been let to Shelburne, and the decision may have been taken as early as Mar. For the history of the Thrales at this period I must be content to refer to *L* iv. 158 and to the acute analysis of all the evidence—multifarious and sometimes contradictory—in C 203–16.

4. His goddaughter.

770.1. W. 20 or Th. 21 Mar. '82.

Thomas Lawrence.

Huntington (undated); copy by Eliz. L, Isham, dated May 1782.—
Works xv, 1789, 499 (dated 21 March 1782).

Nugae anapaesticae in lecto lusae.

Medico Aeger S.

Nunc mihi facilis
Liberiori
Cursu spiritus
Itque reditque;
Nunc minus acris
Seu thoracem
Sive abdomen
Laniat tussis;
Tantum prodest
Tempore justo
Secare venam;
Tantum prodest
Potente succo
Dulce papaver.
Quid nunc superest?
Ut modo tentem
Quantum strictam
Mollia laxent
Balnea pellem.
Cras abiturus
Quo revocarit
Thralia suavis.
Hoc quoque superest
Ut tibi, gentis
Medicae Princeps
Habeam grates;
Votaque fundam
Ne, quae prosunt

770.1.—The date in vol. xv is perhaps a day out; *PM* for 21 Mar. records 'I went to
Mrs. Thrale'. Eliz. L's copy (of the Latin only) is dated 'May—1782'; this is no doubt
a mistake; by 21 May (782.2) J had had time to forget 'some' of the lines. For the
'anapaestic trifles' see *Poems* 198. They celebrate convalescence after bleeding, and
suggest a hot bath before going to Streatham. Lest any innocent reader suspect J
of false quantities, I note that lines 11 and 13 are not anapaestic but iambic, e.g.
sĕcārĕ vēnam.

471

> Omnibus, artes
> Domino desint.
> Vive valeque.

While I was writing this, I had word brought me, that the bath which I had intended to use, is out of order. Is it worth while to look abroad for another, or shall I stay at home. I go to Streatham to morrow.

771. Th. 21 Mar. '82. Edmund Hector (Birmingham).

Address: To Mr Hector in Birmingham. *Postmark*: 21 MR.
Fettercairn.—Boswell 1791, ii. 420 (Hill iv. 146).

Dear Sir

I hope I do not very grossly flatter ⟨myself if⟩ I imagine that You and dear Mrs Careless will ⟨be glad⟩ to have some account of me. I performed the Jour⟨ney to Lon⟩don with very little inconvenience, and came ⟨safe to my⟩ habitation, where I found nothing but ill health, ⟨and of consequence⟩ very little cheerfulness. I then went to ⟨visit⟩ a little way into the Country,[1] where I got a ⟨complaint⟩ by a cold which has hung eight weeks upon ⟨me, and⟩ from which I am at the expence of fifty ou⟨nces of blood⟩ not yet free. I am afraid that I must owe ⟨my recove⟩ry to warm weather, which seems to make no ⟨advance to⟩wards us.

Such is my health which will, I hope soon grow better. In other respects I have no reason to complain. I know not that I have written any thing more ge⟨neral⟩ly commended than the lives of the Poets. and ⟨I have foun⟩d the world willing enough to caress me, if my ⟨healt⟩h invited me to be in much company; but this ⟨season⟩ I have been almost wholly employed in nursing ⟨myse⟩lf.

When Summer comes I hope to see You again, ⟨and⟩ will not put off my visit to the end of the year. ⟨I have⟩ lived so

771.—Dated 1781 in 1791, but placed in 1782. 'A part of this letter having been torn off, I have, from the evident meaning, supplied a few words and half words at the ends and beginnings of lines' JB. A strip about an inch wide has been torn from the outer margin. The supplements, which are not always certain, follow JB's, except where his are manifestly inadmissible. For his omission of the postscripts see Appendix E, II § 1.

1. It is perhaps significant that J does not name S'm. H had met HLT, and must have been familiar with J's way of life.

long in London, that I did not remem⟨ber t⟩he difference of seasons.

Your health when I saw you was much improved ⟨and⟩ You will be prudent enough not to put it in danger. ⟨I ho⟩pe when we meet again we shall all congratulate each other upon fair prospects of longer life, though what are the pleasures of the longest life when placed in comparison with a happy death?

I am dear Sir yours most affectionately
Sam: Johnson

London March 21, 1782 Bolt court, Fleetstreet

Make my compliments to Mr Loyd.

Mrs Thrale has been ill, and though she thinks herself better, in my opinion is not well. Her disorder was a rash, an imperfect struggle for a measley[2] eruption.

772. 28 Aug. n.y. (misplaced by Boswell). Edmund Hector (Birmingham).

Address: To Mr Hector in Birmingham. *Postmark*: 28 AV. Fettercairn.—Boswell 1791, ii. 421 (Hill iv. 147).

Dear Sir

That you and dear Mrs. Careless should have care or curiosity about my health gives me that pleasure which every man feels from finding himself not forgotten. In age we feel again that love of our native place and our early friends, which in the bustle or amusements of middle life were overborn and suspended. You and I should now naturally cling to one another, we have outlived most of those who could pretend to rival us in each other's kindness. In our walk through life we have dropped our companions and are now to pick up such as chance may offer us, or to

771.—2. This word defeated me, but I traced it as best I could. From my tracing and the context Drs. Onions and Sinclair independently guessed 'measley', which is I think almost certainly what J intended.

772.—'Without a date, but supposed to be about this time' (i.e. Mar. '82) JB, who had not noticed the postmark. I agree with Hill that the letter cannot belong to '82, when he could not have described his health as 'not worse'; that it must have been written before HT's death (Apr. '81), otherwise that loss would have been mentioned; and that it does not belong to the lucid interval of some two years from June '79, when his health was so unexpectedly good. Being unable to fix the year I have left the letter in its traditional place.

travel on alone. You indeed have a sister with whom you can divide the day, I have no natural friend left, but Providence has been pleased to preserve me from neglect, I have not wanted such alleviations of life as friendship could supply. My health has been from my twentieth year such as has seldom afforded me a single day of ease, but it is at least not worse, and I sometimes make myself believe that ⟨it⟩ is better. My disorders are however still sufficiently oppressive.

I think of seeing Staffordshire again this autumn, and intend to find my way through Birmingham, where I hope to see You and dear Mrs. Careless well. I am Sir Your affectionate Friend

Sam: Johnson

773. F. 22 Mar. '82. John Taylor.

Not traced; known only from an entry in *PM*: '22 . . . I wrote to Taylor about the pot'.

774. F. 22 Mar. '82. Hamilton.

Not traced; known only from an entry in *PM*: '22 . . . wrote . . . to Hamilton about the Foedera'; '28 . . . Sold Rymer for Davies.'

775. Th. 28 Mar. '82. James Boswell (Edinburgh).

Not traced.—Boswell 1791, ii. 422 (Hill iv. 148).

Dear Sir

The pleasure which we used to receive from each other on Good-Friday and Easter-day, we must be this year content to miss. Let us, however, pray for each other, and hope to see one another yet from time to time with mutual delight. My disorder has been a cold, which impeded the organs of respiration, and kept me many weeks in a state of great uneasiness, but by repeated phlebotomy it is now relieved; and next to the recovery of Mrs. Boswell, I flatter myself, that you will rejoice at mine.

773.—See 767.1, 793.

774.—Hill assumed Hamilton to be WGH. But it might be a bookseller, or any buyer of valuable books.

775.—JB had in several letters 'regretted that I could not come to London this spring, but hoped we should meet somewhere in the summer; mentioned the state of my affairs, and suggested hopes of some preferment; informed him, that as "The Beauties of Johnson" had been published in London, some obscure scribbler had published at Edinburgh, what he called "The Deformities of Johnson".'

What we shall do in the summer it is yet too early to consider. You want to know what you shall do now; I do not think this time of bustle and confusion[1] likely to produce any advantage to you. Every man has those to reward and gratify who have contributed to his advancement. To come hither with such expectations at the expence of borrowed money, which, I find, you know not where to borrow, can hardly be considered as prudent. I am sorry to find, what your sollicitation[2] seems to imply, that you have already gone the whole length of your credit. This is to set the quiet of your whole life at hazard. If you anticipate your inheritance, you can at last inherit nothing; all that you receive must pay for the past. You must get a place, or pine in penury, with the empty name of a great estate. Poverty, my dear friend, is so great an evil, and pregnant with so much temptation, and so much misery, that I cannot but earnestly enjoin you to avoid it. Live on what you have, live if you can on less; do not borrow either for vanity or pleasure; the vanity will end in shame, and the pleasure in regret: stay therefore at home, till you have saved money for your journey hither.

The Beauties of Johnson are said to have got money to the collector; if the 'Deformities' have the same success, I shall be still a more extensive benefactor.

Make my compliments to Mrs. Boswell, who is, I hope, reconciled to me; and to the young people, whom I never have offended.

You never told me the success of your plea against the Solicitors.

     I am, dear Sir, your most affectionate
London, March 28, 1782.   Sam. Johnson.

776. Sa. 30 Mar. '82. Jane Gastrell and Elizabeth Aston (Lichfield).

Pembroke.—Croker's Boswell 1831, v. 25.

Dearest Ladies

The tenderness expressed in your kind letter makes me think it necessary to tell you that they who are pleased to

775.—1. The Ministry had resigned a week earlier.
 2. *L* iv. 148.

776.—On the 29th, Good Friday, J recorded in *PM*: 'A kind letter from Gastrel'.

wish me well, need not be any longer particularly solicitous about me. I prevailed on my Physician to bleed me very copiously, almost against his inclination. However he kept his finger on the pulse of the other hand, and finding that I bore it well, let the vein run on. From that time I have mended, and hope I am now well. I went yesterday[1] to Church without inconvenience, and hope to go to morrow.

Here are great changes in the great World, but I cannot tell you more than you will find in the papers. The Men are got in, whom I have endeavoured to keep out,[2] but I hope they will do better than their predecessors; it will not be easy to do worse.

Spring seems now to approach, and I feel its benefit, which I hope will extend to dear Mrs. Aston.

When Dr. Falconer saw me, I was at home only by accident, for I lived much with Mrs. Thrale and had all the care from her that she could take, or that could be taken. But I have never been ill enough to want attendance, my disorder has been rather tedious than violent, rather irksome than painful. He needed not have made such a tragical representation.

I am now well enough to flatter myself with some hope of pleasure from the Summer. How happy would it be if we could see one another, and be all tolerably well. Let us pray for one another.

I am, dearest Ladies, Your most obliged, and most
humble Servant,
Sam: Johnson.

March 30, 1782. London, Bolt Court, Fleet Street.

777. M. 8 Apr. '82. Frances Reynolds.

Address: To Mrs Reynolds.
Rupert Colomb.—Croker's Boswell 1831, v. 26.

Dearest Madam

Your work is full of very penetrating meditation, and very forcible sentiments. I read it with a full perception of the

776.—1. Good Friday. 2. J had supported Lord North's Government, though he despised it. See Index V, Politics.

777.—Croker printed this from 'Reynolds MSS.' If he saw the original, his text suggests unfamiliarity with J's puzzling hand. 'Ideas of Beauty' became 'plans of Burnaby'. For the 'work' see on 738.

sublime, with wonder and terrour, but I cannot think of any profit from it; it seems not born to be popular.

Your system of the mental fabric is exceedingly obscure, and without more attention than will be willingly bestowed, is unintelligible. The Ideas of Beauty will be more easily understood, and are often charming. I was delighted with the different beauty of different ages.

I would make it produce something if I could but I have indeed no hope. If a Bookseller would buy it at all, as it must be published without a name, he would give nothing for it worth your acceptance.

I am, my dearest Dear, Your most humble servant
Apr. 8. 1782   Sam: Johnson.

778. W. 24 or Th. 25 Apr. '82. Mrs. Thrale.

Sotheby 30 Jan. 1918 (dated 'April'; not seen).—1788, No. 283 (dated 'April' and placed before the letter of 30 April '82).

Madam

I have been very much out of order since you sent me away;[1] but why should I tell you, who do not care, nor desire to know? I dined with Mr. Paradise on Monday, with the Bishop of St. Asaph yesterday, with the Bishop of Chester[2] I dine to-day, and with the Academy on Saturday, with Mr. Hoole on Monday, and with Mrs. Garrick on Thursday the 2d of May, and then—what care you? *what then?*[3]

The news[4] run, that we have taken seventeen French transports—that Langton's lady is lying down with her eighth child, all alive—and Mrs. Carter's Miss Sharpe is going to marry a schoolmaster sixty-two years old.

Do not let Mr. Piozzi[5] nor any body else put me quite out of your head, and do not think that any body will love you like
Your, &c.

778.—Hill argues that since 'Monday' cannot mean 'yesterday' (or J would have said so), and 'Saturday' cannot mean 'tomorrow' (for the same reason), this letter was written on either Wednesday or Thursday.

1. Mr. Clifford calls this a 'quarrel' (C 209). It need not be that; and the words following are, at least ostensibly, jocular.   2. Porteus.

3. 'what then' is not italicized in Maggs catalogue 378, 1163; see on 699.

4. Swift rumour? The *Ann. Reg.* reports, 27 Apr., 'the capture of the Pegasus, and four of the French transports'.

5. 'These words again are of her own fabrication' Baretti; whom I quote only as showing how high feeling ran on this vexed question.

778.1. Th. 25 April ⟨'82 ⟩. Francesco Sastres.

Address: To Mr Sastres at Mr —— Bookseller in Mortimer Street. Oxford Road. *Postmark*: Penny Post Paid T⟨emple⟩ FR. Apr. 26. morning.

Huntington Library.—Hill, *JM* 1897, ii. 454.

Sir

I am very much displeased with myself for my negligence on Monday. I had totally forgotten my engagement to you and Mr ——,[1] for which I desire you to make my apology to Mr.——, and tell him that if he will give me leave to repay his visit, I will take the first opportunity of waiting on him. I am, Sir,

Your most humble servant,

April 25   Sam: Johnson.

779. Tu. 30 Apr. '82. Mrs. Thrale.

Mrs. F. Bowman.—1788, No. 284.

Dearest Madam

I have had a fresh cold and been very poorly. But I was yesterday at Mr Hoole's, where were Miss Reynolds and many others. I am going to the Club.

Since Mrs Garrick's invitation I have a letter from Miss Moore to engage me for the evening. I have an appointment to Miss Monkton, and another with Lady Sheffield at Mrs. Way's.[1]

Three days ago Mr. Cumberland[2] had his third night, which after all expences, put into his own pocket, five pounds. He has lost his plume.

Mrs. Sheridan[3] refused to sing, at the Duchess of Devonshire's request, a song to the Prince of Wales. They pay for

778.1.—The date has been cleared up by Mr. R. B. Haseldon of the Huntington Library and Prof. F. W. Hilles. 26 Apr. fell on a Friday in '76 and in '82; the latter seems the more probable. But for this evidence I should have assigned the letter to '84, in view of 998.

1. Haseldon and Hilles made out 'C . . . . llo'. Miss Balderston suggests that this may be the Irish lawyer Costollo (? Costello) of *Th* 388.

779.—1. I have not identified the Mr. and Mrs. Way named in a letter from Gibbon to Holroyd (quoted by Hill from Gibbon's *Misc. Works* 1814, ii. 79). But Mrs. Holroyd, later Lady Sheffield, was a Miss Way. But see Index II.

2. *The Walloons* ran for six nights. See Hill's note for information on the takings at Drury Lane and the deductions made from the yield of authors' nights.

3. 1788 prints 'S—' and suppresses 'playhouse'.

the playhouse neither principal nor interest; and poor
Garrick's funeral expences are yet unpaid, though the
Undertaker is broken. Could you have a better purveyor for
a little scandal? But I wish, I was at Streatham. I beg Miss
to come early, and I may perhaps reward you with more
mischief.

I am, Dearest and dearest Lady, Your, &c.

Apr. 30.—82   Sam: Johnson.

779.1. W. 1 May '82. Thomas Lawrence.

Address: To Dr Lawrence.

Huntington; copy by Elizabeth Lawrence, Isham.—Boswell 1791,
ii. 418 (Hill iv. 143; quoted but not numbered by Hill in *Letters*,
ii. 251).

T. Laurentio Medico. S.

Novum frigus, nova tussis,[1] nova spirandi difficultas, novam
sanguinosi[2] missionem suadent, quam tamen te inconsulto
nolim fieri. Ad te venire vix possum, nec est cur ad me
venias. Licere vel non licere uno verbo dicendum est;
caetera mihi et Holdero reliqueris. Si per te licet, imperetur[3] nuncio Holderum ad me deducere.

Maijs calendis. 1782

Postquam tu discesseris[4] quo me vertam?

779.2. Th. 2 May '82. Mrs. Thrale.

Address: To Mrs Thrale.

Not traced; copy by C. B. Tinker.—

Dear Madam   May 2—82

No more scandal, but all sorrow. I am very bad. Last
night I bled 16 ounces. To day more is talked of. I could

779.1.—1. 'a fresh cold and cough'. Hill quotes Walpole for the return to 'the depth
of winter' and a famine of coals, for which see 779.4.

2. 'sanguinosi' is an adjective, meaning in medieval Latin 'plethoric'. J uses it as
a noun.

3. The controversy between Macaulay and Croker on this passage may now be
allowed to rest. Croker's translation 'pray tell the messenger to bring Holder to me'
involved a mistranslation of 'imperatur nuncio' (his text), which must mean 'the
messenger is ordered'; but Croker's suggestion in defence, that J wrote 'imperetur',
'let the messenger be ordered', is justified by the original. Elizabeth Lawrence's copy
has 'imperatur'.

4. 'When you are gone', i.e. to Canterbury, whither L retired later in this year.

not go to Mrs. Garrick. Lady Frances[1] not at home. Whether I can go with you to morrow, it is to morrow that must tell. Keep well your dear self. I am

Madam, Your most &c.

Sam: Johnson

779.3. Sa. 4 May '82. Mrs. Thrale.

Address: To Mrs Thrale.
A. E. Newton.—

Dearest Lady

I had a quiet night without opium but am not better. Something more is to be done, and I purpose to see Dr Laurence as soon as I can, and then I hope to be well, and come soon to Streatham. Pray remember me to Miss, if she has not turned me quite out of her heart. I am

Madam, Your most humble Servant

May 4.—82   Sam: Johnson

779.4. Tu. 7 May '82. John Perkins.

O. T. Perkins.—

Dear Sir

Having exhausted my coal cellar, I am induced by the present high price of coals, to solicite from You and the other Gentlemen a favour formerly done me by Mr Thrale, of sending me from your store two chaldrons, for which I will pay you. Be pleased to communicate this request with my respects to Mr Barclay. I am

Sir Your most humble Servant

May 7. 1782   Sam: Johnson

779.5. Tu. 7 May '82. Mrs. Thrale.

Address: To Mrs Thrale.
Rylands.—*R.L. Bull.* Jan. 1932, 35.

Dear Madam

When you left me you know how I was, and, I hope, you do not think that by leaving me you made me better. I took scarcely any thing but physick, and was troubled with a very frequent and violent cough, my lungs however seem to be set at ease. Barley sugar did me some good, but I took

779.2—1. Not identified.

diacodium which gave me quiet but hindred sleep. I think myself upon the whole so much better, that I hope to be soon *sur le pavè*, and then will I try to find Streatham, and then— my dearest Lady—I hope to be better than I have lately been, though I cannot be more,

Dear Madam, Your most humble servant,

May 7. 1782   Sam: Johnson

780. W. 8 May '82. Mrs. Thrale.

Address: To Mrs. Thrale.
Sotheby 10 May 1949.—1788, No. 285.

Madam

Yesterday I was all so bonny, as who but me? At night my cough drove me to diacodium, and this morning I suspect that diacodium will drive me to sleep in the chair. Breath however is better, and I shall try to escape the other bleeding, for I am of the Chymical[1] sect, which holds phlebotomy in abhorrence.

But it is not plenty nor diminution of blood that can make me more or less,

My dearest dear Lady, Your most humble Servant,

May 8. 82.   Sam: Johnson.

I send my compliments to my dear Queeney.

780.1. Th. 9 May '82. Mrs. Thrale.

Address: To Mrs Thrale.
Rylands.—*R.L. Bull.* Jan. 1932, 36.

Dearest Lady   May 9. 1782

Since bleeding and a weak opiate I am more at ease, and my present scheme is to go to the warm bath to morrow, and to Stretham on Saturday.

Poor Dr Laurence followed me home in a chair. He is very bad, but then he can tell of somebody worse.

Keep well, my dearest Lady.

I am &c
Sam: Johnson

780.—1. My physical friends are not able to give any precise meaning to this phrase.

780.2. n.d. Thomas Lawrence.

Huntington Library.—

T. Laurentio Medico. S.

Novum nova mala poscunt auxilia (*sic*). Post sanguinem tuo jussu nuper missum, meliorem valetudinem sperare coepi; pectus interquievit, spirandique vicibus minus impeditis, omnia erant paulo sedatiora.

Nunc vero omnia retro feruntur. Veteres me morbi exagitant, mitiores forsan quam prius, tales tamen ut ijs ferendis vix sim par. Somnus brevis, interruptus, incertus. Somnolentia tamen gravissima. Mihi quidem iterum videtur a chirurgo remedium petendum. Tu vero, Vir doctissime judicabis.

781. W. 15 May '82. ⟨Lancelot St. Albyn.⟩

Address (*GM*): To the Rev. Mr. ——, at Bath.

Not traced.—*GM* 1786, i. 93; Boswell 1791, ii. 423 (Hill iv. 150).

Sir   May 15, 1782.

Being now in the country[1] in a state of recovery, as I hope, from a very oppressive disorder, I cannot neglect the acknowledgement of your Christian letter. The book, called "The Beauties of J——n", is the production of I know not whom:[2] I never saw it but by casual inspection, and considered myself as utterly disengaged from its consequences. Of the passage you mention I remember some notice in some paper; but, knowing that it must be misrepresented, I thought of it no more, nor do I now[3] know where to find it in my own books. I am accustomed to think little of newspapers; but an opinion so weighty and serious as yours has determined me to do, what I should, without your seasonable admonition, have omitted; and I will direct my thought to be shewn in

780.2.—I have placed this letter at a guess. J reports that the improvement following the bleeding 'lately ordered' by L has not been maintained; he suggests further recourse to the knife.

781.—Mr. Robert G. Sawyer of New York possesses a third edition of HLP's *Anecdotes*, which (he writes) 'contains a number of MS. notes by the Rev. Lancelot St. Albyn, from which it is clear' that he was J's correspondent.

1. At S'm.

2. Kearsley's catchpenny anthology perhaps had no ascertainable editor; K may have made it himself, or employed some hack. See Addenda, p. 530.

3. 'now know' *GM*: 'know' 1791.

its true state.[4] If I could find the passage, I would direct you to it. I suppose the tenour is this: "Acute diseases are the immediate and inevitable strokes of Heaven; but of them the pain is short, and the conclusion speedy, chronical disorders, by which we are suspended in tedious torture between life and death, are commonly the effect of our own misconduct and intemperance. To die, &c." This, Sir, you see is all true, and all blameless. I hope, some time in the next week, to have all rectified. My health has been lately much shaken; if you favour this with any answer, it will be a comfort to me to know that I have your prayers.

I am, Sir, your most humble servant,

May 15, 1782.   Sam. Johnson.

782. M. 20 May '82. George Kearsley.

Not traced.—*Beauties of Johnson* 1787 (facsimile); Boswell 1791, i. 116 (Hill i. 214).

Mr Johnson sends compliments to Mr Kearsley, and begs the favour of seeing him as soon as he can. Mr Kearsley is desired to bring with him the last edition of what he has honoured with the name of Beauties.

May 20, 1782

782.1. Tu. 21 May '82. Mrs. Thrale.

Adam.—

Dear Madam

My disorder is, I think, conquered, but it has with the help of its remedies left me in dismal dejection. I have however not totally succumbed, for yesterday I visited Mesdames Reynolds, Horneck, Cholmondely, Biron. It is kind in Miss to come for me. I have seen poor dear Lawrence

---

781.—4. In *The Morning Chronicle* 29 May this appears:

'A correspondent having mentioned, in the *Morning Chronicle* of December 12, the last clause of the following paragraph, as seeming to favour suicide; we are requested to print the whole passage, that its true meaning may appear, which is not to recommend suicide but exercise.

'Exercise cannot secure us from that dissolution to which we are decreed: but while the soul and body continue united, it can make the association pleasing, and give probable hopes that they shall be disjoined by an easy separation. It was a principle among the ancients, that acute diseases are from Heaven, and chronical from ourselves; the dart of death, indeed, falls from Heaven, but we poison it by our own misconduct: to die is the fate of man; but to die with lingering anguish is generally his folly.' JB. The passage is from the 85th *Rambler*.

on Sunday and today, without hope. Heberden attends him.
Such is this World.

I am, Madam, Your most &c

May 21. 1782   Sam: Johnson

782.2 W. 22 May '82. Elizabeth Lawrence.

Maggs Cat. 349 (1916), 1389a (not seen).—Extract in catalogue.

At a visit yesterday, for want of a fire I caught a fresh
cold. I have yet no other symtom than a cough, and that
not violent. . . . Please to ask the dear Doctor (for whom I
pray) whether it be fit to still the cough now in its beginning
with opium. . . .

I wish you would write out for me sometime those short
lines[1] which I sent to the Doctor, for I have forgotten some
of them.

782.3. ⟨Su.⟩ 26 May ⟨? '82⟩. Mrs. Thrale.
Address: To Mrs Thrale.
Houghton.—

Madam

When I came home I took physick with good success. In
the afternoon came Mr Langton, whose company was useful.
In the Evening came Sir Richard, but directed nothing. I
took some buns and negus, and had rather a restless night,
but am better today. I am comforted to find that my disorder is epidemical. Pray come soon. I am Dearest Lady,
your most &c.

May 26.   Sam: Johnson

**783. M. 27 May '82. ⟨The Editor of *The Morning
Chronicle*.⟩**

Harvard. Known to Hill only from an auction catalogue.—

Sir

You are right in your opinion that the misrepresentation
of the passage about Death should be rectified in the paper

782.2—1. 'Nugae anapaesticae in lecto lusae. Medico Aeger S.' See 770.1, and
Poems 198. Each line consists of two feet only, and one line is the single word 'liberiori'.

782.3.—On Mr. Clifford's suggestion I have placed this letter in '82. 'Sir Richard' is
Jebb, who became so in '78, and is not in the letters of any other year (except one in
which he appears as HT's physician). The 'epidemical disorder' would be the cold
and cough of 782.2 and 785.

783.—Doubtless to the editor of *The Morning Chronicle*; see on 781.

in which it appeared; and you are right in your recollection of the paper. Therefore I wish it may now be done.

I have enclosed the letter which I received about it, that you may read it, and return it to me.

I have been for a long time very ill.

I am, Sir, Your humble Servant

May 27. 1782 Sam: Johnson

784. Tu. 28 May '82. ———

Copy by J. E. Hodgson.—Hill 1892.

Sir

I have collected the dates of our business. I shall be at home to morrow morning. I am not well, but hope that you are better. Please to make compliments to all the Company of Wednesday.

I am, dear Sir, Your most &c.

May 28. 1782. Sam: Johnson.

785. M. 3 June '82. James Boswell (Edinburgh).

Not traced.—Boswell 1791, ii. 424 (Hill iv. 151).

Dear Sir

The earnestness and tenderness of your letter is such, that I cannot think myself shewing it more respect than it claims by sitting down to answer it the day on which I received it.

This year has afflicted me with a very irksome and severe disorder. My respiration has been much impeded, and much blood has been taken away. I am now harrassed by a catarrhous cough, from which my purpose is to seek relief by change of air; and I am, therefore, preparing to go to Oxford.[1]

Whether I did right in dissuading[2] you from coming to London this spring, I will not determine. You have not

784.—Possibly to Compton; see 808.

785.—JB says nothing in *Life* of his letter, written 28 May, in spite of J's commendation. Nor is it in his journal, which for 16 May–9 June is very brief, 'the bones of my life' (*BP* xv. 82). In his letter-book it is recorded: '30 May (date 28) in most sincere concern for his illness (copy).' On 8 June he 'was made happy with a noble letter from Dr. Johnson' (*BP* xv. 84).

   1. See *L* iv. 151 for accounts of this visit by Hannah More and Miss Adams.

   2. In 775.

lost much by missing my company; I have scarcely been well for a single week. I might have received comfort from your kindness; but you would have seen me afflicted, and, perhaps, found me peevish. Whatever might have been your pleasure or mine, I know not how I could have honestly advised you to come hither with borrowed money. Do not accustom yourself to consider debts only as an inconvenience; you will find it a calamity. Poverty takes away so many means of doing good, and produces so much inability to resist evil, both natural and moral, that it is by all virtuous means to be avoided. Consider a man whose fortune is very narrow; whatever be his rank by birth, or whatever his reputation by intellectual excellence, what good can he do? or what evil can he prevent? That he cannot help the needy is evident, he has nothing to spare. But, perhaps, his advice or admonition may be useful. His poverty will destroy his influence: many more can find that he is poor, than that he is wise; and few will reverence the understanding that is of so little advantage to its owner. I say nothing of the personal wretchedness of a debtor, which, however, has passed into a proverb.[3] Of riches, it is not necessary to write the praise. Let it, however, be remembered, that he who has money to spare, has it always in his power to benefit others; and of such power a good man must always be desirous.

I am pleased with your account of Easter.[4] We shall meet, I hope, in autumn, both well and both chearful; and part each the better for the other's company.

Make my compliments to Mrs. Boswell, and to the young charmers. I am, &c.

London, June 3, 1782.   Sam. Johnson.

785.—3. Hill quotes *Adventurer* 41: 'the Spanish proverb, "Let him who sleeps too much, borrow the pillow of a debtor".' Prof. F. P. Wilson, an ardent paroemiographer, refers me to James Howell's Παροιμιογραφια 1659, where in a section on Spanish proverbs Howell has 'quien quiere bien dormir que compre la cama de un deudòr', and 'he who desires to sleep soundly, let him buy the boulster of one who died in debt'.

4. 'Which I celebrated in the Church-of-England chapel at Edinburgh . . .' JB. Dr. Pottle has very kindly given me a note on this. There is, he tells me, no evidence that JB ever attended any of the nonjuring chapels of the episcopal church in Scotland, which were at that time distinct from the 'Church-of-England' chapels. But he was addicted to attendance at the latter. He regarded the Presbyterian ministers as not apostolically ordained, and therefore did not accept the Presbyterian communion as a valid sacrament. He would have liked to proclaim himself an Anglican; but fear of his father restrained him.

786. Tu. 4 June '82. Mrs. Thrale.

Rosenbach (1925).—1788, No. 286.

Madam

Wisely was it said by him who said it first, that this world
is all ups and downs. You know, dearest Lady, that when I
pressed your hand at parting, I was rather down. When I
came hither, I ate my dinner well, but was so harrassed by
the cough that Mr Strahan said it was an extremity which
he could not have believed without the sensible and true
avouch[1] of his own observation. I was indeed almost sinking
under it, when Mrs Williams happened to cry out that such
a cough should be stilled by opium or any means. I took
yesterday half an ounce of bark and knew not whether opium
would not counteract it, but remembering no prohibition
in the medical books, and knowing that to quiet the cough
with opium was one of Lawrence's last orders, I took two
grains which gave me not sleep indeed, but rest, and that
rest has given me strength and courage.

This morning to my bedside came dear Sir Richard.[2] I
told him of the opium, and he approved it, and told me, if
I went to Oxford which he rather advised, that I should
strengthen the constitution by the bark, tame the cough
with opium, keep the body open, and support myself by
liberal nutriment.

As to the journey I know not that it will be necessary.
Desine mollium tandem querelarum.[3] This day I dined upon
Skate, pudding,[4] Goose, and your asparagus, and could have
eaten more, but was prudent.

Pray for me, dear Madam, I hope the tide has turned.
The change that I feel is more than I durst have hoped, or
than I thought possible, but there has yet not passed a
whole day, and I may rejoice perhaps too soon. Come and
see me, and when you think best upon due consideration
take me away.

> I am Dear Madam, Your most humble Servant

June 4. 1782 London   Sam: Johnson

786.—1. *Hamlet* I. I.
2. Jebb.
3. Horace, *Odes* II. ix: 'at length these weak complaints give o'er' (Francis).
4. J perhaps meant 'skate-pudding'.

787. Tu. 4 June '82. Mary Prowse (Frome).
Not traced.—*NQ* 4 S. v. 442.

Madam

I have thus long omitted the acknowlegement of your letter and bill—not by levity or negligence but under the pressure of ilness long continued and very distresful. I am now better, but yet so far from health that I have been purposing to seek relief from change of air by a journey to Oxford.

Your health, Madam, I hope allows you the full enjoyment of this blooming season. I have yet been able to derive little pleasure from verdure or from fragrance.

I am, Madam, Your most humble servant
Bolt Court, Fleet Street. June 4, 1782.   Sam: Johnson.

787.1. W. 5 June '82. ⟨? Mrs. Thrale.⟩
Ellery Sedgwick.—

Dear Madam

I have slept in a chair, and am better. When I leave bed, I will do all that the Doctor directs. Your care is a great comfort to me.

                                    I am Madam Your &c
June 5. 1782   Sam: Johnson

787.2. W. 5 June '82. Mrs. Thrale.
A. Houghton.—

Dear Madam

Though Streatham supplies many things which I know not where to find in any other place, You well know it does not answer to change of air. I was yesterday in hope that the poppy would be equivalent to every thing, but having taken it two nights together, I begin to be afraid of it. I have however recovered my appetite and much of my strength. I took my once[1] of bark, but today have taken a laxative, as Sir Richard directed.

787.1.—If it seems unlikely that both this letter and 787.2 were to HLT, my guess is that Miss Lawrence had sent J written instructions from her father. 788.1 shows J reporting on his health to Miss L. But see Addenda, p. 530.

787.2.—1. The reading is I think certain; but J no doubt meant 'ounce', though the spelling 'once' is not recorded in *OED* later than the fifteenth century. See 786.

& bid him observe (with an Air) that my Master had not lost his Stomach—that is the Criterion of a good Constitution in Southwark I believe, so I did not fret at his eating that day. I am called, Dear Sir Farewell, & forget not Your ever much Obliged and

Obedient H: L: T.

663b. Bath. Th. 4 May '80. From Mrs. Thrale.

R 540.96—

Dear Sir   Bath 4: May 1780 Thursday

The Borough people want my Master among them, but he must not come: Southwark is a Scene of Riot and Bustle and it would soon petrify him even to see & hear the Confusion, if he took no active part in it. Now if you think I say this to keep away from my own house, you wrong me, & wrong me cruelly: Mr Thrale is but too willing to get me a fine House in the finest part of the Town, but he is not safe from another Apoplexy, he is not indeed, his Mind if it does not actually wander is enough disposed to do so, & his Appearance among his Constituents would *do him no good*. There is a flutter & a Dejection at Times that will bear no Hurries, though he rides, & breathes pure air in this place, & eats now only of *one* Thing, and much less than ever you saw him eat: Moysey brings him to Rule very tolerably, & we watch him with great Vigilance indeed.

For the rest we live on as we did; & I hope you live on between Starving & Plenty so as to benefit your Health & delight your Friends. You have none however that love & honour you as does Your poor Mistress—Ah Sir! but I am very lowspirited for all I flash away so—Ever faithfully Yours

H: L: T.

664. Su. 7 May '80. Mrs. Thrale (Bath).

Sotheby 30 Jan. 1918 (not seen).—1788, No. 231.

Madam   Bolt-court, Fleet-street, May 7, 1780.

Mr. P⟨erkins⟩[1] has just been with me, and has talked much talk, of which the result is, that he thinks your presence necessary for a few days. I have not the same fulness of conviction; but your appearance would certainly operate in your favour, and you will judge better what measures of diligence and of expence are necessary. Money, Mr. P⟨erkins⟩ says, must be spent; and he is right in wishing that you be made able to judge how far it is spent properly. Perhaps, it is but perhaps, some desire that I have of seeing you, makes me think the better of his reasons. Can you leave Master? Can

664.—Sir Frank MacKinnon suggested that this letter was really written on Saturday 6 May; in that case the 'yesterday' of 665 is correct. See App. F.

1. 'Perkins' HLP (*bis*).

you appoint Mrs. ——[2] governess? If you can, the expence of coming is nothing, and the trouble not much; and therefore it were better gratify your agents. Levy behaves well.

I dined on Wednesday with Mr. Fitzmaurice, who almost made me promise to pass part of the Summer at Llewenny.[3] To-morrow I dine with Mrs. Southwel;[4] and on Thursday with Lord Lucan. To-night I go to Miss Monkton's. Thus I scramble, when you do not quite shut me up; but I am miserably under petticoat government, and yet am not very weary, nor much ashamed.

Pray tell my two dear girls that I will write to both of them next week; and let Burney know that I was *so* angry—

I am, &c.

I know of Mrs. Desmoulines' letter. It will be a great charity.

Let me know when you are to come.

665. M. 8 May '80. Mrs. Thrale (Bath).

Sir Samuel Scott.—1788, No. 232.

Dear Madam

Would you desire better sympathy—At the very time when you were writing I was answering your letter.[1]

Having seen nobody since I saw Mr. Perkins, I have little more to say, than when I wrote last. My opinion is that you should come for a week, and show yourself, and talk in high terms, for it will certainly be propagated with great diligence that you despair and desist, and to those that declare the contrary, it will be answered why then do they not appear? To this no reply can be made that will keep your Friends in countenance. A little bustle, and a little ostentation will put a stop to clamours, and whispers, and suspicions of your friends, and calumnies of your opponents. Be brisk, and be splendid, and be publick. You will probably be received with much favour, and take from little people the opportunity which your absence gives them of magnifying their

664.—2. 'Byron' HLP, an odd guess in view of that lady's condition. See on 658. Lysons's and Malone's 'Montague' is no doubt right.

　3. 'Now selling or sold by his son Lord Kirkwall to Mr. Hughes of Kinmel' HLP.

　4. That is, perhaps, the elder of the two Misses S. But see on 390.

665.—1. This I suppose was a lost letter written on the date of 664.

services, and exalting their importance. You may have more friends and fewer obligations.

It is always necessary to show some good opinion of those whose good opinion we solicite. Your friends solicite you to come, if you do not come, you make them less your friends by disregarding their advice. Nobody will persist long in helping those that will do nothing for themselves.

The voters of the borough are too proud and too little dependant to be solicited by deputies, they expect the gratification of seeing the Candidate bowing or courteseying before them. If you are proud, they can be sullen.

Such is the call for your presence; what is there to withold you. I see no pretence for hesitation. Mr Thrale certainly shall not come, and yet somebody must appear whom the people think it worth the while to look at.

Do not think all this while that I want to see you, I dine on Thursday at Lord Lucan's, and on Saturday at Lady Craven's, and I dined yesterday[2] with Mrs. Southwel.

As to my looks at the Academy, I was not told of them, and as I remember, I was very well, and I am well enough now, and am,

Dearest Madam Your most humble servant

Boltcourt Fleetstreet May 8. 1780   Sam: Johnson.

666. Tu. 9 May '80. Mrs. Thrale (Bath).

Lichfield.—1788, No. 234.

Dear Madam

This morning brought me the honour of a visit from Sir Philip Clerk, who has been to survey Streatham, and thinks it will be long before you can return thither, which he considers as a loss to himself of many pleasant days which your residence might have afforded. We then talked about our Mistress, and ——;[1] and I said you had most wit, and most literature.

Mr. Evans brought me your letter, to which I had already sent the answer, nor have I any thing to add but that the

---

665.—2. A slip, unless either 664 or 665 is misdated.
666.—1. 'Mrs. Montague' HLP, Lysons. The word is obliterated in the MS.

more I reflect, and the more I hear, the more I am convinced
of the necessity of your presence. Your adversaries will be
for ever saying, that you despair of success, or disdain to
obtain it by the usual solicitation. Either of these supposi-
tions generally received ruins your interest, and your
appearance confutes both.

> Cette Anne si belle,
> Qu'on vante si fort,
> Pourquoi ne vient t'elle,
> Vraiment elle a tort.[2]

While you stay away your friends have no answer to give.

Mr. Polhil, as I suppose you know, has refused to join with
Hotham, and is thought to be in more danger than Mr.
Thrale.

Of ——'s[3] letter, I would have you not take any notice,
he is a man of no character.

My Lives creep on. I have done Addison, Prior, Rowe,
Granville, Sheffield, Collins, Pit, and almost Fenton. I
design to take Congreve now into my hand. I hope to have
done before you come home, and then whither shall I go?

What comes of my dear, sweet, charming, lovely, pretty,
little, Queeney's learning? This is a sad long interruption,
and the wicked world will make us no allowance, but will
call us ——.[4]

Lady Lucan says, she hears Queeney is wonderfully accom-
plished, and I did not speak bad[5] of her.

Did I tell you that Scott and Jones[6] both offer themselves
to represent the University in the place of Sir Roger Newdi-
gate. They are struggling hard for what, others think neither
of them will obtain.

I am not grown fat. I did thrive a little, but I checked the
pernicious growth, and am now small as before.

Mrs Strahan is at Bath, but, I am afraid, keeps her room,
if She comes in your way, be civil to her, for She has a great

666.—2. Not traced.

3. 'Pratt' HLP. The traces suggest that the first letter is *T* or *J* and the last *y*.

4. A dash not an erasure.

5. 1788 emends to 'ill'.

6. See Hill's note for details. Both Scott (William, Lord Stowell) and Jones
(William) withdrew; Sir William Dolben and Francis Page were returned.

kindness for me.⁷ I am, Dear Madam, Your humble
servant   Sam: Johnson

May 9, 1780 Bolt-court, Fleetstreet. London

667. Tu. 9 May '80. Thomas Warton.

Not traced.—Croker's Boswell 1831, iv. 311.

Sir   Bolt-court, Fleet-street, 9th May, 1780.
    I have your pardon to ask for an involuntary fault. In a
parcel sent from Mr. Boswell I found the enclosed letter,
which, without looking on the direction, I broke open; but,
finding I did not understand it, soon saw it belonged to you.
I am sorry for this appearance of a fault, but believe me it is
only the appearance. I did not read enough of the letter to
know its purport.
                    I am, sir,
                        Your most humble servant,
                            Sam: Johnson.

667.1. Southwark. F. 19 May '80. Hester Maria Thrale
(Bath).

Address: To Miss Thrale.
Lansdowne.—Lansdowne, *Johnson and Queeney*, 1932, 17.

                            Southwark, May 19, 1780
Dear Madam,   about 5 in the morning
    I am up first in the house; though my Mistress threatened
last night how she would go away this morning without being
seen or heard, yet I shall catch her. She has been very busy,
and has run about the Borough like a Tigress seizing upon
every thing that she found in her way. I hope the Election
is out of danger.
    So far things go on well, but is it not a long time since you
and I sat in a corner together? and is it not likely to be still a
longer time before we shall meet? Such is the lot of mortals
that they can seldom gain one thing but by the loss of another. You are frisking and skipping about Bath, and every

666.—7. 1788 omits the paragraph. For HLT and Mrs. Strahan see on 654.

667. This is the only letter to TW after he and J were estranged (*L* i. 270). See on
215. Unlike the early letters it is not at Trinity.

667.1.—Soon after 9 May HLT and FB left Bath for S'k, returning together on the
19th (C 184).

body talks of pretty Miss Thrale, and proud Miss Thrale, and Miss Thrale in this place, and Miss Thrale in that, but I am all for my own dear Miss Thrale in the Borough, unless I could be with her, and with her I could persuade myself that every place was the Borough. Since we must part, let us be more diligent when we meet again. Endeavour to preserve what you know, and I hope we shall have an opportunity of encreasing our knowledge. In the meantime throw your eyes about you; acquaintance with the world is knowledge, and knowledge very valuable and useful, and when we meet again, you shall tell me what you have seen and heard.

I am, Dearest Sweeting, Your most humble servant

Sam: Johnson

668. Tu. 23 May '80. Joseph Warton (Winchester).

Not traced.—Wooll's *Warton* 1806, 390; Croker's Boswell 1831, iv. 312, from the MS.

Dear Sir   May 23d, 1780.

It is unnecessary to tell you how much I was obliged by your useful memorials. The shares of Fenton and Broome in the Odyssey I had before from Mr. Spence.[1] Dr. Warburton did not know them. I wish to be told, as the question is of great importance in the poetical world, whence you had your intelligence: if from Spence, it shows at least his consistency; if from any other, it confers corroboration. If any thing useful to me should occur, I depend upon your friendship.

Be pleased to make my compliments to the ladies of your house, and to the gentleman that honoured me with the Greek Epigrams[2] when I had, what I hope sometime to have again, the pleasure of spending a little time with you at Winchester.

I am, dear Sir, Your most obliged and most humble servant,

Sam. Johnson.

668.—1. See *Life of Pope* (ed. Hill, iii. 77), where it appears that J had drawn Warburton blank, and that his information on this point came not from the MS. of Spence's *Anecdotes*, but from 'Mr. Langton, to whom Mr. Spence had imparted it'.

2. Mr. Chitty of Winchester informed me that the author was no doubt Huntingford, sub-preceptor at this date. Some of his classical verses were published (*DNB*).

669. Tu. 23 May '80. Mrs. Thrale (Bath).

Address: To Henry Thrale Esq at Bath.
Sotheby 15 Feb. 1926.—1788, No. 235.

Dear Madam

Your letter told me all the good news. Mr Thrale well,
Queeney good, —— pleasing and welcome,[1] and yourself not
so ill but that you know how to be made well; and now
Montague[2] is gone, you have the sole and undivided empire
of Bath, and you talk to many whom you cannot make wiser,
and enjoy the foolish face of praise.[3]

But Montague[2] and you have had with all your adulations
nothing finer said of you than was said last Saturday night of
Burke and Me. We were at the Bishop of St. Asaph's,[4] a
Bishop little better than *your* Bishop; and towards twelve
we fell into talk, to which the Ladies listened, just as they
do to you, and said, as I heard, *there is no rising unless somebody will cry fire.*

I was last night at Miss Monkton's and there were Lady
Craven and Lady Cranburne, and many ladies and few men.
Next Saturday I am to be at Mr Pepys's, and in the inter-
mediate time am to provide for myself as I can.

You cannot think how doggedly I left your house on
Fryday morning, and yet Mrs Abbess gave me some mushrooms; but what are mushrooms without my Mistress?

My Master has seen his handbill; will he stand to it? I
have not heard a word from the Borough since you went
away.

Dr Taylor is coming hastily to town that he may drive his
lawsuit forward. He seems to think himself very well. This
Lawsuit will keep him in exercise, and exercise will keep him
well. It is to be wished that the Law may double its delays.
If Dr Wilson dies, he will take St. Margaret's, and then he
will ⟨have⟩ the bustle of the Parish to amuse him. I expect
him every day. I am, dear Lady, Your most humble servant
May 23. 1780   Sam: Johnson

669.—1. HLP has thoroughly erased the first word, and in 1788 suppressed the three
following. Perhaps J wrote 'Burney'.

   2. Suppressed in 1788.   3. Pope, *Ep. to Arbuthnot*, 212.

   4. HLP suppressed 'St. Asaph's', to conceal the comparison with her favourite
Hinchliffe of Peterborough.

669a. Bath. Tu. 23 May '80. From Mrs. Thrale.

R 540.97—

My Dear Sir   Bath Tuesday 23: May 1780.

I was quite ill when I wrote to you last, but I thought you would be glad I was got back alive: My Master is chearful from the Hopes of Success in his Borough, & I am more & more perswaded that my Journey was right, by seeing him so much happier since he thought there was less Danger of failing in his Election. The Expence is surely not ill bestowed which is spent on the Indulgence of a Desire neither culpable nor absurd in the Mind of a sick Man; and Moysey protests he may be a well Man, if he continues that Care of his Diet with which he boasts to have inspired him. My Friends in this place were glad to see me again: Dear, sweet Mrs Byron was so afraid of dying in my Absence she said: and my Aunt was kind, & Mrs Lambart had taken my Tit with her every where, & says She is the finest young Woman in England for Elegance & Understanding. The truth is She shewed off to more Advantage when I was at a Distance, & I have heard nothing but good of her. She is proud of your Letter and will answer it soon. The Bishop of Peterborough sent Express to Cambridge as soon as I came back, to fetch a Sermon I should like he said—which he preached at the Abbey to please *me*, for he had refused before. See how you have set me up here, well may I be saucy; though the fatigue I had undergone did really lower my Spirits & Health for a Day or two, but all is over now, & I have been in the Cold Bath. The Bishop of Worcester is here & his fine Lady, I met them last night at Mrs Lambart's, but what are they to my favourite Hinchliffes. Lady Dorothy English whom I met at the same house asked very much for you & the Dean of Ossory's Wife is proud of your Remembrance. So we go on. The little musical Girl keeps on with Queeny & I believe we shall get her a Benefit. Let me now bid you farewell, and entreat your continued Regard for Your much Obliged & faithful

                                                                    H: L: T.

670. ⟨? May '80⟩. John Nichols.

Address (not in J's hand): To Mr Nichols.
B.M.—*GM* Jan. 1785, i. 10.

Sir

In reading Rowe in your Edition, which is very impu-dently[1] called mine, I observed a little piece unnaturally and odiously obscene.[2] I was offended, but was still more offended when I could not find it in Rowe's genuine volumes. To

---

670.—1. See *L* iii. 137, iv. 35.

2. Nichols's defence (*GM* 1785, i. 10) is that the peccant 'Epigram on a Lady who shed her water at seeing the tragedy of Cato' (which deserves J's castigation) *was* in Rowe's Works, and that it had been 'transplanted' into the *Miscellanies* published by Pope and Swift. The piece is not in Rowe's *Poems on Several Occasions* (two editions) 1714; it is in the third edition of the same year, in *Poetical Works* 1720, and in later editions.

admit it had been wrong, to interpolate it is surely worse.
If I had known of such a piece in the whole collection I
should have been angry. What can be done?

671. ⟨W. 24 May '80; date added by Nichols.⟩ John
Nichols.

B.M.—*GM* Jan. 1785.

Mr. Johnson is obliged to Mr. Nicol for his communication
and must have Hammond again. Mr. Johnson would be glad
of Blackmore's Essays for a few days.

672. Th. 25 May '80. Mrs. Thrale (Bath).

Bergson.—1788, No. 237.

Dear Madam

Here has been Dr Laurence with me, and I showed him
your letter, and You may easily believe we had some talk
about my Master. He said however little that was new,
except this, which is of great importance, that if ever he
feels any uncommon sensation in his head, such as, heaviness,
pain, or noise, or giddiness, he should have immediate
recourse to some evacuation, and thinks a cathartick most
eligible. He told me a case of a Lady who said she felt a
dizziness, and would bleed; to bleed however she neglected,
and in a few days the dizziness became an apoplexy. He
says, but do not tell it, that the use of Bath water, as far as
it did any thing, did mischief. He presses abstinence very
strongly, as that which must do all that can be done, and
recommends the exercise of walking, as tending more to
extenuation, than that of riding.

——[1] has let out another pound of blood, and is come
to town, brisk and vigorous, fierce and fell, to drive on his
lawsuit. Nothing in all life now can be more *profligater* than
what he is, and if, in case, that so be, that they persist for to
resist him he is resolved not to spare no money, nor no time.
He is, I believe, thundering away. His solicitor has turned

672.—1. 'Taylor' HLP (who kindly suppressed the name in 1788), Lysons.

him off, and I think it not unlikely that he will tire his
Lawyers. But now don't you talk.

My dear Queeny, what a good girl she is. Pray write to
me about her, and let me know her progress in the world.
Bath is a good place for the initiation of a young Lady. She
can neither become negligent for want of observers, as in the
country, nor by the imagination that she lies concealed in
the croud, as in London. Lady Lucan told me between
ourselves how much she had heard of Queeny's accomplish-
ments; she must therefore now be careful since she begins to
have the publick eye upon her.

A Lady has sent me a vial like Mrs Nesbit's vial, of essence
of roses. What am I come to?

Congreve, whom I dispatched at the Borough, while I was
attending the election, is one of the best of the little lives;
but then I had your conversation.

You seem to suspect that I think You too earnest about the
success of your solicitation: if I gave you any reason for that
suspicion it was without intention. It would be with great
discontent that I should see Mr Thrale decline the representation of the borough, and with much greater should I see
him ejected. To sit in Parliament for Southwark is the
highest honour that his station permits him to attain, and
his ambition to attain it is surely rational and laudable. I will
not say that for an honest man to struggle for a vote in the
legislature, at a time when honest votes are so much wanted,
is absolutely a duty, but it is surely an act of virtue. The
Expence, if it were more, I should wish him to despise.
Money is made for such purposes as this. and the method to
which the trade is now brought, will, I hope, secure him
from any want of what he shall now spend.

Keep Mr. Thrale well, and make him keep himself well,
and put all other care out of your dear head.

Sir Edward Littleton's business with me was to know the
character of a Candidate for a School at Brewood in Staffordshire, to which, I think, there are seventeen pretenders.

Do not I tell you every thing? what wouldst thou more of
Man?[2] It will, I fancy, be necessary for you to come up
once again a⟨t⟩ least, to fix your friends, and terrify your

672.—2. Perhaps a quotation.

enemies. Take care to be informed as You can of the ebb or flow of your interest, and do not lose at Capua the victory of Cannæ. I hope I need not tell You, dear Madam, that

I am Your most humble Servant,

Thursday May 25 1780   Sam: Johnson.

No. 8 Boltcourt, Fleetstreet London.

Look at this and learn.

673. Tu. 23 May '80. Richard Farmer (Cambridge).

Fettercairn.—Boswell 1791, ii. 317 (Hill iii. 427).

Sir   May 23. 1780

I know your disposition to forward[1] any literary attempt, and therefore venture upon the liberty of entreating you to procure from College or University registers, all the dates or other information which they can supply relating to Ambrose Philips, Broom, and Gray who were all of Cambridge, and of whose lives I am to give such accounts as I can gather. Be pleased to forgive this trouble from, Sir,

Your most humble Servant
Sam. Johnson.

Please to direct the papers to W. Strahan Esq. in New-street.[2]

674. Tu. 30 May '80. Henry Thrale (Bath).

Bergson.—1788, No. 238.

Dear Sir

You never desired me to write to You, and therefore cannot take it amiss that I have never written. I once began a letter in which I intended to exhort You to resolute abstinence, but I rejoice now that I never sent, nor troubled You with advice which You do not want. The advice that is wanted is commonly unwelcome, and that which is not wanted is evidently impertinent.

The accounts of your health and of your caution with which I am furnished by my Mistress are just such as would be wished, and I congratulate You on your power over your-

---

673.—There is no mention in the *Lives* of any information supplied by F. See 683.
1. 'second' 1791—a very easy misreading.
2. JB omitted the postscript; see Appendix E, ii § 1.

self, and on the success with which the exercise of that power has been hitherto rewarded. Do not remit your care, for in your condition it is certain, that security will produce danger.

You always used to tell me, that We could never eat too little, the time is now come to both of us in which your position is verified. I am really better than I have been for twenty years past, and if You persist in your present laudable practice, you may live to tell your great grandchildren the advantages of abstinence.

I have been so idle that I know not when I shall get either to You, or to any other place, for my resolution is to stay here till the work is finished, unless some call more pressing than I think likely to happen should summon me away. Taylor, who is gone away brisk and jolly, asked me when I would come to him, but I could not tell him. I hope however to see standing corn in some part of the earth this summer, but I shall hardly smell hay, or suck clover flowers.

I am, Dear Sir, Your most obliged and most humble Servant,

London May 30, 1780   Sam: Johnson

674a. Bath. Sa. 3 June ⟨'80⟩. From Mrs. Thrale.

R 540.98—

My Dear Sir   South parade Saturday 3: June.

You say Mr Thrale would not open a Letter directed to me for the World, but here has he been for a full Week fretting over a most extraordinary Epistle sent to me by our poor Friend Sam: Dickinson who desires to be *my* Clerk, as he hears Mr Thrale now leaves all the Business to me. This nonsense my Master open'd in an evil Hour—like the listening Scheme—and found nothing but his own Misery, yet one pities him: he was at last forced to give me my Letter that I might give the good crazy Man an Answer. How unfit he is Dear Creature! to enter at all into Business one may see, and how hard we do all labour to keep up that Temperance by which alone he ever can be totally reinstated.

Do you remember one Colonel Campbell who used to be much about us here four Years ago? he remembers you well, & makes many Enquiries, he was much struck with your Conversation: this Colonel Campbell said one Day when we were all together here in the year 1776, & my Master was stuffing down stewed Lamprey at a valiant Rate—prythee Thrale what dost thou eat these odious black Things for? why thoult eat thyself into an Apoplexy by & by. This Talk it is impossible not to recollect, but Mr Thrale's Shyness of the

Man half shocks me too, and Campbell not aware of it I suppose calls to him Yesterday Morning across a public breakfast Table—Well! why you look as fresh as ever now Thrale, you'll eat a bit of that *Conger* again now I suppose. Oh my sweet Master how abashed he did look. I was very sorry for him, but Burney said it was better so.

Every body is going, Mrs Byron, Mrs Lambart, all the folks: Sir James Caldwall has shone enough—he must go to his Aphelion now. Mrs Montagu has written me another Long Letter. She is very good & very kind, and flatters very delightfully. What shall I do to shew my Consequence? Here is Lord Mulgrave waiting & here is Dr Finch, I will make them stay for their Dinner while I tell you how sincerely I am Dear Sir Your Faithful and Obedient Servant

H: L: T.

675. Tu. 6 June '80. Mrs. Thrale (Bath).

Newton.—1788, No. 239.

Dear Madam

You mistake about Dr Taylor's claim upon the Abby; the Prebends are equal, but the senior Prebendary has his choice of the livings that are in the gift of the Chapter, of which St Margaret's is one; which if Wilson dies, he may take if he pleases. He went home lusty and stout; having bustled ably about his Lawsuit, which at last, I think, he will not get.

Mr Thrale, you say, was pleased to find that I wish him well, which seems therefore to be a new discovery. I hoped he had known for many a year past that nobody can wish him better. It is strange to find that so many have heard of his fictitious relapse, and so few of his continual recovery.

And you think to run me down with the Bishop[1] and Mrs Carter, and Sir James,[2] and I know not whether you may not win a heat now the town grows empty. Mrs Vesey suspects still that I do not love them since that *skrimage*.[3] But I bustle pretty well, and shew myself here and there, and do not like to be quite lost. However I have as many invitations to the Country as you; and I do not mind your breakfasts, nor your evenings.

Langton is gone to be an engineer at Chatham, and I

675.—Hill remarks on J's silence, in this letter and 676, about the riots, which were already at their height; see 677.

1. The Bp. of Peterborough is mentioned in 669a; I find no mention of Mrs. Carter. A letter is evidently missing in which HLT made her 'mistake' about JT. 'run down' is not, I think, 'disparage', but (as we now say) 'beat me to it'.

2. 'I have forgotten who Sir James was' HLP. Probably the 'Sir James Caldwall' of 674a.   3. See 657.

suppose you know that Jones and Scot[1] oppose each other for what neither will have.

If Mr Thrale at all remits his vigilance, let the Doctor[2] loose upon him. While he is watched he may be kept from mischief, but he never can be safe without a rule, and no rule will he find equal to that which has been so often mentioned of an alternate diet, in which at least in this season of vegetation, there is neither difficulty nor hardship.

I am, Dearest Madam, Your most humble servant

Sam: Johnson

London No 8 Bolt court Fleetstreet June 6. 1780

Mind this, and tell Queeney.

676. Tu. 6 June '80. John Taylor (Ashbourne).

Address: To the Reverend Dr Taylor in Ashbourne Derbyshire.
Ernest Sadler.—Hill 1892.

Dear Sir

Just as You went away you asked me whether I thought Mercury would do you any good. I never had considered it before, but the mention of it made an impression upon me, and I am of opinion, that as your disorders apparently arise from an obstructed circulation, Mercury may help you. I would have you try it cautiously, by adding two grains of calomel to your pill at night. Thus taken, it will remain in your body all night, and will be directed downwards in the morning. So small a quantity can have no sudden effect good or evil, but if in a Month You think yourself better continue it, if worse, leave it off, and rid yourself of it by a brisk purge. I hope it will do good. It will add very little to the bulk of your pill, and taste it has none, and as it is combined with a purgative it can never accumulate. Let me know whether you take it or not.

Be sure, whatever else You do, to keep your mind easy, and do not let little things disturb it. Bustle about your hay and your cattle, and keep yourself busy with such things as give you little solicitude.

I am, Sir, Your affectionate &c[1]

June 6. 1780 London　　　　　　　Sam: Johnson

675.—1. See 666.
　　　2. See 654.

676.—1. Possibly 'S^t', i.e. 'Servant'.

677. F. 9 June '80. Mrs. Thrale (Bath).

Lichfield.—1788, No. 240; Boswell 1791, ii. 317, an extract (Hill iii. 428).

Dear Madam

To the question who was impressed with consternation[1] it may with great truth be answered that every body was impressed, for nobody was sure of his safety.

On Friday the good Protestants met in St George's Fields at the summons of Lord George Gordon,[2] and marching to Westminster insulted the Lords and Commons, who all bore it with great tameness. At night the outrages began by the demolition of the masshouse[3] by Lincolns Inn.

An exact Journal of a week's defiance of Government I cannot give you. On Monday Mr Strahan who had been insulted spoke to Lord Mansfield, who had I think been insulted too, of the licentiousness of the populace, and his Lordship treated it as a very slight irregularity. On Tuesday night they pulled down Fielding's[4] house and burnt his goods in the Street. They had gutted on Monday Sir George Savile's[5] house but the building was saved. On Tuesday evening, leaving Fielding's ruins they went to Newgate to demand their companions who had been seized demolishing the Chapel. The Keeper[6] could not release them but by the Mayor's[7] permission which he went to ask, at his return he found all the prisoners released, and Newgate in a blaze. They then went to Bloomsbury and fastened upon Lord Mansfield's house, which they pulled down and as for his goods they totally burnt them. They have since gone to Cane Wood,[8] but a guard was there before them. They

677.—An edition of Johnson's letters is hardly the place for a history of the Gordon Riots. Hill's long notes, with their quotations from Walpole, are, however, very good reading.

1. J presumably answers a question in a lost letter. HLP perhaps drew on that letter for her published letter dated 10 June: 'perhaps you will ask, *who is consternated?* as you did about the French invasion'. See C 449.

2. Lord George was the head of the Protestant Association.

3. The 'Sardinian Chapel', attached to the house of the Sardinian minister in Lincoln's Inn Fields.

4. Sir John, the blind magistrate, who lived in Bow Street.

5. Sir George Savile had introduced the bill for Catholic toleration; his house was in Leicester Fields.

6. Akerman.   7. Brackley Kennet.

8. Canewood or Caen Wood, Lord Mansfield's house by Hampstead Heath.

plundered some papists I think, and burnt a Masshouse in Moorfields the same night.

On Wednesday I walked with Dr Scot to look at Newgate, and found it in ruins, with the fire yet glowing. As I went by, the protestants were plundering the Sessionshouse at the old Bailey. There were not I believe a hundred, but they did their work at leisure, in full security, without sentinels, without trepidation, as Men lawfully employed, in full day. Such is the Cowardice of a commercial place. On Wednesday they broke open the Fleet and the King's bench and the Marshalsea, and Woodstreet counter and Clerkenwell Bridewell, and released all the prisonners.

At night they set fire to the Fleet, and to the King's bench, and I know not how many other places; You might see the glare of conflagration fill the sky from many parts. The Sight was dreadful. Some people were threatned, Mr. Strahan moved what he could, and[9] advised me to take care of myself. Such a time of terrour You have been happy in not seeing.

The King said in Council that the Magistrates had not done their duty, but that he would do his own, and a proclamation was published directing us to keep our Servants within doors, as the peace was now to be preserved by force. The Soldiers were sent out to different parts, and the town is now at quiet.

What has happened at your house[10] you will know, the harm is only a few buts of beer, and I think, you may be sure that the danger is over. There is a body of Soldiers at St Margaret's hill.[11]

Of Mr. Tyson I know nothing, nor can guess to what he can allude, but I know that a young fellow of little more than seventy is naturally an unresisted conqueror of hearts.

Pray tell Mr. Thrale that I live here and have no fruit, and if he does not interpose, am not likely to have much, but I think, he might as well give me a little, as give all to the gardiner.

Pray make my compliments to Queeney and Burney.

I am Madam Your most humble servant

June 9. 1780 London　　　　　　　　　　　　Sam: Johnson

677.—9. The words 'moved . . . and' were omitted in 1788; perhaps this was not an accident; for Strahan's susceptibility see on 654.

10. For the attack on the Brewhouse see *Tb* 437, *Queeney Letters* 1934, 133, C 186, and below.

11. In S'k.

678. Sa. 10 June '80. Mrs. Thrale (Bath).

Sotheby 30 Jan. 1918 (not collated).—1788, No. 242; Boswell 1791, ii. 318, an extract (Hill iii. 429). Maggs catalogue 417, 2838, an independent text.

Dear Madam   June 10, 1780.

You have ere now heard and read enough to convince you, that we have had something to suffer, and something to fear, and therefore I think it necessary to quiet the solicitude which you undoubtedly feel, by telling you that our calamities and terrors[1] are now at an end. The Soldiers are stationed so as to be every where within call; there is no longer any body of rioters, and the individuals are hunted to their holes, and led to prison; the streets are safe and quiet; Lord George was last night sent to the Tower. Mr. John Wilkes was this day with a party of soldiers in my neighbourhood, to seize the publisher of a seditious paper.[2] Every body walks, and eats, and sleeps in security. But the history of the last week would fill you with amazement, it is without any modern example.

Several Chapels have been destroyed, and several inoffensive papists have been plundered, but the high sport was to burn the Jayls. This was a good rabble trick. The Debtors and the Criminals were all set at liberty, but of the Criminals, as has always happened, many are already retaken, and two Pirates have surrendered themselves, and it is expected that they will be pardoned.[3]

Government now acts again with its proper force; and we are all again under the protection of the King and the Laws. I thought that it would be agreeable to you and my master to have my testimony to the publick security; and that you would sleep more quietly when I told you that you are safe.

I am, dearest Lady, Your, &c.

678.—This letter I have seen though I was not able to collate it. I have a note that in the last paragraph J wrote not 'law' but 'Laws'. I have restored some capitals from the Maggs text.

1. 'horrors' Maggs.
2 William Moore.
3. Hill has a note on the pirates' case.

679. M. 12 June '80. Mrs. Thrale (Brighthelmston).

Sotheby 4 June 1908 (not seen); 1788, No. 243; Boswell 1791, ii. 318, an extract (Hill iii. 430).

Dear Madam   London, June 12, 1780.

All is well, and all is likely to continue well. The streets are all quiet, and the houses are all safe. This is a true answer to the first enquiry which obtrudes itself upon your tongue at the reception of a letter from London. The publick has escaped a very heavy calamity. The rioters attempted the Bank on Wednesday night, but in no great number; and like other thieves, with no great resolution. Jack Wilkes headed the party that drove them away. It is agreed, that if they had seized the Bank on Tuesday, at the height of the panick, when no resistance had been prepared, they might have carried irrecoverably away whatever they had found. Jack, who was always zealous for order and decency, declares, that if he be trusted with power, he will not leave a rioter alive. There is however now no longer any need of heroism or bloodshed; no blue riband[1] is any longer worn.

——[2] called on Friday at Mrs. Gardiner's, to see how she escaped or what she suffered; and told her, that she had herself too much affliction within doors, to take much notice of the disturbances without.

It was surely very happy that you and Mr. Thrale were away in the tumult; you could have done nothing better than has been done, and must have felt much terrour which your absence has spared you.

We have accounts here of great violences committed by the Protestants at Bath;[3] and of the demolition of the masshouse. We have seen so much here, that we are very credulous.

Pray tell Miss Burney that Mr. Hutton called on me

679.—1. Hill quotes Walpole, who on 7 June was 'decking myself with blue ribbons like a May-day garland' for protection.

2. 'Mrs. Byron' HLP, once more (see 658, 664) casting that lady for a very unlikely part. The Hon. Mrs. Byron, *née* Trevannion, would not be calling on a widow of Snow Hill. 'Lady Lade' Lysons, no doubt rightly; she was a City merchant's widow. HLP was no doubt misled by 'affliction'; but Lady L was afflicted too, by the health and behaviour of her son.

3. HLT had written that 'the flames of the Romish chapel are not yet extinguished' and that 'the mob had always an idea of my husband's being a concealed Papist'.

yesterday, and spoke of her with praise; not profuse, but very sincere, just as I do. And tell Queeney, that if she does not write oftener, I will try to forget her. There are other pretty girls that perhaps I could get, if I were not constant.

My Lives go on but slowly. I hope to add some to them this week. I wish they were well done.

Thus far I had written when I received your letter of battle and conflagration.[4] You certainly do right in retiring; for who can guess the caprice of the rabble? My master and Queeney are dear people for not being frighted, and you and Burney are dear people for being frighted.[5] I wrote to you a letter of intelligence and consolation; which, if you staid for it, you had on Saturday; and I wrote another on Saturday, which perhaps may follow you from Bath, with some atchievement of John Wilkes.

Do not be disturbed; all danger here is apparently over: but a little agitation still continues. We frighten one another with seventy thousand Scots to come hither with the Dukes of Gordon and Argyle,[6] and eat us, and hang us, or drown us; but we are all at quiet.

I am glad, though I hardly know why, that you are gone to Brighthelmstone rather than to Bristol. You are somewhat nearer home, and I may perhaps come to see you. Brighthelmstone will soon begin to be peopled, and Mr. Thrale loves the place; and you will see Mr. Scrase; and though I am sorry that you should be so outrageously un-roosted, I think that Bath has had you long enough.

Of the commotions at Bath there has been talk here all day. An express must have been sent; for the report arrived

679.—4. What purports to be this letter is No. 241 in 1788, dated 'Bath, 3 o'Clock on Saturday morning, June 10, 1780' (FB 'made me date my letter so'). This document is certainly not genuine as a whole; but Hill is unkind in implying that she knew no better than to write 'Procrastes'; in some copies of 1788 an errata-leaf corrects the misprint. She announces their intention to escape to B'n, and in a postscript adds: 'I wrote you a long letter this morning, or more properly yester morning, and said we were going to Bristol, but you must not mind that.'

5. The words 'and you . . . frighted' were omitted in Hill's edition by homoeoteleuton. 'Miss Burney is frighted, but she says better times will come. . . . Mr. Thrale seems thunderstricken, he don't mind any thing; and Queeney's curiosity is stronger than her fears' HLT in the letter of '10 June' quoted above.

6. J's jocular apprehensions from the Duke of Gordon, Lord George's brother, are intelligible. I do not see how the Duke of Argyle, a stout Hanoverian, comes into the picture. The Protestant riots had begun in Scotland.

many hours before the post, at least before the distribution of the letters. This report I mentioned in the first part of my letter, while I was yet uncertain of the fact.

When it is known that the rioters are quelled in London, their spirit will sink in every other place, and little more mischief will be done.

I am, dear Madam, Your, &c.

680. W. 14 June '80. Mrs. Thrale (Brighthelmston).

Sotheby 4 June 1908 (not seen).—1788, No. 244.

Dear Madam   London, June 14, 1780.

Every thing here is safe and quiet. This is the first thing to be told; and this I told in my last letter directed to Brighthelmstone. There has indeed been an universal panick, from which the King was the first that recovered. Without the concurrence of his ministers, or the assistance of the civil magistrate, he put the soldiers in motion, and saved the town from calamities, such as a rabble's government must naturally produce.

Now you are at ease about the publick, I may tell you that I am not well; I have had a cold and cough some time, but it is grown so bad, that yesterday I fasted and was blooded, and to day took physick and dined: but neither fasting nor bleeding, nor dinner, nor physick, have yet made me well.

No sooner was the danger over, than the people of the Borough[1] found out how foolish it was to be afraid, and formed themselves into four bodies for the defence of the place; through which they now march morning and evening in a martial manner.

I am glad to find that Mr. Thrale continues to grow better; if he is well, I hope we shall be all well: but I am weary of my cough, though I have had much worse.

I am, &c.

680.—1. Hill quotes from *Ann. Reg.* a letter in which the Adjutant-General commended the 'very useful, and at the same time unexceptionable association' formed at S'k.

681. Th. 15 June '80. Mrs. Thrale (Brighthelmston).

Sotheby 18 Jan. 1918 (not seen).—1788, No. 245.

Dear Madam   London, June 15, 1780.

Last night I told you that I was not well; and though you
have much else to think on, perhaps you may be willing
enough to hear, that by the help of an opiate, I think myself
better to-day.

Whether I am or am not better, the town is quiet, and
every body sleeps in quiet, except a few who please themselves with guarding us now the danger is over. Perkins
seems to have managed with great dexterity. Every body,
I believe, now sees, that if the tumult had been opposed
immediately, it had been immediately suppressed; and we
are therefore now better provided against an insurrection,
than if none had happened.

I hope you, and Master, and Queeney, and Burney, are all
well. I was contented last night to send an excuse to Vesey,
and two days ago another to Mrs. Horneck; you may think
I was bad, if you thought about it; and why should you not
think about me who am so often thinking about you, and
your appurtenances. But there is no gratitude in this world.

But I could tell you, Doris, if I would;
And since you treat me so, methinks I should.

So sings the sublime and pathetick Mr. Walsh.[1] Well! and
I will tell you too. Among the heroes of the Borough, who
twice a-day perambulate, or perequitate High-street and the
Clink, rides that renowned and redoubted knight, Sir
Richard Hotham. There is magnanimity, which defies every
danger that is past, and publick spirit, that stands sentinel
over property that he does not own. Tell me no more of the
self-devoted Decii, or of the leap of Curtius.[2] Let fame talk
henceforward with all her tongues of Hotham the Hatmaker.

I was last week at Renny's conversatione, and Renny got

681.—1. *Eclogue* ii in *Letters and Poems, Amorous and Gallant* 1692, 114: 'Yet
I cou'd tell you, fair One, if I wou'd, | (And since you treat me thus, methinks I
shou'd) | What the wise *Lycon* said.' There is no Doris in the poem, but there is a
Chloris.

2. Curtius and the Decii are naturally coupled as types of heroic self-sacrifice.
But J might recall Dryden's *Parallel of Poetry and Painting* (Ker ii. 130): 'Curtius
throwing himself into a gulph, and the two Decii sacrificing themselves for the
safety of their country.'

her room pretty well filled; and there were Mrs. Ord, and Mrs. Horneck, and Mrs. Bunbury, and other illustrious names, and much would poor Renny have given to have had Mrs. Thrale too, and Queeney, and Burney: but human happiness is never perfect; there is always *une vuide affreuse*,[3] as Maintenon complained, there is some craving void left aking in the breast. Renny is going to Ramsgate; and thus the world drops away, and I am left in the sultry town, to see the sun in the crab, and perhaps in the lion,[4] while you are paddling with the Nereids.

I am, &c.

682. F. 16 June '80. Frances Reynolds.

Rupert Colomb.—Croker's Boswell 1831, iv. 319.

Dear Madam

I answer your letter as soon as I can, for I have just received it. I am very willing to wait on you at all times, and will sit for the picture,[1] and, if it be necessary, will sit again, for whenever I sit, I shall be always with you. Mr Langton has already read the volume,[2] and had returned it, when you took it.

Do not, my Love, burn your papers. I have mended little but some bad rhymes. I thought them very pretty, and was moved in reading them. The red ink is only lake and Gum, and with a moist sponge will be washed off.

I have been out of order, but by bleeding and other means am now better. Let me know on which day I shall come to you.

I am dear Madam, Your most humble servant
Sam: Johnson.

June. 16.–80. Bolt court, Fleetstreet

Today I am engaged, and only to day.

681—3. 'Tous les états laissent un vide affreux': letter quoted by Voltaire, *Siècle de Louis XIV* ch. 27. The spelling *vuide* is common.

4. The sun enters the Crab 21 June, the Lion 22 July. J did not get away until Oct.

682.—1. See *L* iv. 453.

2. Perhaps an early copy of some of the *Lives* now printing. See 690.

683. F. 16 June '80. John Nichols.

Address: To Mr Nicol.

B.M.—*GM* Jan. 1785.

Sir

I have been out of order, but by bleeding and physick think I am better, and can go again to work.

Your note on Broome[1] will do me much good. Can you give me a few dates for A. Philips? I wrote to Cambridge about them, but have had no answer.[2]

I am Sir Your humble servant,

June 16. 1780   Sam: Johnson.

684. W. 21 June '80. Mrs. Thrale (Brighthelmston).

Sotheby Jan. 1918 (not seen).—1788, No. 246.

Dear Madam   Wednesday, June 21, 1780.

Now you come to a settled place[1] I have some inclination to write to you; for in writing after you there was no pleasure. All is quiet; and that quietness is now more likely to continue than if it had never been disturbed. ——'s case, if it be not affected, is ridiculous; but there is in the world much tenderness where there is no misfortune, and much courage where there is no danger.

My cold is grown better, but is not quite well, nor bad enough now to be complained of. I wish I had been with you to see the Isle of Wight; but I shall perhaps go some time without you, and then we shall be even.

What you told me of Mr. Middleton frighted me; but I am still of my old opinion, that a semivegetable diet will keep all well. I have dined on Monday and to-day only on peas.

I suppose the town grows empty, for I have no invitations; and I begin to wish for something, I hardly know what: but I should like to move when every body is moving; and yet I purpose to stay till the work is done, which I take little care to do. *Sic labitur ætas.*[2]

683.—1. Anecdotes of Dr. Broome, from Mr. Nichols's 'Select Collection of Poems', are in *GM* June 1780, 269.

2. From Farmer, see 673.

684.—1. 'We made a dawdling journey cross the Country to Brighton'—by way of Salisbury; they reached B'n on the 18th. *Th* 437, C 185.

2. Hill refers to Ovid, *Ars Am.* iii. 65, cito pede labitur aetas, 'age glides swiftly'.

The world is full of troubles. Mrs. ——3 has just been with me to get a chirurgeon to her daughter; the girl that Mrs. Cumins rejected, who has received a kick from a horse, that has broken five fore-teeth on the upper side. The world is likewise full of escapes; had the blow been a little harder it had killed her.

It was a twelvemonth last Sunday since the convulsions in my breast left me. I hope I was thankful when I recollected it: by removing that disorder, a great improvement was made in the enjoyment of life. I am now as well as men at my age can expect to be, and I yet think I shall be better.

I have had with me a brother of ——,4 a Spanish merchant, whom the war has driven from his residence at Valencia; he is gone to see his friends, and will find Scotland but a sorry place after twelve years' residence in a happier climate. He is a very agreeable man, and speaks no Scotch.

Keep Master to his diet, and tell him that his illwillers are very unwilling to think that he can ever sit more in parliament, but by caution and resolution he may see many parliaments. Pay my respects to Queeney and Burney. Living so apart we shall get no credit by our studies; but I hope to see you all again some time. Do not let separation make us forget one another.

I am, &c.

685. Tu. 4 July '80. Mrs. Thrale (Brighthelmston).

Newton.—1788, No. 247.

Dear Madam

You are too happy for any body but yourself to travel in such pretty company,1 and leave every thing safe behind you, and find every thing well when you arrive, and yet I question if you are quite contented, though every body envies you.

684.—3. 'Lennox' HLP.

4. 'Boswell' HLP, Lysons, Malone. JB quotes this passage *L* iii. 434, with a note: 'Mrs. Piozzi has omitted the name, she best knows why.' HLP in a note in her copy of the 1816 *Life* protests she had never heard the name. This seems hardly credible; but if she did not look at her own book she might be at a loss. For JB's letter introducing his brother to J see *L* iii. 433.

685.—1. HLT had gone from B'n to S'm with FB, who thence returned home; HLT went back to B'n taking 'Susan & Sophy to spend their Holydays there'. *Th* 438, FB's *Diary* i. 406–9.

Keep my Master tight in his geers, for if he breaks loose the mischief will be very extensive.

Your account of Mr Scrase[2] and of Miss Owen is very melancholy, I wish them both their proper relief from their several maladies. But I am glad that Queeney continues well and hope she will not be too rigorous with the young ones, but allow them to be happy their own way, for what better way will they ever find?

> C'est que l'Enfant toûjours est homme;
> C'est que l'homme est toujours Enfant.[3]

I have not seen or done much since I had the misfortune of seeing you go away. I was one night at Burney's. There was Pepys, and there were Mrs Ord, and Paradise, and Hoole, and Dr Dunbar of Aberdeen, and I know not how many more. And Pepys and I had all the talk.[4]

To day called on me the Dean of Hereford,[5] who says that the barley harvest is likely to be very abundant. There is something for our consolation. Don't forget that I am, Dear Madam, Your most humble servant

London. July 4. —80   Sam: Johnson.

686. M. 10 July '80. Mrs. Thrale (Brighthelmston).

Newton.—1788, No. 248.

Dear Madam

If Mr. Thrale eats but half his usual quantity, he can hardly eat too much. It were better however to have some rule, and some security. Last week I saw flesh but twice, and I think fish once, the rest was pease.

You are afraid, you say, lest I extenuate myself too fast, and are an enemy to Violence, but did you never hear nor read, dear Madam, that every Man has his *genius*, and that the great rule by which all excellence is attained, and all success procured is, to follow *genius*, and have you not observed in all our conversations that my *genius* is always in

---

685.—2. He was 'too ill to see even me'—HLT to FB 29 June (*Diary* i. 406). HLP expands the 'S—' of 1788 to 'Seward'. For Miss Owen see 686.

3. Not traced.

4. FB wrote to HLT 8 July: 'he . . . talked all the talk, affronted nobody, and delighted everybody. I never saw him more sweet, nor better attended to by his audience'. *Diary* i. 410.

5. Wetherell.

extremes, that I am very noisy, or very silent; very gloomy, or very merry; very sour or very kind? and would you have me cross my *genius* when it leads me sometimes to voracity and sometimes to abstinence? You know that the oracle said follow your *genius*.[1] When we get together again but when alas will that be? you can manage me, and spare me the solicitude of managing myself.

Poor Miss Owen[2] called on me on Saturday, with that fond and tender application which is natural to misery when it looks to every body for that help which nobody can give. I was melted, and soothed and counselled her as well as I could, and am to visit her tomorrow.

She gave a very honourable account of my dear Queeney, and says of my Master that she thinks his manner and temper more altered than his looks, but of this alteration she could give no particular account; and all that she could say ended in this, that he is now sleepy in the morning. I do not wonder at the scantiness of her narration, she is too busy within to turn her eyes abroad.

I am glad that Pepys is come,[3] but hope that resolute temperance will make him unnecessary. I doubt, he can do no good to poor Mr. Scrase.

There is now at Brighthelmston a Girl of the name of Johnson, She is a Granddaughter to Mr Strahan; I wish, you could properly take a little notice of her.[4]

I stay at home to work, and yet do not work diligently, nor can tell when I shall have done, nor perhaps does any body but myself wish me to have done, for what can they hope I shall do better? yet I wish the work was over, and I was at liberty. And what would I do if I was at Liberty? Would I go to Mrs Aston and Mrs Porter, and see the old places, and sigh to find that my old friends are gone? Would I recal plans of life which I never brought into practice, and hopes

---

686.—1. I looked for 'indulge genio' or the like, without success. But see Addenda, p. 530. Mr. Rendall suggests that J was thinking of Plutarch's *Life of Cicero*, ch. 5: ἐρομένῳ γὰρ αὐτῷ τὸν ἐν Δελφοῖς θεόν, ὅπως ἂν ἐνδοξότατος γένοιτο, προσέταξεν ἡ Πυθία τὴν ἑαυτοῦ φύσιν ἀλλὰ μὴ τὴν τῶν πολλῶν δόξαν ἡγεμόνα ποιεῖσθαι τοῦ βίου. 'The Pythia bade him take his own nature, not public opinion, as his guide in life.'

2. 'O—' in 1788. At B'n she had been 'fishing for Health in the Sea', *Tb* 438.

3. Two or three words are erased after 'come'.

4. This paragraph was omitted in 1788; see on 654.

of excellence which I once presumed, and never have attained?
Would I compare what I now am with what I once expected
to have been? Is it reasonable to wish for suggestions of
shame, and opportunities of sorrow?

If you please, Madam, we will have an end of this, and
contrive some other wishes. I wish I had you in an Evening,
and I wish I had you in a morning, and I wish I could have a
little talk, and see a little frolick. For all this I must stay, but
life will not stay.

I will end my letter and go to Blackmores life, when I have
told you that

I am, Madam Your most humble servant
Sam: Johnson.

London. July 10. 1780

686.1. Th. 13 July '80. Robert Lowth.

Bodleian.—*Bodleian Library Record* i. 12, Dec. 1940, 199.

My Lord

If what I am about ⟨to⟩ lay before your Lordship has any
thing of impropriety or intrusion, I entreat that it may be
imputed to no other cause than my inability to contend with
the importunity of a friend in distress.

Mr Percival Stockdale, who has lately applied to your
Lordship for orders, is of opinion that some testimony from
me will promote his suit, and I can declare that I believe
his intention to be that which he professes of going immediately to Jamaica. He cannot therefore without culpable
duplicity show a title to a curacy, since he does not intend
to serve a cure in this country. Is he not, my Lord in much
the same state as a Clergyman ordained for the American
Mission?

He has now a Curacy within his reach, but he wishes rather
to try his fortune in Jamaica, and if he has the honour of
being examined, he will be found, I believe a better scholar
than is often sent to the plantations. Though he is not rich,
he is not distressed, nor likely, in any case, to bring disgrace
upon the order by indigence.

686.1.—With this letter is preserved the good bishop's careful copy or draft of his
reply, in which he explains at length why Stockdale's application could not be entertained. See *BLR*, loc. cit.

It is time for me now to apologise for myself. I hope your Lordship will not be offended, for I write with the submission and respect of one that honours your learning, and reverences your authority.

I am, My Lord, Your Lordship's most obedient and most humble servant

Sam: Johnson

Bolt court, Fleet street. July 13. 1780

686.2. Tu. 18 July '80. Hester Maria Thrale (Brighthelmston).

Address: To Miss Thrale.

Lansdowne.—Lansdowne, *Johnson and Queeney*, 1932, 19.

My dear Charmer,   London, 18 July 1780

I take your correspondence very kindly, and blame myself for not answering you with more punctuality, as well because I would be exemplary as because I would be civil. But don't leave me off, but continue to do right, though I do wrong, and perhaps you may in time mend me.

Pray tell Mr. Thrale that last week I dined once upon peas, and three times upon a gooseberry pie, and that none of the best; and that I hope to grow yet for a time less and less. Tell him that he must come back with all the health that he can get to face the world, which has some difficulty to believe that he is alive, and obstinately refuses to think that he is well.

Yesterday we were disappointed at Mrs. Horneck's of the Burneys, for Mrs. Burney was taken ill; how ill, I know not, for I need not tell you that at Burney Hall a little complaint makes a mighty bustle.

Mrs. Williams continues at Kingston, and says that her friends are very kind to her. She is right to pick a little variety as she can.

From the Borough or from Streatham I have never heard since my Mistresses departure, nor unless Mr. Evans has called, seen any common friend except the Burneys.

You, dear Madam, I suppose wander philosophically by the seaside, and survey the vast expanse of the world of waters, comparing as your predecessors in contemplation have done its ebb and flow, its turbulence and tranquility to the vicissitudes of human life. You, my Love, are now in the time of flood, your powers are hourly encreasing, do not lose the time. When you are alone read diligently, they who do not read can have nothing to think, and little to say. When you can get proper company talk freely and cheerfully, it is often by talking that we come to know the value of what we have read, to separate it with distinctness, and fix it in the memory. Never delight yourself with the dignity of silence or the superiority of inattention. To be silent or to be negligent are so easy, neither can give any claim to praise, and there is no human being so mean or useless, but his approbation and benevolence is to be desired.

I wonder when we shall meet again. I know not when I shall get at liberty, and wish my work done, that I may do something which I am not now doing, but then as now I intend to be,

my Sweetest, Your most humble servant

Sam: Johnson

687. Th. 27 July '80. Mrs. Thrale (Brighthelmston). Adam.—1788, No. 249.

And thus it is, Madam, that you serve me. After having kept me a whole week hoping and hoping, and wondering and wondering, what could have stopped your hand from writing, comes a letter to tell me that I suffer by my own fault. As if I might not correspond with my Queeney, and we might not tell one another our minds about politicks or morals, or any thing else. Queeney and I are both steady and may be trusted, we are none of the giddy gabblers, we think before we speak.

I am afraid that I shall hardly find my way this summer into the Country though the number of my lives now grows less. I will send you two little volumes in a few days.[1]

As the Workmen are still at Streatham, there is no likelihood of seeing you and my Master in any short time, but let

687.—1. FB wrote to HLT 16 Aug. 'Dr. Johnson . . . has delighted me with another volume of his "Lives",—that which contains Blackmore, Congreve, &c., which he tells me you have had.' *Diary* i. 417. The lives of B and C were not ultimately in the same volume; J had early sheets bound as they were ready.

my Master be where he will so he be well. I am not, I believe any fatter than when you saw me, and hope to keep corpulence away, for I am so lightsome, and so airy, and can so walk, you would talk of it if you were to see me. I do not always sleep well, but I have no pain nor sickness in the night. Perhaps I only sleep ill because I am too long abed.

I dined yesterday at Sir Joshua's with Mrs Cholmondely, and she told me, I was the best critick in the world, and I told her, that nobody in the world could judge like her of the merit of a Critick.

On Sunday I went with Dr Lawrence and his two Sisters in law to dine with Mr Gawler at Putney. The Doctor cannot hear in a coach better than in a room, and it was but a dull day, only I saw two Crownbirds, paltry creatures, and a red Curlew.

Every Body is gone out of town, only I am left behind and know not when I shall see either Naiad or Dryad; However it is as it has commonly been I have no complaint to make but of myself. I have been idle, and *of Idleness can come no goodness.*[2]

Mrs Williams was frighted from London as you were frighted from Bath. She is come back, as she thinks, better. Mrs Desmoulins has a disorder resembling an asthma, which I am for curing with calomel and Jalap, but Mr Levet treats it with antimonial wine. Mr Levet keeps on his legs stout, and walks, I suppose ten miles a day.

I stick pretty well to diet, and desire My Master may ⟨be⟩ told of it, for no man said oftener than he that *the less we eat the better.*

Poor Stockdale[3] after having thrown away Lord Craven's patronage and three hundred a year, has had another disappointment. He procured a recommendation from Lord George Germaine to the Governer of Jamaica, but to make this useful something was to be done by the Bishop of London[4] which has been refused. Thus is the world filled with hope and fear and struggle and disappointment.

687.—2. 'Of idleness comes no goodness.' Ray's *Proverbs* 1678, 161.

3. There are three blanks in 1788; 'I have forgotten all these people completely' HLP. Stockdale tells the story in his *Memoirs* ii. 209.

4. Lowth, see 686.1.

Pray do you never add to the other vexations any diminution of your kindness for,

Madam, Your humble servant

July 27. 1780 London.   Sam: Johnson

688. Th. 27 July '80. Lord Westcote.

Not traced.—Croker's Boswell 1848, 650.

My Lord   Bolt Court, Fleet Street, July 27, 1780.

The course of my undertaking will now require a short life of your brother, Lord Lyttelton. My desire is to avoid offence,[1] and to be totally out of danger,[2] I take the liberty of proposing to your lordship, that the historical account should be written under your direction by any friend you may be willing to employ, and I will only take upon myself to examine the poetry. Four pages like those of his work,[3] or even half so much, will be sufficient. As the press is going on, it will be fit that I should know what you shall be pleased to determine. I am, my Lord, Your lordship's most humble servant,

Sam: Johnson.

689. F. 28 July '80. Lord Westcote.

Not traced.—Croker's Boswell 1848, 650.

My Lord   Bolt Court, Fleet Street, July 28, 1780.

I wish it had been convenient to have had that done which I proposed. I shall certainly not wantonly nor willingly offend; but when there are such near relations living, I had rather they would please themselves. For the life of Lord Lyttelton I shall need no help—it was very public, and I have

688.—This letter and 689 are mentioned in the *Hist. MSS. Comm. Report* ii. 37 as among the Lyttelton papers. Lord Cobham told me that there were no Johnson letters at Hagley in his time. (Fire destroyed part of the library in 1934, but spared the MSS.)

1. It was perhaps already known that J could not write a sympathetic life of the Good Lord Lyttelton. But he hardly took the best way to be 'totally out of danger'. The suggestion that four pages, or two pages, might suffice was likely to cause offence; and 689 suggests that W's reply showed that he had taken some offence and looked for more. But see 690. The crown of the offence was the picture of 'poor Lyttelton': his *Dialogues* 'were kindly commended by the Critical Reviewers, and poor Lyttelton with humble gratitude returned his acknowledgements in a note which I have read; acknowledgements either for flattery or justice'. For J's quarrel with Mrs. Montagu, who reigned in the Lyttelton circle, see *L* iv. 64, and Letters 884, 891.

2. I have put a comma here in place of a full point.

3. Perhaps, as Hill suggests, his historical work on Henry II, in 4 vols. 4⁰. But J perhaps wrote 'works' or 'Works'; there was a collected edition 1774. See 698.

no need to be minute. But I return your lordship thanks for your readiness to help me. I have another life in hand, that of Mr. West,[1] about which I am quite at a loss; any information respecting him would be of great use to,

　　　my Lord, Your lordship's most humble servant,

　　　　　　　　　　　　　　　　　　Sam: Johnson.

689.1. M. 31 July '80. Charles Burney (Oxford).

Address: To Dr Burney at the Golden Cross in Oxford.
Bodleian (endorsed 'From Dr Johnson July 31st 1780 N°. 7').—

Dear Sir　　　　　　　　　　　　　　　　　　July 31. 1780

　You did very kindly in letter know[1] that You are at Oxford. You may do me a great favour if You can find in the libraries the Liber Londinensis,[2] as I remember a small quarto printed perhaps in the first years of Henry the eighth; it is a miscellany containing among other things the Nutbrown Maid republished by Prior.[3]

　If you find it I beg you to transcribe literally the prophecy[4] which is there and which lately Swift put in his works. If there is any preface or note or any thing relating to it please to copy the whole, and tell nobody about it. Make my compliments to the Ladies.[5] I am, Sir, Your most humble Servant

　　　　　　　　　　　　　　　　　　Sam: Johnson

689.—1. Gilbert West's mother was a Lyttelton. Perhaps J got no information from that family. 'The intelligence which my enquiries have obtained is general and scanty.' J had perhaps forgotten that Westcote had proffered intelligence and had been told none was wanted. See 698.

689.1.—1. J was perhaps in two minds—between 'letting me know' and a reference to CB's 'letter'.

　2. This is Richard Arnold's chronicle, which 'Conteyned the names of the baylifs ... of the cite of London' (*CBEL* i. 823; thought to have been printed at Antwerp 1503). See below.

　3. As 'Henry and Emma'.

　4. The reference to Swift suggests that the reference is to his 'Prophecy of Merlin' (a squib, though it deceived some readers as of genuine antiquity). I do not understand 'lately'. The real Prophecy of Merlin is not in the early editions of Arnold's Chronicle, nor in Gough's edition of 1811. On the other hand 'The Nutbrown Maid' is very unlikely to have found its way into any other chronicle. Mr. K. B. McFarlane suggests that J might have seen a book in which Arnold and *The Byrth and Prophecy of Merlin* (1510) were bound together. Whatever J wanted, he does not seem to have found it; Swift's 'Prophecy' is mentioned in the Life of Swift ¶ 35, but with no reference to an ancient model.

　5. Dr. Scholes cannot tell me who the ladies were.

690. Tu. 1 Aug. '80. Mrs. Thrale (Brighthelmston).
Adam.—1788, No. 250.

Madam

I had your letter about Mr. Scrase and Miss Owen, but there was nothing to which I had any answer or to which any answer could be made.

This afternoon Dr. Lawrence drank tea, and as he always does, asked about Mr. Thrale; I told him how well he was when I heard, and, he does not eat too much said the Doctor, I said, not often, and the return was, that he who in that case should once eat too much, might eat no more. I keep my rule very well, and, I think, continue to grow better.

Tell my pretty dear Queeney that when we meet again, we will have, at least for some time two lessons in a day. I love her, and think on her when I am alone, hope we shall be very happy together; and mind our books.

Now August and autumn are begun, and the Virgin takes possession of the sky. Will the Virgin do any thing for a man of seventy? I have a great mind to end my work under the Virgin.[1]

I have sent two volumes to Mr. Perkins[2] to be sent to you, and beg you to send them back as soon as you have all done with them. I let the first volume get to the Reynolds's,[3] and could never get it again.

I sent to Lord Westcote about his Brother's life, but he says he knows not whom to employ, and is sure I shall do him no injury. There is an ingenious scheme to save a day's work or part of a day, utterly defeated. Then what avails it to be wise?[4] The plain and the artful Man must both do their own work.—But, I think, I have got a life of Dr Young.[5]

Susy and Sophy have had a fine Summer, it is a comfort to think that somebody is happy. And they make verses, and act plays.[6]

690.—1. The reign of Virgo ends 22 Sept. J had then not ended his work, see 707.1.

2. A bound book, even a little one, could not be sent by post. No doubt such things as fruit and vegetables were regularly sent from S'k or S'm to B'n by carrier. Jane Austen's family used to send letters 'with the cheese'.   3. See 682.

4. Perhaps a quotation, but I have not found it, unless indeed it is a confused recollection of ''tis folly to be wise' in Gray's Eton ode.

5. By Herbert Croft.

6. HLT to FB 29 June: 'Susan and Sophy have taken to writing verses—'tis the

Mrs Montague is, I think, in town, and has sent Mrs Williams her annuity, but I hear nothing from her, but I may be contented if I hear from you, for

I am, dear Madam Your most humble Servant

London Aug. 1. 1780   Sam: Johnson.

691. Tu. 8 Aug. '80. Mrs. Thrale (Brighthelmston).

Huntington.—1788, No. 251.

Dear Madam

What do you scold so for about Granville's Life, do You not see that the appendage[1] neither gains nor saves any thing to me? I shall have Young's life given me to spite You.

Methinks it was pity to send the girls to school, they have indeed had a fine vacation, dear Loves, but if it had been longer it had been still finer.

Did Master read my Books? You say nothing of him in this letter, but I hope he is well, and growing every day nearer to perfect health. When do You think of coming home?

I have not yet persuaded myself to work, and therefore know not when my work will be done. Yet I have a mind to see Lichfield. Dr Taylor seems to be well. He has written to me without a syllable of his lawsuit.

You have heard in the papers how ⟨Sir John Lade⟩[2] is come to age, I have enclosed a short song of congratulation, which You must not show to any body. It is odd that it should come into any bodies head. I hope You will read it with candour, it is I believe, one of the authours first essays in that way of writing, and a beginner is always to be treated with tenderness.

My two Gentlewomen are both complaining. Mrs Desmoulins had a mind of Dr Turton, I sent for him, and he has prescribed for Mrs Williams, but I do not find that he promises himself much credit from either of them.

I hope it will not be long before I shall have another little volume for You, and still there will be work undone. If it were not for these lives I think I could not forbear coming

fashion of the school they say.' *Diary* i. 407. 'Susan is . . . quite a Scholar for ten Years old.' *Th* 449.

691.—1. See on 653.

2. 'Sir J. Lade' HLP, Lysons, which fits the meagre traces of the erasure. For the 'song' see *L* iv. 413, *Poems* 196.

to look at You, now You have room for me. But I still think to stay till I have cleared my hands.

Queeney is not good. She seldom writes to me, and yet I love her, and I love you all, for

I am, Madam, Your most humble servant

Aug. 8. 1780   Sam: Johnson.

692. M. 14 Aug. '80. Mrs. Thrale (Brighthelmston).

Newton.—1788, No. 252.

Dear Madam

I hope my dear Queeney's suspicions are groundless. Whenever any alteration of manner happens, I believe, a small cathartick will set all right.

I hope you have no design of stealing away to Italy[1] before the election nor of leaving me behind you, though I am not only seventy, but seventy-one. Could not you let me lose a year in round numbers. Sweetly, sweetly, sings Dr Swift[2]

> Some dire misfortune to portend,
> No enemy can match a friend.

But what if I am seventy two, I remember Sulpitius[3] says of Saint Martin (now that's above your reading), est animus victor annorum, et senectuti cedere nescius. Match me that among your young folks. If you try to plague me I shall tell you that according to Galen[4] life begins to decline from *thirty five*.

But as We go off others come on: Queeney's last letter was very pretty, what a Hussey she is to write so seldom. She has no events, then let her write sentiment as you and I do, and sentiment you know is inexhaustible.

692.—1. In an undated letter to Mrs. Lambart HLT reported her husband's spirits 'so much increased that he is all on Fire for a Journey to Italy'—from which she herself shrank (C 187). The idea was perhaps revived by their growing intimacy with Piozzi at B'n.

2. 'On the Death of Dr. Swift': 'Some great misfortune to portend, | No Enemy can match a Friend.'

3. Sulpitius Severus, *Epist.* iii: 'Sub signis tuis militabo; et quamvis optata sit seni missio post laborem, est tamen animus' &c.: an old man longs for ease, yet the Spirit will not be conquered by old age.

4. *Comm.* 3 in *Hippocr. aphorismos*, 29: ἰστέον δὲ ὅτι ἡ ἀκμαστικὴ ἡλικία λε΄ ἔτεσι περιγράφεται, ἡ δὲ παρακμαστικὴ μθ΄: porro sciendum est quod vigens aetas triginta quinque annis circumscribitur, declinans autem quadraginta octo. For J's verses on HLT's thirty-fifth birthday see *Poems* 177.

If you want events here is Mr Levet just come in at four-score from a walk to Hampstead, eight miles in August. This however is all that I have to tell you, except that I have three bunches of grapes on a vine in my garden, at least this is all that I will now tell of my garden.

Both my females are ill, both very ill, Mrs. Desmoulins thought that she wished for Dr Turton, and I sent for him, and then took him to Mrs Williams, and he prescribes for both, though without much hope of benefiting either. Yet Physick has its powers, you see that I am better, and Mr. Shaw will maintain, that he and I saved my Master. But if he is to live always away from us, what did we get by saving him? If we cannot live together let us hear, when I have no letter from Brighthelmston, think how I fret, and write oftener; you write to this body and t'other body,[5] and nobody loves you like

Your humble servant

Aug. 14. 1780   Sam: Johnson.

693. M. 14 Aug. '80. Mary Prowse (Frome).

Address: To Mrs Prowse at Berkley, near Frome Somersetshire. *Post-mark*: 14 AV.

Rosenbach (1925).—*NQ* 45. v. 441.

Madam

For the loss which you have suffered I will not recall your grief by the formality of condolence. I believe all to whom Mrs Prowse was known, consider the world as deprived by her departure of a very bright and eminent example.

The allowance which she was pleased to make towards the maintenance of the unhappy girl, has been long discontinued, how long, I really do not know, and am afraid of favouring myself by a conjectural account.

Not knowing whether the payment was witheld by negligence or intention, I sometimes purposed to have written to the Lady, but never did it. Perhaps your accounts can set you right.

692.—5. 't'other body' is 'corrected' in 1788 to 'to that'.

693.—Miss Prowse's endorsement is: 'Not finding in my Mother's Books any acct. of the money having been paid for six years I sent him the whole arrears.' The 'unhappy girl' was Phoebe Herne.

It may be, Madam, in your power, to gratify my curiosity. Your servants, I suppose, go frequently to Froome,[1] and it will be thought by me a favour if you will be pleased, to bid them collect any little tradition that may yet remain, of one Johnson,[2] who more than forty years ago was for a short time, a Bookbinder or Stationer in that town. Such intelligence must be gotten by accident, and therefore cannot be immediately expected, but perhaps in time somebody may be found that knew him.

The great civility of your letter has encouraged me to this request.

The money which your excellent Mother's liberality makes payable to me, may be remitted by a note on a Banker, or on the Bank, to,

Madam, Your most humble Servant,

Sam: Johnson

Bolt court (not Johnson's), Fleet Street, London.
Aug. 14. 1780

694-5. ⟨'80.⟩ To John Nichols.

Address: To Mr Nicol
B.M.—*GM* Jan. 1785 (as if two letters, the second beginning 'I should').

There is a copy of verses by Fenton on the *first Fit of the Gout*, in Popes Miscellanies, and I think, in the last volume[1] of Drydens. In Pope's I am sure.

693.—1. Hill remarks the inconsistency of this spelling with that of the direction. 'Froome' is phonetic. It was not until the nineteenth century that printers imposed uniformity on our spelling. J's spelling is somewhat less uniform than the spelling of printed books in his time, it has its inconsistencies and irregularities; see Index VII. But it is in general fairly consistent. In spelling proper names, however, he makes little attempt at consistency, and he would probably have asserted the right to spell them as he chose.

2. Probably J's brother Nathaniel; see references in Index II.

694-5.—1. I could not be sure whether J wrote 'volume' or 'volumes'. The verses 'On the first Fit of the Gout', not included in the *Poets* 1779, were appended to the *Life of Fenton*, and in 1790 were transferred to the *Poets*. Prof. Nichol Smith tells me they are not in the posthumous volumes (1704, 1709) of 'Dryden's Miscellany'; what J means by 'Popes Miscellanies' is not too clear; I have not explored the eleven volumes to which 'Miscellanies in Prose and Verse' were 'ultimately extended' (*CBEL* ii. 300). The verses are in *Oxford and Cambridge Miscellany Poems* (n.d., Jan. 1708) 373; this is Fenton's Miscellany; the Dedication is signed by him. It is not certain that the verses are his; Nichols, *Select Collection of Poems* 1780, iii. 175, says they were probably by Knightly Chetwood.

389

I should have given Fenton's birth to *Shelton*[2] in Stafford-shire, but that I am afraid there is no such place.

The rest I have except his Secretaryship of which I know not what to make.

When Lord Orrery was in an office Lewis[3] was his Secretary. Lewis lived in my time; I knew him.

The Gout Verses were always given to Fenton, when I was young, and he was living.

Lord Orrery told me that Fenton was his Tutor, but never that he was his Father's Secretary.

Pray let me see the Oxford and Cambridge &c., if you are sure it was published by Fenton, I shall take notice of it.

696. ⟨? '80.⟩ John Nichols.

Address: To Mr Nicol
B.M.—*GM* Jan. 1785.

Mr. Johnson desires Mr. Nicols to send him
   Ruffhead's Life of Pope.
   Popes Works
   Swifts Works with Dr. Hawkesworths life
   Lyttelton's Works.
and with these he hopes to have done.
   The first to be got is Lyttelton.

697. John Nichols.

B.M.—*GM* Jan. 1785.

Mr. Johnson being now at home desires the last leaves of the Criticism on Popes Epitaphs, and he will correct them. Mr. Nichol is entreated to save the proof sheets of Pope because they are promised to a Lady[1] who desires to have them.

694-5.—2. 'He was born near Newcastle in Staffordshire.' So the *Life*. But J's scepticism was ill-founded; Shelton is near Newcastle-under-Lyme, and was indeed F's birthplace.

   3. 'He [Fenton] was a while secretary to Charles earl of Orrery in Flanders' (*Lives* ed. Hill ii. 258). In a note on 'old Mr. Lewis' in the *Life of Swift* (Hill iii. 28) Hill remarks 'not Erasmus'. He seems to have been mistaken, see Mr. Harold Williams in *RES* Jan. 1945, 56.

697.—1. FB. It was her father's idea, but he 'left to his daughter the risk of the petition'. A hint was enough; she was invited to 'Choose your poet'. *Memoirs of Dr. Burney* ii. 178.

698. Wednesday ⟨16 Aug. '80⟩. John Nichols.

B.M. (the date 16 Aug. in another hand).—*GM* Jan. 1785.

Sir

I expected to have found a Life of Lord Lyttelton pre-fixed to his Works.[1] Is there not one before the quarto Edition? I think there is —— if not, I am, with respect to him, quite aground.

Wednesday

699. F. 18 Aug. '80. Mrs. Thrale (Brighthelmston).

Sotheby 30 Jan. 1918 (not seen).—1788, No. 253. Extract in Maggs catalogue 417, 2842, an independent text.

Dear Madam,   August 18, 1780.

I lost no time, and have enclosed our conversation.[1] You write of late very seldom. I wish you would write upon subjects,[2] any thing to keep alive. You have your Beaux, and your flatterers, and here am poor I forced to flatter myself, and any good of myself I am not very easy to believe, so that I really live but a sorry life. What shall I do with Lyttelton's Life? I can make a short life, and a short criticism, and conclude. Why did not you like Collins, and Gay, and Blackmore,[3] as well as Akenside?

I am, Madam, Your, &c.

699.1. F. 18 Aug. '80. Thomas Lawrence.

Address: Dr Lawrence.

Rosenbach (1927); endorsed by HLT 'Dr Johnson to Dr Lawrence Father to Sir Soulden Lawrence concerning Mr Thrale's health.'—

Fryday night Aug. 18 1780

I have read the account and do not like it—It looks like the forerunner of some disorder—To advise at this distance

698.—1. There seems to be no Life of Lyttelton earlier than Phillimore's, 1845. See on 688, 690.

699.—1. See 699.1.

2. 'subjects' is italicized in 1788 but not in Maggs, which enhances the suspicion that some underlines are due to HLP.

3. In her letter dated 'August 20' (1788, No. 254) HLT writes 'Blackmore's life is admirable; who says I dont like it? I like all the Whig lives prodigiously: Akenside's best of the little ones.'

699.1.—This is I suppose J's record, enclosed with 699, of his 'conversation' with L, which would be conducted in writing because of L's deafness.

is difficult—As he thinks himself well, he will do nothing.—Gentle purges will be of great use, and if his pulse be quick and hard, I would advise to take a little blood, by a little I mean ten ounces—He is a large Man.

700. M. 21 Aug. '80. James Beattie (Aberdeen).

Address (Boswell): To Dr. Beattie, at Aberdeen.
Not traced; copy by Beattie, Isham.—Boswell 1791, ii. 321 (Hill iii. 434).

Sir,

More years than I have any delight to reckon have past since you and I saw one another; of this however there is no reason for making any reprehensory complaint. Sic fata ferunt.[1] But methinks there might pass some small interchange of regard between us. If you say, that I ought to have written, I now write, and I write to tell you, that I have much kindness for you and Mrs. Beattie, and that I wish your health better and your life long. Try change of air, and come a few degrees southwards; a softer climate may do you both good; Winter is coming on; and London will be warmer, and gayer, and busier, and more fertile of amusement, than Aberdeen.

My health is better, but that will be little in the ballance when I tell you that Mrs. Montagu has been very ill, and is, I doubt, now but weakly. Mr. Thrale has been very dangerously disordered, but is much better, and I hope will totally recover. He has withdrawn himself from business the whole summer. Sir Joshua and his Sister are well, and Mr. Davies has had great success as an authour[2] generated by the corruption of a bookseller. More news I have not to tell you, and therefore you must be contented with hearing, what I know not whether you much wish to hear, that I am

Sir Your most humble servant,
Sam. Johnson.

Bolt court, Fleetstreet, Aug. 21. 1780.

700.—1. Virgil, *Aen.* ii. 34 (ferebant): 'So the Trojan destiny requir'd' (Dryden).
    2. JB in a note refers this to D's *Memoirs of David Garrick*. For his bankruptcy see 573. J might recall Dryden's *Defence of an Essay of Dramatic Poesy*: 'The Muses have lost him [Sir Robert Howard], but the Commonwealth gains by it; the corruption of a poet is the generation of a statesman.'

701. M. 21 Aug. '80. James Boswell (Edinburgh).

Not traced.—Boswell 1791, ii. 322 (Hill iii. 435).

Dear Sir,

I find you have taken one of your fits of taciturnity, and
have resolved not to write till you are written to; it is but a
peevish humour,[1] but you shall have your way.

I have sate at home in Bolt-court, all the summer, thinking
to write the Lives, and a great part of the time only thinking.
Several of them, however, are done, and I still think to do the
rest.

Mr. Thrale and his family have, since his illness, passed
their time first at Bath, and then at Brighthelmston; but I
have been at neither place. I would have gone to Lichfield, if
I could have had time, and I might have had time, if I had
been active; but I have missed much, and done little.

In the late disturbances, Mr. Thrale's house and stock
were in great danger; the mob was pacified at their first
invasion, with about fifty pounds in drink and meat; and at
their second, were driven away by the soldiers. Mr. Strahan
got a garrison into his house, and maintained them a fortnight; he was so frighted that he removed part of his goods.
Mrs. Williams took shelter in the country.

I know not whether I shall get a ramble this autumn; it is
now about the time when we were travelling. I have, however, better health than I had then, and hope you and I may
yet shew ourselves on some part of Europe, Asia, or Africa.[2]
In the mean time let us play no trick, but keep each other's
kindness by all means in our power.

The bearer of this is Dr. Dunbar, of Aberdeen, who has
written and published a very ingenious book, and who I think
has a kindness for me, and will when he knows you have a
kindness for you.

I suppose your little ladies are grown tall; and your son is
become a learned young man. I love them all, and I love
your naughty lady, whom I never shall persuade to love me.
When the Lives are done, I shall send them to complete her

701.—1. JB in fact wrote, 24 Aug., while this letter was on its way. For his defence
of himself, in his letter of 6 Sept., see *L* iii. 438.

2. *Not* America, as JB remarks.

collection, but must send them in paper, as for want of a pattern, I cannot bind them to fit the rest.[3]

     I am, Sir, Your most affectionately

London, Aug. 21, 1780.   Sam. Johnson

702. Th. 24 Aug. '80. Mrs. Thrale (Brighthelmston).

Adam.—1788, No. 255.

Dear Madam

 I do not wonder that you can think and write but of one thing. Yet concerning that thing you may be less uneasy, as you are now in the right way. You are at least doing, what I was always desirous to have you do, and which when despair put an end to the caution of men going in the dark, produced at last all the good that has been obtained. Gentle purges, and slight phlebotomies are not my favourites, they are popgun batteries,[1] which lose time and effect nothing. It was by bleeding till he fainted that his life was saved. I would however now have him trust chiefly to vigorous and stimulating catharticks. To bleed is only proper when there is no time for slower remedies.

 Does he sleep in the night; if he sleeps, there is not much danger, any thing like wakefulness in a man either by nature or habit so uncommonly sleepy would put me in great fear. Do not now hinder him from sleeping whenever heaviness comes upon him. Quiet Rest, light food, and strong purges will I think, set all right. Be you vigilant, but be not frighted.

 Of M[r] R——[2] I very well remember all but the name. 'He had a nice discernment of loss and gain.' This, I thought, a power not hard to be attained. What kept him out then

---

701.—3. Mrs. B's set was no doubt that sold in the Auchinleck sale of 1893. In the catalogue (Sotheby 23–6 June) it is described as 67 volumes (vol. 51 missing) in 'calf extra, full gilt backs', with no indication of lack of uniformity. No doubt she employed a skilful binder. Where are the volumes now?

702.—1. Hill suggests that J may have recalled the phrase 'popgun artillery', which in the Dictionary he quotes from his favourite Cheyne.

2. J's dash, not an erasure. Doubtless the Rushworth of 702*a*, some interloper who had worked on HT's speculative proclivity. In the published letter dated 20 Aug. she writes: 'We had a visit yesterday from Mr. R——; whom perhaps you remember, perhaps not.'

must keep him out now, the want of a place for him. M^r
P——³ then observed that there was nothing upon which
he could be employed. Matters will never be carried to
extremities. M^r P—— cannot be discharged, and he will
never suffer a superiour. That voluntary submission to a
new mind, is not a heroick quality; but it has always been
among us, and therefore I mind it less.

The expedition to foreign parts you will not much encourage, and you need not, I think, make any great effort to
oppose it, for it is as likely to put us out of the way to mischief as to bring us into it. We can have no projects in Italy.⁴
Exercise may relieve the body, and variety will amuse the
mind. The expence will not be greater than at home in the
regular course of life. And we shall be safe from Brownes and
Guilds,⁵ and all instigators to schemes of waste. Si te fata
ferant, fer fata⁶ ——

The chief wish that I form is, that Mr Thrale could be
made to understand his real state, to know that he is tottering
upon a point, to consider every change of his mental character as the symptom of a disease; to distrust any opinions
or purposes that shoot up in his thoughts; to think that
violent Mirth is the foam, and deep sadness the subsidence
of a morbid fermentation; to watch himself, and counteract
by experienced remedies every new tendency, or uncommon
sensation. This is a new and an ungrateful employment, but
without this self examination he never can be safe. You must
try to teach it and he to learn it gradually, and in this my
sweet Queeny must help you; I am glad to hear of her
vigilance and observation. She is my Pupil.

702.—3. 'Perkins' HLP (*bis*), no doubt rightly. The erasures are so thorough that I
could see no trace, as is usual, of the top of the *k*.

4. See 692. She had deprecated the scheme in hers of 20 Aug.: 'Oh no, let us be
miserable in the old places.'

5. 'B—— and G——' 1788. Mr. Adam prints 'Brewers and Guilds'. HLP is silent.
I read the first word as 'Browne' or 'Brownes', and Lysons has 'Brown'. He did not
fill the second blank, but the reading is not in doubt. Both words are, I suppose,
names of 'projectors'.

6. The late Edward Bensly referred me to George Buchanan's poem, *Epigrammata*
i. 62: Si te fata ferunt, fer fata: ferere. Ferentes | Fata ferunt: rapiunt, si minus illa
feras. Buchanan was translating the Greek Anthology (*Anth. Pal.* x. 73): Εἰ τὸ φέρον
σε φέρει, φέρε καὶ φέρου· εἰ δ' ἀγανακτεῖς καὶ σαυτὸν λυπεῖς, καὶ τὸ φέρον σε φέρει.
The sense is, roughly, 'Grin and bear it; if you don't, it will get worse'.

I suppose the S——y[7] scheme is now past; I saw no great harm in it, though perhaps no good. Do not suffer little things to embarrass you. Our great work is constant temperance and frequent very frequent evacuation, and that they may not be intermitted conviction of their necessity is to be prudently inculcated.

I am not at present so much distressed as you, because I think your present method likely to be efficacious. Dejection may indeed follow; and I should dread it from too copious bleeding for as purges are more under command, and more concurrent with the agency of Nature, they seldom effect any irremediable change. However we must expect after such a disease, that the mind will fluctuate long before it finds its center.

I will not tell you, nor Master, nor Queeney how I long to be among you, but I would be glad to know when we are to meet, and hope our meeting will be cheerful. I am,

Dearest Lady Your most humble servant

Sam: Johnson

Aug. 24. 1780 London.

702a. Brighthelmston. Th. 24 Aug. ⟨'80⟩. From Mrs. Thrale.

R 540.99.—

Dear Sir　　　　　　　　　　Brighthelmston Thursday 24: Aug.

My Master's Spirits are quieter, & he sleeps better, and Pepys did right to racket him so I suppose, for it has mended him apparently, but he lost more than twelve Ounces of Blood, & took such rough Catharticks that he all but fainted from the Violence of their Operation: his Head is prodigiously cooled by these proceedings, and all will be well again.

I have cleared the place of Mr Rushworth too, and am once more tolerably easy, & at leisure to say I am sorry for the bad News, if it be true. We shall have ever so many Wretches breaking our Debt this Winter, and laying their Calamities to this Misfortune. New Taxes too I suppose, for this fine Harvest will encourage them not to spare the Brewers, and nobody left to drink our Beer, so we may contract our Quantity without Thanks to our Prudence. But here is ill humour enough for one Day, Farewell Dear Sir and keep well & good humoured yourself, and then there will be some Comfort still left for your Obliged and Faithful

H: L: T.

702.—7. 'Shelly' HLP, see 703a. The traces support her.

703. F. 25 Aug. '80. Mrs. Thrale (Brighthelmston).

Not traced.—1788, No. 256.

Dear Madam   London, August 25, 1780.

Yesterday I could write but about one thing. I am sorry to find from my dear Queeney's letter to-day, that Mr. Thrale's sleep was too much shortened. He begins however now, she says, to recover it. Sound sleep will be the surest token of returning health. The swelling of his legs has nothing in it dangerous; it is the natural consequence of lax muscles, and when the laxity is known to be artificial, need not give any uneasiness. I told you so formerly. Every thing that I have told you about my dear master has been true. Let him take purgatives, and let him sleep. Bleeding seems to have been necessary now; but it was become necessary only by the omission of purges. Bleeding is only for exigences.

I wish you or Queeney would write to me every post while the danger lasts. I will come if I can do any good, or prevent any evil.

For any other purpose, I suppose, now poor Sam: may be spared; you are regaled with Greek and Latin, and you are *Thralia Castalio semper amata choro*;[1] and you have a daughter equal to yourself. I shall have enough to do with one and the other. Your admirer has more Greek than poetry; he was however worth the conquest, though you had conquered me. Whether you can hold him as fast, there may be *some dram of a scruple*,[2] for he thinks you have full tongue enough, as appears by some of his verses; he will leave you for somebody that will let him take his turn, and then I may come in again: for, I tell you, nobody loves you so well, and therefore never think of changing like the moon, and *being constant only in your inconstancy*.[3]

I have not dined out for some time but with Renny or Sir Joshua; and next week Sir Joshua goes to Devonshire, and

---

703.—1. For the verses by 'Michell, the Boy who won the prize at Cambridge', here quoted, see *Th* 447. I have failed to discover whether his prize-poem was published in any *Carmina Comitialia* or the like.

2. *Twelfth Night* III. iv ('no dram').

3. Cowley, 'Inconstancy' (in 'The Mistress'): 'The *World* 's a *Scene* of *Changes*, and to be | *Constant*, in *Nature* were *Inconstancy*.'

Renny to Richmond, and I am left by myself. I wish I could say *nunquam minus*, *&c.*,[4] but I am not diligent.

I am afraid that I shall not see Lichfield this year, yet it would please me to shew my friends how much better I am grown: but I am not grown, I am afraid, less idle; and of idleness I am now paying the fine by having no leisure.

Does the expedition to Sir John Shelly's go on? The first week of September is now at no great distance; nor the eighteenth day, which concludes another of my wretched years. It is time to have done.

I am, &c.

703a. Brighthelmston. Su. 27 Aug. ⟨'80⟩. From Mrs. Thrale. R 540.100—

Brighthelmston Sunday 27: Aug.

God be praised my dear Sir, all Danger is wholly over, the Pulse is got down from 92—I said 82—to 70, and every thing goes on in the beaten Track. My Master sleeps like those old Heroes who were canonized for sleeping, and even Queeney sets *her* Heart at rest.

You are very kind, offering to come so; but we are going to the Shelleys tomorrow, continue however the direction of Letters to Brighthelmstone. I am at the Top of the World here, that I am, & saucy enough most likely. Stephen Fuller who was I think my greatest Favourite, asked me how I, who kept you Company at home, could bear the Society I was in here: I could only reply they were the best I could get, and of high Rank if that was all. Every body says how well you are, and I shall eternally say how good & kind you are: never compare yourself with perfection, but look as Boswell says at other people's Friends, and think not those Years wretched which have at least been spent on the Improvement of others, though you have perhaps left yourself unimproved.

God grant you my dear Sir many and many Years, and give you Grace to please him; and so far to satisfie yourself as may enable you chearfully to continue your Course. I am most truly Yours

H: L: T.

703.1. M. 28 Aug. '80. Hester Maria Thrale (Brighthelmston). Lansdowne.—Lansdowne, *Johnson and Queeney* 1932, 21.

My dear Charmer,   London, 28 Aug. 1780

I am very much obliged to you for your pretty letters. On Saturday I opened my letter with terrour, but soon found

---

703.—4. Scipio Africanus described himself as 'nunquam minus solum quam quum solus esset': Cato, quoted by Cicero *De Officiis* iii. 1: 'never less solitary than when he was alone' (Burton in the *Anatomy*).

that all is mending. Every thing that I have ever proposed for Mr. Thrale has been found right in the event. We must all combine, as propriety shall permit, to impress him with the true opinion of his danger, for without that he will naturally be negligent of himself, and inattentive to his own sensations. Dr. Laurence is of opinion that the tendency to an apoplexy might always be perceived by one who knew how to distinguish it, and if it was perceived at any distance it might be certainly prevented. But if we cannot teach him to watch his own state of body, we must all watch for him as we can.

It is well for me that a Lady so celebrated as Miss Thrale can find time to write to me. I will recompense your condescension with a maxim. Never treat old friends with neglect however easily you may find new. There is a tenderness which seems the meer growth of time, but which is in ⟨fact⟩ the effect ⟨of⟩ many combinations; those with whom we have shared enjoyments, we remember with pleasure, those with whom we have shared sorrow, we remember with tenderness. You must already have begun to observe that you love a book, or a box, or an instrument that you have had a great part of your life, because it brings a great part of your life back to your view. You can never say that your[1] a very late acquaintance; you can only like, or only admire. As others stand to you, must you stand to others, and must therefore ⟨know⟩ that no new acquaintance much love you, and therefore if you quit old friends for them, you slight those who love you more in favour of those that love you less. This I hope you will remember, and practice, though far the greater part forget it, and therefore have no friend, as none they deserve.

I have been very grave, but you are a very thinking Lady. We shall now meet in a little time, I hope again, and love each other better and better.

Now am I turning to the second leaf just as if I was writing to your Mamma.

Dr. Burney and Fanny and Sophy[2] are gone to be happy

703.1.—1. The sense is clear.
2. Probably (as Dr. Scholes tells me) Sophia Elizabeth, d. of Esther B (CB's d. by his first wife), who in '70 married her cousin Charles Rousseau B. Sophia was their fourth child, so she might be five or six in '80.

with Mr. Crisp, and Mrs. Burney and Susan are left at home, and I am to go see them; indeed I have no other visit to make hardly, except that blind Mrs. Hervey has sent me a peremptory summons to dine with her on Thursday, and I have promised to go lest she should think me intentionally uncivil; and you know, I am the civillest creature in nature.

Seward called on me two days ago, to get help for a poor woman. This is all the news you can have from

Madam, Your most humble servant,

Sam: Johnson

704. W. 30 Aug. '80. Charles Lawrence (Cambridge).

Address (Vol. xv): To the Reverend Charles Lawrence. St. John's College, Cambridge.

G. Wells.—*Europ. Mag.* May 1785, Boswell 1791, ii. 323, 'to a young clargyman' (Hill iii. 436); *Works* xv (1789), 496, 'To the Reverend Charles Lawrence . . . republished from the original.'

Dear Sir

Not many days ago Dr. Lawrence shewed me a Letter in which you make kind mention of me. I hope therefore you will not be displeased that I endeavour to preserve your good will by some observations which your letter suggested to me.

You are afraid of falling into some improprieties in the daily service, by reading to an audience that requires no exactness. Your fear, I hope, secures you from danger, they who contract absurd habits, are such as have no fear. It is impossible to do the same thing very often without some peculiarity of manner, but that manner may be good or bad, and a little care will at least preserve it from being bad; to make it very good there must, I think, be something of natural or casual felicity which cannot be taught.

Your present method of making your sermons seems very judicious. Few frequent Preachers can be supposed to have sermons more their own, than yours will be. Take care to register some where or other the authours from whom your several discourses are borrowed, and do not imagine that you shall always remember even what perhaps you now think it impossible to forget.

My advice however is, that you attempt from time to time an original sermon, and in the labour of composition do not burden your mind with too much at once, do not exact from yourself at one effort of excogitation, propriety of thought and elegance of expression. Invent first and then embellish. The production of something where nothing was before, is an act of greater energy, than the expansion or decoration of the thing produced. Set down diligently your thoughts as they rise in the first words that occur, and when you have matter you will easily give it form. Nor perhaps will this method be always necessary, for by habit your thoughts and diction will flow together. The composition of sermons is not very difficult; the divisions not only help the memory of the hearer but direct the judgment of the writer, they supply sources of invention, and keep every part in its proper place.

What I like least in your letter is your account of the manners of the parish; from which I gather that it has been long neglected by the Parson. The Dean of Carlisle,[1] who was then a little rector in Northamptonshire, told me, that it might be discerned whether or no there was a Clergyman resident in a parish, by the civil or savage manners of the people. Such a congregation as yours stands in much need of reformation, and I would not have you think it impossible to reform them. A very savage parish was civilized by a decayed gentlewoman who came among them to teach a petty school. My learned friend Dr. Wheeler of Oxford, when he was a young man had the care of a neighbouring parish for fifteen pounds a year which he was never paid, but he counted it a convenience that it compelled him to make a sermon weekly. One woman he could not bring to the Communion, and when he reproved or exhorted her, she only answered that she was no scholar. He was advised to set some good woman or man of the parish a little wiser than herself to talk to her in language level to her mind. Such honest, I may call them holy artifices must be practised by every Clergyman, for all means must be tried by which souls may be saved. Talk to your people, however, as much as you can, and you will find that the more frequently you

704.—1. Percy.

converse with them upon religious subjects, the more willingly they will attend, and the more submissively they will learn. A Clergyman's diligence always makes him venerable. I think, I have now only to say that in the momentous work that you have undertaken I pray God to bless you. I am, Sir, Your most humble Servant,

Sam: Johnson.

Bolt court Aug. 30, 1780.

705. Sa. 9 Sept. '80. Viscountess Southwell (Dublin).

Address (Malone): To the Right Honourable Lady Southwell, Dublin.

Sotheby 3 Aug. 1858 (not seen).—Malone's Boswell 1804, iii. 476.

Madam

Among the numerous addresses of condolence which your great loss must have occasioned, be pleased to receive this from one whose name perhaps you have never heard, and to whom your Ladyship is known only by the reputation of your virtue, and to whom your Lord was known only by his kindness and beneficence.

Your Ladyship is now again summoned to exert that piety of which you once gave, in a state of pain and danger, so illustrious an example;[1] and your Lord's beneficence may be still continued by those, who with his fortune inherit his virtues.

I hope to be forgiven the liberty which I shall take of informing your Ladyship, that Mr. Mauritius Lowe, a son of your late Lord's father, had, by recommendation[2] to your Lord, a quarterly allowance of ten pounds, the last of which, due July 26, he has not received: he was in hourly hope of his remittance, and flattered himself that on October 26 he should have received the whole half-year's bounty, when he was struck with the dreadful news of his benefactor's death.

May I presume to hope, that his want, his relation, and his merit, which excited his Lordship's charity, will continue to

---

705.—1. Malone notes that this was 'an extremely painful surgical operation', which she endured without 'allowing herself to be tied to her chair'.

2. 'my recommendation' Hill: a reading for which I find no authority.

have the same effect upon those whom he has left behind;
and that, though he has lost one friend, he may not yet be
destitute. Your Ladyship's charity cannot easily be exerted
where it is wanted more; and to a mind like your's, distress
is a sufficient recommendation.

I hope to be allowed the honour of being,

> Madam, Your Ladyship's most humble Servant,
>
> Sam: Johnson.

Bolt-court, Fleet-street, London, Sept. 9. 1780.

706. W. 13 Sept. '80. William Strahan.

Address: To William Strahan, Esq.
Sotheby 19 April 1918 (not seen).—Hill 1892.

Sir,

Having lost our Election[1] at Southwark we are looking for
a Borough less uncertain. If you can find by enquiry any seat
to be had, as seats are had without natural interest, you will
by giving immediate notice do a great favour to Mr. Thrale.
The messenger shall call to-morrow for your answer. There
are, I suppose, men who transact these affairs, but we do not
know them. Be so kind as to give us what information you
can.

> I am, Sir, Your humble servant,
>
> Sam: Johnson.

Sept. 13, 1780.

706.1. ⟨? Sept. '80.⟩ Lord North.

Rosenbach (1927); endorsed by HLT: 'By D[r] Johnson a Copy of a
Letter to be written To Lord North *a very short* Time before M[r]
Thrale's death'.

My Lord

I have lost the election at Southwark, but am still desirous
of a seat in parliament. Your Lordship knows my opinions
and my practice, and therefore I hope I may without any

706.—1. HT's fate was already certain. When the poll closed on 15 Sept. the figures
were: Hotham 1,177, Polhill 1,025, Thrale 769.

706.1.—I print this document, because I believe it unpublished, though it can hardly
be called a letter of J's. I have not included e.g. the address to the electors, also
written for HT and published *L* iii. 440.

impropriety desire a recommendation to some Borough where I may be chosen, through the influence of Government, at my own expence. I do not mean to stand a contest, but to receive a nomination, such as Mr Elliot who has been long my friend, could give me.

Your Lordship by appointing a time at which you can see me, will very much oblige, my Lord,

707. Sa. 23 Sept. '80. Samuel Hardy.

Address (Hill): To the Reverend Samuel Hardy.
Not traced.—Hill 1892.

Sir,

I should be very sorry to be thought capable of treating with neglect or disrespect such a Man as You, or such an attempt as yours. I certainly wrote my opinion[1] such as it was, long ago. I did not value it enough to keep a copy, and therefore must now tell it again, when the remembrance of your arguments is weakened by time.

You will be pleased, Sir, to recollect that I professed myself unskilful in Biblical criticism; my profession was very sincere, and I am far from desiring to obtrude my notions as decisive.

I admitted without difficulty your *prophesy by action*, all types are prophesies of that kind. But I know not whether the admissions[2] of such prophesies will support your interpretation as there seems to be no action done.

Whether your explication or that which is generally received be considered as true, the use and importance of the Sacrament is the same, and therefore I cannot think the question such as in the present disposition of the world can properly or usefully be moved. Why should you run the hazard of being wrong, when Religion gains nothing by your being right?

707.—Hill quotes Hardy as maintaining, in *The Scripture-Account of . . . the Holy Eucharist*, 1784, 'that the sixth chapter of St. John is to be *primarily* interpreted of the *Eucharist*'; the miracle of the loaves and fishes being 'a *Prophecy by Action*'.

1. J had perhaps given an opinion to a bookseller, who might communicate it to the author.

2. Perhaps 'admission'.

Your arguments from the Old Testament do not appear to me to have any force, or to be applied with any probability to your present purpose. You will gain more upon the reader by omitting them, and trusting only to the passage in itself and to general reasoning. And if you publish your thoughts I think it best to give them the appearance rather of enquiry and conjecture than of assertion and dogmatism.

Once more, Sir, I do not pretend to decide the question which was new to me, and of which I have not perhaps the previous knowledge necessary to the examination. Enquire of men more learned in the Scriptures. You have from me the respect due to all diligent searchers after sacred Truth, and my wishes that you may be long able to continue your studies, to your own improvement, and instruction of others.

I am, Sir, Your most humble Servant,
Sam: Johnson.

Bolt Court, Fleet Street, Sept. 23, 1780.

707.1. M. 16 Oct. '80. Mrs. Thrale.

Address: To Mrs. Thrale.
University of California.—Dixon Wecter in *Mod. Lang. Notes* Nov. 1941, 528.

Dear Madam   Oct. 16, 1780

Gell and Smith[1] never came. The Steyning[2] affair was undertaken by one Mr. Jones, a Shoemaker, an old inhabitant of the King's Bench, of whom Mr Robson had that morning given me the character.

Pray let me know when it is that we *must* go. I will keep the day, but if it could be Saturday I should be glad, but the difference after all will be little more than that of burthening the luggage cart[3] with more books or with fewer, yet I wish it could be Saturday, but make no effort about it, only let me know as soon as ever you can.

707.1.—1. Mr. Wecter conjectures that Gell may be Philip G of Derbyshire, Smith Henry S, HT's cousin. He makes no guess at the activities of Mr. Jones.
2. J's diary records a visit, 10 Nov. '82, to Steyning in Sussex. But the name in the text may be a surname.
3. To take heavy baggage to B'n. The life of Pope was still to write.

I have seen Captain Burney and his cargo. You may remember, I thought Banks had not gained much by circumnavigating the world.

I am, Madam, your most &c.

Sam: Johnson

708. Tu. 17 Oct. '80. James Boswell (Edinburgh).

Not traced.—Boswell 1791, ii. 328 (Hill iii. 441).

Dear Sir

I am sorry to write you a letter that will not please you, and yet it is at last what I resolve to do. This year must pass without an interview;[1] the summer has been foolishly lost, like many other of my summers and winters. I hardly saw a green field, but staid in town to work, without working much.

Mr. Thrale's loss of health has lost him the election; he is now going to Brighthelmston, and expects me to go with him, and how long I shall stay I cannot tell. I do not much like the place, but yet I shall go, and stay while my stay is desired. We must, therefore, content ourselves with knowing what we know as well as man can know the mind of man, that we love one another, and that we wish each other's happiness, and that the lapse of a year cannot lessen our mutual kindness.

I was pleased to be told that I accused Mrs. Boswell unjustly, in supposing that she bears me ill-will. I love you so much, that I would be glad to love all that love you, and that you love; and I have love very ready for Mrs. Boswell, if she thinks it worthy of acceptance. I hope all the young ladies and gentlemen are well.

I take a great liking to your brother. He tells me that his father received him kindly, but not fondly; however, you seem to have lived well enough at Auchinleck, while you staid. Make your father as happy as you can.

You lately told me of your health: I can tell you in return, that my health has been for more than a year past, better

708.—1. JB had written four letters, in Aug., Sept., and Oct., from three of which he prints extracts. He had suggested a meeting at Carlisle, especially eligible if Percy should be in residence, or at York, in the neighbourhood of which city he proposed to visit his 'Yorkshire Chief' Bosville (*L* iii. 438, *BP* xiv. 128).

than it has been for many years before. Perhaps it may please God to give us some time together before we are parted.

I am, dear Sir, Yours, most affectionately,
Oct. 17, 1780.   Sam. Johnson.

709. Brighthelmston. Th. 26 Oct. '80. John Nichols.

Address: To Mr Nicol
B.M. (Brighthelmston added to date in another hand).—

Sir

I think you never need send back the revises unless something important occurs. Little things, if I omit them, you will do me the favour of setting right yourself. Our post is awkward as you will find, and I fancy you will find it best to send two sheets at once.

I am, Sir, Your most humble servant
Oct. 26. 1780   Sam: Johnson

710. Sa. 9 Dec. '80. Mary Prowse (Frome).

Rosenbach (1925).—*NQ* 45. v. 441.

Madam

I return you very sincere and respectful thanks for all your favours. You have, I see, sent guineas when I expected only pounds.

It was beside my intention that you should make so much enquiry after Johnson.[1] What can be known of him must start up by accident. He was not a Native of your town or country, but an adventurer who came from a distant part in quest of a livelihood, and did not stay a year. He came in 36. and went away in 37. He was likely enough to attract notice while he staid, as a lively noisy man, that loved company. His memory might probably continue for some time in some favourite alehouse. But after so many years perhaps there is no man left that remembers him. He was my near relation. The unfortunate woman for whom your excellent Mother

709.—If revises were sent to B'n by post J would now have to pay for them, unless Nichols could get them franked by Strahan or another.

710.—See on 693.
    1. See Index II, Nathaniel Johnson.

has so kindly made provision is, in her way, well. I am now sending her some cloaths. Of her cure there is no hope.

Be pleased, Madam, to accept the good wishes and grateful regard of,

Madam, Your most obedient and most humble Servant,
Decr 9. 1780   Sam: Johnson.

711. Sa. 30 Dec. '80. William Vyse (Lambeth).

Address (Malone): To the Reverend Dr. Vyse, at Lambeth.
Not traced.—Malone's Boswell 1807, iii. 480.

Sir

I hope you will forgive the liberty I take, in soliciting your interposition with his Grace the Archbishop: my first petition[1] was successful, and I therefore venture on a second.

The matron of the Chartreux is about to resign her place, and Mrs. Desmoulins, a daughter of the late Dr. Swinfen, who was well known to your father, is desirous of succeeding her. She has been accustomed by keeping a boarding school to the care of children, and I think is very likely to discharge her duty. She is in great distress, and therefore may properly receive the benefit of a charitable foundation. If you wish to see her, she will be willing to given an account of herself.

If you shall be pleased, Sir, to mention her favourably to his Grace, you will do a great act of kindness, to,

Sir, Your most obliged And most humble Servant,
December 30, 1780.   Sam: Johnson.

711.1. ⟨1780.⟩ Charles Allen (Rochester).

Not traced.—Shaw's *Memoirs* of Johnson 1785, 156.

Sir

Mr. William Shaw, the gentleman from whom you will receive this, is a studious and literary man; he is a stranger, and will be glad to be introduced into proper company; and he is my friend, and any civility you shall shew him, will be an obligation on, Sir, your most obedient Servant

Sam. Johnson

711.—1. For De Groot, see 531.

711.2. ⟨Late '80 or early '81.⟩ John Nichols.

Address: To Mr Nicol.

B.M.—Boswell 1791, ii. 361 (Hill iv. 58, overlooked in *Letters*).

Sir

This life of Dr Young was written by a friend[1] of his son. What is erased[2] with black is expunged by the author, what is erased with red is expunged by me, if you find any thing more that can be well omitted I shall not be sorry to see it yet shorter.[3]

711.3. ⟨?'80.⟩ George Fletcher.

Not traced; described in Shaw's *Staffordshire* i. 323.

'The rev. George Fletcher, rector of Cubley in Derbyshire, informed me, that the Doctor had formerly applied to him for extracts relative to his father and his family, who are registered as the natives of that village.'

712. M. 29 Jan. '81. Warren Hastings (India).

B.M.—*GM* June 1785, misdated 9 Jan.; Boswell 1791, ii. 370, with the same date (Hill iv. 70). See Addenda, p. 531.

Sir

Amidst the importance and multiplicity of affairs in which your great Office engages you I take the liberty of recalling your attention for a moment to literature, and will not prolong the interruption by an apology which your character makes needless.

Mr. Hoole, a Gentleman long known and long esteemed in the India house, after having translated Tasso, has undertaken Ariosto. How well he is qualified for his undertaking he has already shown. He is desirous Sir, of your favour in promoting his proposals, and flatters me by supposing that my testimony may advance his interest.

It is a new thing for a Clerk of the India house to translate

711.2.—1. Herbert Croft.

2. 'crossed' (*bis*) 1791.

3. One may surmise that Nichols left it alone; the *Life* is just half the length of Swift's, and much longer than Thomson's.

711.3.—I owe this to Mr. Reade (*Reades* 125 and R iii. 5), who places it 'c. 1780', the year in which J addressed similar inquiries to Miss Prowse (693).

712.—For Hastings's reply to J's former letters, see on 367. I have found no reply to 712. *Ariosto* was dedicated not to Hastings (as Hoole no doubt hoped) but 'To Harry Verelst Esq.'.

Poets. It is new for a Governour of Bengal to patronise Learning. That he may find his ingenuity rewarded, and that Learning may flourish under your protection is the wish of, Sir,

Your most humble servant,

Jan. 29. 1781   Sam: Johnson

712.1. Th. 1 Mar. '81. Lord Lucan.

Not traced.—*Morning Herald* 8 June 1792, communicated by 'A.B.'.
Address (*Morning Herald*): To the Right Honourable Lord Lucan.

My Lord,
Seldom has the cloudy atmosphere of my existence been more agreeably brightened, than by the notification which your Lordship has been pleased to make to me of the approaching nuptials of your daughter. Gerard Hamilton, indeed, I now find, meant to give me some dark intelligence of it; but Gerard, who like Pope, is *un politique aux choux et aux raves,*[1] and thought it necessary on an occasion of such moment, to be more than usually oracular, wrapt up his meaning in such a mystery of phrase, that it remained in total obscurity, and like most of the Delphick predictions, is discovered only by retrospection from the known event.

Of Hibernian heraldry, I have no exact knowledge; and he who does not know, should be cautious how he speaks. Yet I think my friends Madan and Leland, and I believe too Lord Charlemont, have told me, that though the Bards of Ierne did not sing the pedigree of Bingham, as one of the greatest in that land of Kings, they sung it as sufficiently ancient, to entitle its head to

712.1.—I have not identified 'A. B.', and the late Lord Lucan could not help me. His ancestor's youngest daughter was Anne Bingham. But 'A. B.' is in all probability, as often, a conventional anonym. His or her covering letter is as follows:

Mr. Editor,
It is said that we are obliged to a Lady of quality, for a copy of Dr Johnson's admirable letter to Lord Thurlow; and I am one of those who think that all who are possessed of the Letters of our great moralist, should liberally communicate them to the public. As Mr Boswell has given us a rich store of his illustrious friend's epistolary correspondence, I send you the following letter to Lord Lucan, on occasion of the marriage of his Lordship's daughter, and shall be happy to see it in the modern Xenophon's next edition. I am, Sir, Your most humble Servant A. B.

The letter is in some respects strikingly unlike J's manner. If it were a forgery, or an improvement on a genuine original, we must credit the writer with intimate knowledge of the persons named.

1. That is, one who makes a mystery of the simplest domestic affairs. Prof. Donald F. Bond of the University of Chicago writes: 'I have always quoted this as Lady Bolingbroke on Pope. But I cannot trace it very definitely. I thought surely that Audra would have it, in his *L'Influence française dans l'œuvre de Pope.* He says (p. 110): "Lady Bolingbroke qui, raillant son amour de la mystification et des stratagèmes puérils, l'a si joliment défini, paraît-il, 'un politique aux choux et aux raves...'"' and refers in a footnote simply to Elwin-Courthope, III, 4; and Elwin there gives no reference whatever.' See *L* iii. 324 for J's use of the phrase.

rank high among the *Generosi*, and to be fit to be enrolled among the *Nobiles*. That honour he has now had by the favor of a King;[2] who, if his Majesty does not always meet with gratitude, has done more to deserve it, than almost any Monarch of any race of our Princes. Let the *Progenies Binghamia*, however, be still higher than I perhaps, from erroneous information, or imperfect reminiscence, have been led to rate it; the lustre cannot be so great, but that an additional ray from the splendour of *Spencer*, will yet be visible in the blazon.

At the *Club*, it is not our custom to drink toasts. We have but one, of which *Roma Eterna* might long ago have taught us the vanity—*Esto Perpetua*.[3] But this event, I suppose, will produce an extraordinary one—'*To the felicity of Lord and Lady Althorpe*'. Boswell no doubt, as '*confirmation strong*', of his honest zeal will pour a large libation of wine; and though I should in the words of a Poet,[4] very familiar to the noble Bridegroom, exclaim '*Ἄριστον μὲν ὕδωρ*'—and make the pure element my beverage, I trust that no congratulations will be more sincere than those of

My Lord, Your Lordships most obedient, And most humble Servant,
Bolt-Court, Fleet-street, March 1, 1781.   Sam. Johnson

713. M. 5 Mar. '81. William Strahan.

Address: To William Strahan Esq
Adam.—Hill 1892.

Sir

Having now done my lives I shall have money to receive, and shall be glad to add to it, what remains due for the Hebrides, which you cannot charge ⟨me⟩ with grasping very rapaciously. The price was two hundred Guineas or pounds;[1] I think first pounds then Guineas. I have had one hundred. There is likewise something due for the political pamphlets,

712.1.—2. Lord Lucan did not think his ancestor had received any later 'favor' from the Crown than his barony of '76; the earldom dates from '95.

3. *Esto perpetua* was and is the only Club toast (Hawkins, *Life* 1787, 424). The phrase is said to have been first used, of Venice, by Paolo Sarpi, J's old friend Father Paul.

4. Pindar, *Olymp.* i. 1. The famous tag, 'Water is Best', is inscribed on the façade of the Pump Room at Bath. The writer has accented ἄριστον wrongly.

713.—1. See on 622. Hill assumed the reference to be to the *Lives*, for which the agreed payment was 200 guineas, *L* iii. 111. But the context suggests rather that the reference is to the *Journey*. The Newton copy of the *Journey* (436 in the sale, Parke-Bernet 15 May 1941) included an autograph receipt: 'March 16 1776 I received of Mr Rivington by the hand of Mr Strahan one hundred pounds Sam: Johnson £100. 0. 0.' So far so good. But if I am right, Strahan was strangely dilatory; for on 22 Jan. '84 J signed a receipt for £150 'in full for the copyright of my Journey to the Hebrides' (facsimile in R. A. Austen-Leigh, *The Story of a Printing House* 1912). The imminence of the '85 reprint may have been a cause of the extra payment.

which I left without bargain to your liberality and Mr Cadel's.
Of this you will likewise think that I may have all together.
I am, Sir,

Your humble servant

March 5. 1781   Sam: Johnson

714. M. 5 Mar. '81.   ⟨Thomas Cadell.⟩

Adam.—Known to Hill only from an auction catalogue.

Sir

In making up my account for the lives, I desire that you
will satisfy Mr Dilly for a set of Poets and lives which he sent
on my account to Mrs Boswel, and a set of lives sent by him
to Lord Hailes.

I am glad that the work is at last done.

I am, Sir, Your humble servant

March. 5. 1781   Sam: Johnson

714.1. Th. 8 Mar. '81.   Margaret Owen (Penrhos).

Address: Miss Owen at Penrhos near Shrewsbury.
National Library of Wales.—*Western Mail* 1 Aug. 1938.

Madam

Though I have omitted to answer your letter I have not
forgotten it, nor betrayed it. I have kept your secret, and
pitied your situation. If I could send you any ⟨thing⟩ more
useful than pity, I should be in more haste to write. I can
only repeat the advice which I formerly gave You, to act as
well as You can, and to suffer those evils which you cannot
help to take as little hold as is possible of your thoughts. You
will tell me that you cannot look on the disgrace of your
family, and the waste of an ancient estate without great
distress of mind. And what you say must be allowed to have
great weight; but every passion is stronger or weaker as it is
more or less indulged and what I recommend to You is not
insens⟨ib⟩ility, but a constant endeavour to divert your
thoughts by reading, work, and conversation, and when You
are alone to compose them by trust in God.

Write to me with full confidence whenever You are

714.1.—For Miss Owen's troubles with a mad and drunken brother, see *Tb* 818.

inclined, You shall have a more speedy answer. I sincerely wish you well, and should think it great happiness to contribute in any manner to your ease, and tranquillity.

If you find that your presence does any good endeavour to continue it, but if not, take care of yourself, and retire from the sight of evil which you cannot hinder, and which wears out your life in misery.

All is not happiness in other places. Mr Thrale's apoplexy has much weakened him, and though in my opinion, he may live many years, he will, I fear, always be weak and put into danger by slight irregularities. I am, for my part, better than when You knew me, and I am with great sincerity Madam, your affectionate and most humble servant,
Boltcourt Fleetstreet, March 8. 1781   Sam: Johnson.

714.2. Th. 8 March '81. Lucy Porter (Lichfield).

Address: To Mrs Lucy Porter in Lichfield.
Maggs 1947 (copy by them).—

Dear Madam,

It is indeed a long time since I wrote to you, I have been taken up more than I needed with some little employment, and have neglected you and my other friends. But I did not quite forget you. I hope as the spring advances your health will improve, and that before oisters go out of season you will be able to eat other meat. I hope you receive the weekly barrel[1] which I have ordered since I knew that your stomack was so much disordered. If I can send any thing else that will do you good, I shall be very willing. Take care of yourself.

I missed last year my annual visit to my own country, and I hardly went any whither else. I hope this year to make myself amends. My health has lately fluctuated a little, but I am still better than when you saw me last. Poor Mr. Thrale has had many strokes of an apoplexy, and is very feeble, but I think in no immediate danger. Mrs. Thrale and Miss are well. Pray for me, and may God bless you.

Make my compliments to all my friends. Tell Miss Adey

714.2.—1. Of oysters, see 605.

that I will write to her; and give my sincere respects to
Mr. Pearson.

        I am, dear Love, Your most humble servant,
London, March 8, 1781.   Sam: Johnson.

715. W. 14 Mar. '81. James Boswell (Edinburgh).

Not traced.—Boswell 1791, ii. 370 (Hill iv. 71).

Dear Sir

    I hoped you had got rid of all this hypocrisy of misery.[1]
What have you to do with Liberty and Necessity? Or what
more than to hold your tongue about it? Do not doubt but
I shall be most heartily glad to see you here again, for I love
every part about you but your affectation of distress.

    I have at last finished my Lives, and have laid up for you a
load of copy,[2] all out of order, so that it will amuse you a long
time to set it right. Come to me, my dear Bozzy, and let
us be as happy as we can. We will go again to the Mitre, and
talk old times over.

        I am, dear Sir, Yours, affectionately,
March 14, 1781.   Sam. Johnson.

716. W. 4 Apr. '81. Joshua Reynolds.

Yale.—Boswell 1791, ii. 379 (Hill iv. 84).

    Mr. Johnson knows that Sir Joshua Reynolds and the other
Gentlemen will excuse his incompliance with the Call, when
they are told that Mr. Thrale died this morning.
Wednesday.

715.—1. JB had written in Feb. 'complaining of having been troubled by a recur-
rence of the perplexing question of Liberty and Necessity'. His journal shows that he
had been reading Monboddo and Kames, and 'sunk into dreadful Melancholy, so
that I went out to the wood and groaned'. Volusenus *de animi tranquillitate* and
Montesquieu comforted him somewhat; 'but still the Arguments for Necessity were
heavy upon me. I saw a dreary nature of things.' His spirits rose at the prospect of
his Jaunt, and on 10 Mar. 'I was active and animated and full of hope. How very
different from the dreary metaphysical Wretch that I had been!' *BP* xiv. 156, 164.

    2. See *L* iv. 36, 480. Only two Lives, Pope and Rowe, seem to have survived.

716.—For Thrale's death and J's sense of his loss, see the many quotations and
references in *L* iv. 84.

717. Th. 5 Apr. '81. Mrs. Thrale (Brighthelmston).

Address: To Mrs Thrale at Brighthelmston Sussex. *Postmark*: 5 AP.
Newton.—1788, No. 257.

Dearest Madam

Of your injunctions to pray for You and write to You I
hope to leave neither unobserved, and I hope to find You
willing in a short time to alleviate your trouble by some other
exercise of the mind. I am not without my part of the
calamity. No death since that of my Wife has ever oppressed
me like this. But let us remember that we are in the hands
of him who knows when to give, and when to take away, who
will look upon us with mercy through all our variations of
existence, and who invites ⟨us⟩ to call on him in the day of
trouble.[1] Call upon him in this great revolution of life, and
call with confidence. You will then find comfort for the past,
and support for the future. He that has given You happiness
in marriage to a degree of which without personal knowledge,
I should have thought the description fabulous, can give
You another mode of happiness as a Mother, and at last the
happiness of losing all temporal cares in the thoughts of an
eternity in heaven.

I do not exhort You to reason yourself into tranquillity, we
must first pray, and then labour,[2] first implore the Blessing
of God and ⟨then employ⟩[3] those means which he puts into
our hands. Cultivated ground has few weeds, a mind occu-
pied by lawful business, has little room for useless regret.

We read the will to day, but I will not fill my first letter
with any other account than that with all my zeal for your
advantage I am satisfied, and that the other executors, more
used to consider property than I, commended it for wisdom
and equity. Yet why should I not tell You that You have

717.—'Mrs. Thrale's usual reaction to death was to run away. This time, not waiting
for the funeral, she hurried with Queeney immediately to Streatham and from there
to Brighton.' C 199. It should be remembered that women were not expected to
attend funerals. Cassandra Austen in 1817 did not go to her sister's. Sir Frank
MacKinnon referred me to passages in Woodforde's diary which on the whole suggest
that relatives, and especially women, did not attend: i. 109, 295; ii. 8, 86, 213; iii.
54, 233; iv. 25.

1. Psalm l. 15.

2. J may have had in mind some variation on the theme *laborare est orare*, for
which see King's *Class. Quotations*.

3. These words were added in 1788. The lacuna was due to J's inadvertence.

five hundred pounds for your immediate expences, and two thousand pounds a year with both the houses and all the goods?[4]

Let us pray for one another, that the time whether long or short that shall yet be granted us, may be well spent, and that when this life which at the longest is very short, shall come to an end, a better may begin which shall never end.

I am, Dearest Madam, Your most humble Servant
London Apr. 5. 1781   Sam: Johnson

718. Sa. 7 Apr. '81. Mrs. Thrale (Brighthelmston).
A. Houghton.—1788, No. 258.

Dear Madam

I hope You begin to find your mind grow clearer. My part of the loss hangs upon me. I have lost a friend of boundless kindness at an age when it is very unlikely that I should find another.[1]

If You think change of place likely to relieve you, there is no reason why You should not go to Bath, the distances are unequal, but with regard to practice and business they are the same. It is a day's journey from either place, and the Post[2] is more expeditious and certain to Bath. Consult only your own inclination, for there is really no other principle of choice. God direct and bless You.

Mr Cator[3] has offered Mr Perkins money, but it was not wanted. I hope we shall all do all we can to make you less unhappy, and You must do all you can for yourself. What we or what You can do will for a time be but little, yet certainly that calamity which may ⟨be⟩ considered as doomed to fall inevitably on half mankind, is not finally without alleviation.

It is something for me that as I have not the decrepitude

717.—4. For HT's will see C 200.

718.—1. Nearly half a line is here so heavily erased that I could read nothing.

2. Hill notes that the post went to Bath daily, Sundays excepted, to B'n, at this time of year, four days a week only. There are many complaints of the slowness and irregularity of the B'n post.

3. Cator, who was one of HT's executors, no doubt offered to advance money for the conduct of the business. HLP wrongly supplies 'Crutchley' for the 'C—' of 1788.

I have not the callousness of old age. I hope in time to be less afflicted.

I am Madam, Your most humble Servant,

April. 7. 1781   Sam: Johnson.

719. M. 9 Apr. '81. Mrs. Thrale (Brighthelmston).
A. Houghton.—1788, No. 259.

Dearest Madam

That You are gradually recovering your tranquillity is the effect to be humbly expected from trust in God. Do not represent life as darker than it is. Your loss has been very great, but You retain more than almost any other can hope to possess. You are high in the opinion of mankind; You have children from whom much pleasure may be expected, and that you will find many friends You have no reason to doubt. Of my friendship, be it worth more or less, I hope You think yourself certain, without much art or care. It will not be easy for me to repay the benefits that I have received, but I hope to be always ready at your call. Our sorrow has different effects, you are withdrawn into solitude, and I am driven into company.[1] I am afraid of thinking what I have lost. I never had such a friend before. Let me have your prayers and those of my dear Queeny.

The prudence and resolution of your design to return so soon to your business and your duty deserves great praise, I shall communicate it on Wednesday to the other Executors. Be pleased to let me know whether you would have me come to Streatham to receive ⟨you⟩, or stay here till the next day.

I am Madam, Your most humble servant,

London Apr. 9. 1781   Sam: Johnson.

720. Tu. 10 Apr. '81. William Vyse.
Address (Malone, now lost?): To the Rev. Dr. Vyse at Lambeth.
Adam.—Malone's Boswell 1811, iii. 480.

Revd Sir

The Bearer[1] is one of my old Friends, a man of great

719.—1. JB was in L'n, and they met at dinner on 6 and 7 Apr. *L* iv. 87–8.

720.—1. Macbean; J 'by the favour of Lord Thurlow, got him admitted a poor brother of the Charterhouse'. *L* i. 187.

Learning, whom the Chancellor has been pleased to nomin-
ate to the Chartreux. He attends his Grace the Archbishop[2]
to take the oath required, and being a modest scholar, will
escape embarrassment if you are so kind as to introduce him;
by which you will do a kindness to a Man of great merit, and
add another to those favours which have been already conferred by you on

Sir, Your most humble servant,

Bolt court, Fleet street, Apr. 10. 1781   Sam: Johnson

721. W. 11 Apr. '81. Mrs Thrale (Brighthelmston).

Adam.—1788, No. 260.

Dear Madam

I am glad to hear from my dear Miss, that you have
recovered tranquillity enough to think on bathing but there
is no disposition in the world to leave you long to yourself.
Mr Perkins pretends that your absence produces a thousand
difficulties which I believe it does not produce. He frights
Mr Crichley. Mr Cator is of my mind that there is no need
of hurry. Perkins has disclosed to Mr Crichley his appetite
for partnership, which he has resolved not to gratify. I
would not have this importunity give you any alarm or
disturbance, but to pacify it come as soon as you can prevail
upon your mind to mingle with business. I think business
the best remedy for grief as soon as it can be admitted.

We met today and were told of mountainous difficulties,
till I was provoked to tell them, that if there were really so
much to do and suffer, there would be no Executors in the
world. Do not suffer yourself to be terrified.

I comfort you, and hope God will bless and support you, but
I feel myself like a man begining a new course of life. I had
interwoven myself with my dear Friend. But our great care
ought to be that we may be fit and ready when in a short
time we shall be called to follow him.

There is however no use in communicating to you my
heaviness of Heart. I thank dear Miss for her letter.

I am Madam Your most humble servant

London Apr. 11. 1781   Sam: Johnson

720.—2. Cornwallis.

722. Th. 12 Apr. '81. Mrs. Thrale (Brighthelmston).
Clifton College.—1788, No. 261.

Dearest Madam

You will not suppose that much has happened since last
night, nor indeed is this a time for talking much of loss and
gain. The business of Christians[1] is now for a few days in
their own bosoms. God grant us to do it properly. I hope
you gain ground on your affliction. I hope to overcome mine.
You and Miss must comfort one another. May you long live
happily together. I have nobody whom I expect to share my
uneasiness, nor, if I could communicate it, would it be less.
I give it little vent, and amuse it as I can. Let us pray for
one another. And when we meet, we may ⟨try⟩ what fidelity
and tenderness will do for us.

There is no wisdom in useless and hopeless sorrow,[2] but
there is something in it so like virtue, that he who is wholly
without it cannot be loved, nor will by me at least be
thought worthy of esteem. My next letter will be to
Queeney.

　　　　I am, Madam, Your most humble servant
London Apr. 12. 1781　　　　　　　　Sam: Johnson.

723. Th. 12 Apr. '81. Lucy Porter (Lichfield).
Address: To Mrs Lucy Porter in Litchfield. *Postmark*: 12 AP.
Fettercairn.—Boswell 1791, ii. 382 (Hill iv. 89).

Dear Madam

Life is full of troubles, I have just lost my dear friend
Thrale. I hope he is happy; but I have had a great loss. I
am otherwise pretty well, I require some care of[1] myself, but
that care is not ineffectual, and when I am out of order I
think it often my own fault.

The Spring is now making quick advances; as it is the
season in which the whole world is enlivened and invigorated,
I hope that both You and I shall partake of its benefits. My

722.—1. The following Sunday was Easter. See *L* iv. 88 for J's 'ingenious defence
of his dining twice abroad in Passion-week'; on both 11 and 12 Apr. he dined with a
bishop.
　2. 'Johnson never grieved much for anything. His trade was wisdom.' Baretti.

723.—1. 'care' 1791, 'care of' 1793. The correction may suggest that JB went back
to the original.

desire is to see Lichfield, but being left Executor to my Friend, I know not whether I can be spared but I will try, for it is now long since we saw one another, and how little we can promise ourselves many more interviews, we are taught by hourly[2] examples of mortality. Let us try to live so as that mortality may not be an evil. Write to me soon, my Dearest; your letters will give me great pleasure.

I am sorry that Mr Porter has not had his Box but by sending it to Mr Mathias, who very readily undertook its conveyance, I did the best, I could, and perhaps before now he has it.

Be so kind as to make my compliments to my Friends, I have a great value for their kindness, and hope to enjoy it before the summer is past. Do write to me. I am, dearest Love,

Your most humble Servant

London Apr. 12. 1781   Sam. Johnson.

724. Sa. 14 Apr. '81. Mrs. Thrale (Brighthelmston).

Address: To Mrs. Thrale at Brighthelmston Sussex. *Postmark*: 14 AP. Adam.—1788, No. 262.

Dear Madam

My intention was to have written this day to my dear Queeney, but I have just heard from you, and therefore this letter shall be yours. I am glad that you find the behaviour of your acquaintance such as you can commend. The world is not so unjust or unkind as it is peevishly represented, those who deserve well seldom fail to receive from others such services as they can perform, but few have much in their power, or are so stationed as to have great leisure from their own affairs, and kindness must be commonly the exuberance of content. The wretched have no compassion, they can do good only from strong principles of duty.

I purpose to receive you at Streatham, but wonder that you come so soon.

I sent immediately to Mr Perkins to send you twenty pounds and intended to secure you from disappointment by

723.—2. J perhaps had in mind Horace, *Odes* IV. vii: 'Immortalia ne speres, monet annus et almum | quae rapit *hora* diem.' This would explain 'hourly', which seems otherwise a surprising hyperbole.

inclosing a note in this, but yours written on Wednesday 11th came not till saturday the fourteenth, and mine written tonight will not come before you leave Brighthelmston, unless you have put Monday next for Monday sevennight, which I suspect as you mention no alteration of your mind. I am,

Madam, Your most humble servant
Sam: Johnson

725. M. 16 Apr. '81. Mrs. Thrale.
Copy by C. B. Tinker.—1788, No. 263.

Dear Madam

As I was preparing this day to go to Streatham according to the direction in your letter of the 11th which I could not know, though I suspected it, to be erroneous, I received two letters of which the first effect was that it saved me a fruitless Journey. Of these letters that which I perceive to have been written first has no date of time or place, the second was written on the 14th, but they came together.

I forebore, because I would not disturb you, to tell you that last week Mr ——[1] came to talk about partnership, and was very copious. I dismissed him with nothing harsher than, *that I was not convinced*.

You will have much talk to hear. Mr C——[2] speaks with great exuberance, but what he says, when at last he says it, is commonly right. Mr Robson made an oration flaming with the terrifick, which I discovered to have no meaning at all; for the result was that if ⟨we⟩ stopped payment we should lose credit.

I have already so far anticipated Mr Scrase's advice, as to propose to the Executors advantages — which Mr. —— thinks too liberal. 'Mr Perkins says that the trade will produce in profit 12000£ a year; for the first four thousand

725.—Prof. Tinker noted that the paper is torn between the postscript and the subscription. I do not think this affects the text. For the activities of J and HLT in managing the brewery, for Perkins's aspirations to partnership, for the negotiations leading to the sale, and for the sale itself, see C 200, *Tb* 491, Hayward 1861[2], ii. 47, FB's *Diary* ii. 34, *L* iv. 86.

    1. 'Perkins' HLP, Lysons.
    2. 'Cator' HLP, Lysons. FB gives a copious illustration of Cator's illiterate and garrulous talk (*Diary* ii. 47-8).

725]   MRS. THRALE *M. 16 Apr.* '81

which will come of itself, P. shall have 200£; for the second
four thousand P. shall ⟨have⟩ 400£, and for the third four
thousand which will give yet a higher proof of good management, P. shall have 600£. If the trade gains much, P. shall
gain much even to 1200£ a year.' This connects his interest
with ours. It has however not —— mentioned to him, and
such profit, I suppose, will make him afraid to leave us.[3]

I have written to Mr Robson to send the will. There were
two copies, but I know not who has them.

You are to receive five hundred pounds immediately. Mr
Scrase shall certainly see the will, if you and I go to Brighthelmston on purpose, which if we have any difficulty, may
be our best expedient.

I am encouraged, dearest Lady, by your Spirit. The season
for *Agnes*[4] is now over. You are in your civil character a man.
You may sue and be sued. If you apply to business perhaps
half the mind which you have exercised upon knowledge and
elegance, you will need little help, what help however I can
give you, will I hope, be always at call.

(Make my compliments to Mr Scrase)

I am Madam Your most humble Servant

London Apr. 16. 1781   Sam: Johnson.

726. M. 16 Apr. '81. John Nichols.
Address: To Mr Nicol.
B.M. (the year in another hand).—*GM* Jan. 1785.

Mr Johnson desires Mr Nicol to send him a set of the last
lives,[1] and would be glad to know how the octavo edition
goes forward.

Monday Apr. 16

725.—3. This paragraph was omitted in 1788. HLP's first intention was to print
it in a disguised form, and she erased a number of words. 'Mr. —' is no doubt Cator;
'have' is an inadvertent omission, not an erasure; for the last blank 'yet been' is the
obvious supplement, but Prof. T. thought the first word *not* 'yet'; perhaps 'been
yet', but why should such words be erased? The blank is a short one, perhaps of
one word only.

4. 'agues' 1788 ; "Tis Agnes not Agues; we had a hack joke of calling a creeping
woman Agnes after Molière's Ecole des Maris. See a note to the Tatler, Octavo
Edition, No. 3 p. 25.' HLP. See on 558.

726.—1. Vols. 5–10 of the *Prefaces*.

727. Tu. 17 Apr. '81. Mrs. Thrale (Brighthelmston).

Address: To Mrs Thrale at Brighthelmston Sussex. *Postmark* illegible.
Adam.—1788, No. 264.

Dear Madam

Mr Norris (Mr Robson's Partner) promised to send the
will tomorrow, You will therefore have it before you have
this letter. When you have talked with Mr Scrase write
diligently down all that you can remember, and where you
have any difficulties ask him again, and rather stay where
you are a few days longer, than come away with imperfect
information.

The executors will hardly meet till you come, for we have
nothing to do, till we go all together to prove the will.

I have not had a second visit from M^r ——¹ for he found
his discourse to me very unavailing. I was dry, but if he
goes to —— he will be overpowered with words as good as
his own. S—— appears a very modest inoffensive Man, not
likely to give any trouble. The difficulty of finding Executors
Mr Scrase has formerly told you, and among all your acquaintance except Pepys whom you pressed into the service and
who would perhaps have deserted it, I do not ⟨see⟩ with
whom you could have been more commodiously connected.
They all mean well, and will, I think, all concur. [half a
line erased.]²

Miss told me that you intended to bathe; it is right, all
external things are diversions; Let her bathe too. I regain
that tranquillity, which irremediable misfortunes necessarily
admit, and do not, I hope, think on what I have lost, without
grateful recollection of what I have enjoyed. I am
              Dear Madam Your most humble servant
London. Apr. 17. 1781   Sam: Johnson

727.1. Tu. 17 Apr. ⟨? '81⟩.

Not traced.—A bookseller's catalogue, reference mislaid. Possibly
the same as 727; but 727 is fully dated.

727.—1. HLP supplies the names: Perkins, Cator, Smith, Pepys. Smith is Henry S,
HT's cousin and executor. Pepys (legible, though erased, and in 1788 reduced to
'P—') is William Weller P. 'When Mr. Thrale made his will . . . October 1779. he
kindly asked me who I would appoint Joint Executors with myself—I named Johnson,
Cator, and Pepys.' *Th* 418.

2. The erasure, I think, conceals 'Yet keep' (the rest defeated me).

727.2. Th. 19 Apr. '81. Hester Maria Thrale (Brighthelmston).

Address: To Miss Thrale at Brighthelmston Sussex.
Lansdowne.—Lansdowne, *Johnson and Queeney* 1932, 23.

My dearest Miss   London, 19 April 1781

This is the last night on which I can write to Brighthelmston, and therefore I resolve to pay the letter which I owe to you, for I would not have you think that I want either tenderness or respect for you.

We are now soon to meet, our meeting will be melancholy, but we will not give way too long to unprofitable grief. The world is all before us[1]—and Providence our Guide. Life has other duties, and for you, my dearest, it has yet, I hope, much happiness. The Friendship which has begun between us, may perhaps by its continuance give us opportunities of supplying the deficiencies of each other. I hope we shall never lose the kindness which has grown up between us. The loss of such a Friend as has been taken from us encreases our need of one another, and ought to unite us more closely. I am,

my dear Love, Your most humble servant
Sam: Johnson

728. M. 23 Apr. '81. Margaret Strahan.

Fettercairn.—Boswell 1791, ii. 389 (Hill iv. 100).

Dear Madam

The Grief which I feel for the loss of a very kind friend is sufficient to make me know how much You must[1] suffer by the death of an amiable son,[2] a man of whom, I think, it may be truly said, that no one knew him who does not lament him. I look upon myself as having a friend, another friend taken from me.

Comfort, dear Madam, I would give You if I could, but I know how little the forms of consolation can avail. Let me however counsel you not to waste your health, in unprofitable sorrow, but to go to Bath, and endeavour to prolong

727.2.—1. *Paradise Lost*, at the end.
728.—1 'must' om. 1791.   2. William S the younger.

your own life, but when we have all done all that we can, one friend must in time lose the other.

    I am, Dear Madam, Your most humble servant

Apr. 23. 1781   Sam: Johnson.

729. M. 7 May '81. Mary Prowse (Frome).
Address: To Mrs Prowse.
Rosenbach (1925).—*NQ* 4 S. v. 441.

Madam

    Having lately had a melancholy occasion to search my Chest for mourning, I found in one of the pockets this tattered letter, which seems to prove that you have remitted to me more money than was due.

    You see, Madam, that I was paid, or might have been paid by your good Mother to –76. It is not likely that I neglected to call on the Banker, yet it is possible, but the Bankers books will clear the question. I am willing to suppose that I received it, for it would be hard that Charity should be cheated.

    In a few weeks will be published with my name some Lives of the Poets,[1] of which if you will be pleased to favour me by accepting a copy, I beg that you will let me know to whom in London I may send them, that they may be conveyed to you.

    I am, Madam, Your most humble Servant,

                             Sam: Johnson.

N.B.[2] *Bolt Court* Fleet Street London. May 7 1781.

729.1. Sa. 12 May '81. John Taylor (Ashbourne).
Address: To the Reverend Dr Taylor in Ashbourne Derbyshire
Postmark: 12 MA.
Owen D. Young.—

Dear Sir

    You went out of town without giving me any notice, and considering the state of your health, I did not think you to

729.—See 693.
    1. The octavo edition in four volumes. The book was sold at Sotheby's 17 Nov. 1948, 878. The inscription 'Mary Prowse 1781 The Gift of the Author' is not in J's hand.
    2. Mrs. P had probably written to Johnson's Court. See on 739.

blame, but why you have since given me no account of your-self I cannot discover, for I hope your disorders are not grown worse.

Dr Butter talked to me of writing you some directions for your diet, and other parts of regimen; I called at his door lately but did not find him, if he has sent you any advice, be sure to try it. I have just lost one friend by his disobedience to his physician; let me not lose another. If Butter has for-gotten or delayed his purpose, let me know, that I may remind or quicken him. But write to me immediately. Neither you nor I can now afford to lose time.

I have by negligence and indulgence lost something of the health which I had regained, but I purpose to fall again to work. But I am not near so bad as you have known me. Whether I can come down into the country soon I know not, but having missed the journey last year, I seriously desire to see my old friends this summer. Of old friends you know how few are left to a Man past seventy, and how much danger there is that every year should make them fewer. I have lately heard that Charles Congreve is dead. I am sorry that in his last years I could not love him better. But he had put himself to nurse, a state to which an old Man is naturally tempted, and which he should resolutely disdain, till his powers really desert him.

I am, Sir, Yours affectionately

London. May 12. 1781   Sam: Johnson

729.2. ⟨May '81.⟩ John Nichols.

B.M.; written on part of a letter addressed to Johnson at Bolt Court by Thrale, with a Brighthelmston postmark; the date added in another hand.—*GM* Jan. 1785.

An
Account of the Lives and Works
of some of the most eminent
English Poets, by &c.

———————

The
English Poets
biographically and critically considered
by Sam: Johnson,

Let Mr Nicol take his choice or make another to his mind.[1]

729.3. Tu. 22 May '81. Mrs. Thrale.

Rylands.—*R.L. Bull.* Jan. 1932, 34.

Dear Madam

I will be ready for you when you call, do not let that trouble you. It does not appear that Mr B: want⟨s⟩ to see us separately from Mr C: He wants to see us all together, as he must sometime do, and nothing is necessary but to commission Mr Perkins to let him know that we shall all be *ready* to meet him, upon any time which he shall appoint. Mr P. has probably something to say, respecting his own particular hopes and fears, which he naturally wishes to tell you, and which it can do you no harm to hear, but we shall perhaps to morrow hear it together, for, next to you, he, I believe, thinks me his friend.

In a negotiation of such importance we must expect something of artifice, but less has yet appeared than is practiced upon much slighter occasions. Keep P. in as good humour as you can. Much must depend upon his representation.— Remember that you are to call to morrow for,

Madam, Your most humble servant,

May. 22. 1781   Sam: Johnson

729.4. M. 28 May '81. Mrs. Thrale.

Address: To Mrs Thrale.
National Library of Scotland.—

Madam

I shall have on tuesday an opportunity of making it up[1] with Beattie, and therefore beg your permission to stay here

---

729.2.—1. Nichols chose neither of J's alternatives. The 1781 edition is *The Lives of the Most Eminent English Poets; with Critical Observations on their Works*. This may have been modelled on the Dublin reprint, 1779, of the first four volumes of the *Prefaces: The Lives of the English Poets; and a Criticism on their Works*.

729.3.—The initials are for Barclay, Perkins, and either Cator or Crutchley. Crutchley is perhaps the more likely, for FB's diary shows him much at S'm in May and June, and HLP writes (*Tb* 17 May): 'Mr. Crutcheley lives now a great deal with me.'

729.4.—1. There is no occasion to assume a quarrel; J may have seen less of B than he thought due to an old friend.

till I wait on you at the Borough on Wednesday. I am,
Madam, Your most obedient,

May 28. 1781   Sam: Johnson

730. Sa. 2 June '81. John Perkins (Southwark).
Address: To Mr Perkins in Southwark.
O. T. Perkins.—Boswell 1793, ii. 373 (Hill iv. 118).

Sir

However often I have seen You, I have hitherto forgotten
the note, but I have now sent it, with my good wishes for the
Prosperity of you and your Partner,[1] of whom from our
short conversation I could not judge otherwise than
favourably.

I am Sir Your most humble Servant

June 2, 1781   Sam. Johnson.

730.1. W. 6 June '81. Frederick Augusta Barnard.
Kroch, Dec. 1949 (not seen).—Text in catalogue.

Sir

I have sent you the remaining Lives, and as I must complete those which His Majesty was pleased to accept, I beg
that you will favour me with one of the volumes, that the
additional part may be bound uniformly. My booksellers
have not behaved very well, and therefore, I have not been
able to accomodate my friends as I wish. You must excuse
me yourself, and save my credit with any that may blame me.

I am, dear Sir, Your most hum^ble servant

Sam: Johnson.

730.2. Sa. 9 June '81. Lucy Porter (Lichfield).
Address: To Miss Lucy Porter.
Sotheby 15 April 1929.—Croker's Boswell 1831, v. 1 (overlooked by
Hill).

Dear Madam.

I hope the Summer makes you better. my disorders which
had come upon me again, have given way to medicine, and
I am a better sleeper than I have lately been.

The death of dear Mr Thrale has made my attendance
upon his house necessary, but we have sold the trade which

730.—1. Barclay.

we did not know how to manage, and have sold it for an hundred and thirty thousand pounds.[1]

My lives are at last published, and you will receive them this week by the carrier.

I have some hopes of coming this Summer amongst you for a short time. I shall be loath to miss you two years together. But in the mean time let me know how you do. I am,

dear Madam, your affectionate servant
London. June 9. 1781   Sam: Johnson

731. Su. 10 June '81. John Nichols.

Address: To Mr Nicol.
B.M.; the last sentence is a distinct note, undated.—*GM* Jan. 1785.

Sir

My desire being to complete the sets of lives which I have formerly presented to my friends, I have occasion for few of the first volumes, of which by some misapprehension I have received a great number, which I desire to exchange for the latter volumes. I wish success to the new edition. I am,

Sir, Your most humble Servant,
June 10 1781   Sam: Johnson

Please to deliver to Mr Steevens a complete set of the lives in 12mo

Sam: Johnson

732. Sa. 16 June '81. Bennet Langton (Rochester).

Address: To Captain Langton in St Margarets Rochester. *Postmark*: 16 iv.
Fettercairn.—Boswell 1791, ii. 409 (Hill iv. 132).

Dear Sir

How welcome your account of yourself and your invitation to your new house was to me, I need not tell you, who consider our friendship not only as formed by choice but as matured by time. We have been now long enough acquainted to have many images in common, and therefore to have a source of conversation which neither the learning nor the wit of a new companion can supply.

730.2.—1. The precise figure was that given by J in 732, £135,000; so *L* iv. 86.

My Lives are now published, and if you will tell me whither I shall send them that they may come to you, I will take care that You shall not be without them.

You will perhaps be glad to hear, that Mrs. Thrale is disencumbered from her Brewhouse, and that it seemed to the purchaser so far from an evil, that he was content to give for it an hundred and thirty five thousand pounds. Is the Nation ruined?

Please to make my respectful compliments to Lady Rothes, and keep me in the memory of all the little dear family, particularly pretty Mrs Jane.[1]

I am Sir Your affectionate humble Servant
Bolt court June 16 1781　　　　　　　　Sam: Johnson.

733. Sa. 23 June '81. Joshua Reynolds.
New York Public Library.—Boswell 1793, iii. 391 (Hill iv. 133).
Dear Sir

It was not before yesterday that I received your splendid benefaction.[1] To a hand so liberal in distributing, I hope nobody will envy the power of acquiring.

I am, dear Sir, Your obliged and most humble servant,
June 23, 1781.　　　　　　　　　　　　Sam. Johnson.

734. M. 25 June '81. Frances Reynolds.
Address: To Mrs Reynolds.
Rupert Colomb.—Croker's Boswell 1831, v. 4.
Dear Madam

You may give the books to Mrs Horneck, and I will give you another for yourself

I am afraid there is no hope of Mrs Thrale's custom for your pictures but, if you please, I will mention it. She cannot make a pension out of her jointure.

I will bring the papers myself.

I am, Madam, Your most humble servant,
June 25. 1781　　　　　　　　　　　Sam: Johnson.

732.—1. 'Jenny', though here elevated to the dignity of 'Mrs.', was only five years old.

733.—1. The context in the *Life* suggests that J was not the beneficiary; this was an example of the vicarious charity which he so vigorously practised.

734.—Hill quotes Northcote's *Reynolds* i. 202 (of the octavo edition) for FR's having bought some fine pictures very cheaply in Paris. She no doubt, as Croker supposed, wanted to sell her collection, and thought HLT might pay for them with an annuity.

735. M. 2 July '81. ⟨John Perkins.⟩
Not traced.—Hill 1892.

Sir

Mrs. Thrale has informed me of the iron resolution of Mr.
Cator and Mr. Crutchley. They have law on their side, and
cannot be opposed. What then can be done? If time will do
any thing for you, that you may apply to your friends, I will
struggle for that. I think Mr. Barclay's interest so much
requires your concurrence and assistance, that if you cannot
procure security, he must help you. His difficulties are only
niceties. Do not be bashful, use all the efforts that you can.

                I am, Sir, Your humble Servant,
July 2, 1781.   Sam: Johnson.

I shall come to you this morning, but I will meet Mrs.
Thrale to-morrow about twelve.

736. M. 9 July '81. Frances Burney.
New York Public Library.—*Early Diary* of F.B. 1889, i. 169.

Dear Madam,

Pray let these books be sent after the former to the gentleman whose name I do not know.

                I am, Madam, Your most humble servant,
July 9, 1781.   Sam: Johnson.

736.1. Tu. 10 July '81. ———
Donald S. Tuttle.—

Dear Sir

I am desired by Mrs. Lennox to solicit your assistance.
She is in great distress; very harshly treated by her husband,
and oppressed with severe illness. Do for her what you can,
You were perhaps never called to the relief of a more powerful mind. She has many fopperies, but she is a Great genius,

735.—Perkins had perhaps hoped that the executors would advance part of the
purchase-money. FB noted, 2 July, HLT's 'generosity' to Perkins: 'even to the
lending all her own money that is in the stocks'. *Diary* ii. 72.

736.—The nameless beneficiary was William Bewly, 'the Broom gentleman'. See
FB's *Early Diary*, loc. cit., and *L* iv. 134.

and nullum magnum ingenium sine mixtura[1] I hope—you
will call on her to morrow. She lives at the house of Pauson,
Pewterer, in Queen street, Westminster. I am

Sir Your most humble Servant,

July 10, 1781.   Sam: Johnson

737. Tu. 17 July '81. Thomas Astle.

Address (T.A.'s copy): To T. Astle Esq[r].
Not traced; copy for JB, Isham—Boswell 1791, ii. 410 (Hill iv.
133); Nichols, *L.A.* 1812, iii. 205, perhaps from an independent
source.

Sir

I am ashamed that you have been forced to call[1] so often
for your books, but it has been by no fault on either side.
They have never been out of my hands, nor have I ever been
at home without seeing you, for to see a man so skilful in the
Antiquities of my Country, is an Opportunity of improvement not willingly to be missed.

Your Notes on Alfred[2] appear to me very judicious and
accurate, but they are too few. Many things familiar to you
are unknown to me and to most others, and you must not
think too favourably of your readers, by supposing them
knowing you will leave them ignorant. Measure of Land,
and value of Money, it is of great importance to state with
care. Had the Saxons any gold Coin?

I have much curiosity after the Manners and Transactions
of the Middle Ages, but have wanted either Diligence or
Opportunity[3] or both.[4] You Sir have great Opportunities,[5]
and I wish you both Diligence and Success.

I am, Sir, &c.

July 17th 1781.   Sam. Johnson.

736.1.—1. 'nullum magnum ingenium sine mixtura dementiae fuit'—'great wit is
sure to madness near allied'—Seneca *de Tranquillitate* 17. 10.

737.—1. 'send' 1812. J's 'call' might easily enough be misread 'send'; his 'fend'
could hardly be misread 'call'.

2. Astle's book was not published until '88 (see Index II).

3. J puts his finger on the defects which prevented his becoming one of the greatest
of all scholars. There was also, of course, a better reason; he had a loftier vocation.
It is tempting to apply his own doctrine that genius may be determined in any
direction: he might, for instance, given 'diligence and opportunity', have been great
as a librarian, as a book-collector, or as a bookseller.

4. 'in both' Astle and 1791; 'or both' 1793, 1812.

5. 'opportunity' 1812.

737.1. Tu. 17 July '81. Charles Dilly.

Anderson Galleries, 13 May 1918 (not seen).—

A request for copies of the *Rambler* and the *Lives*.

738. Th. 28 June '81. Frances Reynolds.

F. W. Hilles (see Addenda, p. 530); Malone's copy, Bodleian; a copy by Mary Palmer, the late A. H. Hallam Murray.—Malone's Boswell 1811, iv. 143; Northcote's *Life of Reynolds* 1818, ii. 115; Croker's Boswell 1831, v. 4, 1848, 697.

Dearest Madam

There is in these ⟨f. pages, or remarks⟩[1] such depth of penetration, such nicety of observation, as Locke or Pascal might be proud of. This I desire you to believe is my real opinion.

However, it cannot be published in its present state. Many of your notions seem not to be very clear in your own mind; many are not sufficiently developed and expanded for the common reader: it wants every where to be made smoother and plainer.

You may by revisal and correction make it a very elegant and a very curious work. I am, my dearest dear, Your affectionate and obedient servant,

Bolt-Court, June 28, 1781.   Samuel[2] Johnson.

738.1. M. 6 Aug. '81. John Perkins.

Address: To Mr Perkins.

O. T. Perkins.—

Dear Sir

I have a mind to go for a few weeks into the Country, and

738.—I follow Malone. For a different text, dated 21 July, see Hill, who followed Croker's version of 1848. Croker's note is: 'I print this hyperbolical eulogy from the original in the *Reynolds Papers*, but Mr. Malone, who first produced it, gives it with variations so great in the expressions, and so small in the meaning, that I preserve it as a curious instance of falsification, without so far as I can see any object.' The true explanation is doubtless something less sensational. The work referred to is no doubt a version of FR's 'Essay on Taste', which Northcote (*Reynolds*, ii. 115 in the octavo edition) describes and quotes; 'it was privately printed, but was never published'. I have not seen a copy of this print.

1. Malone's supplement. If I read it right as 'f', it may stand for 'forsan', which M uses frequently in notes in his copy of 1788; but it may be 'f' for 'scilicet'.

2. This is unique in my experience; J always signed 'Sam:'.

shall be glad to borrow thirty pounds of your house, for which if you are willing, I will wait upon you on Monday. I am,

Sir, Your most humble Servant,

Bolt court. Aug. 6. 1781   Sam: Johnson

739. M. 24 or Tu. 25 Sept. '81. Thomas Patten.

Not traced; copy by Harwood (*c.* 1820) at Pembroke.—*GM* Apr. 1819.

Dear Sir

It is so long since we passed any time together, that you may be allowed to have forgotten some part of my character, and I know not upon what other supposition, I can pass without censure or complaint the ceremony[1] of your address. Let me[2] not trifle time in words, to which while we speak or write them we assign little meaning. Whenever you favour me with a Letter, treat me as one that is glad of your kindness, and proud of your esteem.

The papers[3] which have been sent for my perusal, I am ready to inspect if you judge my inspection necessary or useful; but indeed, I do not, for what advantage can arise from it? A Dictionary consists of independent parts, and therefore one page is not much a specimen of the rest. It does not occur to me that I can give any assistance to the Author, and, for my own interest, I resign it into your hands, and do not suppose that I shall ever see my name with regret where you shall think it proper to be put.

I think it, however, my duty to inform a writer who intends so great an honour, that in my opinion, he would better consult his interest by dedicating his Work to some powerful and popular neighbour, who can give him more

739.—1. Patten's letter is in *GM*. He writes: 'Nothing would more highly gratify my taste and my pride than a correspondence with my dear and honoured friend Johnson; but could I conceive myself worthy of so rare a gratification, I should tremble at the price to be paid for it, conscious that my finances would fall far short of paying it', and more, much more, in the same strain. For J's dislike of such ceremony see 3.2.

2. J perhaps wrote 'us'. Cf. 609, where Hill read 'us' as 'me'.

3. Thomas Wilson's *Archaeological Dictionary*, published in '82 and dedicated to J. The dedication of books to a mere scholar was unusual. It is true that the bucolic Taylor had that honour, see 296. But he was a rich man. See, however, 811.1. For other books dedicated to J see *L* iv. 421, 519, 554.

than a name. What will the world do, but look on and laugh when one scholar dedicates to another?

If I had been consulted about this Lexicon of Antiquities while it was yet only a design, I should have recommended rather a division of Hebrew, Greek, and Roman particulars, into three volumes, than a combination in one. The Hebrew part at least, I would have wished to separate, as it might be made a very popular book, of which the use might be extended from men of learning down to the English Reader, and which might become a concomitant to the Family Bible.[4]

When works of a multifarious and extensive kind are undertaken in the country, the necessary books are not always known. I remember a very learned and ingenious Clergyman, of whom, when he had published Notes upon the Psalms, I enquired what was his opinion of Hammond's Commentary, and was answered, that he had never heard of it. As this gentleman has the opportunity of consulting you, it needs not be supposed that he has not heard of all the proper books; but unless he is near some Library, I know not how he could peruse them; and if he is conscious that his *supellex*[5] is *nimis angusta*, it would be prudent to delay his publication till his deficiences may be supplied.

It seems not very candid to hint any suspicions of imperfection in a Work which I have not seen, yet what I have said ought to be excused, since I cannot but wish well to a learned man, who has elected me for the honour of a Dedication, and to whom I am indebted for a correspondence so valuable as yours. And I beg that I may not lose any part of his kindness, which I consider with respectful gratitude. Of you, dear Sir, I entreat that you will never again forget for so long a time,

Your most humble servant,

Sam: Johnson.

N.B.[6] Bolt-court, Fleet-street, Sept. 24, 1781.

739.—4. I have not been able to determine what edition J means, if indeed he intended so to limit the term. The B.M. Catalogue lists 'family' Bibles from 1777. The (unrevised) B.M. Catalogue gives 1780 as the date of Paul Wright's illustrated folio (which is undated). J may have referred to that imposing work.

5. Apparently a conflation of two familiar tags, Persius iv. 52 *curta supellex* 'scant furniture' and Juvenal iii. 165 *res angusta domi* 'a narrow income'.

6. 'N.B.', unless indeed it is a misreading of 'No. 8', calls attention to J's change of address; elsewhere he dates 'Bolt Court, not Johnson's'. See 729.

739.1. M. 24 Sept. '81. John Taylor (Ashbourne).
Address (defective): . . . Dr Taylor . . . Ashbourne Derbyshire.
B.M.—

Dear Sir

All the expedients which you propose are so peremptorily rejected, that I see not what advice can be given you. Nothing seems to remain but that you write immediately[1] to the Duke, by which you will offend his Unkle, and what hope you can have of his acting not only without advice, but contrarily to it, you must consider. If you write, I can suggest no more than you have already, nor can much more be urged.

Mr Barker, who must know the family, seems to despair which is a great discouragement; and indeed it is hard to persist long in importuning men to do what they say they cannot do, and what indeed they cannot do but by indirect and artificial means, which they have not zeal enough to seek, and which can hardly be expected from friendship merely political. However, if you can recollect any other train of interest by which they might proceed, I would have you mention it, with pressing urgency,[2] for I think you have nothing to fear more than disappointment of this preferment.

But let your health be your great care; suffer not vexation to lay hold upon your mind. I am glad to hear that you grow stronger. Be alone, or unemployed as little as you can. Remember that your disappointment is one of the common incidents of life, and if it is not seen to depress you, will supply no triumph to your enemies. I still intend to visit you. I am, dear Sir, affectionately yours

Sept. 24. 1781 London   Sam: Johnson

739.2. M. 8 Oct. '81. John Perkins.
Address: To Mr Perkins.
O. T. Perkins.—

Dear Sir

I have received the notes, and have signed and sent the acknowledgement.

739.1.—1. That is, without intermediary, 'directly'. Cf. 518: 'His acquaintance is with the Lord Cavendishes, he barely knows the young Duke.' For 'immediately' see on 486.

2. See Addenda, p. 530.

I hope You found all your family well, and particularly my[1] little Boy, make my compliments to them all. I am
   Sir, Your obliged and most humble servant
Oct. 8. 1781   Sam: Johnson

740. M. 15 Oct. '81. —— Lowe.

Adam; known to Hill only from an auction catalogue.

Sir

 I have put Mr. Kearsley's note into the hands of Mr Allen to whom I owe rent; if any assistance of yours is necessary, you will certainly give it. If something is not done before my return, I think his last proposal such as leaves him very little claim to tenderness. I am, Sir Your most humble servant Sam: Johnson
Oct. 15. 1781

740.1. M. 15 Oct. '81. Lucy Porter (Lichfield).

Address lost. *Postmark*: 15 oc.
Houghton.—

Dear Madam

 You bade me send You word when I was to be at Lichfield. I am this day going to Oxford, where I shall probably make very little stay, and shall come forward by Birmingham. I hope to be with You in less than a Week, and to find You and all my other friends well. I am,
   Dear Madam, Your most humble Servant,
London Oct. 15. 1781   Sam: Johnson.

739.2.—1. 'my' suggests a godson. I cannot find a Sam Perkins; but see Index II.

740.—Hill knew this letter only from a catalogue, which described it as to 'Mr. Lowe' and paraphrased the first sentence. The catalogue has 'he owes rent'; Hill therefore supposed the letter to be to 'the needy Mauritius Lowe'. Mr. R. F. Metzdorf reports that there is nothing in or (now) with the letter to show to whom it was addressed.

 The 'note' which J handed over to his landlord was no doubt a negotiable instrument; I have no suggestion to make why K owed J money; it was doubtless *not* a payment in respect of *The Beauties of Johnson.*

741. Oxford. W. 17 Oct. '81. Mrs. Thrale.

Sotheby 30 Jan. 1918 (not seen; copy by R. B. Adam).—1788, No. 265.

Dear Madam

On Monday evening arrived at the Angel Inn at Oxford Mr Johnson and Mr Barber without any sinister accident.

I am here why am I here? on my way to Lichfield, where I believe Mrs Aston will be glad to see me. We have known each other long, and, by consequence, are both old, and she is paralytick, and if I do not see her soon, I may see her no more in this world. To make a visit on such considerations is to go on a melancholy errand. But such is the course of Life.

This place is very empty[1] but there are more here whom I know, than I could have expected. Young Burke has just been with me, and I have dined to day with Dr Adams, who seems fond of me. But I have not been very well. I hope I am not ill by sympathy, and that you are making hast to recover your plumpness and your complexion. I left you *skinny and lean.*[2]

To morrow, if I can, I shall go forward, and when I see Lichfield, I shall write again.

Mr Parker[3] the Bookseller sends his respects to you I send mine to the young Ladies.

I am, Madam, your most humble Servant

Oxford, Oct. 17. 1781   Sam: Johnson

741a. Southwark. W. 17 Oct. '81. From Mrs. Thrale to J at Oxford (forwarded to Lichfield).

Address: Doctor Sam: Johnson at [Oxford erased] Litchfield. *Post-mark*: 17 OC. *and* LITCHFIELD.

R 540. 101—

Dear Sir

I write from the old Compting house Desk in the Borough, whither we are all summon'd to receive 5000£ in order to pay Debts &c. Mr Cator and M^r

741.—A careful statement of the motives of this 'ramble', with good resolutions for its conduct, is in *PM*.

1. See references in Index IV. The date seems late; Michaelmas Term began on 10 Oct. 'Full Term' began on the Sunday after the first Congregation. But in '81 the Registrar failed to keep any Convocation records.

2. I have mislaid Mr. Adam's copy (which, however, I had collated) and cannot be sure that it shows 'skinny and lean' as underlined; the Sotheby catalogue italicizes 'skinny' only; Maggs Catalogue 381, 1883, has no italic. See on 699.

3. HLT had no doubt made his acquaintance in '74.

Crutchley are disputing across me this Moment, the first of these Gentlemen
seem to think the Money now bought into the Stocks belongs to the Children,
the last is all for me. But here is another Defalcation: the Oxfordshire Estate
which Mr Thrale *justly thought nothing of*, turns out but 300£ a Year at least,
& scarcely that: . . . My Income will therefore be a good deal less than I
thought for, in Consequence of which I shall lay down a Pair of my Horses
in the first Place, for I will not run out. Barclay & Perkins are excessively
civil, & do all in their Power to accomodate us: I feel a real Kindness for the
people, & 'tis comical to see how they help battle Mr Cator for my Privileges.
This Letter will scarce catch you at Oxford, yet I cannot help writing. I sent
to Bolt Court two days ago to ask if you were well enough to set out, for my
heart misgave me—about that *general Gravedo*.

Nobody has been at Streatham since you left it but Sir Richard Jebb, who
came merely to shew his Regard, or *pay his Respects* as little George Angel says.

Farewell my dear Sir, and keep your Health. I will write to Lichfield, and
am ever with all possible & Affectionate Regard Your faithful Sert
Southwark Wednesday 17. Oct. 1781.   H: L: Thrale

741b. Streatham. Th. 18 Oct. '81. From Mrs. Thrale to J at Lichfield

Address: Doctor Samuel Johnson at Mrs Lucy Porter's Lichfield.
Postmarks: PENNY POST PAID *and* 19 OC.
R 540. 102—

My Dear Sir   Streatham Thursday 18. Octr/81
  You bid me not wait for a Frank, so I will write without; while Sir Philip
is mending his Pen to make up a Letter to send with the freed Cases I beg'd
of him. Cator & Crutchley & I met at the Borough yesterday, & got some
money out of our Successors to pay our Debts; the particulars of our Conversation I wrote to you, but directing my Letter to Oxford it might come thither
too late for you perhaps, & you would not know how I sent to Bolt Court to
see whether you went or no; how my Coadjutors tell me I must have only
1200£ a Year instead of 1600£, how I find my possessions in Oxfordshire
diminish upon close Inspection from 450£ a Year to 300£ & how in Consequence of all these Informations I have sent off a Pair of my Horses.

  Other News have I none to balance the bad I have been telling, except a
fine Letter from Mrs Montagu may be reckoned something of an equivalent;
Presto is once more recovered from the Wounds Kam gave him too, & that is
some Consolation.

  Miss Burney has not yet taken Wing, but I fancy She will go soon; I expect
Mrs Strickland in about a fortnight, & the D'Avenants will not now be long
away. Tell me Dear Sir how you feel, and how Change of Place affects you.
Sir Richard Jebb is the only Person that has been here since you left us—he
asks about your Health with an affectionate Earnestness, & does not like your
complaining of *general Gravedo*. Queeney sends her best Respects. I am always
Your most faithful and most Obedient

                    H: L: Thrale.

742. Lichfield. Sa. 20 Oct. '81. Mrs. Thrale.

Gabriel Wells.—1788, No. 266.

Dear Madam

I wrote from Oxford, where I staid two days; on thursday I went to Birmingham, and was told by Hector that I should not be well so soon as I expected, but that well I should be. Mrs. Careless took me under her care, and told me when I had tea enough. On fryday I came hither and have escaped the postchaises[1] all the way. Every Body here is as kind as I expected, I think Lucy is kinder than ever. I am very well. Now We are both valetudinary, we shall have something to write about. We can tell each other our complaints, and give reciprocal comfort and advice as—Not to eat too much —and—Not to drink too little, and we may now and then add a few strictures of reproof. And so we may write and write, till we can find another subject. Pray make my compliments to all the Ladies great and little.

I am, Madam Your most humble Servant

Lichfield. Oct. 20. 1781   Sam: Johnson

742a. Streatham. Su. 21 Oct. ⟨'81⟩. From Mrs. Thrale to J at Lichfield.

Address: Doctor Samuel Johnson at Mrs Lucy Porter's Lichfield.
Postmark: 22 oc.
R 540. 103—

I received your Letter from Oxford dear Sir, and thank you for it: no need to wonder *why you* are at Oxford? it ought to be a Place you should delight in going to; but then you ought to be fondled as you call it by higher Mortals than —— no Degree of Scholarship can give real Dignity to a Mind naturally feeble; do you remember the old remark I used to be so happy with—'that setting Jewels in Lead only obscured the Lustre of the Stone, & made the possessor ashamed on't.

I saw   yesterday—*he* is an Oxford man, Oh me! what a tedious Creature it is, if Lady Lade had heard him pur so, She would have been sure he did not know a *Word* of *Latin*.

I am sorry that you are not well: I was many Years before I felt Sickness, but it is now in no haste to leave me, I must be still Leaner before I venture to grow fat; I have now pass'd seven Weeks completely without one comfortable Meal & I think seven more must be so spent before I recover.

Count Mannucci has written me a very long and very kind Letter on the *Change of my Existence*! he mentions you with grateful Tenderness, & says in

742.—1.. He had been lucky in finding 'accidental vacancies in passing coaches' (401).

his Foreigners English, that he recollects *your last Embracements with a sweet Commotion.*

Perkins dines with me today; he too reflects on your Kindness to him in a Manner that makes me half jealous somehow—he says there is *one* good Person in this World that knows how to be generous & friendly.—[I hoped he knew that there were *two*]. We have dined at Cator's & met the —— of ——;[1] his Lady is vastly more agreeable than himself. She press'd Acquaintance with me, & now we shall visit. I will write no more till I get a Frank, because this is the third Letter; but I beg or command or do any thing to get another from you to say you are safe at Lichfield, & that the Lady at Stow Hill has Life enough left to enjoy the Comforts of your friendship. Farewell, and wherever you go, love nobody better than Your truly faithful and Obligd Servant

H: L: Thrale

Hester sends her Respects.
Sunday 21. October Streatham.

743. Lichfield. Tu. 23 Oct. '81. Mrs. Thrale (Streatham).
Address: To Mrs Thrale at Streatham Surrey. *Postmark*: 26 oc.
Adam.—1788, No. 267.

Dear Madam   Lichfield Oct. 23. 1781
I had both your letters, and very little good news in either of them. The diminution of the Estate though unpleasing and unexpected must be borne because it cannot be helped, but I do not apprehend why the other part of your income should fall short. I understood that you were to have 1500 L yearly from the money arising from the sale, and that your claim was first.

I sincerely applaud your resolution not to run out, and wish you always to save something, for that which is saved may be spent at will, and the advantages are very many of having some money loose and unappropriated, if your ammunition is always ready, you may shoot advantage as it starts, or pleasure as it flies. Resolve therefore never to want money.

The Gravedo[1] is not removed, nor does it encrease, my nights have commonly been bad. Mrs Aston is much as I

742a.—1. Heavily erased; the first word might, I thought, be 'Bishop'. Evidently HLP thought of publishing this letter; in the end she preferred the very elaborate document dated 'Nov. 2' and numbered 270 in 1788.

743.—1. See 741a, b. Gravedo is the Common Cold. But J's 'general Gravedo' was something more. Hill consulted Sir Norman Moore, who quoted Heberden, who 'had known such an habitual gravedo followed by palsy, and by asthma'.

left her, without any new symptoms, but between time and Palsy wearing away. Mrs Gastrel is brisk and [and] lively.

Burney told me that she was to go, but you will have my dear Queeney, tell her that I do not forget her, and that I hope she remembers me. Against our meeting we will both make good resolutions, which on my side, I hope to keep, but such hopes are very deceitful. I would not willingly think the same of all hopes, and particularly should be loath to suspect of deceit my hope of [my hope of] being always,

Dearest Madam, Your most humble servant,

Sam: Johnson

743a. Streatham. W. 24 Oct. ⟨'81 ⟩. From Mrs. Thrale to J at Lichfield.

R 540. 104.—

Dear Sir　　　　　　　　　　　　　　　　　　Streatham 24: October.

I have got a Frank at last to thank you for your Letters in, that you may at least have my Consolation & Advice gratis: that you are very well is really a delightful hearing, and somehow you had contrived to lower my Spirits about your Health in such a manner, that I did not hope any News of that Sort—at least not with Confidence. I am not yet well at all; but so sullen, that if I have at last lost my Health—the Companion of my Youth—why I will even resolve to do like Zachary Pearce I think—fill out one Glass to the pleasing Memory of her that is departed—& never name her more. Nothing vexes me but my Folly in writing to Oxford. I wonder where that Letter is gone to. Our Pond by the Summer House is got so low for want of Rain, that I fear'd the first Frost would destroy all the Gold Fish, so with Daniel's Concurrence and Assistance we drew the Pond today, & thinned the Number by carrying twenty to the Spring Pond which can never be dry. We dar'd not trust them in the Canal for fear of the Perch, & besides there will scarcely be Water enough in that by Christmas to cover the Fish if it is actually settled there should come no Rain at all. I intended that Queeney should have recorded this Event, but She says you did not bid her write to you; and you *used* to *bid* her write to you.

Mrs Porter is a sweet Lady; if She will accept my Complim^s pray do me the favour to give them her.

Perkins is ill, not ill but broken somehow; & looking like a Man that would not live two years: this is not my Conceit, I hear it from every body, Servants & all: Dear heart! how shocking it is, that if the Ship does with hard fighting weather the Storm, it is at last almost sure to sink in the Harbour. But so all the Poets Lives say, & tho' Perkins has very little poet's Stuff in him I trow—Yet he will die, just like the best of them. Adieu dear Sir, and live long and happily with Your Obliged and Faithful Friend

H: L: Thrale.

drawn some attention, for Lord and Lady Lucan sent to
enquire after me. This is all the news that I have to tell You.
Yesterday I dined with Mr Strahan, and Boswel was there.
We shall be both to morrow at Mr Ramsays. Now sure I
have told you quite all, unless you yet want to be told that
                    I am, Madam, Your most humble Servant,
Oct. 11. 1779 London   Sam: Johnson.

633. Sa. 16 Oct. '79. Mrs. Thrale (Brighthelmston).

Bergson.—1788, No. 214.

Dear Madam

The advice given You by Dr Pepys agrees very exactly
with my notions. I would not bleed but in exigencies.
Riding and cheerfulness will, I hope, do all the business. All
alive and merry, must be my Master's motto.

How did you light on your specifick for the tooth-ach?
You have now been troubled with it long. I am glad you are
at last relieved.

You say nothing of the *Younglings*, I hope they are not
spoiled with the pleasures of Brighthelmston, a dangerous
place, we were told, for *children*. You will do well to keep
them out of harm's way.

From the younglings let me pass to a Veteran, You tell me
nothing of Mr Scrase; I hope he is well and chearful and
communicative. Dos Mr Thrale go and talk with ⟨him⟩[1]
and do You run in and out? You may both be the better fo
his conversation.

I am sorry for poor Thomas,[2] who was a decent and civil
Man. It is hard that he should be overwhelmed by a new
comer. But *Thou by some other shalt be laid as low.*[3] Bowen's
day may come. A finer shop may be erected, kept by yet a
finer man, and crouded by greater numbers of fine Gentlemen and fine Ladies.

My Foot gives me very little trouble, but it is not yet well.
I have dined since You saw me not so often as once in two

633.—1. Omitted at the end of a page.
    2. For the supersession of bookseller T by bookseller B see 636 and FB's *Diary* i. 259.
    3. *Rape of the Lock* v. 98.

days. But I am told how well I look, and I really think I get more mobility. I dined on Tuesday with Ramsay, and on Thursday with Paoli, who talked of coming to see you, till I told him of your migration.

Mrs. Williams is not yet returned; but discord and discontent reign in my humble habitation as in the palaces of Monarchs.[4] Mr Levet and Mrs Desmoulins have vowed eternal hate. Levet is the more insidious, and wants me to turn her out. Poor Williams writes word that she is no better, and has left off her physick. Mr Levet has seen Dr Lewis, who declares himself hopeless of doing her any good. Lawrence desponded some time ago.

I thought I had a little fever some time, but it seems to be starved away. Bozzy says, he never saw me so well. I hope, You will say the same when You see me, methinks it ⟨will⟩ be pleasant to see you all, there is no danger of my forgetting You. Only keep or grow all well, and then I hope our meeting will be happy.

> I am, Dear Madam, Your most humble Servant
Oct. 16. 1779   Sam: Johnson

634. Tu. 19 Oct. '79. Frances Reynolds.

Sotheby 5 June 1929.—Croker's Boswell 1831, iv. 288.

Dearest Madam

You are extremely kind in taking so much trouble. My foot is almost well and one of my first visits will certainly be to Dover Street.

You will do me a great favour if you will buy for me the prints of Mr Burke, Mr Dyer, and Dr Goldsmith, as you know a good impression.

If any of your own pictures be engraved, buy them for me. I am filling a little room with prints. I am, Dear Madam, Your most humble Servant,
Oct. 19. 1779.   Sam: Johnson

633.—4. Perhaps a reminiscence of Horace, *Odes* i. iv: Pallida mors aequo pulsat pede pauperum tabernas/Regumque turres, 'pauper's cot and prince's hall' (Marris).

635. Tu. 19 Oct. '79. John Taylor (Ashbourne).

Address: To the Reverend Dr Taylor in Ashbourne Derbyshire. *Post-mark*: 19 oc.
Loyd.—*NQ* 6 S. v. 461.

Dear Sir

When I found that the Deanery had given You no uneasi-ness I was satisfied,[1] and thought no more of writing. You may indeed very well be without it, and ⟨I⟩ am glad to find that you think so yourself. You have enough, if you are satisfied.

Mr Thrale, after whose case you will have a natural curiosity, is with his family at Brighthelmston. He rides very vigourously, and runs much into company, and is very angry if it be thought that any thing ails him. Mrs Thrale thinks him for the present in no danger. I had no mind to go with them, for I have had what Brighthelmston can give, and I know not they much wanted me.

I have had a little catch of the gout; but as I have had no great opinion of the benefits which it is supposed to convey, I made haste to be easy, and drove it away after two days.

Publick affairs continue to go on without much mending, and there are those still who either fright themselves or would fright others with an invasion;[2] but my opinion is that the French neither have nor had in any part of the summer a number of ships on the opposite coast equal to the transpor-tation of twenty or of ten thousand Men. Such a fleet cannot be hid in a creek, it must be easily visible and yet I believe no man has seen the man that has seen it. The Ships of war were within sight of Plymouth, and only within sight.

I wish, I knew how your health stands. My Friends con-gratulate me upon my looks, and indeed I am very free from some of the most troublesome of my old complaints, but I have gained this relief by very steady use of mercury and purgatives, with some opium, and some abstinence. I have eaten more fruit this summer than perhaps in any since I was

635.—1. The paragraph is erased in the MS. The deanery was apparently that of Rochester, which had been filled in June (Hill, quoting Le Neve's *Fasti*). For JT's erasures see Appendix D.

2. See Hill for entertaining extracts (Lord Carlisle, Susan Burney, Mrs. Barbauld) showing that some people were alarmed, others, like J, imperturbable.

twenty years old, but though it certainly did me no harm, I know not that I had any medicinal good from it.

Write to me soon. We are both old. How few of those whom we have known in our youth are left alive. May we yet live to some better purpose.

I am, Sir, your most humble Servant,
London Oct. 19. 1779   Sam: Johnson.

635.1. Tu. 19 Oct. '79. Lucy Porter (Lichfield).
A. F. Somerset (not seen).—

636. Th. 21 Oct. '79. Mrs. Thrale (Brighthelmston).
Adam.—1788, No. 215.

Dear Madam

Your treatment of little Perkins was undoubtedly right; when there is so strong a reason against any thing as unconquerable terour, there ought surely to be some mighty reason for it, before it is done. But for putting into the water[1] a child already well it is not very ⟨easy⟩ to find any reason strong or weak. That the nurses fretted will supply me during life with an additional motive to keep every child, as far as is possible, out of a Nurse's power. a Nurse made of common mould will have a pride in overpowering a child's reluctance. There are few minds to which tyranny is not delightful; Power is nothing but as it is felt, and the delight of superiority is proportionate to the resistance overcome.

I walked yesterday to Covent Garden, and feel today neither pain nor weakness. Send me, if you can, such an account of yourself and my Master.

Sir Philip[2] sent me word that he should be in town, but he has not yet called. Yesterday came Lady Lucan, and Miss Bingham, and she said it was the first visit that she had paid.

Your new friend Mr Bowen who has sold fifty sets,[3] had but thirty to sell, and, I am afraid, has yet a set or two for a friend. There is a great deal of fallacy in this World. I hope

636.—1. For sea-bathing so late in the year see 585.1*a*.
   2. Jennings Clerk.
   3. Of 'Johnson's Poets'. See 637.

you do not teach the company wholly to forsake poor Thomas.

The want of company is an inconvenience, but Mr Cumberland is a Million, make the most of what you have. Send my Master out to hunt in the morning, and to walk the rooms in the evening, and bring him as active, as a stag on the mountain back to the Borough. When he is in motion he is mending.

The young ones[4] are very good in minding their book. If I do not make something of them *'Twill reflect upon me, as I know not my trade,*[5] for their parts are sufficiently known, and every body will have a better opinion of their industry than of mine. However, I hope when they come back to accustom them to more lessons.

Your account of Mr Scrase gives me no delight. He was a friend upon all occasions, whether assistance was wanted from the purse or the understanding. When he is gone our barrier against calamity is weakened, and we must act with more caution, as we shall be in more danger. Consult him, while his advice is yet to be had.

What makes Cumberland[6] hate Burney. Delap is indeed a rival, and can upon occasion *provoke a bugle,*[7] but what has Burney done? Dos he not like her book?

Dr Burney has passed one Evening with me. He has made great discoveries in a library at Cambridge, and he finds so many precious materials, that his Book must be a Porters load. He has sent me another sheet.

I am, Dearest of all dear Ladies. Your most humble servant

London. Oct. 21. 1779　　　　　　　　　Sam: Johnson

636.—4. 'Miss Thrale and Miss Burney, to whom Dr. Johnson taught Latin. Miss Burney was, however, bid to leave it off by her Papa, who thought it Mannish, he said, in women, to learn dead languages. Queeney went on' HLP. For FB's own view see on 621.

5. See on 892.

6. There is a great deal about the Cumberlands in FB's diary of this visit. She gives this account of his rudeness: 'All the folks here impute the whole of this conduct to its having transpired that I am to bring out a play this season; for Mr. Cumberland ... is ... notorious for hating and envying and spiting all authors in the dramatic line. ... he deserves not to hear of my having suppressed my play' (i. 264). Delap was also a playwright.

7. I can make nothing of this.

636.1. Th. 21 Oct. ('79). Frances Reynolds.

Address: To Mrs. Reynolds.

Rupert Colomb (endorsed by F.R. 'Dr Johnson believe in 79'; she wrote first '80' but erased it).—

Dear Madam

I want no company but yours, nor wish for any other. I will wait on you on Saturday, and am so well that I am very able to find my way without a carriage.

      I am Dear Madam Your most humble Servant

Oct. 21   Sam: Johnson

637. M. 25 Oct. '79. Mrs. Thrale (Brighthelmston).

Bergson.—1788, No. 216.

Dear Madam

Let me repair an injury done by misinformation to Mr. Bowen. He had at first indeed only thirty, that is, two shares;[1] but he afterwards purchased two shares more. So all that he says, I suppose is true.

On Saturday I walked to Dover street,[2] and back. Yesterday I dined with Sir Joshua. There was Mr. Elliot of Cornwal, who enquired after my Master. At night I was bespoken by Lady Lucan, but she was taken ill, and the assembly was put off. I am to dine with Renny to morrow.

I hope Mr. Thrale scours the country after the early horn, and at night flutters about the rooms and once a day makes a lusty dinner. I eat meat but once in two days, at most but four times a-week, reckoning several weeks together, for it is neither necessary nor prudent to be nice in regimen. Renny told me yesterday that I look better than when she knew me first.

It is now past the Postman's time and I have no letter, and that is not well done, because I long for a letter, and You should always let me know whether You and Mr Thrale and all the rest are, or are not well. Do not serve me so often, because your silence is always a disappointment.

Some old Gentlewomen at the next door are in very great distress. Their little annuity comes from Jamaica, and is

637.—1. This does not enable us to determine the number printed; a 'share' might be almost any fraction of the whole.   2. To visit FR.

therefore uncertain, and one of them has had a fall, and both are very helpless, and the poor have few to help them. Persuade my Master to let me give them something for him. It will be bestowed upon real Want.

I hope all the Younglings go on well, that the two eldest are very prudent, and the rest very merry. We are to be merry but a little while, Prudence soon comes to spoil our mirth. Old times have bequeathed us a precept directing us to *be merry and wise*,[3] but who has been able to observe it.

There is a very furious fellow[4] writing with might and main against the life of Milton.

I am Madam Your most humble Servant,
Oct. 25. 1779 London   Sam: Johnson.

638. M. 25 Oct. '79. Elizabeth Aston (Lichfield).
Pembroke.—Croker's Boswell 1831, iv. 291.

Dearest Madam

Mrs. Gastrel is so kind as to write to me, and yet I always write to you, but I consider what is written to either as written to both.

Publick affairs do not seem to promise much amendment, and the nation is now full of distress. What will be ⟨the⟩ event of things, none can tell, we may still hope for better times.

My health which I began to recover, when I was in the country, continues still in a good state, it costs me indeed some physick, and something of abstinence, but it pays the cost. I wish, dear Madam, I could hear a little of your improvements.

Here is no news. The talk of the invasion seems to be over. But a very turbulent Session of Parliament is expected; though turbulence is not likely to do any good. Those are happyest who are out of the noise and tumult. There will be no great violence of faction at Stowhill, and that it may ⟨be⟩ free from that and all other inconvenience and disturbance, is the sincere wish of all your friends. I am,

Dear Madam, Your most humble servant,
Oct. 25. 1779 Bolt court, Fleet street.   Sam: Johnson.

638.—3. A maxim found in Heywood's *Proverbs* 1546 and often elsewhere.
    4. Not identified.

639. W. 27 Oct. '79. James Boswell (Chester).

Not traced.—Boswell 1791, ii. 307 (Hill iii. 413).

Dear Sir,

Why should you importune[1] me so earnestly to write? Of what importance can it be to hear of distant friends, to a man who finds himself welcome wherever he goes, and makes new friends faster than he can want them? If, to the delight of such universal kindness of reception, any thing can be added by knowing that you retain my good-will, you may indulge yourself in the full enjoyment of that small addition.

I am glad that you made the round of Lichfield with so much success: the oftener you are seen, the more you will be liked. It was pleasing to me to read that Mrs. Aston was so well; and that Lucy Porter was so glad to see you.

In the place where you now are, there is much to be observed; and you will easily procure yourself skilful directors. But what will you do to keep away the *black dog* that worries you at home? If you would, in compliance with your father's advice, enquire into the old tenures, and old charters of Scotland, you would certainly open to yourself many striking scenes of the manners of the middle ages. The feudal system, in a country half barbarous, is naturally productive of great anomalies in civil life. The knowledge of past times is naturally growing less in all cases not of publick record; and the past time of Scotland is so unlike the present, that it is already difficult for a Scotchman to image the œconomy of his grand-father. Do not be tardy, nor negligent; but gather up eagerly what can yet be found.

We have, I think, once talked of another project, a History of the late insurrection in Scotland, with all its incidents. Many falsehoods are passing into uncontradicted history. Voltaire,[2] who loved a striking story, has told what we could not find to be true.

You may make collections for either of these projects, or for both, as opportunities occur, and digest your materials

639.—1. JB had written 22 Oct. 'Two lines from you will keep my lamp burning bright'. His letter is full of the hospitalities of L'd and Chester.

2. J and JB had no doubt, when in Scotland, looked at the account of Prince Charles Edward in chapters 24 and 25 of the *Siècle de Louis XV*. Voltaire's editor concedes that it is inaccurate in detail.

at leisure. The great direction which Burton has left to men disordered like you, is this,[3] *Be not solitary; be not idle:*[4] which I would thus modify;—If you are idle, be not solitary; if you are solitary, be not idle.

There is a letter for you, from

Your humble servant,

London, Oct. 27, 1779.   Sam. Johnson.

640. Th. 28 Oct. '79. Mrs. Thrale (Brighthelmston).

Houghton.—1788, No. 217.

Dear Madam

Some days before our last separation, Mr Thrale and I had one evening an earnest discourse about the business with Mr Scrase. It is indeed in a state of convalescence a melancholy affair, yet I am desirous that it may ⟨be⟩ despatched, while You may have the help of so much experience and understanding. I see no objection to entailing the Oxfordshire estate.[1] For myself, You may be sure I am very willing to be useful; but surely all use of such an office[2] is at a very great distance. Do not let those fears prevail which you know to be unreasonable, a will brings the end of life no nearer. But with this we will have done, and please ourselves with wishing my Master multos et felices.[3]

C——L——[4] accuses * * * * of making a party against her play. I always hissed away the charge, supposing him a man of honour, but I shall now defend him with less confidence. Nequid nimis. Horace says, that nil admirari is the only thing that can make or keep a man happy. It is with equal truth the only thing that can make or keep a man honest.

639.—3. 'is this' add. 1793, om. 1791. The change may be JB's, or his printer's.

4. At the end of *The Anatomy of Melancholy.*

640.—1. 'It is indeed ... estate' om. 1788. The 'estate' was Crowmarsh, bequeathed ultimately to Q (C 200).

2. Of executor.

3. *Scil.* 'annos', 'many happy years'. The phrase, which recurs 912, is perhaps not a classical quotation.

4. 'Charlotte Lennox' and 'Cumberland' HLP, Lysons, Malone, which fits the traces; in the first word *l* and *tt* are probable, in the last there are four ascenders in the right places. If this is right, 'C——' below is no doubt 'Charlotte'. So Lysons. HLP's gloss is 'Burney'; perhaps, forgetting the context, she read 'C—' as 'Charles'; but J never so names CB. For the quarrel see *L* iv. 10; J's desertion of Cumberland was due, I suppose, to his envy of FB, see on 636.

315

The desire of fame not regulated, is as dangerous to virtue as that of money. I hope C—— scorns his little malice.

I have had a letter for * * * *,[5] which I have inclosed. Do not lose it, for it contains a testimony that there may be some pleasure in this World; and that I may have a little of the little that there is, pray write to me. I thought your last letter long in coming.

The two younglings; what hinders them from writing to me. I hope they do not forget me.

Will Master give me any thing for my poor neighbours? I have had from Sir Joshua and Mr. Strahan; they are very old Maids, very friendless, and very helpless.

Mrs Williams talks of coming home this week from Kingston, and then there will be *merry doings*.[6]

I eat meat seldom, and take physick often, and fancy that I grow light and airy. A man that does not begin to grow light and airy at seventy, is certainly losing time, if he intends ever to be light and airy.

I dined on Tuesday with ⟨Renny⟩[7] and hope her little head begins to settle. She has however some scruples about the company of a Lady whom she has lately known. I pacified her as well as I could. So no more at present but hoping you are all in good health as I am at this time of writing (excuse haste).[8]

I am, Dearest, dearest Lady, Your most obedient Servant
Oct. 28. 1779 London   Sam: Johnson.

640.1. Su. 31 Oct. '79. Robert Chambers (Calcutta?).
Adam.—

Dear Sir
Your long letter and Lady Chambers's pretty journal gave

640.—5. J might send a letter, entrusted to him, that HT might frank it; but 'do not lose it' precludes that. Hill guessed that J wrote 'from Boswell'. He in fact wrote 'for', but that might be a slip; the word following may be 'Bozzy'—there is a trace of what may be a final *y*. JB's letter from Chester fits J's description, and the L'd gossip in it would amuse HLT. HLP cannot help us; her note is 'I forget who'. For 'for' and 'from' see 640.1.

6. The phrase recurs 744.

7. 'Miss Owen' HLP. She did not notice that on Monday J had told her (637) 'I am to dine with Renny tomorrow'.

8. J is perhaps recalling the epistolary manner of one of his retainers, or of one of HLT's. Or is he quoting a *Polite Letter-writer*?

me great delight, and I intend a long answer[1] for which the bringer[2] of this letter cannot stay, for he goes away to morrow. I believe it will please you to hear that my health has within this last half year been improved very perceptibly to myself, and very visibly to others. I am not without hope of seeing you again.

I am very glad that you have thought it proper to show some countenance to Mr Joseph Fowke. I always thought him a good Man, and I loved him as long as I knew him. Do not let him be oppressed so far as you can protect him.

Mr Levet, and Miss Williams are still with me; Levet is stout, but Williams is declining. I will not tell you more of my domestick affairs, because I reserve from[3] my long letter. The reason for which I now write, is that this young adventurer may have an opportunity of seeing you, and some kind of right to such notice as you can properly take of him, as the son of an ingenious man, and an amiable woman who were known to,

Dear Sir Your faithful humble servant

Oct. 31. 1779 Bolt court, Fleet street.   Sam: Johnson

641. Tu. 2 Nov. '79. Mrs. Thrale (Brighthelmston).

Sotheby 30 Jan. 1918 (not seen).—1788, No. 218.

Dear Madam   London, Nov. 2, 1779.

This day I thought myself sure of a letter, but so I am constantly served. Mr. Cumberland and Mrs. * * * *,[1] and Mrs. Byron, and any body else, puts me out of your head; and I know no more of you than if you were on the other side of the Caspian. I thought the two young things were to write too; but for them I do not much care.

On Saturday came home Mrs. Williams, neither better nor worse than when she went; and I dined at ⟨Lord Lucan⟩'s,[2]

640.1.—1. This if it was written is lost.

2. I cannot identify this 'young adventurer'. He can hardly be Chauncy Laurence, who (see 329.1, 367) had gone to India in '73, and whose parents were both alive in '79 (note 'were known' in the concluding sentence).

3. 'reserve' is blotted but is clear; 'from' is blurred, and Mr. Adam at one time read 'for', which is perhaps what J wrote or intended. For the possible confusion of the two words see 640.

641.—1. 'forsan Montague' Malone; HLP is silent. I do not find Mrs. M in FB's B'n diary.   2. So HLP.

and found them well pleased with their Italian journey. He took his Lady and son, and three daughters. They staid five months at Rome. They will have now something to talk of.

I gave my poor neighbour[3] your half guinea, and ventured upon making it two guineas at my master's expence. Pray, Madam, how[4] do I owe you half a guinea?

I dined on Sunday with Mr. Strahan, and have not been very well for some little time. Last night I was afraid of the gout, but it is gone to-day.

There was on Sunday night a fire at the north end of London-bridge, which has, they say, destroyed the water-work.[5]

Does Mr. Thrale continue *to hunt in fields for health unbought*?[6] If his taste of former pleasures returns, it is a strong proof of his recovery. When we meet, we will be jolly blades.

I know not well how it has happened, but I have never yet been at the B⟨urney⟩s.[7] ⟨The Doctor⟩ has called twice on me, and I have seen some more sheets—and away we go.

                        I am, &c.

642 Th. 4 Nov. '79. Mrs. Thrale (Brighthelmston).

Sotheby 30 Jan. 1918 (not seen).—1788, No. 219.

Madam   London, Nov. 4, 1779.

So I may write and write, and nobody care; but you can write often enough to Dr. Burney. Queeney sent me a pretty letter, to which ⟨Burney⟩[1] added a silly short note, in such a silly white hand, that I was glad it was no longer.

641.—3. Perhaps 'neighbours'; see 637, 640.

    4. J perhaps wrote 'now'; his initial *n* often has its first stroke so tall as to resemble an ascender.

    5. Hill quotes Dodsley's *London* for the 'water-engine' contrived 'to supply the citizen with Thames water', and for the fire refers to *GM* 1779, 562.

    6. 'Better to hunt in fields for health unbought / Than see the doctor for a nauseous draught': Dryden, *Lines to John Driden.*

    7. For the first blank HLP and Lysons supply 'Burneys'. For the second HLP has 'Burney and yᵉ Doctor', which ignores the singular 'has' and the fact that 'Burney', i.e. FB, was with her at B'n. 'The Doctor' Lysons, who probably looked at the MS.

642.—1. Suppressed in 1788; 'Fanny' HLP. FB has preserved her postscript: 'P.S. Dr. Johnson's other pupil a little longs to add a few lines to this letter,—but knows too well that all she has to say might be comprised in signing herself his obliged and most obedient servant, F.B.: so that's better than a long rigmarole about nothing' (*Diary* i. 278).

I had heard before that ⟨Cumberland⟩² had lost not only ten thousand, as you tell me, but twenty thousand, as you with great consistency tell Dr. Burney; but knowing that no man can lose what he has not, I took it little to heart. I did not think of borrowing; and indeed he that borrows money for adventures deserves to lose it. No man should put into a lottery more than he can spare. Neither D——, however, nor B——³ have given occasion to his loss.

Notice is taken that I have a cold and a cough; but I have been so long used to disorders so much more afflictive, that I have thought on them but little. If they grow worse, something should be done.

I hear from every body that Mr. Thrale grows better. He is *columen domus*;⁴ and if he stands firm, little evils may be overlooked. Drive him out in the morning, lead him out at night, keep him in what bustle you can.

Do not neglect Scrase. You may perhaps do for him what you have done for * * * *.⁵ The serious affair⁶ I do not wonder that you cannot mention;⁷ and yet I wish it were transacted while Scrase can direct and superintend it. No other man, if he shall have the same skill and kindness, which I know not where to find, will have the same influence.

Sir Philip never called upon me, though he promised me to do it. Somebody else has laid hold upon him.

I live here in stark solitude. Nobody has called upon me this live-long day; yet I comfort myself that I have no tortures in the night. I have not indeed much sleep; but I suppose I have enough, for I am not as sleepy in the day-time as formerly.

I am, &c.

642.—2. 'Cumberland' HLP here and at 645, where she *prints* 'C——'.

3. 'B——' is certainly Beauclerck, see on 645. 'D——' is obscure. Hill, not knowing the clue to 'B——', naturally thought of 636, and guessed Delap and Burney. But that quarrel does not fit this picture; 'given occasion to his loss' is itself obscure; it is perhaps a quotation.

4. Cf. 487 'he is the pillar of the house'.

5. 'Sir Philip' HLP (i.e. Jennings Clerk).

6. HT's will.

7. To HT.

643. F. 5 Nov. '79. Elizabeth Aston (Lichfield).

Pembroke.—Croker's Boswell 1831, iv. 292.

Dearest Madam

Having had the pleasure of hearing from Mr. Boswel that he found you better than he expected, I will not forbear to tell you how much I was delighted with the news. May your health encrease and encrease, till you are as well as you can wish yourself, or I can wish you.

My Friends tell me that my health improves too. It is certain that I use both physick and abstinence, and my endeavours have been blessed with more success than at my age I could reasonably hope. I please myself with the thought of visiting you next year in so robust a state that I shall not be afraid of the hill between Mrs. Gastrel's house and yours, nor think it necessary to rest myself between Stowhill and Lucy Porter's.

Of publick affairs I can give you no very comfortable account. The Invasion has vanished for the present as I expected. I never believed that any invasion was intended.

But whatever we have escaped we have done nothing, nor are likely to do better another year. We, however, who have no part of the nation's welfare entrusted to our management, have nothing to do but to serve God, and leave the world submissively in his hands.

All trade is dead, and pleasure is scarce alive. Nothing almost is purchased but such things as the buyer cannot be without, so that a general sluggishness and general discontent are spread over the town. All the trades of luxury and elegance are nearly at a stand. What the Parliament when it meets will do, and indeed what it ought to do is very difficult to say.

Pray set Mrs. Gastrel, who is a dear good Lady, to write to me from time to time, for I have great delight in hearing from you, especially when I hear any good news of your health.

I am, Dear Madam, Your most humble Servant,
Sam: Johnson.

London, Bolt-court, Fleet-street. Nov. 5, 1779.

644. Su. 7 Nov. '79. Mrs. Thrale (Brighthelmston).
Adam.—1788, No. 220.

Poor Mrs Byron[1] I am glad that she runs to you at last for shelter, give her, dear Madam, what comfort you can. Has any calamity fallen upon her? Her husband, so much as I hear, is well enough spoken of, nor is it supposed that he had power to do more than has been done. But Life must have its end, and commonly an end of gloomy discontent, and lingering distress.

While you are vigorous and spritely you must take into your protection as many as you can of those who are tottering under their burden. When You want the same support, may you always find it.

I have for some time had a cough and a cold, but I did not mind it; continuance however makes it heavy, but it seems to be going away.

My Master, I hope, hunts, and walks, and courts the Belles, and shakes Brighthelmston. When he comes back frolick, and active, we will make a feast, and drink his health, and have a noble day.

Of the Lucans[2] I have never heard since. On Saturday after having fasted almost all the week, I dined with Renny. For Wednesday I am invited by the Veseys, and if I am well, purpose to go. I imagine there will be a large company. The invitation is to dine and spend the evening. Too much at a time. I shall be in danger of crying out with Mr Head[3] *catamaran* whatever that may mean, for it seemed to imply tediousness and disgust. I do not much like to go, and I do not much like to stay away.

Have you any assemblies at this time of the year, and does Queeny dance? and does Burney[4] dance too? I would have Burney dance with Cumberland, and so make all up.

644.—1. 'Byron' HLP, Lysons, Malone. Not even the initial is in 1788, so that Hill could only guess. As so often, he guessed right, seeing that a letter from HLT to FB, 'Streatham, Saturday', which appears in the *Diary* s.a. '81 (ii. 4), belongs in fact to '79: 'In the midst of my own misery I felt for my dear Mrs. Byron's; but Chamier has relieved that anxiety by assurances that the Admiral behaved quite unexceptionally, and that, as to *honour* in the West Indies, all goes well.'

2. See 641.

3. Hill quotes Hayward (1861², ii. 81) for a long story of this 'low Irish parasite', whose real name was Plunkett, and of the occasion which provoked his ejaculation.

4. Burney and Cumberland are in 1788 reduced to their initials.

Discord keeps her residence in this habitation, but she has for some time been silent. We have much malice, but no mischief. Levet is rather a friend to Williams, because he hates Desmoulins more, a thing that he should hate more than Desmoulins is not to be found.

I hear, but you never tell me anything, that you have at last begun to bathe. I am sorry that your toothach kept you out of the Water so long, because I know you love to be in it.

If such Letters as[5] this were to cost you any thing, I should hardly write them, but since they come to you for nothing, I am willing enough to write though I have nothing to say, because a sorry letter serves to keep one[6] from dropping totally out of your head, and I would not have you forget that there is in the world such a poor Being as

Madam, Your most humble servant

London. Nov. 7. 1779   Sam: Johnson

645. M. 8 Nov. '79. Mrs. Thrale (Brighthelmston).
Mrs. F. Bowman.—1788, No. 221.

Dear Madam

You are a dear dear Lady. To write so often, and so sweetly makes some amends for your absence. Your last letter came about half an hour after my last letter was sent away, but now I have another. You have much to tell me, and I have nothing to tell you; yet I am eager to write because I am eager for your answer.

I thought Cumberland[1] had told you his loss. If it be only report, I do not much credit it. Something perhaps he may have ventured, but I do not believe he had ten thousand pounds, or the means of borrowing it. Of B⟨eauclerc⟩[2] I suppose the fact is true that he is gone, but for his loss, can any body tell who has been the winner? And if he has lost a sum disproportionate to his fortune, why should he run away when payment cannot be compelled?

644.—5. J wrote 'are', corrected in another hand.
   6. It is difficult to say whether J wrote 'one' or 'me'.
645.—1. See 642.
   2. HLP supplies 'Burke' in 642, 'Dick Burke' here, for the 'B——' of 1788. Here my collator, with nothing to prompt him, read the letters conjecturally as 'Bamdon' or 'Bamclon', marking *B* and the ascending stroke as certain. This pointed to 'Beauclerc' (and so Lysons), which was clinched when later 645.1 came to light.

Of Sir Thomas[3] I can make no estimate, but if he is distressed I am sorry, for he was in his prosperity civil and officious.

It has happened to ——[4] as to many active and prosperous men, that his mind has been wholly absorbed in business, or at intervals dissolved in amusement, and habituated so long to certain modes of employment or diversion, that in the decline of life it can no more receive a new train of images than the hand can acquire dexterity in a new mechanical operation. For this reason a religious education is so necessary. Spiritual Ideas may be recollected in old age, but can hardly be acquired.

You shall not hide Mrs. * * * *[5] from me, for if she be a feeler, I can bear a feeler as well as you, and hope that in tenderness for what she feels from nature, I am able to forgive or neglect what she feels by affectation. I pity her as one in a state to which all must come, and I think well of her judgement in chusing you to be the depository of her troubles, and easer of her bosom. Fondle her and comfort her.

Your letters have commonly one good paragraph concerning my Master, who appears to you and to every body to mend upon the whole, though your vigilance perceives some accidental and temporary alterations, which however, I am willing to hope are more rare and more slight than they were at first. Let him hunt much, and think little, and avoid solitude. I hope time has brought some company whom you can call now to your table. Does he take to ——?[6] Does he love her, as you profess to love——? with a fifth part of the kindness that she has for me. I am well rewarded for what I have taught you of computation, by seeing our friendship divided into factions;[7] so we stand, do we? as 2. to 10. a pretty appearance upon paper, and still prettier in the heart. Well —go thy ways old Jack.[8]

Of the capture of Jamaica[9] nothing is known, nor do I

645.—3. 'Mills' HLP, Malone ('forsan').   4. 'Scrase' HLP, *recte.*

5. 'Byron' HLP, 'Biron' Lysons.

6. 'Byron, Fanny Burney' HLP. Lysons fills the first blank 'Burney', perhaps by inadvertence, leaving the second unfilled.

7. 'fractions' HLP. My collator passed 'factions', but J probably wrote or intended 'fractions'.   8. *1 Henry IV*, II. iv.

9. Hill quotes Walpole for conflicting rumours. The island was not in fact taken.

think it probable or possible. How the French should in a few days take from us an Island, which We could not in almost a century take from a few fugitive Negroes whom the Spaniards left behind them, is not easily imagined. If you stay much longer in Sussex you may perhaps hear that London is taken.

We have a kind of epidemick cold amongst us, of which I have had my part, but not more than my part, and I think myself growing well. I have lived very sparingly, but shall have some dinner to day, and Baretti dines with me.

I am, Dearest Madam, Your most humble Servant,
London. Nov. 8. 1779   Sam: Johnson.

645.1. Th. 11 Nov. '79. Hester Maria Thrale (Brighthelmston).

Lansdowne.—Lansdowne, *Johnson and Queeney* 1932, 12.

Dear Madam,   London, 11 Nov. 1779
Your first letter was kind, and your second kinder. It is fit that I should now take my turn to write though I have not much to tell you.

Yesterday I dined at Mr. Vesey's with Lord Lucan and Mr. Pepys. After dinner came in Lady Lucan and her three daughters, who seem all pretty people. In the evening there was Lord Maccartney who had been taken by D'Estaigne in America, and stripped by him almost naked. D'Estaigne took from him ⟨his⟩ Lady's picture because I suppose it was set with stones. He is here now upon parole. He seems in some degree a literary man.

Lady Edgecomb was another of the company. The talk was for a while about Burney's book, and the old objection to the Captain's[1] grossness being mentioned, Lady Edgecombe said that she had known such a captain.

Do not tell this to Burney for it will please her, and she takes no care to please me.

Of the rest I did not know all. Swinburne, the Spanish traveller, I think, was there, but he did not speak or I did not hear him.

Not a word was said all day upon publick affairs. None

645.1.—1. Captain Mirvan, R.N.

care to present the condition in which we now are to their own minds, by expressing their hopes and fears or enquiring into those of others.

What can be come to my Mistress, when going into the sea disorders her. She was used to be quite amphibious, and could hardly be kept out of any water that she could get at. I am however not pleased with the change, and hope to see her original disposition prevail again.

Beauclerc ran no further than home, and is now, I hear, at his own house, perhaps Cumberland's distresses are in the same degree. When stories of this kind are told you, receive them with indifference, and do not by telling them seem to be pleased, but attend to them as traces of character, and hints for inquiry.

The last line of your letter was worth all the rest, if we can get and keep my Master well, we will try to shift for ourselves.

> I am, My dearest, Your most humble servant,
> Sam: Johnson

Your first letter had no date of time or place, the last had only time. Use to date fully. Mamma is negligent too.

646. Sa. 13 Nov. '79. James Boswell (Edinburgh).

Not traced.—Boswell 1791, ii. 310 (Hill iii. 416).

Dear Sir

Your last letter was not only kind but fond. But I wish you to get rid of all intellectual excesses, and neither to exalt your pleasures, nor aggravate your vexations, beyond their real and natural state. Why should you not be as happy at Edinburgh as at Chester, *In culpa est animus, qui se non effugit usquam.*[1] Please yourself with your wife and children, and studies and practice.

I have sent a petition[2] from Lucy Porter, with which I leave it to your discretion whether it is proper to comply. Return me her letter, which I have sent that you may know

646.—1. Horace, *Ep.* i. xiv. 13: 'For in the mind alone our follies lie, / The mind that never from itself can fly' (Francis). 'non . . . usquam', 'nowhere' seems to be an early conjecture for the reading of the MSS., 'non . . . unquam', 'never'.

2. 'Requesting me to inquire concerning the family of a gentleman who was then paying his addresses to Miss Doxy' JB. For particulars see *L* iii. 536.

the whole case, and not be seduced to any thing that you may afterwards repent. Miss Doxy perhaps you know to be Mr. Garrick's niece.

If Dean Percy can be popular[3] at Carlisle, he may be very happy. He has in his disposal two livings, each equal, or almost equal in value to the deanery; he may take one himself, and give the other to his son.[4]

How near is the Cathedral to Auchinleck,[5] that you are so much delighted with it? It is, I suppose, at least an hundred and fifty miles off. However, if you are pleased, it is so far well.

Let me know what reception you have from your father, and the state of his health. Please him as much as you can, and add no pain to his last years.

Of our friends here I can recollect nothing to tell you. I have neither seen nor heard of Langton. Beauclerk is just returned from Brighthelmston, I am told, much better. Mr. Thrale and his family are still there; and his health is said to be visibly improved; he has not bathed, but hunted.

At Bolt-court there is much malignity, but of late little open hostility. I have had a cold, but it is gone.

Make my compliments to Mrs. Boswell, &c.

I am, Sir, Your humble servant,

London, Nov. 13, 1779.   Sam. Johnson.

647. Tu. 16 Nov. '79. Mrs. Thrale (Brighthelmston).

Bergson.—1788, No. 223.

Dear Madam

Pray how long does a letter hang between London and Brighthelmston. Your letter of the 12th I received on the 15th.

Poor Mrs. Byron[1] is a feeler. It is well that she has yet power to feel. Fiction durst not have driven upon a few months such a conflux of misery. Comfort her as You can.

646.—3. JB had written 7 Nov.: 'I am told at my inn, that he is very *populous* (popular).'
4. No son of P's lived long enough to attain holy orders.

5. JB had written: 'It is divinely cheering to me to think that there is a Cathedral so near Auchinleck.' A. was 83 miles from Carlisle by the Dumfries road. On 22 Nov. (see on 655) JB replied that the distance was 'scarcely a hundred miles', so that he could start on a Saturday, attend the Cathedral service on Sunday, and be at home on Monday night.

647.—1. Erased in MS., but fairly clear; see 644, 645.

I have look⟨ed⟩ again into your grave letter. You mention
trustees. I do not see who can be trustee for a casual and
variable property, for a fortune yet to be acquired. How can
any man be trusted with what he cannot possess, cannot
ascertain, and cannot regulate? The trade must be carried
on by somebody who must be answerable for the debts
contracted. This can be none but yourself, unless you deliver
up the property to some other agent, and trust the chance
both of his prudence and his honesty. Do not be frighted,
Trade could not be managed by those who manage it, if it had
much difficulty. Their great Books are soon understood, and
their language

> If Speech it may be call'd, that speech is none
> Distinguishable in number mood or tense[2]

is understood with no very laborious application.

The help which you can have from any man as a trustee
you may have from him as a friend, the trusteeship may give
him power to perplex, but will neither encrease his benevolence to assist, nor his Wisdom to advise.

> Living on God, and on thyself rely.[3]

Who should be trustee but You for your own and your
Children's prosperity? I hope this is an end of this unpleasing speculation, and lighter matters may take their
turn.

What Mr Scrase says about the Borough is true, but is
nothing to the purpose. A house in the Square[4] will not cost
so much as building[5] in Southwark, but buildings are more
likely to go on in Southwark, if your dwelling is at St.
James's. Every body has some desire that deserts the great
road of prosperity, to look for pleasure in a bye-path. I do
not see with so much indignation Mr Thrale's desire of being

647.—2. Milton, *PL* ii. 667: 'If shape it might be called that shape had none, /
Distinguishable in member, joint or limb'.

3. Not traced.

4. It was not until Jan. '81 that they moved into a furnished house in Grosvenor
Square (*Tb* 478, *L* iv. 72, C 194–8).

5. 'In the midst of publick & private Distress, here is my mad Master going to
build at the boro' House again:—new Store Cellars, Casks, & God knows what. I
have however exerted myself & driv'n off his Workmen with a high Hand.—Is this
a Time as Elijah say'd, for oliveyards, & Vineyards? & Men Servants and Maid
Servants?' (*Tb* 391).

the first Brewer, as your despicable dread[6] of living in the borough. Ambition in little things, is better than cowardice in little things, but both these things however little to the publick eye are great in their consequences to yourselves. The world cares not how you brew, or where you live, but it is the business of the one to brew in a manner most advantageous to his Family, and of the other to live where the general interest may best be superintended. It was by an accidental visit to the borough that you escaped great evils last Summer. Of this folly let there be an end, at least, an intermission.

I am glad that Queeny danced with Mr Wade. She was the Sultaness of the evening, and I am glad that Mr Thrale has found a riding companion whom he likes. Let him ride, say I, till he leaves dejection and disease behind him, and let them limp after him an hundred years without overtaking him. When he returns let me see him frolic and airy, and social, and busy, and as kind to me as in former times.

You seem to be afraid that I should be starved before you come back. I have indeed practiced abstinence with some stubbornness, and with some success, but as Dryden talks of *writing with a hat*,[7] I am sometimes very witty with a knife and fork. I have managed myself very well, except that having no motive, I have no exercise.

At home we do not much quarrel, but perhaps the less we quarrel, the more we hate. There is as much malignity amongst us as can well subsist, without any thought of daggers or poisons.

Mrs ⟨Laurence⟩[8] is by the help of frequent operations still kept alive, and such is the capricious destiny of mortals, that she will die more lamented by her husband, than I will promise to Usefulness, Wisdom, or Sanctity. There is always something operating distinct from diligence or skill. Temple[9]

647.—6. On 5 Jan. '80 she noted: 'We are settled once more in Southwark the place I most abhor: but if residing there will contribute to my Husband's Ease or Entertainment—my Duty shall make it Pall Mall to me' (*Th* 416).

7. 'Thus they out-write each other with a Hat' (Prologue to *The Conquest of Granada*).

8. 'Laurence, Wife to yᵉ Dr' HLP, which fits the faint traces of the erasure.

9. After naming the chief 'ingredients' of heroic virtue, Temple adds: 'These ingredients advantaged by Birth, improved by Education, and assisted by Fortune,

therefore in his composition of a hero, to the heroick virtues adds good fortune.

I am, Dearest Lady, Your most humble servant
London Nov. 16. 1779.   Sam: Johnson

648. Sa. 20 Nov. '79. Mrs. Thrale (Brighthelmston).
Leverton Harris.—1788, No. 224.

Indeed, Dear Madam, I do not think that you have any reason to complain of Mr. ——, or Mr. ——.[1] What I proposed is, I suppose unusual. However Mr. Thrale knows that I have suggested nothing to you that I had not first said to him. I hear he grows well so fast that we are not likely to try whose way is best, and I hope he will grow better, and better, and better, and then away with executors and executrixes. He may settle his family himself.

I am not vexed at you for not liking the Borough, but for not liking the Borough better than other evils of greater magnitude. You must take physick, or be sick; you must live in the Borough, or live still worse.

Pray tell my Queeney how I love her for her letters, and tell Burney[2] that now she is a good girl, I can love her again. Tell Mr. Scrase that I am sincerely glad to hear that he is better. tell my Master that I never was so glad to see him in my life, as I shall be now to see him well, and tell yourself that except my Master nobody has more kindness for you, than[3]

Dear Madam Your most humble servant
London. Nov 20. 1779   Sam: Johnson.

649. Th. 2 Dec. '79. Lucy Porter (Lichfield).
Not traced.—Hill 1892 (part only); *JM* 1897, ii. 450.

I have inclosed Mr. Boswells answer.[1]

I still continue better than when you saw me, but am not

seem to make that noble composition'. 'Of Heroick Virtue', in *Miscellanea* Part ii, 1690 (Essay III p. 2).

648.—1. The erasures are thorough, and HLP is silent; but I think the first name is 'Thrale'; it is the right length, and the one visible ascender is in the right place for the *l* of 'Thrale'. The second is almost certainly 'Scrase'.

2. She had writen to him, for the first time, 16 Nov. See Appendix H.

3. After this word is a gap, possibly an original flaw in the paper, but it looked like an erasure of two or three words.

649.—1. To 646. See on 655.

just at this time very well, but hope to mend again. Publick
affairs remain as they were. Do not let the papers fright you.

I have ordered you some oisters this week, which I hope
you will get, though your oisters have sometimes miscarried.
Write when you can. I am, My dear, Your humble servant,
Dec. 2, 1779.　　　　　　　　　　　　　　　Sam: Johnson

649.1. Th. 9 Dec. '79. Mrs. Thrale.

Sotheby 26 Apr. 1869 (not seen).—Extract in catalogue.

(Approving highly of the adoption of whey diet; notices Mr. Thrale's
illness.)

He must be nursed through the winter, and the Spring I
hope will restore him.

Of publick affairs if I knew any good, I would tell you,
but good seems to be very far distant. Nothing is to be seen
but dejection and poverty.

649.2. Sa. 25 Dec. '79. Hester Maria Thrale (Streatham).

Address: To Miss Thrale at Streatham.
Lansdowne.—Lansdowne, *Johnson and Queeney* 1932, 14.

25 Dec. 1779

Pray, my dear Love, take the first opportunity of sending
me my watch, which I left at the Bed. I hope there is no
need of telling you, that I wish you all, every good of the
season, and of every Season.

I am, dear Sweet, Your most humble servant,

Sam: Johnson

649.3. W. 29 Dec. '79. Hester Maria Thrale (Streatham).

Address: To Miss Thrale
Lansdowne.—Lansdowne, *Johnson and Queeney* 1932, 15.

Dear Love,　　　　　　　　　　　　　Wednesday, Dec. 29

I wrote to you some days ago to send me my watch which I
forgot; and you have not sent it, which is not kind. Let me
have it as soon as ever you can.

I am, dear Love, Your humble servant,

Sam: Johnson

650. Th. 20 Jan. '80. Thomas Lawrence.

Address (JB's copy): To Doctor Lawrence.
Maggs Cat. 258 (1910), 526 (not seen).—Extracts in catalogue; *Europ. Mag.* Apr. 1789, xv. 282; *Works* xv, 1789, 494; Boswell 1791, ii. 311 (Hill iii. 419).

Dear Sir,

At a time when all your friends ought to shew their kind-ness, and with a character which ought to make all that know you, your friends, you may wonder that you have yet heard nothing of me.

I have been hindred by a vexatious and incessant cough, for which within these ten days, I have bled once, fasted four or five times, taken physick five times and opiates I think six. This day it seems to remit.

The loss, dear Sir, which you have lately suffered, I felt many years ago; and know therefore how much has been taken from you, and how little help can be had from consola-tion. He that outlives a wife whom he has long loved, sees himself disjoined from the only mind that had the same hopes, and fears, and interest; from the only companion with whom he has shared much good or evil, and with whom he could set his mind at liberty to retrace the past, or anticipate the future. The continuity of being is lacerated. The settled course of sentiment, and action is stopped, and life stands suspended and motionless till it is driven by external causes into a new channel. But the time of suspense is dreadful.

Our first recourse in this distresful solitude, is perhaps for want of habitual piety, to a gloomy acquiescence in necessity. Of two mortal Beings one must lose the other. But surely there is a higher and a better comfort to be drawn from the consideration of that Providence which watches over all; and belief that the living and the dead are equally in the hands of God, who will re-unite those whom he has separated, or who sees that it is best not to re-unite them.

I am Dear Sir Your most affectionate and Most humble Servant,
Jan. 20. 1780.   Sam: Johnson.

650.1. F. 25 Feb. '80.   ⟨? George Colman.⟩

Sotheby 7 Dec. 1900 (not seen).—Sotheby Catalogue.

The honour of being supposed to have some degree of your favour has exposed me to a request which I know not well how to reject. I am desired to solicit from you the resignation of Mr. Walpole's Tragedy, which was stolen from Mr. Hardinge, and by you found upon a stall. The appearance of negligence by which it was lost has made Mr. Walpole very angry, and you may restore peace to our friends by a very small concession, for the piece having satisfied your curiosity is to you of very little value. If you will be ⟨so⟩ kind as to give me the credit of restoring it to the owner I will take care that your civility shall not be without the praise that belongs to it, and I cannot but think that what Mr. Hardinge asks of you, is what you would expect with reason in the like case.

651. ⟨Early '80.⟩ John Nichols.

B.M. (two notes, combined by Nichols in publication).—*GM* Jan. 1785.

Mr. Johnson purposes to make his next attempt upon Prior, at least to consider him very soon, and desires that some volumes published of his papers, in two vols 8vo may be procured.

The turtle and sparrow can be but a Fable.[1] The Conversation I never read.

652. ⟨Early '80⟩. John Nichols.

B.M. (two notes, combined and wrongly paragraphed by Nichols in publication).—*GM* Jan. 1785.

Dr. Warton tells me that Collins's first piece is in the G: M: for August, 1739.[1] In August there is no such thing.

650.1.—The Hardinge of this letter is no doubt George H. I learn from Mathias, *The Shade of Alexander Pope* 1799, that he had 'a villa called Ragman's Castle, at Twitnam', and was thus Walpole's neighbour. There seems to be no reference to the episode in W's letters, though there are many to his fears lest *The Mysterious Mother* should be surreptitiously published.

651.—1. J had written (*Prior* ¶ 54) 'Of these Tales there are only four.' From JN's note to this letter in *GM* it appears that he had questioned that statement. J replies that 'The Turtle and Sparrow' and 'The Conversation', though styled 'Tales', are so only in name.

652.—1. Though J rejects the lines 'To Miss Aurelia C——r, on her weeping at her

Amasius was at that time the poetical name of Dr *Swan* who translated Sydenham. Where to find Collins I know not.

I think I must make some short addition to Thomson's sheet, but will send it to-day.

653. ⟨Early '80⟩. John Nichols.
Address: To Mr Nicol.
B.M.—*GM* Jan. 1785.

Sir

In examining this Book I find it necessary, to add[1] to the life the preface to the *British Enchanters* and you may add, if you will, the notes on *Unnatural Flights*.
Friday.   I am, Sir, &c.

654. Th. 6 Apr. '80. Mrs. Thrale (Bath).
Newton.—1788, No. 225 (misdated 1779 but not misplaced).

Dearest Lady

You had written so often. I have had but two letters from Bath, and the second complains that the first which you call so many, was neglected and you pretend to be afraid of being forgotten. I wonder what should put you out of my mind, you say rightly, that I shall not find such another, for there is not, if I had the choice of all, such another to be found.

sister's wedding', they are, at the end of his *Life*, 'added here' (added, that is, to the poems in 'Johnson's Poets') 'from *The Poetical Calendar*' (Fawkes and Woty) as 'Mr. Collins's first production'; and they have appeared in many editions. Hill points out that the real 'first piece'—'When *Phoebe* form'd a wanton smile'—is in *GM* for *October* 1739, 545. It is signed Delicatulus. The 'wrong' poem is in *GM* Jan. 1739, 41, signed *Amasius*. Warton's mistake is explained by the fact that there is another poem by 'Amasius' in the August number, 436.

653.—1. See the *Life of Granville* ¶ 30: 'His poetical precepts (in the *Essay upon Unnatural Flights in Poetry*) are accompanied with agreeable and instructive matter, which ought not to have been omitted in this edition.' These notes, and the preface to *The British Enchanters*, were appended, accordingly, to the *Life*. The words 'which ought not' &c., were omitted in the four-volume edition of the *Lives*, 1781; Hill (*Lives* ii. 296) notes that 'In the second edition the Appendage was omitted, being transferred to *Eng. Poets*'. I do not fully understand this; the 'appendage' may, indeed, have been included in a corrected issue of the *Poets* of 1779; but I know of no such reissue. It is included in the *Poets* of 1790; if it did not appear earlier, then the 'transference' was prospective.

654.—The false date in 1788 is no doubt a printer's error; 654 is the first letter of '80 in that collection, and the printer repeated '1779' from habit. The correspondence while the Thrales were at Bath, April–June, is illustrated by FB's full chronicle. They arrived 31 Mar. and took lodgings 'upon the South Parade' (*Diary* i. 305).

It is happy both for you and Mrs. Montague that the fates bring you both to Bath at the same time. Do not let new friends supplant the old, they who first distinguished you have the best claim to your attention; those who flock about you now take your excellence upon credit, and may hope to gain upon the world by your countenance.

I have not quite neglected my Lives. Addison is a long one but it is done. Prior is not short, and that is done too. I am upon Rowe, who cannot fill much paper. If I have done them before you come again, I think to bolt upon you at Bath, for I shall not be now afraid of Mrs. Cotton.[1] Let Burney take care that she does me no harm.

The diligence of Dr Moisy I do not understand, about what is he diligent. If Mr Thrale is well, or only not well because he has been ill, I do not see what the Physician can do. Does he direct any regimen, or dos Mr Thrale regulate himself? or is there no regularity among you? Nothing can keep him so safe as the method which has been so often mentioned, and which will be not only practicable but pleasant in the Summer, and before Summer is quite gone will be made supportable by custom.

If health and reason can be preserved by changing[2] three or four meals a week, or if such a change will but encrease the chances of preserving them, the purchase is surely not made at a very high price. Death is dreadful, and fatuity is more dreadful, and such strokes bring both so near, that all their terrours ought to be felt. I hope that to our anxiety for him, Mr Thrale will add some anxiety for himself.

Seward called on me one day, and read Spence.[3] I dined yesterday at Mr Jodrel's in a great deal of company. On Sunday I dine with Dr Lawrence, and at night go to Mrs Vesey. I have had a little cold, or two, or three, but I did not much mind them, for they were not very bad.

Make my compliments to my Master, and Queeney, and

654.—1. They had spent the afternoon of 1 Apr. 'with some relations of Mrs. T.', who included 'Mrs. C——, an ugly, proud old woman, but marvellous civil to me' (*Diary* i. 305).

2. See on 659, 'alternate diet'.

3. The MS. of the *Anecdotes*, the use of which J acknowledges in his *Advertisement*, see *L* iv. 63. (In the quotation from Walpole, in Hill's note on this passage, 'genius' is a misprint for 'guinea'.)

Burney, and Mrs. Cotton, and to all that care about me, and more than all—or else.

Now one courts you, and another caresses you, and one calls you to cards, and another wants you to walk, and amidst all this pray try to think now and then a little of me, and write often. Mrs. Strahan[4] is at Bath, but I believe, not well enough to be in the rooms.

I am Dearest Madam Your most humble Servant

Apr. 6, 1780   Sam: Johnson.

655. Sa. 8 Apr. '80. James Boswell (Edinburgh).

Not traced.—Boswell 1791, ii. 312 (Hill iii. 420).

Dear Sir

Well, I had resolved to send you the Chesterfield letter; but I will write once again without it. Never impose tasks upon mortals.[1] To require two things is the way to have them both undone.

For the difficulties which you mention in your affairs I am sorry; but difficulty is now very general: it is not therefore less grievous, for there is less hope of help. I pretend not to give you advice, not knowing the state of your affairs; and general counsels about prudence and frugality would do you

654.—4. Mentions of the Strahans in 666, 686, 877 are suppressed in 1788. This is no doubt connected with the fact that Strahan and Cadell were HLP's publishers. Mrs. S's visit to Bath is not mentioned in *Th*; perhaps HLT failed to pay her any attention there.

655.—This time it was J who kept JB in suspense. JB tells us (*L* iii. 418) that he wrote 22 Nov. and 21 Dec. '79, 1 Jan. and 13 Mar. '80, and summarizes both pairs of letters. That of 22 Nov. has survived, because J sent it to LP (see 649), and Prof. Tinker in his edition of JB's letters prints it (199a) from the MS. in his possession. It reported favourably 'concerning the family of Miss Doxy's lover' (see 649), and replied to J's strictures (646) on JB's enthusiasm for Carlisle. The letter of 21 Dec. is reported thus: 'that I had repeatedly begged of him to keep his promise to send me his letter to Lord Chesterfield, and that this *memento*, like *Delenda est Carthago*, must be in every letter that I should write to him, till I had obtained my object.'

1. I suspect the text of this passage. JB had 'imposed' two 'tasks' upon J; J was to send him the Chesterfield letter and (*L* iii. 418) to 'return me Goldsmith's two poems, with his lines marked' (see *L* ii. 478). J complains of the double imposition. I can find no point in 'mortals'. If it means merely 'people' (which is unlikely?) it seems in itself pointless, for J and JB frequently imposed tasks on each other and gladly executed them, and it has no relation to what follows ('to require two things', &c.). I see no solution. I have indeed suggested (*TLS* 4 Mar. 1939, 140) that 'mortals' might conceal 'intervals'; but I am unable to suggest any satisfactory reconstruction.

little good. You are, however, in the right not to increase your own perplexity by a journey hither; and I hope that by staying at home you will please your father.

Poor dear Beauclerk—*nec, ut soles, dabis joca.*[2] His wit and his folly, his acuteness and maliciousness, his merriment and reasoning, are now over. Such another will not often be found among mankind. He directed himself to be buried by the side of his mother, an instance of tenderness which I hardly expected. He has left his children to the care of Lady Di. and if she dies, of Mr. Langton, and of Mr. Leicester, his relation, and a man of good character. His library[3] has been offered to sale to the Russian ambassador.

Dr. Percy, notwithstanding all the noise of the news-papers, has had no literary loss.[4] Clothes and moveables were burnt to the value of about one hundred pounds; but his papers, and I think his books, were all preserved.

Poor Mr. Thrale has been in extreme danger from an apoplectical disorder, and recovered, beyond the expectation of his physicians; he is now at Bath, that his mind may be quiet, and Mrs. Thrale and Miss are with him.

Having told you what has happened to your friends, let me say something to you of yourself. You are always com-plaining of melancholy, and I conclude from those complaints that you are fond of it. No man talks of that which he is desirous to conceal, and every man desires to conceal that of which he is ashamed. Do not pretend to deny it; *manifestum habemus furem*;[5] make it an invariable and obligatory law to yourself, never to mention your own mental diseases; If you are never to speak of them you will think on them but little, and if you think little of them, they will molest you rarely. When you talk of them, it is plain that you want either praise or pity; for praise there is no room, and pity will do

---

655.—2. Also 'jocos'. From the poem by the Emperor Hadrian 'Dying, to his soul': 'No more with wonted humour gay' (Byron).

3. Malone notes that it was sold 'by publick auction . . . for 5011*l*'.

4. 'By a fire in Northumberland house, where he had an apartment' JB. In a note in one of his books P recorded that it 'was thus piteously burnt in the fire which con-sumed my Library at Northumbd. House in 1780'. *RES* 23, 89 (Jan. 1947), 45. This book, however, was only charred at the edges, a loss which J might not much regard.

5. 'We have the undeniable thief.' A similar legal maxim is 'habemus confitentem reum: the culprit has confessed the crime'. JB reports one of his letters of this year as stating 'that I had suffered again from melancholy'.

you no good; therefore, from this hour speak no more, think no more about them.

Your transaction with Mrs. Stuart[6] gave me great satisfaction; I am much obliged to you for your attention. Do not lose sight of her; your countenance may be of great credit, and of consequence of great advantage to her. The memory of her brother is yet fresh in my mind; he was an ingenious and worthy man.

Please to make my compliments to your lady, and to the young ladies. I should like to see them, pretty loves.

I am dear Sir, Yours, affectionately,

April 8, 1780. Sam. Johnson.

656. Sa. 8 Apr. '80. Lucy Porter (Lichfield).

D. F. Pennant.—Croker's Boswell 1831, iv. 303.

Dear Madam

I am indeed but a sluggish Correspondent, and know not when I shall much mend; however I will try.

I am glad that your oisters proved good, for I would have every thing good that belongs to you; and would have your health good that you may enjoy the rest. My health is better than it has been for some years past, and, if I see Lichfield again, I hope to walk about it.

Your Brother's request I have not forgotten. I have bought as many volumes as contain about an hundred and fifty Sermons which I will put in a Box,[1] and get Mr. Mathias to send him. I shall add a Letter.

We have been lately much alarmed at Mr Thrale's. He has had a stroke like that of an apoplexy, but he is at last got so well as to be at Bath, out of the way of trouble and business, and is likely to be in a short time quite well.

I hope all the Lichfield Ladies are well, and that every thing is prosperous among them.

655.—6. JB had written 20 Sept. '79: 'Your Amanuensis Stewart's sister has been so obscure that I have not yet discovered whether she be dead or alive, but I shall pursue the inquiry.' (*L* iii. 399, *BP* xiii. 305, 312, and App. B.) We hear no more of this 'transaction', but see references in Index II. The spelling 'Stewart' (1793), may be JB's correction of 'Stuart' (1791).

656.—1. We hear of the box again 723, a year later (not, as Hill inadvertently says, four days later). If it was the same box it was tardy; but Leghorn, where Porter flourished, was a long way off. For LP's reply to this letter see Addenda, p. 529.

A few months ago I sent you a little stuff gown, such as is all the fashion at this time. Yours is the same with Mrs Thrale's and Miss bought it for me. These stuffs are very cheap, and are thought very pretty.

Pray, give my Compliments to Mr. Pierson, and to every body, if any such body there be, that cares about me.

I am now engaged about the rest of the lives, which I am afraid will take some time, though I purpose to use despatch, but some thing or other always hinders. I have a great number to do, but many of them will be short.

I have lately had colds, the first was pretty bad with a very troublesome and frequent cough, but by bleeding and physick it was sent away. I have a cold now, but not bad enough for bleeding.

For some time past, and indeed ever since I left Lichfield last year, I have abated much of my diet, and am, I think, the better for abstinence. I can breathe and move with less difficulty, and I am as well, as people of my age commonly are. I hope we shall ⟨see⟩ one another again sometime this year.

I am Dear Love Your humble Servant

London. April 8. 1780.   Sam: Johnson.

656.1. Sa. 8 Apr. '80. Hester Maria Thrale (Bath).
Address: To Miss Thrale.
Lansdowne.—Lansdowne, *Johnson and Queeney* 1932, 16.

My dear Love,   London, 8 April 1780
    It is well that you are all housed safe at last. By this journey you are sure to escape some danger. My master will be out of the way both of political and commercial tumults and hurries, and I hope that change of air, and proper proportions of exercise and rest may produce some actual good.

As for such younglings as you, a new place is always a good place, unless it be eminently bad. The great pleasure of life is the influx of novelty, and probably for that reason only our earliest years are commonly our happiest, for though they are past under restraint, and often in a very unpleasing course of involuntary labour, yet while every hour produces something new, there is no deep impression of discontent.

Therefore, my charming Queeny, keep your eyes and your ears open, and enjoy as much of the intellectual world as you can. If Ideas are to us the measure of time, he that thinks most, lives longest. Berkley[1] says that one man lives more life in an hour, than another in a week; that you, my dearest, may in every sense live long, and in every sense live well is the desire of

Your humble servant
Sam: Johnson

657. Tu. 11 Apr. '80. Mrs. Thrale (Bath).

Newton.—1788, No. 226.

Dear Madam

On Sunday I dined with poor Lawrence who is deafer than ever. When he was told that Dr Moisy visited Mr Thrale he enquired, for what? and said that there was nothing to be done, which Nature would not do for herself. On Sunday evening I was at Mrs Vesey's and there was enquiry about my Master, but I told them all good. There was Dr. Barnard of Eaton, and we made a noise all the evening, and there was Pepys, and Wraxal till I drove him away. And I have no loss[1] of my mistress, who laughs, and frisks, and frolicks it all the long day, and never thinks of poor Colin.[2]

If Mr Thrale will but continue to mend we shall, I hope, come together again, and do as good things as ever we did, but perhaps you will be made too proud to heed[3] me, and yet, as I have often told you, it will not be easy for you to find such another.

Queeney has been a good Girl, and wrote me a letter; if

656.1.—1. J probably had in mind, as Prof. Aaron suggests to me, *Siris* § 109: 'it being manifest, that one man, by a brisker motion of his spirits and succession of his ideas, shall live more in one hour, than another in two.'

657.—1. This is I suppose bravado. The possibility occurs that J wrote 'news'. For confusion of *n* and *l* see 103, where the first editor read 'content' (J meant 'be content') as 'recollect', and 206, where 'collected' was read as 'connected.' See also on 641. But I failed to note any discrepancy when I collated this letter many years ago.

2. Rowe's 'Colin's Complaint': 'Then to her new love let her go; | And deck her in golden array; | Be finest at every fine show | And frolic it all the long day.' Colin recurs later in this letter, and see 547.

3. If J wrote 'need' (for his *h* and *n* see on 641) I failed to detect it.

Burney[4] said she would write, she told you a fib. She writes nothing to me. She can write home fast enough. I have a good mind not to let her know, that Dr Bernard, to whom I had recommended her novel, speaks of it with great commendation, and that the copy which she lent me, has been read by Dr Lawrence three times over. And yet what a Gypsey it is. She no more minds me than if I were a Brangton.[5] Pray speak to Queeney to write again.

I have had a cold and [and] a cough, and taken opium, and think I am better. We have had very cold weather, bad riding weather for my Master, but he will surmount it all. Did Mrs Browne make any reply to your comparison of business with solitude, or did you quite down her? I am much pleased to think that Mrs. Cotton thinks me worth a frame, and a place upon her wall. Her kindness was hardly within my hope, but time does wonderful things. All my fear is, that if I should come again, my print would be taken down. I fear, I shall never hold it.

Who dines with you? Do you see Dr. Woodward or Dr. Harrington? Do you go to the House[6] where they write for the myrtle? You are at all places of high resort, and bring home hearts by dozens; while I am seeking for something to say about men of whom I know nothing but their verses, and sometimes very little of them. Now I have begun however, I do not despair of making an end. Mr. Nicols holds that Addison is the most *taking* of all that I have done. I doubt they will not be done before you come away.

Now you think yourself the first Writer in the world for a letter about nothing. Can you write such a letter as this? So miscellaneous, with such noble disdain of regularity, like Shakespeare's works, such graceful negligence of transition like the ancient enthusiasts.[7] The pure voice of nature and

657.—4. 'Dr Johnson . . . has not yet received a scrawl I have sent him. He says Dr. Barnard, the provost of Eton, has been singing the praises of my book, and that old Dr. Lawrence has read it through three times within this last month.' FB's *Diary* (13 Apr.) i. 316.

5. The Branghtons are the vulgar 'cits' in *Evelina*. For the story of J's comparison of JB to a Branghton see FB's *Memoirs of Dr. Burney* ii. 193, quoted by Hill on this letter.   6. Lady Miller's.

7. J is perhaps thinking of Pindar, whose abrupt transitions were a commonplace of criticism. Prof. Dodds refers me to 'Longinus' 33. 5; the supposed obscurity of Gray's *Odes* of 1758 had made the theme familiar.

of friendship. Now of whom shall I proceed to speak? Of whom but Mrs. Montague, having mentioned Shakespeare and Nature does not the name of Montague force itself upon me? Such were the transitions of the ancients, which now seem abrupt because the intermediate idea is lost to modern understandings. I wish her name had connected itself with friendship, but, ah Colin[8] thy hopes are in vain, one thing however is left me, I have skill to complain, but I hope I shall not complain much while you have any kindness for me. I am,

Dearest and dearest Madam Your most humble servant
Apr. 11. 1780 London   Sam: Johnson.
You do not date your letters.

658. Sa. 15 Apr. '80. Mrs. Thrale (Bath).

Adam.—1788, No. 227.

Dearest Madam

I did not mistake D[r] Woodward's[1] case, nor should have wanted any explanation. But broken[2] is a very bad word in the city.

There has just been with me D[r] Burney, who has given. What has he given? Nothing, I believe, gratis. He has given fifty seven lessons this week. Surely this is business.

I thought to have finished Rowe's life today, but I have five or six visitors who hindred me, and I have not been quite well. Next week I hope to despatch four or five of them.

It is a great delight to hear so much good of all of you. Fanny tells me good news of you, and you speak well of Fanny, and all of you say what one would wish of my Master. And my sweet Queeny, I hope is well. Does she drink the Waters? *One glass* would do her as much good as it does her father.

You and M[rs] Montague must keep M[rs] Cotton[3] about

657.—8. 'What though I have skill to complain, | Though the Muses my temples have crown'd . . .? | Ah, Colin! Thy hopes are in vain, | Thy pipe and thy laurel resign, | Thy false one inclines to a swain | Whose music is sweeter than thine.' See note 2 above.

658.—1. Not explained.

2. 'broken' and 'city' are underlined in the MS., I think by HLP. The words were not italicized in 1788.

3. Erased, and suppressed in 1788; 'Byron' HLP—a very bad guess. See 664, 679.

you, and try to make a Wit of her. She will be a little unskilful in her first Essays, but you will see, how precept and example will bring her forwards.

Surely it is very fine to have your powers. The Wits court you, and the Methodists[4] love you, and the whole world runs about you, and you write me word how well you can do without me, and so, go thy ways poor Jack.[5]

That sovereign *glass of water* is the great medicine; and though his legs are rather too big, yet my Master takes a glass of water. This is bold practice. I believe, under the protection of a glass of water [of water] drank at the pump, he may venture once a week upon a stew'd lamprey.[6]

I wish you all good, yet know not what to wish you which you have not. May all good continue and encrease. I am

Madam Your most humble servant,

April 15. 1780   Sam: Johnson

You owe me Silver Ϝ:[7]

659. Tu. 18 Apr. '80. Mrs. Thrale (Bath).

Newton.—1788, No. 228.

Dear Madam

Of the petticoat Government[1] I had never heard. Of the Shakespeare[2] I was once told by Miss Laurence, and that is all that I know of it. I have not seen nor heard of any body

658.—4. I do not find any record of association with Methodists in Bath, except the Mrs. Browne of 657. In the published letter dated 9 May (1788, No. 233) she writes: 'the Methodists love you, says my dear Mr. Johnson. I do hope that my amiable friend Mrs. Browne *does* love me.'

5. 'old Jack'; see on 645.

6. 'Johnson thought little of the power of remedies, and less did he think on the power of stewed lampreys to hinder all remedies from being efficacious' HLP. The first is a surprising judgement. For HT's addiction to lampreys see Hayward 1861[2], ii. 41.

7. HLP omitted the postscript, which perhaps she did not understand. I have not found an explanation of J's symbol, except a suggestion that it might be the roman numeral 40, i.e. 'forty shillings'.

659.—1. J writes of petticoat government in the ordinary sense in 664; and he often writes of HLT's 'government' of himself. That does not seem to fit this context. Hill plausibly suggests that 'Petticoat Government' was the title of a current pamphlet (John Dunton had so named one in 1702). But I have not found such a pamphlet.

2. Sir Edmund Chambers suggested the possibility of a reference to the 'version of an alleged lost ballad on Sir Thomas Lucy cited by Edward Capel in his *Notes to Shakespeare*' (published 1783 but in print earlier).

that has seen the wonders. You may be sure I should tell you any thing that would gratify your curiosity, and furnish you for your present expences of intellectual entertainment. But of this dramatick discovery I know nothing.

I cannot see but my Master may with stuborn regularity totally recover. But surely though the invasion has been repelled from life, the waste it has made will require some time and much attention to repair it. You must not grow weary of watching him, and he must not grow impatient of being watched.

Pray, of what wonders do you tell me? You make verses, and they are read in publick,[3] and I know nothing about them. This very crime, I think, broke the link of amity between Richardson and Miss Mulso, after a tenderness and confidence of many years. However you must do a great deal more before I leave you for Lucan or Montague, or any other charmer, if any other charmer would have me.

I am sorry[4] that you have seen Mrs. Walmesley. She and her husband exhibited two very different appearances of human Nature.—But busy, busy, still art thou.[5]—He prevailed on himself to treat her with great tenderness, and to show how little sense will serve for common life, she has passed through the world with less imprudence than any of her Family.

Sir Philip's[6] bill has been rejected by the Lords. There was, I think, nothing to be objected to it, but the time at which it was proposed, and the intention with which it was projected. It was fair in itself, but tended to weaken government, when[7] it is too weak already.

Scrase[8] is doubtless pleased with the payment of your debts. My Master, if I understand him right, talked of putting the other eight thousand pounds into the Bank, till it could be commodiously received. I wish it were done. I love that

659.—3. See 660.1*a*.

4. J probably intended 'not sorry'.

5. Thomson, 'Fortune': 'But busy, busy still are thou | To bind the loveless, joyous vow, | The heart from pleasure to delude, | To join the gentle to the rude.'

6. Jennings Clerk. For the fortunes of his 'Contractors' Bill', which became law in '82, see Hill's note; and for FB's account of J's vacillation on the subject, see the same note, or FB's *Diary* for '79, i. 180.

7. J perhaps wrote 'where'; the two words are often hardly distinguishable.

8. The sentences following, to the end of the paragraph, were suppressed in 1788.

money should be in the Bank, and I love that debt should be discharged.

. . .⁹ has no business about you, but to be taught. Poor B⟨iron⟩'s¹⁰ tenderness is very affecting. Comfort her all you can. I sincerely wish her well. Declining life is a very awful scene.

Please to tell Mr. Thrale, that I think I grow rather less, and that I was last week almost dizzy with vacuity. I repeat my challenge to alternate diet,¹¹ and doubt not but both of us by adhering to it may live more at ease, and a much longer time.

Though I am going to dine with Lady Craven,

I am Madam Your most humble servant

London. 18 April. 1780   Sam: Johnson.

660. See next page.

661. W. ⟨19 Apr. '80⟩. Charles Burney.
Address (Hill): To Dʳ Burney—or any Burney.
Not traced.—Hill 1892 (misplaced).

Mr. Johnson received an invitation from Mrs. Ord for to-morrow, and having forgotten her street, desires to be informed where she lives. If Dr. Burney goes to-morrow, Mr. Johnson will call on him, and beg the favour of going with him.

Wednesday.

659.—9. 'I forget' HLP. I could not read the erasure.
    10. 'Biron' Lysons, 'Byron' HLP. Mrs. B's son, 'Captain George Byron, is lately returned from the West Indies, and has brought a wife with him from Barbadoes, though he was there only three weeks . . . a pleasant circumstance for this proud family! Poor Mrs. Byron seems destined for mortification and humiliation; yet such is her native fire . . . that she bears up against all calamity' (FB's *Diary* i. 324). 'Poor Mrs. Byron is very far from well . . . but her charming spirits never fail her' (ibid. i. 310). See also 660.1a.
    11. The term recurs, and should seem to be technical. My medical advisers do not recognize it as such, but have no doubt that it means abstinence from meat on alternate days. See 654, 'changing meals'.

661.—Hill, not noticing the days of the week, placed this letter after 660. Since J spent the evening with Mrs. Ord on 'Thursday' 20 April (see 662), 661 was written on 'Wednesday' 19 April.

660. Th. 20 Apr. '80 (misdated 1778, cf. 660.1). John Taylor (Ashbourne).

Address: To the Rev Dr Taylor in Ashbourne Derbyshire.

Gabriel Wells.—*Morrison Autographs* 1885, ii. 343.

Dear Sir

The quantity of blood taken from you appears to me not sufficient. Thrale was almost lost by the scrupulosity of his Physicians, who never bled him copiously till they bled him in despair; he then bled till he fainted, and the stricture or obstruction immediately gave way, and from that instant he grew better.

I can now give you no advice but to keep yourself totally quiet, and amused with some gentle exercise of the mind. If a suspected letter comes, throw it aside till your health is reestablished; keep easy and cheerful company about you, and never try to think but at those stated and solemn times when the thoughts are summoned to the cares of futurity, the only real cares of a rational Being.

As to my own health, I think it rather grows better, the convulsions which left me last year at Ashbourne have never returned, and I have, by the mercy of God, very comfortable nights. Let me know very often how you are, till you are quite well.

   I am, Sir, Your affectionate humble servant,

London April 20 1778   Sam: Johnson.

660.1. Th. 20 Apr. '80 (misdated 1778, cf. 660). Mrs. Thrale (Bath).

Adam.—1788, but cancelled in proof. Broadley, *Dr. Johnson and Mrs. Thrale* 1910, 114, from the proofsheets then in his possession.

Dear Madam

Being to go dine with your favourite Hamilton, and to pass

660.—Hill saw that this letter must belong to '80; it refers to HT's illness of June '79, and to J's release from 'convulsions', which is fixed by *PM* 18 June '80 as having been granted him 'this day last year'. Hill had not seen 660.1, which has the same erroneous date; it refers to the evening spent with Mrs. Ord, which is fixed by 662 as Th. 20 Apr. '80. The reference to CB's fifty-seven lessons (see 658) is equally decisive. The error is surprising. We know that J wrote his diary for '82 in the blank spaces of a printed calendar for '65 (*L* iv. 504). Now if he looked at such a calendar on this occasion, believing that it could tell him the day of the month, he might mechanically copy its year.

661.1.—For the date see on 660.

the evening with Mrs Ord, I write before your letter comes to me, if there comes any letter. I have not indeed much to say but inclose one from Lucy, and another from Taylor, keep them both for me.

I do not think they bled Taylor enough. Mr Thrale was saved by it, and I hope he will steadily remember that when evacuation is a cure, plenitude is a disease, and abstinence the true and only preventive.

I owe Miss Thrale and Miss Burney each a letter which I will pay them.

Dr Burney gave fifty seven lessons last week, so you find that we have recourse to musick in these days of publick distress. Do not forget me. I am,

Dearest Madam, Your most humble servant
London. Apr. 20. 1778   Sam: Johnson
You never date your letters.

660.1a. Bath. Th. ⟨20 Apr. '80.⟩ From Mrs. Thrale.
R 540.93—

Dear Sir   South parade Thursday Morning
I *do* tell my Master how you starve & grow less, and even faint with hunger; but I protest I do not think that Method would be right for *him*, and all the Medical People positively say it would be wrong: the alternate Diet is a better plan, more rational and more feasible, I should like to see that established.

I am this moment come from my Dear Mrs Byron. She like Mr Thrale is mending visibly, but She will not survive another Fit of Illness when it comes I think. Her tenderness, & Reliance on me are affecting indeed, yet She will not do what I wish her in positive Things; her Mind stronger and more vigorous than her Fellow pupil Sir Philip's, is not half as docible and easy of Conviction. She has such quick Sensibility however, & such fine Understanding her Virtue is more valuable: He is with his Lady in Hampshire, forgetting his Contractor's Bill.

I have seen Mr Jerningham the poet & heard him sing Songs to his Harp: all his hearers so worship'd him and he so gaped for the Incense, I actually ran sulky & would not say a Word—he revenged himself last night at the Play, by chatting with Mrs Cook of Norfolk as they call her in preference to me, and then all *my* Worshippers wondered. Wits are much esteemed here I can tell you, but *such Esteemers!* as Mrs Montagu says.

The Verses that were publickly read was only The Old Tale of the three Warnings: a Man who gave publick Lectures upon Reading gave that as one of the Specimens. No Breach of Confidence there, except in suffering any body to tell on't except myself. Will Miss Reynolds let you drink Tea with her after dining at Lady Craven's? She is a much more culpable Creature than poor Abington. Where do you get your large Gilt paper Dear Sir? I never saw such but in your Letters.

When your Work is done I hope you will come among us; but if after all my puffing you should at last find me like poor Relhan at Brighthelmston sucking my Hat, or twirling my Thumbs! Oh that would be bad enough, but the worst is we have no spare Apartment in our Lodging.—Hester's sore Eyes continue to mortifie & to confine her, but Moysey who felt her Pulse today would not order her to lose blood.

Farewell my Dear Sir, & never love us less than you do. I am most truly Your Faithful and Obedient Servant

H: L: Thrale.

661. W. ⟨19 *Apr.* '80⟩. Charles Burney. See above, after 659.

661.1. (? Sa.) 22 Apr. Lucy Porter (Lichfield).
Address: To Mrs. Lucy Porter Lichfield. Franked by Thrale. *Postmark*: 22 AP.
Fettercairn.—

Dearest Madam

Now the days grow longer and the weather warmer, I hope that, notwithstanding your presages, your health will mend, and your strength increase. Continual disorder of body is but an uncomfortable State, but I am afraid that in the latter part of life much health is not often to be expected. My nights are very restless and tedious, and my days for want of Sleep often heavy. I do not find that I am worse or better by changing air, and therefore it is with no great expectation of amendment that I make every year a journey into the country. But it is pleasant to visit those, whose kindness has been often experienced.

661.—Hill placed this letter conjecturally from the reference to Mrs. Ord in 662, and his conjecture is confirmed by 660.1. He seems to have overlooked the fact that 20 April 1780 was a Thursday; 661 should properly precede 660.

661.1.—JB in his list of the letters to LP (Abbott, *Catalogue* p. 249) notes of this: 'No date but in Summer 1784.' He overlooked the frank. Prof. Abbott conjecturally assigned it to '80, the latest possible year. This requires two assumptions: (1) that J sent it, in a cover, to Bath to be franked; (2) that the letter as we have it, with direction and postmark on p. 4, went from Bath to L'd by L'n; otherwise it could not bear a date-stamp. This seems decisive against '80; but I see no means of choosing between several years in which J might 'hope' to visit L'd in May. JB's omission of this letter might be due to uncertainty about its date; see also on 983.1, and (on JB's omissions in general) App. E, II § 5.

I hope to see Lichfield about the middle of May in my way to Derbyshire, and perhaps in June at my return homewards. If you want any books, let me know that I may procure them for you. Make my compliments to Mrs Cobb and all my friends. I am, Dear Madam Your humble Servant

Sam: Johnson

662. Tu. 25 Apr. '80. Mrs. Thrale (Bath).

Not traced.—1788, No. 229.

Dear Madam

Mr. E—— and Mr. P——[1] called on me to-day with your letter to the electors,[2] and another which they had drawn up, to serve in its place. I thought all their objections just, and all their alterations proper. You had mentioned his sickness in terms which gave his adversaries advantage, by confirming the report which they already spread with great industry, of his infirmity and inability. You speak, in their opinion, and in mine, with too little confidence in your own interest. By fearing, you teach others to fear. All this is now avoided, and it is to take its chance.

How do you think I live? On Thursday I dined with Hamilton, and went thence to Mrs. Ord. On Friday, with much company at Reynolds's. On Saturday, at Dr. Bell's. On Sunday, at Dr. Burney's, with your two sweets[3] from Kensington, who are both well; at night came Mrs. Ord, Mr. Harris, and Mr. Greville, &c. On Monday, with Reynolds, at night with Lady Lucan; to-day with Mr. Langton; to-morrow with the Bishop of St. Asaph;[4] on Thursday with Mr. Bowles; Friday, ——;[5] Saturday, at the Academy; Sunday, with Mr. Ramsay.

I told Lady Lucan how long it was since she sent to me; but she said I must consider how the world rolls about her. She seemed pleased that we met again.

662.—1. 'Evans and Perkins' HLP.

2. Parliament was not dissolved until Sept.; but the government had been defeated in the House, and an earlier dissolution was expected.

3. HLT had left Susan and Sophy at school in Kensington.

4. Shipley.

5. The blank is, I suppose, J's, not an erasure by HLP.

The long intervals of starving I do not think best for Mr. Thrale, nor perhaps for myself, but I knew not how to attain any thing better; and every body tells me that I am very well, and I think there now remains not much cause for complaint: but O for a glass, once in four-and-twenty hours, of warm water! Can warm water be had only at Bath, as steam was to be found only at Knightsbridge.[6] Nature distributes her gifts, they say, variously, to show us that we have need of one another; and in her bounty she bestowed warm water upon Bath, and condemned the inhabitants of other places, if they would warm their water, to make a fire. I would have the young ladies take half a glass every third day, and walk upon it.

I not only scour the town from day to day, but many visitors come to me in the morning; so that my work makes no great progress, but I will try to quicken it. I should certainly like to bustle a little among you, but I am unwilling to quit my post till I have made an end.

You did not tell me in your last letter how Mr. Thrale goes on. If he will be *ruled, for aught appears, he may live on these hundred years.*[7] Fix him when he comes in alternate diet.

> I am, dearest Lady, Your, &c.

London, April 25, 1780.

Now there is a date; look at it.

662a. Bath. F. 28 Apr. ⟨'80⟩. From Mrs. Thrale.

Address: Doctor Johnson Bolt Court Fleet Street London. *Postmark*: 1 MA. Franked by HT.

Fettercairn (*Cat.* 1451).—Boswell 1791, ii. 314, suppressing the names Cotton and Aston (Hill iii. 421).

I had a very kind letter from you yesterday, dear Sir, with a most circumstantial date. You took trouble with my circulating letter Mr. Evans writes

662.—6. See *L* v. 286 for this story. JB's original journal for 5 Oct. '73 shows that its heroine was Mrs. Langton.

7. Swift, 'On the Death of Dr. Swift': 'Had he been rul'd, for ought appears, | He might have liv'd these twenty years.'

662a.—'I shall present my readers with one of her original letters to him at this time, which will amuse them probably more than those well-written but studied epistles which she has inserted in her collection, because it exhibits the easy vivacity of their literary intercourse. It is also of value as a key to Johnson's answer, which she had printed by itself, and of which I shall subjoin extracts' JB. For HLP's account of the matter see on 663.

me word, and I thank you sincerely for so doing: one might do mischief else not being on the spot.

Yesterday's evening was passed at Mrs. Montagu's: there was Mr. Melmoth, I do not like him *though* nor he me; it was expected we should have pleased each other! he is however just Tory enough to hate the Bishop of Peterborough for Whiggism, and Whig enough to abhor you for Torism.

Mrs. Montagu flattered him finely so he had a good afternoon on't. This evening we spend at a concert! poor Queeney's sore eyes have just released her, she had a long confinement and could neither read nor write; so my master treated her very good-naturedly with the visits of a young woman in this town a taylor's daughter, who professes musick, and teaches so as to give six lessons a day to ladies at five and threepence a lesson—Miss Burney says she is a great performer, and I respect the wench for getting her living so prettily: she is very modest and pretty-mannered, and not seventeen years old.

You live in a fine whirl indeed; if I did not write regularly you would half forget me, and that would be very wrong—for I *felt* my regard for you in my *face* last night, when the criticisms were going on.

This morning it was all connoisseurship; we went to see some pictures painted by a gentleman-artist, Mr. Taylor of this place: my master makes one, every where, and has got a good dawling companion to ride with him now Captain Cotton who married Miss Aston. He looks well enough, but I have no notion of health for a man whose mouth cannot be sewed up—Burney and I and Queeney teize him every meal he eats, and Mrs. Montagu is quite serious with him; but what *can* one do? he will eat I think, and if he does eat I know he will not live. It makes me very unhappy, but I must bear it. Let me always have your friendship. I am most sincerely dear Sir Your faithful servant,

Bath, Friday, April 28.   H. L. T.

663. M. 1 May '80. Mrs. Thrale (Bath).

Not traced.—1788, No. 230; Boswell 1791, ii. 315, an extract (Hill iii. 423).

Dearest Madam

Mr. Thrale never will live abstinently, till he can persuade himself to abstain by rule. I lived on potatoes on Friday, and on spinach to-day; but I have had, I am afraid, too many dinners of late. I took physick too both days, and hope to fast to-morrow. When he comes home, we will shame him, and Jebb shall scold him into regularity. I am glad, however, that he is always one of the company, and that my dear

663.—'This is the Ans. to a letter of my own wch. I wd. not publish, but wch. Mr. Boswell bought of black Francis for ½ a Crown and printed in his Life of Johnson' HLP. In 1816 (see *L* iii. 536) she calls her letter 'the famous letter with which Boswell threatened us all so'. See 662*a* and Appendix E, II § 5.

Queeney is again another. Encourage, as you can, the musical girl.[1]

Nothing is more common than mutual dislike where mutual approbation is particularly expected. There is often on both sides a vigilance not over benevolent; and as attention is strongly excited, so that nothing drops unheeded, any difference in taste or opinion, and some difference where there is no restraint will commonly appear, it[2] immediately generates dislike.

Never let criticisms operate upon your face or your mind; it is very rarely that an author is hurt by his criticks. The blaze of reputation cannot be blown out, but it often dies in the socket; a very few names may be considered as perpetual lamps that shine unconsumed. From the author of Fitzosborne's Letters[3] I cannot think myself in much danger. I met him only once about thirty years ago, and in some small dispute reduced him to whistle; having not seen him since, that is the last impression. Poor Moore the fabulist was one of the company.

Mrs. Montague's long stay, against her own inclination, is very convenient. You would, by your own confession, want a companion; and she is *par pluribus*,[4] conversing with her you may *find variety in one*.[5]

At Mrs. Ord's I met one Mrs. B——,[6] a travelled lady, of great spirit, and some consciousness of her own abilities. We had a contest of gallantry an hour long, so much to the diversion of the company, that at Ramsay's last night, in a crowded room, they would have pitted us again. There were Smelt, and the Bishop of St. Asaph, who comes to every place;[7] and Lord Monboddo, and Sir Joshua, and ladies out of tale.

The exhibition,[8] how will you do, either to see or not to

663.—1. 'Now the great Mrs. Miles then Jenny Guest' HLP, see 662*a*.

2. 1791 omits the redundant word.   3. Melmoth, see 662*a*.

4. Mr. Vernon Rendall tells me that 'Nec pluribus impar' was Louis XIV's motto.

5. *Spectator* 470: 'For here the false inconstant Lover, | After a thousand Beauties shown, | Does new surprising Charms discover, | And finds Variety in One' (Addison).

6. 'Judge Buller's Lady. She is alive still. 1803' HLP.

7. J may intend censure of the bishop. See *L* iv. 75 for his disapproval of Shipley and Porteus 'for going to routs, at least for staying long at them'.

8. The Royal Academy this year for the first time held its exhibition at Somerset House, 'quite a Roman palace' (Walpole, quoted by Hill).

see! The exhibition is eminently splendid. There is contour, and keeping, and grace, and expression, and all the varieties of artificial excellence. The appartments were truly very noble. The pictures, for the sake of a sky light, are at the top of the house; there we dined, and I sat over against the Archbishop of York.[9] See how I live when I am not under petticoat government.

London, May 1, 1780.   I am, &c.

Mark that—you did not put the year to your last.[10]

663a. Bath. W. 3 May '80. From Mrs. Thrale.

R 540.95—

Dear Sir   Bath Wednesday 3: May 1780.

As far as shaming will do we work pretty hard at my Master here; Mrs Montagu interests herself for him quite tenderly, complains to Moysey when She sees him eat to much, & sends him hither to say in worse Language, but not less forcible—what She says, and you write in the most elegant Terms.

If says the Dr Mr Thrale will not mind the wisest Man & Woman in the World—let him listen to the foolishest; here's not an Apothecary's Prentice in this Town, but what can see that he's *knockt down* like a *Cock at Shrove Tide*; & all by over feeding: For God's Sake dear Sir do not *stun* your Senses so; neither Sir Richard Jebb nor I can restore them you when they are lost. To all this Burney adds constant teizing, and *I* who know him best, do protest that he never lived so temperately since I lived with him.—he does really not eat much, & will probably never eat less, it is therefore I think so ill of his Situation.

I heard of your Prowess at Lord Lucan's—a Friend of Mrs Byron's was there, & was never so entertained She said: I likewise heard of you at the Burney's, & it was very kind to tell me yourself the gay Afternoon you spent at Ramsay's; I shall hear of that thro' Smelt's Daughter I dare say.

Mrs Montagu & I meet somewhere every Night; People think they must not ask one of us without the other, & there they sit gaping while we talk: I left it to her for the first fortnight & She harangued the Circles herself; till I heard of private Discussions why Mrs Thrale who was so willing to talk at other Times, was so silent in Mrs Montagu's Company—then I began, and now we talk away regularly when there is no Musick, & the folks look so stupid, except one or two who I have a Notion lie by to laugh, & write Letters to their Sisters &c. at home about us.

We are this moment going to the play. Sir Richard Hotham is busy in the Borough it seems, & spends Money very liberally, but it will not do I think; one of our principal Friends there came to Bath t'other day, partly to bring us Intelligence, & partly I believe to see & make a Report of Mr Thrale, for he examined deeply into the State of his Health: I asked the Man to dinner,

663.—9. Markham.   10. 662*a*.

I have no mind of a journey but know not whether I can escape it. I shall let you know how we go on. I dined today on Veal pie.

I am Madam, Your most humble

London June 5. 1782.   Sam. Johnson.

Compliments to dear Queeny Love.

787.3. F. 7 June '82. Mrs. Thrale.

Address: To Mrs. Thrale.
Rylands Library.—R.L. *Bull.* Jan. 1932, 36.

Dear Madam

I had such a night, that there are few better. My cough is very much abated, but now I am risen, I feel little alacrity, but that may return. I took physick yesterday of the strongest sort, which made me uneasy, but, I think, did me good.

I have no mind of a journey, and had rather not go. If you please to call on me, you will find me

Madam Your most humble servant,

June 7. 1782 London   Sam: Johnson

787.4. F. 7 June '82. Frances Burney.

Marchioness of Crewe. (Endorsed 'No. 3'.)—

Madam

For some time past there has been often at my House, a young Man whose name is Mara; He is without employment or provision, and therefore is very desirous of going to Sea, as a servant of the Captain. His behaviour is without reproach, he is of pleasing manners, and regular conduct, and capable, I suppose, of any business included in clerkship. I have taken an interest in his success, and beg of you, dear Madam, to engage him to Captain Burney, before his number is full. Do for us what you can. I am, Madam, Your most humble Servant Sam: Johnson

June 7. 1782 Boltcourt. Fleetstreet

788. Sa. 8 June (misdated July) '82. Mrs. Thrale.
Address: To Mrs Thrale.
H. Murdock.—1788, No. 292.

Dear Madam

Perhaps some of your people may call to morrow. I have this day taken a passage to Oxford for Monday. Not to frisk as you express it with very unfeeling irony, but to catch at the hopes of better health. The change of place may do something. To leave the house where so much has been suffered affords some pleasure. When I write to you, write to me again and let me have the pleasure of knowing that I am still considered as,

     Madam, Your most humble servant
Saturday July 8. 1782   Sam: Johnson.

788.1. Su. 9 June '82. Elizabeth Lawrence.
Address: To Miss E. Laurence.
Liebert.—

Madam

Be pleased to let me know the state, whatever it be, of dear Dr Laurence. Is he attended by any clergyman?

Let him know, if it be proper, that I have been much dejected by this long illness, but think myself slowly recovering. I am going to morrow to Oxford, to try change of place. The Doctor has my prayers and I desire his. I am, Madam
      Your most humble servant
June 9. 1782   Sam: Johnson

789. Oxford. Tu. 11 June '82. Mrs. Thrale.
Sotheby 30 Jan. 1918 (not seen).—1788, No. 298 (misdated 1783 and misplaced accordingly).

Dear Madam,   Oxford, June 11, 1783.

Yesterday I came to Oxford without fatigue or inconvenience. I read in the coach before dinner. I dined moderately, and slept well; but find my breath not free this morning.

Dr. Edwards, to whom I wrote word of my purpose to come, has defeated his own kindness by its excess. He has

gone out of his own rooms for my reception,[1] and therefore
I cannot decently stay long, unless I can change my abode,
which it will not be very easy to do: nor do I know what
attractions I shall find here. Here is Miss Moore at Dr.
Adams's, with whom I shall dine to-morrow. Of my adventures and observations I shall inform you, and beg you to
write to me at Mr. Parker's[2] bookseller.

I hope Queeney has got rid of her influenza, and that you
escape it. If I had Queeney here, how would I shew her all
the places.[3] I hope, however, I shall not want company in
my stay here.

I am, Dear Madam, Your, &c.

789.1. Oxford. Tu. 11 June '82. Sir Richard Jebb.

Address: To Sir Richard Jebb Bar^t in Westminster. *Postmark*: 12 IV.
Sotheby 17 Feb. 1930.—

Dear Sir

I came to Oxford yesterday without fatigue in the common coach. I have now more appetite than I venture to
gratify, and sleep with very little inconvenience. My cough
though very much abated is still troublesome, and takes
every opportunity of an open door or a cold blast, to put
my breast in motion. If I have any wrong tendency it is to
costiveness, though I do not now take the bark, but this
indisposition is easily counteracted. My breath is still short
and laborious.

This account, dear Sir, I thought it proper to give You,
because I have sufficient reason for believing that you have

789.—1. See Hill for a conjecture as to J's rooms in Jesus College.

2. The famous bookshop at the north end of 'the Turl', almost directly opposite
Jesus College, did not become 'Parker's' until 1798; J's Parker had his shop some way
off in Logic Lane. J perhaps gave Parker's as his address thinking that he might move
elsewhere in O'd when Edwards had had enough of his company.

3. In her published letter dated 'Bath, June 15, 1783', which purports to answer
789 (which HLP had misdated and misplaced), HLT (or HLP) writes 'It would have
been a fine advantage indeed could she have seen Oxford now in your company'—
and so forth, leading up to a poetical quotation. Hill pointed out that HLT could
not write this in '83, in which year J did not visit O'd. It has been argued that he
may have contemplated a visit then; but this is to stretch the arm of coincidence to
an incredible length. Again, HLP's letter is not merely misdated, for part of it is
applicable to '83 and not to '82.

some kindness for me, for which I beg you to accept my sincere thanks.

I am, Dear Sir, Your obliged humble servant,
June 11. 1782   Sam: Johnson
Oxford, at Mr Parker's, Bookseller

790. Oxford. W. 12 June '82. Mrs. Thrale.
Thomas L. Stix.—1788, No. 287.

Dear Madam

My Letter[1] was perhaps peevish, but it was not unkind, I should have cared little about a wanton expression, if there had been no kindness.

I find no particular salubrity in this air,[2] my respiration is very laborious. My appetite is good and my sleep commonly long and quiet. But a very little motion disables me.

I dine today with Dr. Adams, and tomorrow with Dr. Wetherel, and yesterday Dr. Edwards invited some Men from Exeter College whom I liked very well. These variations of company help the mind, though they cannot do much for the body. But the body receives some help from a cheerful mind.

Keep up some kindness for me; when I am with you again, I hope to be less burdensome, by being less sick.

I am, Dearest Lady, Your most humble Servant
Oxford. June 12. 1782   Sam: Johnson

791. Oxford. Th. 13 June '82. Mrs. Thrale (Streatham).
Address: To Mrs Thrale at Streatham Surry. *Postmark*: 14 IV.
C. Tildesley.—1788, No. 288.

Dear Madam

Yesterday a little physick drove away a great part of my cough, but I am still very much obstructed in my respiration and so soon tired with walking, that I have hardly ventured one unnecessary step. Of my long illness much more than

790.—1. 788. Hill conjectured 'any kindness'; 'no unkindness' is a better emendation, but I think none necessary. The 'kindness' is his, not hers, and he means 'If I had not loved you, I should not have resented your unfeeling irony.' Cf. 895, 'What did I care, if I did not love you?' I am (later) confirmed by the MS.

2. Hill quotes local authorities for the 'salubrity' of Oxford. One claims that 'the soil is dry, being on a fine gravel'. It is true there is gravel; there is also clay, and two rivers. The modern tendency is to represent the climate as worse than it is.

this does not remain, but this is very burthensome. I sleep pretty well, and have appetite enough, but I cheat it with fish.

Yesterday I dined at Dr. Adams's with Miss Moore, and other personages of eminence. To day I am going to Dr. Wetherel, and thus day goes after day, not wholly without amusement.

I think not to stay here long; Till I am better it is not prudent to sit long in the libraries, for the weather is yet so cold, that in the penury of fuel[1] for which we think ourselves very unhappy, I have yet met with none so frugal as to sit without fire.

                    I am, Madam, Your most humble Servant
Oxford. June 13. 1782   Sam: Johnson.

Poor Davis complained that he had not received his money for Boyle.[2]

791.1. Oxford. Th. 13 June '82. John Taylor.
Columbia University.—

Dear Sir

You will receive in this cover some letters written to me by Miss Collier, to which I really know not what answer to make. The Children are my near relations, and I would not spare any thing that could properly be done. I have not written to her, because I know not if I fully understand the business, and because I was afraid lest Mr Flint should be made more their enemy by our correspondence. I would write to Mr Flint, but that I know not well what topicks to urge. Consider the matter and tell me what to do as soon as You can. I am Dear Sir Your most &c
June 13. 1782   Sam: Johnson

792. Oxford. M. 17 June '82. Mrs. Thrale (Streatham).
Address: To Mrs Thrale at Streatham Surry.
Sotheby 15 Feb. 1926.—1788, No. 290.

Dear Madam

I have found no sudden alteration or amendment, but I am grown better by degrees. My cough is not now very

791.—1. See on 779.1.   2. No doubt a book sold by D, cf. 774.

troublesome to myself nor I hope to others; my breath is still short and encumbered; I do not sleep well, but I lie easy. By change of place, succession of company, and necessity of talking, much of the terrour that had seized me seems to be dispelled.

Oxford has done, I think, what for the present it can do, and I am going slyly to take a place in the coach for Wednesday, and on Thursday you or my sweet Queeney will fetch me [on Thursday], and see what you can make of me.

To day I am going to dine with Dr Wheeler and to morrow Dr Edwards has invited Miss Adams and Miss More. Yesterday I went with Dr Edwards to his living. He has really done all that he could do for my relief or entertainment, and really drives me away by doing too much.[1]

　　　　I am, Madam, Your most obedient servant
June 17. 1782 Oxford　　　　　　　Sam: Johnson.

When I come back to retirement it will be great charity in you to let me come back to something else.

792.1. M. 24 June '82. William Langley.
Not traced.—Quotation in Langley's letter to Johnson 14 Feb. 1783: *GM* Dec. 1878, 700.

Dr Taylor has engaged in their affair, and therefore it will be fit to let him act alone.

792.2. M. 24 June '82. James Burney.
Morgan Library.—
Sir

The Bearer is the young Man whom I have taken the liberty of recommending to your kindness. He is the son of a Clergyman very regular in his conduct, and decent in his manners. He will serve You I hope with diligence and fidelity, and I shall think myself favoured by your acceptance of his endeavours.

I congratulate You, Sir, upon your fine ship, and sincerely wish You all possible good. You have suffered hardships

792.—1. Hill was informed that in the two weeks covering J's visit, Vice-Principal Edwards's battels rose from an average of ten shillings to £2. 16s. 3d. and £4. 1s. Some of his colleagues also launched out. J styled E 'my convivial friend'.

792.2.—See 787.4.

sufficient, and I hope the time of recompense is not far distant. I am, Sir, your most humble Servant
London June 24. 1782   Sam: Johnson

792.3. Tu. 2 July '82. Elizabeth Lawrence.
Not traced; copy by R. B. Adam.—
Madam
    My remembrance of the kindness with which I was always treated by dear Dr Lawrence, and of the pleasure which his company has so often afforded me, makes me desirous of knowing from time to time the state of his health and of his mind. That such a mind should be so eclipsed produces very melancholy reflections. Perhaps he may have some happier intervals. Let me know how he goes forward, and let him know, if you can, with how much solicitude I enquire after him, and with how much earnestness I wish him better.
    Be pleased to make my compliments to all the Ladies.
        I am, Madam, Your most humble servant,
London. July 2. 1782.   Sam: Johnson

793. M. 8 July '82. John Taylor (Market Bosworth).
Address: To the Revd Dr Taylor in Ashbourne Derbyshire (redirected to Market Bosworth Leicestershire). *Postmarks*: 8 and 9 IY.
A. T. Loyd.—*NQ* 6 S. v. 461.
Dear Sir
    You are doubtless impatient to know the present state of the court. Dr Hunter whom I take to have very good intelligence has just left me, and from him I learn only that all is yet uncertainty and confusion.[1] Fox, you know, has resigned Burke's dismission is expected. I was particularly told that the Cavendishes were expected to be left out in the new settlement. The Doctor spoke, however, with very little confidence, nor do I believe that those who are now busy in the contest can judge of the event. I did not think Rockingham of such importance as that his death should have had such extensive consequences.

793.—1. Rockingham's death on 1 July was followed by the resignation of Fox and Lord John Cavendish, Chancellor of the Exchequer, on 5 July, and of Burke a few days later.

Have you settle⟨d⟩ about the silver coffeepot? is it mine or Mrs Fletcher's?[2] I am yet afraid of liking it too well.

If there is any thing that I can do for Miss Colliers,[3] let me know. But now You have so kindly engaged in it, I am willing to set myself at ease.

When you went away, I did not expect so long absence. If you are engaged in any political business, I suppose your operations are at present suspended, as is, I believe, the whole political movement. These are not pleasant times.

I came back from Oxford in ten days and was almost restored to health. My breath is not quite free but my cough is gone.

I am, Sir, Your most &c

London, July 8, 1782.   Sam: Johnson

793.1. M. 8 July '82. Richard Chambers (Newcastle).
Address: To Mr. R. Chambers in Newcastle Northumberland.
Sotheby 17 March 1930.—

Sir

Your solicitude for your Brother is such as a Brother like him deserves and might expect. I make this haste to tell you that I think the danger over. He will not be recalled this Session, and when the parliament meets again, there is likely to be other business. He will doubtless resign the place which has exposed him to censure; and when he no longer offends there will be no thought of animadversion. He was very well supported, and Smith was forced to confess that the house was generally on his side. He is, by the recal of Impey, now chief Justice, and, I do not see any reason why he may not enjoy his place till he wishes to return unless a new system of government should be formed and even then I know not why he should not be the first man to be consulted and employed. I am

Sir Your humble Servant

Sam. Johnson

London. July. 8. 1782 Boltcourt, Fleetstreet.

793.—2. See 767.1.
3. J is capable of 'Colliers' for Collier, but he usually writes of the girls in the plural, and here probably means 'Misses Collier', see 795.

793.2. Su. 14 July '82. Frances Reynolds.

Address: To Mrs Reynolds.
W. R. Batty.—

Dear Madam

If You are at home, and desirous of seeing me, I will wait upon You, but it is too late now to carry the letter that we talked of. If it will be equally convenient to You, I will come on Monday about noon. I am, Madam,

Your humble Servant

July 14.—82   Sam: Johnson

794. M. 22 July '82. Elizabeth Lawrence (Canterbury).

Address: To Mʳˢ Eliz. Laurence in Castle St. Canterbury.
Copy (source not now known).—Boswell 1791, ii. 418, an extract from a copy (now Isham) by E. L. (Hill iv. 144).

Madam

I was not without suspicion of the cause why my letter was not answered sooner.

Mʳ John Laurence had called and given me part of the account contained in your letter, he has been here today the second time, and has just left me. His cough is abated, but his voice seems hoarse, and I advised him to a mild vegetable diet.

You will easily believe with what gladness I read that you had heard once again that voice to which we have all so often delighted to attend. May you often hear it. If we had his mind and his tongue we could spare the rest.

I am not vigorous, but much better than when dear Dʳ Lawrence held my pulse the last time. Be so kind as to let me know from one little interval to another the state of his body. I am pleased that he remembers me, and hope it never can be possible for me to forget him.

Make my compliments to all the ladies.

I am Madam Your most humble servant

July 22. 1782. London.   Samuel Johnson.

795. M. 22 July '82. John Taylor (Market Bosworth).
Address: To the Reverend Dr Taylor at Market Bosworth Leicester-
shire. *Postmark*: 22 IY.
A. T. Loyd.—*NQ* 6 S. v. 461.

Dear Sir

I do not hear that the Cavendishes are likely to find their
⟨way⟩ soon into publick offices, but I do not doubt of the
Duke's ability to procure the exchange for which he has
stipulated, and which is now not so much a favour as a
contract. Your reason for the exchange I do not fully
comprehend, but I conceive myself a Gainer by it, because,
I think, you must be more in London.

Mr. Burke's family is computed to have lost by this
revolution twelve thousand a year. What a rise, and what a
fall. Shelburne speaks of him in private with great malignity.

I have heard no more from the Miss Colliers. Now you
have engaged on their side, I am less solicitous about them.
Be on their side as much as you can, for you know they are
friendless.

Sir Robert Chambers slipped this session through the
fingers of revocation, but I am in doubt of his continuance.
Shelburne seems to be his enemy. Mrs. Thrale says they
will do him no harm. She perhaps thinks there is no harm
without hanging. The mere act of recall strips him of eight
thousand a year.[1]

I am not very well, but much better than when we parted,
and I hope that milk and summer together are improving
you, and strengthening you against the attack of winter.

        I am Dear Sir Your most affectionate
London July 22 1782   Sam: Johnson.

796. Su. 28 July '82. John Perkins.
Address: To Mr Perkins.
O. T. Perkins.—Boswell 1793, iii. 415 (Hill iv. 153).

Dear Sir

I am much pleased that You are going a very long Journey,
which may by proper conduct restore your health and prolong your life.

795.—1. See 793.1. According to authorities cited by Hill, C's salary was £6,000.
There might be perquisites.

Observe these rules

1 Turn all care out of your head as soon as you mount the chaise

2 Do not think about frugality, your health is worth more than it can cost.

3 Do not continue any day's journey to fatigue.

4 Take now and then a day's rest.

5. Get a smart seasickness if you can.

6 Cast away all anxiety, and keep your mind easy.

This last direction is the principal; with an unquiet mind neither exercise, nor diet, nor physick can be of much use.

I wish You, dear Sir, a prosperous Journey, and a happy recovery, for[1] I am

Dear Sir Your most affectionate humble Servant

July 28. 1782   Sam: Johnson

797. Sa. 3 (misdated 4) Aug. '82. John Taylor (Market Bosworth).

Address: To the Reverend Dr Taylor in Ashbourne Derbyshire (redirected to Market Bosworth Leicestershire). *Postmark*: 3 AV. National Library of Scotland.—Morrison Catalogue 1885, ii. 343.

Dear Sir

The refusal of Mr Dixie, if it be peremptory and final, puts an end to all projects of exchange.[1] You may however, if your friends get into power, obtain preferment. But do not be any further solicitous about it; leave the world a while to itself.

I now direct to Ashbourne, where, I suppose, you are settled for a while, and where I beg you to do what you can for the poor Colliers.

I have no national news that is not in the papers, and almost all news is bad. Perhaps no nation not absolutely conquered has declined so much in so short a time. We seem to be sinking. Suppose the Irish having already gotten a free trade and an independent parliament, should say we will have a King, and ally ourselves with the house of Bourbon, what could be done to hinder or to overthrow them?

796.—1. 'for' om. 1791.

797.—1. See 795.

Poor dear Dr Lawrence is gone to die at Canterbury. He has lost his speech, and the action of his right side, with very little hope of recovering them.

We must all go. I was so exhausted by loss of blood, and by successive disorders in the beginning of this year that I am afraid that the remaining part will hardly restore me. I have indeed rather indulged myself too much, and think to begin a stricter regimen. As it is my friends tell me from time to time, that I look better, and I am very willing to believe them. Do you likewise take care of your health, we cannot well spare one another.

I am, dear Sir, Yours affectionately,

London Aug. 4. 1782   Sam: Johnson.

798. M. 12 Aug. '82. John Taylor (Ashbourne).

Address: To the Reverend Dr Taylor in Ashbourne Derbyshire.
Postmark: 13 AV.
Morgan Library.—Hill 1892.

Dear Sir

I calculate this letter to meet you at Ashbourne, whither I hope you are well enough to come according to your purpose. And I write to warn you very carefully against useless and unnecessary vexation. To be robbed is very offensive, but you have been robbed of nothing that you can feel the want of. Let not the loss, nor the circumstances of the loss take any hold upon your mind. This loss will in a short time repair itself, but you have a greater loss, the loss of health which must be repaired by your own prudence and diligence, and of which nothing can more obstruct the reparation than an uneasy mind.

But how are you to escape uneasiness? By company and business. Get and keep about you those with whom you are most at ease, and contrive for your mornings something to do, and bustle about it as much as you can. If you think London a place of more amusement come hither, or take any other kind of harmless diversion, but diversion of some kind or other you cannot at present be without. To muse and think will do you much harm, and if you are alone and at leisure, troublesome thoughts will force themselves upon you.

Be particularly careful now to drink enough, and to avoid costiveness; you will find that vexation has much more power over you, ridiculous as it may seem, if you neglect to evacuate your body.

I have now had three quiet nights together, which, I suppose, I have not for[1] more than a year before. I hope we shall both grow better, and have a longer enjoyment of each other.

I am, Dear Sir, Yours affectionately,
August 12. 1782. London   Sam: Johnson

798.1. Sa. 17 Aug. '82. ⟨?   ⟩.
Bodleian—William Cotton, *Reynolds's Notes on Pictures* 1859, 73 (headed 'Dr. Johnson to ——').
Sir
When the sheet that relates to the publication of the *English*[1] *Iliad* comes to hand, be so kind as to keep it till we can talk together. There is a passage in the Life of Bowyer upon which we should confer. I am Sir Your most humble servant
Aug. 17. 1782   Sam: Johnson

799. Sa. 17 Aug. '82. John Taylor (Ashbourne).
Address: To the Reverend Dr Taylor in Ashbourne Derbyshire.
Postmark: —AV.
Tregaskis (1923).—Hill 1892.
Dear Sir
Though I follow you thus with letters, I have not much to say. I write because I would hear from you the state of your health and of your mind. Upon your mind in my opinion your health will very much depend, and I therefore repeat my injunction of bustle and cheerfulness. Do not muse by

798.—1. A word erased after 'for', probably 'eighteen'. Eighteen months is approximately the duration of his illness as stated 801.

798.1.—The recipient might, in spite of the reference to 'the Life of Bowyer', be Nichols himself; but how should the letter escape from those retentive hands? In *Anecdotes of Mr. Bowyer* 1782, 502–3, details of the editions of the *Iliad* are given, and ¶¶76–9 of J's *Life* are quoted. See Hill's edition for the material changes made by J in the edition of 1783.

1. It is unlikely that J underlined 'English'; in the first edition of the Life of Pope, 1781, the phrase is printed 'English *Iliad*'.

yourself; do not suffer yourself to be an hour without something to do. Suffer nothing disagreeable to approach you after dinner.

Of the publick I have nothing to say, there seem to be expectations of a violent session when the factions meet. Nor have I much to say of myself but that I think myself freed from all the supervenient distempers of this year, and as well as when I was with you. My great complaint now is unquietness in the night.

Do not let me write again before I am told how you do. It is reasonable that you and I should be anxious for each other; our ages are not very different, and we have lived long together.

I am, Dear Sir, Your affectionate &c

Aug. 17. 1782   Sam: Johnson

Do not fret.

800. M. 19 Aug. '82. George Strahan.

Address: To the Reverend Mr Strahan.
Sotheby 11 Feb. 1929.—Hill 1892.

Sir

I have not yet read your letter through and therefore cannot answer it particularly. Of what you say so far as I have read all is I think, true but the application. What I told him[1] of your discontent on many occasions was to not[2] provoke him but to pacify him, by representing that discontent of which he complained so much, not as any personal disrespect to him but as a cast of mind which you had always had. Your discontent on many occasions has appeared to me little short of madness, which however I did not tell him. Then your uneasiness at Oxford was a weak thing which passed for an instance by which I do not see how he could be inflamed. The whole tendency of what I said was this, 'He is you say discontented, if he is, it is not by any personale disesteem of you, he is apt to be discontented.'

As to the matter of the money I am much of the mind that you have represented. But I did not think nor think now

800.—1. George's father.
        2. Sic in MS.

that I said any thing that would hinder your father from any act of liberality.

You may be sure, I am sure, I had no intention to hurt you, and if I have hurt you, nothing that I can do shall be omitted to repair the hurt.

You may well be at a loss to conjecture why I should injure you, whom certainly I have no reason to injure, and whom I would suffer much ⟨rather⟩³ than injure by design, and shall be very sorry if I have done it by that train of talk which I was drawn into without design and almost without remembrance. If I have really done you harm I shall live in hope of doing you sometime as much good, though good is not so easily done.

I am Sir, Your most, &c

Aug. 19. 1782   Sam: Johnson

801. Sa. 24 Aug. '82. James Boswell (Edinburgh).

Not traced.—Boswell 1791, ii. 425 (Hill iv. 153).

Dear Sir

Being uncertain whether I should have any call this autumn into the country, I did not immediately answer your kind letter. I have no call, but if you desire to meet me at Ashbourne, I believe I can come thither; if you had rather come to London, I can stay at Streatham; take your choice.

This year has been very heavy. From the middle of January to the middle of June I was battered by one disorder after another; I am now very much recovered, and hope still to be better. What happiness it is that Mrs. Boswell has escaped.

My 'Lives' are reprinting, and I have forgotten the authour of Gray's character:¹ write immediately, and it may be perhaps yet inserted.

Of London or Ashbourne you have your free choice; at any place I shall be glad to see you. I am, dear Sir,

your, &c.

Aug. 24, 1782.   Sam. Johnson.

800.—3. Hill's conjecture. Dr. Onions tells me the passage will not make sense without some supplement.

801.—1. Temple. The acknowledgement was made in the edition of 1783.

802. M. 26 Aug. '82. Elizabeth Lawrence (Canterbury).

Address: To Mrs Eliz Laurence in Castle Street Canterbury. *Postmark*: 26 av.

Adam; copy by E. L. Isham.—Boswell 1791, ii. 425 (Hill iv. 144).

Madam   August 26 1782

I am much delighted even with the small advances which dear Dr Lawrence makes towards recovery. If we could have again but his mind and his tongue, or his mind and his right hand, we would not much lament the rest. I should not despair of helping the swelled hand by electricity, if it were frequently and diligently applied.

Let me know from time to time whatever happens. I hope I need not tell you how much I am interested in every change.

Please to make my compliments to all the Ladies.

I am, Madam, Your most humble servant

Sam: Johnson

I am much better than I was when you last saw me.

803. Sa. 7 Sept. '82. James Boswell (Edinburgh).

Not traced.—Boswell 1791, ii. 426 (Hill iv. 154).

Dear Sir

I have struggled through this year with so much infirmity of body, and such strong impressions of the fragility of life, that death, wherever it appears, fills me with melancholy; and I cannot hear without emotion, of the removal of any one, whom I have known, into another state.

Your father's death had every circumstance that could enable you to bear it; it was at a mature age, and it was expected; and as his general life had been pious, his thoughts had doubtless for many years past been turned upon eternity. That you did not find him sensible must doubtless grieve you; his disposition towards you was undoubtedly that of a kind, though not of a fond father. Kindness, at least actual, is in our power, but fondness is not; and if by negligence or imprudence you had extinguished his fondness, he could not at will rekindle it. Nothing then remained between you but

803.—JB had written from Auchinleck 30 Aug. 'that my honoured father had died that morning' (*L* iv. 154). In his journal he does not mention J, but records 'Up all night . . . writing letters in a giddy state' (*BP* xv. 121).

mutual forgiveness of each other's faults, and mutual desire of each other's happiness.

I shall long to know his final disposition of his fortune.

You, dear Sir, have now a new station, and have therefore new cares, and new employments. Life, as Cowley seems to say,[1] ought to resemble a well ordered poem; of which one rule generally received is, that the exordium should be simple, and should promise little. Begin your new course of life with the least show, and the least expence possible; you may at pleasure encrease both, but you cannot easily diminish them. Do not think your estate your own, while any man can call upon you for money which you cannot pay; therefore, begin with timorous parsimony. Let it be your first care not to be in any man's debt.

When the thoughts are extended to a future state, the present life seems hardly worthy of all those principles of conduct, and maxims of prudence, which one generation of men has transmitted to another; but upon a closer view, when it is perceived how much evil is produced, and how much good is impeded by embarrassment and distress, and how little room the expedients of poverty leave for the exercise of virtue; it grows[2] manifest that the boundless importance of the next life, enforces some attention to the interests of this.

Be kind to the old servants, and secure the kindness of the agents and factors; do not disgust them by asperity, or unwelcome gaiety, or apparent suspicion. From them you must learn the real state of your affairs, the characters of your tenants, and the value of your lands.

Make my compliments to Mrs. Boswell; I think her expectations from air and exercise are the best that she can form. I hope she will live long and happily.

803.—1. 'seems to say' should naturally imply that Cowley's language is obscure, which it is not. But J may refer to the hypothetical expression of his quotation, which is from the 'Ode upon Liberty': 'If Life should a well-order'd Poem be | (In which he only hits the white | Who joyns true Profit with the best Delight) | The more Heroique strain let others take, | Mine the Pindarique way I'le make.'

2. So 1793; 1791 has 'its sorrows'. We have here a rare example of a 1793 correction, clearly editorial, of a document printed in 1791. One cannot be sure that the correction was made by reference to the original, and the corruption of 'it grows' to 'its sorrows' does not seem very easy; 'it becomes' would perhaps more easily be so misread.

I forget whether I told you that Rasay[3] has been here; we dined cheerfully together. I entertained lately a young gentleman from Corrichatachin.[4]

I received your letters[5] only this morning. I am, dear Sir, yours, &c.

London, Sept. 7, 1782.   Sam. Johnson.

804. See before 815.

805. Sa. 21 Sept. '82. James Boswell (Edinburgh).

Not traced.—Boswell 1791, ii. 427 (Hill iv. 155).

In answer to my next letter, I received one from him, dissuading me from hastening to him as I had proposed; what is proper for publication is the following paragraph, equally just and tender.

One expence, however, I would not have you to spare: let nothing be omitted that can preserve Mrs. Boswell, though

803.—3. Macleod. J noted in his diary under 11 Aug. 'Raasa. Hoole'.

4. Doubtless a Mackinnon. 'Corrichatachin' is a correction 1793 of 'Coriatachat' 1791. J no doubt wrote 'Coriatachan' (as in his *Journey*). The late Prof. Fraser confirmed me in the opinion that this was a phonetic spelling; J did not hear the guttural *cb*.   5. 'letters' should probably be 'letter'.

805.—The date is given in J's diary now in the Bodleian. After his father's funeral JB rejoined his wife in Edinburgh. They went to Auchinleck on 17–18 Sept. In spite of her illness JB intended to go to London 24 Sept. He proposed delay, but she 'thought I had better go now and be back for business. I parted with her sorry. But Dr. J's wisdom was highly requisite.' On 25 Sept., however, having started, he was overtaken by the news of 'a violent fit of spitting of blood' and 'rode home in agitation'. On 27 Sept. he 'got a letter (805) from Dr. Johnson which settled me not to go'. (For J's advice to JB see his description of it, to JT, in 807.) *BP* xv. 124–5. JB's 'next letter' (*L* iv. 155), that is, a letter of *c.* mid-Sept., to which 805 replied, is not in the journal.

But a further letter to J of 1 Oct., not mentioned in the *Life* nor recorded in JB's journal, is preserved among the Malahide papers and is printed *BP* xv. 248. JB's unpublished Register describes this letter, and proves that he kept a copy of it. Dr. Pottle, however, tells me that the physical nature of the Malahide document, which was folded as a letter was folded, all but proves that it is not the copy but the original. My guess is that JB failed to use this letter in the *Life* because he had mis-laid it, and that it has survived for the same reason, whereas the letters used in the *Life* were kept together and, so far as is known, perished together. In this letter JB tells J the whole story: how he 'hovered here, in fluttering anxiety to be with you', and finally set out only to return, and was finally 'settled' when 'your most excellent letter forcibly dissuading me from *deserting my station* arrived'. The three words in italic are no doubt quoted from the missing part of 805. 'My Wife', JB goes on, 'was so affected by your letter that she shed tears of grateful joy, and declared she would write to you herself. Accordingly you have enclosed the spontaneous effusion of her heart, which I cannot doubt will interest you.' In the *Life* (iv. 155) JB describes this 'effusion': 'My wife was now so much convinced of his sincere friendship for me, and it should be necessary to transplant her for a time into a softer climate. She is the prop and stay of your life. How much must your children suffer by losing her.

806. Sa. 21 Sept. '82. John Taylor (Ashbourne).
Address: To the Reverend Dr Taylor in Ashbourne Derbyshire.
Sotheby 31 March 1875 (not seen).—Hill 1892 (from a copy).

Dear Sir,

Your letter about a week ago told me that your health is mended. Health is the basis of all happiness [of] this world gives. Your loss[1] likewise seems to be less than I had feared.

Of the probability of Shelburne's continuance[2] I can make no judgment. Sickness has this year thrown me out of the world; but I think myself growing better.

The proposal of Miss Colliers seems to be wild. If I understand it right, they wish that he should lend them money, that they may sue him for the estate.

I hope to[3] let them know that if they send me their Grandfather's will, I will get some opinion upon it.

If they want money to procure it from the registry I will repay you what you advance as far as ten pounds.

Take great care of your health. Let nothing disturb you. Particularly avoid costiveness, and open no letter of business but in the morning.

If you would have me write to Mr. Langley,[4] about Miss Colliers, let me know. I will do anything for them that is proper.

I am, Sir, Yours affectionately,

Sept. 21, 1782. Sam: Johnson.

regard for her, that, without any suggestion on my part, she wrote him a very polite end grateful letter'. As Dr. Pottle remarks (*BP* xv. 244), JB here refers to her letter 'in such a style that one thinks he is going to print it'. Perhaps that was his intention. He may have expected to find it. Instead, however, the words 'grateful letter:' (the colon may be significant?) are followed in the *Life* by the text of J's letter to Mrs. B of 7 Dec. (804, see below before 815) which is misdated 7 Sept. All we have of Mrs. B is her rather colourless letter of thanks dated 20 Dec. and printed *L* iv. 157. Finally, Dr. Pottle's correction of the date of 804 explains J's silence about Mrs. B in 815, which would otherwise be very strange. There is, it is true, a suppressed passage in that letter; but JB would not have suppressed a reference to his wife's health.

806.—1. By robbery, 798. 2. As prime minister. It lasted till 5 Apr. '83.
  3. Perhaps J wrote 'you'.
  4. The owner of the letter, who sent Hill a copy, read this doubtfully as 'Hayley' or 'Layley'. Hill's 'Langley' is certain.

806.1. Th. 3 Oct. '82. Philip Metcalfe.

Not traced.—Boswell 1791, ii. 429 (Hill iv. 170); overlooked by Hill in 1892.

Mr. Johnson is very much obliged by the kind offer of the carriage; but he has no desire of using Mr. Metcalfe's carriage, except when he can have the pleasure of Mr. Metcalfe's company.

807. Th. 3 (misdated 4) Oct. '82. John Taylor (Ashbourne).

Address: To the Reverend Dr Taylor in Ashbourn Derbyshire. *Postmark*: 3 oc.
A. T. Loyd.—*NQ* 6 S. v. 462.

Dear Sir

To help the ignorant commonly requires much patience, for the ignorant are always trying to be cunning. To do business by letters is very difficult, for without the opportunity of verbal questions much information is seldom obtained.

I received, I suppose, by the coach a copy of Dunn's will, and an abstract of Mr. Flint's marriage settlement. By whom they were sent I know not. The copy of the Will is so worn, that it is troublesome to open it, and has no attestation to evince its authenticity. The extract is, I think, in Mr. Flint's own hand, and has not therefore any legal credibility.

What seems to me proper to be done, but you know much better than I, is to take an exemplification of the will from the registry. We are then so far sure. This will I entreat you to read, if it be clear and decisive against the Girls, there can be no farther use of it. If you think it doubtful send it to Mr. Madox, and I will pay the fee.

When the will is despatched the marriage settlement is to be examined, which if Mr. Flint refuses to shew, he gives such ground of suspicion as will justify a legal compulsion to shew it.

It may perhaps be better that I should appear busy in this matter than you, and if you think it best, I will write to Lichfield that a copy of the will may be sent to you, for I would have you read it. I should be told the year of Mr. Dunn's death.

I think[1] the generosity of Mr. Flint somewhat suspicious.

807.—1. J originally wrote 'Both You and I think'. The erasure may be JT's, for whose erasures in J's letters see App. D.

I have however not yet condemned him nor would irritate him too much, for perhaps the Girls must at last be content with what he shall give them.

My letter, which you shewed to Miss Collier, she did not understand, but supposed that I charged her with asking money of Mr. Flint, in order to sue him. I only meant that her proposal was to him eventually the same, and was therefore, as I called it, wild.

I hope your health improves. I am told that I look better and better. I am going, idly enough, to Brighthelmston. I try, as I would have you do, to keep my body open, and my mind quiet.

I hope my attention grows more fixed. When I was last at your house I began, if I remember right, another perusal of the Bible[2] which notwithstanding all my disorders I have read through except the Psalms. I concluded, the twenty second of last month. I hope for as many years as God shall grant me, to read it through at least once every year.

Boswels Father is dead, and Boswel wrote me word that he would come to London, for my advice. ⟨The⟩[3] advice[4] which I sent him is to stay at home and ⟨busy⟩ himself with his own affairs. He has a good es⟨tate con⟩siderably burthened by settlements, and he is himself ⟨....⟩ in debt. But if his Wife lives I think he will be prudent.

I am, Sir, Yours affectiona⟨tely⟩
London Oct. 4. 1782   Sam: Johnson.

808. Su. 6 Oct. '82. James Compton.

Address (Malone): To the Reverend Mr. Compton.
Not traced.—Malone's Boswell 1811, iv. 225.

Sir

I have directed Dr. Vyse's letter to be sent to you, that you may know the situation of your business. Delays are incident

---

807.—2. For J's perusal of the Bible, 'a very great part of which I had never looked upon', in '71–'72, see *PM* 18 and 26 Apr. '72, *L* ii. 495. Direct quotation is not frequent in the *Life* or the letters, nor, I think, in the works. But his familiarity with many parts of the Bible, in several versions, is clear enough.

3. The paper is torn at the edge. The restoration is simple except for a word, which cannot be long, before 'in debt'. The fragment of the first letter suggests a *d*, and my guess is 'deep'.   4. See 805.

808.—For J's assistance to C see Hawkins 530 quoted by Hill, and below, 811.1, 835.

to all affairs; but there appears nothing in your case of either superciliousness or neglect. Dr. Vyse seems to wish you well.

I am, Sir, your most humble servant,

Oct. 6, 1782.   Sam: Johnson.

809. Brighthelmston. Th. 10 Oct. '82. George Strahan (Islington).

Address: To the Reverend Mr Strahan at Islington London.
Sotheby 11 Feb. 1929.—Hill 1892.

Sir

When I called last week, to do a little business in New Street, I found the difference between you and your Father still subsisting, and though I have reason to think you sufficiently prejudiced against my advice, I will, without much anxiety about my reception, suggest some reasons, for which, in my opinion, you ought to make peace as soon as you can.

All quarrels grow more complicated by time, and as they grow more complicated, grow harder to be adjusted.

When a dispute is made publick by references and appeals, which neither your Father nor you have enough avoided there mingles with interest or resentment a foolish feint of honour. Perhaps each part would yield, were not each ashamed.

Your dispute has already gone so far, that the first concession ought to come from you, since you may without any disgrace yield to your Father, and your Father will hardly yield to you, but with some dishonour to both.

You might therefore properly make the first advances, even if your Father were in the wrong, of which, if I understand the question, you will find it difficult to convict him.

When a Man is asked for money which he does not owe he has a right to enquire, why the demand is made.

When you tell him that you ask for money because you want it, he may again very reasonably enquire why you are in want who have already much more than is generally appendant to your station.

To this question it is my advice that you give a calm, decent, and general answer. Neither your Friends wish, nor, I suppose, your Father wishes that you should show bills and receipts, though of those you need not be ashamed, for nobody suspects your expences of anything vitious, but that you should tell in a manly and liberal way why your income falls short of your desires.

With a general account, such as may liberally give him the victory, your Father will probably be satisfied, and this account it will be prudent rather to write than to give in person, though to a written account there may be objection. You will use your discretion.

My serious, and whatever you may think, my friendly advice is that you make haste to reconciliation. Those who encourage either to persist, mean ill to one of you, perhaps without meaning well to the other, or without much malice or any kindness divert themselves with your discord, and are quietly amused by guessing the event.

I am, Sir Your most humble Servant
Brighthelmston Oct. 10. 1782   Sam: Johnson.

810. Brighthelmston. Th. 10 Oct. '82. John Nichols.

Address: To Mr Nicol.
B.M.—*GM* Dec. 1784, 893; Boswell 1791, ii. 430, extract (Hill iv. 161).

Sir

While I am at Brighthelmston, if you have any need of consulting me, Mr. Strahan will do us the favour to transmit our papers under his frank. I have looked often into your Anecdotes,[1] and you will hardly thank a lover of literary history for telling you that he has been informed and gratified.

I wish you would add your own discoveries and intelligence to those of Dr Rawlinson, and undertake the Supplement to Wood.[2] Think on it.

I am, Sir, Your humble servant,
Brighthelmston Oct. 10. 1782   Sam: Johnson.

810.—1. Of Bowyer.
2. For Rawlinson's MS. collections see *L* iv. 161.

811. Brighthelmston. Th. 22 Oct. '82. Mauritius Lowe.

Address: To Mr Lowe.

Adam.—Croker's Boswell 1831, v. 35.

Sir

I congratulate you on the good that has befallen you. I always told you that it would come. I would not however have you flatter yourself too soon with punctuality. You must not expect the other half year at Christmas. You may use the money as your needs require, but save what you can.

You must undoubtedly write a letter of thanks to your benefactor in your own name. I have put something on the other side.

I am, Sir, Your most humble servant,

Oct. 22. 1782 Sam: Johnson

811.1. Brighthelmston. Th. 24 Oct. '82. James Compton.

Address: To the Reverend Mr Compton. In the post to Mrs Williams.

Harvard.—J. T. Fields, *Underbrush*, Boston 1877, 17.

Sir

Your business, I suppose, is in a way of as easy progress as such business ever has. It is seldom that event keeps pace with expectation.

The Scheme of your book I cannot say that I fully comprehend. I would not have you ask less than an hundred Guineas, for it seems a large octavo.

Go to Mr Davies in Russel Street, show him this letter, and show him the book if he desires to see it. He will tell

---

811.—On the verso is J's draft of L's acknowledgement. It was no doubt addressed to Lord Southwell.

My Lord

The allowance which you are pleased to make me, I received on the . . . by Mr Paget. Of the joy which it brought your Lordship cannot judge, because you cannot imagine my distress. It was long since I had known a morning without solicitude for noon, or lain down at night without foreseeing with terrour the distresses of the morning. My debts were small but many; my creditors were poor and therefore troublesome. Of this misery your Lordship's bounty has given me an intermission. May your Lordship live long to do much good, and to do for many what you have done for

My Lord Your Lordships &c
Lowe

811.1.—I cannot find that Compton ever published a book.

You what hopes you may form, and to what Bookseller You should apply.

If You succeed in selling your book, You may do better than by dedicating it to me.[1] You may perhaps obtain permission to dedicate it to the Bishop of London or to Dr Vyse, and make way by your book to more advantage than I can procure You.

Please to tell Mrs Williams that I grow better and that I wish to know how she goes on. You, Sir, may write for her to, Sir, Your most humble servant

Octr 24. 1782   Sam: Johnson

811.2. Brighthelmston. Th. 24 Oct. '82. William Strahan.

Address: To William Strahan Esq M.P. in London. Stamped FREE. Morgan Library.—

Sir

I am very much obliged by your kind enquiries. When I came hither I was so breathless and encumbred that I stopped four times to rest between the inn and the lodging, a space perhaps as great as from your house to Black Friers. I can walk better now. We have a deep Well, when I came I suffered so much in letting down the bucket, that I never tried to pull it up. But I have done both to day with little trouble. By such experiments I perceive my own advances. I have likewise much easier nights. I have evacuated much, but without bleeding, and have lived sparingly. The success of my endeavours has really been beyond my hopes. This is a place where one lives much one's own way, and one is not much hindred in a regimen.

I hope dear Mrs Strahan and you are both well and will long continue well.

                              I am Sir your humble servant
Oct: 24. 1782   Sam: Johnson

811.1.—1. For dedication to a scholar see on 739. In his diary for '82, now in the Bodleian, J records two lost letters: 9 Sept. 'to Vyse about Compton', 7 Nov. 'to Compton'.

812. Brighthelmston. M. 28 Oct. '82. John Nichols.

Address: To Mr Nicol.
B.M.; the sentence printed by Nichols as a postscript is on a separate scrap of paper.—*GM* Dec. 1784, 893, and Jan. 1785, 11; Boswell 1791, ii. 430, extract dated 20 Oct. (Hill iv. 161).

Dear Sir

You somehow forgot the advertisement[1] for the new Edition. It was not enclosed.

Of Gay's letters[2] I see not that any use can be made, for they give no information of any thing. That he was member of the philosophical Society is something, but surely he could be but a corresponding member. However not having his Life here I know not how to put it in, and it is of little importance.

What will the Booksellers give me for this new Edition? I know not what to ask.[3] I would have 24 sets bound in plain calf, and figured with number of the volumes. For the rest they may please themselves.

I wish, Sir, you could obtain some fuller information of Jortin, Markland, and Thirlby. They were three contemporaries of great eminence.

I am Sir, Your most humble servant

Oct. 28, 1782   Sam: Johnson
    This is all that I can think on therefore send it to the press, and fare it well.[4] Sam: Johnson.

812.—1. That is, no doubt, a proof of the 'Advertisement' to the 1783 *Lives*.

2. No use was made in the new edition of letters, or of G's membership of 'the philosophical society', which Hill supposed to be the Spalding Society, of which Nichols records that 'John Gay esq. lepidissimus poeta' was a member.

3. J's receipt for £100 'for Revising the last Edition', dated 19 Feb. '83, was in the Morrison collection. Hill notes that below this receipt is pasted the following paper in his writing: 'It is great impudence to put Johnson's Poets on the back of books which Johnson neither recommended nor revised. He recommended only Blackmore on the Creation and Watts. How then are they Johnson's? This is indecent.'

4. Nichols explains in a note that this was the 'advertisement', i.e. copy for it. This does not contradict the first sentence of the letter, for we do not know the date of the 'postscript'.

812.1. Sa. 9 Nov. '82. Mrs. Thrale (Brighthelmston).

Address: To Mrs Thrale.
Copy by C. B. Tinker.—

Madam   Saturday Nov 9, 1782
  Mr Metcalf has found so many places worthy of curiosity
in our way, that we cannot find our way home to day. I hope
to wait on you to morrow. I am,
                          Madam, Your most humble Servant
                                              Sam: Johnson.

813. Brighthelmston. Th. 14 Nov. '82. Joshua Reynolds.

Address: To Sir Joshua Reynolds in London. *Postmark* illegible.
Fettercairn.—Boswell 1791, ii. 430 (Hill iv. 161).

Dear Sir
  I heard yesterday of your late disorder,[1] and should think
ill of myself if I had heard of it without alarm. I heard likewise of your recovery which I sincerely wish to be complete
and permanent. Your Country has been in danger of losing
one of its brightest ornaments, and I, of losing one of my
oldest and kindest Friends, but I hope You will still live long
for the honour of the Nation, and that more enjoyment of
your elegance, your intelligence, and your benevolence is
still reserved for, Dear Sir, Your most affectionate and most
humble Servant
Brighthelmston Nov. 14. 1782   Sam: Johnson

814. Brighthelmston. Th. 14 Nov. '82. William Strahan.

Address: To William Strahan Esq M. P. London. *Postmark* illegible.
Adam.—Hill 1892.

Sir
  Your kindness gives you a right to such intelligence relat-
ing to myself as I can give you.
  My Friends all tell me that I am grown much better since

812.1.—FB records 'Thursday' (7 Nov.) 'Mr. Metcalf called upon Dr. Johnson, and
took him out an airing'. She does not record their more ambitious excursion of
8–10 Nov. to Arundel, Chichester, Cowdrey, Petworth, &c. (*Diary* ii. 177, *L* iv. 506).
There is no mention of M in *Tb*, in which the autobiographical part is very scanty
for this visit to B'n. But Fanny is full of him.

813.—1. 'A slight paralytic affection' Northcote, *Reynolds* (1818) ii. 131. FB wrote
28 Dec.: 'But how, my dearest Susy, can you wish any wishes about Sir Joshua and
me? A man who has had two shakes of the palsy!' (*Diary* ii. 218).

my arrival at this place. I do not for my own part think myself well, but I certainly mend.

I shall not stay here above a week longer,[1] and indeed it is not easy to tell why we stay so long, for the company is gone.

Last Fryday or Saturday there was at this place the greatest take of herrings that has been ever known. The number caught was eight lasts, which at eight thousand a last, make eight hundred thousand.[2]

I am Sir Your most humble servant

Brighthelmston Nov. 14. 1782   Sam: Johnson

Make my compliments to dear Mrs Strahan

814.1. Sa. 30 Nov. '82. Mrs. Thrale.
Address: To Mrs Thrale.
Rylands.—R. L. *Bull.* Jan. 1932, 37.

Madam

Nothing that you say has any other effect upon my opinion, than to make me rest in the sullen conclusion that what is past is past. You have only turned uncoined silver into silver coined.[1]

Your fathers case[2] and yours have an essential difference which I cannot now explain, but will try to do it if ever you will hear me. With regard to my self I am obliged to you for thinking my quiet worth an apology.

I am Dearest, dearest, Your most humble servant

Nov. 30. 1782   Sam: Johnson

814.2. Tu. 3 Dec. '82. John Perkins.
Address: To Mr Perkins.
O. T. Perkins.—

Dear Sir

Macqueen had, as I find, two volumes of the Rambler, and

814.—1. They left for Argyll Street 20 Nov. FB's *Diary* ii. 184.
    2. Sic in MS.

814.1.—1. J's diary for 30 Nov. has the laconic entry 'Plate sold'. This must be HLT's, for why should he sell his own? HT's will had left her S'm for life only, but its contents absolutely. For her financial stress see C 214–15.

    2. This perhaps refers to Lady Salusbury's claim, which rested on a transaction in which HLT's father was concerned. See C 19, 211, and J. D. Wright, *Unpublished Letters to and from Dr. Johnson* 1932 (the corrected reprint), 44.

814.2.—I have not identified Macqueen; Scot may be 'our Neighbour Scott' of *Th* 220. The application to Perkins suggests that the books belonged to the S'm library, not to J's own.

two of Burnet's History. They make sets imperfect, and therefore I wish Mr Scot could be so kind as to enquire after them, and recover them.

I was much delighted to see you so well yesterday. I am, Sir,

Your humble Servant
Dec.ʳ. 3. 1782   Sam: Johnson

804. Sa. 7 Dec. '82. Margaret Boswell (Edinburgh).
Not traced.—Boswell 1791, ii. 427, misdated 7 Sept. (Hill iv. 156).
Dear Lady

I have not often received so much pleasure as from your invitation to Auchinleck. The journey thither and back is, indeed, too great for the latter part of the year; but if my health were fully recovered, I would suffer no little heat and cold, nor a wet or a rough road to keep me from you. I am, indeed, not without hope of seeing Auchinleck again; but to make it a pleasant place I must see its lady well, and brisk, and airy. For my sake, therefore, among many greater reasons, take care, dear Madam, of your health, spare no expence, and want no attendance that can procure ease, or preserve it. Be very careful to keep your mind quiet; and do not think it too much to give an account of your recovery to Madam, your, &c.
London, Sept. 7, 1782.   Sam. Johnson.

815. Sa. 7 Dec. '82. James Boswell (Edinburgh).
Not traced.—Boswell 1791, ii. 427 (Hill iv. 156).
Dear Sir

Having passed almost this whole year in a succession of disorders, I went in October to Brighthelmston, whither I came in a state of so much weakness, that I rested four times

804.—For the date see on 805, and add J's diary for 7 Dec.: 'I wrote to Mr., Mrs. Boswel, and Dr. Taylor'. Mrs. B's reply 20 Dec. is printed *L* iv. 157. For her earlier letter see on 805; it no doubt seconded JB's invitation to J, in his letter of 1 Oct., to visit Auchinleck in that month.

815.—J's complaint of JB's silence suggests that he had forgotten JB's very long letter of 1 Oct. (see on 805), or had forgotten that (as appears) he had not answered it. The suppressed passage, however, may have been his answer to JB's request for his 'counsel at large' on the proper behaviour to his 'injusta noverca' Lady Auchinleck.

in walking between the inn and the lodging. By physick and abstinence I grew better, and am now reasonably easy, though at a great distance from health. I am afraid, however, that health begins, after seventy, and often long before, to have a meaning different from that which it had at thirty. But it is culpable to murmur at the established order of the creation, as[1] it is vain to oppose it. He that lives, must grow old; and he that would rather grow old than die, has GOD to thank for the infirmities of old age.

At your long silence I am rather angry. You do not,[2] since now you are the head of your house, think it worth while to try whether you or your friend can live longer without writing, nor suspect after so many years of friendship, that when I do not write to you, I forget you. Put all such useless jealousies out of your head, and disdain to regulate your own practice by the practice of another, or by any other principle than the desire of doing right.

Your œconomy, I suppose, begins now to be settled; your expences are adjusted to your revenue, and all your people in their proper places. Resolve not to be poor: whatever you have, spend less. Poverty is a great enemy to human happiness, it certainly destroys liberty, and it makes some virtues impracticable, and others extremely difficult.

Let me know the history of your life,[3] since your accession to your estate. How many houses, how many cows, how much land in your own hand, and what bargains you make with your tenants.

* * * * * *

Of my 'Lives of the Poets', they have printed a new edition in octavo, I hear,[4] of three thousand. Did I give a set to Lord Hailes? If I did not, I will do it out of these. What did you make of all your copy?[5]

Mrs. Thrale and the three Misses are now for the winter,

815.—1. 'as', in J, is hardly ever purely causal; it means' in proportion as' or the like. There is therefore no temptation to read 'as culpable'.

2. That is, 'You do not, I trust'; unless indeed J wrote 'Do you not', meaning an imperative, and was ignorantly corrected. For the charge cf. 626.

3. JB did not reply until Jan. See on 827.1.

4. The comma might mislead a modern reader. 'I hear' applies to the number printed only.

5. The MS. of the *Lives*, see 715.

in Argyll-street. Sir Joshua Reynolds has been out of order, but is well again; and I am, dear Sir,

your affectionate humble servant,

London, Dec. 7, 1782. Sam. Johnson.

815.1. Sa. 7 Dec. '82. John Taylor (Ashbourne).

Address: To the Reverend Dr. Taylor in Ashbourne Derbyshire. *Postmark*: 7 DE.

Rosenbach (1925).—

Dear Sir

I went in October to Brighthelmston in a very feeble state, but I grew better, and though not well, have much less to complain of.

I now am willing to resume the offices of life, and particularly to do what I can for my Cousin Colliers. You sent me a will and recommended to me to carry it to Counsel which I am willing to do, but do not, till you have instructed me know what is expected from the will, nor what question I am to ask.

You will therefore, dear Sir, recollect the affair, and give me what instruction you can, for I am very much in dark, not being used to business, and not having much investigated the case now before us.

Do not let your law come, however, without some account of your health. As you might have suspected of me, I suspect of you, that silence is no good sign, and am afraid that you are not well. Take care of yourself. We have outlived many friends, let us keep close to one another

I am, dear sir, Your most affectionate

London Dec. 7. 1782 Sam: Johnson

815.2. Sa. 7 Dec. '82. Richard Clark.

No address, but endorsed 'Dr Johnson to Richard Clark Esq[r] now Chamberlain of London', with date 1816.

Earl Waldegrave.—

Dear Sir

If you are not engaged by any previous solicitation, I hope you will be pleased to favour the Bearer . . . Collet, in his petition for the place of Tollgatherer on the Bridge. He

has been long known to me, is an honest Man, and has great difficulty to support his family. I am, Sir, your most humble servant
Boltcourt. Dec. 7. 1782   Sam: Johnson

816. M. 9 Dec. '82. John Taylor (Ashbourne).
Address: To the Reverend Dr Taylor in Ashbourne Derbyshire.
Not traced.—Facsimile in Morrison Catalogue 1885, ii. 343.
Dear Sir
    Your letter contained almost an answer to that which You had not received.
    Take great care of your health. I am sorry that You are still subject to unprovoked disorders; but now You are better, be very tender of yourself. Had You been costive? or had any thing disturbed You? I have but two rules for you, keep your body open, and your mind quiet.
    Sickness concentrates a man's attention so much in himself, that he thinks little upon the affairs of others. Now I have a little gleam of health, I have the business of the Miss Colliers almost to begin. I do not know what it is that Mr Flint offers. Make me as much Master of the business as You can, yet I am afraid of giving you trouble. I would write to the Miss Colliers if I knew how. Shall I send my letter under cover to You, or to any other person? Miss Collier writes well, and can perhaps tell me something of importance. Let me know what I shall do.
    Take a scrupulous and diligent care of your health, that we may yet have a little comfort in each other.
                    I am Sir Yours most affectionately,
London December 9. 1782   Sam: Johnson.

816.1. M. 9 Dec. '82. Mrs. Thrale.
Not traced. Described in J's diary.—

    J noted in his diary (now in the Bodleian) for 9 Dec. 'I wrote to Taylor and to Mrs. Thrale, querulous'; and for 10 Dec. 'Soft ans. from Thrale'.

816.1.—I include this lost letter because it has the rare distinction of a description by the writer.

817. W. 11 Dec. '82. William Strahan.

Sotheby 11 Feb. 1929.—Hill 1892.

Sir

In your letter there is no need of alteration it may serve its purpose very well as it is, but if you change any thing, I think you may better say nothing of his cloaths, for if you allow him five suits in two years, they will cost near 45£ and the other 25£ will easily go for linen shoes and all other parts of cloathing.

Suppose you concluded your letter with some thing like this.

You express your desire of seeing me, and therefore I think it ⟨...⟩ to let you know, that whenever you bring with you that respect and gratitude to which I am entitled, you shall find me no longer

Your offended &c.

This is all that occurs, except that perhaps it were as well not to insist on a minute knowledge of the wife's expences, but to blame the first article as indistinct, without requiring it to be reformed.

I am, Sir, Your most humble Servant,

Decʳ 11. 1782   Sam: Johnson

817.1. W. 11 Dec. '82. Mrs. Thrale.

Morgan library.—

Madam

You are very kind to think so well of so little as I am doing, or can do. It was not till today at noon that Mr Norris brought me the writing of which Lord Ashburton required the perusal. He accompanied it however with other papers, I think, very properly. The whole bundle I sent this day to his Lordship, and when he has leisure, shall hear from him; but that leisure it is fit that I should wait.

817.—See 809.

817.1.—The letter is endorsed by FB: 'This Letter from Dr. Johnson to Mrs. Thrale was kindly sent to me at the time she received it; and was never reclaimed.' The letter is also marked 'Nᵒ. 6', which probably shows its place in FB's collection of J's letters; we have four to herself. It is perhaps surprising that HLT should show (FB does not claim that she gave) such a letter even to a devoted slave; but *Cecilia* was too much for her impulsive nature.

I am glad of Cator's intelligence, and am inclined to think him right. Therefore, dear Lady, hope the best. The best is indeed very bad, so bad that hope can hardly be joined with it. Let us however remember with gratitude that the worst, is but vexation, it will not be distress.

We had yesterday a very crouded Club. St Asaph, Fox, Bourk, Althrop,[1] and about sixteen more. And the talk was of Mrs Siddons.[2] Can you talk skilfully of Mrs Siddons? I had nothing to say. There was talk of Cecilia,—and I did better.

Then I went to the Painters distribution of prizes.[3] Sir Joshua made his Speech. The king is not heard with more attention.

I have very sorry nights, and therefore but chearless days. But I hope things will mend with us all. Let me continue to be,

Dear Madam, Your most humble Servant

Dec. 11. 1782   Sam: Johnson

817.2. M. 16 Dec. '82. Mrs. Thrale.

Address: To Mrs Thrale.
Rylands.—R. L. *Bull.* Jan. 1932, 37.

Madam

My purpose was to have shared the gayety of this evening,[1] and to have heard, Ye Gods! and to have seen,[2] but a very dreadful night has intervened, and [and] as want of sleep has made me very sleepy, it remains for me to dream if I can of Argyle Street.

I am Madam, your most &c

Monday evening December. 16. 1782   Sam: Johnson

817.1.—1. Althorpe; the pronunciation is 'Altrop'. Jane Austen writes 'Ibtrop' for Ibthorpe.

2. 'The Town has got a new *Idol*—Mrs. Siddons the Actress.' *Tb* 554.

3. JR's twelfth 'Discourse to the Students of the Royal Academy on the Distribution of the Prizes' was delivered 10 Dec.

817.2.—1. FB gives an account of this 'very full assembly at Mrs. Thrale's', but does not mention J (*Diary* ii. 202). 'I am all the Mode this Winter' *Tb* 553, but HLT does not record this occasion.

2. Not traced.

817.3. Tu. 17 Dec. '82. Mrs. Thrale.

Address: To Mrs Thrale.

Rylands.—R. L. *Bull.* Jan. 1932, 38.

Madam

I am really very much disordered, and know not how to get better; but am trying the old way.—Thou know'st my *old ward*[1]—I hope you are well after all your fatigue of talking—or of hearing, if of that you suffered any.

I am, Madam, Your most humble servant

Dec. 17. 1782   Sam: Johnson

817.4. W. 18 Dec. '82. Mrs. Thrale.

Address: To Mrs Thrale.

Rylands.—R. L. *Bull.* Jan. 1932, 38.

Dearest Madam

I have been bad, and am something better; perhaps to be worse and better, and never to be well, is what now remains. Perhaps yet a little more.

Mr Cator was with me this morning to enquire about Lord Ashburton, I told him what I have told you, and let him know that I took care to live within call, but that the hurry into which he must be put by the fire in his chambers would naturally divert his attention.

I have not been wanting. I wrote him a respectful note upon the accident. Our papers are at his House.

I may perhaps not be long before I come and see you. Dum spiro, spero. That's my maxim, what d'ye say to that now?

Mr Cator still thinks that our adversaries are not eager of more law, and that they may yet accept the six[1] thousand.[2] I am apt to think that he may be right.

I am Madam Most cordially your &c

Dec. 18. 1782   Sam: Johnson

817.3.—1. *1 Henry IV*, ii. iv. 215.

817.4—1. Mr. Wright printed *six'ⁱ*, but his comma is, I think, merely the dot over the *i*, and what looks like *t* may be an accidental mark.

2. They seem to have accepted £7,500. C 214.

818. F. 20 Dec. '82. Mrs. Thrale.

Address: To Mrs Thrale.
Rosenbach (1927).—1788, No. 293.

Dear Lady   ·

I hope the worst is at last over. I had a very good night, and slept very long. You can hardly think how bad I have been, while you were in all your altitudes, at the opera,[1] and all the fine places, and thinking little of me. Sastres has been very good. Queeney[2] never sent me a kind word. I hope however to be with you again in a short time, and shew you a man again.

I am, Madam Your most obliged and most humble
                                            Servant,
Dec. 20. 1782   Sam: Johnson

818.1. Sa. 21 Dec. '82. Hester Maria Thrale.

Address: To Miss Thrale.
Lansdowne.—Lansdowne, *Johnson and Queeney* 1932, 28.

Dearest Love,   Dec. 21, Shortest day, 1782

I am grown better by the old way, but the contest has been very stubborn. I have tasted no land animal since Sunday, but I will venture a little tomorrow, and hope to be among you ere long.[1]

You are very kind in writing. Never omit those little ceremonial notices, they nourish friendship, at very small expence. I would therefore have you practice them through life rather superfluously than penuriously.

Please to tell my Mistress that I hear nothing yet from Lord Ashburton, and, after what has happened,[2] do not think it proper to importune him.

I am, dearest Sweeting, Your most humble servant.
                                        Sam: Johnson

818.—1. FB records 19 Dec. 'She and her daughter carried me to the opera house'. *Diary* ii. 203.

2. The appeal was not in vain, see 818.1.

818.1.—1. On 27 Dec. FB 'dined with Mrs. Thrale and Dr. Johnson, who was very comic and good humoured'. HLT 'gave up her visit [to Mrs. Ord] in order to stay with Dr. Johnson'. *Diary* ii. 215.

2. See 817.4.

819. Th. 26 Dec. '82. Joshua Reynolds.

Sotheby 10 May 1875, 22 July 1922 (not seen). Described in 1875 catalogue.

'Declining an invitation on account of illness.'

819.1. Th. 26 Dec. '82. Mrs. Thrale.

Rylands.—R. L. *Bull.* Jan. 1932, 39.

Dear Madam

I had not passed the door since I left you, before yesterday morning. That I dined out was the consequence of a very early invitation and much importunity.[1]

In the afternoon I was seized with a fit of convulsive breathlessness such as I think you have never seen, but I fell at asleep before the fire and awaked somewhat better. But my nights are very restless, and life is very heavily burthened. I am afraid of opium and the methods which succeeded so well at Brighthelmston have not now had the same effect.

I have this day seen Mr Allen, Hoole, Compton, Walker, and Cambridge. But I have not seen those of whom I once hoped never to have lost sight.

This is the time of good wishes I hope, ye all know that you have those of, dearest, and dearest Madam,

Your most humble servant,

Dec. 26. 1782   Sam: Johnson

819.2. Sa. 28 Dec. '82. Mrs. Thrale.

Address: To Mrs Thrale.

Harvard.—

Dear Madam

I am very poorly, and am going home.[1] when I get a little better, I will be with you again, in the mean time think on me a little, and be certain that you will think on nobody, who thinks oftener on you. I am,

Madam, Your most &c

Decemb. 28. 1782   Sam: Johnson

819.1.—1. Perhaps he dined with his neighbour Allen.

819.2.—1. I suppose J wrote this from some place, not Bolt Court, where HLT knew him to be.

819.3. M. 30 Dec. '82. Mrs. Thrale.

Sotheby 30 Jan. 1918 (not seen).—Description in catalogue.

'About attending a meeting of executors.'

820. Tu. 31 Dec. '82. Thomas Wilson (Clitheroe).

Address (Boswell): To the Reverend Mr Wilson, Clitheroe, Lancashire. Not traced; copy by Wilson, Isham.—Boswell 1791, ii. 430 (Hill iv. 162); Wilson, *Archaeological Dictionary* ed. 2, 1793.

Reverend Sir

That I have so long omitted to return you thanks for the honour conferred upon me by your Dedication, I intreat you with great earnestness not to consider as more faulty than it is. A very importunate and oppressive disorder has for some time debarred me from the pleasures, and obstructed me in the duties of life. The esteem and kindness of wise and good men is one of the last pleasures which I can be content to lose; and gratitude to those from whom this pleasure is received, is a duty of which I hope never to reproach myself with the final neglect. I therefore now return you thanks for the notice which I have received from you; and which I consider as giving to my name not only more bulk, but more weight; not only as extending its superficies, but as increasing its value. Your book was evidently wanted, and will, I hope, find its way into the schools, to which, however, I do not mean to confine it; for no man has so much skill in ancient rites and practices as not to want it. As I suppose myself to owe part of your kindness to my excellent friend Dr. Patten,[1] he has likewise a just claim to my acknowledgements, which I hope you, Sir, will transmit. There will soon appear a new edition of my Poetical Biography;[2] if you will accept of a copy to keep me in your mind, be pleased to let me know how it may be conveniently conveyed to you. The present is small, but it is given with good will by, Reverend Sir,

Your most obliged and humble servant

Sam. Johnson.

Dec. 31, 1782. Bolt Court Fleet Street London

820.—JB does not tell us when he got this letter; his copy, no doubt by Wilson, was found at Malahide. W retained the original; I have therefore preferred his readings where they differ from JB's: 'so long' for 'long', 'reproach myself' for 'be reproached'; 'schools' for 'school'.

1. See 739.   2. This copy was sold in 1921 (*L* v. 508).

821. Tu. 31 Dec. '82. John Taylor (Ashbourne).

Address: To the Reverend Dr Taylor in Ashbourne Derbyshire. *Postmark*: 31 DE.

A. T. Loyd.—*NQ* 6 S, v. 462.

Dear Sir

Your last little note was very unsatisfactory. That a silly timorous unskilful Girl has behaved improperly, is a poor reason for refusing to tell me what expectations have been raised by the will, and what questions I must ask the Lawyers, questions which if you do not like to answer them I must ask elsewhere, and I am unwilling to mingle this affair with any name that you may hear with disgust.[1]

This, my dear Sir, is the last day of a very sickly and melancholy year. Join your prayers with mine, that the next may be more happy to us both. I hope the happiness which I have not found in this world, will by infinite mercy be granted in another.

I am, dear Sir, Yours affectionately,

Dec. 31. 1782   Sam: Johnson.

821.1. ⟨? '82.⟩ Thomas Wilson.

Not traced.—*Works* of Thomas Wilson (the elder) 1782, xvi.

'The most eminent literary character of this kingdom . . . (in a letter to Dr. Wilson) expresses his high approbation of Bishop Wilson.' . . .

To think on Bishop Wilson with veneration is only to agree with the whole Christian world. I hope to look into his books with other purposes than those of criticism, and after their perusal NOT ONLY TO WRITE, BUT TO LIVE BETTER.

821.—1. The name that would displease JT ('disgust' was a much milder term than it now is) was that of Langley. See 823.

821.1.—I owe this letter to a note by Mr. P. B. Gove in *RES* xvi. 64, Oct. 1940, 455. The capitals are doubtless not J's.

373. Mr. Metzdorf reports the discovery in the Adam collection of a fifth version, in a hand not identified; at the foot J has written 'I believe this is a true copy—I have it only in my memory.' The wording is very close to the original, except that J had forgotten the sentence about his reverence for truth. It is not Shaw's lost MS.

380 and 505. The inscription in Monboddo's copy is 'This Book was sent to me by the Authour D^r. Samuel Johnson to be presented to Lord Monboddo. James Boswell.' It looks as if JB had forgotten or mislaid the 'list' sent him by J in Feb. '75. See *L* iii. 102 for the story of the presentation.

380.1. JR's nephew Samuel Johnson writes to his sister Elizabeth 9 March '75 (Radcliffe, op. cit. above p. 13).

I believe I writ you about the Prologue which Cousin Jo was desir'd to write. When He had finish'd it He to the great mortification receiv'd a note from Dr. Johnson of which the following is a copy.

Mr Johnson sends his compliments to Mr. Palmer and is sorry for the trouble which has been taken by him in making the Prologue. He need not proceed as Mr. Hoole thinks himself oblig'd to use that which he has.

The prologue was for *Cleonice*.

397.1. n. 1. Dr. Pottle corrects me. J means that he could have 'taken the place' for Friday if he could have been sure his clothes would come as in fact they did.

431. In the Isham collection is a leaf of copy in which JB has written 'Take in his [no doubt the original] of 27 August, leaving out last line page first from You never to the end of the paragraph and putting three or four stars ****. Take in his of 30 August. These two 27 & 30 August are attached to this leaf.'

458. The MS of the *Life* shows that JB wrote 'on the 29'; the next line of his MS is partly erased, and words written between the lines contain the word 'melancholy' so written that the top of the *h* has obscured the tail of the 9.

463. JB wrote in his copy two descriptions that do not appear in 1791:

1. 'Part of a Letter from Dr Johnson to Dr Wetherel Master of University College Oxford containing the science of Bookselling.' JB's copy does not contain the 'Dear Sir' which in 1791 disguises the fact that only part of the letter is given.

2. On a separate scrap of paper: 'Dr Johnson to Mr Wetherell about establishing Mr Carter as riding master at Oxford.'

JB's original intention was to give Douglas's name; he had written a foot-note 'Now Bishop of Carlisle'.

486. Dr. Pottle plausibly suggests that J wrote 'I am sincerely sorry', deploring pregnancy in 'a world full of troubles'. HLT replies protesting that a son is all she has to live for. J in 488 (which Dr. Pottle regards as the reply to 488*a*) says he concurs; he meant no more than that, since it is so, 'cheerfulness is reckoned a good thing'. The evidence of the 'Children's Book' is not decisive.

491. I learn from Dr. Powell that in the other copy—in Lord Crawford's collection—are these words:
Rerum, sive naturalium, sive civilium, elegans, at gravis scriptor.

502 (152). The relevance of 'real sorrow' does not appear; J presumably alludes to something in JB's letter of 21 Oct. that is not quoted in *L*.

505, n. 1. My note was written in ignorance of the latest discoveries at Malahide, the full range of which is not known to me. In so far as the finds were of J letters, they confirm the view that the copy for the letters printed in the *Life* was reassembled in three classes: originals of J to JB (still missing); originals of J to others (Fettercairn); copies of J to JB and others (found, in part, in the latest Malahide hoard). See Appendix B.

570. Dr. Powell reminds me that Adams, the Master of Pembroke, was like Gwynn a Shrewsbury man. He was perhaps J's correspondent.

574.1. William Adams (Oxford). Tu. 7 Apr. '78.
Historical Society of Pennsylvania.—
Dear Sir
    When I travelled in Scotland, I was one Night at the House of a Minister named Macaulay, who had been sent to visit the Island of St. Kilda, and under whose name the last account of it is published. In our evening's conversation I gave an account of the University of Oxford, and excited first in the Lady and then in the Minister a desire of having their Son educated amongst us. They were content that he should be a Servitor, and I promised my endeavour in his favour. This promise is now claimed, and I take the liberty of soliciting your assistance. If you have any vacancy I hope you will please to receive him, if You are full, it will be a great favour if you will enquire after a vacancy in any other house.
                    I am Sir Your most obedient and most humble Servant
                                            Sam: Johnson
Boltcourt, Fleetstreet Apr. 7. 1778

575. JB added to his copy 'The foregoing is an exact copy . . . James Boswell'.

598. The two books 'left'—i.e. at Hussey's house?—were probably of J's own writing. The reference is not to a bequest.

610.1. See 229.2 (i. 442).

Tu. 27 Apr. '79. Edmund Burke (London).

No address or postmark.

Earl Fitzwilliam.—

Dear Sir

I flatter myself that you will not be offended that I solicit a favour. The Vicar of Coventry[1] whose case I have enclosed is my friend, and his petition is in my opinion not only just but modest. His business will be brought before a committee to morrow, and I beg your attendance and patronage. I am,

Sir, Your most obedient and most humble servant Sam. Johnson Apr. 27, 1779.

610.1.—1. The 'Vicar of Coventry' is no doubt J's friend Rann (see Index II), who was V. of Holy Trinity Coventry from '73. The archivists of the House of Commons have no record of any Committee affecting him in '79. The appeal of Joseph Rann and another v. Hughes (Josiah Brown, *Reports of Cases in Parliament*, second edition, iv. 27) does not seem to be relevant. I am indebted to officials of both Houses of Parliament for their kind researches.

656. I had overlooked LP's reply, 15 April, to this letter—her only known letter. See Appendix H. She thanks J for the gown, which she had only guessed to be his present, and inquires if it came from London; for if so 'the carrior has cheat'd me' by charging 2s. 2d.

662, n. 4. 'On Wednesday who, do you think, dined at the Bishop's? Dr. Johnson and Ld. Montboddo. Johnson was silent at dinner, loquacious after it. Montboddo could hardly get in a word and was indignant, nor has his indignation yet ceased. A strong invective against Musick was poured forth by Johnson, which would have diverted you, as it did me, though neither you nor I are insensible to the charms of melody.' (Sir) William Jones to Viscount Althorp, 29 April 1780 (*Althorp MSS.* Communicated by Dr. Powell).

686. 'Indulge genio' is in Persius, v. 151: Indulge genio, carpamus dulcia, nostrum est/quod vivis.

712. See i. 429, note on 353. I find that there are in B.M. three holographs of this letter, dated 29 Jan. & 12 June '81, 21 Jan. '82. I have seen a letter of Hastings's own in triplicate, each MS bearing the name of a different ship. Though J no doubt rewrote from memory, the variations in his MSS are very slight. My text is substantially JB's.

738. Since my text and note were beyond recall, Prof. F. W. Hilles has sent me a copy of the original, addressed 'To Mrs Reynolds' and dated July 21. The obvious explanation of the puzzle, that J wrote substantially the same letter on 28 June and 21 July, seems precluded by the close verbal correspondence of the two documents. However that may be, our sole original is as below.

Dearest Madam

There is in these such force of comprehension, and such nicety of observation as Locke or Pascal might be proud of. This I say with intention to have you think that I speak my opinion.

They cannot however be printed in their present state. Many of your notions seem not very clear in your own mind, many are not sufficiently developed and expanded for the common reader; the expression almost every where wants to be made clearer and smoother. You may by revisal and improvement make it a very elegant and curious work.

I am, Dearest Dear, Your most humble servant

July 21. 1781   Sam: Johnson.

For *An Enquiry concerning the Principles of Taste*, 1785, see Prof. Clifford's edition, Augustan Reprint Society, 27, Los Angeles, 1951.

739. Dedication to a private man was less uncommon than I—perhaps than J?—had supposed. I have noted John Kirkby, *English and Latin Grammar* 1746, dedicated to Gibbon's father (Gibbon, *Autobiog.*); Thomas Francklin's *Demonax* 1780, dedicated to J himself (*L* iv, 479); V. J. Peyton's French Dictionary 1764, dedicated to J— W— (*sc.* John Wilkes).

739.1. 'with pressing urgency' seems not to suit the context. It occurs that J might intend 'without', that is 'I do not press you to urge it'.

760. Hill's assumption was natural; but the text of Thompson's answer (now in the Hyde collection) makes it clear to whom J had written.

781. See A. T. Hazen's argument, *Mod. Philology* 35 (Feb. 1938), 289, in favour of William Cooke as compiler of *The Beauties*.

787.1. Prof. Clifford suggests that Dr. Lawrence was perhaps too ill (788.1) to 'direct'. If the letter is to HLT, the doctor is Jebb, see 782.3.

874.1. The address is not preserved, but see L ii. 380. J and JB were much together on 7 April, and recalled their tour of '73. But JB does not seem to have got a copy of this letter.